MODERN
Tackle Craft

C. BOYD PFEIFFER

LYONS & BURFORD, PUBLISHERS
New York

To my wife JACKIE,

who gave me the time to work on this book,
the inspiraton to begin it,
and the constant encouragement to complete it.
Hopefully, her faith in this effort will be justified,
as was her faith in the original TACKLE CRAFT.

NOTE TO THE READER

I have made every effort to describe tackle-making methods that are easy and safe. Familiarity with tools is important in any craft, and no less so in making fishing tackle. In the making of some tackle—such as the molding of lead sinkers, bucktails, tin squids, and soft plastic lures—improper techniques may prove to be extremely dangerous. As a result, I describe methods of tackle-building that are safe if directions are followed; and, along the way, I warn readers of any possible dangers.

However, neither the author nor the publisher can assume responsibility for any damages or injuries resulting from construction, molding, repair, or formation of tackle described in this book, or for products used without due care,

This book on tackle craft is as complete as I can make it. I have tried to include all of the types of tackle that can easily be made in any home workshop. Obviously, there are some special methods of tackle-making and even some special tackle items with which I am not familiar. While I am unable to enter into extensive correspondence with readers, I would be delighted to hear of new and different tackle items or tackle-making methods. Readers can contact me through the publisher.

Lyons & Burford, Publishers,
31 West 21 Street,
New York, New York 10010.

Printed in the United States of America

10 9 8 7 6 5 4 3 2 1

Design by Ruth Kolbert

Library of Congress Cataloging-in-Publication Data

Pfeiffer, C. Boyd.
Modern tackle craft / by C. Boyd Pfeiffer.
p. cm.
Includes bibliographical references and index.
ISBN 1-55821-184-5
1. Fishing tackle. I. Title.
SH447.P47   1993   92-29639
688.7 '91 — dc20   CIP

Acknowledgments

Books are only rarely the work of a single mind. This book—both the first edition, TACKLE CRAFT, and this greatly expanded edition, MODERN TACKLE CRAFT—is no exception. For more than forty years I have been experimenting with making fishing tackle and have at various time made and used all of the types of gear mentioned in this book.

However, along the way I have picked others' brains, and I have constantly learned of new methods, tricks, tips, and types of tackle that can be built by the home craftsman. Fortunately for the tackle craftsman, more and more information on tackle building is increasingly available. Magazine articles, books, pamphlets, booklets, and other information published; videos, films, and tips on the TV fishing shows have all been helpful. For this, a general debt of gratitude is owed and gratefully acknowledged.

Many companies and individuals in those companies have helped immensely in this and other projects. Thus, much thanks go to the following:

Ande for the use of knot illustrations.

AFTCO Manufacturing Co. and Bill Shedd for the loan of materials used for photos.

B.D. Classic Enterprises for materials used for photos.

Bead Chain Tackle and Pete Renkert for permission to use the size charts of their products.

Bellinger Reel Seats for the loan of materials for photos.

Berkley and Company and Mike Fine for permission to use their line art on knots and snells and terminal tackle.

Cortland/Rodon for the loan of products used for photos.

DNY Marketing for the loan of materials and sizing charts for their products.

Do-it and Jerry Bond for the loan of materials and permission to use certain charts.

Dupont Stren for the use of their charts on knots and snells.

Environmental Technology, Inc., and Ed LaFley for information on their casting resins for making offshore trolling lures, and for samples used for photography.

Flex Coat and Roger Seiders for materials used for photos.

The Gaines Company and Tom Eggler for materials used for photos.

Gamakatsu for sizing charts for their hooks.

G. Loomis for guide-spacing charts for use with their rod blanks.

Gudebrod, Inc. for materials for photos and for permission to use size charts of their products.

Hilts Molds and Roy Hilts for the loan of materials and permission to use certain charts.

J. Kennedy Fisher for guide-spacing charts for their rod blanks.

Lakeland, Inc. for permission to use size charts of their lure components.

Lamiglas for information and blanks for photo purposes and guide-spacing charts.

Mason Tackle Company and Chip Powell for materials and permission to use some sizing charts.

M-F Manufacturing and Bob Maserang for materials used for photos.

Perfection Tip for the loan of materials and permission to use size charts of their products.

Mildrum Manufacturing Co. and Ted Benson for the loan of guides used for photos.

O. Mustad and Son, USA, for hooks for photos and hook-size charts.

St. Croix and Jeff Schluter for materials used for photos.

Sage for guide-spacing charts for use with their rod blanks.

Sevenstrand Tackle Corp. and Bill Goodman for permission to use artwork on the proper crimping of leader sleeves.

Glenn Struble for the loan of materials used for photos.

Talon for guide-spacing charts for use with their rod blanks.

Tri-peek International, Inc., for photo samples and information on their EasyWeld micro flame torch and products for welding.

Witchcraft Tape Products for photo samples.

VMC for sizing charts for their hooks.

The Worth Company and David Worth for materials for photos and permission to use size charts of their lure components.

The Wright and McGill Company and Gene Wilson for permission to use size charts of their hooks.

Special thanks must be singled out for Cam Clark, Roy Hilts, and Jerry Bond. Cam Clark, the editor for *RodCrafters*, the magazine of the organization started by Dale Clemens, was unstinting in his cooperation, friendship, and help in providing me with photo models of the many decorative wraps and weaves that he has made on rods and which serve as samples for his courses on rod building. He has my sincere thanks for the time and tips that he shared with me.

Jerry Bond of Do-It and Roy Hilts of Hilts Molds both rendered yeoman service by reading the chapter on molding bucktails. Both were generous in their kind comments and their welcome constructive criticism. I thank them both for the time they took for this thankless task.

In addition, special thanks go to good friends who have served for years—decades really—as a sounding board for my ideas and theories, who have and shared freely with their ideas and constructive criticisms, suggestions, and comments. Thus, special thanks for the friendship and help over the years go to Chuck Edghill, Norm Bartlett, Lefty Kreh, Ed Russell, Irv Swope, Joe Zimmer, and others.

My wife Jackie also deserves special mention. When the first TACKLE CRAFT was completed, she thought that she had seen the end of books from me and that her days of retyping my chicken scratches of writing were over. It was five books later before we bought a word processor and retired her from being a word processor of books, magazine articles brochures, and other efforts— 21 years of making my bad-looking stuff look good. For that, and for her constant reassurances in this and faith in me in this difficult field of freelance writing, I thank her. She was and is my best critic and my best inspiration.

Thanks also go to my children—Debbie, Greg and his wife Kathy, and Jeff, for their understanding over the years of this time-consuming profession and their help in many ways. Also, to my father and mother who, while not anglers, instilled early in me a love for the outdoors and encouraged me to seek my own path in life. To all of them, my thanks.

Finally Nick Lyons, Peter Burford, and all their fine staff at Lyons & Burford deserve special thanks and recognition for taking on such a monumental task, sticking with it—and me—through delays and more delays past original deadlines while I struggled to bring this monster into being. The manuscript and photo package—like the original—grew far larger than any of us anticipated, and far larger than the original TACKLE CRAFT.

Contents

Introduction

There are four good reasons for making your own tackle. It is a fun hobby; it can save you money over the cost of commercially available equipment; it allows you to make custom tackle unavailable elsewhere; and it helps you to become a better angler. That last deserves some explaining. I've found, as have others, that by making your own tackle you understand it better—understand what it takes to make an effective rod or lure or tackle accessory. It also helps through a subconscious realization that you have spent only a fraction of the cost of equivalent commercial gear. As a result, you begin to fish deeper, cast into more difficult structure, fish the "impossible" places. Yes, you lose some of your home-made tackle, but as a result of fishing where others won't, you also catch more fish, bigger fish, more often.

Tackle-crafting can be as comprehensive as you want, or involve only one type of lure or tackle part. It can be simple—with little outlay of money and minimal expenditure of time—or it can be as complex and expansive as you wish.

And there never seems to be enough written on the subject—either in books or magazine articles. My book TACKLE CRAFT, of which this is a greatly updated, expanded, and completely re-written version, was the only one at the time covering both lures and rods. Many books are out of date, out of print, or deal only with rods or lures—not both. In contrast, you can find a couple of dozen books on fly tying for every book on some form of tackle building. And as a result, flies, bass bugs, and similar lures tied by means of standard fly-tying methods and with a fly-tying vise and tools will not be dealt with here. Excellent publications on these subjects would make any such addition superfluous.

Perhaps you have considered making your own lures and rods in the past but never actually tried it. Often, those who have yet to try it think that tackle-making will take too much skill or too many tools. Nothing is further from the truth. With only two pair of pliers (which you might already have) you can make any of the standard spinner designs on the market, in addition to originating new designs. Without any tools you can wrap a rod. The standard rod-wrapping support and thread-tension devise is nice but not absolutely necessary. And you can make any soft-plastic lures with only the molds required. Other simple tools found on any home workbench allow you to make wire rigs and spreaders, wood plugs (carve them with a pocket knife), assemble spoons, and make spinnerbaits and buzzbaits. With the proper molds and melting pots, it is easy to make any type of sinker or bucktail.

Note that while several chapters cover tools, each chapter includes a listing of both the basic tool needs and additional helpful tools that might be desired for that chapter.

Making tackle is fun. It is associated with fishing and allows all of us to remain active in our sport, even when seasons or conditions don't allow it. Thus, it is great as a wintertime hobby and recreational craft that pays dividends once on the water.

The degree of skill required for making fishing tackle varies with the type of tackle being made and the degree of perfection required in the lure or rod. I've seen some rods and lures that are truly works of art and as fine examples of the craftsman's skill as can be found. I've also seen lures and rods that looked like rejects after the last day of a flea market. What both have in common is that they catch fish. The slight flaw in the paint job on a wood plug, the molding error in a soft plastic lure, the imperfect tail tied on a bucktail, or the badly wrapped guide on a rod might affect how you or others feel about the tackle; it won't likely affect tackle performance or fish caught.

This is not to endorse sloppy workmanship, but only to suggest that while your skills and results in making tackle will improve over time, the first lure, rod, or tackle accessory made will no doubt work well enough to catch fish.

Making tackle also saves you money. Just how much is difficult to say, but some ideas are suggested in each chapter. For example, if you mold sinkers from lead wheel weights that you get free from a gas station, the only cost is the mold which is quickly amortized. Carving wood plugs often allows you to make lures that are one-tenth or less the cost of store lures—the only expense is in the hardware and paint. Assembly is all that is required for making spinners and for some types of spinnerbaits and buzzbaits. Expensive offshore lures are easy to make if you invest a little in time and imagination to develop the right molds and inserts of these big-game lures.

Rods can be built at little cost when compared to commercially equivalent models and all tackle can be customized as you wish. Thus, you can design your own lures, try different plugs, spinners and spoons, make rods with different guide and handle arrangements, or designed with complex thread wraps.

One point about this book. It does not take each model, design, and shape of lure or rod in turn and give specific instructions and blueprints for making that particular size and shape of lure or rod. It does provide extensive and detailed information on all sorts of methods of designing, making, and modifying lures and rods. Most chapters list variations of lures that can be made following the basics outlined in that chapter. Methods of making some lure types that are not yet commercially available are also described. Thus, this book is designed to expand your thinking, open your imagination, and teach you basic tackle-building skills that will allow you to make anything that you can think of.

As a result, this book has some repetition—

deliberately so. For example, tools and how to make some tools are covered in the first two chapters. But each chapter on a lure or rod-construction method also covers tools. Thus, while there is some repetition, it is done deliberately so that each chapter will stand alone—or almost alone—to save you from repeatedly having to refer to other sections or chapters for more information. The purpose is to aid the reader, perhaps at the expense of slightly more bulk and repetition.

And while this book has a beginning, middle, and end, there is no end to tackle building. Just today I was talking to Dick French of Dale Clemens Custom Tackle and learned of a new computer program that allows you to pre-plan weaving of thread in decorative rod wraps. You need a 286 or higher IBM computer or clone to do it, but with a mouse you can draw the design on a computer screen, print it out, and the program will plan the thread wraps for the diameter of the rod, even adjusting if you decide to change thread size.

Also, at this time, the craft company Aleene's has introduced a granular plastic material that can be heated in boiling water and then shaped into any design you wish. It comes in many colors and is available at craft and hobby stores. To date, I haven't yet figured out how to use this for making lures, but something will occur to me, or to someone else. A similar product is available in sheet form, lending itself to the idea of making spoons or other flat-lure shapes.

I am not advocating making lures to sell. Tackle-making should be fun and the complexities of operating a successful tackle business are too extensive to cover here. If contemplating this, be sure to read Appendix B first.

This book is meant to increase your fishing and fishing-related pleasure—the personal pleasure you have with our sport. I hope that you will get as much enjoyment reading and learning from MODERN TACKLE CRAFT as I have had in preparing it. More importantly, I hope that you have as much fun in making and experimenting with your own fishing tackle as I have in making mine.

—C. Boyd Pfeiffer
June 1992

1

Tools and Materials

INTRODUCTION ∎ BENCH OR WORKTABLE ∎ VISE ∎
LIGHTING ∎ HAMMERS ∎ HAND SAWS ∎ ELECTRIC SAWS ∎
DRILLS ∎ DRILL PRESSES ∎ TWIST DRILL BITS ∎ PLIERS ∎
METAL SNIPS ∎ FILES ∎ SOLDERING IRON ∎ POP-STYLE
RIVETER ∎ ELECTRIC GRINDER ∎ ELECTRIC SANDER ∎
LATHE ∎ WIRE FORMERS ∎ REAMERS ∎ DIVIDERS ∎ RULE ∎
ANVIL ∎ GATE CUTTER ∎ LEADER-CRIMPING PLIERS ∎
FLY-TYING TOOLS ∎ ROD-WRAPPING TOOLS ∎ THREAD
TENSION DEVICES ∎ CURING MOTOR ∎ HANDLE SEATER ∎
TAPERED REAMER ∎ TIP-TOP GAUGE ∎ BURNISHER ∎
TORCH ∎ SCALPEL ∎ DIAMOND WRAP TOOLS ∎ MASKING
TAPE ∎ SAFETY EQUIPMENT

INTRODUCTION

Proper tools are the secret to doing any job well. A repairman who comes to your house to fix a dishwasher, TV, oven, or hot water heater always has a well-equipped tool box. A carpenter or cabinetmaker could not begin construction of anything without the proper woodworking tools. By the same token, the tackle tinkerer must have the proper tools to construct the many types of fishing tackle. Fortunately, the basic tools needed for making most fishing tackle are not expensive or hard to get. In all likelihood, you will already have a number of the required tools, or can improvise others. Many can be made, as outlined in Chapter 2. And it is important to realize early on that much tackle requires a minimum of tools,

materials, and skills to make.

It is not necessary to collect or buy all the tools listed before you begin making fishing tackle and lures. You may be interested only in two or three types of lures or accessories and will never need the tools required for making other lures. Each chapter lists both the minimally required tools and those tools that are not required but that will make the job easier — or perhaps be required for major jobs or larger-scale operations. If you plan to make all of the tackle covered in this book, you will ultimately need or want most or all of the *basic* tools listed. You may in time wish to get some of the optional or extra tools to make some tasks easier or less time-consuming In all cases, you *must* have and use the basic safety equipment listed for each chapter and type of tackle.

Otherwise, look at the materials list at the beginning of each chapter for suggestions on required tools before heading to the tackle shop or hardware store. Try where possible to substitute the same or similar tools that you may already have on hand.

BENCH OR WORKTABLE

You will need a place to work and to hold tools, materials, and finished products. This can be as simple as a small TV tray to hold the parts and materials for making a few spinners; on the other hand, you will want a sturdy workshop bench to saw out wood-plug bodies, make gaffs, and wrap rods. When molding plastic lures (worms), lead sinkers, lead bucktails, jig heads, tin squids, and the like, you may not be able to work where you wish, but may have to work in the kitchen where you will have access to heat for melting materials and to ventilation for dissipating any resulting fumes. In other cases, you may want to work on a camp stove on an outdoor picnic table for the same purposes. Whatever your circumstances, a small square or rectangle of thin plywood, Masonite, scrap kitchen countertop material (laminate), aluminum sheet, or large asbestos kitchen heat pad will be necessary to catch spilled metal or plastic, saving the kitchen counter or picnic table from possible scarring. If you are unwelcome in the kitchen or at the picnic table, there are several other options. One is to use a propane torch or stove in your workshop. The second is to use a hot plate in your workshop to melt the soft plastic used in making worms and grubs. A third is to get a self-contained electric heater and melting pot for melting the lead for bucktail and sinker molding. A must for melting lead is to have a *sturdy* workplace. If you use a heavy furnace that must be bolted down for security and safety, you will not be able to work with a sheet of plywood over the kitchen counter, but must have a sturdy worktable.

I use several types of workbenches when making tackle. I have a long sturdy workbench — 8 feet by 3 feet — made from two-by-fours that are upended, through-bolted, and mounted with a heavy machine vise. For heavy work, it is as sturdy as a bomb shelter and just about as heavy. Two similar but lighter-weight workbenches of equal size flank this central bench. One contains a small specialized lathe I use for turning rod handles, rod parts, butt caps, wood plugs, and some metal parts. The other is kept free for any overflow of work from the main bench. This last workbench is also ideal for mounting rod-wrapping tools, fly-tying vises, and similar temporary tools. I have a completely separate fly-tying table and work area. For lead molding, I use a small sturdy workbench where I can bolt down any furnaces and cover the wood top with sheet metal for an easy cleanup.

I use yet another, smaller, square workbench as a repository for power tools: a grinder, sander, small drill press, small Dremel lathe for turning lures, and small band saw. Bins underneath this bench hold hand power tools, such as several power drills, a saber saw, and a circular saw. For some tackle work, such as the maintenance, modification, and repair of reels, I have a separate small workbench (about six-by-two feet) in my rod, reel, and lure tackle-storage room. I also have a fly-tying bench that sometimes doubles as a workbench for making small lures such as spinners, and is also used for tying tails on bucktails and jigs and for rigging small trolling lures.

Over or near each workbench I mount perfboard (Peg-Board is a brand name) for hanging tools, reels, special parts, small power tools, and so on. The variety of styles and lenghts of hooks available make it possible to hang up almost any tool or part. Both 1/8- and 1/4-inch-thick perfboard are available, with the 1/8-inch sufficient for most tackle applications.

VISE

A vise is a necessity for holding wood in order to cut it to the right sizes and shapes for making plugs, for holding sheet metal when making spoons, and for clamping materials for similar drilling and cutting operations.

Woodworkers' vises are ideal for holding wood because they have special large wood-faced jaws that prevent damage to the wood being held. Most mount below or flush with the workbench top. A machinists' vise mounts on top of the bench and has machined steel jaws. Most have a swivel base for turning the vise, and others can also be turned at an angle to vertical. Those that are a permanent mount are best, but some smaller vises that clamp (like a C-clamp) onto a table or workbench are also quite adequate for most tackle-crafting.

I like the machinists'-style vise. It has more versatility of movement and plenty of clamping power. In most cases, even when working with

Middle section of author's workbench: note perf-board on back wall to hold tools, and drawers under workbench for tools and materials. At the far end of the bench (far right) is a small rod-building lathe for turning handles, etc.

wood, any scarring that the jaws might cause will be cut or sanded away as you finish a plug body, smooth a spoon-blade blank, or polish other materials. Also, it is easy to make jaw-covering faces of wood, composition material, aluminum, or copper. I like the soft-metal aluminum or copper faces because they can easily be cut to shape and size to fit over the jaws, and are easily replaced as desired.

LIGHTING

Proper lighting over any work area is essential. Without it, doing good work is impossible, and in some cases even dangerous. If you can't see well, you can't cut or drill well or make good tackle. I like the double fluorescent "shop lights" sold in any hardware or general store or major outlet such as WalMart, K-Mart, Sears, or Wards. Two-foot, four-foot, and eight-foot lengths are available. I use a bank of four-foot-length lights, which

are sold everywhere at reasonable prices. If I had it to do over again, I would go with the eight-foot size, even though the bulbs are harder to handle and obtain. Fluorescent lights come in a variety of different colors, from cool white to warm-spectrum light. Get the type of light you prefer. I find the cool white to be somewhat harsh, although the warm light may be too warm for some tastes. I like the soft white best. In any case, for uniformity of lighting, be sure to use bulbs of the same shade.

One tip is to mount the main lights over the front edge of the workbench for the best general lighting, and to use supplemental lighting such as incandescent-bulb swingarm lights for spot-lighting.

On small workshop projects, a small swingarm or gooseneck lamp with a 60- or 75-watt bulb may be adequate. Small high-intensity lights are also good for this and for getting a large amount of light into a small area.

HAMMERS

Hammers are not needed for much tackle-craft work. They are needed for hammering out metal to make spoon blades, for getting a hammered finish on a spoon, for any task where you have to use a drift (a punching tool), or for making some of the tools that will be suggested later.

For most work, ball-peen hammers are best because you do not need the claw (to pull nails) found on carpenters' hammers. You can pick a variety of sizes: Ball-peen hammers are rated by the weight of the head, from about 4-ounce through 6-, 8-, 10-, 12-ounce and heavier sizes. Cross-peen hammers are also useful for making straight marks on metal lures because the cross-peen has a wedgelike (chisel) end opposite the hammer face.

If you have a carpenters' hammer, you can certainly make do in most cases. Other types of useful hammers are the soft-face hammers (either plastic or hard rubber or one of each) and brass-head hammers that are soft enough not to scratch metal surfaces. Both styles are ideal for making spoon blades. A wood mallet also has uses and for tackle-crafting can sometimes double for some of the above hammer types.

To maximize striking force when forging spoon blades (hammering them into a concave shape) consider dead-blow hammers. These hammers are made with lead shot in the hollow head to minimize rebound and maximize striking force. They are relatively expensive, however, so be sure you are serious about making your own blades before purchasing one.

HAND SAWS

Saws are not needed in most tackle-crafting, although there are some exceptions. Some of these exceptions are:
- Cutting wood for carving your own wood plugs. Use a regular crosscut saw (usually you will be cutting across the grain when sawing long lengths of square cross-section material into plug- or lathe-lengths). Coping saws and keyhole saws also work well.
- Cutting rod blanks when you want to chop a blank at the tip or butt to make a rod of a different action. Use a hacksaw with a very fine blade (32 teeth per inch is best). Often, a regular hacksaw is too large and bulky. A small saw that consists only of a handle to hold the blade is best, and is easy to handle.

- Cutting metal to fashion spoons, squids, and other similar lures. Use a hacksaw, regular style (with frame), with a metal cutting blade (24 or 32 teeth per inch).

ELECTRIC SAWS

Electric saws are also helpful for tackle-crafting, but unless you are into a large-scale operation, they are usually not worth buying just for making tackle. If you have one or more for other purposes, or buy one for several types of household chores and also use it for tackle-crafting, so much the better. Some possibilities and their uses include:
- *Band saw.* Large band saws cost well into the hundreds of dollars, but smaller ones with 8-, 10-, or 12-inch throats (the distance between the blade and the edge of the tool equals the width of the material that can be handled) are ideal. Small bench-top styles are good and can usually be found in hardware and variety stores and through mail-order outlets. Used ones sold through newspaper ads or in flea markets are also good bets. It is important to get one that has or uses a narrow blade of about 1/4-inch, because blade width controls the radius of any cut that can be made. Since these are ideal for cutting out the plug shapes from square wood blanks, a thin blade makes it possible to make sharp-curve-radius cuts.

Different types of cutting blades used for tackle-crafting. The three to the left are hacksaw blades; that to the right is an X-Acto saw. Fine-tooth blades such as those with 50 teeth per inch (far right) or 32 teeth per inch (second from right) are required for cutting rod blanks.

- *Scroll saw.* This will also cut the shape of a plug from a wood blank, but if making any but the smallest plugs, it is not best. Most scroll saws are designed to work with 3/8- to 1/2-inch-thick material, usually far thinner than the 1 1/2-inch thickness of most plugs. They are okay for wood up to 3/4-inch thick, but the thicker the wood the slower the work, and the greater the possibility of blade breakage, crooked cuts, and work chattering because the blade binds up.
- *Saber saw.* This has a reciprocating blade, like the scroll saw, but is heavy-duty enough for general work. Often saber saws are used in construction or home repairs for light cutting. Because they usually have a large gap around the blade, they cannot be mounted upside down and used as a stationary saw. They are okay for general cutting and for sawing wood to length for use in a lathe or for carving.

DRILLS

Either an electric or hand drill is useful for drilling holes in spoons or spinner parts, making pilot holes in wood or plastic plugs, and also for making molds. Although small single-speed non-reversible 1/4-inch drills are often available very cheaply, the best are variable-speed reversible 3/8-inch chuck drills. With these you can use the fastest speed for wood, moderate speeds for metal, and slow speeds for plastic (so that you do not burn or melt the material).

Rechargeable electric drills allow you to work without cords anywhere you want, and are fine for tackle-crafting projects. So are Dremel or Dremel-type rotary tools, which are small high-speed tools with specialized chucks for holding small drill bits, sanding discs, router bits, sanding drums, and stones. These are particularly good for working on the small parts used in tackle-building. A wide range of accessories is available for Dremel tools, and several different models of Dremel tools are available.

DRILL PRESSES

Drill presses are stand-mounted drills. Most have a variety of speeds or different speed settings, and come with a 3/8-inch or larger chuck. Many are expensive and mounted on floor stands, but smaller, inexpensive tabletop styles are ideal for tackle-making.

As with band saws, the larger drill presses have a larger throat for taking larger chunks of mate-

Example of small drill press useful for tackle-crafting. This has had a drill-press vise added to hold parts securely — a must for serious drill-press work.

rial, but this is seldom a problem for the small-scale work of making tackle. If you use a drill press, be sure to get and use a drill-press vise that will mount to the work base and hold the work as a bench vise does. Several types and sizes are available, some will hold work at various angles, and some are relatively inexpensive.

There are also brackets designed to hold standard hand-operated electric drills, and these are fine for simple tasks. They are not as accurate or capable of repeat work as are the true drill presses. Similarly, there is a fine bracket that holds a Dremel tool, in effect making a miniature drill press out of it.

TWIST DRILL BITS

Twist drill bits are also needed, of course, usually in small sizes for drilling pilot holes and through-drilling plugs for hook hangers for salt-water fishing.

Twist drills come in several sizing configurations: Most come in fractional-inch sizes, ranging down to about 1/16-inch, sometimes to 1/64-inch. These are used by most home craftsmen, carpenters, and machinists. Letter sizes are used in the machine trades and are usually larger, ranging from A (small, .234-inch, or slightly smaller than 1/4-inchh) to Z (the largest at .413-inch, slightly less than 1/2-inch). Numbered drill bits, also used in the machine trades, range from 80 (the smallest, at .0135-inch, and smaller than 1/64-inch) to 1 (the largest at .228-inch, or slightly smaller than 1/4-inch). The most useful for tackle crafters will be the fractional sizes, because the precise sizes used for machining are seldom if ever required in making rods, lures, or tackle. The most useful sizes are usually between 1/32- and 1/8-inch.

For making plugs with through-wire construction, in which a wire runs through the length of the plug, you will need longer drill bits. (Wood and especially balsa plugs need through-wire construction to prevent the loss a strong or toothy fish in case the fish shatters the plug. The through-wire construction, in which all hooks are attached to the same wire or plate as the line tie, prevents fish loss. Most saltwater and muskie/pike plugs are made this way.)

Long drill bits are often called aircraft or electricians' bits, and unlike standard bits, in which the drill length varies by the drill size (diameter), they come in standard 6-inch and 12-inch lengths. In most cases, the 6-inch length is adequate for drilling end-to-end through a plug. The longer drill bits can be used but are more difficult to stabilize.

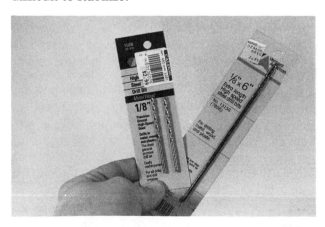

A longer drill bit (right) compared to standard bits (left) of the same diameter. The longer bits, sometimes called aircraft or electrician's bits, are available in many diameters and in 6-inch and 12-inch lengths.

PLIERS

Several types of pliers are needed, and these will be among your most useful tools. Large combination pliers (slip-joint or arc-joint pliers in which the pivot point is adjustable) can be used to hold lures during painting processes, while adding split rings and lips and hook hangers, and while drilling holes. Large-jaw pliers opened wide can be used to hold hot jig and sinker molds. In general, smaller pliers are better for most tackle-making jobs. The best is a pair of small round-nose pliers to form eyes in wire when making spinners, spinnerbaits, buzzbaits, some trolling rigs, and similar lures. These pliers come in various sizes, from about 4 1/2 inches and larger, and have round tapered jaws to allow any size eye to be formed in the wire.

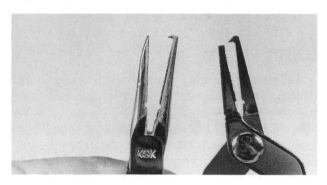

Split-ring pliers — to the left a precision plier, to the right an inexpensive pair. They have a small tooth on one jaw to open the split ring for adding hooks and parts. The author modified the pair on the left by grinding down the non-toothed jaw to work with small split rings.

Sometimes sets of pliers and wire cutters can be found in hardware, electronic, or hobby shops. Often these sets include four or five tools, such as tapered round-nose pliers, diagonal wire cutters, end-cutting wire cutters, long-nose pliers, and flat-nose pliers. All are very handy for the tackle tinkerer. If you do not get a set like this, it will still be necessary to have a pair of wire cutters in addition to the round-nose pliers listed above. Some sets or combinations include different types of pliers and cutters, including extra-long-nose pliers, bent-nose pliers, and wide-jaw pliers.

Of the cutters, diagonal wire cutters are best because they will cut closer to the spinner or lure body than will end-cutting cutters. Even with diagonal wire cutters, however, there are differences in the placement of the jaw's cutting edges. Some are shaped so that the edge of the jaw is flush with the pliers, to minimize tag ends. Others are made so that the edges of the jaws are inset slightly. The best are those with flush cutting jaws. Wire cutters are good not only for cutting excess wire in making spinners, but also for cutting lead from molded jigs and sinkers.

Cheap long-nose pliers are helpful in painting. With these, you can hold a lure by the lip, line tie, or wire and paint it by dipping or spraying. The advantage, particularly with spraying, is that you will not get your hands covered with paint. Use cheap pliers for this, since you are not concerned about precision or quality workmanship as long as the pliers hold well—and, of course, they will become covered with paint.

Compound-action parallel-closing pliers are useful for many purposes. Originally made under the Bernard Sportmate label, many brands are available today in several different sizes. They are ideal when holstered in a belt sheath for fishing (I would not be without a pair), but are also handy for much tackle-making. The parallel-acting jaws will hold nuts securely, and all these pliers have very strong wire cutters to cut wire, screw eyes, or even hook shanks. Although they are most useful when fishing, I also particularly like the Donnmar stainless steel fisherman's pliers and the lightweight FF-1 pliers by Sports Tools for many tackle-crafting needs.

Vise grips or locking pliers are particularly good for tackle-making. I like the Vise-Grip brand because they are sturdy and a number of different styles and sizes of pliers are available. Basically, this type of pliers locks when closed, and the locking tension is adjustable by means of screw. A simple lever unlocks the pliers to release the gripped object. For both fishing and tackle-making I particularly like small long-nose styles, which make it easy to grip small lures and parts.

Split-ring pliers are specialized pliers for opening split rings. They have a tapered flat jaw in combination with a second jaw that overlaps the first slightly and has a small tooth at the end by which split rings can be pried apart. The Worth Company makes these in an inexpensive flat model and two sizes of better-quality pliers. They are ideal for adding hooks to hook hangers via split rings or for replacing hooks on any lure.

Metal Snips

Snips for metalworking will be needed only if you plan to make your own spoons from sheet metal or cut sheet metal for spinner blades or

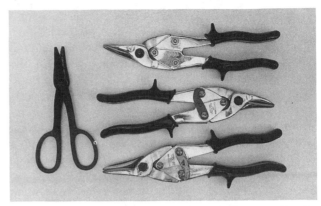

Sheet-metal snips. Left are duck-billed snips. To the right are three styles of aviation snips: right-cutting, left-cutting and straight-cutting. Some snips incorporate all three cuts in one tools.

accessories (metal tackle boxes or lure boxes, for instance). If the metal you plan to work with is thin (under 20-gauge), regular duckbill snips will work fine. Several sizes are available, with the smallest usually the cheapest and easiest to use for making lures.

For cutting heavier-gauge metal, for spoons and such, you will need the heavier leverage of aviation snips, sometimes called compound leverage snips. These snips, which usually have about a 12:1 power ratio or leverage advantage over regular snips, are available in both inexpensive and high-quality tools. The inexpensive are often designed as "all-in-one" tools, in which one snip will cut in any direction. The better-quality snips are made with specifically designed jaws to cut in a certain direction. Thus, of the high-quality snips you will need three, or a complete set: one each to cut straight, left, and right. Keep in mind that one of the all-purpose inexpensive snips will cost about a quarter of the price of one set of three better snips. As with the dead-blow hammers for forming spoon blades, these are not really economical unless you plan on cutting a large number of spoon blades.

Files

Several files will be needed for a variety of tackle-making operations. Coarse flat files are used for shaping spoons, roughing out wood plugs, filing points on gaffs, and similar tasks. Medium files give a smoother finish in these same operations and can also be used for the preliminary shaping of rod grips. Fine-tooth files are useful to remove the flash (excess lead) from molded jigs and bucktails, making and finishing molds, sharpening hooks, and filing down guide feet for a smooth fit on a rod blank. It also helps to have files in several configurations, including flat and half-round. The half-round files are perhaps the best because you get one flat side and one round side, which is good for shaping the concave parts of wood plugs and similar tasks.

Fine files are very handy for a variety of tackle tasks and often come in sets. I have a set of a dozen that includes flat, triangular, round, half-round, oval, knife, and other shapes. Often these are called needle-style or Swiss-style files. Some come with handles, others do not.

For making your own rods with cork handles, be sure to get a rat-tail file that can be used to ream out the holes in cork rings to fit the rod you are building exactly. (A good substitute for this, however, is a reamer.)

Wood rasps are good for initial rough work on cork rod grips and wood-plug bodies. One rasp, usually a half-round, is sufficient for most jobs. The best length for most files, with the exception of the small set of fine files, is about 8 to 10 inches. Smaller files are difficult to work with, larger ones just overpower the work and job.

If you plan to work extensively on tackle and to make your own lures and rods, you may want some special files and accessories. All-purpose files will do most jobs, but since they are not specifically designed for use on lead, aluminum, or brass, they tend to clog up quickly when used on these metals. For these, special open-tooth files are available that are designed to work with softer metals and not clog up.

Be sure to buy a file cleaner, often called a file card. These are small, flat cleaners that have very short, tempered metal bristles for cleaning particles from file teeth.

One additional file/rasp tool is used with an electric drill, but serves the purpose of a rasp or file. This is the rotary file and rasp that, when fitted onto the end of a bit extension, allows you to rasp out holes in foam grips. The small rotary bit fits into the extension, and this in turn fits into the drill.

Soldering Iron

A soldering iron will be helpful in making spoons and some specialized lures in which spoon and spinner blades are used. An electric soldering iron with a small tip, the type used in radio and electronics work, is best. Often small soldering irons like this come in kits with several tips, or

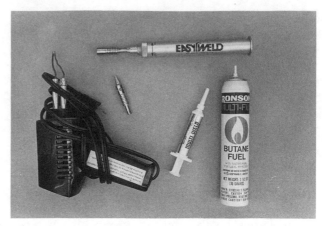

Examples of flame and gun soldering tools. The gun to the left has a fine tip for working with lures; the flame torch at top right fills with butane and provides a small flame for welding.

with optional tips for specific tasks available.

With a soldering iron, you can solder hooks to spoon blades, hooks to spinner blades to make small ice-fishing lures, and weight blades with solder to make a heavier lure or to change the action of a blade.

Pop-Style Riveter

Pop riveters, those that rivet from one side of a piece of material, are ideal for some tackle tasks. They allow you to rivet the eye of a hook into the hole drilled into a spoon to make a fixed-hook spoon. They can also be used for repairing reel seats in which the metal swaged hood becomes loose on the barrel, or for fastening together triple-wing buzzbait blades of your own design. Those that take the smallest-size rivets, with 1/8-inch shanks, are most useful.

Electric Grinder

Electric grinders are not required, but can be used to smooth and polish spoon blades, to sharpen tools, and to accomplish similar tasks. Most useful are the small hobbyist-size grinders with two wheels of about a 5- or 6-inch diameter.

Electric Sander

Electric sanders will do some of the same things electric grinders do. They will not easily sharpen many tools, but can be used for polishing and fine-shaping spoon blades, sanding wood plug bodies, and removing flash from molded-lead sinkers and jig heads. There are a number of types of bench sanders (the type you will want, if you get one) including belt and disc sanders. I like the belt sanders best because they allow sanding against the firm support of the flexible belt. Many of these hobby-type tools include both a belt and disc sander.

LATHE

Even inexpensive machine lathes are priced high for the use you get from them in tackle-building, but there are some specialized rod-building lathes on the market, along with small hobby woodworking lathes, that can be used for rod-building and lure-turning. When you are rod-building, a lathe is ideal for turning handles and grips, and even for rod-wrapping if it can be run at a very slow speed. For making lures, lathes are ideal for turning wood plugs. If you are considering one for turning handles for rods, remember that you must turn the handle and *then* glue it onto the rod, or get a lathe that has a through-center tail stock or a long-enough bed to allow you to place the entire rod blank into the lathe. The through-center tail stock will allow you to run the rod blank above the handle, through rollers or a centering bearing, to support the rod and keep

it from whipping around as the lathe turns the handle.

There are other lathe possibilities. One is a small Dremel Moto-Lathe that, while not large enough for rod work, is ideal for turning wood plugs. This model used to be widely available, but has recently been taken off the market. Some might still be available through secondhand shops or flea markets. The Dremel was available alone or in a kit with tools and accessories.

Small substitute lathes are also sometimes seen. One inexpensive possibility is a wood-turning attachment to be used with any hand electric drill. In essence, it is a bench-mounted clamp that holds the drill upside down but horizontal by means of a special bracket and large hose-type clamp, with a small bed and tail stock for holding the work. You can find this attachment in hardware stores, catalog hardware houses, and stores such as Sears and J. C. Penney. One in a current Sears catalog will hold work up to 16 inches long and 4 1/2 inches in diameter—ideal for turning handles separate from the rod and for turning any size wood plug.

WIRE FORMERS

Several types of wire formers are available.

Examples of two lathes for hobby and tackle-crafting work. The large lathe in the foreground was designed for rod work, the small Dremel lathe (now discontinued by the company) is ideal for turning a plug bodies.

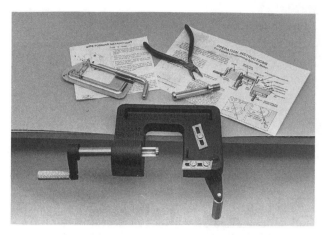

Several types of wire formers are available for making spinner and spinnerbait forms. The Cabela's tool in the foreground clamps to a workbench, is relatively expensive, and designed for heavy, continuous work. An extra, revolving shaft head is also shown. The wire-forming tool (left) from the Worth Company does simple tasks on light wire. The round-nose pliers to the right are also useful for most tasks. The two wire-forming tools come with instructions.

Some are small inexpensive tools that allow the forming of various types of eyes in most spinner and spinnerbait wires. They are great for the lure-maker who has trouble using pliers to make eyes or who does not want to use pliers. One model looks like a screwless C-clamp, and with a turn of the handle will make a variety of wire forms, eyes, and bends.

Larger, more expensive wire formers are bench-mounted and come with attachments or have accessories available for making eyes and bends in different-size wire. Different collets are available for different wire-size ranges. One such tool available from several mail-order companies (Hille, Cabela) is of sturdy cast iron, and will clamp to any table or workbench up to 1 3/4 inches thick by means of two screw clamps. With two handles working in opposite planes, it will make virtually any type of spinner or wire eye, bend, snell, or wire form. Collets available for this include those for wire from .018- through .025-inch, .026- through .029-inch, and 0.30-through .035-inch. Although relatively expensive, these tools are extremely versatile for any serious tackle-maker.

REAMERS

Reamers are available from any hardware store and will usuallly ream holes from 1/8- to 1/2-inch. They are ideal for enlarging the holes in cork rings to fit onto rod blanks. I like them better than rat-tail files because they are easier and quicker to use.

DIVIDERS

Dividers as used by carpenters are useful to transfer dimensions from one part of a piece of work to another. Thus, they are ideal for checking the dimensions of both sides of a wood plug, the length of a guide wrap on both sides of a rod guide, or the length of wire in a spinner. Straight dividers are ideal and much better for most tasks than inside or outside calipers.

RULE

A rule, or ruler, as this tool is commonly called, is necessary for measuring parts in lure- or rod-building. The best ones are those of plastic or metal with measurements in both inches and millimeters. Short, 6-inch rules are ideal for measuring lure parts; larger, 18- to 24-inch rules are better for measuring handles and guide spacing on rods. One small rule that is ideal for rod work has an "0 center" mark and inches or millimeters measured out from this center point. These rules are made by the C-Thru Ruler Company and are ideal to mark the center position of a taped-down guide to assure that the guide wraps on both feet are of equal length. They are available at stationery and drafting-supply stores.

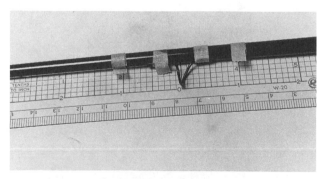

One type of rule that is ideal for tackle building, since it has a center "0" that makes it easy to mark the center of the guide ring and to indicate identical marks for beginning wraps.

Two types of small hobby anvils for swaging lures, hammering scale marks on spoons, etc.

ANVIL

If you are planning to make a number of spoons from scratch, a small anvil will be handy. Several sizes are available in hardware and hobby stores. Get one that has a horn at one end for working with odd shapes.

GATE CUTTER

Although called a "gate cutter" by companies such as Do-It and Hilts Molds, these are really specialized cutters for stripping wire. As a gate cutter used for removing the sprue from lead castings, they should be used only for lead or plastic and for not the heavy hard wire used in fishing.

LEADER-CRIMPING PLIERS

These are specialty pliers that are used to close the leader sleeves used in rigging heavy leaders, big-game leaders, and similar rigs requiring leader

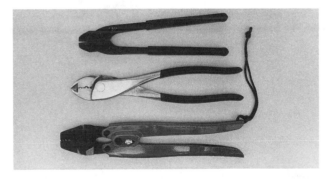

Pliers designed to crimp leader sleeves. At bottom is the cup-opposing-cup style, at center an example of the point-opposing-cup style. Each takes a different type of sleeve.

sleeves. Several types are available. One type is the cup-opposing-cup style, used for crimping oval sleeves. The point-opposing-cup style is designed for working with round sleeves only. Each style of crimping pliers *must* be used with the correct style of sleeve, otherwise the sleeves can be damaged, and the crimp made poor and weak.

These pliers come in a number of different styles, including small hand pliers for simple crimping operations, or larger, compound-action pliers that are preset for a given force for a certain style of sleeve: This type is best when working with large sleeves such as are used for the heavy leaders and riggings for offshore big-game fishing. They are the type preferred for crimping and making 250- to 400-pound test leaders of wire or mono for billfish and such.

FLY-TYING TOOLS

Special fly-tying tools are available and very useful for some aspects of tackle-building. A fly-tying vise is a must for bucktails, other types of tied tails on spinnerbaits and buzzbaits (though these are an exception to the slip-on tails usually used), fur and feather tails tied on spinner hooks, and other tied tails for various lures. Other accessories used in fly tying are useful as well.

FLY-TYING VISE

Fly-tying vises are designed to hold a hook, on which various materials are tied. Vises are commonly used in all aspects of fly tying but are also very useful for trying bucktails and dressed hooks for spinners and plugs. The cost of a vise ranges from very inexpensive to several hundred dollars. The simple inexpensive ones work fine for tackle-building.

Be sure you get a vise with jaws that will open wide enough to hold the largest hook on which you wish to tie materials. Some vises have separate jaws for different hooks, while others advertise that they will securely hold any hook from a size 28 through a 5/0. Failure to use a vise with jaws that will hold the large-sized hooks can result in sprung jaws, a broken vise, and insecure clamping of the hook.

Most vises are available on either a pedestal base or a clamp base. The pedestal bases are ideal if you are going to move around the house — tying bucktails on the basement workbench, on a TV table in the family room, on an office desk, or on any surface to which you cannot clamp or do not wish to scar.

The clamp-on vises are sturdier and as a result of the adjustable clamp do allow up and down adjustment of the vise head for more comfortable tying.

OTHER FLY-TYING ACCESSORIES

An entire mini-industry has been built around the various types of fly-tying vises and fly-tying tools and accessories. Although these are most useful for true fly tying and are less necessary for the more basic bucktails and hook tying, they are still handy to have. Some accessories to consider include:

Bobbin holders. These are small arms that are usually attached to the vise post and hold the thread on a bobbin out of the way. They are useful for holding the thread clear while winding hackle when tying dry flies or palmered-hackle bodies.

Bobbins. Any fly or bucktail can be tied using thread cut from a spool, but a bobbin that holds and guides the thread makes tying easier, allows more precise thread work, reduces thread waste, creates constant thread tension, and causes less fatigue. Many companies make bobbins in various styles (metal and nongrooving ceramic tips), in different sizes for different spools (Gudebrod makes two bobbin sizes), and in different tubing lengths. If you are serious about bobbins, it helps to have one for each thread color or thread size you use.

Bodkins. Bodkins are nothing more than a metal point on a handle and are used for picking out thread and adding head cement to a wrap to secure it. They are handy for many tackle tasks and are easy to make (See Chapter 2).

Half-hitch tools. To finish off any wrap, you must use a half-hitch or whip-finish. Special tools are available to make these tasks easier. Half-hitch tools are usually double-ended, with a different head on each end to fit different hooks. They can only be used on the heads of hooks in back of the eye and will not work on any wrap in which you have to bring the thread over part of the lure or jig, as with bucktail heads. For this, you must use a freehand half-hitch finish.

Whip-finisher. Whip-finishers are more complex to use and require some practice, but they allow a tier to finish a wrap with a whip-finish. As with half-hitch tools, they can only be used on a wrap that is finished on the hook shank just in back of

the hook eye. They cannot be easily used with lead heads or other lures.

Hackle pliers. These are small, spring-operated clamps that hold hackle for winding around a hook shank. They are useful for wrapping hackle on some special jigs such as crappie flies (really jigs) and similar hackled jig heads. Several styles and sizes are available.

Details on all these tools can be found in the many books available on fly tying, and purchase is easy through any fly-fishing shop or through the many mail-order catalogs that vater to fly tiers. Some of the mail-order companies listed in Appendices F and G include fly-tying tools and materials; other sources can be found through the various fly-fishing magazines, such as *Fly Fisherman, American Angler, Fly Rod and Reel, Salt Water Fly Fishing,* and *Trout.*

There are also special tools made exclusively for rod-building, which usually are only available from tackle shops or mail-order component-parts outlets.

ROD-WRAPPING TOOLS

These are available in both manual and electric models. The manual models range from simple wood racks with notches at each end to hold the rod and a thread tension device attached to the base, to more sophisticated tools of aluminium or with special attachments or features for wrapping or other rod-building tasks. Some locally made

Small rod-wrapping tools are available from many suppliers. This example—from Flex Coat—contains felt-protected "V" blocks and sewing-machine-style tension devices. An extension for long blanks is also shown.

house brands are available from tackle shops and mail-order companies, and D. H. Thompson and Netcraft both have simple clamp-on rod-wrapping tools available.

Electric models usually include a power supply, a built-in chuck to hold the rod, and a base with one or several additional rod supports; the device is controlled by a foot-pedal rheostat control for adjustment of thread-wrapping speed. Often the base is on a rack that will slide back and forth, enabling the rod-builder to sit in one spot and wrap, sliding the rod and motor base along the rack as needed to wrap each guide.

Some simple manual rod winders are inexpensive, while some of the variable-speed, aluminum-base, aluminum-chuck, roller-rod-support machines are very expensive. Some of these come with optional slow-rpm curing motors. Details on any of

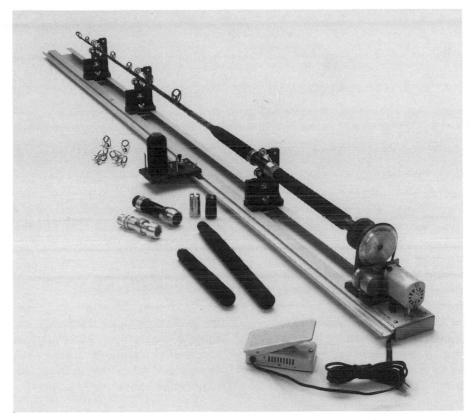

Many companies make power wrappers that are controlled by a foot pedal and turn a blank on rollers for fast, easy wrapping. This one is by Pacific Bay.

Another example of a power rod wrapper, with foot pedal. This one by Flex Coat has felt-covered "V" blocks for the blank.

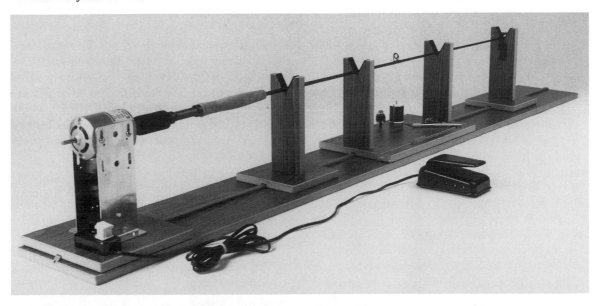

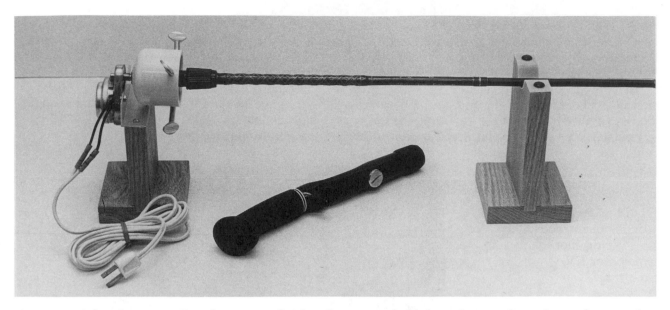

A commercial curing motor that, by means of a thumb screw to hold the rod, turns the rod at a slow speed to prevent sagging of the finish.

these can be found in catalogs, although you can also make your own simple machines, as noted in Chapter 2.

In considering any of these, get as many catalogs as you can and examine features and prices to determine the features you want and what you can afford.

One important feature with manual machines is the ability to adjust the position of the thread tension device and one-end rod support. It also helps to be able to get an additional single rod support for working with long blanks or one-piece blanks. However, you can make your own additional support or jury-rig a support if necessary. These adjustments, however, make it possible not only to wrap any guide, but also to do the small decorative wrap on the end of a tip-top or the combination decorative/hoop-strength wrap required for self-ferrules.

For electric models, make sure the motor has a secure chuck, either a thumb screw or a self-centering chuck, so that you can hold any rod. If working with complete rods in which the handle has been attached, there is an advantage to working with thumb screws or a nonself-centering chuck: This will allow you to mount rods in the chuck that have an offset angle (some trigger-style rods), as well as any of the pistol-grip-handle rods. If working on long rods such as one-piece or long two-piece surf sticks, you may need extension base sections to hold the whole rod and to allow wrapping guides at one end. If this is a possibility,

consider the length of the base when buying the machine and explore the possibility of obtaining extra extensions if needed.

THREAD TENSION DEVICES

These are available as separate items from most parts outlets. They are usually the thread tension device used in sewing machines, adapted for thread-wrapping. These can be bought at sewing and fabric stores in addition to tackle and mail-order houses.

CURING MOTOR

Curing motors are a necessity for building rods today because all of the best finishes are thick epoxy or polyurethane, which require constant slow rotation once applied to the blank to prevent the finish from sagging and dripping. For these, a curing motor is a must.

Curing motors come either DC- (battery operated, either one or two D or C cells) or AC-operated. Motors typically range from about 4 to 10 rpm, although a slightly slower or faster speed also works. All include some form of chuck to hold the rod. Chuck variations include simple rubber butt caps that can be fitted onto the motor and adjusted to any rod, a simple three-jaw chuck of thumb screws, or self-centering chucks of rubber or aluminum (these are most like a lathe chuck). Some chucks are nothing more than a heavy rubber membrane stretched over a rotating cup, and the rod or rod blank is mounted in a hole in the center of the membrane. This thick membrane, almost like a automobile tire tube, holds the rod securely enough for the slow rotation.

These tools usually come with, or have as an option, a support for the other end of the rod. The best are those that are AC-operated.

HANDLE SEATER

Handle seaters are easy to make (see Chapter 2), but are also available from some tackle shops and component houses. In essence it is a board with one or more holes, by which a synthetic (Hypalon or EVA) grip can be pushed into place on a blank.

TAPERED REAMER

These are long reamers with a grit finish for tapering cork grips and rings. Most are about 18 inches long and come in several size grits.

TIP-TOP GAUGE

Gauges are available from tackle shops and component-parts houses. The only one that I know of is made by Mildrum and consists of a small plastic rule with assorted holes and nubs that make it possible to measure both tip-top (the end guide on a tube) and rod-blank-tip sizes from 4/64 through 32/64. In the sizes indicated, it can also measure metal ferrules.

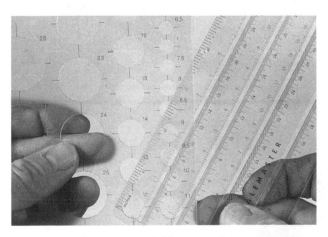

Various scales are available to make rod-wrapping thread designs easy. These are two scales used for lining up decorative butt wraps on rods. The circle template is used to line up decorative wraps on the rod; the straight scales to measure for those wraps.

BURNISHER

This is a small tool, usually plastic, to help smooth guide wraps and to close or prevent any gaps in the thread. Good substitutes include plastic-barrel ballpoint pens or similar devices.

TORCH

Small alcohol or butane torches are available and useful in removing bubbles from thread-wrap finishes by the application of quick heat. They are also helpful in removing and replacing tip-tops. In addition, small butane torches are available for welding and soldering operations, such as fastening hooks to small ice-fishing blades or larger spoons. Some of these torches, such as the butane Micro Flame Torch & Soldering Iron, made by Tri-Peek International, Inc., are designed specifically for small-flame hobby work and are ideal for tackle-crafting purposes. The torch is easily filled from butane fuel injectors and comes with flame and soldering tips. Solder, such as the Tri-Peek Aluminum Weld and their Multi-Weld (for soldering everything but aluminium, magnesium, and pot metal) is available for these tools.

ALCOHOL LAMP

An alcohol lamp is very useful for wrapping rods. The side of the flame can be used for singing the thread wrap to remove any small fuzzy areas, and to make finishing easier. These lamps are also useful to heat a tip-top before attaching it to a rod tip with a heat-set cement or one of the several ferrule cements made for this purpose.

A particularly nice one is a needle sterilizer.

SCALPEL

This, along with its disposable replacement blades, is ideal for cutting excess thread in rod-wrapping. If you have a choice in blades, choose the #11, which is sharply pointed and has a flat cutting edge, ideal for tackle-craft and rod work.

DIAMOND WRAP TOOLS

These are available to help in making and laying out diamond, chevron, and other decorative wraps. The tools consist of templates that allow the positioning of diamond or chevron marking points on four sides of a rod (such as in the Diamond Master from Pierson's Tackle Crafters), along with right-angle gauges for checking the initial crossing threads after the first wrap is laid down.

MASKING TAPE

Masking tape in 1/8-, 1/4-, 3/8-, and 1/2-inch thicknesses is available from some tackle-parts catalogs, art stores, hobby shops, automotive supply shops (where it is used for pin-striping), and stationery stores. It is ideal for determining and laying out the guide spacing on rods and for masking fine parts of lures for painting. The 1/8-inch size is best for holding guides while rod-wrapping; the 1/2-inch size is best for masking lures for painting.

SAFETY EQUIPMENT

Basic safety equipment is a must for safe tackle-building, especially when power tools are used or when lead is molded. Drilling, sawing, grinding, sanding, and lathe operations frequently throw off small bits of wood and metal and dust. To prevent injury to your eyes, wear safety goggles during these and all other shop and tackle-making operations. This is especially important when cutting spinner wire, drilling, cutting and making spinner blades and wire riggings, and making and hammering spoon blades. Safety goggles are inexpensive and good insurance.

A shop apron is also handy for all workshop tasks — from painting to molding lead bucktails to working with power tools. Pick a good long apron that will protect you and your clothes.

When molding bucktails and sinkers, wear heavy gloves to prevent burns. Either heavy work gloves or, preferably, welders' gloves, should be worn. If you carefully follow the directions on molding with lead, you will seldom if ever have a problem or spill. In thirty years of tackle-making and molding sinkers and bucktails, I have never had a serious spill. Even if such a spill occurred, it is unlikely that it would spill on your hands, but the added protection of gloves is definitely worthwhile. In addition, when working to make lots of lures, the ladles, pots, and molds will become hot. Gloves make handling these items easy and comfortable.

Since spray painting is used for finishing many lures, it is worthwhile to invest in a small breathing mask fitted with removable, replaceable filters. (Most of the excess spray paint can be trapped by using a "paint box," as outlined in Chapter 15.) It is also handy to have some disposable rubber or plastic gloves on hand. These make it easy to paint without having to clean up afterwards. The disposable gloves are sturdy enough for painting and can be thrown out after use.

It is also important to have adequate ventilation, preferably an exhaust fan. These precautions and suggestions concerning ventilation and

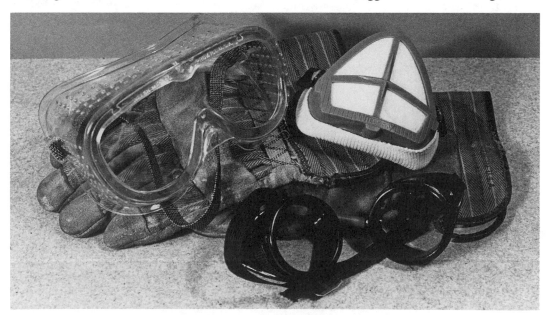

Safety equipment is very important in tackle crafting. The heavy gloves are useful for holding molds and ladles when pouring sinkers and bucktails; the face mask for painting and the goggles for most shop and hobby operations for eye protection.

the use of a breathing mask are just as important for molding lead lures and sinkers and molding soft plastics as they are for painting. See the chapters on these lures for specific suggestions.

The important thing is to use any and all safety equipment possible. This means not only the above equipment, but any other you learn about. Equally important is common sense in using power tools. Basically, this means removing any jewelry, ties, loose sweaters, or loose jackets, rolling up your sleeves, and wearing a work apron. This will prevent any jewelry or clothing from becoming caught in power tools with damaging or tragic results. When using a power tool, be sure to read, understand, and follow the directions and safety rules for that tool. The general suggestions and ideas on the use of power tools here and in subsequent chapters are in addition to — not in place of — the basic operations and safety information supplied by individual manufacturers, suppliers, and dealers.

Remember that you do not need all of the equipment mentioned — or most of it — to make much of your own tackle. (The one exception is safety equipment). The discussion above is meant as a comprehensive overview of the tools you might want to consider using, if you already have them on hand, or buying, if you get heavily into one type of tackle-making where these tools can save time and, eventually, money.

There are substitutes for some of these tools that amount to almost no-cost replacements. These are covered in the next chapter, along with directions for the construction of some specialized tools for rod- and tackle-making that you cannot find.

2

Substitute Tools and Tools to Make

INTRODUCTION ▪ SMALL VISE OR FLY-TYING VISE ▪
WIRE FORMER ▪ PIGTAIL WIRE FORMER ▪ ANVIL ▪ METAL
FINISHING STAMPS ▪ BOBBIN ▪ ROD WRAPPERS ▪
ROD-HANDLE GLUING CLAMP ▪ CORK HANDLE REAMERS ▪
CURING MOTOR ▪ BURNISHER ▪ HANDLE SEATER ▪
DECORATIVE-WRAP LAY-OUT TOOLS ▪
DECORATIVE-WRAP-ALIGNMENT CHECKER ▪ WRAP
FINISHER ▪ TENSION HOLDER

INTRODUCTION

A friend of mine who was active in fly-tying and teaching fly-tying to kids, related the story of a small boy who wanted to learn to tie but did not have the money for a vise. In class he was all right because vises were provided, but at home he had a problem. His imaginative solution was to take two large washers, thread a large screw through them, and secure the screw into a scrap of wood. When fastened tightly, the two washers would hold a fly-tying hook securely. When the screw was loosened with a screwdriver, the finished fly could be removed and a new hook added. Presto —a practical, no-frills fly-tying vise, one that could be used for fly-tying or securing jig heads for tying on tail material.

While few of us experience such limited means, there are ways to cut costs and make do without buying every tool in sight. Some suggestions follow.

SMALL VISE OR FLY-TYING VISE

One possibility for a simple vise is to use locking pliers (Vise-Grips) for holding jig heads for tying, spoons for drilling holes, and similar vise work. Clamp the pliers or Vise-Grips into a regular bench vise to secure them. In addition, there are locking pliers that have a C-clamp type of arrangment built into the handles so that the tool can be clamped onto a table or workbench and used to hold tackle parts.

WIRE FORMER

One way to make a wire former to form eyes of all types in wire of all sizes does not even require round-nose pliers. Hammer a nail or two into a block of wood and cut the head off the nail with a hacksaw. File the cut smooth and remove any burrs. Removing the head of the nail allows you to remove a wire eye once you form it. Since the nail will determine the size of the eye, you can make different formers for different-size eyes, as needed. You can also make such wire formers with several nails in several positions for specific wire-forming tasks. The best method for making these is to hammer two nails into a block of wood with only a space to accommodate the thickness of the wire separating them. That way the shafts of the two nails will hold the end of the wire in place while you wrap the wire around one of the nail shafts to form an eye.

To make this handy tool, choose a nail for the eye size you desire and hammer it into a block of wood. (Scraps of end-grain two-by-fours or two-by-sixes are ideal for this.) Saw off the head. Then place the wire next to the hammered-in nail, place another nail close to the wire so that the space between the two heads is just large enough for the chosen wire size. Hammer this second nail straight into the wood and remove its head. The

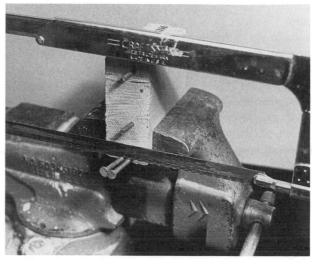

Sawing the nails off to complete the wire former. These are custom-made for each type of wire form.

second nail provides a leverage point for bending the wire around the main nail. Also, when you are forming a wrapped eye, it allows you to make the shoulder bends that are necessary to form the eye on center with the wire shaft.

This style of wire former is also ideal for making bends in larger wire, such as household or hobby copper or brass wire, for through-wire hook hangers for use in saltwater or balsa plugs, for making hook lears for saltwater bottom rigs, and for making large eyes for sinkers and tin squids.

To make a wire former to form simple eyes with larger wire, you will need two nails hammered in side by side, as above. To make simple "omega"-shape wire eyes for squids and sinkers, you will need three nails hammered in a V shape so that the central nail can be used to form the eye and the two side nails used to form the flare that will hold the eye in the sinker/squid.

To make a longer figure-eight shape for sinkers or squids, you will need five or six nails hammered in a larger V for the additional bends in the wire. Spaced-out nails can be used to make similar bends in combination with other eyes on the wire, as in making the additional necessary eyes for hook lears in bottom rigs. (A hook lear is a wire or plastic form used to offset a snelled hook from the main line of a bottom rig so that it will not tangle and will present the bait better.)

As you make these wire-formers, other combinations of bends and wire rigs will come to mind. In cutting off the nail heads, remember that shorter nail lengths are best, because leverage that will weaken the nail positions will increase as the

Nails hammered in the end grain of a block of wood make for easy-to-construct wire formers for making sinker eyes, hook lears, bottom spreaders, and similar heavy wire rigs. The nail heads are sawed off to allow removal of the wire, once formed.

wire is bent higher above the wood base. Also, consider making some nails longer or shorter than others to facilitate the working and bending of the wire around the nails. Both common and finishing nails will work for this, although the common nails are usually heavier (thicker) in a given length and size. Special nonbending hardened nails, such as are used for concrete work, are also good for this purpose, although most are not smooth (rough or fluted finishes are common), making it more difficult to remove the finished wire rigs and eyes. Because these nails are hardened, it is also more difficult to cut off the heads.

PIGTAIL WIRE FORMER

A pigtail swivel functions just like a snap swivel except that in place of the snap there is a pigtail-wrapping of wire. Thus, any attachment to it is made by threading along the pigtail — like an open spring — to hold the lure or hook or to place the swivel as a slide swivel on a line for a fish-finder rig.

The tool to make this is a simple one. You will need wire former to make an eye in which the ends of the wire cross at right angles. Then one end of the wire is held straight while the other end is wrapped in an open-spring wrap. The tool for this consists of a steel or aluminum rod about 1/4- to 3/8-inch in diameter, though you can make any size you wish. (You can even make it of wood.) Drill a hole straight through the center of the rod, then cut out half of the rod about 3/4 to 1 inch from one end. The result is a round rod, flat at one end, with a hole straight through it.

To make the pigtail former, the appropriate diameter of metal rod is center-drilled and then sawed longitudinally in half, as shown here.

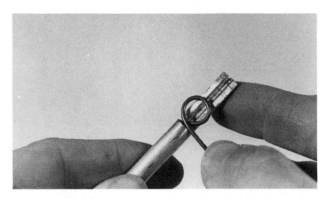

Once the eye is completed, the shaft is inserted into the hole through the pigtail former and the wire bent around the main part of the rod. As a result, this eye must be formed before any changes are made to the other end of the wire.

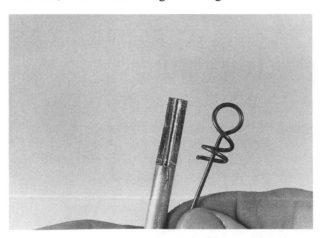

Pigtail wire former and the resultant eye (here shown in larger-than-normal size for clarity). The pigtail eye allows for addition or removal of rigs without opening and closing snaps.

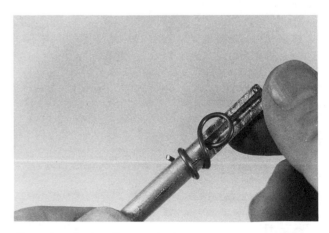

Completed pigtail wire before being removed from the wire former.

The pigtail end is then made in any wire rigging by sliding one end of the wire into the hole, holding the open eye flat on the flattened area of the rod and up against the shoulder, then wrapping the rest of the wire around the round portion of the rod to form the open pigtail. Remove the wire from the tool, cut off any excess, and finish by using a standard wire former to make a closed eye, adding a swivel (if desired) as you do so.

Anvil

An anvil is helpful in forming spoon and spinner-blade blanks. Since anvils that are sold commercially seldom have the shapes you need to hammer into the spoon blade, you are often better off making your own shaping form from a wood block. Hard wood is best, although soft wood like pine will also work. (Soft wood will not last as long, however.) To make a wood form, first determine the shape you want in a spoon blade and use a chisel or gouge to cut this shape into the block. Usually you will want to cut it slightly deeper than the curve you want because the spoon metal will have some bounce to it. Once you get the rough shape, you may wish to smooth it using a router, ball-head stone, or file bit in a drill or Dremel Moto-Tool.

If you don't have the tools for cutting out a round, smooth shape, you may be able to hammer it, using a regular carpenters' or ball-peen hammer. Lacking this, you can use an old teaspoon or tablespoon, repeatedly heating it to red hot and burning it into the wood to create a depression. Routers and rotary files for electric drills and drill presses also work well for this. You may wish to make several depressions for different spoon sizes and shapes.

To make hammered finishes on the convex side of a spoon blade, you need a raised area on which to hold the spoon while you work with a chisel or stamping device. To hammer stampings while holding the spoon on a flat surface or iron anvil would only tend to flatten it. To make a round end on which to hold a spoon for this (like a horn on an anvil), you can use several sizes of wood dowel: Round off the end with a grinder, sander, or wood rasp, and glue the dowel into a hole of the same size on your wood-block anvil. The dowel should only be raised about 1/2- to 1 inch above the flat surface of the block. An electric drill or brace and bit will drill these holes easily. Half-inch, 3/4-inch, 1-inch, and 1 1/2-inch dowels

Using a grinding stone to cut depressions into a block of wood to serve as templates for hammering spoons.

are ideal sizes for this purpose.

Another possibility is to use a wood darning egg (the kind used to darn socks and available at sewing supply stores). Cut the egg into several parts that can be glued onto the anvil or fitted on a short length of dowel that is glued to the anvil.

Metal Finishing Stamps

In addition to using the nail sets and various commercial punches described in Chapter 8, you can make your own stamps to obtain certain finishes or markings. Use short lengths of steel rod in 1/8-, 1/4-, and 3/8-inch diameters, or hardened nails. File the ends into different shapes. These shapes can include sharp or blunt chisel ends, curves (to simulate fish scales), dots,

Stamping tools can be made from nails and other steel rods. These allow stamping of markings into metal blades.

Xs, and +'s. First file the rod or nail to a flat blunt end, then use a file or grinder to remove excess material to get the shape you want. The stamps are used exactly as are punches and nail sets (described in Chapter 8) to make markings on metal.

BOBBIN

Bobbins are used to hold thread for fly-tying and jig-making, in the latter to tie tails onto the bucktail and jig heads. Both types of bobbins are really the same and are used for the same basic purpose. We'll consider the bobbin a tool in this section.

To make a bobbin from coat-hanger wire, cut

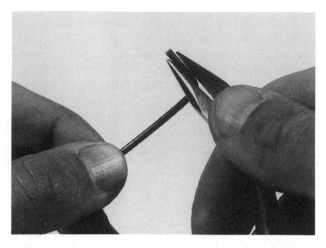

First bend made in coat-hanger wire.

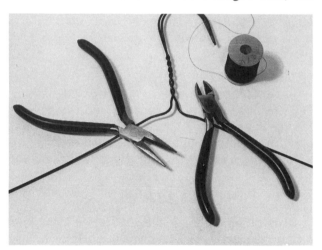

Tools and materials required for making a simple bobbin with which to wrap tail materials on bucktail bodies and treble hooks.

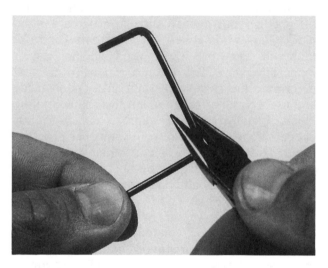

Second bend made in coat-hanger wire.

the hook from the wire with wire cutters. (Compound-action wire cutters are best for this heavy wire.) Straighten the wire. Next, make a right-angle bend about 1/2-inch from one end. Then make a second right-angled bend (to form a J shape) about 1 1/2 to 2 inches from the first. Consider the width of the spool to be placed in the bobbin and make a loop in the wire with pliers so that the loop centers on about one-half the width of the spool. Cut the end of the wire. To determine the spot to cut, measure the length of the wire from the center of the loop to the end of the wire at the bend. For example, if you make the first bend 1/2-inch from the end of the wire, the second bend 2 inches from the first bend, and there is 3/4-inch of wire from the second bend to the loop, add these figures together to make the cut 3 1/4 inches from the loop.

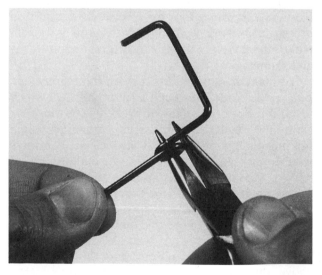

Loop in wire is made for the thread to run through while winding thread.

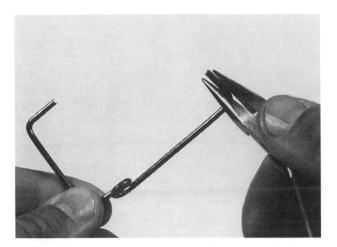

Third bend in wire.

Completed bobbin with thread through loop.

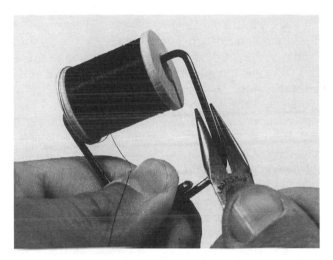

Fourth bend in the wire is made with the spool in place. The tension on the spool is adjusted by the degree of bend in the wire.

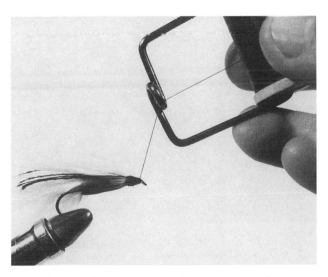

Completed bobbin being used to wrap thread.

To complete the bobbin, make a right-angle bend 1/2-inch from the end of the wire and a final bend two inches from the first. In completing this bend, place the spool of thread into the two open end posts and sharply angle the final bend to create tension on the side of the spool. Tension can easily be adjusted in this way.

A modification of this can be done by making additional bends from the center point to make an extended loop arm for more control of the thread. These extended arms can be twisted to keep them from opening or left parallel so that a rubber band can be used to help control tension on the thread spool.

Another type of bobbin that is ideal for wrapping jigs and bucktails was developed by angler Keith Walters of Bozman, Maryland. Keith used lamp parts and strap iron to make a simple but effective bobbin. To make one, Keith suggests using the heavy strap iron made for hanging radios in cars and trucks. Bend the strap iron into a C shape, with the top and bottom of the C just wide enough to bracket the spool of thread. Midway between these two parallel straps, drill a hole that is large enough to accommodate a short length (3 to 5 inches) of the threaded tubing used for lamp fixtures. Fasten one end of the threaded tubing into the hole in the bracket, using a nut on one side of the bracket to hold the threaded rod, a pull-chain finial nut on the other. Add another pull-chain finial nut to the other end of the tubing. This smooth end, normally used for a pull-cord or chain in a lamp, protects the thread on both ends of the tubing. To hold the thread spool in place, use a bolt and nut or wing nut.

ROD WRAPPERS

There are dozens of types and variations of tools for wrapping guides on rods. They range from the simple to the highly complex — and expensive. The simple methods and tools are best for those who will make just one or two rods or repair a guide or two. Good basic manual or electric rod wrappers are ideal for the serious rod-builder, while those who are into custom rod-building as a part-time business or for a tackle shop or fishing club can go with the expensive multipurpose wrappers. Some ideas include:

One easy, no-cost way to wrap rods involves only a teacup, a telephone book or books, and two sheets of clean typing paper. Work at a kitchen or card table and place the rod-wrapping thread in the cup or a bowl. This will keep it from rolling around on the table or off onto the floor. Next, run the thread through a phone book, using a sheet of clean typing paper over each of the opposing pages to prevent the thread from becoming soiled by the inks. Tension is controlled by how deeply the thread is run through the book or by how many additional books are placed on top of the book holding the thread. Hold the rod and wrap it by rotating it in your hands, pulling the thread through the book. The disadvantage of this method is that the thread is not visible where it begins to lay down on the rod, making gaps or errors more likely than with some other methods.

An alternative to the above is to locate a comfortable open-back chair, place the teacup behind the chair, run the wrapping thread between two sheets of typing paper on the chair seat, and sit on it. Wrap the rod by turning it in your hands, and control the thread tension by shifting your weight. An alternative to this is to run the thread between clean sheets of paper placed in the center of a telephone book, which is placed on the floor with the thread running under the chair legs and up in front of you.

For either of the above methods, it is possible to make a support for the rod so that you do not grow tired holding it in midair. There are several possibilities for this, all without cost. One is to obtain a long corrugated-cardboard box, cut out most (but not all) of the front and back, and cut a deep V notch in each end. The notch will hold the rod while you turn it, and the open front allows room for your hands. If you are working from the teacup on a table, you will need a slot or gap in the back of the box for passage of the thread. Note that you can't cut the front or back out completely, because this would eliminate support for the ends holding the rod. You must also leave some support at the corners.

Another method is to use a length of coat hanger bent into a lowercase "h" shape and the two parallel arms bent to clamp tightly onto a work bench or table. The other end — the upper part of the h — can be curved or bent into a shallow V to hold the rod. Two of these tools — one on each side of you — will be needed.

For a more permanent but still dirt-cheap rod-wrapping tool, use a scrap piece of wood shelving cut into three pieces: two short ones of the same length and one longer. Fasten the two short pieces to the long piece, which should be 18 to 24 inches long. Before nailing or screwing the ends on the base, cut a sharp V notch into the top end of each to hold the rod.

To keep the rough wood from scratching a fine blank, you must add a protective surface to these V cuts. One possibility is to use protective self-adhesive felt, available from craft and hobby stores, and cut it into strips to cover the V's. I like using smooth plastic: Use any thin plastic from a flat food container (I use one-gallon milk containers, but other containers work just as well), cut strips the width of the V's, and tack the strips in place. Make sure that the tacks are high on the V so that they will not touch the rod blank. These plastic strips are very smooth, and in years of using them, I have never scratched a blank. If you use felt, check periodically for wear and replace when necessary.

A fancier alternative is to use rollers for the rod. You can use simple 2-inch-diameter casters, sometimes called tray casters. These come on a

"V" cuts in the upright supports used to support a rod. Such supports, mounted on a base, can support a rod when using a curing motor. The plastic strips prevent scratches in the rod blank.

short post so that they can be easily mounted on top of any board or on a block that in turn can be mounted on a 3/8-inch aluminum rod (available from the do-it-yourself aluminum section of hardware stores), then mounted in a standard clamp-on fly-tying base. This allows vertical adjustment of the rollers, and the rollers will turn to prevent scratching of the rod. If the bases are mounted as closely as possible, most brands of casters will end up with about 1/8-inch clearance between the two rollers. Since the rollers are plastic and are injection-molded with a seam line down the center, I like to sand the seam off with sandpaper and then cover the rollers with narrow masking tape (1/4-inch, available at art supply stores or some tackle parts mail-order houses). The masking tape provides a soft base and also some tooth to keep the rollers turning as you turn the rod, at the same time protecting the rod from the hard-plastic seam line.

The wood bases by their length only allow support of the rod at predetermined places, so there is a possibility that you might have to wrap a guide in such a position that a previous guide will interfere with turning the rod because it will hit at the notch. (Naturally, the clamp-type supports with the rollers can be positioned anywhere on a table edge.) There are many solutions to this. The first is to make one end movable with two 1/2-inch-long dowels glued into its bottom, to fit into a series of matching holes drilled into the base at various positions.

Another possibility is to make a base with two strips of wood with a slot in between that will take an L-shaped wood end. A bolt and washer/wing nut through the base of the L will hold the end support at any desired position. Simpler but similar is a plain wood base with an L-shaped support end that can be clamped with a C-clamp to a workbench. Two of these will allow any type of rod and support positioning. Naturally, with any of these systems, measurements have to be adjusted so that both ends are level with the base. This allows wrapping on a horizontal plane. If one end is not adjusted properly, rods with a steep taper might be difficult to wrap. In all cases, only one end needs to be adjustable or movable.

There are several ways to make a tension device for this tool. One is to mount a screw eye into the central base and run thread on a bobbin though the eye. The screw eye will hold the thread in place and the bobbin will create the tension. Another possibility is to acquire a thread tension device made for sewing machines, available from

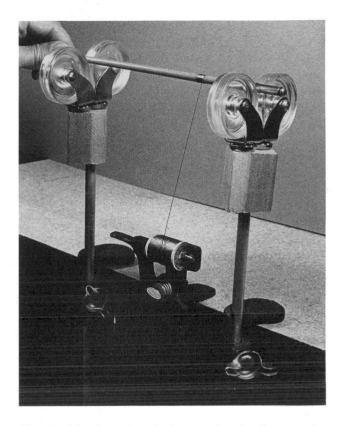

Simple thread-tension devices and rod rollers can be easily made. Here, fly-tying clamps are used to support 3/8-inch rod, which in turn holds short wood blocks into which are mounted plastic chair rollers. While not shown, it is best to wrap the rollers with two layers of masking tape to protect the rod and for grip for easy rolling. The thread-tension devise is a standard commercial style that also clamps to the work table.

sewing and fabric outlets. A third possibility is to mount a flat head machine bolt from underneath the base (drill a hole) and mount the spool on the bolt, adjusting tension with a compression spring, available at hardware stores, between two washers and fastened securely with a wing nut or double locking nuts. The best fasteners are the lock nuts that have a small nub of plastic or rubber in the threads that will allow the nut to be turned, but will lock it in place to prevent slight movements. Lacking this, you may find periodic adjustment necessary to maintain tension, because the turning thread will tend to tighten or loosen the tension, depending upon the relation of the turning spool to the thread direction.

Another possibility for a tension device that I like best, even though it requires mounting the tool over the edge of the table and clamping it in

Homemade thread-tension device for wrapping rods. Made of extruded aluminum, this will clamp to any table. The thread tension is adjusted from underneath using eye bolts, springs, and wingnuts. It will hold any size thread spool. Similar devices can be made from wood shelving.

place, involves the use of two 3-inch eye bolts, two compression springs, two washers, two wing nuts, and one thin rod or 4-inch shoulder bolt and wing nut. To make this tool, drill two holes 3 inches apart in the center of a flat board. (This base need be nothing more than a piece of scrap wood that you can clamp to the table with C-clamps.) Make the holes about 1 inch from the front edge of the wood scrap. Run the eye bolts through these holes, and underneath the base mount one compression spring, washer, and wing nut on each eye bolt. Mount the thread on the thin rod or the long bolt that you have run between the two eye bolts. This way, tension can be adjusted from underneath and is never affected by the turning of the thread spool, as can happen if the spool is mounted on a bolt.

In making this device, try to get eye bolts (I use 1/4-20 thread, but any size will work) that have small eyes so that small spools of rod-wrapping thread can be used. Large eye bolts are often too large for this purpose. If you can't get small eye bolts, you can still use this system by fastening a small block of wood between the two eye bolts to elevate the thread and create tension. An alternative is to go with smaller-thread-diameter eye bolts, since smaller-diameter wire has smaller eyes. Either 3/16- or 1/8-inch-diameter eye bolts will work. Because the spool will be turning on the edges of the eye bolts, use a small sheet of plastic (such as was cut from milk bottles for the rod holders) with punched holes for the eye bolts to hold it in place. This will also smooth the tension for easy, effortless guide wrapping.

Electric rod wrappers can be made with jury-rigged parts from other tools, from sewing machine parts, from parts available from some catalogs. Basically, they include a block to hold a simple three-jawed drill or lathe chuck; a motor controlled by a rheostat (speed control) floor pedal; and a bed, usually of rails holding adjustable roller supports to support the rod and an adjustable-tension device. There are endless variations of these, some with the motor and bed riding on a separate bed of rails so that the whole rod-wrapping assembly can slide along the rails, eliminating the need for the rod-builder to move to make each successive wrap.

ROD-HANDLE GLUING CLAMP

When you are making cork handles and grips, a rod-handle gluing clamp is a handy, inexpensive, easy-to-make, and easy-to-use tool. A gluing clamp makes it easy to clamp the cork rings of a handle together until the glue cures, prior to shaping, and to make sure there is a good, tight bond between each cork face.

There are two basic ways to make one. The first involves two 2 × 1 × 5-inch strips of wood, two 1/4-20 threaded rods, six nuts, two wing nuts, and two washers to fit the threaded rods. The threaded rods can be other diameters if you like, and their length should be based on the length of the handles you are making. The threaded rod can be anything from 12 inches long (usually too short unless you are making handles separate from the rod and adding them later) to 36 inches long (necessary only for surf rods, where you will be gluing the grips directly onto the rod blank).

Drill a hole into the center of each of the wood strips to accommodate the rod blank. Make the size of the hole appropriate to the diameter of the blanks you are using. Drill two more holes— one above and one below the center hole—to fit the threaded rods. Attach one end of each of the threaded rods into the outer holes in one of the wood strips, using two nuts to lock them into place.

Ream out the two outer holes in the other wood strip so that the threaded rods will slide easily through them. Slip the second wood strip onto the threaded rods, and fasten with washers and the wing nuts.

The cork rings are added to the blank to build up the rod handle. Then the base of the gluing clamp is slipped over one end of the blank and the wood strip is seated against the cork rings at one

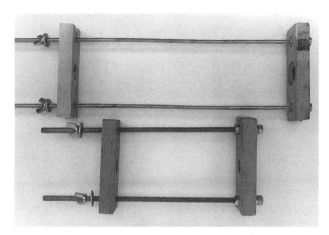

Two lengths of cork-handled clamps using threaded rod, scrap wood, nuts, and wing nuts.

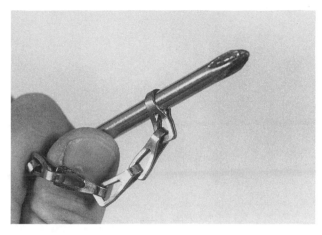

To make an adjustable cork clamp, first open up a chain link to fit onto an eye bolt.

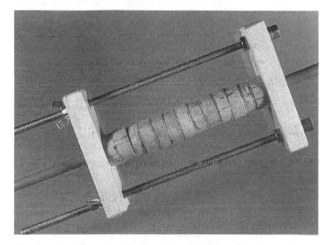

Cork grip clamped in homemade handle clamp.

Open eye bolt to accept chain link for adjustable part of the cork clamp.

end of the handle. Slip the other wood strip (at the opposite end of the gluing clamp) over the rod blank and onto the threaded rods, add the washers and wing nuts, and tighten the second wood strip to draw the cork rings together for curing.

One disadvantage of this tool is that if you are making a short handle with long threaded rods, you will have to turn the wing nuts a lot to get tension on the cork grips. A solution to this is to modify the tool as follows: Use two strips of wood as above, but on one of them cut slots completely though the wood from each end to the two side holes. Use a large saw blade to cut a groove into the top of this end over the top of each hole (center of the slot).

Instead of threaded rods, use two chains of any length desired. Any light chain will work well provided that it will fit through the sawed slot. (I like safety or sash chains.) You will also need two 4-inch-long eye bolts (1/4-20), two washers, and

Adjustable part of the cork clamp. The rod blank can fit through the center hole and the wingnuts adjust the pressure on the cork grip.

Fixed end of the cork clamp where the hitch-pin clips are placed in the chain to adjust for the length of the cork grip.

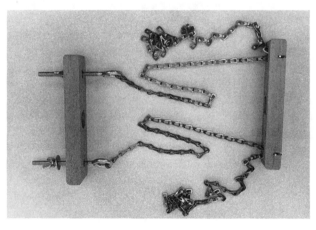

Completed cork clamp with chain, hitch-pin clips, and adjustable eye bolt.

two wing nuts to fit them, along with two hitch-pin clips. Fasten the end of each chain to the eye bolts by opening the eye bolt and sliding a link in place before closing the bolt. Also, lightly ream out the holes at the one end so that the eye bolts will slide easily.

To use the tool, run the wing nuts down to the end of the threaded eye bolts. Slip the hitch-pin clips through the chain links at the appropriate length for the rod grip you are making. Slip the rod blank into the center holes of each wood strip, slide the chain into the slot in one wood strip, slip a hitch-pin clip into the chain and into the groove in the wood strip to hold the chain in place. Tighten the cork clamp by turning the wing nuts to draw the clamp together.

The advantage of this is that it is quick and easy to use. After clamping a short fly-rod grip of only 6 inches, it is easy to remove and readjust by moving the hitch-pin clips to clamp a 24-inch-long

surf handle. The only turning required is no more than the length of the threaded eye bolts. Naturally in all of this, it is necessary to make the handle before the reel seat is added, or to lengthen the gluing clamp so that the reel seat is included, drawing up the cork handle against one end only.

Another possibility is to use a modification of a carpenters' pipe clamp. These tools are sold in sets, with the sliding part of the clamp and the threaded adjustable part—you provide the pipe. Thus, the clamp can be made any length and is usually reserved for larger clamping jobs. If you have one (don't buy one just for clamping rod handles), it is possible to use a small C-clamp to hold a wood yoke on each end. These yokes should be cut from short lengths of shelving and a deep U should be cut into one end. Use the C-clamp to hold the wood yoke onto the existing clamp surface and place the rod with the handle cork in between these yokes.

Another possibility if you have one and want to make a permanent cork clamp is to weld a similar-shaped yoke of steel onto the clamp faces. If you use flat steel for these additions, you can still use the pipe clamp for general carpentry tasks as well as for a cork clamp.

Take care to use only slight pressure, because these clamps are capable of great force. Too much pressure, regardless of the type of clamp used, will only squeeze the glue out of the adjoining cork faces and may even deform the cork rings.

CORK HANDLE REAMERS

Standard, commercially available reamers are not long enough, nor do they have a gentle enough taper to ream out an entire cork handle. Long reamers are necessary for shaping the hole in a cork handle made on a threaded rod and then fitted to a rod blank, or when using commercially available preformed cork grips.

There are several ways to make these reamers. The best base for such a reamer is a scrap piece of rod blank about 18 inches long. It is best to make several sizes, or diameters, for reaming out cork grips for different-size rods. One way is to cut thin strips (about 1/2-inch wide) of coarse sandpaper from a sheet. Run these over the edge of a table to "break" the backing paper so that it will not crack or split when wrapped around the scrap rod blank. Coat the entire scrap blank with a 24-hour epoxy glue. Then, starting at one end, spiral-wrap the sandpaper strips around the reamer blank to completely cover it. An alternative method is to clamp down both ends of the sandpaper strips, backing up, and then coat the backing with epoxy glue. Then spiral-wrap the strips around the reamer, covering it completely or leaving gaps between the strips where the blank will show. This latter is really the best of the two methods, because it will leave spiral channels for cleaning out the cork dust as you work the reamer. If you were to coat the blank with glue and then spiral-wrap leaving these spaces, you would fill up these channels with glue and reduce the effectiveness of the tool.

A third method of making a reamer is to coat grit directly onto a glue-coated rod blank. To do this, you will need abrasive grit. Some commercial-style hardware stores sell grit such as is

Cork reamers can be made from scraps of blank and strips of coarse sandpaper. Here, a rule is used to cut strips of sandpaper from a sheet. The strips are then glued onto the tapered blank to make the reamer.

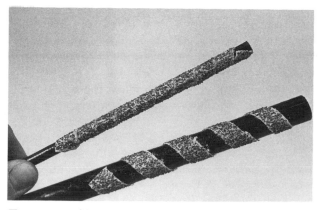

Two types of homemade reamer. The one on top has a solid wrapping of coarse strips of sandpaper, the one on the bottom has grooves between the sandpaper to clear the cork dust while working.

used on sandpaper, but alternatives are plain sand (such as is found at fresh- or salt-water seashores or beaches, or used to fill a child's sandbox) and sand-blasting sand. The one problem with natural sand is that it will vary widely in size and sharpness. Many of the particles will be rounded and thus less effective for reaming. Sand-blasting sand is sharp and comes in various grades, but unfortunately it is only available in large quantities—like hundred-pound bags! Perhaps a call to a sand-blasting company could get you a pound or two.

To make a reamer this way, spread the grit out evenly on a sheet of wax paper. Then coat the scrap rod blank with epoxy glue. Make it a thin coating so that it does not run, or use some of the gel-type glues that are more viscous. You can coat the entire blank or use a spatula or craft stick to coat it in a spiral, leaving channels, or coat it in rings to leave segmented channels. Once you have it coated this way, press the reamer down into the grit on the wax paper, lifting, turning, and pressing it back down in the grit to get complete coverage. Roll it lightly in the grit and then set it aside to cure overnight. In use, some grit will come off initially, but after this stage the reamer should be good for many handle-shapings.

CURING MOTOR

Curing motors are required to properly cure the finish on rod wraps when modern epoxy and urethane finishes are applied. These finishes are thicker than the varnish used in the past, and will sag and drip if the rod is not supported horizontally and turned for several hours until the finish cures. Commercial curing motors are available, but you can build your own.

You will need a slow-turning motor such as those used for rotisserie spits for barbecues, slow-clock or timing motors, or similar motors. The best are those that have a turning speed of 1 to 20 rpm and are AC-style, so that you do not have to continually buy batteries. They must have enough power or gearing to turn the heaviest rod that you might build. I like rotisserie motors. They are heavy duty, work well, and are often purchased inexpensively at flea markets, or acquired from neighbors who are throwing out an old grill. In all cases, you will have to jury-rig a system for holding the butt end of the rod. How you do it will depend upon the motor.

Some motors, such as the rotisserie-style, have a blind square hole, others have a short shaft, still

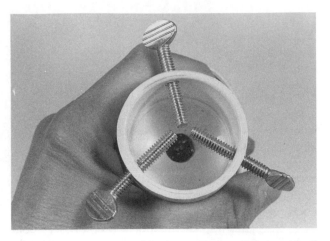

Thumb screws in a PVC pipe end cap make an ideal holder for a rod-curing motor. The cap must be mounted onto a low-rpm motor for curing rods. The plastic is easy to drill and tap for these thumb screws.

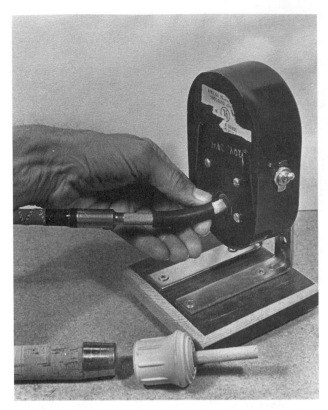

Curing motor made from a low-rpm rotisserie motor from a barbecue grill, with a wooden blind wedge in the square hole, and rubber tubing to connect with the butt on a casting rod. Other types of attachment can be used, as shown by the crutch tip (to hold the rod blank or butt cap) mounted on a wooden dowel in the foreground.

others end in small gear wheels. For the blind square hole, you can cut down a dowel and blind-wedge in into the hole (place a wedge in the square hole so that forcing or driving the dowel into the hole will wedge it into place).

For gears or shafts, the best system is usually to glue a rod-holding device onto the shaft or to fasten a rod-holding device onto a block of wood that in turn can be drilled to fit onto a gear or shaft. One way to do this is with a series of rubber butt caps fitted to different blocks of wood that can be force-fitted onto the shaft, or with a block permanently glued or fastened to the motor butt and fitted with a threaded rod and wing nut to hold butt caps punched with an appropriate-size hole.

Another possibility is to use a standard plastic PVC end cap, or similar metal cap, and to drill and tap for thumb screws at three points placed equidistant around the perimeter. For this, I like 1/4-20 thumb screws, and a 3/16-inch tap drill will

work fine. Once the holes are drilled and tapped, add the thumb screws. For use, adjust the thumb screws to hold the finished rod.

Another alternative is to use a standard PVC end cap fitted onto the rotating motor and a hose clamp to hold a piece of slightly stretched tire-inner-tube tubing or similar rubber. Before adding the rubber membrane, punch a hole in its middle through which the end of the rod can be inserted when the hole is stretched. This system is fine for light rods like fly rods, but is not as good when heavy guides, such as are found on offshore rods, might create enough torque in the rod to cause it to slip.

BURNISHER

Burnishers are available commercially, but easy substitutes to smooth thread wraps and close thread gaps include plastic pens, discarded felt-tip markers, or any other similar small, smooth tool. In all cases, use only the smooth skin of the tool to smooth the wraps — not the point.

HANDLE SEATER

Handle seaters are used to push synthetic grips into place on a rod. They can be made several ways. One way is to use a 1 × 2 × 15-inch board. Drill a 1-inch hole through the center, and to one side drill additional holes measuring 3/4-inch and 3/8-inch. To the other side, drill 1/2- and 1/4-inch holes. Any of these holes can be used to push the grip into place. Pick the hole size that's just barely

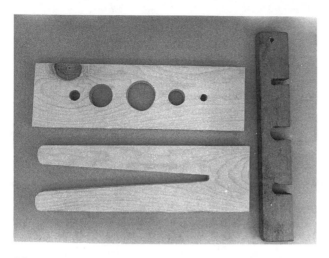

Three types of handle seaters that will work for foam or cork grips.

larger than the diameter of the rod at the top of the handle. To use, the handle seater is placed over the rod blank after the foam grip is placed on the blank. Use both hands to push the seater down and slide the grip down the blank. Handle seaters are necessary because the diameter of any synthetic grip must be smaller than the diameter of the blank in order to hold properly on the blank.

Another way to make the same basic tool is to use a board with a central hole of about 1 to 1 1/2 inch, and to use this as a brace against another piece of wood that contains smaller holes of 1, 3/4-, 1/2-, 3/8- and 1/4-inch. I have even made seaters with a rotary wood "wheel," on which the holes are drilled. The wheel is screwed to the wood board so that the small holes are lined up with the larger hole in the board, and the tool is pushed down to move the handle into place.

DECORATIVE-WRAP LAY-OUT TOOLS

Tools for laying out diamond, chevron, and similar wrap patterns can be purchased, though they are not made for this purpose. For example, a circle template will have a number of different circles, most with marks to indicate the four quadrants. By placing the circle template on the blank at the handle and selecting a circle of the same size as the blank, it is possible to lay out 180- or 90-degree marks for single or double diamond and chevron wraps. It is best to first wrap the blank above the handle with masking tape on which to make the quadrant marks. Then slide the template hole in place, making sure that it is the right-size hole with a snug fit. Line up one of

the quadrant marks with the center of the reel seat and mark the masking tape with the two or four quadrant marks, as desired. Remove the template and wrap the blank again with masking tape just above where you want the decorative wrap to end. Repeat at this spot (using a small template circle) and make two or four more marks, making sure they are completely aligned with the original marks.

One easy way to check this is to use a strong overhead light (fluorescent lights are good) that will make a streak or reflection of light running the length of blank. Hold the rod and your head steady and rotate the blank to line up the streak of light with the mark made at the handle. I find that it helps to close one eye to do this. Then, without moving your head or the rod, run your eye to the upper wrap of masking tape and rotate the circle template to line up the quadrant mark with the streak of light. Check several times and then mark the masking tape. Once these marks are made, it is simple to use a rule to line up the respective quadrant marks and to make the blank with small marks, at which points the initial threads should cross.

It is also possible to buy special rulers (from stationery, drafting, and art-supply stores) that have individual marks for various measured distances. These rulers, for example, have specific scales for measurements of 3/16-, 5/16-, 5/8-inch, and so on, as well as the more common 1/4, 1/2-, and 3/4-inch spacings. Thus, they make it easy to space out the decorative wrap without the calculations that are required when using regular rules.

DECORATIVE-WRAP-ALIGNMENT CHECKER

An easy decorative-wrap-alignment checker is easily made from a right-angle piece of clear plastic. This is used to line up the initial crossing threads of such wraps. The clear plastic makes it possible to line up the crossing threads with the sharp bend. Clear-plastic angles are available in several widths and lengths as wallpaper and paint outside-corner protectors manufactured for homes and offices.

WRAP FINISHER

The standard method of finishing rod wraps is to loop the thread, wrap over the loop, cut the end of the thread, and place it through the loop,

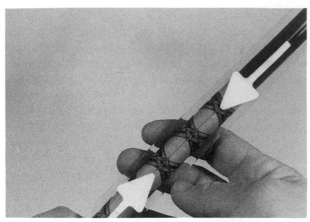

Clear corner edging with checking decorative wraps. The optical line formed by the sharp bend in the clear plastic (arrows) makes it easy to check the wrap alignment.

pulling the loop through to the tuck the thread under the last wraps.

The problem is that making these turns after laying down a loop of thread often causes the loop to spiral and tangle around the blank and guides. You can prevent this by making a simple wrap finisher. It consists of nothing more than short strips of hook-and-loop fastener, a small eyelet or rivet, and a short length of monofilament. To make it, cut a length of hook-and-loop fastener about 3 to 4 inches long. Cut one end square and the other end into two opposing angles. Making these angle cuts will allow a small tag end to stick out for easy opening of the finisher.

Use an awl to poke a hole through both sides of the square-cut end, and insert and seat a small eyelet. These eyelets are sold in kits in sewing-supply stores. If you don't have or don't want to get these eyelets, you can use a rivet, or sew the two parts, or even glue them. Through the eyelet, or attached to that end, add a small loop of monofilament fishing line. Place the knot at the eyelet or close to this position. Use a mono size relative to the size of the thread used and the pressure used to wrap the guide in place. I find that 10- to 12-pound test mono works well, but lighter or heavier line can be used if desired.

To use, first wrap to the point where the loop is wrapped down. At this point, open the hook-and-loop fastener and secure it around the rod blank with the loop end over the wraps. Then wrap over the mono for the desired number of turns. Cut the end of the thread, tuck it through the mono loop, and pull the loop through to pull the thread under the previous wraps. Remove the wrap finisher until it's needed on the next guide.

TENSION HOLDER

This really isn't the best name for this simple tool, but it lacks better description. A tension holder allows you to maintain tension on an incomplete thread wrap on a rod when you have to leave the wrapping bench. If you don't use something like this, or don't tape the thread down (a messier alternative), the thread wrap will lose tension.

A tension holder is nothing more than a piece of wire with two sharp bends in each end. One end must be covered with rubber or plastic tubing before bending. The tubing creates friction on the rod to prevent it from rotating back and losing thread tension. The hook on the other end holds a sinker of any type. Usually two to four ounces is a good weight, although you might want more for big rods where heavier thread and more tension is used. You can also bend this hook into an eye to permanently attach the weight.

I have made these from plastic-coated coat hanger wire, stiff utility wire (or plain coat hanger wire) with a slip-on plastic or rubber tubing, and from utility wire coated with the latex rubber dip sold and used for coating tool handles.

Keep one on your wrapping table. To use, slip the sinker onto the hook and place the rubberized hook on the rod next to the wrapping thread.

This simple tension holder maintains basic tension on the thread wrap while wrapping a rod should you have to leave the wrapping bench. The plastic-coated wire will not hurt the rod; weight prevents the rod from turning and the tension form slipping.

3

$\mathcal{S}pinners$

INTRODUCTION · TOOLS · SPINNER PARTS AND
MATERIALS · STEPS IN BUILDING A TYPICAL SPINNER ·
CORRECTING PROBLEMS · VARIATIONS IN SPINNER
DESIGN AND CONSTRUCTION · FIGURING SPINNER
WEIGHTS · SPINNER KITS

Basic Safety Requirements
Goggles
A clean, clear place to work

Basic Tools
Needle-nose or round-nose pliers with side
cutters

Helpful Tools
Small round-nose pliers
Diagonal wire cutters or compound-action
pliers with wire cutters
Wire former (commercial or homemade)
Worth split-ring pliers
Compound-leverage fishing pliers

INTRODUCTION

Spinners are among the most popular and
effective lures for a wide range of freshwater
gamefish. That they are not used more widely in
salt water is probably more a function of rust and
corrosion than of a lack of their ability to catch
fish. Spinners predate many other lures. Some
catalogs of the 1890s prominently displayed them;
the Wilkinson Co., a distributor of the time, shows
Pflueger's Success Luminous Spoon. Although
called a spoon, this was really a spinner design
with a straight shaft and fluted fish-head-pattern
blade that revolved around the shaft on a clevis.
The lure was equipped with a feather-dressed
treble hook. Similar "spoons" (really spinners in
today's parlance) are shown in earlier catalogs.

Mepps, makers of some of the best-known spinners, recently (in 1988) celebrated their fiftieth anniversary in the U.S. Mepps began here in 1939, before the big influx of spinning in the late 1940s and early 1950s. It was probably the influx of spinning tackle, however, that tremendously increased the popularity of these small light lures, since spinning tackle made them easy to cast. Previously, they were mostly trolled.

Today, spinners retain their high popularity and effectiveness. In all their variety of colors, styles, sizes, shapes, and finishes, they are among the best of lures for almost all types of freshwater gamefish, and some saltwater gamefish as well. Unfortunately, these small hunks of metal are also relatively expensive. And to be fished well, they must be fished deep. This means more fish, but it also means more lost lures, because the treble hooks of typical spinners catch easily on underwater snags.

By making your own spinners, you can reduce a substantial part of the cost of these lures, and as a result find yourself fishing more effectively as your concern over losing them lessens.

TOOLS

Many anglers avoid tinkering with spinners because of false notions about either the complexity of making them or the tools required. Many anglers think that a complex, expensive wire former is required to bend and form the eyes on the spinner shafts. Few of us fish so much as to be able to afford such expensive equipment to make only one type of lure. Although this tool (sold by Cabela's and other companies) is handy and will make wire-forming very easy, the only tool really required is a pair of round- or needle-nose pliers with built-in side cutters, and a pair of diagonal wire cutters if the pliers lack this feature. And in fact, as noted in Chapter 2, you can avoid this expense by making a simple wire former from nails and a block of wood, reducing the tool cost to zip.

The pros and cons of each type of tool you can use (*not* must have!) are as follows.

Production wire formers. The Tacklemaker, available from some tackle shops and a number of mail-order suppliers, is one of these. It clamps to the table, has bins to hold parts, and uses different collets or heads for working with different-size wires. Wire ranges, in fractions of an inch, for this are .018 to .025, .026 to .032, and .033 to .040. Two handles adjust to make different types of eyes and bends in wire. This tool is ideal but relatively expensive.

Wire former. These smaller wire formers are available from many shops and catalogs, and are relatively inexpensive. They look like a C-clamp with an adjustable handle that can be turned to form simple wraps and bends, including wrapped eyes. They will not handle wire smaller than .020.

Commercial wire former making a wrap in a spinner wire. This is used for high-production spinner-making. Interchangeable rotating shafts are available for different sizes of wire.

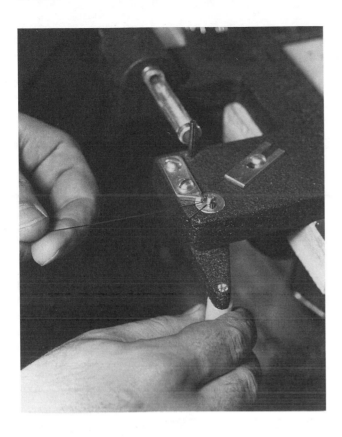

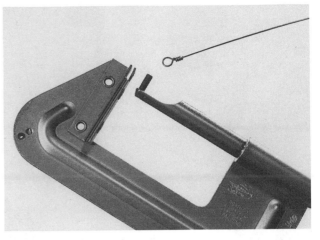

Worth wire former can be used to make several different types of eyes and bends in spinner wire.

Separate handle on the commercial wire former makes various "R" and "Omega" type bends in wire, along with bends for snap-closure and coil-spring fasteners.

Tack-L-Tool. This wire former from Netcraft also has a handle for turning wrapped eyes and other bends, and can be used freehand or mounted to a worktable. Like the small wire formers, it is inexpensive.

Needle-nose pliers. These will work and are listed simply because they are more common in most shops than are the preferred round-nose pliers. The singular disadvantage of these is that the two jaws are not round but half-round, making it almost impossible to get a completely round eye in a spinner. They are okay to use if you have

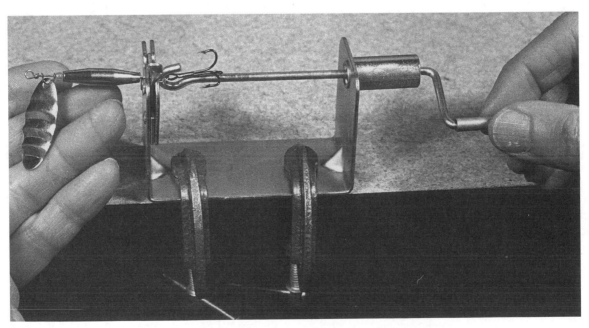

Netcraft wire former clamps to table, as show, to make spinner-making easy.

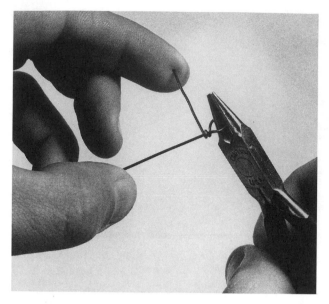

Most spinner-making tasks can be done with a pair of roundnose pliers, as show, and wire cutters.

them, since any slight irregularity in the eye will not affect fishing performance or reduce the number of strikes possible.

Round-nose pliers. These are preferred over needle-nose pliers simply because both jaws are completely round and thus will make a perfectly round eye in any wire. In most cases, these jaws are tapered so that, by using different parts of the jaws, different-size eyes can be formed.

Wire cutters. These are only necessary if you do not have wire cutters built into your pliers or wire formers. Some form of wire cutter (built-in or separate) is necessary to cut off excess wire after finishing a spinner. The best are those with flush diagonal cutters, although the compound-leverage action of fishing pliers will cut easier, though not as close to the shaft.

Split-ring pliers. These are available through tackle shops and parts catalogs. Several styles are available from Worth, including an inexpensive pair and two sizes of precision pliers. All styles work the same in that they have a small tooth over the end of the tapered jaw, the tooth making it possible to pick up and open any size of split ring for adding to a wrapped eye or hook. One modification that I like to make is to slightly sharpen the tapered jaw and to reduce the size of the tooth to make it easier to pick up the split rings.

SPINNER PARTS AND MATERIALS

As a general rule, spinners consist of a shaft, clevis, spinner blade or blades, body or beads, hooks, and tail dressings. The shaft, with an eye at each end, holds the body or beads and the clevis, which in turn holds the rotating blade. A hook is attached to the lower eye. Specific parts and details are as follows.

SPINNER SHAFTS

These are usually made of straightened piano wire or stainless steel wire. If you plan to fish in salt or brackish water, get the stainless steel shafts. They cost a little more than tinned piano-wire shafts, but are readily available. Any slight cost difference is worth it.

For standard spinners, there are several types of eyes on the shafts. Shafts are available in several lengths, usually ranging from 3 inches to 8 inches. While wire sizes of .024 to .030 are typical of most shafts, some range up to .035 and larger.

Shafts are available in straight lengths, with a single (one end) wrapped eye, or with an open eye (closed with a spring and used to change hooks and parts), self-lock-snap shafts (in which the eye has a formed spring lock), and swivel shafts (which have a barrel swivel eye at one end built into the shaft).

The straight lengths must have all eyes formed. They are best only if you plan to form some different eyes or make some of the variations of spinners to be discussed later. Straight wire is also available in longer lengths (usually about 18 inches) or in coils that are about 16 inches in diameter and sold on a per-pound basis. The wire is often available this way in stainless steel, tinned piano wire, or brass wire. Usually the spring coils are tempered so that there is no curve or curl. Use caution if the coils are not spring-tempered, because usually it will be impossible to straighten out these lengths.

The wrapped-eye shaft is the most useful for making most typical spinners, because the eye can be used for the line tie and the rest of the body and blade added to the shaft, with the hook added to an eye that is formed to complete the spinner.

The open-eye, also called a spring-closure eye, has an eye with the end bent parallel to the main shaft and closed by means of a short (1/4- to 1/2-inch-long) spring. These are ideal for those lures where you wish to change hooks, add lure dressing to hooks, add additional wire or second hooks for

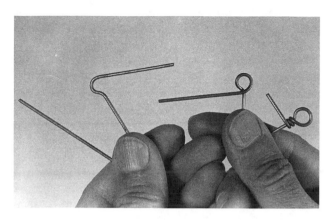

Methods of making a simple wrapped eye. From left to right, beginning with straight shaft, to first and sceond bend, completed eye and wrapped eye. Eye must have excess wire trimmed after this final stage.

minnow or bait rigs, or add a spinner to the front of a lure or fly.

The self-lock-snap type (also called a self clip or safety-lock-wirc shaft) is similar to the open-eye but has a small right-angle hook on the end of the open eye so that the eye can bc closcd by snapping it on the shaft. It also allows changing parts, hooks, and riggings, but does not require the spring closure.

Swivel shafts are rated by the size of the swivel, ranging from a number 10 (small) through a num-bcr 3 (large) swivel, and come in lengths from 3 to 5 inches. There is a wrapped rotating eye coming from one end of the barrel in this swivel; the shaft (usually brass) emerges from the other end.

With the exceptions of the swivel shafts that are made of brass, shafts are springy and are made of tinned or stainless steel. With the various dia-

Types of wire eyes used for making spinners. Shafts are available with these eyes formed. Left to right: coil-spring closure, wrapped eye and snap closure.

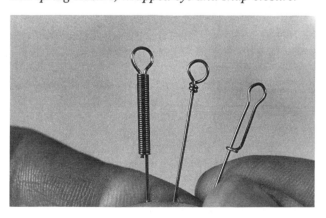

meters ranging from .026 to .040, you can make spinners with stiff shafts or light-wire shafts that will vibrate. All of this wire is strong, so go for the lightest wire to increase vibration. However, in some styles, the light bendable wire can some-times cause binding of turning parts. This is parti-cularly true of double-blade styles, to be discussed later. Also, tough fish will bend and sometimes ruin light-wire spinners.

In ordering wire, order enough to make the lures you want, because quantity purchases will reduce cost. Also, be sure to order wire not only with the best type of eye for your purposes, but also of the proper length. Realize that you will need some wire to work with in making the eye. Usually one to two inches extra is sufficient. Thus, for a one-inch-long spinncr, get 3-inch-long wire; for a 2-inch spinner, 4-inch wire; and for a 3-inch-long spinner, 5-inch wire. This will give you enough to form the eye, make the wraps or closure type that you want, and cut off the excess.

The best way to buy all spinner shafts is in lots of onc hundred or more, since this will give you the best pricing. Also, to avoid getting a lot of different shafts, it is often best to get spinner shafts in the longest length that is practical and useful, even if you will be making some short spinners. That way, you can get a larger bundle (at a lower cost) of, say, 6-inch shafts, rather than getting one hundred each of 3-inch, 5-inch, and 6-inch shafts, all for different-size spinners.

Clevises

These should also be bought in lots of a hundred each, although if you'll be working with different-size blades, you may wish to get two or morc sizcs. Clcvises come in several styles, in-cluding folded, stamped-stirrup, wire-stirrup, and fast-change styles.

The folded type is made by stamping out sheet metal in an O shape and then folding it over into a U shape with the holes formed by the fold of the metal in the upper part of the U. The shaft runs through these holes, and the bend of the U holds the spinner blade. I do not like the folded clevises for spinners because I feel the broader folded portion of metal might create more water resis-tance, and thus slightly interfere with blade rota-tion. However, many manufacturers use folded clevises on their commercial spinners, so my fears are probably more fanciful than factual. The folded types are best on monofilament worm rigs, because the folded wire will wear less on the monofilament used in these rigs. (Worm rigs are covered in Chapter 12, Miscellaneous Lures.) Five sizes are available, in both nickel finish and polished brass.

Stamped clevises are made from an I-shaped piece of metal with a hole punched in each end. They are bent into a U shape so that the thin edge of metal cuts the water smoothly as the blade turns. The shaft runs through the two holes in the ends, which are parallel once bent into the U shape.

Wire clevises are similar, but with a round wire and the ends forged flat and punched. Of the three, these have the nicest appearance close up, although the fish probably won't care. Usually the stamped and wire clevises are available in nickel finish, and four sizes. Most sizes in all clevises run from 0 or 1 to 3 or 4; the larger the number, the larger the clevis.

Some clevises are a fast-change style to allow for changing spinner blades at will. One of these types is of plastic in two sizes and several colors. It has a plastic collar through which the shaft runs, and a tiny clip into which spinner blades can be fastened. There is also a fast-change wire clevis, in a U shape, but with a small open spring on each end. This spring allows for changing the clevis, but works best on flexible cable or mono rather than the stiffer wire used in spinners.

In choosing any type of clevis, it is important to choose the proper size for the size of the spinner blade you will use. For rapid and easy spinning you want the smallest one possible, but too small a clevis may cause the blade to bind against the shaft. Unfortunately, there is no easy way to check this. If in a store, get a sample clevis, blade, and

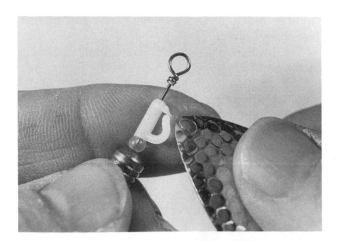

Quick-change clevis makes it possible to quickly change spinner blades while fishing.

shaft, and temporarily assemble them to check for binding.

It is possible to make your own clevises, although most of these will be of a large size. You will need safety chain (sometimes called "sash chain"), which has a fold-over oval link. By cutting these links out to make separate brass ovals, it is possible to fold the ovals into a clevis.

The easiest way to do this is to cut a slot into a wood board, then lay the link across it and use a thin chisel, hacksaw blade, or similar device to form the oval link into a folded U. Use a nail of the size required to form a wire sleeve, and place it into the slot. Use flat-jaw pliers or clamp the rest of the folded oval in a vise to form a flattened U around the nail. Remove the nail to use the clevis.

Note that I said this was possible — not easy or economical. In fact, with the low cost of clevises, this is just unnecessary work. The only real reason for making them is if you wish to use a clevis on a relatively larger-diameter wire form or for a heavy-duty spinner made on thicker than normal wire, where normal clevises won't work.

Blades

Blades come in such a bewildering array of styles, sizes, colors, finishes, and shapes that an orderly description is all but impossible. It used to be that standard spinner blades included the Indiana, Colorado, and willowleaf styles. Today, these are joined by Badger styles, fluted trolling, regular trolling, Chopper (a fat, bowling-pin type of shape), in-line, French style, spin true, ripple, rotoblade, June Bug, bent-edge (the Presto from Netcraft), and swing styles.

Colorado. A basic fat style of spinner blade found on many lures. As a result of its fat shape, it will spin at a pronounced angle from the shaft when on a spinner.

Indiana. A slightly thinner style of spinner blade, but still with a rounded end. It will also spin at an angle from the shaft, but not as much as in the Colorado.

Willowleaf. Looks like a leaf from a willow tree. Has a pointed end. These spin very close to the shaft of a spinner when they rotate.

Badger. A shape that is slightly thicker or fatter than the Indiana, but not nearly as fat as the Colorado. Some companies use this term for a thinner, lightweight blade in the Colorado and Indiana styles.

Regular trolling blades. These are like fat willow-

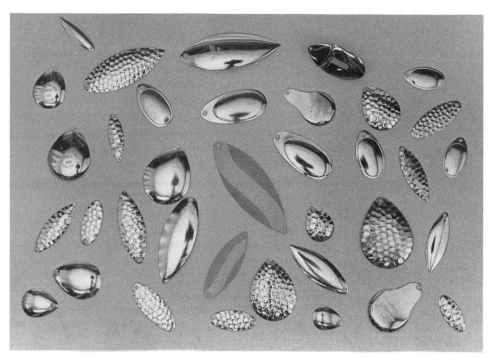

Many different blades are available for making spinners and spinnerbaits.

leaf blades, but are designed for trolling rigs. They really belong in the chapter on miscellaneous lures, but are included here because they can be used for spinners.

Fluted trolling blades. Like regular-trolling blades, but with a slightly scalloped edge.

Chopper blades. These are made by one company and are available through tackle dealers in kit form. They are used in a popular brand of spinnerbaits. The blades have a figure-eight shape, or a shape like a schmoo, if you remember L'il Abner.

In-line blades. These are relatively new to component parts, although a similar blade has been

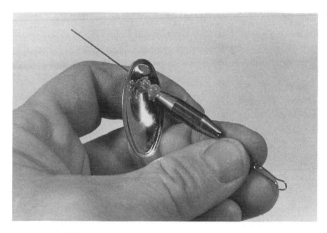

Through-blade spinner. These special blades do not use a clevis; the shaft goes through a hole part way down the blade. The blade still rotates rapidly.

used for years on a popular spinner. It consists of a fat, egg-shaped style of blade, but with a hole about a quarter of the way back from the head end instead of at the edge. A clevis is not used with this blade because the shaft runs through the hole. A unique style with lots of vibration.

French style. These blades have a forged, raised bevel, similar to the blade used in a popular spinner. They are called Spem blades in some catalogs.

Spin-true blades. These, along with the Roto-spins, have an angled blade and an additional bent extension arm that holds the blade at a specific angle. The shaft runs through the hole at the top end of the blade and the extension arm in order to achieve this fixed position and rotation.

Rotospin blades. Like the spin-true blades, but in a slightly fatter shape.

June Bug. These blades have a stamped-out extension arm (stamped from the middle of the blade) through which the shaft runs to hold the blade at a specific angle.

Bent-edge. Also called Presto blades, these have a slightly bent or cupped edge. This employs one of the tricks of the bass-fishing pros, who often bend the edges of their spinner blades to get more vibration, noise, and action from spinners and similar spinner-blade lures.

Swing blades. These blades are slim and uniform throughout, unlike the Colorado or Indiana blades that are tapered at the top like an egg.

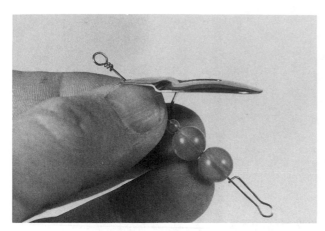

Example of June bug spinner used often for bait-fishing. The snap-closure shaft allows for adding a straight-eye, long-shank hook for holding worms, leeches, minnows, etc.

These are most like a willowleaf with the ends rounded off. They are a copy of a blade used on a well-known lure.

Ripple blades. These are like swing blades and about the same shape, but with horizontal ripples or bends in the blade for added flash and attraction.

All these blades require clevises, with the exception of the in-line style, in which the shaft runs through the hole in the blade, and the fixed-position blades such as the Rotospin and June Bug.

Sizes

Blades sizes range widely. Numbers are used to indicate size for each blade style, although the length of a number 4 willowleaf (about 1 7/8 inches) is not the same as a number 4 Colorado (about 1 1/4 inches). Sizes range from small 00 and 000 designations that are about the size of a little fingernail, up to 6s, 7s, and 8s (the maximum size number varies with the blade style) that can be as long as 3 7/8 inches. There are also occasionally half-sizes, such as a 3 1/2 or 4 1/2. The size must be compatible with the total lure, clevis, and beads or body. The larger the blade, the larger the clevis needed to prevent binding. Also, larger bodies are usually used with large blades.

Finishes and Colors

All spinner blades come in specific finishes, some in painted colors. Most are metallic, with a nickel finish the most popular. Other popular finishes include copper, brass, gold-plate, and two-tone finishes, although nickel/copper is most popular. These are polished finishes, but the same finishes are also available in hammered blades.

Both hammered and smooth-polished blades are available in baked-on painted finishes. These can include a variety of colors such as, but not limited to, red, chartreuse, black, orange, green, blue, purple, and white. Combinations are available with one color on one side and a second on the other, or with a metallic finish on one side and paint on the other. Blades with painted spots, stripes, scale patterns, herringbone stripes, and other patterns are also commonly available.

In addition to this, I have on occasion seen plastic blades in opaque-colored and translucent-colored finishes. The translucent-finish blades usually have some glitter in them for added flash. Because these blades are lighter, they throb far less in the water and have less of a strobelike flash from the reflective surface. They have a completely different action.

Plastic blades come in typical colors, such as chartreuse, hot pink, green, glitter chartreuse, glitter red, glitter blue, pearl, glitter purple, and glitter brown, in standard shapes such as the Colorado and Indiana.

Pearl blades used to be widely popular, but today are less-often seen. They are available for making your own spinners. They are cut from shell and drilled and shaped like other spoons. Usually limited sizes and shapes are available, with sizes 00 through 3 in the Indiana style most popular.

It is possible to make your own blades by cutting handles off lightweight teaspoons and tablespoons or hammering out blades from light metal using the techniques listed in Chapter 8. In addition, you can use other items for blades. One example is the brightly colored plastic fingernails sold in cosmetic departments. In truth, though, they are usually too expensive to seriously consider, since so many other metallic-finish and painted blades are available specifically for tackle-making.

BEADS

Beads are used to make up a wide variety of commercial spinners, and perhaps the most popular and well-known of this style is the C. P. Swing. Brass beads are used in this lure.

Beads come in a wide variety of sizes, styles, colors, and materials, so that the choices and

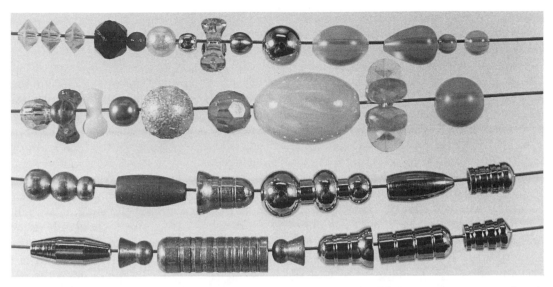

Beads and bodies available for making spinners and other tackle. Top two rows are beads; bottom two rows are various spinner bodies.

combinations are really infinite. Examples of bead styles include:

Solid brass beads. These are just what the name says — solid brass, polished and with a hole drilled through to allow slipping onto the spinner shaft. Typical hole sizes are about .052- to .063-inch, plenty large enough for any spinner shaft (usually .024 to .035) and often large enough for the larger-diameter shafts (often .040) used for spinnerbaits, buzzbaits, and similar jig-spinner forms. Typical sizes range from 1/8- though 11/32-inch, in 1/32-inch increments. They are commonly available in both polished brass and nickel plate.

Hollow brass beads. These are hollow brass, and thus are lighter in weight. Because of the way they are made, they often have a slightly larger hole than the solid brass beads, but come in both a lacquered brass and a nickel finish. The sizes are usually the same as those found in the brass beads.

Salmon red beads. These are translucent beads in a salmon red or bright pink color and are widely popular for a number of spinners, either as the main beads to make up the body, as attractor beads added at one end of the spinner, or as a small bearing for the clevis in place of the "unies" made for this purpose.

Often these are called "flourescent" or "fire" beads to indicate their color, although fluorescence can be found in many colors.

While all salmon beads are smooth and polished, several shapes are available, including round, oval, and pear. Unlike the brass beads,

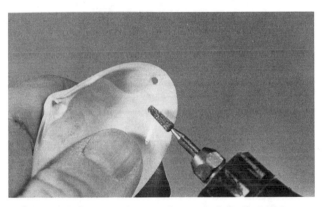

Spinner blades can be made out of shell, but is not recommended because of the high percentage of breakage. Here, the eye is formed using a small high-speed grinding tool.

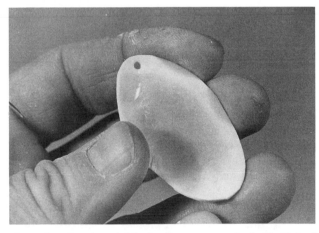

Completed spinner blade from natural shell. Grind the blade shape after drilling the hole, since breakage is most likely to occur when drilling.

which all seem to be measured in fractional inches, these and most other beads are measured in millimeters. Round beads range in size from 2 1/2 to 10 mm. Oval beads are listed by millimeters in two dimensions, with typical sizes being 3 × 6, 5 × 7, 6 × 8 1/2, 7 × 10, and 8 × 11 1/2. Pear beads also are measured in two dimensions, ranging from 4 × 5 1/2, 5 1/2 × 8, 8 × 11 1/2, 8 × 16, and 12 × 18. These are also called teardrop shape or teardrop beads.

Translucent beads. These are like the salmon beads, but are in other colors, such as yellow, light green, blue, and sometimes others. They are usually available only in round shapes, but in the full range of sizes.

Faceted plastic beads. Like the translucent beads, but with cut sides or facets for added sparkle. Only available in the round shape in all the typical sizes, and in blue, red, yellow, purple, and gold.

Opaque beads. These are also usually available only in polished round shapes, but come in opaque colors including black, dark green, blue, yellow, and red. Sizes usually range from 3 through 10 mm.

Luminous beads. These are not flourescent, which is a bright color, but are glow-in-the-dark, or phosphorescent. They are charged by light and will glow for some time after exposure. In color they are usually on off-shade, yellowish ivory or sick yellow. In the dark they glow yellow, although other colors are possible and available. Sizes range from 3 to 10 mm. It is now possible to make glow-in-the-dark items in other colors, so this capability might show up in beads as well.

Pearl beads. Although these are plastic, they have a pearl finish and range in size from 3 to 10 mm.

Round glass beads. Glass beads are not as widely used as they once were, but they are a translucent bright red, somewhat like the salmon beads. Typical sizes are from 4 through 10 mm, with prices, particularly in the smaller sizes, much higher than for plastic beads.

Faceted glass beads. These are also red, but with cut sides for more flash and sparkle. Otherwise, in price and size they are about the same as are the round glass beads.

Tee beads. Tee beads are made of plastic, usually in three colors: yellow, blue, and fluorescent red. The shape comes to a point like a thin six-sided pyramid. Because they are larger than other beads, they are often used on larger spinners and sometimes on offshore trolling lures.

Plated plastic beads. Plated beads are plastic that is plated a gold or silver color. Sizes from 3 to 8 mm are available.

In addition to the beads described, there are lots of variations that can be found through art and craft stores and mail-order outlets. I am fortunate in having a craft store near me, and I find lots of additional parts for making spinners and other lures. Some of the beads I've discovered include:

Tri-beads. These are triangle-shaped—looking somewhat like stubby propellers—with a center hole for threading on the shaft. They will stack up on the shaft, and make for a neat body when used this way. Several sizes of these plastic beads are available, along with a wide variety of opaque and translucent colors. In the larger sizes I like them not only for larger spinners, but also for small or thin offshore trolling lures (see Chapter 11). These are also beginning to show up in the tackle-component catalogs for larger spinners or as beads used as spacers for offshore skirted trolling lures.

Starflake beads. These look like stylized snowflakes with six "wings" or projections from the center hole. Most are large—the smallest I have seen was 12mm, the largest 25mm. The smaller sizes are fine for spinners, the larger for offshore trolling lures and other uses.

Floating beads. These are designed for adding to a snelled hook to float a lure or to make a "floating" jig head. They are medium-sized floating beads available in a variety of colors including luminous (glow-in-the-dark) purple, coral, green, black, and red. The two sizes available are 3/8- and 1/2-inch in diameter. They can be added to spinners when you want to reduce the total weight of the lure for casting on certain tackle, or to help float a lure up off of the bottom to prevent snagging or loss.

Bodies. Although beads work fine to make up the body of a typical spinner, there are larger body forms that accomplish the same purpose. In some cases several are used, just as they are on commercially made spinners. They come in brass, lead, or plastic.

Brass bodies. These are solid brass, but are available in a polished-brass or polished-nickel finish. There are no names for the many shapes available, but suffice it to say they are identical or similar to those used in standard commercial spinners. Torpedo shapes are the most popular and are available in about six sizes and weights. Little ones are about 5/8-inch long and weigh

5/64-ounce; the largest sizes are about 1 1/4 inches, weighing 7/32-ounce.

In addition, there are various lengths and shapes that look like little bullets or lead-bullet castings; small, pointed, tapered bodies; those that resemble strung beads; and some odd shapes that defy description. Prices range widely, depending upon the number bought, the finish, and the size and complexity of the shape.

In general, the nickel-finish bodies are more expensive than the solid brass. These bodies often have a small slot in one end so that the spinner wire can be bent to lock the body in place when making the lures in reverse (tail to line-tie) fashion.

Lead bodies. These are usually available both unpainted and painted, the latter in a wide variety of colors. Both come in 1- or 1 1/8-inch lengths and .1875-ounce (1 inch) or .250-ounce (1 1/8-inch) weights. They have holes large enough for any size wire.

Plastic bodies. Plastic bodies are similar to the brass or lead bodies. Most common are those in a small tapered shape (like a cigar) that is about 1- to 1 1/2-inches long. In addition, you can get similar small plastic "beads" from art and craft shops, sometimes sold as spaghetti beads. Those that I have used measure about 3/4-inch long and come in bright colors, as do the fishing-tackle plastic bodies. Any of these can be used as a single complete body on a spinner, or in combination with beads, brass bodies, or other parts. Similar craft beads with a larger hole, called pony beads, are also available, but in general are not as useful because of the large hole size. They will work better on offshore lures, though.

HOOKS

Treble hooks are used on most typical spinners, but single or double hooks can also be used. In all cases, use good hooks such as those made by Mustad, Eagle Claw, VMC, Gamakatsu, Tiemco, or similar brands. Many variations in treble hooks are available, including shank length (standard, short, and long), finish (bronze, gold, japanned, nickel, cadmium, tinned), point style (curved, beaked, or straight). In addition, treble hooks come with fixed eyes or with sliced eyes in which the hook can be added to a fixed, permanent hook hanger and the hook eye closed with pliers. From a standpoint of tradition at least, most spinners use bronze-finish, standard-shank-length, straight- or curved-point trebles.

Dressed treble hooks are available from some companies, which allows you to make dressed spinners without the need to tie your own bucktail, fur, or feathers onto bare trebles. These dressed trebles are more expensive than plain trebles, but they are time-savers and avoid the need for a fly-tying vise or other tools required to tie dressed hooks.

Double hooks can be used, and their one main advantage is that the construction of the hook is such that they can be slid off the spinner eye and changed or replaced as required. Single hooks require a straight eye, since a turned-up or turned-down eye will not allow the hook to hang straight in the current — it will kink to one side. Open-eye single hooks, Siwash style, will also work, and can be closed onto a spinner eye with pliers.

Among the several advantages of single hooks on spinners (or any lure) are that they are easier to unhook from toothy fish (using the necessary pliers, it is easier and quicker to remove one hook than several), and that single hooks can usually be used in larger sizes than trebles without upsetting the balance of the lure. Also, larger single hooks are usually stronger when landing large fish.

OTHER PARTS

Depending upon the style of spinner, there are other parts to consider. These include:

Unies. These are tiny metal (nickel or brass) beads that are made specifically to serve as a bearing for the rotating clevis. This does not mean that you have to use these as a bearing, but for maximum reflection and action of the blades, you should use a small bead if not using a uni or two. Since these are small, only one size is available and color is not important. Although plastic unies can be used, metal is usually best, because with heavy fishing and constant wear, the plastic can become worn from the constantly turning clevis.

Coil springs. These are used as a closure and lock for the open-eye type of shaft. Several sizes are available and used according to the shaft size chosen. The Worth Company lists their .045-inch diameter coils for wire from .020 to .022, their .051-inch coils for wire from .024 to .026, and their .064-inch coils for wire diameter from .028 to .032.

Coil lengths range from 1/4- to 1 inch and come in tinned wire or stainless steel. The price is usually the same for either material.

Split rings. Split rings are used for a wide variety of purposes in making lures, primarily for attaching hooks to lures, as line ties, to connect lure parts, and to add attractors such as spinner blades or plastic teasers. Split rings come in stainless steel, tinned wire, or brass; in small to large sizes (0 to 12); and in lightweight or heavyweight wire. The smallest (size 0) from one catalog are .165-inch (about 1/6-inch) in diameter, and the largest size (12) is about .740-inch (3/4-inch) in diameter. Split rings are just like the familiar split-ring key rings in that they are a double wrap of spring wire that can be twisted onto a hook or lure.

Tubing. Tubing in many colors is used as an attractor on spinners and can be found on many commercial brands. Red is most common, although other colors, including white, yellow, green, pink, black, and blue can be used. Most is vinyl plastic tubing about 1/8-inch in diameter, and is usually sold by the foot. In use, small pieces are cut (usually about 3/8- to 5/8-inch long) and slipped over the treble-hook shank before the spinner is completed. The colored tubing must be short enough to fit over the shank without binding the eye so that the hook will swing free. An exception to this is that some anglers will use a slightly longer length of tubing so that they can slide it up over the spinner-shaft eye and hook eye to bind the two together and keep the hook in line with the spinner shaft. (There are other ways to do this, which we'll explore later in this chapter.)

Lure flippers. These are small pieces of plastic placed onto the spinner-shaft eye along with the hook eye and used for dressing up the lure, as does the attractor tubing. There is some variety in shape but not in color of those that are commercially available. Most are translucent red with a hole punched at one end, and several small sizes in egg, oval, or fishtail shapes, are available. They can be added to any lure using a split ring. Sometimes they are called "tail tags."

Skirts. Skirts, because of their large size, are not usually used on spinners; they are usually reserved for the larger spinners used for pike, muskie, and similar large fish. They must be put on before the hook is permanently attached to the spinner shaft or else used with a snap-lock spinner shaft that allows removal of the hook for adding or removing skirts (or tubing or tail tags) at will.

STEPS IN BUILDING A TYPICAL SPINNER

Although the listing of all these spinner parts can sometimes be confusing, the construction of a spinner is simplicity itself. Take, for example, a standard spinner, such as one with a brass swing blade, body of brass beads, and treble hook.

First, pick a shaft of the wrapped-eye type that is about 5 inches long, for ease of handling. The wrapped eye will be the "line eye" or line-tie end of the lure. Next, take a stamped or wire clevis and put it through the hole in the end of the blade. (It is a good idea to remember to use as small a clevis as possible in all spinners. The small clevis will spin better and start easier than will those in larger sizes. However, in no case should the clevis be so small as to permit the spinner blade to bind against it or the spinner shaft.)

Now hold the blade, with the clevis through the hole, and place the spinner shaft through the holes in the clevis. Check now to be sure that the concave side of the blade is next to the spinner shaft when the blade hangs against the lower part of the shaft. If the blade is on backward, remove the shaft from the clevis and replace it correctly, in the opposite direction, with the concave side of the blade resting next to the shaft.

Next, add the body parts to the shaft. Since in this typical lure the body is made up of brass beads, select the size and number of beads to go on the shaft first. Depending upon the blade size and the size of the beads chosen, this might be three, four, or five beads. In general, all bodies should be about the length of the spinner blade as it hangs down against the shaft. You can vary from this, of course, but it's a good general rule. Regardless of the size of the beads chosen, select a small brass bead to rest against the clevis and to serve as a bearing for easy rotation of the blade and clevis.

An alternative to this is to first use one or two of the small brass or nickel unies that are designed as bearings for the clevis. Another alternative is to use a tiny red glass bead as a bearing. In the case of making a spinner with body parts or with large beads, you will have to use one of these options anyway (small brass bead, uni, or small glass bead) as a bearing for the clevis. This will provide a relatively frictionless surface allowing the clevis to turn freely. (As described before, plastic beads may wear in time and are not recommended for this use.)

The rest of the body in our typical spinner is built up of larger, then successively smaller, beads to give the body an overall cigar shape or taper. Naturally, you do not have to go with this shape and can use beads in any configuration or size arrangement you want—running from small to

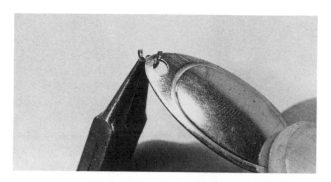

Making a spinner: Placing the blade on the clevis.

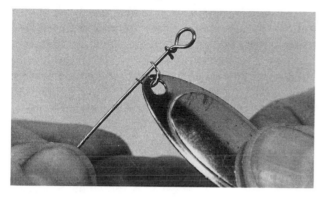

Making a spinner: Adding the clevis with blade to the wrapped eye shaft.

Making a spinner: Adding beads (and/or body) to the shaft.

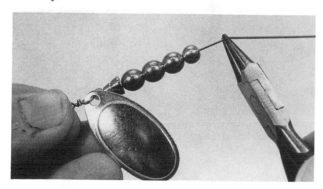

Making a spinner: Making the first bend in the wire to complete the spinner.

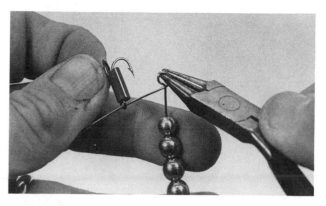

Making a spinner: Completed eye. Adding the hook onto which colored tubing has been added.

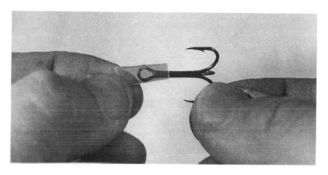

Colored tubing can be used on any treble hook, as shown, to add to the attractiveness of the lure.

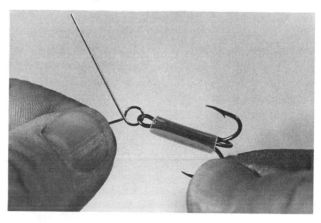

Treble with colored tubing on eye before the eye is wrapped.

large, large to small, in an hourglass shape, or any other combination or variation. The total length should be such that the spinner blade and bottom bead will rest at about the same spot.

Beneath the last bead, leave about 3/8-inch to 1/2-inch of clearance. This clearance is important, because without it parts of the spinner body and clevis may bind between the two shaft eyes once the spinner is completed and the lower hook eye is wrapped.

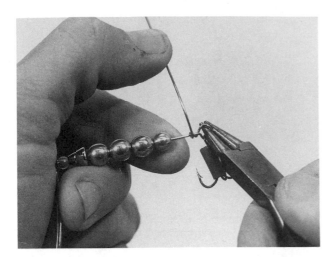

Making a spinner: Wrapping the eye.

Completed spinner.

At this 3/8- to 1/2-inch clearance point, use your round-nose pliers to bend the shaft sharply. If the round-nose jaws are tapered, hold the wire by the end of the jaws to make a relatively sharp bend. Then reposition the jaws so that you are holding the wire higher up on the jaws (on the more rounded part of the jaws). Hold the free end of the wire just beneath the body parts. Bend the free end of the wire completely (360 degrees) around the one jaw. To do this you will first be able to make an approximately 270-degree bend, at which point you will have to readjust the position of the wire in the jaws to continue the bend. When complete, the free end of the wire will cross over the sharp bend made previously. At this point, add any attractor tubing or skirt material to the treble hook. To add attractor tubing, first measure the shank length of the treble hook exclusive of the eye and hook bends.

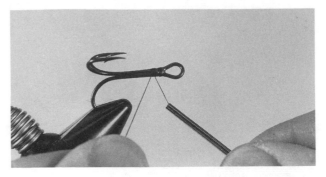

Other ways in which hooks can be decorated, including dressing with a wrapped-on fur tail. Here, the treble hook is held in a fly-tying vise and wrapped with thread.

Over-wrapping the fur to be added to the hook. Note that the fur completely surrounds the hook shank.

Using scissors to trim the excess fur forward of the hook shank.

Wrapping the fur in place and building up a solid protective layer of thread.

Finishing the wrap with a series of half hitches.

Completing the dressed hook with a coat of protective finish (nail polish, epoxy, or fly head, cement) on the wrap. Several coats are required.

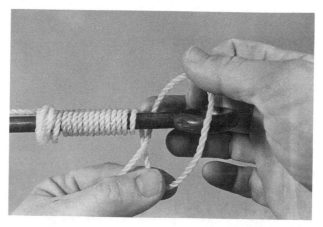

Details of completing thread wrap on dressed hooks. Here, a half hitch is placed on the hook. Several of these are used to secure the thread.

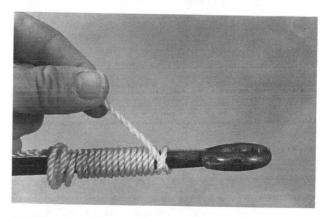

Half hitch pulled up into place.

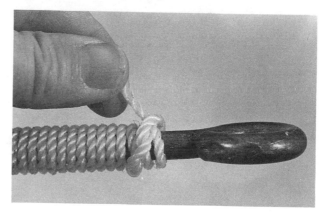

Several half hitches in place to secure thread. (A large cord is used in these photos for clarity.)

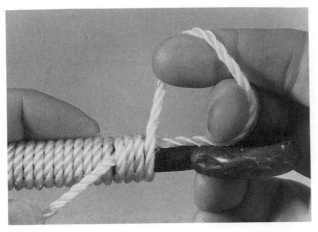

Making the whip finish by wrapping around the thread and hook shank with a loop. Four to five turns are taken this way.

Whip finish pulled up tight.

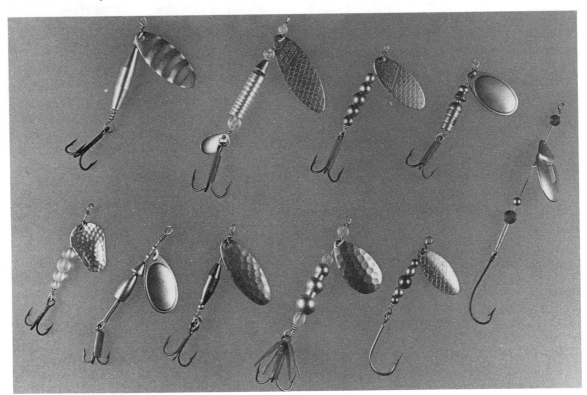

Examples of finished standard spinners.

Cut the tubing to this length with scissors and slip it over the eye of the treble hook. If using a skirt, slip it on the same way. To dress a treble hook with fur or feathers, tie the materials on using fly-tying methods or the methods described for finishing a bucktail in Chapter 4.

Next, slip the eye of the hook onto the free end of the wire, and take care to carefully push the hook eye past the previous wire bend and onto the formed eye for completion. If you plan to add a tail tag or lure flipper, add it at this time. Now hold the end of the shaft and the end of the hook (and lure flipper, if used) securely with pliers and carefully (watch the hook points!) wrap the free end of the wire tightly around the shaft of the spinner. Make two turns. If the loose end of the wire is long enough, you can do this by hand; otherwise, another pair of pliers will help. To make sure that the turns are tight, hold the wire (by hand or with pliers) as close to the spinner shaft as possible. After making the two turns, clip off the excess wire with wire cutters.

Caution. Be sure you are wearing your goggles when cutting off this surplus wire. Hold the spinner over a wastebasket and aim the end of the wire toward the bottom, because the cut portion will fly off. This can be dangerous unless you follow the above directions exactly. One other way to prevent this is to hold the spinner in your palm and use two fingers to hold the shaft to be cut as you use your other hand on the wire cutters.

When you've finished, you will have an imitation of a well-known spinner that is effective for trout, crappie, bass, pike, sunfish, walleye, and other gamefish.

CORRECTING PROBLEMS

Sometimes, after completing a spinner, you will find that the blade will not work or spin as expected. There can be several causes for this. One may be that you did not allow enough clearance on the shaft between the parts, so that the clevis binds and does not turn. Another possibility, particularly for Colorado and similar fat blades that spin at a larger angle to the shaft, is that too small a clevis might cause the blade to bind on the shaft.

It is best of course, to check carefully before the eye is wrapped to prevent such problems.

Problems in making spinners include eyes not tightly wrapped and clevises bound against body (both at right) and using too small a clevis on a blade so that the blade binds against the shaft (left).

However, if the lure is complete, try lightly squeezing the clevis with pliers to give a tiny amount of additional play of the parts on the spinner shaft. This will also give the blade more play on the clevis. Generally, the two ends of the clevis can be squeezed together about one-half of the normal spread without adversely affecting the clevis action. Squeeze too much, of course, and the clevis will bind on the shaft or blade and ruin the spinner. This procedure works best only with stamped or wire clevises—not the folded style that are difficult to bend this way.

Another problem can occur if the bearing bead or uni has a small rough spot that prevents the blade from turning freely. Try to check this before bending the wire to complete the shaft. If the bearing bead is plastic, you might be able to use a knife blade to remove the rough spot. Otherwise, the only solution is to cut the spinner shaft and salvage the usable parts for the next lure.

Sometimes the eyes will not end up in a straight line with the shaft of the spinner. Although this is more of a perceived than a real problem, you can correct it by adjusting the eye position. Place needle-nose pliers on the shaft next to the eye and tapered round-nose pliers on the eye. Bend both slightly until they are properly lined up.

VARIATIONS IN SPINNER DESIGN AND CONSTRUCTION

While the previously described method can be used for making dozens of different spinners using different body, blade, shaft, and hook combinations, there are other ways to make spinners, and other spinner designs you can utilize. Some possibilities and variations include the following.

BODY TYPES

In addition to the bead construction noted, it is possible to use lead, plastic, brass, or nickel bodies for the same purpose. In one sense this is even simpler, because many of these bodies are large enough to be used singly. In other cases, you will want to combine several smaller body styles to make up the body on a spinner shaft. Many popular commercial lures are made this way.

Bodies can also be combined with beads, and different color combinations of bodies and beads can be used. Regardless of the type of body used, you will still need a small bearing bead or uni directly beneath the clevis and above the body for proper blade turning.

PROPELLER SPINNERS

These are spinners that use propeller blades in place of the clevis and a single blade. As such, they are subject to spinning and line twist (as are almost all spinners—homemade and commercial). They are built the same way as outlined above, but with the propeller blade taking the place of the spinner blade and clevis. For proper turning, you still need a uni or bearing bead under the propeller.

Example of propeller of spinner in which simple propeller blade is used on shaft.

KEEL SPINNERS

Spinners spin—and cause line twist. One way to prevent this is to use a body shaped like a keel. Unfortunately, there are no keel-shaped spinner bodies that I know of. There are two solutions to this, however. One is to use a keel-sinker mold and modify it so that you can use an insert pin (more about this in Chapter 4). This insert pin will run through the length of the mold cavity to make a sinker with a hole completely through its long axis, rather than with an eye at each end. Painted a bright color over a base coat of white, this is ideal for use as a spinner body.

Another alternative is to use a regular keel sinker, paint it for use as a body, and use it in line with other parts to make up a unique spinner. In this, the painted sinker will be the body, attached to a treble hook with a split ring at the tail eye. The forward eye will be attached by a split ring to a short shaft spinner holding the spinner blade, clevis, and a bearing bead or uni or two. In essence, this becomes an in-line-parts combination spinner, although in the water it will resemble a standard spinner. The keel will prevent twisting, but the keel shape of the body might interfere with the blade on spinners where the blade spins close to the body axis. Check for this by trying a

prototype in running water, or use a wide-spinning blade such as a Colorado or Indiana. Willowleaf blades usually spin too close to the shaft to be useful in this variation.

Another way to make a keeled spinner is to start to make a typical spinner, but don't clip the wire on completion. Instead, make a sharp right-angle bend with the wire, add a small egg sinker to make the lure a preferred fishing weight, make another right-angle bend in the wire, and add a small snap hook (J-shaped) at the end. Use this J-shaped hook over the main spinner shaft to hold the weight to the spinner shaft but definitely behind the bearing uni or first bead. As an alternative, you can wrap the remaining wire around the main spinner shaft for a permanent lock. In doing either of these variations, be sure to start with long-enough wire and to leave extra clearance for the extra space on the shaft required by the snap lock or wire wrap. As with the keel sinker, it is also important to leave room for blade clearance and turning.

Coping with Twist

A keel spinner or variation is one way to cope with line twist, but it's not the only way. Another way is to add a swivel to the upper end of the spinner. This will help, but is best if it is a ball-bearing swivel, since this is the freest-moving. It is also far more expensive than regular swivels. In using one, you will probably want to start with straight wire (no formed eyes or bends) to build the swivel right on the upper eye. Some ball-bearing swivels have a small split ring as an eye on each side. For these, you can start with an eyed shaft, threading the split ring onto the spinner eye. An alternative, if you are making a spinner using a coil-spring (open) spinner shaft or one with a snap lock, is to build the spinner in reverse, starting with the hook end and ending up with the wrapped eye formed with the swivel in place. As has been mentioned, shafts with built-in swivels are available, but none have built-in ball-bearing swivels.

Another possibility is to make the spinner with a longer-than-normal wire shaft (about 1 to 1 1/2 inches longer than normal). Thus, you will have about 1 to 1 1/2 inches of extra play on the shaft when the spinner is complete. Then use pliers to bend the upper part of the shaft at about a 60-degree angle to the main shaft. This offsets the center of pull on the turning of the blade, reducing, if not completely eliminating, spinner

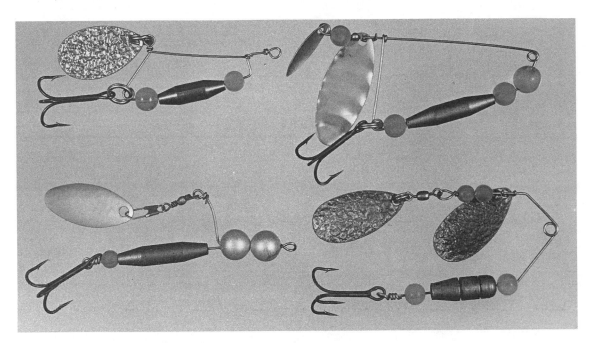

Keeled spinners are designed to reduce or eliminate line twist.

Here a keeled spinner has been made by using the end of the spinner wire to add a small egg sinker which will serve as the keel.

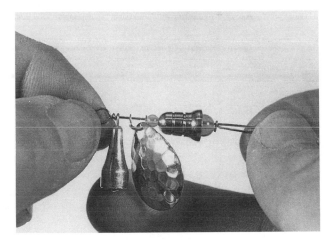

Keel added to the forward part of a spinner using the same technique as above and using a small bullet worm weight. Check all such additions carefully to make sure they do not interfere with hooking or blade rotation.

Left: Using extra length of wire to make a spinner in which the forward wire is bent to the side. This will also reduce or eliminate line twist.

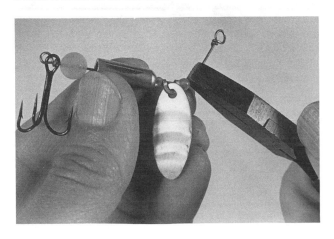

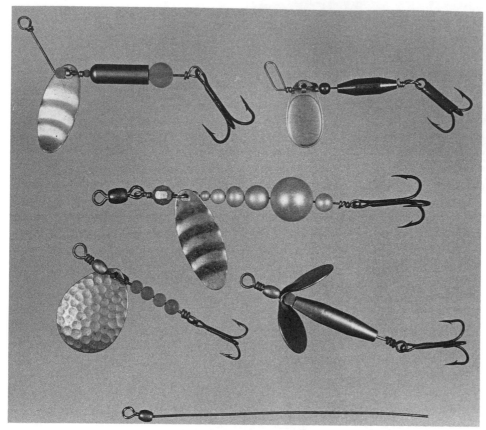

Spinner with bent shaft to prevent line twist, and spinners made with swivel eyes (bottom of photo), also to reduce line twist.

twist. You must have the wire offset for this to work. Within reason, the more offset the wire, the less the possibility of line twist. In all cases, be sure to leave enough clearance in the main shaft for the blade to turn. If you wish to have a specific length of bent wire at the front of the spinner blade, make this bend first and then build the spinner normally.

REVERSE-BUILT SPINNERS

The only reason to reverse-build a spinner is if it is simpler than building it from the head down. An example would be if you were making spinners with the open loop (coil-spring closure) or snap lock for changing hooks and parts, or adding the spinner in a combination with another lure. You could make the spinner from the top down and form the open or snap-lock ends with pliers, but the wrapped eye is simpler and just an easy to do at the upper end as at the hook end. You can buy spinner shafts with the open loop or spring-lock closure eye for the lower end. In fact, it is really easier to make them in reverse and wrap the upper eye, since a hook is not attached and in the way in this method.

Another reason to make reverse-built spinners is for the use of the tapered brass bodies that have a slot in the end of the body. In this case, you can build the lure from the tail up, beginning with an open-loop eye, adding a treble hook, and then slipping the tapered body over both wires. Take

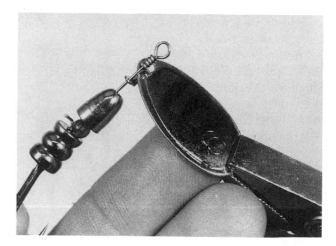

Example of reverse-built spinner in which the hook and body are added first and built up from the bottom, the blade/clevis added last, the wrapped eye completing the lure.

the short end of the wire and bend it sharply into the slot in the upper part of the body. Since these bodies are usually longer than the end of the wire on manufactured open-eye shafts, you may wish to make this eye from straight lengths of wire. However, there is no problem with making this type of spinner on the open-loop eye shafts because the spinner will be plenty strong enough without the wire folded into the body slot. Once you've added the body and bended the wire, clip off the excess and then continue to add body parts, ending with a uni or bearing bead, the blade on a clevis, and finally wrapping a line-tie eye in the upper end of the shaft.

Of course, even without a slotted body you can build spinners this way. By the same token, the presence of a slot in a body does not mean that you *have* to build it this way. You can make them the same way as is described for the typical spinner.

Yet another reason for building in reverse is if you are making an odd-shape spinner that will be easier to build from the tail up than from the line-tie down. Three types of shafts with eyes are available. A close examination of any spinner style or design will suggest the best way to build it and the best type of shaft to use.

FORWARD-WEIGHTED SPINNERS

Forward-weighted spinners have a weight ahead of the spinner blade to get the lure down deeper. This type of lure, whether called a spinner, forward-weighted spinner, weight-forward spinner, or forward-weighted spinnerbait, is often used for walleye and other deep-water-species fishing.

Although the commercial lures use special heads for the front of this kind of lure, you can make the same lures. Blanks with molded-in heads on a straight wire are sometimes available through tackle and mail-order shops. In addition, some companies (Do-It in particular) have molds with which you can mold your own heads. Do-It, for example, makes five different molds of Erie jig spinners, keel spinners, and walleye spinners that have the lead head up front and the rest of the lure built on a .030-inch-diameter wire. A variety of lures can be made from these heads or molds. (Techniques for molding these can be found in Chapter 4.)

Lacking blanks with heads, you can use an egg sinker that is threaded onto the wrapped-eye shaft, using the wrapped eye for the line-tie.

Because the egg sinker pressing against the clevis will stop blade rotation, place a sharp right-angle bend into the wire. Using needle-nose pliers, make another right-angle bend so that the shaft ends up with a small step, or Z bend, in it right behind the egg sinker. Then build the spinner normally using blades, clevises, beads, or body parts, and ending with a single, double, or treble hook.

An alternative to this is to use a small drop of solder or epoxy glue on the main shaft just forward of the rear blade to prevent binding by the egg sinker.

A lot of these lures (especially for walleye) are fished with bait. To make a bait rig using a long-shank single hook that is removable, make the same lure in reverse, using an open, coil-spring, or snap-lock loop, and leaving clearance for blade-turning and so that the sharp bends will prevent the forward weight from binding the blade. If desired, paint the egg sinker or dress it up a bit with the addition of fore and aft colored beads.

Making a forward-weighted spinner by adding an egg sinker to the spinner shaft first. Excess wire locks the sinker in place to prevent the blade from binding.

Example of completed forward-weighted spinner.

Another method is to use a small keel sinker with a modified mold and insert pin (as mentioned above for preventing twist) and slip this onto the shaft as a body. This is more typical of the shape found in these spinner bodies, and will help to keel the lure and prevent line twist.

Some years ago, another type of weight-forward spinner appeared on the market. It looked like a standard spinner but with the addition of a long, skinny, dull black weight on the forward part. This part was not meant to attract fish; it was there to get the lure down deep while it appeared to be a normal spinner. Spinners with different-length forward weights were designed for different depths and types of fishing. You can do this also, using the same procedure described and substituting several small egg sinkers, hollow

pencil lead (available for West Coast steelhead fishing or constructed with special sinker molds), several thin clinch-on sinkers, pinched-on split shot, or a series of brass beads. If you use beads, or if the sinkers are bright, paint them black or dark gray to reduce the apparent bulk and size of the lure. You will still have to make the right-angle bends in the wire between the forward part and the spinner parts to prevent blade-binding.

Another way is to make two separate parts: one the slim sinker portion with two eyes; the second the spinner. The two are joined at the eyes. Yet another possibility is to make the forward sinker portion with an eye at one end and a coil-spring open eye or snap-lock eye at the other. This way, any length or weight sinker can be placed on any spinner.

SPINNERBAIT WIRES

These are safety-pin style of spinnerbait wire that is made with a snap-lock or open-coil spring-wire shaft bent into a safety-pin shaft and ending with one or two spinner blades. With the easy-attach end, it is made to convert any jig into a spinnerbait. The central eye in the middle of the "safety pin" replaces the eye of the jig for line attachment.

To build one, add the coil spring to the shaft (if using one) and use round-nose pliers to make a complete circular eye in the middle of the wire. When this part is complete, the wire ends should be at about a 60- to 90-degree angle, although this can be adjusted for your fishing as desired. At the end of the wire, make a wrapped eye around a swivel. (The swivel allows the blade to turn freely and spin.) Use a split ring to attach a spinner

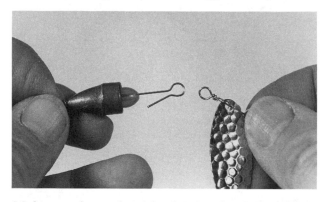

Making a forward-weighted jointed spinner. Here, the weight forward part is on one shaft with a coil-spring closure fixed with a red tapered bead. The blade-and-hook part (or a standard spinner) is added here.

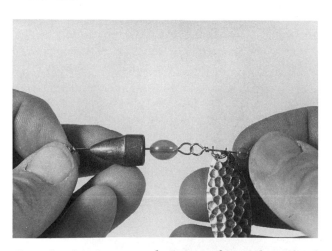

Completed spinner made into a forward-weighted style with the addition of the sinker section.

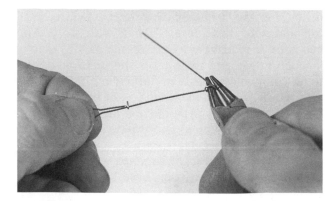

Making the safety-pin bend in a spinnerbait wire for adding to a jig.

blade to the swivel to complete this lure accessory. To add two spinner blades to the shaft, first thread on a blade and clevis, add a bead or two (again, these bearing surfaces are important for blade movement), and complete. Depending upon the angle that the wire and lure come through the water, the forward blade (on the clevis/shaft) may not completely rotate, but will flash and turn from the water resistance. These can be made any size to match any size jig.

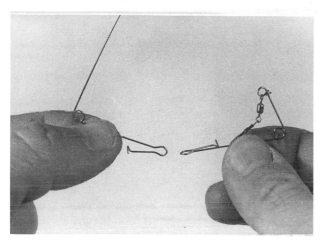

Partially completed spinner-jig form (left) and completed form (right), prior to blade being added.

BAIT SPINNERS

Bait spinners are nothing more than spinners designed for use with worms, minnows, leeches, or similar long, swimming baits. As a result, most are built with an open-coil spring or spring-lock closure, and thus are made in reverse order from the typical spinner. They also usually use long-shank single hooks. Be sure to use a straight eye (not turned up or down) to prevent kinking. Some rigs use two single hooks: a smaller one to lip-hook a minnow or hold a piece of pork rind; a larger, longer-shank hook to body-hook the minnow or serve as a main trailer hook. Both are attached to the same spinner eye.

DOUBLE SPINNERS

These use two spinner blades, both on clevises, and both on the same shaft. One is forward of the other, making for a longer spinner. To make one, begin with the wrapped eye and add the clevis and blade as for a typical spinner. Add some bearing beads or unies, make a right-angle bend, then make a second bend close to the first using needle-nose pliers. The result is small Z-shaped bend like that used for the weight forward spinner

Examples of different spinner rigs to fit on a jig. Top left, blade on shaft with clevis; top right, twin blades with snap for jig attachment; bottom, single blade on swivel attached with coil spring fastener to jig.

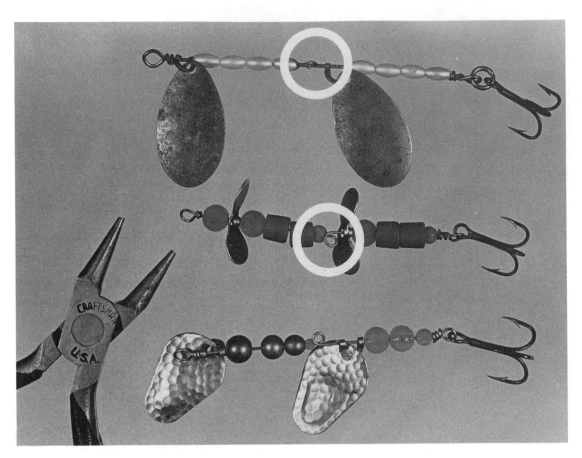

Making double spinners: Methods to prevent binding of the rear spinner blade by the forward components include a drop of solder on the shaft (top photo) and an eye wrapped in the center of the shaft (center). A sharp kink (two bends) in the wire will accomplish the same thing.

described above. Then add the second spinner blade and clevis and the body to complete the lure. Remember that failure to add the slight crimp or bend to the shaft just ahead of the second blade will cause water pressure on the forward blade to bind the second blade.

An alternative to the sharp bends is to add a small drop of solder or epoxy glue to serve as a stop for the forward blade and beads. Spinners can be made like this with two blades and one body, or two of each (almost like two spinners on one shaft), or even three blades, if desired. The variations are endless, but with each addition of a blade or body, the spinner gets longer.

SPINNERBAIT SPINNERS

In general, spinnerbaits (covered in Chapter 6) are larger and formed by casting lead on a special hook/wire form. Paint, skirts, and spinner blades are added to the lead bodies. Tiny spinnerbaits,

which I call "minibaits," or variations of spinner-baits can be made by using spinner-making techniques and parts. This results in smaller lures for small-fish populations and spinnerbaits that can be cast on ultralight tackle.

These are made just like the spinnerbait wire that is added to jigs, except that you make them with a small body of spinner parts, usually bodies or brass beads for weight. Begin with a straight (no eyes or forms) shaft, and make a wrapped eye around a swivel. Use a split ring to add a spinner blade to the other eye of the swivel. Using as much shaft as you like (you can make short-arm or long-arm spinnerbaits, as you prefer) make a complete eye bend in the wire, with the free end about 60 to 90 degrees to the upper arm. Add the body parts or beads desired for the body of the minibait. Form the wrapped eye as described for the typical spinner, adding the treble, single, or double hook at the same time.

If you wish a straight, single, fixed hook in line

Mini-spinnerbait formed of spinner components on spinner wire.

with the minibait, there are several ways to do this. One is to use red tubing to hold the free-swinging hook in line with the body. Another way is to use the minibait wire and thread it through the eye of the single hook, then wrap the wire around the shank of the hook. It helps to solder this in place. Make sure that the hook point is up (pointed toward the spinner blade) in all mini-baits, just as in spinnerbaits.

It is also possible to make two-blade minibaits by adding a second blade to the main shaft with a clevis and some bearing beads to help the blade rotate. Because the purpose of any of these is to make spinnerbaits smaller in size and weight than the 1/8-ounce minimum weight available commercially or from molding heads, use small light-weight beads and brass spinner bodies together with small blades in the 00 to 1 sizes.

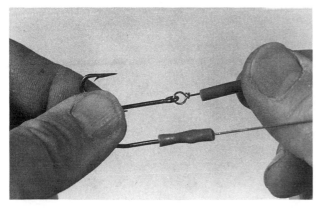

One way to keep a hook straight on a spinner wire is to use a small piece of rubber tubing slipped onto the spinner wire and then over the hook eye/spinner eye.

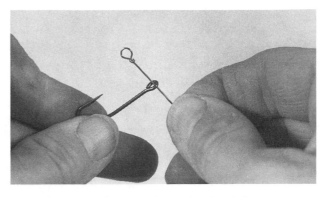

It is also possible to make a fixed solid connection between a spinner wire and hook. First slip the spinner wire through the hook eye in a downward direction as shown.

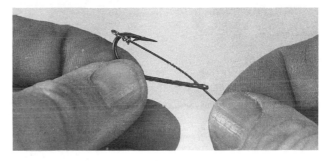

Next, slip the wrapped wire eye over the hook point.

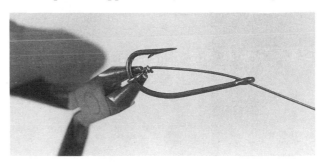

Continue, slightly bending as shown.

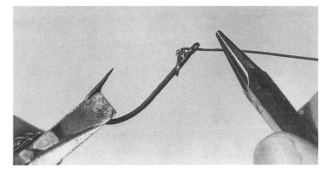

Force the two eyes close together (pull one with pliers with other in vise, or bend eye as shown) to make fixed connection.

Bend wire shaft up and parallel with hook shank to complete.

SPLIT-RING SPINNERS

These do not have rotating spinner blades on a shaft. Instead, the spinner blade is attached to a split ring, usually with a swivel in front and a treble hook in back. Usually, large split rings are used, and some of these have two blades, one on each side of the hook. Split-ring spinners were once widely used and are not often seen now, but they will still catch fish.

As mentioned, it is possible to use this method to make keeled and other combination spinners. Attach the blade-and-hook combination to the rear of a painted keel sinker to make a variation of a weight-forward spinner or spinnerbait.

Two types of Coloado spinners. The one on the left has two swivels (standard construction), the one on the right only one.

FIXED-BLADE SPINNERS

These spinners look much like regular spinners in the water, but they do not use a clevis, and the blade is always at a fixed angle. Typical fixed blades are the June Bug blade and various Roto-spin blades. All have arms (Rotospin from the top, June Bug from the center blade), so that the shaft goes through two holes in the blade to hold it at a fixed angle to the main shaft. They all rotate well and are popular; the June Bug spinner is widely used for fishing bait on a hook attached to the open-coil spring eye at the rear.

TAIL SPINNERS

These are nothing more than a variation of a standard spinner in which the blade is at the rear of the body. In making them, the body is built forward on the wire shaft, and the shaft is crimped or fixed with solder to provide clearance so that the rear blade (on a clevis) will spin. It is best to use fat blades (like the Colorado or badger) that will spin at an angle to the shaft so as not to hit the hook just behind the blade.

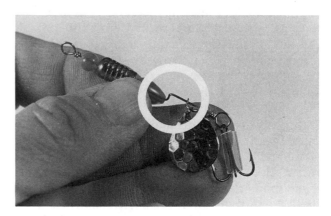

Another method of making a forward-weighted spinner using a spinner body on the shaft first, making two sharp bends as shown to prevent the blade from binding, then adding the spinner blade and finally the hook on a wrapped eye.

MAKING OTHER SHAFT FORMS

Although you can buy wires with wrapped eyes, snap-lock eyes, and open coil-spring eyes, you can also make your own. The wrapped eye was described in the typical spinner construction.

To make a snap-lock eye, first make sure you have enough wire. Begin by making a sharp bend in the wire with needle-nose pliers or the ends of tapered round-jaw pliers. Then use the larger-diameter portion of the pliers jaw to form an eye, bending the wire 360 degrees. Hold the eye with the tips of the round-nose jaws or with the needle-nose pliers and make a sharp bend so that the end of the wire is almost parallel to the main shaft. At this point the wire will look like the outline of a keyhole. About 1/2-inch up from this point, with the finest tips of the round-nose pliers make a tiny J shape in the wire. This J should be at right angles to the plane of the two wires, not in line with them. Then use the needle-nose or round-nose pliers to make a sharp bend so that the J can be snapped over the main shaft. At this point it will be easier to clip off the remaining wire, using proper safety precautions as described earlier.

To make an open coil-spring-eye form, follow the same procedure, but do not make the J shape at the end. Clip the wire to about a 1/2- to 5/8-inch length, measuring from the sharp bend above the eye. Use a coil spring on the main wire shaft to close it. (Often this coil spring must be added first, before making the bends.)

FIGURING SPINNER WEIGHTS

You may not need or be concerned with weights for your spinners, because most spinners are light and cast with light or ultralight spinning or spin-cast tackle. The component-parts companies may or may not list the weights of all of the parts, although they do sometimes list the weight of the brass beads and bodies in fractional ounces. If you are concerned about the weight of the total lure, there are several ways to determine it. One is to compare your finished spinner in size and style to an existing commercially made spinner for which you know or can determine the weight. This won't be exact, but will usually be close enough for figuring tackle needs.

The second method involves weighing the parts in quantity. In doing this, get a good postage scale and add parts to the scale until you reach a weight in ounces. Count the items and figure the fractional weight of each item. Do this with each item and convert the resulting fractions to a common denominator to determine the total weight of the lure. You can do this more accurately with a grain or powder scale, if you like. Also, for measuring beads, you may want to use a small cup (reset the scale to zero when doing this) to keep them from rolling off the pan.

A third possibility is to make up a quantity of identical lures, add them to the scale until one ounce is reached, then count the number of lures to determine the fractional weight.

SPINNER KITS

The most widely known kit for making spinners is available from Worth, though the company calls it the "Lure Making Kit." It includes a wire former, paints for finishing bodies, and enough shafts, clevises, swivels, coil springs, snaps, blades, bodies, and hooks to make at least twenty-five lures. Naturally, the paint and wire former, plus the excess parts, can be used for making spinners of varying design with additional parts.

Other companies have spinner kits available, too. For example, Cabela's has two kits containing spinner blades and crane-snap swivels for quick-change convenience. These kits are primarily designed for spinnerbait blade changes, but can be used for spinners as well. Some companies sell kits with tools and paints, others with parts only. Jann's, Hille, Netcraft, Reed, Midland, and others all carry spinner parts.

4

Bucktails And Jigs

INTRODUCTION ▪ TYPES OF MOLDS ▪ HOOKS ▪ SOURCES OF LEAD ▪ HEAT SOURCES ▪ SAFETY ▪ MOLDING TECHNIQUES ▪ MOLDING STEPS ▪ FINISHING MOLDED BUCKTAILS ▪ WRAPPING TAILS ON LEAD HEADS ▪ JIG COMPONENTS AND KITS

Basic Safety Requirements
Goggles
Welders' or heavy gloves for handling molds, pots, ladles
Respirator mask
Apron
A clean, clear, sturdy countertop on which to work, preferably covered with sheet metal

Basic Tools
Old cooking pot
Cheap gravy ladle or large serving spoon
Bucktail molds
Fly-tying vise, machinists' vise, or C-clamp
Hot pads
File

Helpful Tools
Plumbers' melting pot
Plumbers' ladle
Gate cutters or shears
Wire cutters
Ingot molds
Heavy pliers
Electric-element hand-held melting pot
Electric bottom-feed furnace
Split-ring pliers
Compound-leverage fishing pliers
Spinner-making tools may be useful for some assembly and modifications

INTRODUCTION

If asked to choose one lure for all types of fishing, many expert anglers would name the lead-headed jig, or bucktail. Time and experience have proven that this lure, in all its many variations of size, shape, tail, and modifications, can effectively imitate saltwater baitfish, eels, squid, crabs, and freshwater minnows, crayfish, hellgrammites, stone cats, and similar baits.

Commercial bucktails and jigs come in tiny 1/80-ounce sizes and giants that weigh up to 24 ounces. While all of these lures are basically lead heads molded on a hook, those used in salt water are generally called bucktails, while those used in fresh water are called bucktails or jigs. All of them are essentially the same: a lead head on a special hook with a skirt or tail. Some variations are manufactured (and possible when making your own) with lips, tail spinners, jointed bodies, and the like.

Skirts on these simple lures can include bucktail, (hence the name), other furs, artificial furs (FisHair), craft fur (similar to FisHair and available from craft, fabric, and hobby shops), feathers, saddle hackle, frayed polyproplyene rope, fine strands of nylon (UltraHair), Living Rubber, strands of dynel (similar to nylon), and marabou. Vinyl skirts, soft-plastic grubs, minnows, soft-plastic skirts, vinyl skirts, trailer tails, crawdad tails, plastic frogs, salamanders, eels, and shrimp are possible slip-ons for some types of jig heads. Most of these latter jigs and bucktails have special collars with one or more barbs designed to hold the soft-plastic addition in place.

Most jig or bucktail types have different names. Sometimes the same lure will have different names in different geographical areas. In addition, molds for the same type of head may have different names according to the manufacturer. Typical bucktails include:

Banjo-eye bucktails. With bulging eyes, for use in saltwater and striped-bass fishing along the mid-Atlantic Coast. Often trolled and tied with a straight-fur (bucktail or similar artificial fur) tail. Often heavy; this will vary, however, from 1/4-ounce to 8 ounces.

Crappie killers. Small, usually with a round head, often tied with a chenille body or palmered (hackle-wrapped) chenille body and marabou tail for added action. Used for crappie; also used in a variety of sizes for many other gamefish. Often 1/80- to 3/8-ounce in size.

Shad darts. Small tapered, lead heads with sloping fronts, originally designed for American and hickory shad, but used for a variety of panfish, sunfish, and crappie. Usually about 1/32- to 3/4-ounce.

Bullet-head or bullet-nose bucktails. Molded with a bullet head for a long streamlined look, and usually used in salt water. Sizes from 1/4-ounce to 4 ounces.

Glider or slider heads. Made with a flat horizontal head for slider fishing with a short worm or grub tail. Also used to make bonefish jigs for shallow-water flats saltwater fishing. Mostly small, about 1/16- to 3/4-ounce.

Lima bean, Upperman-style, or flat-head jigs. These have a slim vertical, round, or egg shape when seen from the side, and are very popular for saltwater fishing because they sink rapidly and are easy to work.

Commercial bucktails range in price from a few cents for small, inexpensive, simple styles to several dollars or more for the large, heavy, saltwater bucktails or those with glass-eye inserts, special tails, or similar more-complex features. These same lures can be home-molded and tied for a fraction of the commercial cost.

Molding bucktails takes only the proper mold, a few hooks, some lead, and an old file. To finish and tie up the bucktail takes only the tail material, thread, paint, and a vise of some sort for clamping the hook in place while tying on the tail materials. These supplies serve as a bare minimum. A ladle and special melting pot or hand-held electric furnace are better for melting lead than are the old soup ladle and cooking pot sometimes used. Also, wire cutters are handy to easily remove the lead sprue that is attached to the head from the molten lead that was poured through the sprue hole or gate of the mold. Special gate cutters in two sizes are available from manufacturers such as Do-It and Hilts Molds. These are sometimes spring-loaded, have cushioned plastic grips, and will shear lead sprue close to the jig head. One important point: They are *not* to be used for cutting wire.

TYPES OF MOLDS

Commercially molded jigs and bucktails are made in several ways. One is to use a round two-part mold (much like two pie plates, but made of special rubber) and a centrifugal molding machine to spin the molten lead from a central sprue hole out into all the cavities. The molded result, before the jigs are cut out, resembles a lead

Various types and brands of bucktail and sinker molds, by Hilts Molds, Do-It Corp., and Li'l Mac.

wagon wheel complete with spokes and with a large lead arbor — the molded jig heads comprise the outer rim. This is not for the home craftsman; the cost of the machinery is very high and is designed for large-quantity production work. Commercial molders also use heavy-duty precision single-cavity aluminum molds fed by a bottom-feeding furnace. A number of molds are used in rotation so that a high commercial production output is possible.

For the home craftsman, the molds available commercially are usually two-piece, made of aluminum or aluminum alloy, and have one or more lure cavities. These cavities form the lure when the molten lead is poured into them through a tapered funnellike opening called a sprue hole, gate, or down-gate.

At one time, molds for fishermen were different from those for the small commercial operation. Today that separation is disappearing as more and more fishermen are making their own tackle and using precision molds that produce high-quality lures. For example, mold costs from Do-It and Hilts Molds, both major manufacturers of molds for the home craftsman and small business, are well within the range of any sportman. Some tackle craftsmen have a dozen or more molds for making different bucktail heads. Do-It, Hilts Molds, L'il Mac, and others also have molds that make multiple lures of the same weight that

are better for those selling lures or needing only one size for specialized fishing.

Thus, a typical mold from Do-It for making a round-head jig — model JNR-6-A — will make one each of 1/80-, 1/64, 1/32-, 1/16-, 1/8-, and 1/4-ounce heads. The production molds make all heads of the same size, such as in the similar model 1249 mold, which makes seven 1/32-ounce round-head jigs. Other Do-It production molds, such as the 1250, 1251, and 1252, make seven 1/16-, 1/8-, and 1/4-ounce lures, respectively. The same applies to Hilts Molds, in which the model LMRH-M will make one each of 1/32-, 1/16-, 1/8-, 1/4-, 3/8-, and 1/2-ounce round-head, collared, and barbed jig heads. The LMRH-32-6 will make six each of the above heads, all in a 1/32-ounce size. Hilts Molds has similar multiple-cavity, single-size molds for other sizes, through 1/2-ounce. The difference is not really in the quality of the mold or of the jigs produced, but in the variety of lures made. Most fishermen will want a variety of head sizes, and the standard molds allow this with the purchase of one mold in place of a half-dozen.

All modern molds from companies such as Do-It, Hilts Molds, and others are top quality and designed to produce lures without flash or fins. ("Flash" and "fins" are molders' terms for excess metal that leaks from the mold where the two mold halves join.) When or if this occurs, it must be filed off or removed to make top-grade bucktails. This work is unacceptable for the commercial molder and a nuisance for the home craftsman. It is far more cost efficient in terms of time to buy only those molds that will produce top-quality, flash-free results.)

Molds come in several different designs. Pinned molds are the least expensive, but also the most difficult to work with. They consists of two flat sides with a registration pin-and-socket arrangement to hold the two halves together and line them up properly for good registration. They must be clamped together with C-clamps, spring clamps, or otherwise held securely each time a lure is molded. They are made in two separate halves, usually with a pin on one side of each mold half that fits into a socket on the other half as the mold is closed. To their advantage, pinned molds usually form very good lures with little flash.

But while these molds are somewhat inconvenient to use, they are inexpensive and mold lures just as well as any other type of mold. However, the clamping and unclamping of the mold is time-consuming and makes it difficult to turn out a number of lures quickly, particularly when the mold starts to get hot from repeated pourings. One way to speed up this operation when using pinned molds is to use a pair of woodworkers' spring-loaded gluing clamps to hold the halves together. If using gluing clamps, be sure to remove the vinyl tip protectors, or the hot molds may burn them.

Another type of mold has two clamps, one on each side of the mold, the clamps holding the two halves together for pouring. Otherwise they are just like the pinned molds, and do have pins and sockets for proper registration of the two half-cavities. A variation of this is a design in which one side is hinged and the other spring-clamped. Because of the hinge on these molds, registration pins may be absent. In most cases, there is at least one pin and socket on the opposite side of the hinge to keep the parts aligned.

The most popular and widely available molds are those that are hinged and handled. These are my personal favorites because they are easy to work with and produce excellent results. The hinge holds the two halves in perfect alignment, and the two handles make it easy to hold the mold together for quick and efficient operation. Registration pins — usually on the handle side — also help to align the two halves for perfect lures. The only slight disadvantage is that the handles can

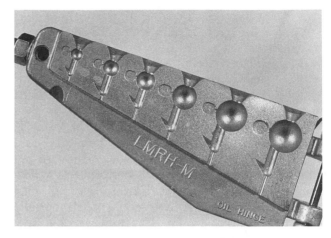

Another example from Hilts Molds showing a ball-head jig designed to take a grub tail. (The barb molded into the collar holds the grub in place.)

quickly get uncomfortably hot. This is more theoretical than actual, because most molds have heavy wood or plastic handles. Those that have metal handles are easily handled with heavy gloves to prevent discomfort. Also, all molds get hot in use, and, in fact, for the best results should be gently heated before use to prevent incomplete castings.

The number of cavities in a mold is often determined by the size of the mold blank. Thus, a mold to make small jigs might contain as many as eight cavities. A mold for larger lures, such as one to make 3- and 4-ounce spearhead jigs from Do-It might have only two cavities (one of each size), while the Hilts Molds Scampee Bullet Nose and

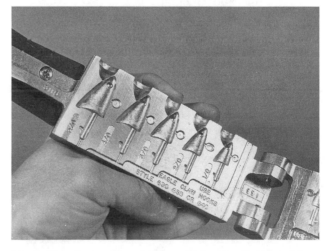

Example of arrowhead jig mold by Do-It Corp. Note that the hook style and different sizes of hooks are noted on the mold and that the mold produces different sizes of heads.

Big Bullet Nose jig molds have only single cavities for these lures that range from 1/2-ounce to 24 ounces each.

Molds also sometimes require pins, plates, or rods to make holes, slots, or cavities. Those requiring plates and rods are more typical of molds for sinkers that require these parts to make a specific sinker. Plates to make a slot, for example, are required to make split-shot, rubber-core, and pinch-on (clinch-on) sinkers, while rods are required for the holes through egg sinkers, bullet-weight, and similar-type sinkers.

Pins are sometimes required in molds to make weedless jigs and bucktails because the pin produces a socket in the back of the head for gluing in a Y or nylon-fiber weed-guard. Some molds allow you to mold Y- or brush-guards in place, eliminating the need to glue later.

Molds vary widely in the variety of heads they produce, even aside from the many sizes and various shapes. The simplest type will make one or more simple, plain bucktails. Molds are available that make similar simple heads but that are modified with the addition of one or more barbs on the lead collar behind the head: The barbs help hold soft-plastic tails, minnows, grubs, and the like in place. Other molds have circular ribs around the collar or a small ball on the end of the collar to help in tying and holding in place bucktail or other tail materials. Some have sockets on the sides of the head for gluing on plastic or glass eyes for added attraction. Still others include the core pins for molding in weed-guard sockets, or for molding in the weed-guards themselves.

Some jig and bucktail molds take inserts in addition to the hook. These inserts can include the aforementioned Y or nylon weed-guards molded into the head of the lure. Usually these

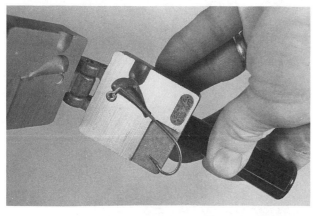

Another example from Li'l Mac, this with the hook in place.

are made of materials that will not melt in the short contact with the hot lead, which makes it easy to mold weedless jigs. Some large molds require insert eyes, to which the line is tied. The large Hilts Molds Bullet Nose jigs require this in the 6- through 24-ounce sizes, since the hook sizes required (10/0 or 11/0) do not come in the bent-shank bucktail style for this mold. Regular hooks are used with the insert eyes added for a line-tie.

Do-It has a bass spin jig (model ARK-3198FS) that uses not only the nylon weed-guard or brass pin insert, but also a length of multistrand wire for adding a spinner blade after finishing the jig. The spinner addition makes it more like a spinnerbait in construction, but the line-tie is still to the hook eye, and the finished lure is fished like a jig.

Do-It has a "blank" mold to allow the home craftsman to make his own head designs, should a specialty head or size not be available from a manufacturer. The Do-It style is a completely blank mold (model 1155) in which the mold can be cut by a tool-and-die maker or machine shop to form the cavity area, hook and eye channels, and the gate and sprue. Because this type of work can be very expensive, get an estimate of any such project before ordering a blank mold. Hilts Molds has a Perfect Replica mold (model PRMOLD) that is a blank mold with a recessed box and four sprues. It is used with the PRMR-1 kit, which consists of two pieces of silicone rubber that have a modeling-clay consistency to allow making a mold from an existing wood, plaster, lead, or similar-material copy lure. The silicone is set by vulcanizing at 375° for forty-five minutes in a regular oven. The frame can be reused, and extra silicone kits are available. (More details are in Chapter 17.)

A blank mold similar to the Do-It model is available from L'il Mac in their model A-3200-1 mold.

In addition to the above assortment of molds, mold replacement parts are available. Do-It and L'il Mac carry and sell replacement wood handles to fit any of their molds, Palmer can supply replacement plastic handles for their molds, and Hilts Molds has replacement bolt-in plastic-covered steel handles for their molds.

I particularly like those molds that have important information engraved or molded into the mold. Both Do-It and Hilts Molds do this, with the information usually including the hook sizes that will fit each cavity (this will vary with the cavity on most hobby molds), the hook style or

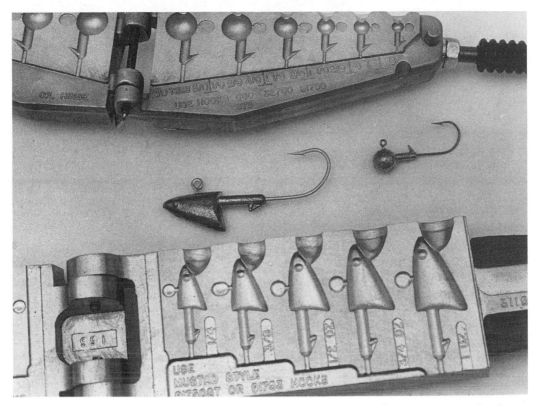

Examples of molds, and the jigs they produce, from Hilts Molds (top) and Do-It Corp. (bottom). Both companies have a wide variety of bucktail, lead lure, sinker and similar molds.

styles that will fit (hook styles vary and are not universally interchangeable between different molds), the weight of the lure molded in each cavity, and so on. Some, such as Do-It, even have

This jig mold from Hilts Molds will mold in the plastic weed guard and make four sizes of jigs. Note the weight, hook style and hook weight imprinted on the mold for ready reference.

a notice on the mold suggesting oiling the hinges periodically! STP or other heavy oils are excellent for this.

HOOKS

Special hooks are required in most molds for bucktails. Exceptions can be found in some lures, such as the very large bucktails for which the special bent hooks are not available, and the specialized lead lures (not really bucktails) that have a lead body, molded-in wire form for the line-tie, and hooks and a tail spinner. These are often called tail spinners generically, and are like the commercially available Little George and similar horse-head and pony-head lures.

Other examples of specialty lures include the slab spoon lure, vertical jigging spoons, structure spoons, and diamond jigs. All of these require wire forms or insert eyes for hook- and line-ties, but usually use standard free-swinging treble hooks instead of the molded-in bucktail single hooks.

Standard bucktail hooks come in a wide variety of sizes and styles, but all of them have a bend

This mold from Li'l Mac is from the company's Midget Mold series, although larger molds for bucktails and sinkers are available.

in the shank near the eye of the hook. In most cases, this bend is at a right angle to the the rest of the hook shank, but some hooks (often the larger sizes) have a 45-degree bend to the shank. Examples of those with the right-angle bend include the Eagle Claw 630 series of hooks, or the Mustad 32760. Those with a partial bend include the Eagle Claw 730 wide-throat flipping hooks, and the Mustad 34185. The sizes of most manufacturers' jig hooks range from about size 12 through 7/0.

In almost all cases, the hook eye is in line with the plane of the hook. In other words, were the hook normal (straight-shank), the hook eye would be flat to the hook bend, not at right angles to it, as are most other hooks. (One exception to this is the style 1623, in which the eye is at right angles to the hook plane and the slight shank bend is near the hook. This is used in the stand-up jig from Do-It, in which the large "foot" of the head holds the hook point up and high.)

These hooks come in regular and extra-heavy wire, round and forged shanks, and various bends, including Aberdeen, Model Perfect, O'Shaughnessy, Sproat, and similar basic hook styles. Hook finishes include bronzed, gold, nickel, cadmium, and tinned. Any of these platings will work in both fresh and salt water, although saltwater use might require a freshwater rinse for jigs molded on bronze or gold hooks. Tinned hooks are often best for salt water.

All are good and reliable, although they vary in their features. For example, light-wire hooks will bend under stress, something that is an advantage

in some freshwater jig fishing where hooks are often snagged and must be pulled free. It is a disadvantage in other types of fishing, primarily in saltwater fishing, where long fights are typical and a light-wire hook can result in a lost fish.

In some cases, standard-style hooks are used. This is usually only done with the very large jigs, such as the Hilts Molds Big Bullet Nose jig in all sizes from 6 through 24 ounces. These jigs take either 10/0 or 11/0 hooks, and specialty jig hooks are not made in these sizes.

It can't be emphasized too strongly that you must use the right hook style for each mold. The eye must fit into a small round depression in the mold, and the hook wire diameter and shape must fit the mold cavity exactly. The right size is also important. Using the right style but too small or too large a size will result in the hook fitting at a cocked angle into the mold. Any of these situations will result in the mold not closing properly or flash forming around the hook shank or the joint of the mold halves.

SOURCES OF LEAD

Lead and lead alloys are available in a variety of forms and mixes and from a number of sources. Pure lead is available from those companies that manufacture molding supplies such as furnaces and molds. Pure lead is soft and as a result will pour and form easily. Plumbing-supply houses also sell pure lead, and it can be bought in better hardware stores.

All service stations that change tires or mount new tires have ample supplies of old lead in the tire weights that come off the wheels. Large stations often sell their weights, but some smaller stations are glad to have them taken off their hands. These weights have a steel bracket in them to clip the lead onto the wheel. In addition, they are often coated with road grease and oil. As a result, the impurities on these wheel weights must be skimmed off the top of the molten metal as slag before the lead can be poured. The metal clip will also melt off and float on the surface of the lead to be skimmed off. These weights are not pure lead but an alloy, usually with some antimony and tin mixed in to make for a harder alloy. They also require a higher heating temperature than pure lead, and as a result will often pour easier. Antimony melts at 1,166° Fahrenheit, lead at 621°. A small percentage of antimony in lead will result in different alloys melting at different temperatures. As a result, lead alloy will handle a little differently during pouring and may not fill small-cavity molds as easily as will the softer pure lead. However, if you can get it free, the price is right and the result will be fine for larger jigs and large sinkers (see Chapter 5).

Other sources of lead are junkyards, scrap-metal yards, lead from lead sheathing and from cable used in telephone wiring. Telephone-wiring sheathing is almost pure lead—about 98 percent pure—although the lead solder used to join sections of pipe or wiring is a lead alloy. Never, never, ever melt down batteries for lead, because all lead batteries contain acid and are extremely dangerous and hazardous to handle. In addition, small batteries (sizes AAA through D are commonly used in toys, flashlights, and electric equipment) may explode if heated over a flame. You may, however, be able to get "battery lead," which has been melted down from batteries by recovery companies, and thus is safe to use.

Your choice of lead might be dictated by cost or availability. If these are not important to you consider the following: Pure lead will melt most easily, will have the least amount of impurities and slag, and will pour most easily for the best filling of all molds, especially small mold cavities. However, because it is soft, it will dent more easily if, during casting, it hits rocks, resulting also in chipped paint. Harder lead alloys with a mix of antimony and tin will not pour as easily, nor will they fill small-cavity molds as well as pure lead, but they will be harder when molded for less painting, chipping, and denting problems when fished around hard structures. There is no right answer to this dilemma, and some commercial manufacturers of jigs, bucktails, and spinnerbaits use pure soft lead while others use harder lead alloys. I use all types of lead and lead alloys, but I try to keep them separate so as not to combine them any further.

HEAT SOURCES

The actual process of molding lead-head lures is a simple one, but one that must be carried out carefully and with forethought for safety and to attain the best results.

While molding bucktails is fun, it must be done safely. Roy Hilts, owner of Hilts Molds, and in the business of manufacturing molds for almost forty years, says: "Never become so confident that you are not scared of it."

The first safety consideration is the place where the molding will be done. The kitchen stove is one

obvious place for melting lead and pouring lures, although Roy Hilts does not like it because of the possibility of lead spilling on countertops, the floor, and the sink. (Molten lead and water *never* mix, and water thrown on a spill can cause explosive splatters of molten lead.)

But I like the kitchen area for several reasons. First, there are several stove burners so that several pots of lead can be kept hot at once. This is important if a large quantity of lead is needed. Second, kitchen stoves always have an exhaust fan nearby. This can be a typical above-stove hood-type exhaust fan, or a fan that exhausts below. Since there can be trace elements of toxic substances in lead (even pure lead), and since lead itself is a toxic substance, a good, high-volume exhaust fan is a must for any melting and molding operation. (If your kitchen or work area does not have a fan or a properly working fan, do not work in the area. Proper exhaust when working around molten lead is crucial to your long-term health. It might also help to open windows on the opposite side of the kitchen for cross-ventilation.

A third advantage to using the kitchen area is that usually there is ample counter or table space for laying out molds, hooks, and the other tools

A more sophisticated molding furnace. The tracks for holding molds and the lever for releasing lead through a bottom opening indicate a bottom feed. While designed mainly for bullet molding, these are used and usually easily adapted for bucktail and sinker casting. Courtesy of Lyman.

and materials required. Of utmost importance in using the kitchen for this purpose, if you want to be allowed in the house again, is to cover all working surfaces with a protective layer of quarter-inch or thicker plywood, thick masonite, thick wood paneling scraps, hot pads, or a similar sturdy, non-heat-conducting material. Do not use anything thin, plastic, or metal (they will usually not protect adequately from the extremes of heat necessary to lead-melting). The best solution is complete coverage with the large-size hot pads made of aluminum or stainless steel. Some are available in sizes up to an 18 × 24-inch rectangle. Several of these over the area immediately surrounding the stove will work fine.

The aluminum or stainless steel pads are really better than scraps of wood, because they make for easier cleanup of any small spills of lead. Lead will stick to wood or similar materials (although it can be pried off them), but when cool it can be lifted easily from most metal surfaces. Completely cover the sink and any wet or moist areas. Also be sure to remove all exposed food and to completely clean all work areas after molding, after removing all the lead and tools, and again before exposing food to the area again. For your family's health, this is a must. *No exceptions!*

If you lack a suitable kitchen area in which to work, it is possible to use other heat sources, such as liquid-fuel camping stoves, propane and butane stoves and torches, some electric hot plates, and outdoor charcoal and propane barbecue grills. Be sure to use them only where safe (outdoor stoves and heat sources are to be used outdoors only), and be sure that you have sufficient sturdy, steady tables or other level-work-surface areas that you can cover and protect as needed. Naturally, these must be used with adequate ventilation and air exhaust, as with the kitchen stove. One advantage of a separate, special workplace is that you can bolt a furnace in place there. You can bolt a furnace to sections of shelving boards and place this on a covered kitchen countertop, but make sure the result is sturdy and stable.

Electric lead-melting furnaces were used in the past by hand-loaders primarily for molding lead bullets, but they are becoming more common for sinker- and bucktail-molding. They eliminate the need for a local heat source because they can be plugged in anywhere, used on regular 120-volt household electric service, and do not use an open flame as do some other heat sources. All these furnaces work with a heating element much like the small immersion heaters that are popular for heating water for tea, coffee, and soup when away from a stove.

Electric melt furnaces are made by Palmer, Hilts Molds, Lee, RCBS, and Lyman. (The latter three are made primarily for bullet molding.) They can range from the small Palmer Hot Pot, which holds four pounds of lead, up to the giant Hilts Molds Ultimate Inferno, which will melt up to 35 pounds of lead at a time on household current. (It does require a y circuit—preferably at least 20 amp—because it uses 1,600 watts.)

The smaller units usually pour from the top as if from a ladle; you pour the lead from the heated container into the mold cavity through the sprue hole. Larger units either bottom-feed through a bottom nozzle or top-pour, but with the ladle supported and balanced for easy pouring. The Ultimate Inferno, for example, is capable of pouring through the top spout or through the bottom 1/8- and 1/4-inch-diameter nozzles and bottom-pour plug. Most of the bottom-pour furnaces are best for smaller-cavity molds, from 1/120-ounce up to about 2 ounces. Larger-cavity molds have larger gates or sprue holes and can be filled easily either with hand-held or frame-supported ladles. One that does have the capability of bottom-pouring large quantities is the 35-pound-capacity Ultimate Inferno from Hilts Molds. Roy Hilts says he can completely fill a five-pound rock-cod-sinker mold through the bottom spout of this furnace.

Many of these electric furnaces have options of top- or bottom-pour capabilities, and replacement elements are available should an electric element burn out over time. One option available for several of the furnaces is mold guides, which can be fitted to the bottom-feed furnace to properly position the mold under the furnace for easy, accurate pouring. The guides are available primarily from those companies making bullet-molding furnaces, although some can be fitted onto different furnace brands.

Most of the better furnaces have a rheostat control to adjust the temperature between perhaps 500° and 800°. This allows proper heating of a variety of lead and lead alloys whose melting temperatures are within these ranges. The smaller, ladle-type electric heaters do not have this capability.

Some melting furnaces are simply electric pots that will melt lead but that require a separate ladle to transfer molten lead from the pot to the mold.

One big advantage of a bottom-feed furnace is that any slag, dross, or impurities will stay on the molten lead's surface, making it less likely that these impurities will mix in with the lead used in the lead heads. Furnaces also provide greater flexibility in working area, because with them you are not confined to the kitchen, but can mold anywhere there is a sturdy work area and a proper electric outlet. Another advantage to furnaces is speed, because when properly set up, and with skill and experience, they make speeds of up to 400 jigs per hour possible. It should be pointed out, however, that these speeds are attainable only with experience. Casting lead heads is not a speed contest, and safety concerns must be paramount at all times.

Naturally, furnaces must be positioned on a firm, sturdy work surface with ample space for molds, hooks, and various safety equipment. Ideally, furnaces should be bolted to the work surface or workbench top.

Many furnace models are available, and some can be expensive, though others, such as the Palmer Hot Pot, are relatively inexpensive. Take your time in considering such a purchase and thoroughly examine all available furnaces to determine the one best suited to your purposes, budget, and production needs.

In addition to kitchen stoves and electric furnaces, other types of heat sources can be used for melting lead. Single- or two-burner camp stoves operating on liquid fuel (like the Coleman models) or small cylinders of propane or butane are also ideal for bucktail-molding. They have the advantage of portability, something definitely not possible with a kitchen stove or when you are limited to a locality with the proper amperage outlet for an electric furnace. As a result, these stoves allow bucktail-molding in an open garage, carport, patio, breezeway, backyard, gazebo, deck, or other outdoor area, or any part of the house, such as a workshop area. Be aware, however, that most parts of the house, even a workshop, will lack the ventilation of a kitchen or the outdoor areas, and ventilation is vital for your long-term health in molding lead.

If you use a camp stove, be sure to match it with a flat-bottom pot to hold the lead. The flat bottom is critical to prevent wobbling and possible spills of molten lead. Pots and matching ladles for melting lead are available from tackle shops, mail-order supply houses for lure-making parts, and hardware stores carrying plumbers' supplies. If you use a large ladle in place of a pot, you will need a rack to support the ladle. These racks are made for gas stoves and are designed to allow a small pot to be used on a larger burner by concentrating the flame to the smaller pot bottom.

Plumbers' pots will vary within a capacity of 5 to 20 pounds of lead: the ladles will hold from 4 to 16 ounces of lead. Bullet-casters' ladles are smaller and more precise, often with two spouts (on opposite sides for both right- and left-hand pourers), and with partitions at the spout to hold back slag. The bullet-casters' ladles usually hold less lead, however — from 1 to 4 ounces — so are less effective when molding larger bucktails.

It is important to use a large-enough ladle or pot. For example, most small pots that can be heated on stoves will hold about 6 to 10 pounds of lead. A ladle might hold 1 to 2 pounds. This sounds like a lot until you start to fill molds. To make 4-ounce bucktails, for example, in a four-cavity mold, 1 pound of lead will be used in one pouring.

The ideal ladle for working from an open pot is the kind (often used by bullet casters) that has a vertical partition across the ladle near the spout. The partition has holes in the bottom so that lead will flow from one side of the partition to the other. This allows only pure lead into the mold, since the slag that floats to the top is kept back by the partition.

If necessary, you can get by with a soup ladle and a discarded cooking pot, but be careful. Make sure these do not have soldered or heat-sealed joints, or handle fastenings that might loosen or weaken with the high heats used in melting lead. Make sure the pot and ladle are sturdy and will hold the weight of lead you will be using. If you are doubtful at all, do not use them. And once you do use them, *never again* use them for food or drink.

SAFETY

Safety in using and handling lead must be paramount in any operation to make bucktails, jigs, and sinkers. The cautions in this chapter are equally important for Chapter 5, "Sinkers and Tin Squids," and must be reviewed before any attempt to make sinkers and tin squids, as well as bucktails.

Safety in molding lead heads must be on several levels. Lead can be a dangerous, toxic substance. In addition, it often contains minute amounts of impurities such as tin, antimony, arsenic, which poisonous, and mercury, the vapor of which is highly poisonous.

Lead has an accumulative effect—it does not easily flush from the body. Lead absorbed over time builds up to higher levels, and too high a level is toxic. Examples of the danger are found in many inner cities, where chilen eat lead-paint chips (lead is no longer used in most paints), and as a result experience mental impairment, as well as other medical problems.

Lead is absorbed into the body when its fumes are inhaled (thus the need for proper venting or outside location when melting lead). The fumes are deposited on the mucous membranes of the nose or mouth and subsequently swallowed, absorbed by ingestion (thus the need for proper hand-washing after handling lead and care around food), or by contact with oil-soluble lead that is absorbed directly into the skin, as in smoking while molding.

Certain safety procedures in handling lead and melting lead are necessary. These include making sure that you work in a properly vented area. This does not just mean a workspace in a large area, or one with passive ventilation, but one (as with the kitchen vent fan) that will actively pull the fumes from the work area and vent them outside. Lacking proper ventilation, work outside.

Do not smoke. Experts warn that smoking while molding is one of the principal ways in which lead can be ingested or absorbed. Lead is transferred to your hands, which in turn is transferred to the cigarette or cigar, which in turn is transferred to your mouth. Also, it is possible that lead could be deposited on the cigarette paper and then burned and inhaled as the cigarette is smoked.

Take your smokes before or after molding and be sure to wash thoroughly as described after molding and before handling any smoking materials.

Do not eat or drink anything while molding lead heads or melting lead. This is a must, because lead will be absorbed onto your hands and can be transferred to food, and thus into your body. Be sure to wash your hands properly and thoroughly after each molding session and before doing anything else. Use *plenty* of soap. The best are the special heavy-duty hand-cleaner soaps that are gritty (such as Lava), and that will thoroughly clean your hands of oil-carried lead or other lead residue.

Wear protective clothing to prevent lead-to-skin contact. Long-sleeve shirts, caps or hats, and gloves are a help. Heavy insulated gloves are particularly good because they aid in safe handling of molds and ladles while minimizing contact with lead or lead-based oils or substances.

In addition to these main concerns over handling and working with lead, there are also the safety concerns of working with the high heat necessary to melt lead. Whether using pure lead or lead alloys, or even pure tin (more on the subject of making tin squids in Chapter 5), molten metals are dangerous if not handled carefully and systematically. Tin melts at 449°, pure lead at 621°. Although it may seem repetitive to you, follow these rules when preparing and working with any molten metal. Note that these rules are in addition to those for safety: They do not replace them.

- Before beginning to mold bucktail heads or sinkers, make sure there is no competing activity in the house. Do not mold when others, particularly children, are in your area or likely to interfere physically or by distraction. Molding requires all of your concentration. Put all pets, including dogs, cats, and anything else in a secure place (basement, bathroom, inside if you are working outside, outside if you are working inside) for the duration of the molding session. Make sure others in the house know about this so that they do not release the pet.

- Make sure you have adequate ventilation if you are working at home. While this is important for safety, it is also important if you want to be allowed back in the house after the molding session is over. Many wives are very unsympathetic to the fumes and odors of lead-molding, but the main reason, of course, is safety.

- Make sure you have a safe, sturdy workplace with a counter of ample size that is properly protected with large hot pads, sheets of plywood, or similar insulating sheets. Make sure that any lead that might spill will be contained so as not to ruin countertops, other equipment, or flooring.

- Use an adequate furnace or heating source. If working with a furnace, camp stove, torch, or barbecue grill not specifically made for melting metal, make sure it is sturdy—not at all wobby—and will not slip or move. Similarly, make sure that any pots used on such stoves are flat-bottomed and stable. (Most are, and the Lee pots have a wide, flat bottom just for this purpose.) Lead is heavy, and a small pot can hold 10 or 20 pounds and be completely uncontrollable if it starts to spill. Make sure you have furnaces and melting pots bolted down properly.

- Work out a plan for your molding, pouring, and handling of hooks and molds. It is usually best to have your steadiest hand control the pouring lead while the other hand holds the mold. If you are right-handed and working with a bottom-feed furnace, it often is best to use your right hand for the furnace controls and hold the jig mold in your left hand to line it up under the furnace spout. If you work with a top-pouring electric furnace, it helps to use your right hand to control the lead and your left to hold the mold handles. If you work with a pot (electric or heated separately) and separate ladle, hold the ladle with your right hand and pour into the mold being held with your left hand. (The latter two suggestions assume you are right-handed. Reverse the directions if you are a southpaw.) All of these methods mean you will need a large working area to the left of the heat source to minimize the amount of movement you will make with a lead-filled ladle or to eliminate crossover where you would have to bring a mold across or in front of the molten lead supply. Naturally, this will be reversed if you are left-handed.

- *Never* cool a mold or lead by dipping it in water, and never have water anywhere near the molding operation. Moisture or water in the melting pot or ladle or dropped into the molden lead will cause the melt to explode violently, and with dangerous and potentially disastrous results.

None of this is designed as scare tactics to keep you from molding your own lead heads. If you have molded lead heads or sinkers before, you already know most or all of these cautions. And if you are new to molding lead heads, most of them will be recognized as just plain common sense. But they are most important commonsense rules.

MOLDING TECHNIQUES

As just mentioned, it is important to have a basic game plan and working arrangement. If you have not molded sinkers before, it helps *before starting* to go through the motions of adding hooks to the mold, closing the mold, pouring the lead, opening the mold, removing the lead heads, cutting the sprue lead from the head, re-adding more hooks, and so on. In other words, the full cycle of molding should be rehearsed to make sure you have enough space, nothing is in the way, and the best arrangement for repeated molding has been prepared.

Plan on making a lot of molded heads at once —this will save time and money. I like to mold lures, but I do not like to prolong the process by molding only a few at a time on repeated days. It's a waste of both time and natural gas, electricity, or other fuel every time the lead is remelted. Once the pot of lead is melted, it is easy to add more ingots to keep the operation going. It is far simpler, more time-efficient, and more economical to mold fifty to two hundred lead heads of a favorite fishing lure at one time, even though such a supply might last for several seasons.

There are no real tricks to molding, but two suggestions to maximize your time are to work with a partner or fishing buddy, and to work with several molds. The reasons are simple. With a two-man operation, it is easy to separate the work as follows: One person is responsible for picking up the prepared molds and filling them with molten lead; the second person is to place the hooks in the molds, to close them, to leave them on their sides and ready for pouring, and to remove the lead heads from the cooled molds. In some cases, it might even help to have two persons doing these latter tasks: one to place hooks in the molds, the other to remove the completed lead heads. Although none of these tasks are difficult, they do take care, especially when adding the hooks to hot molds and removing the still-hot lead heads from the molds. Using several molds allows for a rotation of this process and prevents one mold from getting too hot from repeated use.

If there is any trick to getting good lead heads, it is in having the lead hot and the mold warm. When the lead first melts, it will be a bright, glistening silvery color, almost the sheen of highly polished sterling silver or a brand-new silver-plated spoon. As more lead is added (or as lead ingots or excess sprue is added to replenish the molten lead), the temperature will drop and the lead will turn mushy. It will still be molten, but will have a slushy appearance. I think of it as looking like silver oatmeal or mashed potatoes.

In part, the temperature range will vary with the type of alloy or lead used. Lead with a little (2 1/2 percent) tin will have only a short, 9-degree, temperature range through this slushy stage until it reaches the liquid temperature. An alloy with ninety-five percent lead and five percent tin will have a broader temperature range, 75 degrees, between solid and liquid. A similar alloy of ninety-one percent lead, two percent tin, and seven percent antimony will have a range of 62 degrees, and an alloy of ninety-four percent tin and six percent antimony will have a sixty-four-degree pasty or slushy temperature range.

The lead must be heated beyond this slushy stage to a molten liquid stage before you are able to work with it. It must be hot enough to pour smoothly and rapidly into the mold and to completely fill the cavity or cavities. One way to judge the proper temperature is to heat the lead until it becomes a purplish or golden color. Because this is at a higher temperature, it might bring to the surface some additional impurities, giving the surface a slightly scummy appearance. Too much of a purplish/blue/red hue in the surface sheen indicates that tin is drossing out of the lead (oxides are rising to the surface and separating), and stirring might be required.

These impurities may not matter unless the scum and slag are so excessive that they will interfere with the proper filling of the mold with pure lead. If they do seem excessive, skim off any slag with an old tablespoon reserved for that purpose. Before that, however, try stirring to reintroduce the lighter metals to the alloy mixture.

Take care that you do not overheat the lead, particularly if working with alloys. Excessive heat will tend to separate the metals in the alloys (usually tin and antimony added to the lead), so that fluxing and stirring are necessary. Fluxing, practiced primarily by bullet-casters and involving adding tallow or candle wax to the lead, is smelly and creates excessive fumes. If you do have excessive drossing or scumming indicative of metal separation, fluxing helps. One tip is to use plain candle wax or beeswax, about a 1/4-inch-diameter chunk for 3 pounds of molten lead. Add it carefully to the melt, and immediately touch a match to it to burn off the black fumes that will otherwise result. If doing this, avoid working in the kitchen and creating fumes. Also, try this first on a small scale to get a feel for the extent of the fumes and smoke that can occur. The process *does* help mix two separate metals to make a better mixed alloy.

Stirring will help to mix the metals, which otherwise will tend to separate as a result of their different specific gravities. Lead that is too hot can overheat molds, increase the time it takes the lead heads to cool for removal from the mold, cause a frosty or crystalline appearance on the surface of the lead head, cause lead to run along the seam lines of the mold, and increase the possibility of flash on the completed head.

When molding bucktails, you often don't know the type or percentage of the metals in lead alloys. In most cases, you can get by with scrap lead (usually an alloy), but if problems occur, stick to straight, soft, pure lead. The additions of other metals to the lead will cause various effects — some good, some bad. Tin is very ductile (thus ideal for the old-style tin squids) and lighter than lead, but it will also strengthen the lead. It also alloys easily with lead. Antimony also adds strength to the lead, along with hardness, and might be something to consider when molding lead heads that will be cast around and into rocks. Other substances, such as zinc, aluminum, arsenic (added to older car-battery lead), iron, copper, and nickel, sometimes found in lead alloys do not help in any way.

When alloys are used, it is important to periodically stir the molten lead because the lighter metals will rise to the surface as a dross, and skimming them off may result in losing the positive characteristics the metals add to the alloy.

If you work from a bottom-pour furnace, you will have few problems other than adjusting the spout and feed of the furnace to the quantity of lead needed for the mold used. For this reason, it is best to use molds that fit any mold guides that come with the furnace or that you rig for this purpose, and whose cavity sizes match the amount of lead released from the bottom-pour. In most cases, you will be limited in the amount of lead you can pour. (There are exceptions, such as the Hilts Molds Ultimate Inferno, that will pour any amount of lead through the bottom spout.)

On most bottom-feed furnaces you will not be able to use any molds that have wire or projections (such as spinnerbaits, walleye spinners, bottom-bounce/bottom-walker sinker molds, tail spinners, or molds using large hooks that project from the mold), because they will interfere with placing the nozzle tight to the mold sprue.

The melting pot (electric or stove-heated), provides a ready "stock" of melted lead to pour into the mold. However, unless the pot is designed specifically with a spout and tilting arm or lever, *never* pour from the pot — use a ladle. Unfortunately, many beginners have problems in using a ladle to dip lead from the pot. The problems usually result from using a cold ladle, or one that has been allowed to cool between pours. A cold ladle will rapidly cool the lead even before you can begin to pour it into the mold. There are two solutions: One, if you use a lightweight ladle, keep it in the pot so that the cup of the ladle is always at the temperature of the molten lead; two, use a second burner and rest the ladle on this burner (properly supported and secured, naturally) to heat it and keep the lead it picks up at the proper molten temperature. The hot ladle can easily be refilled from the larger pot. Keep the ladle hot and dry, and never put a cold lable into molten lead.

Similarly, the mold must be kept warm. The mold will eventually become warm through repeated moldings, but when beginning, you must heat the mold on the stove, or warm it by pouring lead into the mold cavities until complete, perfect heads are achieved. If you heat the mold on the stove, use only the lowest heat for a few minutes: Excessive heat will not allow the heads to cool easily and might even warp aluminum molds. Some furnaces, such as the Lyman 20-pound MAG 20 bottom-feeding furnace, have a "warming shelf" to keep molds hot.

If you heat molds by casting heads, do so *without* hooks until perfect results are achieved. The early imperfect heads can be returned to the melting pot or furnace. Use care, because they might leak lead through the channels for the hooks and wire. This will occur where hooks are placed in the cavities for complete heads. I like molds to be just slightly too hot to touch, but experience with your individual molds will dictate the proper working temperature.

While a cold mold or cool lead from a cold ladle will cause imperfect castings, other casting problems can occur, too. Sometimes the sprue hole is not quite large enough to fill the mold cavity before cooling begins to take place. I recall one of my molds that cast four bullet-shaped bucktails, all of the same size. No matter what molten lead temperature I achieved, whether I used alloy or pure lead, how hot the mold or ladle was, or which sprue hole I filled first, one cavity always produced poor, incomplete results. I drilled out the sprue hole slightly to enlarge it and since then the mold has worked fine. If you find this necessary, be very careful that any drilling or reaming is confined to the sprue hole only and does not go deep enough to damage the mold cavity. The best solution is to hold the mold closed in a drill-press vise, and drill straight down, using a stop on the bit or the drill-press arm to prevent cavity damage. If you lack a drill or drill press, you can do this with a razor blade, X-Acto knife, or scalpel, carefully carving away the excess aluminum to enlarge and smooth the gate hole.

Proper and easier molding is achieved by smoking the mold cavities with a flame. A candle flame works fine, as shown here. Molds should be re-smoked when required, usually indicated by incomplete castings or casting with a ripple finish. The smaller the mold cavity, the more important smoking the mold.

Sometimes large cast bucktails will have a rippled surface. One solution to this, and in fact something that should be done with every mold, is to smoke the mold with a candle flame. For some reason, candle-flame smoke will create smoother bucktails (and sinkers) and reduce molding problems. The theory behind this is that the smoke layer creates an insulation that allows the molten lead to flow freely, not forming ripples.

Too hot a mold or lead also creates problems, since this might remove some metals of the alloy (changing the characteristics of the lead head) or create a frosty, crystalline surface, and increase the possibility of flash or fins on the lure edges

Insert pins and brush guards in place, and also held separately.

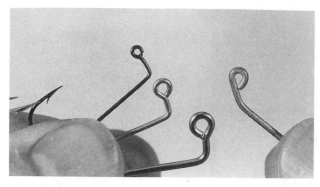

Jig hooks, all with bent shanks, and eyes in plane with the hook bend for easy fitting into the molds. Most have a 90-degree bend as on the left; some hooks have a 60-degree or other bend, as on the right. It is most important to use the right style and size hook recommended by the mold manufacturer.

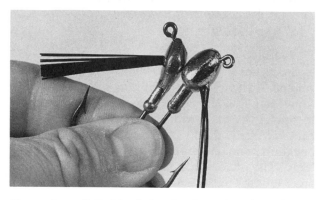

Examples of finished heads (unpainted and un-dressed) with fiber weed-guard (left) and "Y"-shaped weed-guard (right) molded into the lead head.

where the two mold halves come together. This can happen to a slight degree with any mold, but with the high-quality molds of today, with their machined inner surfaces, it is far less likely than with older, less-polished molds. You must avoid this flash, because it requires time and effort to remove it for perfect results. (Other causes of flash are from the mold not completely closing, when the wrong size or style of hook is used, the use of a dirty mold, and lead in the mold hinge from an overpour.

Molding Steps

The actual steps of molding lead heads are simple. First, place the special jig hooks in the mold, taking care that the right brand, style, and size is used for each cavity. After the hooks are properly positioned, close the mold carefully by

bringing the second half over onto the first, which is kept level and horizontal. Hold or clamp the mold halves together securely. If you work in a team and use several or more molds, you may wish to use spring-style carpenters' clamps to hold the molds closed so that the hooks do not slip. If you do this, remove any plastic protective tips, because they might burn.

If you use a bottom-feed furnace, adjust the spout lever or feed to the quantity of lead needed for each mold cavity. Slide or place the mold into the mold guides, and make sure the sprue hole is directly under and in close contact with the furnace spout. Pour the lead into each mold cavity, remove the mold from the furnace, and lay it down. Allow it to cool before attempting to remove the lead heads.

If you will be using a top-pour, trunnion-pivoted furnace, make sure the pot pours well and straight. If necessary, use sturdy blocks of wood as a base on which to support the mold, making sure that the support is at the right height for proper pouring. (This support height might have to be changed with different molds.) This is always helpful, but especially necessary when using molds to make larger bucktails, because a multiple-cavity mold where each cavity makes a several-ounce lure can mean more than a pound of lead will be necessary for one pour.

If you use a ladle, remove it from the pot or stove where it is kept to maintain proper heat for smooth pouring. Usually you can rest the lip of the ladle on the edge of the mold for support, but

Molding requires a high heat to melt lead. If not using an electric furnace or pot, one good source is the kitchen stove, provided that proper safety techniques are used (see text). Note block top holds ladle level and board to the right of the stove to protect the kitchen counter top.

take care in doing this to prevent the ladle from slipping and spilling molten lead. Finish the pour and set the mold aside.

If you work with large lures, you may have to keep the mold upright for a few moments for the lead to cool sufficiently before placing the mold on its side. This can easily be seen by watching the lead in the sprue, which will change from a liquid shiny sheen to a more crystalline, slightly duller surface as it cools. Also, the lead will dip slightly in the center, since the cooling process will usually draw some liquid lead from the sprue area to adjust for the slight shrinkage that occurs when lead cools.

When pouring by any of these methods, make sure the lead does not spill outside the sprue area. If lead laps over the sides of the mold or into the hinge area, it will be difficult or impossible to open the mold without prying or cutting the excess lead free.

If working with a partner on a rotation method with several molds, you should have separate places for the filled molds and those that are ready to be poured. Once a filled mold is cool, open it carefully. At this point, the lead heads will still be hot, so lift them our of the mold with pliers (handling by the sprue only to avoid damaging the body) or with gloves, and place the heads on a hot pad. If you have a mold where the lead heads will fall out, make sure the heads fall onto a soft surface, such as an old folded-up towel, to protect them from damage. This is particularly important with heavy heads when using pure (soft) lead. Once the lead heads are cooled, make sure you do not handle them with your bare hands. This will deposit oils onto the lead, which will interfere with painting the heads. If you use the heads bare, as for slider-fishing, worm-fishing, or grubs or minnow tails, this will not matter. Place more hooks into the mold and you are ready to cast that mold again.

Cut away the excess lead that forms in the sprue hole of each cavity by using wire cutters or special lead-cutting gate cutters. Most of the mold-manufacturing companies sell these special cutters that are to be used only for lead or plastic (not for wire). The excess lead, sometimes called "sprue" after the entrance hole into the mold, can be added to the lead stock pot.

It is best to leave lead in the melting furnaces when you finish, because it will heat the additional lead more rapidly at the next session, saving electricity and lessening the possibility of damage to the heating coils. If you don't want to keep the

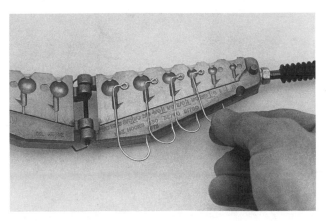

Placing hooks in a mold (Hilts Molds). Normally, the mold would be smoked, but here has been left unsmoked for clarity in the photo.

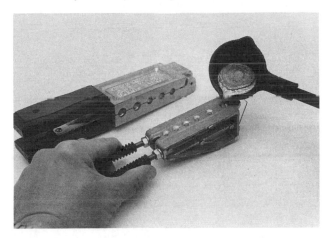

Pouring molds. In all cases, use heavy gloves to hold the ladle, properly support the mold and pour quickly but carefully. The Hilts mold is being poured; the Do-It mold has been filled with hooks and will be poured next. Working in a rotation system like this is more efficient.

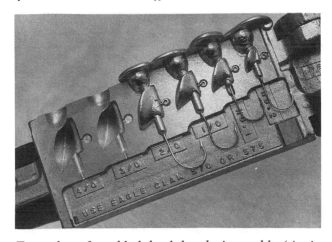

Examples of molded lead heads in mold. (Again molds would normally be smoked.)

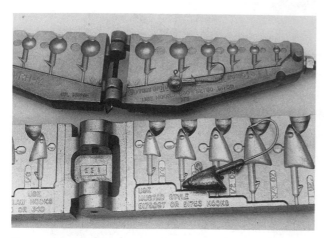

Example of jig heads from two different molds. Top, a Hilts mold; bottom, a Do-It mold.

A large saltwater bucktail head, here removed from a single-cavity smoked mold.

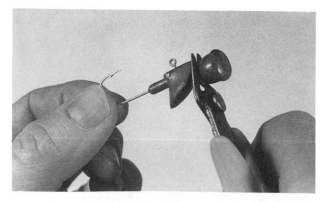

Using gate cutters (available from Hilts Molds, Do-It Corp. and other sources) to clip the sprue from a molded bucktail head.

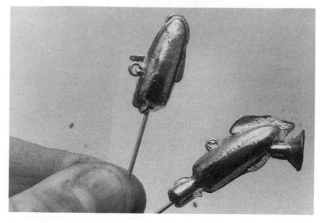

Examples of defective molded heads, as a result of using the wrong hooks, not closing the mold properly, using a mold that is not hot enough, or not smoking the mold.

leftover lead in the pot or ladle when you are finished molding, buy some ingot molds. Pour this lead into them to form small "pigs." Although there is nothing wrong with leaving lead in the pot until the next pouring session, you might still want ingot molds if you get lead in odd shapes and sizes and wish to melt it down into usable bars. If you are using, or wish to keep separate, different alloys, work out a system of marking the pigs with a chisel, scratch awl, or felt-tip marker.

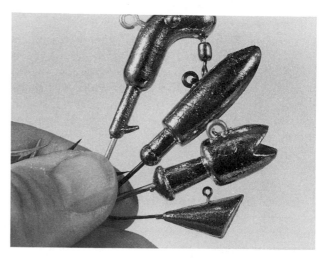

Examples of molded lead heads after being removed from the molds and the sprue cut off.

FINISHING MOLDED BUCKTAILS

Once all the heads have been molded, make sure you handle them only with lightweight gloves. Rubber dishwashing gloves or cotton gardening gloves are fine for this. The gloves prevent the oils

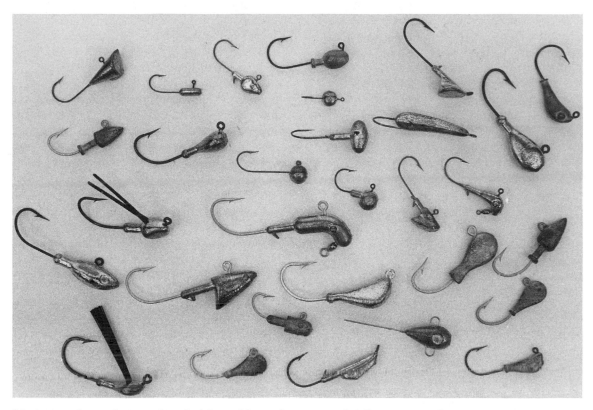

Various styles and sizes of jig heads and lures from several different manufacturers.

from your hands from coating the lead heads and interfering with paint adherence.

There is still work to do before the lure can be tied onto the end of a line. First, check the head carefully, especially the hook eye and the seam line where the two molds halves met. If lead has deposited in the eye, there are several ways to remove it. One is to use a pair of side-cutting wire cutters and gently (do not cut through the hook wire) cut around the base of the eye and twist free any excess lead. Another way is to use a small awl, ice pick, or similar pointed instrument to poke the lead out of the eye. I use an old small screwdriver that I ground down to a four-sided point (like a pyramid) that serves as a coarse reamer to remove lead. Punch-out tools are also made specifically for this task.

Ideally, there should be no flash on the sides of the lure. If there is a small amount, it can be removed with a coarse file. Regular flies are designed to be used with steel and other hard metals, and while they will work on lead, there are special files on the market designed for use with special metals that are more appropriate for this task. There are lead files, brass files, and aluminum files that are made of steel for working on these materials. Flat and half-round shapes are

typically available. Prices are slightly higher than for similar regular files.

If you are turning out a quantity of bucktails and not tying them up immediately, it is still wise to give them a base coat of paint shortly after molding. If the lead heads are not painted, they will slowly oxidize, making paint adherence more

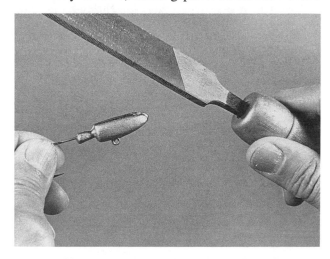

Using a file to smooth any flash from along the joint line of the two mold sides or cavity halves. If the mold is a good mold and if the right size and style hook is used, this is generally not necessary.

difficult. Any quality color paint will work well, although white is preferred because it provides a good base for any light or bright colors painted on later. Until the lead heads are painted, be sure to handle them with gloves to prevent any oils from your skin transferring to the lure, which would interfere with paint adherence.

The choice of paint is a difficult one, because the problem with any lead-head lure is that the paint will chip off if the lure hits a rock. This is true even with most commercially made bucktails. The pros and cons of various types of paint and the methods of using them to paint bucktails and jigs (as well as other lures) are covered in Chapter 16.

After the first coat of paint or primer to prevent oxidation is applied, the lead head can be left indefinitely without finishing. I usually keep a stock supply of different styles and sizes of lead heads on hand, all painted with primer or a base coat of white, to tie up at my leisure or as needed.

WRAPPING TAILS ON LEAD HEADS

To finish a traditional bucktail lure, place the hook of the painted lead head in a vise. A small fly-tying vise works best for this step, and most vises today have interchangeable jaws to adjust to different-size hooks. Lacking that, any small vise or clamp will do in a pinch. Some possibilities here include Vise-Grips (which can be clamped in a larger vise or to a table with a C-clamp, although self-clamping styles are also available), a small clamp-on work vise, or hobby vises.

You will need thread, and, preferably a bobbin to hold the thread. Fly-tying or rod-wrapping

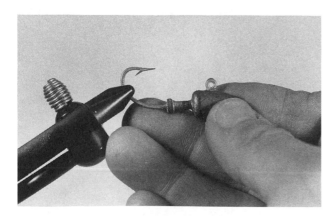

Finishing a jig head involves wrapping the collar with tail materials. The first step in this is to clamp the hook into a fly-tying vise or simple vise substitute.

thread will work fine. Do not use cotton sewing thread—it is too fuzzy to produce good results. The best thread sizes are 2/0 for small bucktails up to about 3/4-ounce; size A for larger bucktails to about 4 ounces; and size D or E thread for anything larger. If making a very thick tail, you may wish to go to a slightly larger thread for the lure size to tie the material down tightly. While you can wrap by holding the spool of thread, it will be far easier to use a bobbin such as is used in fly-tying.

Typical tail materials fur, bucktail, artificial fur, saddle hackles, crinkly nylon, polypropylene fibers (often unraveled from polypropylene rope), marabou, mylar strips, or special materials such as UltraHair, Krystal Flash, and Sparkle Flash. These materials can be used in combination.

Deer tail fur is clipped from the skin for use as the tail material on a jig.

Bucktail heads will differ, some having a completely bare hook shank, others having a molded-in lead collar, some with ridges to help hold the body and tail material or with a slight ball at the end to prevent the material and thread from slipping off.

Begin by wrapping the thread several times around the collar or hook shank. After several turns, wrap the thread back over the previous wraps, in essence tying the thread down with the tension of the overwraps. Continue to wrap, and after several more turns cut off any excess thread. From this point on it will be necessary to maintain tension (though there is an exception at one step) to keep the thread or materials from loosening.

Choose the tail material, cut the proper amount close to the skin or base, and measure it for length

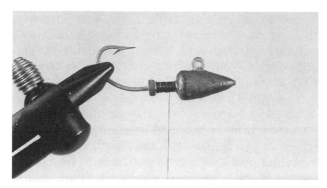

Using standard tying techniques, tie down the thread as shown and build up a base of thread on the jig collar.

on the bucktail head. For best results, the tail should extend past the hook bend. General guides are to make it about one and a half to one and three-quarters the length of the hook shank so that the tail extends well *past* the bend of the hook.

There are two basic ways to add a fur or artificial-fur tail to the lure. One is to take the full bunch of fur and hold it in position on top of the hook shank or collar, spiral several slightly loose wraps of thread around the fur and hook, and pull the thread down tight, continuing to wrap as you do so. While doing this, spiral and push the fur uniformly around the hook so that the entire hook shank or collar is covered with it.

The second method is to use small bunches of the fur and to tie each down tightly in place around the hook shank or collar. These small

Begin by holding the fur over the top of the collar and wrapping the thread over it several times. Rotating the fur before pulling the thread tight will spread the fur uniformly around the collar.

Fur spread uniformly around the jig collar. Excess fur forward of the collar is clipped off with scissors.

Once the excess fur is clipped off, the fur tail is completely wrapped with thread as shown.

sections assure more complete, even coverage, particularly on larger heads. This method takes longer, but usually produces better results for the beginner.

If you make very thick-tailed bucktails on larger heads, the thick fur is often difficult to cut off at the rear of the head. One way to solve this is to cut the fur to length before tying it down, then tie the fur in place so that no subsequent cutting is necessary. Another way is to soak the butt end of the cut fur in hot water for a few minutes to soften it, which will make cutting on the lure easier.

Some lures use only fur as a tail, while others mix fur with saddle hackles, mylar strips, Krystal Flash, or other materials. In these cases, it is usually best to wrap the fur in place before adding the other materials. The reverse is also possible: adding the more fragile materials first and protecting them with a layer of fur.

Completely wrapped tail.

Two-tone fur bodies can be made by tying in two fur bundles—one on top of the hook shank or collar and one underneath. Typical color combinations would be dark on top and light on the bottom (simulating the colors in baitfish) and would include two-tones such as red-white, red-yellow, black-white, black-yellow, red-pink, blue-white, green-white; green-yellow for salt water; and all these combinations along with black-brown, black-red, and black-orange for fresh water.

Some bucktails and jigs require bodies on the hook shank or collar. These are of the "Doll Fly" type, also called crappie flies (really jigs with a lead head). For this almost any plain hook or plain collar (no barbs for soft plastics) can be used. The thread is tied down as above and then wound to the rear of the hook shank. The tail (often marabou) is tied into the rear of the hook shank, just forward of the bend. Once the tail is tied down, the body materials are tied down at the same spot. If a palmered hackle is to be used, it is tied in at this time. Typical body materials include hackle palmered over the body, chenille wrapped around the hook shank, or a combination of both to make a flylike jig.

Once the body material or materials are tied down at the tail, wrap the thread forward and tie down about 1/4-inch behind the ball head. Then the body materials—first the chenille and then the hackle—are wound forward and tied off with the thread. The body materials can be tied in separately or together. Other alternatives are to wrap the tail materials in place with a hackle wrapped in place right behind the head, much as the hackle in a cork bass bug is tied down. Variations of these ties can be used, following fly-tying methods and techniques, but most jigs and bucktails are pretty basic.

Some materials are more difficult to work with than others. Nylon tail material has a tendency to pull out unless it is tied down very tightly. It is a good idea to soak the butt ends of nylon material with a clear fingernail polish or fly-tier's head cement while it is being wrapped on. This will help to hold the nylon in place. Polypropylene tails can be made from a piece of poly rope, the fibers frayed out from the rope and bunched to make a kinky tail. Another way to do this is to tie a short length of the rope in place on the hook shank, threading the hook through the end of the rope to make sure that the fibers are bunched uniformly. Then fray the ends after the rope is securely tied down. An awl, bodkin, needle, fine nail, or similar sharp tool is ideal for this. Fray a little at a time to prevent loosening the material. Bucktails using this material are highly popular and successful, particularly in the Gulf Coast area, where they are advertised and sold as being excellent for ling, the local name for cobia.

Once the tail or body materials are all tied in place, any excess material that laps over the bucktail head must be clipped off square. Do this with fine scissors, or use a razor blade. A razor blade works well to cut around the hook shank or collar, but be sure to avoid cutting thread. At this point, the thread must be tied down and cemented to secure it. To do this, you can finish the thread with half-hitches or with a whip-finish. To make a whip-finish, turn the thread so that you continually wrap over the original wraps, which are then pulled tight.

An easier way to finish the thread is with several half-hitches. Twist the thread to make a half-hitch, pull the knot snug against the body, and repeat several times to secure the thread. After the last one, clip the thread with scissors, and the bucktail is almost finished. If the bucktail was painted completely, you can finish it by protecting the thread with a coat of clear fly head cement, clear nail polish, or even the same paint used on the head of the jig. If you use anything other than paint, take care that you do not cause a reaction between two dissimilar coatings.

If you have not completely painted the head, you can dip it in a second color at this point, covering and scaling the thread wrap also. A second dip may be required (after drying) to completely seal the head. Then the head can be finished by spraying, dipping the forward half of the head, or painting eyes. (Details on painting are covered in Chapter 16.) Eyes can be added in a variety of ways, to be detailed in Chapter 16.

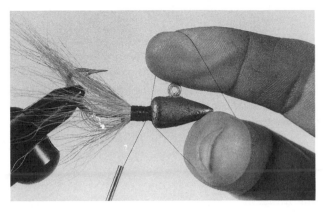

To finish the wrap, use a whip finish, or several half hitches (shown here) to secure the thread. At this point, the head can be painted, either by dipping or brushing. The thread wrap will thus be completely covered, making the wrap and head a uniform color as well as protecting the wrap from moisture.

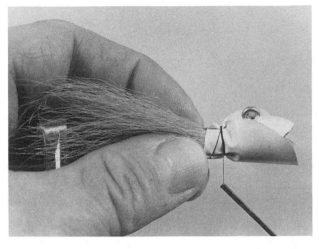

Wrap the collar in place in reverse so that when complete, the collar can be folded back over the thread wrap.

Another way to finish a wrap on a bucktail is to tie in a plastic collar to protect the thread wrap. To do this (here shown on a painted and finished bucktail head) continue the wrap as shown.

Once the collar is wrapped securely, finish the wrap with a whip finish or series of half hitches (shown).

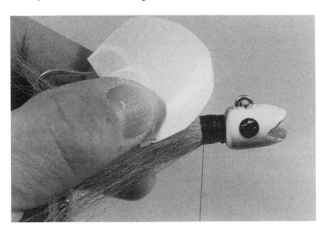

Cut a small piece of flexible vinyl or similar plastic for use as a collar around the wrap.

To protect the thread wraps, coat with fly head cement, nail polish, paint or a similar sealer.

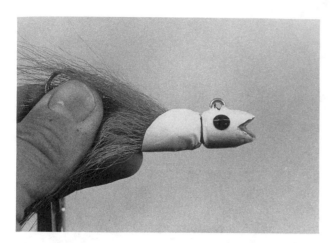

Completed bucktail with the vinyl collar folded back over the thread wrap to protect it and provide additional color to the lure.

Another method of finishing the wrap is to wrap down a small triangular patch of plastic sheeting, leaving the forward part of the triangle pointed forward and uncovered. Once the thread wrap is tied down, protect it with a clear sealer and fold the plastic sheeting back over it. This method is used for many commercial jigs, particularly saltwater models.

JIG COMPONENTS AND KITS

For those who do not wish to mold their own bodies, molded heads are available that can be tied into finished lures. They are available both bare and painted, in most of the sizes and styles available to the home molder using commercial molds.

Cabela's, Netcraft, E. Hille, Jann's, Bass Pro Shops, and other companies sell jig heads this way. Most of those sold bare are used bare with soft plastic grubs, worms, teasers, and plastic minnows.

There is no rule stating you have to paint the jig head, even if you tie on a permanent tail. In fact, most fishermen can relate experiences of catching lots of fish on jigs that are beat-up and missing most or all of their paint. Although I paint my jig heads, my feeling, and the feeling of many, is that it is the action and color of the tail or soft plastic that attracts the fish, not the paint on the lead head.

Jig kits are also available through tackle shops and mail-order companies, the most popular and widely known of which is the Worth kit, comprising twenty-four complete lures from pre-painted heads. This is an ideal, safe way to get youngsters into lure-making.

5

Sinkers and Tin Squids

INTRODUCTION • SINKER-MOLD TYPES • SINKER TYPES AND SIZES • SINKER COSTS • MOLDING TECHNIQUES • METAL SQUIDS • LEAD LURES • FINISHING TIN SQUIDS AND LEAD LURES • COSTS OF METAL LURES

Basic Safety Requirements
Goggles
Welders' or other heavy gloves for handling molds, pots, and ladles
Respirator mask
Apron
A clean, clear, sturdy countertop on which to work

Basic Tools
Old cooking pot
Cheap gravy ladle or large serving spoon
Sinker and/or tin squid molds
Hot pads
File

Helpful Tools
Plumbers' melting pot
Plumbers' ladle
Gate cutters or shears
Wire cutters
Ingot molds
Heavy pliers
Electric-element hand-held ladle
Electric bottom-feed furnace
Worth split-ring pliers
Compound-leverage fishing pliers
Spinner-making tools may be useful for some assembly and modifications

INTRODUCTION

Sinkers can be molded just as easily as bucktail bodies can. In one sense, they are more satisfying for the beginner, because once a sinker is popped from the mold and the excess lead (left from pouring through the sprue hole) is removed, it is ready to use. No finishing, painting, or tying is required.

Sinker molds come in the same styles as do bucktail molds: in pinned, clamped, and hinged-handled models. As with bucktails, the hinged-handled models are the easiest to use and handle. There are some differences between bucktail and sinker molds, however. Not all sinker molds are made of aluminum, as are jig and bucktail molds. Some sinker molds and tin-squid molds have in the past been made of cast iron with machined molding surfaces. Models for molding all types of sinkers are available from the Ed Hain Company (see Appendix G). Because cast-iron molds can rust when not in use, they do require more care and maintenance. Should you have or acquire one of these iron molds, one way to prevent rust is to soak it in a mixture of equal parts of motor oil and kerosene, then stand it on edge to drain (preferably on newspaper) for a few days until it is dry. Make sure it is completely dry before using it.

SINKER-MOLD TYPES

Sinker molds can be separated into several different styles:

No-insert sinker molds. This is my term; by it I mean those molds that do not require any addition of brass eyelets, swivels, rings, wires, core rods, or plates to make holes or slots, as for egg sinkers and pinch-on sinkers. This type of sinker mold casts the eye in lead at the same time the sinker cavity is filled. Styles include molds for bank sinkers, pyramid sinkers, walking sinkers, pencil sinkers, snagless sinkers, bell sinkers, and dollar sinkers.

The big advantage of these types of molds and sinkers is that they are very fast to use because there is nothing to add to the mold before pouring. The only requirements are a hot mold and pourable lead. With these molds, sinkers can be turned out as rapidly as you can safely pour lead into the mold and pop it out again.

Sinker molds with core rods or insert pins. These sinkers also have no brass eyes, swivels, or line-tie inserts added, but do require a core rod (often called a pull pin) or insert plate in the mold to properly form the sinker. Usuallly the brass pull pin has a handle and is infinitely reusable. It is placed into the closed mold and the lead is poured into the cavity. It is pulled out immediately after pouring and will leave a hole in the sinker.

Similarly, sinker molds requiring insert plates leave a slot in the finished sinker. The insert plate is placed in the mold before it is closed and the lead is poured into the cavities. The plate is usually removed with the sinkers attached when the mold is opened, and the sinkers are slipped off the plate.

Examples of sinkers made with a hole using the pull pin include egg sinkers, worm bullet-weight sinkers, pencil sinkers, and commercial net sinkers. Sinkers requiring a slot from the insert plate include pinch-on sinkers, rubber-core sinkers, and split-shot sinkers.

These sinkers are almost as fast to mold as those without any inserts or additions, because the plate or pull pin is easily placed in the mold before or after closing and is the only item to go into the mold. The core rods or plates are supplied with accompanying molds, and replacements are available should they be lost or broken.

Sinker molds requiring eyes. These sinker molds require eyes or an addition to each cavity. Usually these are line-ties, and vary between simple figure-eight brass eyelets, swivels, and special pins or wire forms. Sinkers made this way include bass-casting sinkers, bell sinkers with brass eyelets, cannonball sinkers, cannonball weights for down-rigger trolling, crescent sinkers, pencil sinkers, pyramid sinkers, river sinkers, round concave sinkers, round flat sinkers, in-line trolling sinkers, bead-chain trolling sinkers, keel trolling sinkers, storm sinkers, three-sided pyramid sinkers, bull-dozer sinkers, claw sinkers, silver-dollar sinkers, cushion sinkers, spoon sinkers, banana sinkers, torpedo sinkers, and miniball sinkers.

Usually the brass eyelets, swivels, bead chain, wire forms, and similar inserts are available in bags of one hundred or one thousand of each size. Sometimes they are sold by the pound, with the number per pound varying by the size of the brass eyelet. Swivels are sold by the hundred or by the gross.

When molding some sinkers, wire forms are needed, such as for the straight torpedo or banana-shaped trolling sinkers. These forms are also available by the hundred. Some, such as the Do-It bottom-bouncing sinker, take a long wire form that extends from both ends of the lead and is designed to prevent snagging when fishing lures

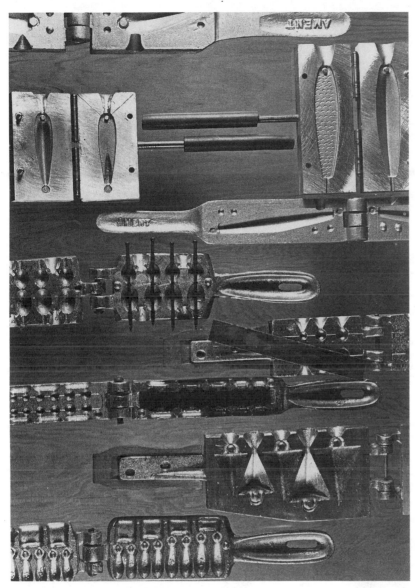

Typical sinker and tin squid molds, including those for egg sinkers, split shot, pyramid sinkers, bank sinkers, and several types of tin squids.

or bait along the bottom.

It is also important to note that with some sinker molds, the sinkers can be cast with either a brass eye or a self-casting lead eye. These molds usually include pyramid, bass-casting, and some trolling styles. Use caution with this, because some lead eyes formed in molds for brass eyes will be weaker.

Most of the sinker molds in the larger sizes will also cast in the lead the size of the sinker in ounces. This is almost always found in bank, pyramid, cannonball, egg, pinch-on, no-snag, walking, and various trolling sinkers. This information may be found on bass-casting, bell, and keel sinkers, but is never found on the small sizes such as worm bullet-weights, split-shot, and small flat sinkers.

In addition, there are also simple molds for

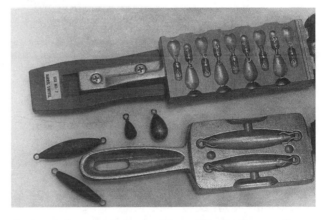

Some sinkers and tin-squid molds require eye forms in the mold. Here, swivels are placed in the mold for molding casting sinkers in a Do-It mold; brass eyes are placed in a trolling-sinker mold.

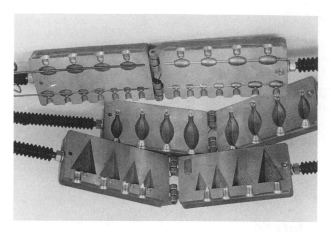

Sinker molds from Hilts Molds including, top to bottom, pyramid, bank and egg sinker molds.

lures and other purposes. Spin jig heads for through-line lures (like a jig, but threaded on the line) and offshore through-leader trolling heads use core rods to make the hole in the lures. Molds for cannonball downrigger weights to 12 pounds, slab-sided structure and casting spoons, duck decoy sinkers, and slingshot pellets are all available from the same companies that make sinker and bucktail molds.

SINKER TYPES AND SIZES

As with bucktail molds, sinker and lure molds come in production types in which all cavities

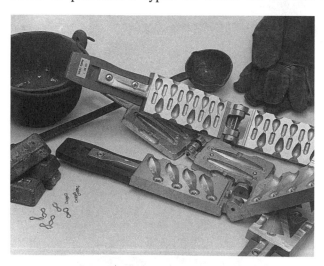

Examples of various sinker and squid molds, three of which are from Do-It, including molds for casting sinker, bank sinker and pyramid sinkers. Also shown are the leave gloves, pot and ladle used when not molding with an electric pot or furnace.

make the same size of sinker or lure, or combination types with assorted or combination cavities that make a range of sizes of a given sinker. In most cases, the molds that make an assortment of sizes are most useful, but if you need only one size of sinker, the production molds will make more of them quicker without wasting additional cavities.

Basic sinker types and the size ranges available in molds include:

Bank sinkers. These are ideal sinkers for much fresh- and saltwater fishing. They are shaped like a tapered hourglass with a molded eye at the top, and are best when fishing around rocks because they tend to remain snag-free. Sizes range from 1/8-ounce up to 20 ounces.

Pyramid sinkers. These are used for sandy-bottom fishing such as surf fishing, and they are very popular on the Atlantic Coast. Both four- and three-sided pyramid-sinker molds are available. Sizes range from 1 through 20 ounces.

Storm sinkers. These are just like pyramid sinkers but with a long, tapered, round point on the end. Sizes range from 2 through 8 ounces.

Bass-casting sinkers. These look like an inverted teardrop with a molded-on swivel. They are popular for much freshwater fishing and some saltwater use. Sizes range from 1/8- through 8 ounces.

Bell sinkers. These are just like bass-casting sinkers in shape, but with a lead molded eye or

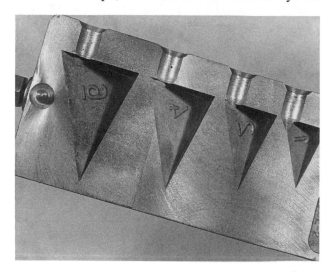

Mold cavities in a Hilts mold. The socket for the sinker eye is on the opposing half of the mold.

brass eyelet for a line-tie in place of the swivel. Sizes range from 1/8- to 2 ounces.

Cannonball sinkers. These are a new design, copied from the heavier cannonball weights used in downrigger fishing. They are round balls with a brass eyelet. Sizes range from 1/2- to 48 ounces (3 pounds).

Bottom-bounce sinkers. These are formed on a wire with a right-angle bend at one end; the wire is formed with two eyes (one at the bend and one at the free end) for fishing the bottom with lures or bait. They are very snagless for river and rocky-bottom fishing. Sizes range from 3/4- to 1 3/4 ounces.

Bulldozer sinkers. These look like a miniature scoop or are shaped like a Y with the eyelet at the junction of the upper part of the arms. They are designed to hold in sand for surf fishing. Sizes range from 1 through 5 ounces.

Claw sinkers. These too are designed for surf fishing on sandy bottoms, and are shaped like a triangle with a projection on the bottom of the triangle and an eyelet at the point. Sizes range from 1 through 8 ounces.

Crescent, banana, and kidney sinkers. These are designed for trolling with a curved shape to prevent line twist. The curved crescent, banana, or kidney shape works like a keel on the line. Eyes are at both ends for tying the sinker between the line and leader. The degree of curve or bend in the sinker is usually relative to the weight and size. Sizes range from 1 through 6 ounces.

In-line, trolling, and torpedo sinkers. These are all similar in that they are shaped like a small, tapered torpedo or cigar with an eye or bead chain on each end. They are designed as trolling sinkers to be placed on the line or between the line and leader. The eyes are centered on the weight so that there is no keel effect as with the crescent, kidney, or banana sinkers. Sizes range from 1 through 24 ounces.

Egg sinkers. These are made with a large hole running through them, and are designed so that the line will run freely to allow a bait-taking fish to run without dragging or feeling the weight of the sinker. As the name suggests, they are shaped like an egg. Sizes range from 1/8- through 11 ounces.

Flat round, dollar, river, round concave, round flat, silver-dollar, and cushion sinkers. All of these are similar, although they will differ individually as to edge types, side shapes, and so on. All are flat like a silver dollar, for which one style is named. Sizes range from 1/4- to 10 ounces.

Split-shot, removable split-shot sinkers. All molds

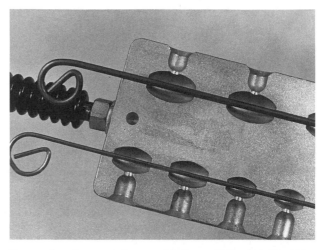

Example of egg-sinker mold from Hilts Molds. The two pins (of different sizes for the different sinkers molded) form the hole through the sinker and are pulled out immediately after molding. Note that to mold all cavities, the mold must be turned over after filling the cavities on one side.

This egg-sinker mold from Do-It uses a handled pin that is placed in one side for pouring, then immediately pulled out and run into the core holes on the other side for molding the cavities on the other side of the mold.

are similar and most require an insert plate, although some do not. They are round with a split or slot in one side to clamp onto the line or leader. Some have "ears" on the side opposite the slot to allow for opening and reuse. Sizes range from 1/64- to 1 ounce. For these or any type of sinker that is clamped onto the line, only soft lead should be used.

Pinch-on sinkers. These have small "ears" on each end on either side of a slot through which the line is run. The ears pinch onto the line to

Egg sinkers and split shot before the pins and insert sheets are removed (normally they would be removed as soon as the lead has solidified). These show how the holes and slots are formed in these sinkers.

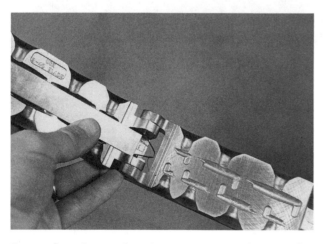

Insert sheet being placed in a Do-It pinch-on sinker mold, which works the same as a split-shot mold to form the slot and sinker "ears."

hold the sinker in position. Sizes include 1/16- through 1 1/2 ounces.

Rubber-core sinkers. These are similar to the pinch-on sinkers in the tapered cigar shape, but have a rubber slug in the center slot that is designed to be turned in order to hold the sinker in place on the line. Sizes range from 1/16- through 1 1/2 ounces. The rubber centers are available from mold manufacturers or from component-parts houses.

Pencil sinkers. These are available fashioned like a solid rod (designed to be slipped into rubber

tubing for snagless bottom fishing) with eyes at both ends, with an eye at one end, or with a hole through the long axis for through-line threading. They are straight-sided and come in sizes from 1 1/4 to 4 ounces. Several diameters are available to fit different tubing, with the most popular 3/16-, 1/4-, and 3/8-inch.

Bullet weights, worm weights. These are used for plastic-worm fishing and are placed on the line in front of the worm. They are like a bullet or round spear point in shape. Sizes that can be molded include 1/8- through 1/2-ounce.

Walking, snagless, and spoon sinkers. The shapes of these vary slightly, but all are flat and wide and tapered, with a molded-in eye at the small end, and are designed for snagless fishing. Sizes range from 1/8- to 4 ounces.

Bullet-weight mold from Li'l Mac, in which the core pins to form the hole in the worm bullet weights go through both halves of the mold rather than in the core hole between the two halves.

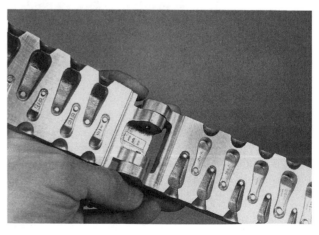

Example of walking-sinker mold from Do-It. Note that the cavities or opposing sides differ.

Rock-cod sinkers. These look like a small brick with one rounded end and range in size from 1 to 5 pounds.

Snag weights. These are not lures, not bucktails, and not sinkers. They are really snatch hooks used to retrieve objects from the bottom and, where legal, to catch fish by snagging. The weight is molded right onto the treble hook. Hook sizes range from 2/0 to 14/0 in trebles; weights are from 1/2- to 8 ounces.

SINKER COSTS

Sinkers become almost free if you mold your own. If you can get lead or lead alloys free from scrap or wheel weights, then your only cost is for the molds and the ladle and furnace, if you use one. If you melt lead in old but sturdy pots and incur only the cost of the molds, the cost of your sinkers amortizes quickly. If you buy the electric pot, ladle, and gate cutters described in Chapter 4, the only other cost is for a mold or molds. Thus, the total cost for a sinker when free lead is available will drop to only a few cents in time. If you forget the basic costs of the molding tools and can get lead for free, then there is no cost for the sinkers other than the cost for eyelets for those sinker types that require them.

Three factors will affect the cost of molding your own sinkers. One, if you mold bucktail heads, the cost of basic equipment such as furnaces and ladles is amortized over the cost of the lures and sinkers; it is not a separate cost. Two, if you mold sinkers requiring insert eyes or wire forms, this cost must be added. Three, if you want to make a lot of different sinker types, then you will need a lot of different molds. One solution to this problem is for friends to band together, each one buying different sinker (or bucktail) molds for the use of all. Fishing clubs can do the same thing, setting aside certain nights for sinker- and bucktail-molding, or loaning out the molds to members as a membership service.

MOLDING TECHNIQUES

Be sure to read and review the section on safety and molding techniques in Chapter 4. The same basic techniques of molding and the steps in working with molten lead and molds is identical for bucktails and sinkers, with only a few differences. Reading and understanding these basic steps as they were outlined earlier is a must before proceeding.

Smoking a mold with a candle flame.

Just as hooks are placed in bucktails molds, some sinkers require the placement of brass eyelets, swivels, or wire forms that are molded into the completed sinker, or of core rods or plates that are used to help form holes or slots.

Although brass eyes are standard for pyramid, bell, keel, and some trolling sinkers, it may be preferable to mold the sinker without them, forming a lead eye instead. (In some molds this is possible, in others it is not — on some molds the manufacturer may list these options; if not, you will have to experiment. It will be quicker, easier, and less expensive if you do not have to use the brass eyes or any forms.)

There is one additional advantage to a lead eye, along with one disadvantage. The advantage of the molded eye in fishing rocky or snaggy areas is that a hung sinker can sometimes be broken off when snagged. A molded-in brass eye will seldom

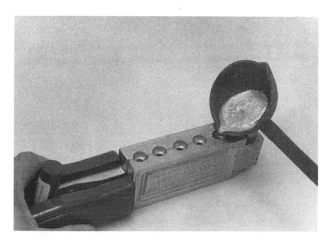

Use care to support the mold when pouring, such as is done here when using a ladle to pour an egg-sinker mold.

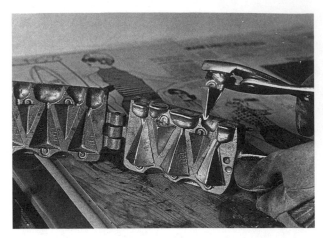

Removing sinkers from sinker mold. Use pliers, as the sinkers (and bucktails when using bucktail molds) will be very hot. Heavy gloves provide protection as well.

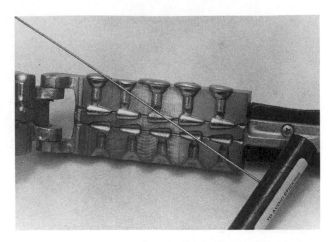

Do-It mold for making worm bullet weights; a pin forms the hole in the sinkers.

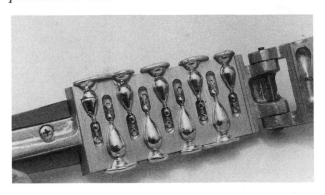

Do-It mold with casting sinkers in place after being molded and before being removed from the mold.

Various sinkers before the sprue (excess lead) is cut off of the sinker. Wire cutters or special lead gate cutters are best for this. Since sinkers are not used as lures, no additional finishing is required.

break. If the lead eye of the sinker breaks, the loss is only an easily made, inexpensive sinker, whereas if brass eyes are used, the line must be cut or broken, possibly resulting in the loss of lure, hook, bobber, or other terminal gear. Some molds are made with this "breakaway" feature in mind. Others have a mold cavity designed to take an eyelet or molded-in eye.

However, if the sinker is tied directly to the line and used continuously, there is some danger that the rough lead in the large molded eye will wear the line, causing it to break. This is not like the loss of a fish or lure, but when it happens, a new sinker must be tied on. One way to avoid this is to tie the line to a large snap for the sinker, or to retie the sinker to the line several times a day, checking for line damage and removing all abraded sections of line.

Generally, the choice of lead or lead alloy for sinkers is even less of a consideration than for

bucktails, since a dented or scrapped sinker can't affect fishing results as might a similarly damaged jig head. However, in the case of split-shot and pinch-on sinkers, you *must* use soft, or pure, lead. Any lead with antimony in it will be harder and will prevent the closing of split-shot or sinker ears, or they might break. Even worse, the hard lead alloy might damage the line, causing breakage with a fish on.

Since a sinker's appearance is not important, you can use several methods to remove the sprue from the sinker. The gate cutters mentioned for bucktail molding are the best, but lacking that, wire cutters, twisting the sprue off with pliers, or using any kind of snip will work.

When molding sinkers and metal lures, make

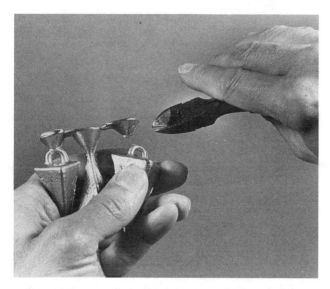

Removing the sprue from a sinker with wire cutters.

sure you have enough lead on hand. Large molds will use lead fast, and some lead sinker molds will use lead at a rate of 2 to 10 ounces for many saltwater sinkers, with some sinkers even requiring 5 pounds of lead.

METAL SQUIDS

Metal squids are used by surf anglers and are widely regarded as one of the best lures for certain surf-fishing situations, either alone or rigged with pork rind, strip bait, or a skirt of some kind. Metal squids or lures can also be used when

inshore-fishing from boats or from piers and jetties, both trolled and cast. Some have fixed hooks, others free-swinging hooks, either plain or dressed with skirt material. Most that are sold commercially today are not cast, but forged and chrome- or nickel-plated.

Although the word "squid" is used, metal or tin squids can resemble any of a large number of small inshore baitfish that come in a variety of different shapes. As a result, tin or metal squids come in both broad short models and long thin lures. The short broad ones imitate herring, killifish, menhaden, mullet, and achovy while the longer thin ones will imitate sand eels, various saltwater minnows, silversides, spearing, and similar fish, including squid.

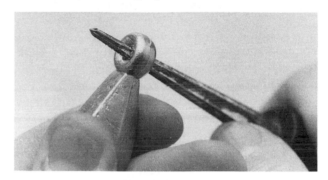

If flash tends to clog the molded-in eyes on some sinkers, a simple wood-working reamer will immediately remove excess lead and smooth the hole.

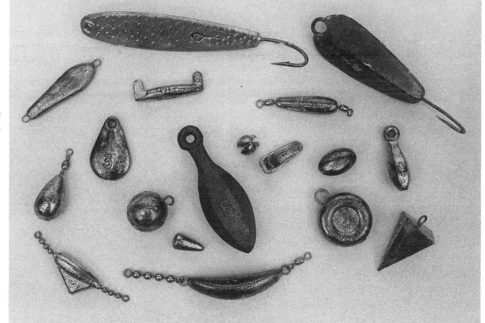

Examples of home-made molded sinkers and tin squids.

While these tin or, perhaps more correctly, metal squid lures can be made of lead or other metals, including zinc, tin squids are perhaps best known and most popular among surf fishermen. The tin used in these lures has the advantage of staying bright (lead dulls rapidly) and bendable, so that an angler can bend the lure to a shape that provides action in the water. Part of this is because tin weighs less than lead, so the lure will twist in the water when bent properly. (The difference in weight is about a five-to-eight ratio, so a tin lure weighing 2 1/2 ounces would weigh 4 ounces if it were made of lead. Of course, this also means you get more lures from a pound of tin.)

An advantage of tin-squid molding is that tin melts at a lower temperature (449°) than lead, so it will not take as long to heat or use up as much fuel to stay at a molten temperature. As with larger trolling sinkers (which they resemble), tin squids require an eyelet on each end or a hook molded into one end of the lure. Those for swinging hooks require a second eyelet, and the hook is added later by means of a split ring or by an open-eye Siwash-style hook.

LEAD LURES

Metal lures can also be molded by using lead or other alloys, although they are usually painted or covered with prism tape later to brighen them because lead is far duller in appearance than tin. Type metal, or linotype metal (a mixture of lead, tin, and antimony), will stay brigher than pure lead, though not as bright as tin.

Lead lures cannot usually be bent to shape for a swimming action, although some very thin, long lures of pure soft lead can be bent for better action in the water.

Lure molds for lead-molding can include the thin tin-squid type, as well as vertical casting and jigging spoons, diamond lures (diamond in cross section and thin like a minnow), casting spoons that resemble the stainless steel jigging spoons, and other slab-sided lures. Some, such as the Hilts Slab Mold (model LM SLAB-W) are even made in a fish shape, complete with fins and tail features. It comes in 1/2- to 5-ounce sizes in both through-line and wire-form (eyelet) styles. Other similar lure molds include the Do-It jigging spoon mold-model JS-3-A and several casting spoon molds.

Molds for making tin lures are not labeled as such, and any mold for making lead items can be used for molding tin. Thus, metal lures of tin or lead or other alloys (even zinc) can be made in any of the aluminum or cast molds from any of the major mold manufacturers.

One-piece molds for tin squids or lead-slab lures are not available commercially, but because these lures are usually flat or slab-sided, one-piece or open-face molds can be made from plaster, silicone molding material, wood, or metal. (Directions for this are found in Chapter 14.)

Using an open-face mold is easy, because there is no sprue hole through which the metal must be poured, no possibility of unfilled parts of the cavity, no possibility of air pockets, no opening or closing of the mold. Naturally, any inserts must be placed in the mold for line and hook attachment, and the hook must be added for fixed-hook lures. The open mold and these inserts do require more careful pouring and special caution to prevent overpouring. Also, since the insert material is lighter than the lead, you might have to hold it in place with a metal carpenters' spring clamp until the lead cools.

Position the mold near the melting tin, pour rapidly, and allow the lead to cool. Open-face molds can be made with a small slot at one end to hold the hook in place. Or the hook can be slipped into the molten tin and held in place briefly until the metal solidifies. Wear heavy gloves or use pliers to hold the hook, because it will become hot.

If you do overpour slightly, you have two choices. One is to dump the mold contents back into the pot for remelting, removing the eyelets and any hooks as the lure melts. If you do this, use pliers to hold the hook point out of the molten metal, and remove the hook from the pot as soon as possible so as not to ruin the temper of the hook. If you suspect the temper has been affected, do not use the hook.

If the overflow is slight, the other solution is to use snips to remove excess flash. Because they have a compound action for cutting heavier metal, aviation snips are ideal for this, although regular sheet-metal snips will work if the metal is soft (pure lead or tin) and not too thick.

FINISHING TIN SQUIDS AND LEAD LURES

Completed slab lures may be used as is if the hook is molded in, or they may be finished with a swinging hook and any dressing. If the lure has two eyelets, then a free-swinging hook must be added. This can be a treble, double, or single, with single hooks used in most lures.

There are several ways to add a hook. Double hooks with separate, double shanks can be slid onto the eyelet or, for more action, slipped onto a split ring added to the eyelet. Single hooks come in an open-eye style that can be attached to the eyelet or a separately added split ring: The hook eye is then closed to secure the hook. Treble hooks are made the same way, with open eyes that can be closed once added to a lure, with a split shank for threading onto an eyelet, or they may be added by means of a split ring. If adding hooks using a split ring, add both the lure eyelet and the hook to the split ring at the same time to reduce any spreading of the split ring and to save time. To do this, use split-ring pliers to first open the ring, then slide the hook, followed by the lure eyelet, on, and finally rotate the split ring while holding both parts to attach them. If you use a single or double hook in which you want the hook points aligned with one side of the lure, align this first before adding the parts.

If you make lures with a dressed hook, do the dressing *before* adding the hook to the lure. You can buy dressed hooks or dress them yourself using fly-tying methods or the methods outlined for tail attachment on bucktails. Basically, clamp the hook in a fly-tying or similar vise, and wrap the thread around the hook and over the previous wraps to hold the thread in place. Use size 2/0 thread for small hooks to size 2 or 4, size A thread for larger hooks to size 4/0 or 5/0, and size D or E (rod-wrapping) thread for larger hooks. Once the thread is tied down, wrap the tail materials of fur, artificial fur, saddle hackle, mylar, nylon, or similar material onto the hook. Make several turns of thread to firmly secure the material, and then clip off any excess in front of the wrap. Finish the wrap and tie it off with several half-hitches or a whip-finish. Protect the wrap with a touch of paint (red is always good), nylon-base nail polish (colored or clear — Sally Hansen Hard as Nails brand is good), or, if you're after toothy fish, epoxy finish.

You can also use rubber or plastic tubing in short lengths or with longer split tails on the hook, and this also must be added before the hook is placed on the lure. Soft-plastic tails such as grubs and worms can be added to the hook later. If you plan this, consider one of the barbed-shank hooks that are designed to hold bait or soft plastic.

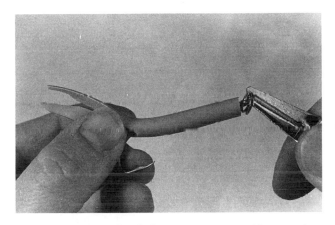

Finishing some lead lures or tin squids requires adding hooks and tail materials. Here, a hook skirted with a split tail of surgical tubing will be added to a small slab lure.

Tail-spinner lead lure complete (painted and hooks and blade attached) on the left; example of a bare molded lure (although a slightly different style) on the right.

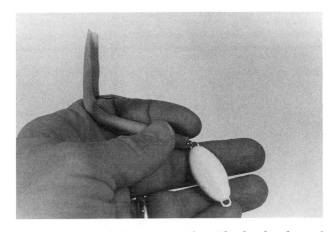

Small slab lead lure, painted, with the hook and surgical-tubing tail added.

COSTS OF METAL LURES

If the metal is free, as it often is in wheel weights, the cost of metal lures can be minimal. Most lure molds with one to four cavities sell for about the cost of a sinker or bucktail mold.

The technique of molding sinkers and tin squids is easy. With the cost of lead sinkers and metal lures constantly rising, molding your own not only makes sense, but saves cents as well. Starting with these easy-to-make tackle items is a natural for anyone who wants to cut the cost of angling while adding to the wintertime or off-season pleasure of tackle craft.

Once sinker or bucktail molding is complete, excess lead can be poured into ingot molds, available from most companies. If using a furnace or electric pot, it often is better to leave excess lead in the pot for rapid heating next time. Check manufacturers' recommendations on this.

6

Spinnerbaits and Buzzbaits

INTRODUCTION ▪ TOOLS ▪ PARTS ▪ MOLDING
TECHNIQUES ▪ FINISHING ▪ SPINNERBAIT ASSEMBLY ▪
BUZZBAIT ASSEMBLY ▪ IN-LINE OR WEIGHT-FORWARD
SPINNER ASSEMBLY ▪ VARIATIONS

Basic Safety Requirements for Molding

Welders' or heavy gloves for handling molds,
    pots, ladles
Respirator mask
Apron
A clean, clear place to work with heavy
    countertop

Basic Tools for Molding

Old cooking pot
Cheap gravy ladle or large serving spoon
Bucktail, spinnerbait, and buzzbait molds
Fly-tying vise, machinists' vise, or C-clamp
Hot pads
File

Helpful Tools for Molding

Plumbers' melting pot
Plumbers' ladle
Gate cutters or shears
Wire cutters
Ingot molds
Heavy pliers
Electric-element hand-held ladle
Electric bottom-feed furnace
Worth split-ring pliers
Compound-leverage fishing pliers
Spinner-making tools may be useful for some
    assembly and modifications

Basic Safety Requirements for Assembly
Goggles
A clean, clear place to work

Basic Tools for Assembly
Needle-nose or round-nose pliers with side cutters

Helpful Tools for Assembly
Small round-nose pliers
Diagonal wire cutters or compound-action pliers with wire cutters
Wire former (commercial or homemade)
Worth split-ring pliers
Compound-leverage fishing pliers

INTRODUCTION

Lures resembling spinnerbaits have been around a long time, but the lure as we know it has been popular and in the same general design since about the early 1900s. In 1917 and 1918 the Shannon Twinspinner, made by the Jamison Company, was an early precursor of the twin-spinnerbait style we know today. Even then there were about a dozen or more variations of this basic style, although the Twinspinner seems to be the most widely remembered today.

Buzzbaits are not that new, but some of the early Al Foss Wigglers from the same period were not unlike the in-line buzzbaits of today. Also similar were the early Fred Arbogast Hawaiian Wigglers, still sold by the Arbogast Company today. The typical J-shaped wire-form buzzbaits appeared about 1940. The in-line buzzbaits appeared at about the same time.

Modern spinnerbaits come in small through large sizes, in single spin, tandem spin (blades in line with each other), and twin spin (two blades with each blade at the end of a separate upper arm), in stiff and flexible (cable) wire, and with a variety of modifications in skirts, blades, and head styles.

Another variation, usually under a separate subcategory, is the in-line or weight-forward spinner. These are designed for bottom-fishing for walleye and are called spinners because they are of a straight-line construction on a weighted-head shaft, even though they have similarities to a spinnerbait. The straight-line construction resembles a standard spinner; the weighted head makes them perform like a spinnerbait. A good argument could be made for either description. They are included here because they require molding the head if you want to make them from scratch, and thus require the same techniques as for making lead-head spinnerbaits and buzzbaits. All these variations, plus many more, can be built into any homemade spinnerbait.

Buzzbaits come in two basic styles. One is the older, less-common, in-line style in which a straight shaft holds the propeller blade or spinner blade, behind which is the weighted head and skirted hook. These are made with the same techniques used for the in-line spinners. The more common buzzbaits are made on a bent-wire form that resembles a J lying on its side, with the longer end of the shaft holding the weighted head and skirted hook, and the upper, or shorter, arm ending with the single or double delta or buzz propeller blades. Some variations include small "clicker" or "clacker" blades on the upright part of the arm that will click against the buzzbait to make a fish-attracting noise. Other unusual variations include side-by-side arms and blades, and various head styles.

Spinnerbaits and buzzbaits are designed primarily for bass, although both work well for a host of other, primarily freshwater, gamefish, including walleye, muskie, pike, and crappie (in small-size lures). There is even a large commercially marketed buzzbait for saltwater big-game trolling.

All of these lures are included in this chapter because they are all built on a wire shaft, have a lead head, a skirt, and one or more metal blades.

TOOLS

Tools for building buzzbaits and spinnerbaits are no different from those used for building spinners and molding bucktails, because buzzbaits and spinnerbaits are in essence a combination of spinner and bucktail parts. To build them from scratch by molding the bodies and assembling the blades and parts, you will need the basic tools listed at the beginning at this chapter. If you have already built jigs and spinners by following the instructions in Chapters 3 and 4, you will have these tools. If you skipped to this chapter first, go back and read Chapter 3 and 4 for ideas and details, and especially for the safety tips and instructions.

Required tools include basic molding tools such as a furnace, pot, ladles, and safety equipment. For assembly, you will need some wire-forming tools such as round-nose or needle-nose pliers, wire cutters, and split-ring pliers.

Parts for making spinnerbaits include wire forms, molded wire-form bodies, blades, hooks, skirts, split rings, swivels, beads, and clevises. In most cases, only round-nose pliers will be needed for assembly.

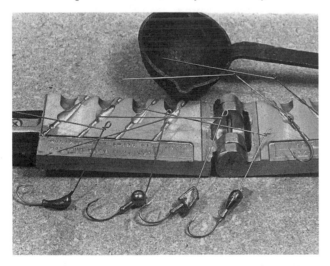

Mold and the spinnerbait forms produced from various molds. The hooks and wires are joined by a hook to prevent pulling apart when fishing.

You do not have to mold your own bodies. You can buy painted or unpainted spinnerbait blanks in sizes from about 1/8 through 3/4-ounces. In these cases, you will not need the tools necessary to mold the bodies or the other required parts.

However, as will be discussed shortly, molding bodies for spinnerbaits is slightly different from molding jig and bucktail heads.

PARTS

Parts will vary with the type of spinnerbait or buzzbait to be made, and many of these parts are already listed in Chapters 3 and 4. Be sure to check these chapters for full details and more information.

Some parts needed for making spinnerbaits and buzzbaits include:

Hooks. Hooks for molding spinnerbaits and buzzbaits are special. First, because these hooks are fastened by the hook eye to the spinnerbait or buzzbait wire, they must be straight-eyed. They are also straight hooks, neither kirbed nor offset, and with a medium-length shank. Although many hooks will fill these basic requirements, special spinnerbait and buzzbait hooks have very small eyes. This is because the hook eye, along with the spinnerbait or buzzbait wire, is molded into a relatively small lead head. Hooks with large eyes (really normal-size eyes for the size of the hook) are more likely to result in incomplete heads or heads with a void or flaw in the side. Typical hooks range in size from about 1 through 5/0.

Stinger hooks are similar, but with a regular eye so that they can be slipped over the point and past the barb of the main spinnerbait hook. Usually a size close to that of the main hook is best.

Wires. You can purchase straight wire lengths or coils of wire for making spinnerbaits and buzzbaits. Straight wires with a small hook on one end to fasten into the hook eye are available in either .035 or .040-inch-diameter wire. Bent wire in the typical two-legged safety-pin form for spinnerbaits, and the J-shaped form for buzzbaits, are also readily available. Bent wire for spinnerbaits is usually lighter than that for standard buzzbaits, but some small-diameter wire for small-size buzzbaits is also available. Typical wire diameters in fractions of an inch for spinnerbaits from several manufacturers are .035, .036, or .040. Buzzbait wire is .035 for the small buzzbaits, .045, .050, .051, or .052 for the larger forms.

In addition, wire forms come in several different styles. Spinnerbait wires are available in a long, twisted eye-form, a long "R" eye form (an open eye preferred by some anglers), and an open R-style "short arm" wire. All of these forms have the small J-shaped bend at the end to attach to the hook in the mold.

Lighter wires are available to make spinnerbaits and buzzbaits with some vibration. Wire of about .022- or .026-inch-diameter will make lures that vibrate; the degree of vibration depends on the type and size of blade or blades used.

If you use straight wire, you will need round-nose pliers, needle-nose pliers, or a wire former capable of working with the wire size chosen to make the several bends necessary for these versatile lures. If there is a choice, stainless steel wire is best for lures because it won't rust, as may tinned wire. Most of the wire currently sold for spinnerbaits, spinners, and buzzbaits is of stainless steel.

Spinnerbait and buzzbait blanks. To eliminate molding the bodies in which the hooks and wire are required, you can buy formed bodies. These usually have a tapered lead head, and come in 1/8- through 3/4-ounce sizes with the hook and wire molded in place. They come unpainted (bare lead), painted in a base coat of white, or painted in finished colors.

Blades, spinnerbaits. Blades for spinnerbaits are the same as those used for spinners, listed in Chapter 3. The same colors, sizes, finishes, and styles are all suitable for spinnerbaits. Thus,

typical blades for spinnerbaits would include the standard willowleaf, Indiana, Colorado, and swing blades, although deep-cut blades, ribbed blades, and fluted blades are getting more popular as this is being written. The several exceptions generally not found on spinnerbaits might be the fixed-angle blades in which no clevis is used and in which the shaft runs straight through the two holes in the blade—the holes and arms designed to hold the blade at a specific angle—and the in-line blades in which the shaft runs through the hole in the single blade set somewhat back from the edge of the blade. Examples would be the in-line spinner blade, June Bug blade, Rotospin blades, and similar types. This does not mean that they cannot be used for spinnerbaits, only that they have seldom been commercially used in these lures.

In most cases, larger blades are used on single-spin spinnerbaits, smaller blades on the twin-spin style, while tandem spinnerbaits usually use one larger blade on the back and a smaller one in front. In tandem spinnerbaits, the blades can be the same style, finish, color, and size, or completely different. In most cases they have an identical finish on both sides of the blade.

Blades, buzzbaits. Buzzbait blades are completely different from the spinner-type of blades on spinnerbaits. Spinner and spinnerbait blades have a tapered elliptical shape with a hole at one end for attachment to the lure. Those for buzzbaits come in several styles of propeller blade. The so-called delta blades are shaped like a big triangle or A, like the delta wing of a supersonic jet or like the wings of a skate or stingray.

The two outer wings of the blades are bent in opposing directions to make the blade spin in the water. Holes formed and stamped in the center keep the blade on the shaft. These blades are almost always used singly, although sometimes a small clicker or clacker blade is used to hit against the front of the delta wing. Different sizes of delta blades are available, with sizes ranging from 1 inch long by 1 1/4 inches wide to 1 5/8 inches long by 1 15/16 inches wide.

Smaller blades, sometimes called counter or counter-rotating blades, also have right-angle bends in the edges of the wings with holes through the center for the shaft. As smaller blades are designed more and more to be used in sets of two, one turns clockwise, the other counterclockwise. The opposite-turning blades make a lot of fuss on the water and counter any tendency of the buzzbait to spin or rotate in one direction. This is

Buzzbait blades come in many styles, colors, finishes, and materials. Shown are four-blade, triple-blade, plastic, metal, delta-wing, cupped-wing, double counter-rotating, and other types of blades.

particularly important on the straight-line or in-line buzzbaits, less so on those using the J-shaped arms. Although spinner blades are often stamped of brass and finished in nickel, copper, brass, or are painted, buzzbait blades are usually nickel-coated brass or aluminum. Most blades are sold individually or, in the case of the counter-rotating blades, in sets of two.

A new innovation is the introduction of sets of two separate wings (blades) that are designed to slide together (back-to-back) on a shaft to make a clattering noise as the blade turns. They are separate to make a loose, clattering, four-blade or quad wing. They are usuallly aluminum and available in several sizes from 1 1/16 inches to 1 3/4 inches in width.

In addition to the metal buzzbait blades, plastic blades are available. These come in several sizes in triple and quad wings molded in each blade. They are usually of the larger delta shapes, designed for one blade per lure. Most have the metal (aluminum) pop-rivet blade collar molded into the rear of the blade, although some do not.

Many colors are available and will vary with the manufacturer. Clear, red, black, white, chartreuse, pink, yellow, and blue are common. The advantage of these blades is that the greater number of wings (three or four as opposed to two) will allow a slower retrieve for the same surface fuss.

Clicker or clacker blades are something new; they were first developed on commercially manufactured lures. These small blades, like a wing or pennant with holes for the shaft, slide on the upright part of the arm and are designed to hit the blade with each revolution. As with the technique of the main blades lightly dinging the shaft on each rotation, these clacker or clicker blades give the lure more noise. Most are of aluminum, with 3/4- and 1-inch lengths standard.

Blade collar. These are really pop-rivet collars used behind the buzzbait blades to create the squeaking sounds characteristic of these lures. Although you can use regular pop-rivet collars, popping out the metal shaft used to pull the rivet tight, it is far better and cheaper to buy these collars in bulk.

Cable. Cable is sometimes used for making spinnerbaits, in imitation of some of the commercially available styles that use flexible wire (cable) for either the entire wire form of the lure, or for the upper arm. Stainless steel cable is best, in sizes from .030 to .040. If you use cable, you will also need crimping pliers and some leader sleeves to form loops in the wire. (Construction is covered later in this chapter.)

Swivels. Swivels are used to allow spinnerbait blades to turn at the end of the arm. This is also possible with buzzbaits, though seldom done.

There are several ways to use swivels, one of which is to attach a swivel to the end of an arm, then attach a blade to the swivel with a split ring. It is also possible to use a snap swivel with the swivel attached to the arm; the snap is used to attach the blade for instant changes of blade color, size, and shape.

Swivels can also be used, though they rarely are, as attachments to the line-tie eye for more action and also to prevent the line from wrapping around the arms of the spinnerbait during fishing.

Clevises. Clevises are used in two ways on spinnerbaits. As with spinners, they are used to hold a spinner blade on the upper-arm shaft in tandem spinners. The smaller front blade will fit on a clevis on the shaft and will flap and wobble. It may not rotate around the shaft, as will a spinner blade on a spinner shaft, although this will depend upon the angle at which the upper arm rides in the water. The rear blade can be fixed the same way, but is more likely to be fixed to a swivel attached to the end of the arm for free rotation and swinging.

Clevises can also be used on the front of the arm at the line-tie position. In this, straight wire must be used or the arm must be straightened so that a large clevis can be slipped in place on the shaft. The use of a clevis here reduces the possibility of the line getting tangled around the arm or blades on a cast or when flipping. Since the clevis can rotate completely around the shaft, such tangles are lessened. For free movement of the clevis, a single bead should be used both above and below it. Otherwise, the clevis might bind on the wire bend and defeat its purpose.

Clevises are not used in buzzbaits, although a substitute for the clacker blade mentioned above is to use a small spinner blade on a clevis, attached to the upright arm: The spinner blade will be struck by the buzz blade on each rotation.

Beads. The same variety of beads used in spinners can be used in spinnerbaits and buzzbaits. Most beads are small and red and are used for bearings and to add a little color to the lure. They are used primarily on tandem spinnerbaits as bearings for the front blade that rotates around the shaft. For this, red-glass and hard-plastic beads are used in small sizes of 2 1/2 to 4 mm. Larger sizes and different colors can be used for special applications.

Unies. Unies, the small special beads used exclusively for bearings, can be used for bearings on clevis-mounted blades in tandem spinnerbaits also.

Snaps. Snaps and snap swivels allow for blade changes on spinnerbaits when they are added to the end of the arm. The snap swivel must be added by the swivel to the arm; the snap is used to hold the blade. For this, snap swivels incorporating regular snaps, interlock snaps, Duo-Lock snaps, or other snaps will work. The smallest possible snaps are best to reduce the bulk of the lure.

Split rings. Split rings have many applications in making spinnerbaits. They are used to connect snap swivels to upper arms, to the front of the lure line-tie for added action, or to attach blades to swivels. Sizes range from the tiny 00 to the larger size 8, but should be as small as possible for the purpose without causing binding or cramping of the parts joined. Polished brass, nickel-plated brass, nickel-plated steel, and zinc-plated steel split rings are all available, and the nickel-plated styles are best for most freshwater applications.

Butt rings. These small rings, also sometimes called jump rings, are not as strong as a split ring

A skirt kit that includes the tool and materials for making rubber skirts for spinnerbaits and buzzbaits. A variety of colors are available.

and should *never* be used for a line-tie or hook attachment. (An exception would be if they are soldered shut for strength.) They are ideal for attaching a spinner blade to a swivel or for some similar, nonstress, task.

MOLDING TECHNIQUES

Molding spinnerbaits is similar to molding jigs and bucktails, but with a difference. The difference is that in addition to placing a hook in the mold, you must also add the spinnerbait wire. Other than that, the molding is about the same.

Make sure the mold has been smoked as described in Chapter 4, for the best results. Preheat the mold, as described for bucktail molds, making sure the mold is hot enough that lead fills the cavity evenly, but not so hot as to be dangerous or warp the mold. The cold metal parts of the hook shank and spinnerbait wire will cool any molten lead rapidly.

Most molds, such as the excellent models by Do-It and Hilts Molds, specify not only the hook type and size required, but also the wire size to be used. In most cases this wire is readily available. You usually can't use larger-diameter wire, because the mold will not close securely and flash will result not only at the wire, but also along the entire joint. You can use smaller-diameter wire, but then you risk lead leakage around the wire. Any such flash formed will affect the appearance, but not the function, of the lure. If desired, it is easily removed.

The wire must be straight to fit into the mold properly, so any wire from coils must be checked and straightened if necessary.

Before using the wire you must make sure you have a small J-shaped bend in the end that fits into the mold cavity, and that the J fits through the hook eye. As listed before, the hook eyes should be small to allow for complete coating of these parts by the lead.

Straight wire is best if you plan to make spinnerbaits or buzzbaits with any special additions, since as clacker blades on the upright arm of a buzzbait or a clevis as the line-tie on the arm of a spinnerbait or buzzbait. Both parts require a relatively straight wire to slide in place. If you use a formed wire, the wire must be opened or straightened, at least partly, to add these parts.

Similarly, cable can be used in place of wire, but the small J-shaped bend on the end is a must to hook the cable into the hook eye in the molded-lead head. It is really best to twist the wire

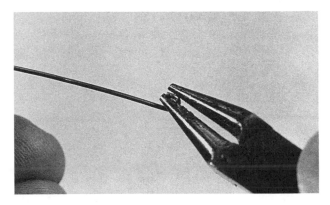

Bending the hook in the wire to mold a spinnerbait or buzzbait. The hook fits over the eye of the hook for a permanent attachment.

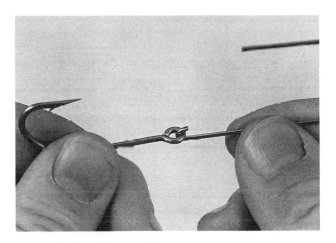

The hook of the wire on a buzzbait (shown here) or spinnerbait hooked onto the eye of the hook.

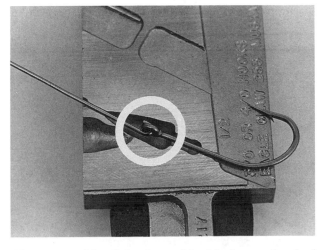

The wire and hook in the mold with the two hooked together. Circle is around the hook parts.

around the eye some so that it is impossible for the cable wire to pull out. Another alternative is to use a leader sleeve to make a closed loop on the hook eye.

If you use formed wire (available from shops and mail-order stores), the line-tie bends and arms will already be formed in the wire. The small J-shaped bend may or may not be formed. Failure to form this bend will assure that the wire will at some point pull out of the lead body, resulting in a lost lure or fish. While remote, that same possibility exists if the J bend is not placed over the hook eye.

Place the wire and hooks into the mold properly, with the wires extending out one side of the mold. In some cases, the hook points and bends may also extend out the other side, making these molds impossible to set down on a table once they are ready to be filled with lead. To provide a steady support for the mold during pouring, use a small block of wood to hold the hinge end of the mold while you hold the handles and pour. An alternative is to use a long block of wood and rest one side of the mold on it. The spinnerbait wires or hook bends will hang down alongside, and clearance must be provided to allow for this. Do not try to pour these molds or any mold without some support. If the wires or hooks extend up (on the gate or sprue-hole side) you may not be able to use a bottom-feed furnace, because the bottom spout must contact the sprue hole. If this is a problem, use a ladle or top-pour furnace.

In some cases, the bend of the hook may extend below the mold and thus make it difficult to get a solid support for the mold. To adjust for this, use a small block of wood, as shown, and rest one side of the mold on this block while pouring lead.

Once the spinnerbait bodies are molded, following the directions in Chapter 4, allow the mold to cool, place it on its side, and open it carefully. If you pry the lead heads out of the mold, do so carefully and do not try to lever them by using the lightweight spinner wire. To do so risks bending the wire to the side of the lure, which can result in an unbalanced spinnerbait. If this does happen, however, it is easy to bend the wire back in line with the body and hook.

Molding spinnerbaits is a little different from molding jigs, as the wires or hooks will extend up into the molding area, as shown. Use basic safe molding procedures for this step.

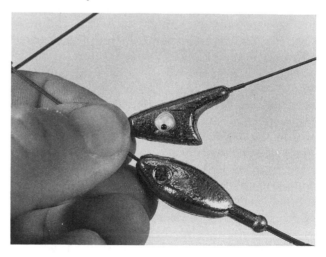

Some spinnerbaits and buzzbaits have molded-in sockets for painted or added eyes, as shown here. For illustrative purposes, the upper example has had a doll eye added, although in normal operation this would only be done after assembling and painting the lure.

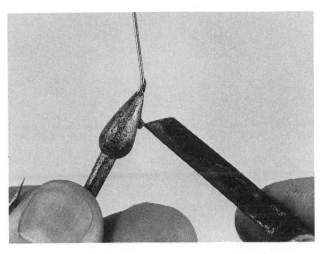

Some imperfections in the lead head might be noticeable after molding. This is easily removed with gate cutters or by filing.

Once the bodies are removed, cut off any excess lead using gate cutters or flush-cut wire cutters. Because spinnerbaits and buzzbaits are painted upon completion, do not touch these lead heads at all until they are at least painted with a base coat of white or primer. As with jigs, handle them with gloves or by the hook (or wire in this case) to keep your skin's oils off the lead.

FINISHING

Finishing spinnerbaits and buzzbaits can be accomplished on several different levels, depending upon how they were molded. If they were molded on straight wires, then the wires will have to be bent into shape for the finished lure, and the lead lure heads painted. If preformed wires were used, then painting only is required, followed by assembly of the blades, beads, and other components. If you formed the lead heads on straight wires, you might want to paint the heads before forming the wires. This might make for easier painting, and the painted heads can be handled while you bend the wire, something that should not be done without gloves to unpainted lead heads.

Painting is thoroughly covered in Chapter 15, but some tips here are important. First, you should paint or at least put a base coat on the lead heads as soon as possible. Paint adherence on any metal is never good, but some factors make this even more difficult on lead. First, the oils from skin contact and handling will prevent good adherence; second, lead will oxidize, and this oxi-

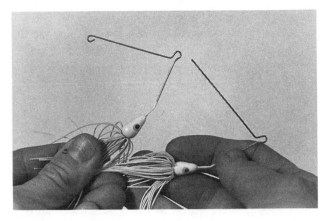

Examples of molded—unfinished and painted—spinnerbait heads.

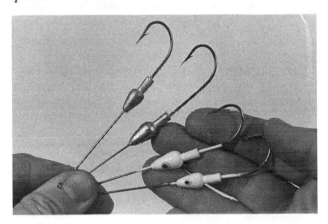

Painted and skirted spinnerbait bodies with the hook formed in the upper arm of one for swivel and blade attachment.

dation will further block good paint adherence.

Bending wire to form it is easy with round-nose pliers. Before doing so, however, decide if you will be adding anything to the wire. For example, if you want anything on the lower arm of a spinnerbait, you must add it before making any bends. The same applies to a buzzbait. If you add a clacker blade to a buzzbait, you will have to make the first line-tie bend and then add the bead, clacker blade, and another bead before making the second bend for the upper arm.

Assuming you are making the bends on a spinnerbait and beginning with straight wire, first decide on the type of line-tie you want. Measure the length of the lower arm and then make the desired bend. If you make an R type of bend in the wire, all of the bending will be on the same plane as the angle of the spinnerbait. Grasp the wire with the pliers and bend the wire through a three-quarter turn upward with the pliers. (By making the bend upward, the wire end will be bent back and toward the hook point.) Hold the wire bend with the pliers, take the end of the wire, and bend it back up again to make the lower part of the R bend. The result is the R, or open-eye, bend.

To make a wrapped eye, measure the length of the wire for the lower arm and grasp the wire with round-nose pliers. Bend the wire *up* past a full turn (about 540 degrees) so that the two parts of the wire cross or touch. In essence, what you are doing is making 1 1/2 complete turns with the eyes on the same plane as the spinnerbait, ending with the upper arm at about a 60- to 90-degree angle to the lower arm. This is the type of eye used on many commercial spinnerbaits.

Another way to make a wrapped eye is to measure the length of the wire for the lower arm and grasp the wire with the pliers. Bend the wire *down* through a 360-degree bend so that the end of the wire overlaps the lower arm. Hold the eye with the round-nose pliers and wrap the end of the wire a full turn around the lower arm so that the end of the wire sticks straight up, in line with the hook and lower arm.

It is also possible to make a wrapped eye by bending the wire *up* a full 360 degrees, but this will end with the upper arm pointing down. To complete the wrap, you then have a choice of making either an additional half-wrap or a 1 1/2-wrap of the wire around the lower arm. The 1 1/2-wrap is more than required, and the half-wrap is not as sturdy as it should be. Thus, the initial downward bend to allow for one complete wrap is best.

Another method is to bend the wire *down* a full 360 degrees around the round-nose plier jaw, then continue bending on the same plane so that the upper wire is angled back over the hook point. There are no tight wraps around the lower wire.

Once the eye is complete and the upper arm is in the upward-angled position, the spinnerbait is ready for assembly. The upper and lower arm should form a 90- to 45-degree angle, but this can be adjusted when the lure is completed.

Buzzbaits are made in two different ways: in-line and bent-arm. If you make the in-line buzzbaits, start with the straight wire (not the wire forms) and keep the wire straight until you're ready to complete the assembly. Making the bent-arm buzzbaits requires using formed wire or bending the straight wire. Bending wire to complete buzzbait forms is very similar to the above instructions, with the R or open-eye almost

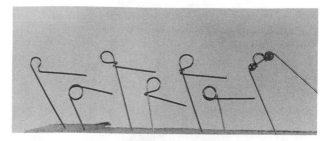

Examples of eyes used for spinnerbaits. The "R" or open eye is to the left; others are examples of various styles and types of wrapped eyes. The one to the right uses a clevis and beads to prevent the clevis from sliding up the arm. Normally identical beads would be used, but for illustrative purposes, one metal and one red plastic bead are used here.

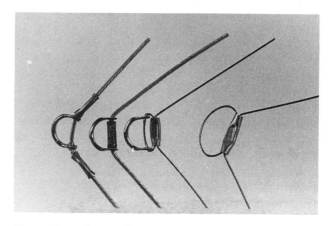

Examples of eyes (line-ties) that can be used when making spinnerbaits of cable. These all use leader sleeves in some way to prevent the line-tie or clevis from slipping.

universally used. The wraps are made exactly as are the eyes for spinnerbaits, but you might find the wire slightly harder to work because buzzbait wire is often thicker than spinnerbait wire.

When completing the buzzbait eye, make sure the upper arm is at a 90-degree angle to the straight lower arm. Once this bend is made, measure the spot where you will make the bend in the upright arm to form the upper arm that is parallel to the main arm and body. This upper arm holds the buzz blade or blades and keeps them in line with the axis of the lure body. This bend can be critical because you need enough clearance for the blade to turn, yet the blade should turn close to the main shaft, particularly if you wish to turn the lure so that the blade lightly dings the wire with each revolution or hits a clacker blade.

To make the bend, use round- or square-jaw pliers and hold the wire securely, bending sharply at the premeasured and marked spot. When bending, make sure the wire is in plane with the hook bend so that the blade runs true with the lure body.

At this point, the lure bodies are ready to assembly into lures.

SPINNERBAIT ASSEMBLY
SINGLE-BLADE SPINNERBAITS

Single-blade spinnerbaits are easy to assemble because they only require adding a blade to the end of the upper-arm wire. First, decide whether you wish a short-arm or long-arm spinnerbait. If you want a short-arm spinnerbait, cut the upper-arm wire accordingly. If you are unsure as to correct length, check some commercial short-arm spinnerbaits to get an idea. Cut for that length, but be sure to allow an additional 1/4- to 3/8-inch for the eye bend to hold the blade.

Any type of blade in any finish and any size can be used, but, in general, single-spin spinnerbaits use larger blades than do twin-or tandem-spin spinnerbaits. In addition to the blade, you will also need a split ring or butt ring and swivel. The split ring or butt ring connects the blade and swivel. If you use a butt or jump ring, you will need two pairs of pliers to spread the ring open, add the swivel and blade, and close the ring again. If you use a split ring, use the correct size. Split rings range from the small size 00 to the large size 8. The split ring must be large enough to prevent binding of the parts. Also, you should use split-ring pliers. These are available in small inexpensive models and in more precise pliers. Either will work well, and both have straight jaws with a small tooth on the end of one jaw, by which the split ring can be separated and opened. Open the split ring with the pliers and add the blade and the swivel to the ring together. Once the blade and swivel are on one of the prongs of the split ring, rotate the split ring while holding the blade and swivel until they both move freely on the ring. Once these parts are connected, use the round-nose pliers on the end of the wire, and bend it into an almost complete circle. Leave enough room to add the swivel, then close the wire eye with pliers.

An alternative to this is to add a snap swivel to the end of the wire by making a bend in the wire.

Adding a blade and swivel together with a split ring and split-ring pliers for attachment to a spinnerbait arm. Here a ball-bearing swivel is used.

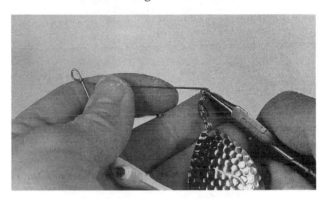

Completing the eye on the upper arm of a spinnerbait to hold the blade and swivel in place. This has been designed as a long-arm spinnerbait.

The same techniques can be used to make a short-arm spinnerbait. The spinnerbait above was modified by cutting back the upper arm and reattaching the blade.

This will allow you to add or change any type, size, style, or finish of blade you want, anytime you want. It is a simple modification, easily done, and allows for increased versatility of this lure.

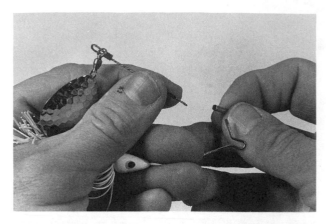

Some kits for making cable-arm spinnerbaits allow attachment of the two parts using leader sleeves, as shown. The sleeve slides onto the cable arm and is then crimped.

Completed cable-arm spinnerbait.

TANDEM-BLADE SPINNERBAITS

Tandem-blade spinnerbaits have two blades on a single shaft. Usually the forward blade is smaller and may be a different style and finish than the larger rear blade. As a result, almost anything goes in two-blade spinnerbaits. The main difference in the two blades is that the forward blade is normally on a clevis and thus may rotate or just swing and flop around to create flash. (There are variations — you can use a swivel or snap swivel here — see directions later in this chapter.) The rear blade is on a swivel or snap swivel and does rotate. To construct these, first choose a clevis that will fit the forward blade and allow clearance for it to rotate or swing. Place the clevis through the hole in the blade. Add one or more small beads or unies to the shaft to serve both as color and also as spacers to prevent the clevis from flopping forward on a cast and jamming against the line-tie eye. These beads can be hollow metal, solid metal, red plastic, or anything you like, but

usually should be small. Do not add too many, or the water pressure on them might impede the movement of the forward blade and clevis. Next, slide the clevis and blade onto the shaft, making sure that the convex side of the blade faces forward when the blade hangs free.

Add two or three more small beads or unies on the shaft to serve as bearings; otherwise, the clevis will bind against the eye in the wire. These beads may be the same color or of a different color and finish from those used to the rear of the clevis. Once these parts are added, finish as above, adding a swivel, split ring, and blade, or snap swivel and blade, to a small eye bent in the end of the wire.

Attaching clevis to a spinner blade for a spinnerbait. Either single- or double-blade (the second blade) spinnerbaits can be made this way, since the blade will still generally rotate completely around the upper arm of the lure.

Two blades on one arm are possible using several different techniques. Here, the main blade is attached normally with a swivel and snap (the snap used for blade changes) while the smaller forward blade is attached to the shaft by a clevis. Beads separate the two blades.

In most cases, the forward, smaller, blade rides close to the rear blade as a result of the few beads added that only provide marginal space between the two blades. This is fine and is how most commercial spinnerbaits are made, but you can space them out farther if you wish by moving the clevis of the smaller blade forward on the shaft. There are several ways to do this. One is to use more beads or unies on the shaft behind the clevis so that they separate the two blades. Another way is to use a small section of thin tubing on the shaft. Empty ballpoint-pen ink tubes; narrow fuel-line tubing for model airplanes (available at hobby shops); the thin spray tubing from cans of demoisturizers; and the thin straws used as coffee stirrers in fast-food places can all be used. Be sure to measure the length of tubing you will need before cutting, and add two or three beads forward of the tubing (between the tubing and the clevis) to serve as bearings for the free-swinging clevis.

Another way to accomplish this is to slide the forward beads, the clevis and blade, and the bearing beads onto the shaft and then make two sharp, close right angle bends—like a modified Z —to keep the bearing beads from sliding up the shaft beyond this point. A drop of solder on the wire shaft at the appropriate point will also provide more spacing, but this is often more trouble to accomplish than the methods just described.

The skirt on a spinnerbait is added in one of several ways. First, any tail material or skirting can be tied on using the fly-tying techniques described

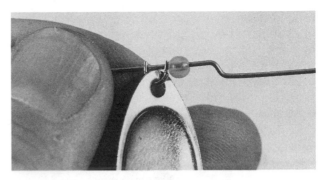

One way to separate several blades is to make two sharp bends in the upper arm as shown to keep the forward blade from sliding back. To do this, first add the blade on a clevis and at least one bearing bead as shown.

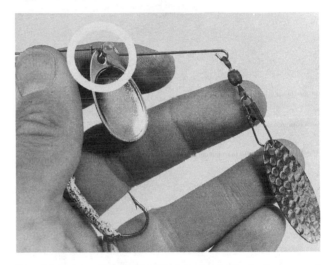

Bend in upper arm of spinnerbait, with circle around the bend and the blade/bead position.

Three ways of making double- or multiple-blade spinnerbaits. Left to right; using a double bent shaft with a bead; using beads; and using thin tubing with beads as separators.

fully in Chapter 4. Second, the living-rubber style of skirting can be added by using the special pliers to open the rubber O-rings: Hold the rubber in place with the pliers, slide the rubber and hook collar into place, and close the pliers to secure the skirt. Then the skirting — in sheet form until cut — is trimmed with scissors to form the living-rubber strands. This material can also be tied in place on spinnerbaits. A final method is not to use any natural or artificial skirting, but a grub tail or worms as a trailer attractant. Usually those with curved tails are best because of the rippling, lifelike action.

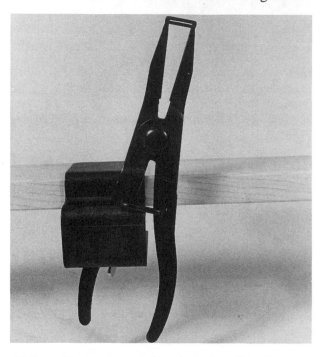

Adding skirts using a skirt tool. Small collars are placed on the thin end tips of the special "pliers" and the handle locked to hold this open position. The table clamp allows easy use of the tool.

The skirt-sheet material through the collar, ready to be positioned and trimmed to form the skirt.

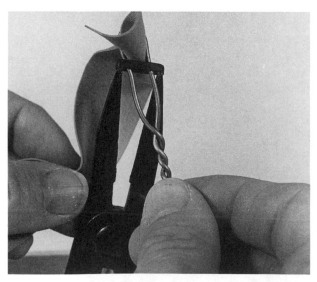

Using a small loop of wire (not supplied; made by the author) makes it easy to bring a length of skirt-sheet material through the rubber collar.

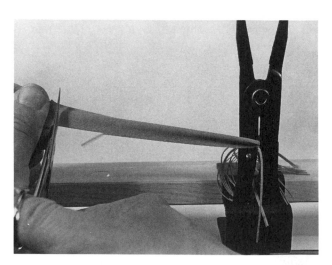

Here, the skirt has been moved to a clamped position on the tool and secured in place with the table clamp. Pulling the sheet material as shown and then trimming separates the sections of the sheet to form the skirt.

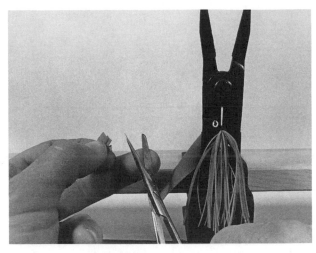

Completed skirt on one side, with the small amount of trimmed material. Trim as little as possible to avoid waste.

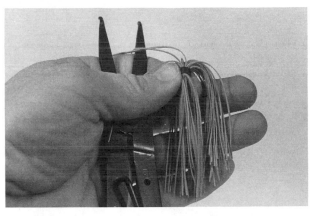

Completed skirt after the second side has been trimmed. Skirt is ready to be added to the spinnerbait or buzzbait.

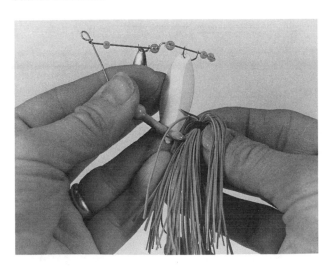

Adding completed skirt to spinnerbait. Rubber collar holds skirt in place and on hook shank.

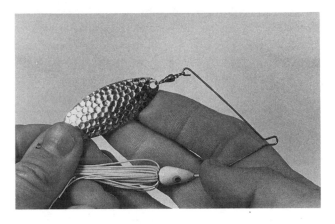

Single-blade spinnerbait with a standard rubber skirt. Skirt is on in reversed fashion, standard for most lures.

Silicone sparkle skirt with a stinger hook added to the lure.

BUZZBAIT ASSEMBLY

BENT-ARM BUZZBAITS

Once the eyes and bends in a buzzbait are formed, the assembly is relatively simple and very much like the assembly of spinnerbaits. The main difference is that buzzbaits use one or two cupped-wing propeller-type blades on the shaft rather than the spinner blades on a swivel or clevis. To make a single-blade buzzbait, first thread a small bead on the shaft. This will prevent the blade from sliding forward and binding against the bend in the upper arm. Next, thread the blade on the shaft. Finally, add a small pop-rivet or blade collar to both serve as a bearing and to make the squeaking sound favored in buzzbaits. (Some plastic buzzbait blades come with a molded-in aluminum collar, thus eliminating this steps.) Once the collar is in place, make a right-angle bend in the shaft, after measuring and marking where you want the blade positioned on the shaft. Use compound-action cutting pliers to cut off any excess wire.

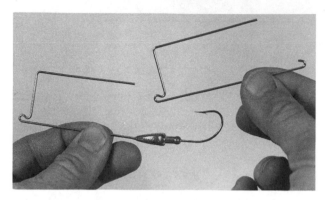

Buzzbaits can be bought molded with wires and hooks, or wire forms can be purchased for use in molds to make these bodies.

Adding a triple-wing delta blade to a buzzbait. A bearing bead is added in back of the blade and then the upper arm bent to hold the parts on the shaft.

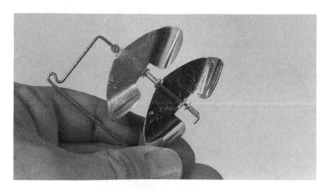

Double, counter-rotating blades on a buzzbait, separated by a sleeve.

Left, buzzbait with single large triple-wing blade; right, a double-wing buzzbait.

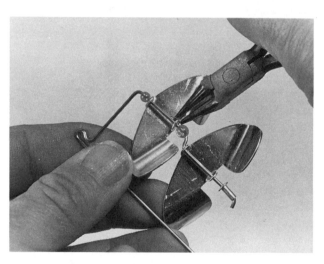

One way to separate the two blades on a double-blade buzzbait is to use the double-crimped bends in the arm, as shown here. If the blade binds slightly, sometimes bending the wire attachment ear, as shown, will help to free it.

IN-LINE BUZZBAITS

In-line buzzbaits work the same way on the surface of the water but are made somewhat differently than the bent-arm buzzers. Because these are built in a straight line with the hook shank and main shaft, the only bending is that of the eye for the line-tie when the lure assembly is completed. Since in-line buzzbaits will have a tendency to rotate, use only the tandem counter-rotating blades, or a large delta blade with a counter-rotating blade in front. Assuming you are working with wire (the hook and wire molded in the lead body), first thread on a small bead as a bearing or spacer, add a blade collar or pop-rivet squeaker, then follow with the large or rear blade. Add several more beads after the rear blade as spacers to make sure the two blades do not hit and bind. Add the second blade, a final bead, and then make a simple loop eye for a line-tie.

The pressure of the first blade against the beads serving as spacers will slightly slow the second or rear blade, but not enough to be noticeable. If you are concerned about this and wish to completely separate the two blades for totally free movement, there are two solutions. One is to make two small, closely spaced right-angle bends in the wire immediately forward of the rear blade to prevent it from sliding back. If you do this, be sure to use a bead or pop rivet as a bearing directly behind each blade. Then add the second blade and finish as above.

The second method of separating the blades is to add a small drop of solder to the wire shaft to prevent the forward blade from sliding back. If you do this, you can add the solder as the lure is being built or after completion. If you do so after completion, be sure to allow enough space and play in the wire for the soldering operation. Also, be sure to provide a pop rivet or bead as a bearing behind each of the blades.

Skirts are added using the same materials and methods described for spinnerbaits: artificial fur, feather, or rubber or plastic skirting material tied in place; a rubber or plastic skirt slipped on; or a soft plastic grub tail or worm slid onto the hook.

IN-LINE OR WEIGHT-FORWARD SPINNER ASSEMBLY

In-line or weight-forward spinners are really a compromise between spinnerbaits and spinners, but since they require a molded-in head, they are included here. Unlike spinners in which all the parts are threaded onto a bare shaft, these lures have molded heads; yet unlike spinnerbaits, they are built in-line. The forward-weight design allows them to be fished on the bottom, and as a result they are popular walleye lures. In essence, they are really like an in-line buzzbait with the blades and body reversed in position and spinner blades instead of buzzbait blades.

Different head designs are available and they also go by names like walleye spinners, Erie spinners, Erie rigs, and keel spinners. Unlike spinnerbait or buzzbait heads that have a wire and hook molded in, these lures are molded on a looped-eye wire, with the loop eye forming the line-tie and the wire then threaded with a spinner blade and ending with a clip eye that allows opening and closing. This clip eye holds a straight-eye hook that can be dressed or that more typically is used to hold bait. Typical baits for these rigs for walleye include minnows, night crawlers, and leeches.

These lures are molded using the same techniques used to mold jig heads, sinkers, spinnerbaits, and buzzbaits. Because the wire used generally extends out the bottom of the mold, special support of the mold, as outlined under the techniques for molding spinnerbait and buzzbait heads, is required.

Once the head is molded, the rest of the lure is ready to be assembled. For this, a bead or two is usually threaded onto the shaft that extends from the rear of the head. This is followed by a clevis and blade. Any spinner blade in any size or finish is possible, but French-style blades in nickel or copper finish are often favored by walleye fishermen. This is followed by two or more beads to serve as spacers and bearings for easy turning of the blade.

The clip is formed by first making a small J-shaped bend in the wire, then making a right-angle bend just above this bend so that the J bend is angled to the side. Finish with a wider bend about one inch up the wire, formed so that J-shaped hook will catch on the main shaft of the wire. This arrangement allows opening and closing for adding or changing hooks.

Hooks should be straight-eyed, and with a slightly long shank. Often Mustad 3366G hooks are used ("G" for the gold finish) because they have unusually large eyes that will swing freely on the end of the spinner and minimize tangling and twisting on both cast and retrieve.

The same methods described for adding skirts to standard spinnerbaits are used for in-line spinnerbaits, if and when skirts are used. Often live minnows or leeches are used in place of a skirt when fishing for walleye.

VARIATIONS

There are a number of possible variations of all of these lures: Some can be done on only one type of lure, while others are applicable to any of them. In fact, some of the following variations are adapted from commercial lures of the present and past. In addition, your own imagination can be applied to any of these lures. You can try many variations, but plan the order of assembly or construction modification necessary to the lure before beginning.

VARIATIONS IN LINE-TIES

The open R eye or the wrapped eye is standard in most spinnerbaits and buzzbaits. Other possibilities include one that I call the "omega eye," which is really a variation of the R eye with an additional bend in the vertical leg of the R to make it like the Greek letter Ω. This is easily done by forming the eye at the proper position, then making a sharp bend away from it on each side to spread the legs of the lure. This is possible on any type of spinnerbait or bent-arm buzzbait.

It is also possible to place a free-swinging clevis on the wire shaft for the line-tie. To do this, start with straight wire, and a small bead as a spacer, then add a large stirrup-style clevis and a second bead. Make a bend below and one above these parts to keep them in place. For spinnerbaits, these can be sharp-angle bends, while on a bent-arm buzzbait the lower arm will have a sharp 90-degree bend, and the upper arm will have a slight bend to keep the clevis from sliding up.

Another variation on buzzbaits is to make a sharp right-angle bend to form the upright arm, add the beads and clevis, and then make two sharp, close-together right-angle bends (like Z's) to keep the clevis from sliding. An alternative is to add the beads and clevis and then add a short length (premeasured) of thin plastic or metal tubing to keep the clevis from sliding up the shaft. In making these, you *must* use the stirrup-style clevis, because the folded types have sharp edges that could cut the line.

A variation similar to the above is to add a swivel for a line-tie. A bead both above and below, as with the clevis, is necessary. Another method of doing this is to add a swivel (no beads) when making a wrapped eye. This is possible on both spinnerbaits and buzzbaits, although both variations are more practical on spinnerbaits. Both methods can be used when constructing spinnerbaits with cable, as will be described later in this chapter. The one variation when using cable is that you must use a crimped-on leader sleeve above and below the clevis or swivel bearing to keep them from sliding on the cable. Bends on flexible cable are not sufficient to keep a clevis or swivel in place.

VARIATIONS IN BLADE POSITION AND NUMBER

The instructions listed above are for generally accepted styles of spinnerbaits and buzzbaits. However, extra blades can be added to spinnerbaits and buzzbaits, and blades can be placed in other than standard positions. An example would be to include extra blades on the upper arm of spinnerbait, each separated by a few beads and spacers, and each on its own clevis to swing around on retrieve. Using this method, it is possible to make three-, four-, and even five-bladed spinnerbaits, with one large blade on a swivel at the end of the arm and all others on clevises on the upper arm. These extra blades can be added to any spinnerbait constructed, whether you work with straight wire and mold the lure or buy unpainted or painted molded heads.

Similarly, it is possible to add small blades to the lower arm of the spinnerbait, although this must be done only with straight wires because the blades and clevises must be added before the wire is bent and the eye is formed.

You can also add a blade to the forward part of the upper arm, make a kink in the wire, then continue as before to make a two- or three-blade style. Another way to separate blades in any two- or three-blade spinnerbait is to use bearing beads next to the clevis, separated by thin plastic or metal tubing.

One easy way to add extra blades to produce a spinnerbait with a wild action is to use a three-way swivel and add a blade (using a jump ring or split ring) to each of two eyes, adding the swivel to the arm with the third eye. The result will be blades that rotate at the same time they move around each other. Either the same or different sizes, styles, and finishes can be used in the choice of the two blades. Typically, different sizes, styles, and colors are used for maximum visual and vibration effects.

Another way to add spinner blades to a tandem spinnerbait is to use a swivel or snap swivel in place of the clevis. For this, thread a bead or two on the upper shaft, add a swivel or snap swivel, then another bead or two (or whatever you wish to used to produce the spacing desired), then finally make the J bend in the wire to finish the spinnerbait with the larger tail blade. Add a small spinner blade to the snap swivel, or use a split ring to join a blade and the swivel eye to complete the lure.

Extra blades are not usually added to buzzbaits, with one exception. This is to add a single spinner

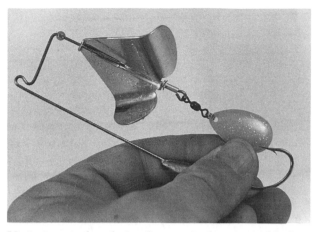

Variations in buzzbaits; here a single spinner blade is attached by a swivel to the end of the buzzbait arm. A standard delta-wing blade is used.

blade to the end of the wire, as in making a single-blade spinnerbait. This is in addition to the single delta or double-counter blades on the typical bent-arm buzzbait, and does give the lure a little additional flash. Usually small blades are used, of any style or finish. A variation of this idea is to add two blades to two eyes of a three-way swivel, attaching the third eye to the end of the arm of the buzzbait. These blades are usually small, but can be of matching or different styles or finishes for endless combinations. Since buzzbait wire is often heavier than spinnerbait wire, take care in forming the eye for these variations. You may have to use heavier round-nose pliers, or to form part of an eye, add the swivel, and then close the

Three styles of separate buzzers which can be added in front of any lure, including spinners, spinnerbaits, spoons, jigs, etc. Left, double-wing counter-rotating blades with a red body in between; center and right, single delta blades. All make it easy to add lures through a snap or coil-spring fastener.

eye with flat-nose pliers. Another technique is to use a small torch to heat and soften the wire, then make the bends while the end of the wire is still hot.

It is difficult to make blade additions to in-line buzzbaits, but one possibility is to thread a regular spinner blade on a clevis (with bearing beads fore and aft), make a slight kink in the wire to prevent pressure on these parts, and then add the single delta or double-counter blades to the shaft. The single spinner blade will rotate while the propeller-type delta or counter blades will spin on the shaft. This will make for a slightly larger, longer, and bulkier-looking lure.

Weight-forward or walleye-style spinners typically have one spinner blade on the shaft behind

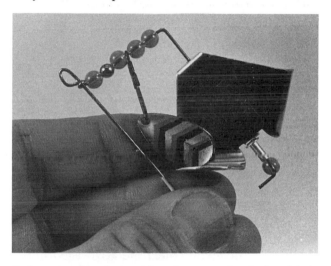

Delta-wing buzzbait with a homemade clicker blade added using a snap and standard spinner blade.

the weighted head, but more can be added. Two blades on clevises are possible, separated by bead spacers, a tubing spacer, or a dot of solder between the two blades. It is also possible to use one or more small propeller blades or even small buzzbait blades, although this is seldom seen. Because these lures are fished on or close to the bottom, the spinner blades that hug close to the shaft are more practical than the broader propeller blades.

Spinner blades placed on the hook are a possibility for all of these lures. Usually small blades are best to add a little flash to the lure. These can be forced over the hook barb, or a folded clevis can be forced over the hook point and barb. Other similar attachments can include small red or other-colored plastic tags, chamois, or the Dri-Rind-type tails and split lengths of red or colored plastic tubing.

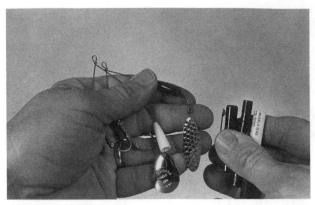

Protecting spinnerbait swivels from weeds and algae is easy by using discarded ball-point pens. The tapered end is used as shown to slide over the wire before the blade is added to the shaft. Use care to make sure that the cut-off pen end will only cover the swivel—not interfere with the blade rotation.

VARIATIONS IN BLADES

Although all of the assembly instructions and examples so far have included the standard commercially available spinner blades in basic styles (mostly willowleaf, Colorado, and Indiana), it is possible to make blades by using the techniques outlined in Chapter 8. Usually, the cost of spinner blades makes this uneconomical.

It is also possible to make different blades such as are now beginning to be seen on some commercial lures. One of these involves a flat rectangular sheet of metal (sheet metal) twisted into a spiral. The resultant spiral causes the blade to rotate when the spinnerbait is retrieved. A hole

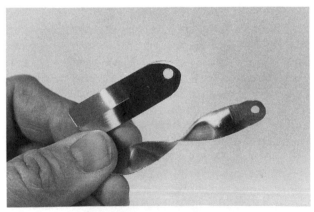

Different types of blades for spinnerbaits can be made using scrap sheet metal. These were made from old damaged award plaques. The one on the left has a split end to form two blades; the one on the right is twisted. Both rotate on their own axis when attached to the end of an arm with a swivel.

punched into the center of one end allows for attachment to a swivel or snap swivel.

Another method involves using a similar flat rectangular sheet of metal and cutting it lengthwise halfway through the metal. Spreading these cut ends in opposite directions results in a propeller blade that will rotate through the water. Punch or drill a hole in the opposite, uncut, end to attach to the spinnerbait. Rectangles of metal about 1/2-inch by 2 inches are best for most of these blades, although any size rectangle can be used.

VARIATIONS IN WIRE FORMS, EYES, ARMS

Arms on spinnerbaits and buzzbaits can be bent at various angles for optimal performance in the water. Often, spinnerbait wire must be bent sharply at the junction with the lead head so that the hook is in line with the retrieve direction of the lure.

Double-arm spinnerbaits, in which one blade is at the end of each arm, can be molded, although this is not typical. One way to do this is to use two wires in the mold that are connected to the hook eye. These wires must be lighter than the wire that would normally be used, or they will not fit or allow the mold to be closed properly, thus causing flash on the lead head. Once these wires are molded in, it is easy to wrap an eye with them, then separate them so they extend to each side of spinnerbait and over the top of the hook. Then, blades can be added to the end of each arm as per the instructions of a single-blade spinnerbait. Though this is seldom seen, blades can also be added to the shaft, using the same lineup of bearing beads, spacers, and clevises as is used for double- or tandem-blade spinnerbaits.

One way to add two blades on double arms is to add a jointed wire to the upper arm with a blade at each end of the wire. To do this, cut back the upper arm, make a slight bend about 3/4-inch from the end and a second bend about 1/4-inch from the first. These bends will be the beginning of a triangle in the end of the wire. Before proceeding, form a tight coil spring in the center of a straight spinner or spinnerbait wire using a wire former or round-nose pliers. Slide this wire onto the straight length of the upper arm and then finish the bend on the upper arm with pliers. Cut any excess wire if necessary. Bend the two end wires at a slight backward angle and add spinner blades to the ends.

Another way to do this is to mold or buy a

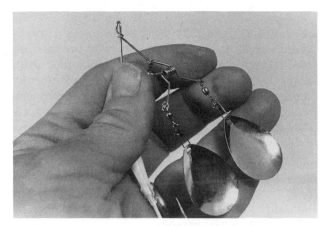

Another method of making a double-arm, double-blade spinnerbait by forming a "stirrup" in the end of a short wire and then adding a double-arm attachment, as shown. The coiled center is made in the same manner as making a spring with round-nose plier; the other bends and arm lengths are easily made.

Making a triple-arm, triple-wing spinnerbait. Doubled spinnerbait wire is placed over the lower arm and up through the line tie. For this, it is best to have the line-tie in a horizontal plane instead of the standard vertical plane.

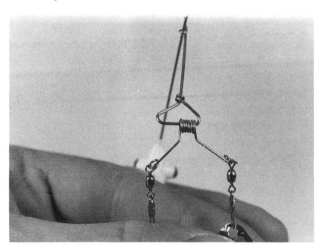

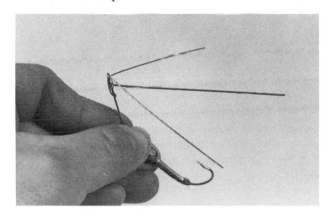

Detail of above to show the various bends and wire forms.

Completed three-arm spinnerbait body in which the two arms have been pulled tight and bent back and at an angle. Single or double blades can be attached to each arm.

standard single-wire spinnerbait wire form and use the upper arm to wrap a very tight multiple wrap (almost like a tension spring). This wrap must be at right angles to the axis of the wire. Run a separate wire through this springlike wrap, center it, and make a slight bend on each side of the wrap. Then the ends of this wire are used for blade attachment to make a free-swinging twin-blade spinnerbait. This method has been used successfully commercially.

You can make spinnerbaits with three arms — a technique just recently seen commercially. To do this, use standard spinnerbait wire to make a typical spinnerbait bend in the wire with a typical looped eye. To add the two additional arms, use thinner, lighter wire and thread the wire through the eye, around the rear of the lower shaft wire, then up through the eye going in the opposite direction of the original wire.

It often helps to make a sharp bend in the light wire so that the two ends are parallel and then to run the two ends up through the eye in opposite directions so that the wires exit the eye in opposite directions. Bend these wires in the plane or direction you wish and add single or double blades to them along with the main central wire.

Another way to do this is to make a wrapped eye but to turn the eye at right angles to the plane of the spinnerbait and run the wires up through this eye or line-tie. The end result is the same in both cases.

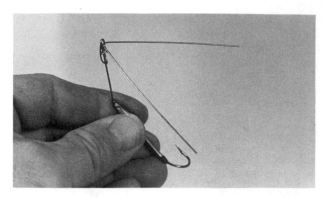

By clipping the center arm of the above arrangement, it is possible to make a double-arm spinnerbait.

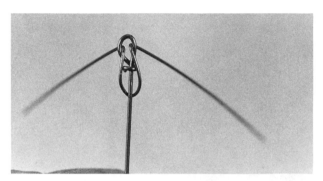

Detail of the double-arm arrangement to show the position of the two added wires. The same would be true for a triple-arm spinnerbait, by leaving the center arm long.

You can make buzzbaits with free-swinging blades so that the buzzbait may be used as a surface lure that will sink and "helicopter" down into a hole. To do this, clip the upper arm of the buzzbait off short and make a simple loop or eye in the end. Then add the buzzbait blade or blades onto a separate wire shaft, and form an eye in it that is attached to the loop in the upper wire arm. The result is a buzzbait that will track straight when used on the surface (like a normal buzzbait) but will swing up from water pressure to helicopter on the fall.

CABLE CONSTRUCTION

Spinnerbaits can be made using cable in place of wire. Any size cable can be used, although nylon-covered cable about twenty- to thirty-pound test is best. You will also need leader sleeves matched for the wire size. You can make an eye or loop on the hook and mold the wire into the lead head, or you can use a standard jig with

the desired head shape and attach the cable to the external hook eye with leader sleeves. To do the first, make sure the cable is secure in the mold so that it will not later pull out. For the latter method, thread a leader sleeve on the end of the cable, thread the cable through the hook eye, and bend it sharply about 1/2-inch from the end. Thread this end back through the leader sleeve and crimp the sleeve to secure.

To make an eye for a line-tie, there are several possibilities. One is to thread the wire through a leader sleeve once, and then once again in the same direction to make a loop of cable. Crimp the leader sleeve to keep the cable from sliding. A variation of this is to thread the cable through a stirrup clevis or swivel before going through the leader sleeve the second time. Use a bearing bead above and below the clevis. Then the clevis or swivel may be used for the line-tie. Thread bearing beads, a spinner blade/clevis, and more bearing beads onto the cable, then cut the cable where you wish the end of the wire to be. Make a leader-sleeve loop at the end and at the same time secure the swivel holding the rear blade.

Another line-tie variation is to thread a leader sleeve on the cable, then a bearing bead, the clevis, a second bearing bead, and a second leader sleeve. Crimp the leader sleeves to hold the clevis in place on the cable.

JIG-SPINNER WIRES

You can use wire to make jig-spinners that are in essence the wire end of a spinnerbait and are designed to be used with a jig to make up a flexible-head spinnerbait. These are available commercially, either as separate wires to use with any jig or as a complete jig-and-spinner wire. In most cases they are used in small sizes, primarily for crappie, panfish, sauger, and white bass. Since they are used with standard jigs, they do not have the smooth tapered heads found on standard spinnerbaits.

To make these, use any spinnerbait or spinner wire. Generally, the lighter, springier wire of about .024-inch to .045-inch in diameter and designed for straight spinners is best, because the completed wire forms must have a catch for jig attachment. Begin by taking a short length (5 to 6 inches) of any light-spring stainless steel wire, and form an open or R-style eye, wrapped eye, or loop eye in the middle of the wire. For the jig attachment, make a spring-closed open eye or clip eye at one end. To make the spring-closed open eye, first slide a coil-spring fastener onto the wire. This is used to lock the open eye in place and the usual fastener inside diameter of .070-inch will fit any wire from .024-inch to .030-inch. One-half inch from the end of the wire, make a small kink using needle-nose pliers. Use the larger end of a pair of round-nose pliers to make a round eye in the wire, ending with a kink on the other side of the round eye so that the eye is centered on the wire shaft. The coil spring can then be slid down over both wires to lock the eye closed, or slid up the wire to expose the open end for removal or the addition of a jig.

To make a clip eye, first bend one end of the wire in a sharp, small J shape. Make a sharp right-angle bend in this wire just above the J, and then a second bend or open eye in the wire about 1/2- to 3/4-inch from the J hook. Make sure this open eye is made so that, when it is complete, the J hook will clip onto the standing wire. This eye also allows the addition or removal of any jig head.

One or two blades and the appropriate hardware are added to the other end of the wire, using techniques already discussed for making one- or two-blade spinnerbaits.

It is also possible to make these spinnerbaits of cable by using cable techniques and a clevis for the line-tie. Since you cannot make a coil-spring open eye or clip eye on the end of the wire, you can use leader sleeves for a permanent attachment to the jig head or to attach a snap that in turn allows attachment and removal of the jig head.

VARIATIONS IN HOOKS

An unusual variation in spinnerbaits is to make them with a large blade and a lot of bearing spacers on the upper arm so that the blade is attached close to the center of the lure or at the fork of the two arms, with the hook attached to the upper arm to make a lure with two opposing hooks, almost like ice tongs. The hook can be soldered to the eye in the wire to keep it from flopping around and snagging on the lower hook. An easier way to do this is to use a short length of rubber or plastic tubing first threaded on the wire, then backed up over the wire/hook-eye joint to hold the hook straight and in place. This type of lure was manufactured a few years ago, with only fair commercial success, but it can be fashioned by any tackle hobbyist.

Some hook variations are obvious. Stinger hooks on spinnerbaits and buzzbaits are well known, although some of the methods of placing them there are not. Any single hook can be placed on any spinnerbait or buzzbait, provided that the eye of the stinger hook is large enough to fit over the barb of the fixed hook. Even this can be adjusted either by slightly opening the eye of the stringer hook or bending down the barb of the fixed hook.

Once you bend down the barb of the fixed hook, you can open it again by prying with a knife blade. You can open the eye of a stinger hook by using wire cutters, using them as prying levers by placing the cutter jaws at the open end of the hook eye and gently squeezing to pry open the eye. Do this with care, because some brittle hook eyes may shatter. Naturally, with this as with all tackle-making operations, use goggles for eye protection. Once it's on the fixed hook, the stinger-hook eye can be closed with pliers.

This method of attaching free-swinging stinger hooks does allow for tangling and snagging, so some means of stabilizing the hook is a must. There are several methods to do this. One is to use a paper or leather punch and punch plastic discs out of a coffee-can, or similar plastic, lid. These discs are then given a center hole with an awl and placed on the fixed hook both above and below the stinger hook. They will help stabilize the stinger hook on the bend of the fixed hook but will still allow it to swing from side to side. A better method is to use a small piece of rubber (preferably) or plastic tubing that will just fit over the eye of the stinger hook. Forcing the eye on the fixed hook with this tubing in place helps to stabilize the hook in line with the lure. An even better method is to use a slightly longer piece of tubing (about 1 1/2 inches) and thread the fixed hook through 1/4-inch of the tubing. Thread the tubing partially onto the fixed hook, place the eye of the stinger hook in the opposite end of the tubing, and then impale this stinger hook on the fixed hook. Slide the tubing up on the shank of the fixed hook to keep the stinger hook in line with the lure at all times.

Some alternatives are to use a small scrap piece of plastic worm over the eye of the hook or a longer 1 1/2-inch length threaded onto the fixed hook, to stabilize the eye of the stinger hook as with the tubing above. In any of these methods, the stinger hook can be point-up or point-down, although point-up is the standard version.

Other possibilities for hooks include using double hooks or treble hooks for stinger hooks, or using these hooks on a short length of heavy leader (usually no longer than 2 or 3 inches) snelled to both the shank of the fixed hook and to the stinger hook.

It is also possible to make lures with free-swinging hooks. This is standard on in-line spinners, and can be added when molding spinnerbaits and buzzbaits by molding the heads with a wire eyelet form (you will have to make these) in the head in place of a hook. Then use a split ring to attach a free-swinging single or double hook. An alternative to this is to use a long wire form and run the wire straight through the head cavity to make a long J-shaped eye in the end. To keep the lead head from sliding on the wire, bend a small kink at the spot that is in the center of the lead head. Then attach the hook to the exposed wire eye.

SKIRTS

Skirts for spinnerbaits and buzzbaits are typically slipped on following the assembly of the arms and blade components in the finished lure. These use the rubber or plastic-fringe skirts that will slip easily onto the collar of any spinnerbait or buzzbait. Exceptions include those skirts that are tied permanently onto the lure, those that use the small rubber O rings that are slid up or rolled onto the collar, and those that use filament rubber.

To tie a skirt on a spinnerbait or buzzbait, apply the same techniques used for tying on jig and bucktail skirts. Begin by wrapping the thread around the lead collar several times, and secure by wrapping over these previous wraps. Continue with several wraps to firmly secure the thread, then tie in the skirt material. Skirt materials of fur, artificial fur, saddle hackle, nylon, mylar, or metalized fibers can all be used. Hold the skirt material over the collar, make several turns of thread around it and do some adjusting to make sure it completely covers the lead collar. Clip off any excess material forward of the collar, wrap completely to cover the skirt material, and tie off with half-hitches. Once the skirt is tied off, finish with fly-tying head cement, clear or colored nylon-based fingernail polish, paint, or epoxy finish.

Filament rubber skirts are made with a special spreading-plier tool, and when finished they are rolled or slid up onto the lure collar.

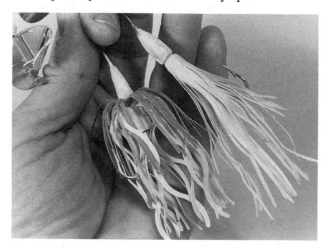

Two methods of adding skirts to spinnerbaits and buzzbaits. Left, reversed style for more bulk and flare; right, standard style that makes for a slimmer profile with less action.

In-line buzzbaits can be made jointed (left) or on a single straight-through wire (right). Any standard buzzbait blade style can be used.

7

Soft-Plastic Lures

INTRODUCTION ▪ TOOLS ▪ MATERIALS ▪ PARTS ▪
GENERAL MOLDING TECHNIQUES ▪ STEPS IN MOLDING
REPRESENTATIVE PLASTIC LURES ▪ TWO- OR MORE
COLOR LURES ▪ MOLDING ROUND LURES ▪ TWO-PIECE
AND ONE-PIECE PLASTER MOLDS ▪ MOLDING IN HOOKS
AND LEADERS, MAKING WORM RIGS ▪ VARIATIONS IN
WORMS AND WORM RIGS ▪ KITS

Basic Tools
Plastic or rubber one-piece molds
Two-piece molds
Injector for two-piece molds
Melting pot
Stirring sticks

Helpful Tools
Hot plate or special melting stove
Special plastic-melting furnace
Gloves
Cooling pan
Pizza cutter
Scissors
Threading needle
Heat-melt-cement electric gun

INTRODUCTION

Many anglers who buy soft-plastic worms, grubs, and minnows are not aware that worms just as soft, just as good, and in a variety of colors and sizes, can be made at home for a few pennies each. And although worms and molds for making them are popular, it is also possible to make a wide variety of soft freshwater and saltwater plastics that include worms of all lengths and styles, curved-tail worms, grubs, shrimp tails, minnows, eels, snakes, spinnerbait tails, frogs, salamanders, lizards, crayfish, egg sacks, and some larger saltwater soft plastics. In addition, it is possible to make your own molds for lures for which molds are unavailable commercially.

Only a few tools and parts are needed, along

Some molds and materials, along with small pots that are sold for the purpose.

with some easy-to-obtain molding plastic, colors, and scents. The procedure is simple, quite safe, and makes it easy to produce quantities of soft plastics in any color and style desired.

TOOLS

The tools needed for making soft-plastic lures include molds, injectors, pots, and stirrers.

Molds. Available molds are made in a shiny hard plastic, a more-flexible shiny plastic, and aluminum. Most are of one piece to facilitate the direct pouring of molten plastic from the pot or ladle. These molds are available from the Lure-Craft, M-F, and Limit companies. Two-piece molds to make round lures by using an injector are available from Hilts Molds.

Open-face molds are just that—open on one side of the mold cavity. While most commercial worms today are injection-molded in round multiple-cavity two-part molds, originally they were made using the open-mold method. The results from one-piece molds are semi-round worms, because the molds are designed to make a worm as close to round as possible.

Two-part molds are made with registration pins and locking plastic C-clamps to hold the two sides together. These molds will form a completely round worm. Hilts is the only supplier of these molds at the time of this writing. Most require an injector tool to squirt the soft plastic into the sprue or gate of the mold. Those that do not require a separate injector have a built-in reservoir on one side of the mold into which a fitted plunger inserts to inject the plastic. These molds are fitted together with wing nuts to hold the two parts together.

Injectors. These are used only with two-piece molds to inject the soft plastic. They work like a simple medical syringe, with a cavity and a plunger that pushes the liquid plastic through a small spout and into the mold.

Plastic-melting stove. These stoves are sold by some companies for melting plastic in pots. In most cases they are identical to small single-burner hot plates. Most have an adjustable rheostat temperature control and will plug into standard 120-volt outlets.

Pouring pan. Any type of small flat-bottom aluminum pan can be used for melting plastic.

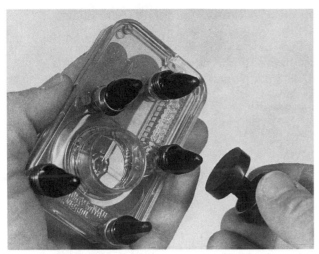

A two-piece mold from Hilts Molds for making round soft plastics. The black spring-loaded pins lock the two parts together and the plunger (right) is used to push molten plastic into the mold through an injection system.

Another Hilts injection soft-plastic mold that uses a separate injection plunger system. The plastic "C" clamps hold the two mold halves together.

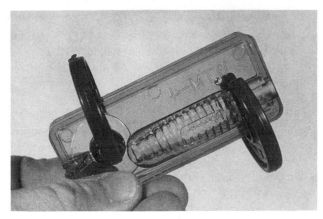

Hilts mold with the two clamps in place.

Inexpensive cookware pots are fine, but some companies have similar or smaller pots for melting smaller quantities of plastic. One pan from Lure Craft, when half-full, will make six to eight worms. It is important to have a flat bottom on these pans, as well as some form of lip for easy pouring. In some cases it helps to use pliers to further accentuate this spout for easy pouring and cleanup.

Stirring sticks. Stirring sticks can be anything, from popsicle sticks, tongue depressors, and plastic straws (although usually these are too weak for good stirring), to scraps of wood or short sections of round wood dowels. The main thing is to have a stick that will allow you to stir completely and thoroughly as the plastic is being heated. It also helps to have some long stirring sticks to stir the liquid plastic in its container before it is poured into the pan for melting.

Glue gun. Glue guns used for regular hot-melt cement are useful for molding plastic lures. With a short "stick" of colored plastic inserted into the open end of the glue gun, and with a follow-up "push stick," it is possible to dress up soft-plastic lures with spots and stripes of different colors using the heated gun to melt and deposit small amounts of the colored-plastic sticks in specific spots on the lure. Lure-Craft even has a four-cavity mold for making the colored sticks to be used in the gun.

Wormizer. This tool, by Missouri Boat Products, is used more for modification and repair of soft plastics than for making lures. It is small, AA-flashlight-sized, tool (and uses one AA battery) with a brass-and-nichrome wire tip for molding, shaping, cutting, customizing, mending, and modifying soft-plastic lures with the heat generated through the tip.

MATERIALS

Materials for making soft plastics include various types of plastic, along with additives. These include:

Liquid plastic. The liquid plastic probably varies from manufacturer to manufacturer, but is basically a milky-white liquid plastic with a petroleum base that turns clear and solid, though soft, when heated. In most cases, melting temperature is about 300° to 350°F. It is usually sold in pint, quart, gallon, 5-gallon, and 55-gallon drum containers.

Unless you want clear lures, the plastic must have color added to it. It can be mixed with additives containing hardener, softener, glitter, and various scents.

Some companies sell different formulas of liquid plastics, such as standard and super soft. The super-soft plastic will make the extra-soft worms popular today. You can make standard plastic soft by adding special softeners.

Softeners. This is also sold in pint through five-gallon containers, and is added to liquid plastic to make softer lures. Although there are no rules as to how much softener to add to liquid plastic, usually a mix of about 1 to 2 ounces of softener to a pint of plastic (a 1:8 or 1:16 ratio) is about right. More or less can be used as desired, or follow specific manufacturer's instructions.

As with liquid plastic, the softener is milky white. Naturally, the softer the lure becomes the more fragile it is, and the more likely it is to tear and become abraded while fishing. Extra-soft lures are a must for some fishing, as in worm-fishing for bass.

Hardener. Also sold in pint through five-gallon containers, hardener is used to make harder, tougher lures. This is often a requirement for saltwater fishing where durability is more important than softness and the fish are not as finicky as are largemouth bass. The hardener is also a milky-white liquid, and it is best to begin with a ratio of 1 or 2 ounces to a pint of plastic. It is usually added to the cold, raw liquid plastic before melting, but be sure to follow specific manufacturer's instructions.

Worm oil. This is not used for molding but in the packaging of worms to make them seem more slippery and lively. Too much will make the worms and the packaging seem slimy, and none at all will make it difficult to remove the worms from a plastic bag. Worms can be soaked in the oil or the oil can be added to the worms when they are packaged.

Colors. Although the liquid plastic is milky in color in the bottle, it becomes clear when melted. As a result, color must be added to the lure. Most available colors are highly concentrated so that a little bit goes a long way. Most companies recommend a starting point of about 1 ounce of color added to 1 gallon of plastic, although more or less can be used.

Colors are available in 1-, 2-, 4-, 16-, and 32-ounce bottles. Some companies sell colors in glass jars, others provide plastic squeeze bottles in the smaller sizes, with dropper spouts for easy application. Typical standard colors include black, blue, green, purple, red, yellow, white, strawberry, watermelon green, pink, brown, silver, orange, natural, avocado green, amber brown, golden yellow, lemon yellow, lime green, strawberry red, motor oil, violet, violet grape, grape, and black grape. Some companies supply colors in both opaque and translucent shades, although the opaque colors can be used in very small amounts to make for very light, see-through translucent lures. Lure-Craft labels their colors with an O or T to indicate the difference, however.

In addition, fluorescent colors are available in red, yellow, blue, green, pink, orange, and purple. These colors are added to the liquid plastic *before* heating (recommended by some companies, insisted upon by others). Standard pearl, along with pearl white, pearl yellow, and pearl silver, are also available to give plastic lures a pearl-like sheen. The pearls are available in liquid or powder forms, of which a small amount (Lure-Craft recommends 1/4-teaspoon to one of their pans half-full of plastic) is added to the plastic or to other colors. The dry pearl can be mixed into clear plastic for a different look.

Glow-in-the-dark pigment is also available to make lures that will glow for awhile after exposure to light. The pigment is available in liquid or powder forms and can be added to paint or to liquid plastic. In addition to the typical yellowish green shade, it is available in other colors, usually yellow and red. Phosphorescent lures have been declared illegal in some areas in the past—be sure to check your local regulations before making lures that glow in the dark.

Glitter. Glitter is nothing more than metal or metalized plastic flake that can be added to any soft-plastic lure. The soft-plastic parts catalogs list a few colors such as silver, gold, blue, black, and green, but it is also available from craft and garment shops (it is used to decorate clothing) in other colors, including pink, yellow, bronze, brown, chartreuse, and purple, usually in 1/2- or 1-ounce bottles. M-F sells it in 4 colors of aluminum, six colors of poly glitter. It can be added to liquid plastic before or after heating.

Glitter can imbue worms with the "salt-and-pepper" look if used in quantity or in larger-size particles. Lure-Craft and Hilts sell glitter in two sizes for this purpose. Lure-Craft lists .015-size squares for normal use and a coarser .035 size for salt-and-pepper worms.

Glitter has other uses: It can be added to wet paint on lures or mixed with a clear sealer and added to plugs. More on these applications is found in Chapter 15.

Scents. Scents can be added to liquid plastic

before or after heating, or to finished worms. Available scents include anise, strawberry, licorice, wild cherry, raspberry, cheddar cheese, and fish. Unless they specifically recommend or state that they will not harm plastic worms, do not use the spray or dip scents that are used in fishing. These in concentration may cause some worms to "melt." Adding scents to a liquid plastic formula or to a bag of worms after molding is counterproductive. They can, however, be sprayed onto a worm during fishing. The scents designed to be used with worms are usually sold in 1-, 2-, or 4-ounce bottles and are highly concentrated; only a few drops per pan of plastic are needed in most cases.

Salt. Standard table salt can be added to liquid plastic. Usually up to thirty percent salt by volume can be added to any soft-plastic lure. As with commercial salt worms, this is supposed to increase strikes.

PARTS

Although no parts as such are required for molding worms or soft-plastic lures, additional parts can be used in assembly or when making rigged lures. Examples would be worm rigs that use molded-in hooks or incorporate blades and beads strung on mono on the rigged lure for added attraction. Most worms used to be made and sold this way, although now most sold for that purpose are designed for specific applications, such as walleye fishing or "do-nothing" bass fishing.

The parts are no different from those used for making spinners. Complete descriptions of these parts can be found in Chapter 3 but here are some generalities.

Mono. Monofilament line, usually about thirty-pound test, is used for the rigging and is molded into the worm. Any mono can be used, and you can choose heavier or lighter pound test as required.

Wire. Wire is seldom used for a worm rigging, but that doesn't mean you can't use it if you so desire. Usually twenty-pound cable, uncoated or nylon-coated, is used for this.

Beads. Beads of plastic, metal, and glass are commonly used for color, flash, and as bearings for blade clevises on worm rigs. A wide range of sizes and types can be found in any lure-parts component catalog. In addition, floating beads are also popular with some rigs, and these are available in a variety of colors. One way to add

beads to worm rings after the fact is with U.S. Tackle Speedo Beads, which can be added or removed at will. They float and come in two sizes.

Blades. Blades vary widely, although typical blades are generally small and of the same type as is commonly used for spinners. These include Colorado, Indiana, and willowleaf styles. Some worm rigs also use propeller blades. These are all small-size and are usually the same blades used for propeller top-water plugs.

Clevises. Clevises for mono or wire rigs should be of the folded style. They have a wider bearing surface on the mono, and thus are less likely to wear through it, as might occur with the thinner stirrup clevises. Several sizes are available, and the size must be chosen to both fit the mono or wire and also to provide clearance without binding for the chosen blade.

GENERAL MOLDING TECHNIQUES

Because you will be working with a hot substance, it pays to use caution when molding soft-plastic lures. Use goggles, wear gloves when working with the hot pans used for melting the plastic, and wear an apron to protect against any spills. You will also need a spacious work area. The same work areas recommended for molding bucktails and sinkers are fine—kitchen, basement, garage, deck or patio, carport, workshop. These should all have some ventilation (for this reason the kitchen is ideal) because there will be some smell and fumes with most soft-plastic molding.

The main work area should have a heat source, lots of counter space, and ventilation. Unlike lead molding, a water source is desirable, since water is used in cooling the pans that hold the hot lures after they are removed from the mold.

The kitchen stove can be used for a heat source, but the key here is to keep the heat low and controlled. Unlike lead molding, where high heat will melt the lead quicker, too much heat when melting the liquid plastic will only scorch the plastic and ruin it—and fill the kitchen with fumes in the process.

If you mold in an area other than the kitchen, a variable-heat (rheostat) one- or two-burner hot plate is an ideal heater. It will allow heating to a controlled temperature, and you can work anywhere there is an electrical outlet. A one-burner hot plate is fine if you make only one color or finish molding in one color before starting another. If you make lures in which two colors are used in a single mold (such as a fire-tail worm) you will need a two-burner model because two pans of liquid color will have to be kept hot at the same time.

Take care in heating, because overheating will lead to noxious fumes and some smoke. Also, the plastic is flammable, so low heating over an electric burner is usually safer than using an open flame.

Because of the possibility of fumes, make sure you have adequate ventilation, using the vent fan in the kitchen or making similar arrangements for fans and open windows in any other part of the house where you might work. Molding outside on a hot plate or camp stove (be careful of the open flames though) is ideal on calm days in mild weather.

Safety is important, because the liquid plastic and any additives will melt in the range from 300° to 350°F. The plastic can burn, though not badly, and it does cool quickly. As with molding lead, consider a breathing mask, goggles, and even gloves.

You will need a shallow pan or cold water to cool the worms or soft-plastic lures. A shallow baking pan or similar container with sides about two inches high is ideal. A large pan is best, because you want the cooling plastic lures to lie naturally in it. If they cool in bent or contorted positions they will remain that way and cannot be used.

Always start with very little color and make a test run of a lure or two to check the color. The color always looks different in a mass of plastic in the pan than it does in a single lure. If you have too little color, you can always add more, and even remelt the test lure if you wish. If you have too much color, you then have to add large quantities of liquid plastic to dilute it. Start with a little color and add more as necessary.

Just as you can remelt a test lure, you can also save and recycle scraps left over from molding, as well as used lures, regardless of the brand. These can be remelted, but you *must* keep colors separate. If you don't, you'll end up with a brownish mud color.

You should lubricate your molds, pans, and injectors, periodically, using only liquid vegetable oil.

If you overpour so that some plastic flows beyond the mold cavity, you can salvage it. First allow the lure to cool and cure properly in the water pan, then lay it open, cavity-side down, and use a pizza-cutter wheel to trim around the edges. This is the fastest method, although trimming also can be done with scissors.

To mold, liquid plastic is poured into a pan, here heated on an electric hot plate. The liquid plastic is milky in color and consistency.

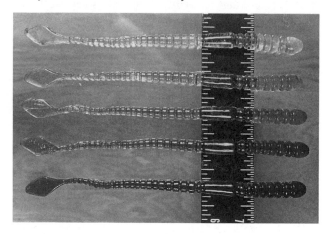

Different shades of worms can be made by using different quantities of color in the liquid plastic. Here the same worm is shown in five different shades.

One problem many plastic molders have is plastic dripping from the spout after pouring. A suggestion for solving this is to use a paper towel, cloth, or small block of cured plastic to mop up any excess dripping plastic. Another possibility is to use a small rubber spatula, used in cake-making to scrape batter out of the bowl. This allows you to scrape up all the plastic and return it to the melting pan. It also helps if you bend the pouring spout to make it more pronounced to reduce or prevent dripping.

The secret of molding good lures is to make sure the liquid plastic is mixed and melted properly. For this, the milklike (both in color and consistency) plastic is added to the pan, and the heat is started low and is then gradually (very gradually) raised as the plastic melts. The plastic will go from the milky liquid to a thicker, somewhat lumpy consistency that is not unlike warm tapioca pudding. Continued heating past this stage brings the plastic to a smooth, syrupy consistency not unlike thick molasses or pancake syrup.

Any hardener or softener should be added at this time, followed by the color (although the fluorescent colors usually must be added before melting), which is mixed in thoroughly, then any scents, glitter, or other additives are added. *Note*: While most scents, glitter, and color are added after the plastic has been melted, be sure to follow the manufacturer's directions. Plastics and additives may differ slightly according to manufacturer, and following directions is critical for good results.

Once the plastic contains the proper additives and you have tested a lure or two for color, you can begin molding. Some general tips are as follows.

- You may find that the larger-size pans often used for melting plastic are too large to use easily for pouring, especially for small molds or fine details. Try using a small implement that you can dip into the main pan to get enough plastic to fill one mold cavity. Some possibilities here are gravy ladles, small aluminum measuring cups (1/4- to 1/2-cup sizes are good), large spoons, and small tuna cans. In all cases, make a pronounced spout or reform the existing spout for good pouring. These smaller containers also allow you to pour closer to the mold, making for greater accuracy.

- Begin pouring at the tail-end of the mold, particularly when making curved-tail worms, grubs, and similar lures. And when molding frogs, crayfish, and similar lures with fine or delicate parts, begin at the smallest parts of the mold cavity, too. This is the preferred method because the liquid plastic will be at its hottest when you begin the pour and will gradually cool as you continue to pour. This is particularly true if you pour from the smaller dipper ladles or pans. You want the hottest, most liquid plastic to fill small cavities; you can easily fill the main cavity of the worm, grub, crayfish, or frog later.

- It is widely known that you cannot mix and then store soft plastics of different colors together. The darker colors will stain or elute into the plastic of lighter shade or color. Even if you mix colors of similar shade — red and orange, yellow and light green — the colors will still tend to mix

Use low heat to melt the plastic, to prevent burning and smells. The plastic will first turn thick and lumpy — like tapioca — then turn thin, clear and smooth. Shown is the "tapioca" stage.

Checking the plastic again, this time heating on a stove. Heating on a stove does have some advantages, since the heat can be controlled more easily. Color is also being added at this stage.

Once the liquid plastic is smooth and the color mixed in, pour into any open-face molds by beginning at one end and working to the other.

Once the molds are completely filled, use a cloth or paper towel to wipe the lip to prevent spills and drips.

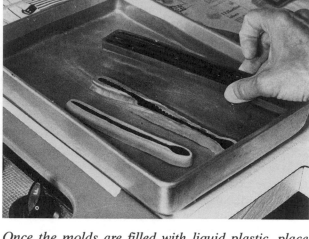

Once the molds are filled with liquid plastic, place them into a shallow pan of cold water to cure.

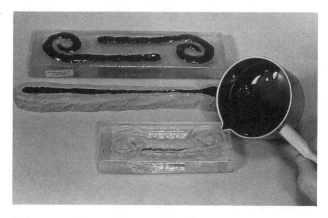

When working with curved-tail or detailed molds or begin filling at the tail or detail areas before filling the main body of the mold.

and muddle slightly. One way to prevent this is to pour clear soft plastic and use glitter as the coloring agent. The mylar or metallic or plastic glitter is trapped in the plastic and cannot stain other lures. Thus, glitter worms of green, blue, red, yellow, gold, and silver can be mixed and stored together.

- Once lures are poured, the mold should be allowed to cool for a few minutes. You can hasten this by placing the mold into the water pan, but this risks getting water into the mold. This is not dangerous, as it is with lead molding, but it will make for deformed lures if all the water is not removed from the mold before the next pour. Once the mold and lure are slightly cooled, you can remove the lure. To do this, use your thumb or finger to roll the

edge of the soft plastic lure up slightly, then grasp the lure carefully and slowly lift and pull it out. Do not use force, because this will lengthen and stretch the final result. Immediately place the lure into the pan of water and make sure it is lying horizontally and straight and is not in contact with other lures. Allow it to cure in the water until it can be handled without bending or deforming. This will take at least a few minutes. If you do get any deformed lures, you can put them back in the melting pot (same color, naturally), once they are thoroughly dry, for remelting.

- For best results, use several molds on a rotation basis. This allows two or three molds and their contents to cure as you pour others, and you will not have to wait to remove a lure from a mold. One person in a team can do this, since there are no hooks added to the mold to slow down the loading and pouring process. (There are ways to mold in hooks, as will be covered shortly.)

- Because these are all open-face molds (there is no closed cavity, which would make a round lure) it helps to slightly overfill the cavity to make for a more rounded result. Although most commercial worms are made in two-part injection molds and come out round, the fact that your worms and grubs have a flat side will not affect your fishing or the fish. In fact, at one time all worms were made in exactly this way.

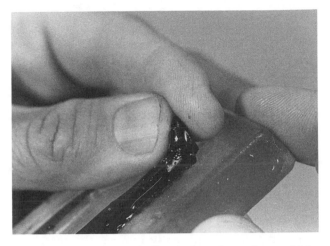

Once the soft-plastic lures are cool enough to remove, pull them out and put them in the water for additional cooling. The cool water also allows them to cool straight, preventing misshapen lures.

Begin to remove a soft-plastic lure from the mold by rolling one end of the lure out of the mold. Then grasp the lure and pull slowly and evenly to prevent stretching the soft plastic.

Lures being removed from the mold.

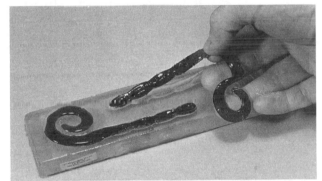

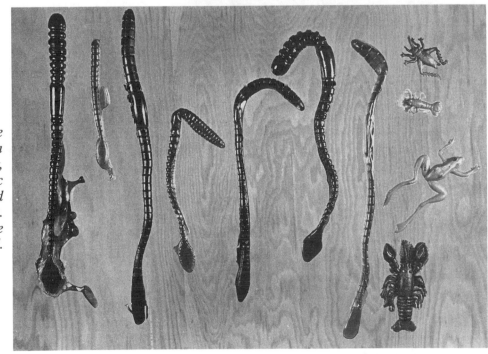

Examples of lures that are bent from being held in a bent position while curing, lures in which the plastic has overflowed the mold cavity, and stretched lures. Some of these can be salvaged.

STEPS IN MOLDING REPRESENTATIVE PLASTIC LURES

The steps in molding soft plastics are simple. Use one of the heat sources outlined above to slowly heat the plastic to a syrupy consistency. Add color, glitter, scent, or other additives when required, usually after the plastic is melted. Use care in pouring, and pour first into the smallest parts of the mold cavity. Thus, fill legs, antennae, tails on worms, or grub tails first, then fill the body to slightly overflowing. Stop pouring, wipe the pan lip to prevent dripping, and place the mold in a large shallow pan of water to cool. Remove the mold from the pan, gently remove the lure, and place it horizontally in the same or another pan of water. Make sure the mold is clean and dry, then prepare to pour another lure.

Another way to cool the mold with the lure without risking getting water in it is to place the mold on top of a tray of ice cubes or a block of ice. Once the lure is slightly cooled, it can be rolled out and floated in a pan of water.

One way to salvage a lure in which the plastic has overflowed the mold is to use a pizza cutter to remove excess plastic.

TWO-, OR MORE, COLOR LURES

Lures can be made of two or more colors, with stipes and dots, or with different-color tails, as follows:

Blue worm with a red tail. For this you will need two pots of plastic, one red and one blue. First pour a small quantity of red plastic into the tail area, immediately place the red pan back on the heater, and fill the rest of the cavity with the blue plastic from the blue pan. The two colors of liquid plastic will meet and fuse.

You may wish to try this in reverse, pouring the blue body first, followed by the red tail. Depending upon how your molds are made, you may find that pouring one way causes more "bleeding" or free-flowing into the other part of the mold cavity, thus not producing results as good. Use the method that works best after trying both. If you do have to scrap some of these lures after a trial run or two, make sure you cut them exactly at the color joint to avoid contaminating one color with another when you remelt them.

This color technique works best with opaque or strong colors or at least an opaque or bright tail. Naturally, it can also be used to make two-color lures with the color joint at any point in the lure. Because some cavities fill from the bottom up, you may have to pour small quantities of each color several times to make for a sharp color separation.

Obviously, this technique can be used with any color combination you desire.

Black worm with white stripe. To do this, use two colors of plastic, white and black, and make them strong or opaque. Pour a thin band of white the whole length of the mold to make the white stripe, and replace the pan of white plastic on the stove. Allow the poured plastic to cool for a minute, then pour black into the mold, filling it to slightly overflowing, as outlined earlier. Any combination of colors can be used.

Green frog with yellow legs and red eyes. Three pots of colored liquid plastic will be needed for this lure, and like the two preceding, the colors should be opaque for the most pronounced, striking results. First pour the yellow legs. Then use a toothpick or nail to remove enough plastic from the red pot to make red eyes in the mold at the proper spots. Allow the legs and eyes to cool slightly, then fill the entire cavity with the green color. Similar methods can be used for molding different colors of fins, gill plates, and eyes on minnow molds, and for various combinations on molds for salamanders, crayfish, jig tails, worms, grubs, and others.

MOLDING ROUND LURES

It is possible to make completely round soft-plastic lures using a two-part mold and a simple method of injection molding. Such molds are available from Hilts (the same company that makes lead jig molds) under their Super Sport label. These molds are strong, clear polycarbonate in two parts, and they are held together with simple plastic C-shaped clips that work like spring clamps. The molds that use the screws and wing nuts come with an open reservoir and plunger to inject plastic into the tail area of the mold cavity. Then, holding the mold and the plunger, raise the mold to a vertical position and press the plunger firmly to fill the rest of the cavity with the plastic. The vertical maneuver is necessary because there are vent holes in the end (the upper end when the mold is in a vertical position), which must be filled with plastic. Stop pressing when the vent holes are full of plastic.

Allow the mold to cool completely in a vertical position before opening the mold cavity. Proper cooling will take about two minutes. There will be some shrinkage of the plastic in the vent holes, but this is normal and necessary to make perfect worms and lures.

Remove the wing nuts and open the mold. Use scissors or a razor blade to remove the excess plastic at the gate and the vent holes. Save this excess plastic and add it to the pan for remelting and reusing. Reassemble the mold for the next injection.

It is possible to make two-color worms or lures with these molds, as follows.

Open the mold and cut off the gate, the plastic at the vent holes, and also as much of the tail as you want to be a different color, without removing the molded lure. Use a razor blade, but cut carefully to keep from damaging the mold. It is best to cut on a slant to create more surface area for good adhesion with the next color. Close the mold, secure it with the wing nuts, add a small amount of a second color of plastic to the cup in the mold, and use the plunger to inject plastic into the tail area of the mold cavity. Then, holding the mold and the plunger, raise the mold to a vertical position and press the plunger firmly to fill the rest of the cavity with the plastic. Allow the plastic to cool, open the mold, and remove the lure.

The rest of the Hilts Super Sport molds use a separate injection system. This allows one injector to be used with a variety of molds to make a variety of lures. In addition, the injector is large enough to hold enough plastic to fill several mold cavities, speeding the operation, particularly if several different molds are used in rotation.

Prepare the liquid plastic. Open the mold and spray the halves lightly with spray vegetable oil. (Do this only occasionally, as needed, to help ease removal of completed lures). Close the mold and secure it with the C-clips provided. Spray the injector cavity and plunger with vegetable oil.

Place the injector cavity on the table (the nozzle will be down) and fill it to within about 1/2-inch of the top with liquid plastic. Insert the plunger and turn the injector over so that the nozzle is up. (If some liquid plastic flows through the nozzle when it is down, remove the plastic carefully.)

Place the mold onto the nozzle tip. (The mold will have one small hole designed to mate with the injector nozzle and one larger hole that is a vertical vent hole.) Place both hands on the mold and push it firmly and slowly down to compress the injector, which will fill the mold. Be sure to use both hands; trying this with one hand could cause you to tip the mold and spill the plastic. Continue pressing down until the vent hole is completely or partially filled. Remove the mold from the injector and set it upright to cool for several minutes.

Use the same injector with more plastic on additional molds until you run out of plastic. Once you are finished, allow the plastic in the injector to set up. Open the injector and remove the solid plastic with a thin bent wire. (A small wire with a hook on one end makes plastic removal easy.) Once the molds are cool, remove the C clamps, open the mold, and remove the lure. If the mold is completely cool, cut off the excess plastic at the gate and vent holes. Add this to the pan for remelting.

Two-colored worms and lures can be made with these molds with a procedure similar to that for the self-contained molds.

Open the mold and carefully (do not hurt the mold) cut off the tail or that part of the worm you wish to replace with a second color. Reassemble the mold and reshoot a second color into the mold. You can make three-color worms by repeating this step a second time to produce a worm with a head, middle, and tail of three different colors.

It is also possible to make gradual color changes of two or more colors in one worm by injecting the mold halfway or one-third with one color and then immediately following with a second injector, previously prepared, with the second, and then even a third, color. Blood-line worms may be created by filling a mold cavity to within one inch of the top with one color, and immediately following with a second color, under pressure, to fill the worm with a contrasting-color center line.

Some Hilts Super Sport molds have three injection gates. These are for three-tail trailers and salamanders. For these molds, first fill the side cavities with liquid plastic, then inject plastic into the bottom gate to completely fill the mold. This allows you to make these lures with flippers and curved tails of a different color than is used on the main body. Use the two-injector technique outlined above.

Hilts also makes a hinged aluminum two-part Scampee mold for making a saltwater twin-tail grub lure using harder plastic, which would be hard to inject without flash or leakage.

TWO-PIECE AND ONE-PIECE PLASTER MOLDS

It is possible to make your own plaster molds for molding worms, grubs, and similar soft-plastic lures. Generally, it is best to use commercial molds, because plaster molds will chip in time and produce less-perfect results. Using methods similar to making plaster bucktails molds, it is possible to make two-piece molds using a commercial round-worm or two-sided lure as a model. (Complete details for making this kind of mold, for worms and bucktails, are described in Chapter 16.)

Using such a mold is similar to the molding of bucktails, except that liquid plastic is used in place of lead. The soft plastic is prepared in the same fashion as for the one-piece molds. Clamp the two pieces of the plaster mold together with several rubber bands. Stand the mold upright, and slowly and carefully pour the liquid plastic into it.

It is extremely important to have the liquid plastic properly prepared, with no lumps that might clog the mold before it is completely filled. A plastic lump will fill the sprue hole, preventing the passage of additional plastic, with the result an unusable, defective lure.

If there is one trick to this pouring, it is to pour the hot liquid plastic carefully down one *side* of the sprue hole and cavity. This allows the plastic to run all the way to the bottom of the mold cavity while also allowing air to escape through the sprue hole. If a lot of plastic is suddenly dumped into the sprue hole, it will clog the hole, preventing the escape of air and impeding the downward flow of the hot plastic. All too often, the plastic will begin to cool and cure before the mold can be completely filled. You can drill or otherwise form a vent hole in the bottom of the mold, and this sometimes lessens the problem but the hole must be large. Otherwise, the liquid plastic will not flow evenly to fill the mold cavity, or an air bubble will

Plaster molds can be used (see Chapter 16—MAKING LEAD AND SOFT PLASTIC LURE MOLDS), but the cavity must be painted to avoid a matte finish on the worm body and leakage of the liquid plastic into the porous plaster. Parts of worms, as shown here, can be used to make "masters" for new types of worm molds.

develop in the center of the worm.

If, after you follow the above instructions carefully, the mold cavity still does not fill with plastic, enlarge the sprue hole. (This operation is detailed in Chapter 16.) I like the sprue hole in a two-piece plaster mold to be about the diameter of the head of the worm. It makes it easy to get perfect lures this way, and the excess plastic that accumulates is easy to cut off and reuse.

Plaster molds must cure in air—to put them into water to cool, as for the plastic and rubber molds, would ruin them. Since the plaster molds are thicker, and since the two-part molds do not allow as much heat exchange, using them is slower than making plastic lures in commercial open-face molds. One solution, particularly since the two-piece molds are inexpensive to make, is to make a half-dozen or so (of the same or different designs) so that you can mold in a rotation system by which the first mold will be cool and the lure cured enough for removal by the time you have poured the last mold. Another alternative is to use two-piece molds alternately with one-piece commercial molds.

Making one-piece plaster molds is also described in Chapter 16. Their use is exactly the same as with rubber and plastic commercial molds, except that they cannot be placed in water for cooling but must be air-cooled and cured, as with the two-piece plaster molds.

These plaster molds can be used to make any type of soft-plastic lure, although they are probably best for making unusual lures for which molds are not available commercially.

MOLDING IN HOOKS AND LEADERS MAKING WORM RIGS

All of the soft-plastic lures described to this point are molded unrigged; that is, without the addition of hooks or snells. Most anglers prefer their lures this way, especially the worms, because it allows specific rigging for specific fishing situations or species sought.

Any soft-plastic lure can be molded with hooks or snells in it and complete worm rigs, with beads and blades, can be made up. Lure-Craft supplies its molds plain, or for a slight additional fee with harness rings that allow hooks and leaders to be molded in place in the lure. Even without harness rings it is possible to mold in hooks on snells. The best way to do this is to buy rubber molds (by Lure-Craft), and slit each end of the mold to hold the leader in place during molding. It is also possible to use a fine saw to cut a slit into the hard-plastic open-face molds for the same purpose.

To mold leaders or snells in place in a mold prepared this way, take an 18- to 24-inch length of fifteen- to thirty-pound test monofilament (it should be stronger than the line used for fishing the lure), and snell a hook to the mono. Leave a long tail of mono that can be secured to the slit in the mold. One, two, or three hooks can be snelled to the hook, depending upon the rig and the length of the worm. Slip the two ends of the mono into the slits at either end of the mold. Position the hooks in the mold cavity. Pour the plastic into the mold in the usual way. The result is a worm, minnow, or other lure with molded-in hooks and leader. This always makes for an exposed hook-point rig, but you can use plain hooks or those with wire weed-guards. Once the lure is removed from the mold, clip the end of the mono at the tail.

To finish the lure, take the longer piece of mono (at the head of the worm or lure) and tie a loop knot or attach a combination of beads and blades. To make a complete rig, add several plastic beads and a propeller blade or spinner blade on a folded clevis. (The folded clevises will work better here than on spinner wire in making spinners.) You can rig these with any size, color, and type of beads and blades, although most are made with about a half-dozen red plastic beads and a single spinner or propeller blade. Finish

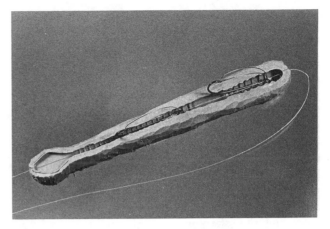

One way of making a rigged soft-plastic worm is to snell hooks with mono and place the mono straight in the mold cavity. Here a rubber mold allows cuttting small slits in each end to hold the mono securely.

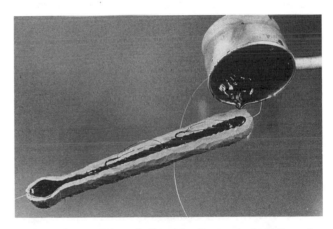

Filling the mold with liquid plastic, imbedding the hook shanks and mono in the plastic lure.

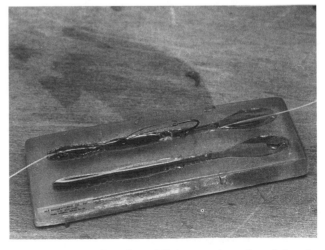

Another example of molding a mono-rigged hook, this time using a hard M-F mold.

with a loop knot, using a figure-eight, perfection loop, or surgeon's loop knot.

Another way to rig worms is after they are molded, using a tip from Bing McClellan, former president of Burke Lures. Bing developed and even sold for a while a worm rigger that consisted of a long needle, with the eye exposed, in a short wood-dowel handle. This tool can be made easily by pushing an upholstery needle or similar needle (check a sewing supply store) into a wood dowel. It allows easy rigging of snelled hooks and Texas rigs placed in the rear of the worm.

To rig this way, run the needle into the worm from the rear, beginning at the point where you want the bend of the hook to be. Run the needle eye out through the head of the worm, thread the monofilament through the needle eye, and pull the needle *back* through the worm body with the mono. Pull the mono out, tie on or snell the hook, and then pull the mono through the worm to properly and carefully position the hook.

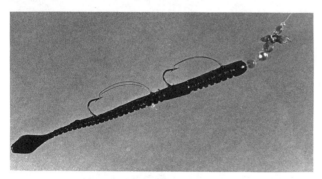

Finished worm with beads and spinner blade rigged on the mono, the mono finished with a loop knot.

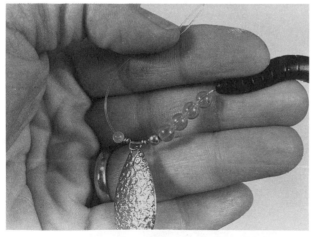

Another example of a spinner blade on a clevis on a worm rig. Beads serve as bearings for the blade of clevis.

Once the worm rig is complete, any excess mono is clipped from the tail of the worm.

VARIATIONS IN WORMS AND WORM RIGS

Variations in molding and making worms and other soft-plastic lures are endless. The most common are variations in color, glitter, scent, and salt. Others include adding softener or hardener. Usually, the bass angler will want a very soft lure, the saltwater angler a tougher, harder lure. Either is possible by the addition of the right liquid enhancer to the basic plastic.

Another variation is to use the same dumbbell lead eyes favored by fly tiers. You will have to choose the mold and/or eyes carefully to make sure that the width of the eyes is equal to the width of the mold. Rubber molds are preferred for this, since they can be adjusted a little to accommodate a tight-fitting set of eyes. The eyes can be painted first, then molded into the lure and either left as is, or the plastic "skin" that usually forms over the eye can be popped off to expose the eyes.

These eyes in different weights can be added to other parts of the worm to add more weight for faster sinking in deep fishing. It is also possible to use lead wire or lead-core trolling line (lead covered by a braided coating) held in place in the slits of the mold as mono would be, and mold the worm around it. This will also add weight for faster sinking, but it will affect the flexibility of the worm somewhat. Different sizes of lead wire (again used by fly tiers) is available for different sink rates. One way to partially control the loss in flexibility is to run the lead-core line or lead wire through the front half or two-thirds of the worm only, leaving the tail free to wiggle.

Although they are usually added after the fact,

it is easy to add one or more of the various plastic or grass worm rattles to molds for incorporation into the lure.

Other longitudinal fibers can be added for various purposes. In translucent worms, a long standard or strands of Krystal Flash, tinsel chenille, tinsel, mylar tubing, or other material from fly-tying, craft, sewing, or hobby shops will add color and flash. The material is held in place in the worm just as is mono, and is clipped close once the worm is removed. Such fibers can be added to unrigged worms or to mono- and hook-rigged worms. If the fibers are strong enough, it is possible to use the long-shank worm-rigger (long needle with dowel handle previously described) to pull the fibers through the molded worm just as line is pulled through to rig a hook in back of the head.

Another variation is the result of a new innovation from one of the commercial worm companies. The Culprit company in 1989 added a small patch of the "loop" portion of hook-and-loop-fastener material to their worms. The small patch, usually about 1 1/2 inches long, catches in the tiny teeth of a largemouth bass to reduce the chances of the fish spitting out the worm and to give more time for the angler to set the hook. You can do the same thing with a small thin patch of this material added to the open side of an open-face worm before the liquid plastic has time to set up and cure. Such patches are easy to cut to size, and add to the effectiveness of any plastic worm or lure.

KITS

Worm kits are available from a number of companies. Lure-Craft has a worm-making kit that includes a special six-cavity mold (two straight worms, one straight grub, one curved-tail worm, one curved-tail grub, and one lizard); one pint each of two different plastic formulas; one bottle (1 ounce) each of red, purple, and black color; 1-ounce bottle of grape Lunker Lotion (scent); and two pouring pans. M-F has a basic worm kit that includes a double-cavity 7-inch curly-tail mold, black and purple color, liquid plastic, and instructions.

Hilts has five different worm-making kits, and each makes a different type of soft-plastic lure. The WTK-1 makes a 7-inch curved-tail worm; the WTK-2 kit makes a 3-inch double-curved-tail trailer; and the DIK-1 kit makes a 6-inch round worm and a 3-inch curved-tail worm. The DIK-2 makes a scorpion flat-tail worm and a 3-inch curved-tail worm; the DIK-3 makes a 3-inch curved-tail grub and a curved-tail scorpion worm. The first two kits have self-contained injector molds, the latter three have two molds each, with separate injector. All five kits include liquid plastic and purple color, and the DIK-1, DIK-2, and DIK-3 kits also contain fluorescent chartreuse color.

Examples of soft-plastic lures made from liquid plastic and simple molds.

8

Spoons

INTRODUCTION ▪ TOOLS ▪ HARDWARE ▪ SPOON CONSTRUCTION AND ASSEMBLY ▪ MAKING SPOON BLADES ▪ STEPS IN MAKING SPOON BLADES ▪ MAKING FIXED-HOOK SPOONS ▪ VARIATIONS IN MAKING SPOONS ▪ MISCELLANEOUS SPOONS AND METAL LURES ▪ SPOON KITS

Basic Safety Requirements

- Goggles
- Gloves
- Apron

Basic Tools For Assembly

- Small round-nose pliers
- Worth split-ring pliers

Basic Tools For Cutting And Hammering Blades

- Tin snips or aviation snips
- Hacksaw
- Files
- Electric drill and bits
- Ball-peen hammer

Helpful Tools

- Jewelers' saw
- Anvil
- Plastic and rubber hammers
- Metal chisels in various sizes
- Nail set
- Punch
- Soldering iron

INTRODUCTION

No special talents or tools are needed to construct spoons that are almost identical to those found in tackle stores—all it takes is a small pair of round-nose or split-ring pliers and the appropriate spoon components. With just this one tool, spoon "blades," treble hooks, split rings, and swivels can be assembled into workable lures in just a few minutes. Of the simplest of the swinging-hook-style spoon, you can probably turn out about five to ten per minute with the right tool and parts.

TOOLS

Serious spoon-makers should invest in a pair of split-ring pliers manufactured by the Worth Company. These pliers have thin, straight jaws with an overlapping "tooth" or hook on the end of one jaw that allows easy opening of a split ring to place it on a lure. The better-quality pliers—available in two sizes—also have a notch farther back on the jaws for crimping leader sleeves and for making wire leaders, and the pointed end can be used to open split shot.

In addition, I like to modify these pliers slightly by grinding the lower (no-tooth) jaw to more of a point to allow me to pick up and work with the smallest sizes of split rings easily. You may wish to slightly sharpen the point of the tooth for the same purpose.

For those with original ideas on making different types of spoons or hard-core do-it-yourselfers, spoons can be made from raw materials. In this case metal snips, aviation (compound-action cutting) snips, a jewelers' saw, several sizes and styles of files, an anvil, a ball-peen hammer, and a soldering iron are all either useful or necessary, depending upon the lure and how it's made.

Standard metal snips or duck-bill snips are fine for cutting light-metal spoon blades, while the compound-action aviation snips are better for cutting out heavier sheet metals. For this you may need several types, because the compound-cutting snips come in straight-cutting, right-cutting, and left-cutting styles. Since few spoons require straight cuts, you may get by with either the right- or left-cutting style.

For very thick metals you will need a small jewelers' saw. In addition, files are necessary to polish and smooth the rough edges of the spoon blades. To shape the blades you will need various hammers, ball-peen hammers, anvils, and wood blocks to form the curves that give the spoon action. Chisels and punches are also useful to give the spoon surface a hammered or scalelike finish.

An electric drill is necessary to drill holes through both ends of the blade for the line-tie split ring and the swinging hook, or to make the holes for fastening a fixed hook. Small bits from

Nail sets, drifts, chisels, and punches can be used to make scale and other marks in the surface of spoons.

Ball-peen hammers hit on the ball, or on the side of the ball, can also make different marks in spoon surfaces.

about 1/16- to 1/8-inch in diameter are best for drilling these holes. A countersink is also helpful to polish the hole after drilling.

A soldering iron with a small tip or a soldering torch with a small flame is handy for soldering hooks onto small spoon blades to make small spoons, jigging spoons, and ice-fishing lures for crappie, panfish, trout, and bass.

HARDWARE

The basic parts of any spoon with free-swinging hooks are the hook, blade, and split rings. For fixed-hook spoons, you will also need a rivet, small bolt, or other means of attachment to hold the hook to the spoon blade.

Many home craftsmen, and some commercial spoon manufacturers, make spoons without a ring, snap, or split ring at the line-tie. It is much better, however, to add a split ring, snap, snap swivel, or soldered jump ring to the line-tie hole. Without such an attachment, the spoon will not have the best movement or action, particularly when tied to heavy line or wire. Even more important, the rough edges of the drilled hole may cut the line while casting or playing a fish. To prevent this, be sure to add some type of additional attachment link to all spoons, or if you use more expensive ball-bearing swivels to prevent line twist, be sure to use them with snaps or split rings to attach to each spoon.

Spoon blades come in a wide variety of sizes and shapes for everything from panfish to muskie and saltwater gamefish. Blades as small as 1 inch and as long as 4 inches are readily available. As with spinner blades, they are available in a variety of finishes, including nickel, brass, gold, copper, and even painted, as with the popular red-and-white-striped pike spoon. This is not the only color available: Many standard and fluorescent colors and combinations are sold.

The cost of a spoon blade varies with the size, thickness, and finish. In almost all cases though, they are about a third to an eighth the cost of a commercial lure. The cost of the hooks and split ring must be added to this, but the total is still small considering the quality you get from these ready-made and finished blades and the little bit of time required to assemble them.

In addition, it is possible to use spinner blades for spoons by drilling a hole in the rear of the blade and rigging it as a swinging-hook lure. These provide greater variety, because they are available in small sizes of about 3/4-inch long to giants of about 3 inches long, in plain and hammered metal finishes, in single- and multiple-shade painted finishes, in fluorescent colors, and painted on one or both sides. These same blades in small sizes, soldered to a single hook and painted or left bright, are ideal fixed-hook spoons for ice and panfish fishing.

Split rings are necessary in all stages of spoon-making for both line-ties and hook attachment. Split rings are not the only possibility, however. You can use jump rings; but because these are not as strong, they must be soldered. You sometimes see soldered jump rings on commercial spoons and lures.

Another possibility is a small snap of some type. The easiest to use are the Berkley Cross-Lok snaps or the Duo-Lock snaps. These can be opened at both ends so that you can add, remove, or replace them at will. Regular snaps and nickel interlock snaps are alternatives. For spoons that rotate and twist the line, snap swivels are the best

choice, with the ball-bearing style the best of those.

Some form of swivel is a must for trolling, and in cases of severe line twist of fast-rotating lures, even ball-bearing swivels may not be enough. In these cases use ball-bearing swivels, but also consider in-line trolling rudders and sinkers between the line and leader to prevent twist.

Ball-bearing swivels are made by the Sampo, Berkley, and other companies, and are usually available in black and bright finishes in many sizes. Solid-ring swivels, split-ring and lock snaps, split rings and safety snaps, solid-ring and coast-lock snaps, and solid-ring pompanette snaps are also manufactured in ball-bearing swivel styles. Swivels alone can be used, fastened as a line-tie to the spoon with a split ring. Some of the ball-bearing styles come with a split ring at each end.

In addition, the Bead Chain Tackle Company makes freely turning swivels, along with single-snap swivels, double-snap swivels, and lock-type snap swivels. These feature the multiple swiveling of the many links of bead chain and are particularly popular in saltwater applications.

Such swivels and fasteners as those from Bead Chain, Sampo, Berkley, and others will add to the cost of the finished lure but more than make up for it by reducing or eliminating line-twist and cut-line problems. If you make lots of spoons and you don't want to add an expensive ball-bearing swivel to each, add the split ring to the spoon and use a ball-bearing snap swivel on the end of the line.

Spoons can be rigged with single, double, or treble hooks, with the single hooks used in swinging or fixed style. For the free-swinging hook the treble is the most popular, although for some western freshwater applications and for much saltwater fishing, heavy-wire single hooks are preferred.

All three types of hooks come in a full range of sizes and styles. Treble hooks range from the tiny #18 up through 5/0 or larger in regular-shank, short-shank, and extra-strong-wire styles. Bronze, cadmium, nickel, gold, tinned, and stainless steel hooks are all available. Standard treble hooks require a split ring in order to be attached to a spoon unless they are one of two styles designed to slip onto a spoon blade. One of these styles has an open eye that is closed with pliers once on the lure. The second type has an open split shank that allows sliding on much as a double hook is slid in place.

Double hooks are formed from one piece of

wire so that the hook can be slipped on or off at any time simply by spreading the two shanks apart to slip on a screw eye or split ring. They range in size from #14 through 5/0 and come in both 90-degree and 120-degree hook-spreads. Most of the finishes listed are available.

Single hooks come in hundreds of variations, many of which can be used for spoons. Generally, spoon hooks must be straight-eye (not turned-up or turned-down), regular length or short, and can be straight or bent to one side (kerbed or offset). Sizes from #22 through 12/0 are available in most of the finishes listed. Siwash single hooks have an open eye that can be slipped onto a spoon blade or split ring and then closed with pliers.

I have changed my mind several times over the years on the use of stainless steel for bait hooks in salt water. I used them at first, then I did not, so that my hooks would more quickly rust out of a lost fish; now I am using them again because recent research indicates that stainless steel is less damaging to fish and is expelled just as quickly. I still think stainless steel is best for lures, including spoons. Spoons aren't usually lost, and if they are lost in a fish are generally hooked in the lip where they are more easily dislodged than is a deeply placed bait hook. The use of stainless steel hooks in saltwater applications also reduces the amount of time required for care and maintenance of lures or for replacing rusted and ruined hooks. If stainless steel is not available or is too costly, tinned hooks are a good substitute.

SPOON CONSTRUCTION AND ASSEMBLY

The construction of a spoon from readily available parts is quite simple. Choose the spoon blade you want for your lure, then choose a hook style and size to match it, and finally choose a split ring to match both parts. The split ring to connect the hook and spoon blade should not be overly large but must be strong enough that it won't pull apart during the strike or the playing of the fish. It should be large enough to provide clearance between the spoon eye and the hook eye without binding.

Use round-nose pliers or, better still, split-ring pliers. If you use round-nose or needle-nose pliers, pull one side of the split ring open and insert one jaw of the pliers into the gap to hold the ring open. Place the open ring on the spoon blade, followed immediately by the hook eye. Hold the two parts (spoon blade and hook) and use the pliers to rotate the split ring until both

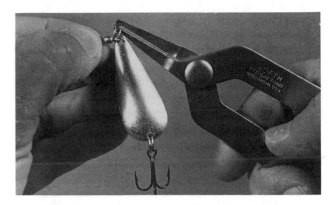

Assembly of spoons from commercially available blanks involves only a set of split-ring pliers to add hooks and line-ties.

parts are completely on the ring and move freely. Turning the split ring through both parts at one time is quicker, and allows you to complete the lure in less time. Also, opening the split ring a second time might tend to deform and weaken it. Be sure to position the hook in the desired direction; the hook point can be positioned on the concave or convex side of the lure. Normally, all swinging-hook lures are positioned on the concave side of the blade, causing them to ride up and be more weedless as the lure wobbles through the water. Using split-ring pliers makes the job easier because the tooth on one jaw allows easy opening of the split ring in order to slide it on the spoon blade and hook.

Once the split ring is on, turn it until all the parts move freely. (An alternative method, though not recommended, is to use a knife blade to open the split ring. This is potentially dangerous, however, because it is easy for a knife to slip and cut.

Assembly of a spoon from a cut and polished stainless-steel teaspoon.

Do not use this method, or use it only as a last resort and with due care for your safety.)

Add a split ring or other line-tie to the other end of the spoon, and the assembly is completed. You can also add a swivel to the line-tie split ring at this point if desired or needed.

MAKING SPOON BLADES

Making spoon blanks, or blades, from sheet metal adds to the complexity of making spoons. Of course, it also reduces cost. The advantage of making blades is that you can be as original as you want, using any type of metal in a wide variety of shapes, thicknesses, sizes, and finishes. The disadvantage is that it is time-consuming and does require some special tools.

Sheet metals that can be used in making spoon blades include copper, brass, steel, stainless steel, and aluminum, along with nickel-, gold-, and silver-plated metals. Of course, other metals or plated finishes may be used, but these are generally too costly or difficult to obtain.

Among the metals listed above, most are not difficult to obtain. Aluminum sheet and 1/8- and 1/4-inch bar stock are available from hardware stores that stock these do-it-yourself metals, often available through the Reynolds or Alcoa companies. Copper sheeting is available from some hobby shops. Copper tubing, which can be hammered to shape, is available from hardware stores and plumbing-supply houses. Brass, steel, and on occasion stainless steel, is sometimes available from hobby shops or hardware stores. Good sources to search for such metals include hobby shops, craft stores, hardware stores, plumbing-supply houses, discount-lumber and home-supply shops, even junkyards. If you are searching for some special material, you might look in the telephone book Yellow Pages under "Metals" or "Scrap Metals." Often, suppliers found there will deal only with large quantities, but on the chance that someone there is a fisherman, you may get lucky and be able to buy a few pounds of what you need.

Obviously, a lure made of any of these metals will have different cutting, polishing, and finishing requirements, as well as different weight and action in the water, than a lure made of another metal. Even so, some generalities about spoon blanks are possible.

Thin sheet metals (nontempered, up to about 20 gauge) can be cut with regular tin or sheet-metal snips. (Naturally, this will vary, because tin snips come with standard and duck-bill cutting blades, and in lengths from short to long. Those with long handles will have greater leverage in cutting, and will thus cut easier than will short-handled models.)

Often these metals are too thin for most spoons, although they are fine for spinner blades and for the very thin dodgers used as attractors in front of a fly, lure, or bait in deep, Great Lakes-style trolling.

For thicker metal that cannot be cut with standard tin snips, there are two other choices. One is to use aviation snips, often called compound-leverage cutters. These exert greater pressure than tin snips because they are designed for greater leverage in cutting. The disadvantage is that three snips are required for complete metal-working: one pair each for straight, right-, and left-handed cuts. If the spoon and spinner blades desired are simple shapes, it is often possible to get by with one set of aviation snips, using them to rough out the metal and finishing with a file, grinder, or sander. For making curves, choose left-cutting snips if you are right-handed and right-cutting snips if you are left-handed. The cuts will be easier to make this way.

Even the aviation snips have limits, however, based in part on the material being cut. Copper, aluminum, and brass, for example, are far easier to cut than is stainless; thus, thicker sheets of these metals can be cut more easily than sheets of steel or stainless. Heavy metals are often used for making thick spoons used for vertical jigging or structure fishing, the so-called structure spoons, jigging spoons, or slab spoons. In large sizes, these are popular for surf fishing. (These can also be cast in tin or lead, as described in Chapter 5, or made other ways, as described in Chapter 12.)

Cutting the heavy metals used to make these spoons for western, saltwater, and deep-lake fishing, is beyond the limits of cutting tools. The best solution, and the second of the choices mentioned earlier, is a fine-blade hacksaw or fine-blade metal saw. One disadvantage of the hacksaw is that the thick blade only allows it to cut straight. The straight cuts require extensive recutting or filing to round off the edges. Small metal or jewelers' saws have narrower blades (1/4-inch on a metal saw, as compared to 1/2-inch or more on a hacksaw blade) and thus can cut a circle of a smaller radius. Thin and wirelike blades are available to fit into a jewelers' saw or hacksaw, and these will cut in any direction to make any shape desired.

Hobbyists who have electric jigsaws with metal-cutting blades will find these a distinct advantage because they cut quickly and are easy to use. But they *are* expensive. If you already have one, consider using it. If not, think long and hard before making such a purchase for the sole purpose of cutting out metal spoon blades and similar work.

STEPS IN MAKING SPOON BLADES
SHAPING THE BLADE

The first step in making any spoon, spinner blade, or flat metal shape, is to determine the desired shape and size of the blade. To do this, draw spoon-blade outlines on paper until you are satisfied with one. To start, you may want to trace some existing blades to get an idea of what you want. In fact, it often helps to trace an existing blade lightly and then alter the shape in heavier strokes as desired. Copy the final shape onto heavier cardboard. (One way to do this is to fasten the paper on the cardboard and use a pin or awl to prick the outline every 1/4-inch or so. Then use the pin pricks in a "connect-the-dot" exercise to draw the shape on the cardboard.)

If the blade is bilaterally symmetrical (with exactly the same shape on both sides), an alternative method will make the final result better. For this, draw a center line on the paper, trace or draw one side of the spoon blade, fold the paper along the center line, and trace the second side from the first. That way, both sides will be absolutely identical. The finished drawing can then be traced on the cardboard.

Once the blade shape is drawn on the cardboard, use sharp scissors to cut it out. The best method is to discard the cardboard cutout piece and use the cardboard sheet with the blade outline as a template. The template can easily be held onto the metal for tracing.

Trace the blade shape into the edge of the metal sheet (to minimize waste) with an awl. Label the template and keep it for future use after you've traced all the blade shapes you need for the moment. Initially, and especially if you will be making a shape different from that used in commercial spoons, you may wish to make only a few blades and test them for action. If the shape performs as you expect, you can easily make more. If not, you have only "wasted" a few pieces of metal (and probably learned a lot about spoon-shaping and construction).

Cut out the spoon blade using tin snips,

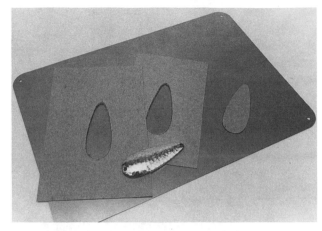

Templates of either the spoon or of the spoon outline can be used to mark and shape spoons. These templates are of cardboard—permanent ones can be made of sheet steel or plastic sheeting.

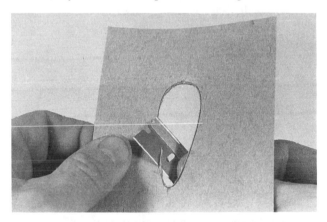

Cutting a sheet of cardboard that will be used as a template for outlining a spoon. This type of template, as opposed to one the actual shape of the spoon, are easier to hold and use when the spoon is small.

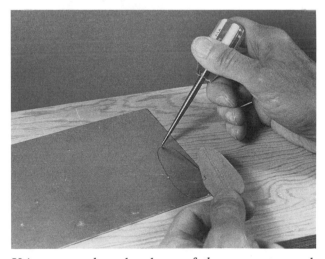

Using a template the shape of the spoon to mark sheet metal for cutting.

For making a template in which the spoon shape is removed, it is easier to cut through the cardboard and along the edge with scissors to make a smooth shape. The cut made in the cardboard is taped before use.

aviation snips, a hacksaw, jewelers' saw, or electric saw. If you use snips, hold them in one hand and the metal in the other, turning the metal and the snips to fashion the curves and shape of the blade. If you use a saw, clamp the metal in a vise. With a metal vise, use some scrap pieces of wood, plastic sheeting, or sheet metal to keep the scored jaws from damaging the spoon blade. Clamp as close as possible to the edge that is to be cut to prevent the metal from bending or chattering as you make the cut.

Cut as close as possible to, or preferably right on, the drawn line. After the initial cut, smooth the spoon blade with a large quick-cutting file. For this, you can work by holding the file and blade in your hands, or clamp the blade in a vise as you

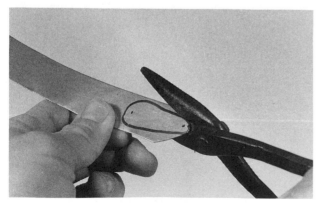

Using duck-bill snips to cut thin metal to make a fluttering-spoon.

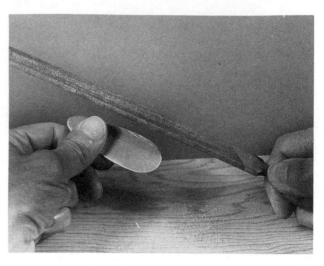

A file, electric sander or grinder makes it easy to smooth the cut edges when making spoons or spinner blades.

file; you can even fasten the file in the vise (protect the teeth with wood scraps) and scrape the edge of the blank against it. This latter method is often best for rounded spoon edges. Use successively finer files to smooth the blade edges, ending with emery cloth or an old, cheap sharpening stone. (If you use a stone, use only an *old* one, because smoothing the spoon edge this way will groove the stone and ruin it for tool- and knife-sharpening purposes.)

DRILLING THE HOLES

Once the blade is shaped and smoothed, the next step is to drill a hole in each end, hammer it into the proper curvature, and finish, if desired, with a hammered, scaled, decaled, or painted finish. It is best to drill both holes in the blade while it is still flat, because it is always easier to work on flat than on rounded or curved metal. A hand drill can be used, although a portable electric drill is better; a drill press is best. In all cases, keep the drill bit at right angles to the blade. Support the blade on a wood scrap in a vise, or clamp or secure it to the drill-press table.

Use a small drill bit, one sized appropriately for the blade size. Usually this will be about 1/16- to 1/8-inch, but it can be varied if desired. Make sure the bits are hardened and designed for metal. (Before starting to drill, use a small punch, awl, or prick-punch to mark the drilling spot and prevent the drill bit from slipping or walking.) In all cases, use a slow speed to prevent the drill bit from "walking" on the metal and to allow it to bite into

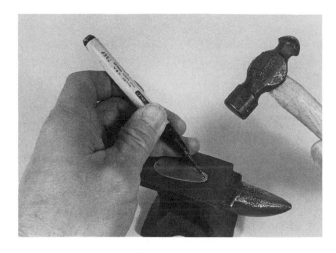

Mark the spot for drilling for the hook and line tie attachments by using a punch on a small anvil. The punch makes a mark that will also prevent the bit from drifting while drilling.

the metal. This is especially important with harder metals such as steel and stainless steel, less so with soft metals such as copper, brass, and aluminum.

Control is easy with a drill press; with a hand electric drill you will have no choice unless the drill has a variable speed control (many today do have variable speed control). In this case, you can hold the trigger lightly for a slow speed. Make sure the hole is large enough for the split ring or hook eye, and that it is close to the edge but not so close that it might pull out. If additional holes are desired for adding glass or plastic eyes, for action or water flow, or for the attachment of

other parts such as small spinner blades, drill these holes now.

Take care to drill both holes exactly on the center line of the spoon unless an erratic wobbling action is desired. You might experiment with off-center drilling, because this can provide interesting results and fish-catching action. It is also possible to drill several holes for the line-tie at several points around the forward edge so that you have a choice when tying the lure and in the resulting action. Generally, the farther the line-tie hole is from the centerline of the lure, the more erratic the action. Remember, however, that you will have to add split rings to all of these holes, or else be sure to use a snap at the end of the line to prevent line damage.

HAMMERING BLADES TO SHAPE

Once the blade is cut, polished, and drilled, the next steps are to add any finishing marks in the metal and to hammer the blade into the desired curve for the best action in the water. Either of these operations can be completed before the other, but there are advantages and disadvantages involved with either choice.

Hammering the curve into the lure first makes it more difficult to add any finishing marks to the convex side of the lure later. It is easy to hammer finishing marks on the concave side of the lure; you can do this while hammering the spoon blade to shape or after it is shape.

To add hammered finish marks to the convex side of the bent spoon requires a special anvil or

Using an electric drill held in a drill-press holder to drill out the hole on a spoon blade. As shown, it is easiest to drill before the spoon is bent to shape.

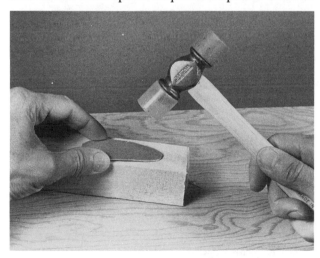

Using a nylon-head hammer to begin hammering a spoon to shape. Hammering on a flat block of wood like this will produce a concave surface in the spoon blank.

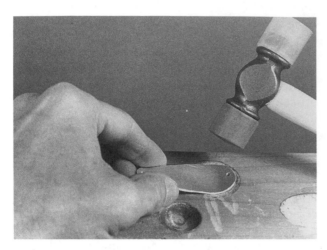

Shallow depressions cut into a block of wood make it easy to deepen the curvature in a spoon blank. Here, the rubber face of the hammer is used to avoid marks on the spoon blank.

Using a nail set to make scale marks on a spoon blank before it is bent into shape with convex and concave curves.

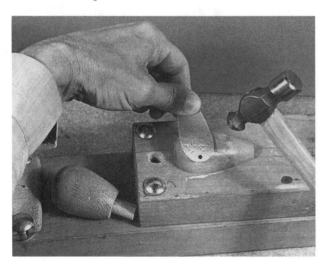

Using a ball-peen hammer to make marks on the spoon blank after it is shaped. To prevent the blank from being hammered flat again, it is necessary to hold the spoon blank on a convex surface—here a darning egg glued to a wood block.

blade into shape. One way, suggested by my friend and fishing buddy Norm Bartlett, is to place the blade on a block of wood, put a large steel ball (like a ball bearing) on the blade where you want curvature, and then hit the ball with a heavy hammer. (Naturally, in this as in all shop operations, be sure to follow safety guidelines and wear goggles.) To accentuate this curve further, first carve (or hammer) a depression into the supporting block of wood so that the spoon blade has a pocket into which it is pressed when the steel ball is hit. Different-size balls can be used for different curves and shapes. It is also possible to place a large concave curve on one end of the spoon blade, then to turn it over and with the

support. You can't hammer in finish marks unless the blade is supported directly under the hammer area or you will just flatten the blade. Even with a special anvil or support, it is difficult to hold the blade on the support while also holding the chisel or marking tool and a hammer.

Hammering the finish first tends to put a curve into the blade, thus putting the finish on the concave side. If you want the finish on the convex side, the finished blade must be hammered flat again and then rebent to the desired shape.

There are several ways to hammer the spoon

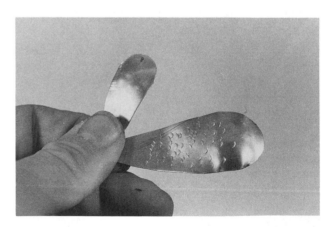

Hammered thin-metal spoon blanks, one with scale marks hammered into it with a large nail set. The half circles are cut into the blade by hammering the nail set at an angle. Though crude, these spoons will have good action in the water and will catch fish.

same or a smaller ball make a reverse curve on the other end.

You can use a homemade wooden anvil with a curved, carved pocket in it and a ball-peen hammer to shape the blade into the proper curvature. For this, small anvils are available from hobby, craft, and hardware shops. Make sure the anvil has a "horn," or curved end, on which to hammer shapes.

You can make your own anvil by using hard wood carved to shape and pinned to a larger wood block for support. One easy way to do this is to use a hardwood darning egg used for repairing socks (if anyone does that any more). Cut the egg in half and pin and glue this half to a larger block of wood.

If you want a smooth finish, or if some other type of finish will be added later on, use a rubber- or plastic-head hammer, working the spoon on a hard flat or shaped wood block, like those described above. Hammer evenly all over the part of the spoon to be curved. The hammering will gradually produce a concavity on the hammered side, so the anvil or block must be concave. With practice, you will be able to hammer spoons into almost any degree or type of curvature, including reverse or S-shaped curves.

HAMMERED AND CUT FINISHES

Although Chapter 15 covers painting and finishing, some types of finishes for spoons are best covered here because they involve hammering and marking methods needing a hammer and anvil.

One easy way to decorate a spoon is to give it a hammered finish, either while forming the curve in the spoon or later, after the spoon is shaped. If the hammered finish is to be on the concave side of the spoon, it is easy to place the spoon on the wood block and hammer until the desired effect is achieved.

If you wish the hammered finish to be on the convex side of the spoon blade, there is a problem. Hammering on the convex side of the spoon will destroy the curve without some support *directly under* the hammered area. For this you can use an anvil or a homemade wood block or similar support. Place the spoon blade concave-side-down on the anvil or support and hammer the finish with a ball-peen or cross-peen hammer. The former will leave small polished marks, although they will vary with the material on which the spoon blade is hammered and the makeup of

the side of the ball-peen head. The cross-peen hammer will leave straight-line marks, much like a chisel. These also will vary with the material used as a base for the hammering operation.

As was previously described, you can hammer the finish on a flat support before the blade is shaped. In this case, a rubber- or plastic-faced hammer must be used for shaping in order to prevent scarring the finish and the blade after decorating.

It is possible to make different kinds of finishes, either before or after shaping. To do this, use punches, nail sets, prick-punches, and chisels to get different effects. A finish of small circles — much like fish scales — is easy to make by hammering in a pattern with a large nail set held at an angle. Made-to-punch (or "set") finishing nails just beneath the surface of wood, a nail set has a small cuplike depression on its face. A similar effect is achieved with a flat-end round punch or drift. A punch, drift, or nail set can be used straight-on (at right angles to the spoon blade) to make various-sized circles, if desired.

Various straight lines and designs on a spoon blade can be made with a cold chisel. Hammer the chisel into the spoon to make parallel lines, herringbone patterns, or random marks as desired.

You can make your own special stamps and punch patterns from hardened nails. Directions are found in Chapter 2.

Spoons and spinner blades can be painted. At one time, most fishermen preferred metalic-finish spoons and blades, but that is changing now. Today, brightly painted spoons and spinners, along with those decorated with glitter or prism tape, are preferred in some areas or for some types of fishing. The painting of spoons, as well as other finishes of tape, glitter, and flocked materials, are discussed in Chapter 15.

MAKING FIXED-HOOK SPOONS

Many spoons are made in which the single, double, or treble hooks are added to the spoon blade with a split ring, and thus swing free. It is also possible to make spoons in which the single hook is fixed to the concave surface of the blade instead of swinging free. This method is used commercially for large trolling spoons, bass-fishing-style weedless spoons, and some surf-fishing spoons. There are no commercial blanks for this, however (there are many for swinging-hook spoons), but blanks can be made in the same way that all spoons blades are cut out from sheet metal.

Once the spoon is cut out, the hole for the hook is drilled to a larger than normal (or larger than needed for a swinging hook) size, through which the hook point is inserted. The metal at the edge of the hole is bent toward the inside, or concave side, of the spoon so that the hook shank will fit through the hole and be straight, or parallel to the spoon blade. This bend must be toward the concave surface of the blade.

Once the hole is drilled and its edge is bent, insert the hook point through it and position the hook eye on the center of the spoon blade, or at a position to allow a good exposure of the hook point. Mark through the center of the hook eye where it falls on the blade with an indelible-ink or felt-tip marker. Remove the hook, clamp the blade to a wood block or into a vise, and drill the marked spot. Use a drill bit that will allow you to fasten the hook eye to the blade with a small rivet (like a 1/8-inch in diameter pop-style rivet), split rivet, or small bolt and nut. Before drilling, make *sure* you have a method of fastening that will fit through the hook eye; match the hole in the spoon to this fastener. Shape the blade and add any finish, if this has not been done previously. Insert the hook, then place the hook eye over the hole in the spoon and fasten, using a hammer for a regular rivet, a pop-rivet tool, or a screwdriver and wrench for the bolt and nut. If possible, use a stainless steel or brass bolt and nut to eliminate or reduce future corrosion problems.

One advantage of using a bolt and nut is that the hook can be changed as desired. Thus, if a hook becomes hopelessly dulled, or the feathers are chewed off a hook by a bluefish, or a hook rusts in the off season, it is easy to replace. If you won't ever replace it, use the rivets, or hammer the end of the small bolt to peen it and make nut-removal impossible.

One additional fastening method is to solder the hook to the spoon blade. This method makes for a weaker connection, however, so use it only as a last resort and check it frequently. If you solder to stainless steel, you will have to use silver solder, which is more difficult to use in most cases, and definitely more costly.

You can also use standard commercial blades by enlarging the rear hole to insert the hook point, bending the metal to allow clearance for the hook shank, and drilling the central hole for the hook-eye attachment. Then proceed as above to finish the assembly.

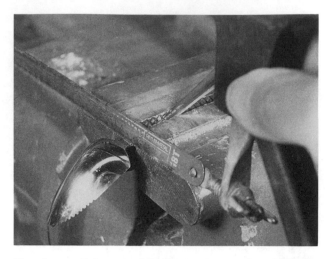

Regular stainless-steel teaspoons can be used for making simple fixed-hook and swinging-hook spoons. Here, a spoon is held in a vise by the handle and cut off with a hacksaw.

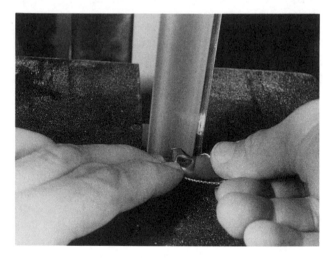

Using a sanding belt to polish the cut edge of the spoon.

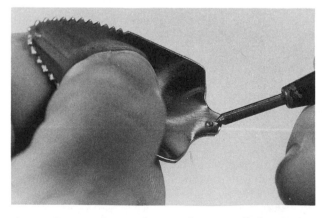

A punch must be used to make a small depression in the spoon blade for drilling, or the bit will drift.

Drilling a spoon for the line-tie attachment split ring using a small hobby drill press.

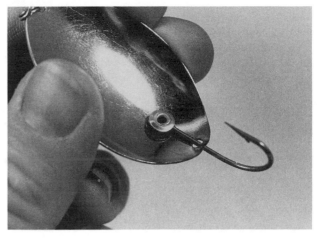

Here a spoon is finished using a pop rivet through a hole in the spoon blank to hold the hook eye in place. Small bolts and nuts can also be used.

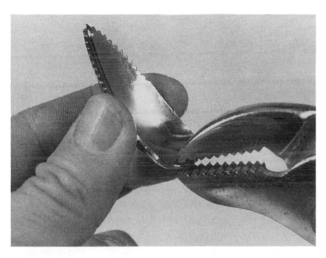

After drilling both ends, use pliers to bend up one end before adding the hook

VARIATIONS IN MAKING SPOONS

Many variations in making spoons are possible. For swinging-hook spoons, add a special worm hook in place of a standard hook. This way, a worm or long grub can be fastened to the spoon Texas-style as an added attraction and also to make the hook weedless. Some commercial spoons have red glass or plastic eyes on each side of the forward part of the spoon. These can be added to a spoon by drilling and making some simple additions. First, decide what size of red plastic or glass eyes you wish to add. Choose a drill bit slightly larger than the eye to drill holes through two premarked spots on the blade. To do this safely and properly, first mark the spot with a felt-tip marker, then use a prick-punch to mark the spots and prevent the drill from walking. Then, with a *small* drill bit, drill the holes on each side, using successively larger bits to expand the hole until the finished size is reached. If it is desired or necessary, polish the hole edges with a larger drill bit or countersink.

Once the final holes are made, mark, punch, and drill tiny holes (1/32- or 1/16-inch will do) immediately ahead and in back of each large hole. Cut light stainless steel wire about 1/2-inch longer than the distance between the small holes that bracket each large hole. Slip the wire through the red eye and bend it in a U or staple shape with the bends precisely at the distance between the holes. Place the ends of this "staple," with the red eye attached, through these small holes (the eye will lodge in the large hole) and use pliers

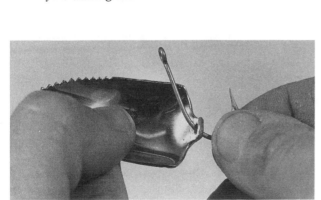

Threading the hook through the folded-up eye for the fixed hook attachment. Once this is done, the position for drilling the hook-eye attachment is marked with a punch.

Drilling holes in the center of the spoon for adding a red plastic bead that will show from both sides.

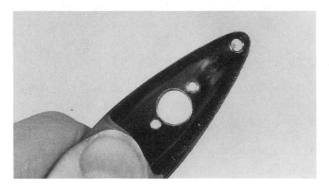

The larger center hole holds the bead; the two smaller holes secure the wire holding the bead.

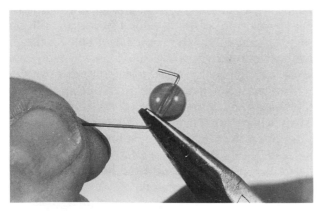

Use pliers to bend the wire once the bead is in place. These bends must correspond with the distance between the two holes.

to secure the ends of the wire to hold the eye in place.

An alternative method of adding eyes is to use glue made for doll eyes, available from craft shops. This involves no drilling—just gluing with a good epoxy glue. Other doll eyes, such as the

The finished lure with the bead in place and wired to the spoon blank. A simpler way to get a similar effect is shown in the top spoon—using plastic craft "jewels" glued to the blade.

snap-on type, can be used for spoons. These eyes have a short stem that is smaller in diameter than the eye, and the eye is held in place with a backing plate that is pushed in place on the stem. To use these for spoons, drill a hole or holes slightly larger than the diameter of the stem. Do not drill any side holes, as for bead eyes. Insert the eye stem through the hole and add the backing plate, pushing it on securely to hold the eye. Then cut off the excess stem. You must leave a little bit of the stem in order for the backing plate to hold. For added security, add some epoxy glue to the stem, or use a soldering iron to melt and flatten the plastic against the backing plate. These bright and colorful eyes can also be glued in place, in which case you can cut the stem off completely.

Another way to add more flash to a spoon is to attach a smaller-size spinner blade—usually a willowleaf—to the forward (line-tie) split ring. Tie the line to the split ring, and the willowleaf blade will hang down and twist, turn, and flash as the spoon is retrieved.

To add small willowleaf or other blades to the tail of the lure, add one to the split ring holding the hook as in the above method. A similar way to do this to some lures is to drill two small holes at the rear of the spoon on either side of the hole made for the swinging or fixed hook. Add small willowleaf blades to these holes using small split rings. (Naturally, other types of spinner blades can be used in these variations, although the willowleaf blade is the most common because of its slim shape.)

Two or more short, stubby spoon blades can be connected with a split ring to make for a long jointed spoon, with the end blade holding the

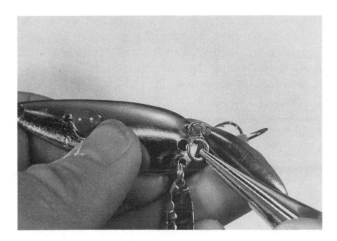

Two small spinner blades have been added to the sides of the back of this spoon for added noise and flash. The split ring for the hook is being added.

Completed lure with plastic tubing on the treble hook.

fixed or swinging hook. A variation of this is to make a jointed spoon. To do this, cut out a long spoon blank or use a standard commercial spoon blade. Cut the spoon blade in half horizontally (or into thirds, if you like), and then round and smooth the cut edges. Drill center holes in these parts and join them with a split ring. Jointed spoons like this can be made using different colors, finishes, metals, shapes, and in swinging-hook or fixed-hook styles. Swinging-hook styles are most common.

Spoons, with either a fixed hook or a swinging hook, can be combined with spinner attachments. To do this, add a spinner wire to the eye of the hook or to the forward split ring and build up the wire with beads (at least one used for a bearing) and a clevis-fitted blade or two.

Any spoon can be made weedless. Swinging-

hook spoons are easily assembled using weedless hooks. These are widely available and have a small wire weed-guard over each point of the hook. For making weedless fixed-hook spoons, use light weed-guard wire. Light-wire weed-guard wire is available from most component-supply houses. It averages about .016-inch in diameter, but ligher or heavier wire can be used—some as light as .012 or as heavy as .020. Even-heavier wire could be used for heavy muskie-style spoons or saltwater spoons. Form the wire into a small circle at the end. Fasten this circle onto the spoon blade when fastening (by bolt, rivet, or solder) the hook eye to the spoon blade. Once this is done, use pliers to bend the wire close to the bolt eye so that the wire bends back over the point of the hook. Clip the wire at about the end of the hook bend.

To make a double weed-guard, use the same wire and bend a length into a V. Fasten the bend of this V at the eye of the hook as above and bend both wire stems back over each side of the hook point. Clip where desired. To avoid wasting wire, figure the length that will be required and cut it to length in advance.

Any hook on any spoon can be dressed with fur, feathers, or similar artificial materials. Use standard fly-tying or bucktail-making methods (see Chapter 4) to tie in the materials, wrap off the thread, and secure the wrap with fly-head cement or sealer. If you dress fixed-hook spoons, be sure you make the dressing sparse for easy fastening of the hook to the spoon blade.

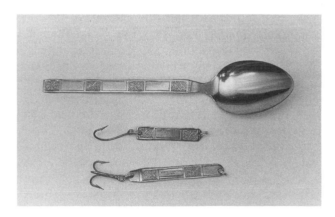

Two lengths and sizes of structure-type spoons made from the handle of a teaspoon. The spoon handle has been cut into two lengths and drilled for swinging-hook and line-tie split rings. By choosing spoons with the right handle, it is possible to get several lures from each spoon.

Two structure spoons made from a spoon handle. Single, double or treble hooks can be used, undressed as shown or dressed with feathers, fur, or surgical tubing.

Whether you are making fixed-hook or swinging-hook spoons, the hook should be dressed separately and before it is added to the spoon.

Stinger hooks can be added to spoon hooks just as they can to spinnerbaits and buzzbaits, and standard or stinger hooks can be dressed with fur, nylon dressing, artificial fur, or feathers for more attraction.

MISCELLANEOUS SPOONS AND METAL LURES

In addition to the standard types of free-swinging and fixed-hook spoons, there are other metal lures that fall loosely into the spoon category and are easily made. For example, small-diameter copper tubing and similar small conduit can be cut into 2- to 6-inch lengths, hammered flat, drilled at each end, and fitted with hardware. This is easy to do with a hacksaw blade to cut the tubing, a hammer to flatten it, a drill to make the holes, and a file to round and polish the ends.

A variation of this type of tube lure can be made by hammering the tube only partially flat, leaving the other end with a round or elliptical cross-section. You can leave it this way for maximum action or fill it with molten lead (see Chapters 4 and 5 for details on molding) for more weight to get the lure deeper or to achieve more casting distance.

Instead of filling the hollow end with lead, you can glue in some open-cell foam, being careful not to seal off the end, so that while you are fishing the foam can be filled with various fish scents that will leach out into the water for more attraction.

Another possibility is to hammer both ends flat, leaving the center hollow and round; before the second end is flattened, fill the tube with rattles for weight and sound. Different rattles will make different sounds: lead shot makes a dull sound, steel ball bearings make a heavy, sharp sound, and glass or plastic beads (the lightest of these materials) make a light, sharp sound.

The same type of tubing in a larger size can be cut on a sharp diagonal to create a wobbling type of swinging-hook lure. Square, rectangular, or round bar stock can be cut on the diagonal to make a heavy slab-sided lure. It will, however, take time to cut through the bar stock with a fine-tooth (metal) hacksaw blade. Old discarded knife and other utensil handles can be used for spoons after a hole is drilled in each end for the line-tie and hook. Best are those bulky handles that will result in a lure resembling some of the vertical jigging and structure spoons.

SPOON KITS

Unlike those for some other lures, kits for spoons do not seem to be readily available. However, many companies, including Jann's (the Tackle Box), Netcraft, Cabela's, Hille, and others have spoon blades that are simple to finish with the addition of a hook and split ring. At this time, Cabela's does have one spoon kit in which parts are provided for fifteen bright salmon trolling spoons. The kit includes spoon blades, split rings, and treble hooks.

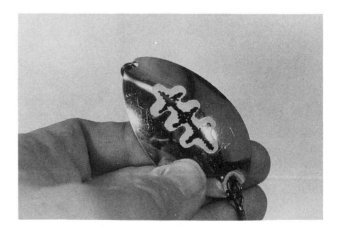

A simple way to finish a simple spoon is with self-adhesive decal stickers, available in many shapes and colors from several manufacturers.

9

Wood Plugs

INTRODUCTION ▪ TOOLS ▪ PLUG HARDWARE ▪
WOOD PLUG BODIES ▪ WOOD STOCK FOR MAKING WOOD
BODIES ▪ CARVING WOOD BODIES ▪ USING POWER TOOLS
TO MAKE WOOD BODIES ▪ THROUGH-WIRE AND PLATE
CONSTRUCTION ▪ SEALING AND PAINTING ▪ ADDING
PLUG HARDWARE ▪ VARIATIONS IN MAKING WOOD
PLUGS ▪ PLUG-MAKING KITS ▪ COSTS

Basic Safety Requirements
Safety goggles
Carpenters' apron
Work gloves

Basic Tools For Assembly
Small screwdriver
Pliers
Split-ring pliers

Basic Tools For Carving
Pocket knife
Sandpaper
Countersink

Helpful Tools For Carving
Electric drill
Wood rasp
Long-shank electricians' or aircraft drill bits
Electric-drill routers (such as Dremel Moto-Tool)
Lathe
Lathe chisels
Band saw
Carpenters' saw
Knife
File set   Calipers
Sandpaper, assorted grades   Rule
Glue   Awl
Contour gauge   Saw

INTRODUCTION

When I was a boy, plugs were almost all wood and sold for about seventy-five to eighty-five cents each. That was pretty steep for a lad with a paper route as his only souce of income. Today, though I am making more money, plugs cost an average of about three to six dollars, more for saltwater models. I'm not sure that I am that much better off.

One solution is to make your own. The advantages of the savings, custom finishes, special shapes and sizes, and similar features are offset only by the time it takes to make the plugs.

At one time, all plugs (today called crankbaits, particularly in bass-fishing circles) were made of wood. Then, from the introduction of the early plastic plugs in the 1940s until recently, most were made of plastic. There were always some wood-plug holdouts such as Smithwick, A. C. Shiner, the popular Rapalas and their balsa imitations, Bagley, and so on. Today however, there is a resurgence of wood plugs, with outdoor-magazine articles noting not only the nostalgic interest in wood plugs of the past, but also the effectiveness of wood plugs of the present. Wood plugs for both fresh and salt water are available from Heddon, Poe's, Gibbs, Acme, Dennis Gilmore, Ozark Mountain, Capt. Andy, Gags Grabbers, Arbogast, Fudally Tackle, Great American Fishing Supply Co., Luhr Jensen, Martin Tackle, Mouldy's Tackle, Nica, Smithwick Bait, Stidham

Enterprises, Strike King, Suick Lures, and Trader Bay. Wood is back, maybe bigger than ever.

There are several ways to go in making your own wood lures. Some preshaped wood-plug bodies are available. These are easy to paint and assemble into finished plugs. It is also possible to buy wood blanks—wood blocks cut into the widths and lengths most practical for making wood-plug bodies; you can get your own wood boards and cut them to size to end up with similar wood blocks. With either of the latter two alternatives, there are further choices between carving out the finished plug with a pocket or carving knife or turning it on a lathe. Once they're at the finished-shape stage, the painting and final assembly is the same for all plugs.

TOOLS

The tools required vary, depending on the method chosen for making the plugs. If you work only with preshaped wood-plug bodies, then you may need a small screwdriver to insert the screws used to attach the hook hangers and plate holders on some lures; for plugs that require only screw eyes for the line-tie and hook hangers, even this will not be needed. If you use long screw eyes for work with hard wood, you may want a drill and small drill bits to predrill holes in the plug for the screw eyes.

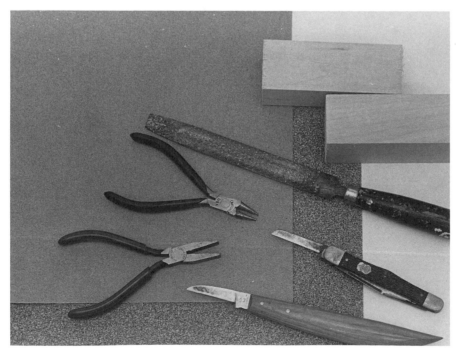

Tools and materials needed for hand-carving wood plugs. The blocks of wood are stock for making plugs. Tools include various carving and pocket knives, pliers, rasp, and several grades of sandpaper.

At the other extreme, a start-from-scratch plug-builder could equip himself with a lathe to turn out lures quickly or with nothing more than a pocket knife. If you have a lathe, this is an easy way to turn out plug bodies with a round shape. The best lathes for this would be relatively large, with a universal or self-centering chuck (all three jaws close at once with one operation) for working with round stock such as large dowels or closet rods, or a four-jaw chuck (each jaw is operated independently) for holding square stock such as the wood boards and blocks previously described.

It helps if the lathe has a through-center head, which allows stock to be held and passed through the head and jaws of the lathe. This way, it is possible to seat round stock in the jaws, turn one plug body of the shape desired, cut it off with a cutting tool, open the jaws to move the stock up, and repeat the process. However, a tail stock must be used at all times to hold the free end.

Small hobby-style lathes may also be used, because the swing (clearance between the center of the lathe and the bed) and the length of stock they allow are large enough for any fresh- or saltwater plug. Small lathes like this are sometimes available inexpensively, and used lathes are sometimes available through classified ads.

If they are not supplied with the lathe, special chisels to cut the wood must be obtained. Many styles are available, but you can probably get by with four or five, including a gouge, round-nose, skew, spear-point, and parting tool. The gouge is used for roughing wood to general shape and for rounding off square stock. The round-nose, skew, and spear-point are all used for the final shaping of the stock, and the parting tool is used to cut off the stock when it is completely finished.

Sandpaper is useful for finishing wood-plug bodies. Special lathe sandpaper in narrow (1 to 1 1/2 inch) widths and long coils makes it possible to tear off a strip and work while the lathe runs — in effect turning the stock against the sandpaper — instead of the other way round.

Kits are available with which a drill handle is held up in a clamp, which in turn mounts on a board or benchtop for lathe work. Some of these are just simple clamps; the better ones include a simple tail stock and tool-rest. These are not common, but they are available. Although they will not do precision work, these small drill clamps are okay for limited use in making wood-plug bodies.

A drill with long bits (called electricians' or aircraft bits) is handy for making plugs that require through-wire construction, in which a strong cable or wire runs through the plug to prevent loss to toothy or destructive fish. The bits are available in 6- and 12-inch lengths; the 6-inch lengths are suitable for all but the longest plugs.

A hand saw is also useful for making wood

Steps in carving a wood plug go from carving plug shape on wood stock (left), to rough carving (middle), and sanded body (right). Parts and sample of finished lure are shown.

plugs. It is possible to use a template to trace an outline on two sides of the wood-plug blank (of square stock) and then use the band saw to saw out the blank to the desired shape. The result is a squared-off plug in the general shape desired. To finish, it is easy to remove the corners of the rough cut with a carving knife, whittling knife, pocket knife, rasp, sandpaper, or sanding wheel, or a combination of these.

For finishing rough cuts or carving a wood plug from scratch, carving, pocket, and whittling knives are fine, even if time-consuming to use. The best are those with straight blades for straight cuts. Many styles of small wood-handled carving knives are available at hobby shops, and some special whittling knives have similar straight blades. Folding knives should have a locking blade for safety.

Electric belt sanders are handy for finishing and forming plugs. To form the bodies, such as when removing the corners from sawed stock, use coarse sandpaper; finish with finer sandpaper.

Other tools to consider include a countersink for recessing a slight depression in the wood to hold the screw eye or a cup washer for a line-tie or hook hanger. A carpenter's contour gauge is also handy. These are tools that, through a series of thin pins held in a special bracket, allow exact duplication of a shape that can then be traced onto a block of wood or used to make a reusable template. Thus, if you have rough-carved a plug that seems to have great action, you can trace it to make more plugs exactly like it. It is best not to trace commercial lures. Some now have design copyrights or are otherwise protected. You could probably get away with it for your own use, but as soon as you give some to friends or sell to a local shop you could be in violation of the law, not to mention being liable for the excise tax on lures. (For more details on this problem, see Appendix B.)

Calipers are a good second choice for checking plug dimensions. A wood saw is a possibility if you are cutting wood to make your own blocks, and is necessary if you cut a slot in a plug for through-wire construction or add a metal plate for this same purpose.

Plug Hardware

All plugs require hardware. For wood plugs, this can include everything from simple screw eyes or hook hangers to hold the hook, to some sort of bill or lip to make surface lures wobble or diving lures dive deep. Screw eyes come in nickel-plated brass or stainless steel, and the nickel-plated is the more common. Use the stainless steel style for saltwater plugs. Both closed-eye and open-eye styles are available: the closed-eye is used for the line-tie, the open-eye for attaching the hooks. (Although it's seldom done, you can use closed-eye screw eyes and open-eye hooks — trebles, doubles, or singles — on the completed plug.)

Both styles of screw eyes come in a variety of lengths and wire thicknesses, and the length and wire thickness are related. For example, in one catalog the smallest screw eye (open or closed) with a 1/4-inch-long shank is made of 0.041-inch-diameter wire, while the larger sizes, ranging from 3/4-inch to 1 1/4-inches, are of 0.072-inch-diameter wire.

Generally speaking, the longer screw eyes will hold better, although the wood used for the plug also has a definite bearing on screw-eye strength. Do not confuse these small screw eyes with the larger hardware-style eyes that are available at hardware and variety stores. The screw eyes for plugs are much smaller, are made specifically for plug and lure construction, and have thin wire and small eyes for hook attachment.

The proper screw-eye length for the size and type of plug varies with the size of fish the plug is meant to attract and the type of wood used in its construction. Generally, the harder the wood the shorter the screw eye required; the softer the wood the longer the shank necessary to hold in the wood. In general, a 1/4-inch shank length should be used only in the smallest plugs, used for relatively small fish. Screws with a 1/2-inch or 3/4-inch shank length are better for standard bass, walleye, pike, big bass, and catfish plugs. For larger fish, go with the 1 1/4-inches lengths, and beyond that, or for saltwater use, employ through-wire or plate construction to hold hooks.

If you work with hard wood and a long shank, you will need to drill a pilot hole. The best pilot holes for the smallest screw eyes of .041 or .051 wire are 1/32-inch (.031250), and for the larger screw eyes of .057, .063, or .072 wire, drill a pilot hole of 3/64- or 1/16-inch (.046875 or 0.062500, respectively).

The cost of screw eyes is minimal, and because they are used in all plugs, they should be ordered by the hundred. I order only the open-eye hooks because it is easy to close them for line-ties with pliers at the same time I add hooks. This will reduce your inventory of screw eyes, particularly if

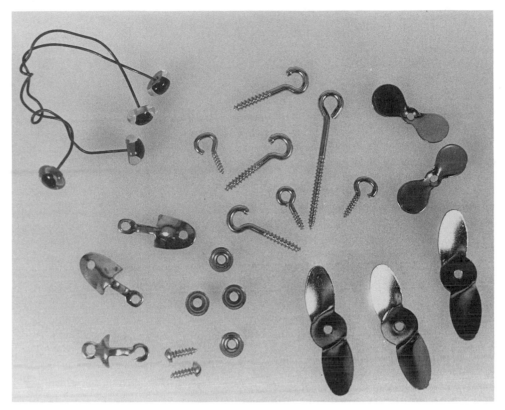

Parts for assembling wood plugs. Included are glass eyes, open and closed screw eyes, propellers, cup washers, and hook hangers.

you need different lengths for different-size plugs. Fortunately, they are inexpensive, although the stainless steel screw eyes are more expensive than the nickel-plated styles.

Screw eyes are often used with cup washers, although this is not absolutely necessary. Cup washers look like tiny regular washers bent into a bowllike shape. Disc washers are similar, but look like small derby hats with a hole in the top. A countersink depression is necessary for the cup washers, and a straight-sided, shallow drilled hole is necessary for proper seating of the disc washers.

The washers supposedly give the plug a more "finished" look, but they also have an important role. They help to limit the swing or movement of the hooks, thus preventing or reducing the instances of the hook points scratching the paint finish. The disc washers are more effective in this regard than are the cup washers. Usually the disc washers are used in the belly of the plug, where free-swinging hooks can causes the most damage, and cup washers are used for the line-tie and the tail hook.

Cup and disc washers are usually made of nickel-plated brass and range in size from 11/64- to 1/4-inch in diameter. The depths usually range

from 1/16-inch for the cups to 3/16-inch for the discs, and the hole diameter is about .072- or .082-inch, enough to accommodate the largest screw eye.

Hook hangers are small devices in the shape of a bent gardening trowel. They are designed to hold a hook and limit its forward swing, and are held in place with two small screws. Their main advantage is that of sharply limiting the forward movement of the hook to help prevent it from tangling with other hooks on the plug or from swinging forward and catching the line. Hangers are usually available in two or three sizes and are made of nickel-plated brass. They are inexpensive, although slightly more costly than screw eyes and cup washers.

The screws used for hook hangers and for lips and bibs (to be described presently) are nickel-plated steel, usually in a 1/4- or 3/8-inch shank length and about the same price as the hook hangers.

Plates, bibs, lips, and bills are plastic or metal devices that are used to add to the action of any lure. Those that create more surface splash on top-water lures are often called "plates," "scoops," or "bibs." They are usually screwed into the plug at an angle so that any jerk or movement of the lure will create surface splashing, gurgling, or popping. Those devices used to control the depth and movement of underwater crankbaits are usually called "lips" or "bills." Some are metal, attached with small screws (the same kind used for the hook hangers listed above). The line-tie is sometimes attached to the lip other times it's a screw eye in the nose of the plug. Metal lips are usually nickel-plated steel or brass.

Plastic lips are available and are usually made of Lexan or a similar tough, clear plastic. They are set into slots cut into the plug body to control the depth to which a lure will run. The size of the bill and the degree of the angle it makes with the long axis of the plug determines the general depth to which the plug will run. Short bills and those at a pronounced angle to the axis will run shallow; long or larger bills set almost parallel to the axis will run deep.

Connectors are often used for greater movement in plugs: The connector is a loose attachment to the line-tie that prevents a tight knot from impeding the movement of the lure. Connectors should *always* be used in the case of lips with punched-out holes for line attachment. The edges of the holes are sharp and may cut any line tied through the holes. Connectors can include a wide variety of attachments such as split rings, welded jump rings, figure-eight attachments, connector links, Berkley or Duo-Lock snaps, and so on. The most common attachments are the split rings, figure-eight connectors, and connector links. All are commonly used on commercial deep-diving lures. Connector links are generally not used on top-water plugs unless there is a punched hole in the bib or scoop, in which case a split ring is the best connector.

Hooks for plugs, top-water lures, and crankbaits must be chosen with care. Treble hooks are most often used, but double hooks and single hooks are sometimes found on commercial plugs and used on homemade ones for specific purposes.

Treble hooks are made by all the hook manufacturers, including Mustad, Eagle Claw, VMC, Gamakatsu, and Tiemco. Sizes range from the tiny 14 and smaller up through the huge 6/0, and even larger. Obviously, there is a full range for making any size or type of lure. The most popular sizes for freshwater lures will be from #10 through 1/0, and big-water freshwater (salmon, muskie) sizes might go to 3/0. For salt water some plugs might carry hooks to 5/0. Finishes include solid stain-

less steel (ideal for saltwater plugs), bronze-, and nickel-plated styles. Both straight and curved (beak) points are available, and the hooks also come in short or regular shank lengths. The short shank lengths are best where a separate split ring is used between the screw eye or hook hanger and the hook eye, because the split ring will add some length to the total hook arrangement.

Split rings for treble-hook attachment are usually not necessary unless you are replacing hooks on a commercial plug with molded-in hook hangers, or adding a hook to through-wire or plate-style construction for a saltwater or big-water plug. Even in these cases, it is possible to use open-eye treble hooks. Mustad makes an open-eye hook that can be added to any hook hanger and the eye then closed with pliers. Mustad also manufactures a split-shank treble hook that can be slid in place just as are continuous-wire double hooks. Treble hooks range widely in price, depending upon their size, finish, and style.

Double hooks are less often used for wood plugs. They are sometimes used for top-water lures, with the two hook points up to the rear, so that when the plug is moved the hooks will tend to ride up close to the plug body and not hang up on weeds. In fact, some bass pros, when encountering a weedy section that they want to fish with a top-water plug, will use compound-action cutter/ pliers to cut off the forward point of a treble to provide the same weedless action of a double hook. These double hooks have a split shank so that the hook can be slid in place onto any hook hanger, screw eye, or split ring. They are *not* like the solid-shank salmon double hooks used for fly tying. Both nickel- and bronze-plated styles are available, in sizes ranging from about #16 through 3/0. Prices range depending upon style and size.

Single hooks are rarely used in plugs, although there are some notable exceptions. Some bass anglers will use single hooks with wire weed-guards to fish crankbaits or top-water lures in weedy areas. Some saltwater anglers prefer single hooks for the improved hooking power (usually a single hook one size larger than the appropriate treble hook is used) and because they are easier to unhook from fish, a particular advantage when toothy critters such as barracuda, mackerel, or bluefish are being sought.

Eyes on lures have become increasingly popular, particularly since some biological reports indicate that gamefish seem to react to the eyes of prey, and that prey species often have large eyes, obviously for spotting danger and predators. Eyes for wood plugs can take all manner of forms. Small round-head tacks are useful for eyes, and in fact were the type of eyes first used on wood plugs at the turn of the century, before glass eyes became available and popular. Map tacks—small, round-headed plastic pins used for marking maps and business reports—are also good. They will stick out with a pop-eyed effect, although if this is not desired it is easy to use a small drill or countersink to cut a recess for one-half of the plastic bulb. Because they are plastic and come in many colors, tacks do not have to be painted and can be added after the plug is completely finished.

Glass eyes are available from some mail-order outfits. They come on a wire shaft with one eye on each end. The shaft is cut so about 1/4-inch of wire with the attached eye is inserted into the plug at the appropriate spot.

Decal and self-adhesive eyes are available from those companies that make vinyl and prism tapes for decorating lures. These eyes are added after the plug is complete and painted.

Craft stores and some tackle-supply houses sell "wiggle eyes," which are flat-back clear-front "bubbles" containing a small black pupil that rattles around in the bubble. Sizes range from a tiny 2 mm up to 1 1/2 inches, which is best used as inserts in clear plastic for offshore lures.

Stemmed eyes used for craft dolls are solid plastic with a stem and metal backing plate that holds them on the doll or stuffed animal. They are good for wood plugs when small-enough sizes can be found, since a hole drilled in the wood allows the stem to be easily glued in place.

Eyes can be carved into a plug. One easy way is to hammer a dull round punch into the wood.

WOOD PLUG BODIES

Some wood plugs are available to the tackle-builder. Mail-order houses sometimes stock them, and local tackle shops may have some that are locally made. Usually these plug bodies are round in cross section and are mass-produced on assembly-line lathes in the same way round table legs are produced.

Most are of white cedar or basswood, although other woods can be and are used. Typical lures from recent catalogs include chuggers, shallow divers, jerk or stick baits, and jointed divers. Usually these are nicely sanded and finished and ready for assembly. In some cases it does help to touch up the ends (end grain), where they were held in the lathe and might be a little rough.

WOOD STOCK FOR MAKING PLUG BODIES

A large variety of wood types is used to make commercial wood plugs. These include cedar, California cedar, sugar pine, basswood, teak, birch, oak, balsa, African odom, abachi, jelutong, and ponderosa pine. Basswood, cedar, and sugar pine seem to be the most common, especially for freshwater plugs. All three are easy to work, finish well, hold screws and attachments securely, are easy to seal and paint, and float well for top-water and floater-diver plugs. Balsa is very popular for some commercial lures but requires care in finishing. Although it is soft and easy to work and carve, it is also difficult to finish. In addition, it requires special consideration in attaching screw eyes, with through-wire construction recommended. It also requires special care in sealing and painting, because the soft wood requires more than the normal number of coats to protect the lure and prevent nicks and cuts that would swell the wood and ruin the lure.

Harder woods, such as birch, oak, and teak, are sometimes used, most commonly with saltwater plugs that are subject to more abuse than are freshwater models. These harder woods are more difficult to carve and finish, sometimes are more resistant to scaling, and do require pilot holes for screws and screw eyes to prevent the screw eye from twisting off or splitting the wood. For saltwater plugs, through-wire construction is often used anyway, even with these tough woods, so this is not a consideration. Any of these woods—and others—can be used for making plugs at home.

Homemade plugs can be cut from small blocks of wood obtained from lumberyards, hardware stores, hobby shops, tackle stores, and fishing-tackle mail-order supply houses. One such mail-order/retail operation carries small basswood blocks that range in size from 3/4 x 3/4 x 3 inches to 1 x 1 x 6 inches and that may be used for a variety of plug styles and sizes.

Cedar is the traditional plug wood, and was used at the turn of the century for those venerable old plugs by Heddon, Shakespeare, South Bend, and others. White cedar, although now more scarce than it once was, is still available in the small sizes required by lure carvers. Some companies offer small blocks about 1 x 1 x 4 to 1 x 1 x 6 inches long. It is also possible to get it in wide boards of 4 to 8 inches in width, and 1-inch, 2-inch, or 3-inch thicknesses, which can be ripped (sawed) to size.

Other woods are available in similar-size widths and thicknesses from hardware, lumber, and specialty wood shops. To try exotic woods, find a specialty wood shop that caters to a wood-carving and furniture-making clientele. They often will have scraps (though they still charge for them) in small sizes of exotic woods with which you can experiment. Some such shops advertise in the specialty wood-carving/furniture-making magazines.

Wood dowels are also a possibility for plugs but work best only if you have a lathe or band saw, or both. Wood dowels are available in 3-foot lengths, ranging from very thin up to the 3/4-, 7/8-, 1-, 1 1/4-, and 1 1/2-inch sizes most useful for plugmakers. Although they come in a round cross section, dowels are very hard and are thus difficult to carve by hand. They are okay to use if you have access to a lathe, because they can be held with a spur center or three-jaw chuck and turned down to the required size and shape. If you don't have a lathe, it is possible to use rotary rasps mounted in an electric drill to shape dowels.

CARVING WOOD BODIES

Anyone can carve plugs or crankbaits from wood blocks using nothing more than a pocket knife or wood-carving knife. Essential to the use of any of these tools is a knowledge of how to work safely with sharp tools, and a sharp blade on the tool of choice. Carving and cutting with the blade worked away from you is mandatory. To maintain a sharp blade, a good sharpening stone, hone, or diamond sharpening steel or hone is as necessary as the knife.

Sharpening instructions come with most good knives and with all of the better sharpening sets. In picking a sharpening set, be sure to choose one that has a fine grit so that it will sharpen the blade properly. Most blades need only a touch-up now and then to bring them back to razor sharpness, so coarse stones and hones are seldom needed. Some sophisticated sharpening sets have special brackets to hold the knife at a set angle to sharpen it properly. These are fine, but if you buy one, check first to be sure that your knife will fit it for proper sharpening. Many of these sets are designed primarily for larger-blade fishing and hunting knives.

Before beginning, first decide on the type, style, and design of the plug to be carved from each stock piece of wood. Random carving on a block in hopes of producing a lure usually results in a pile of wood chips. Before touching the knife to the wood, make templates or determine the exact design you wish to make.

Often, the best way is to begin by copying an existing plug. One easy way to do this is to use a carpenters' contour gauge pressed into the side of a lure to exactly duplicate the shape of the plug. A contour gauge consists of a series of short rods or pins mounted in a clamped bracket. Pushing the contour gauge against anything pushes in the pins to exactly match the shape of the object being copied. In using a contour gauge for plugs, make sure you push it into the centerline or center axis of the plug to copy the full shape and width of the lure.

Carpenter's contour gauges can be used for copying existing plugs to make similar or identical wood plugs. Note however, the cautions concerning trademark registration and patents in Appendix B — Sales of Tackle.

If the plug is not uniformly round, you will have to trace its shape. Sides are almost always symmetrical; the back and belly are often different shapes. Trace these patterns on cardboard, making a different pattern for the top (showing the two sides) and the sides (showing the back and belly). In the case of lures such as stickbaits or top-water chuggers, all sides may be identical in size, requiring only one template.

These templates can be either "positive" (the cardboard piece is in the shape of the lure) or "negative" (the shape of the plug is cut out of the surrounding cardboard). The former is easiest to line up on a block of wood but is harder to handle.

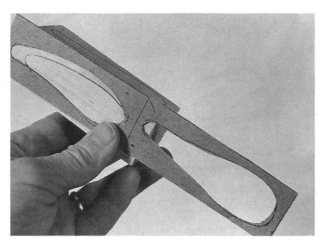

Templates are different for the top/bottom and sides of a plug in all but cigar-shaped surface plugs. Both templates can be made on one sheet of cardboard, as shown, for easy filing of basic designs.

Using a template to trace the design for a wood plug onto the wood stock. The design must be traced on both planes of the wood, as shown.

One tip for making templates is to try a plug first to determine if it will have the action you desire. If it does, you may wish to make templates out of sheet metal for long-term use. To do this, trace the plug's outline from cardboard to the sheet metal — tin or aluminum are both readily available. Then cut the outline out of the metal with tin snips. You may have to begin outside the template area if you're making a negative template, but this will not affect the final result. Flexible sheet plastic also works for this and can usually be cut with scissors. When making templates, whether from cardboard, sheet metal, or plastic, always mark the centerline of the long axis of the plug accurately.

Plugs can be designed freehand, but here it helps to use graph paper to make sure both sides of the plug design are symmetrical. First, draw a centerline on the graph paper, mark the length of the plug, and let your imagination go wild. When drawing outlines, however, use simple shapes and lines as much as possible. Wildly varying shapes and curves are difficult to carve and usually are no more effective in catching fish than simple shapes are.

One other way of making or testing an outline is to draw one side from the centerline, fold the paper in half on the centerline, then trace the other half of the pattern on the other side of the paper. It also helps to use a rule or precise calipers to check the dimensions.

Once the outline is traced to cardboard and the cardboard is cut for either a negative or positive template, prepare the wood block. First find the centerline of the plug by drawing diagonal lines from corner to corner on each end of the block.

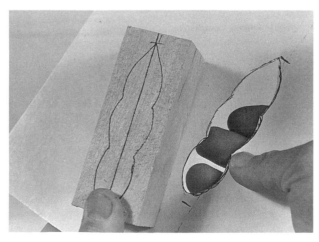

Plug template with tracing made on wood stock.

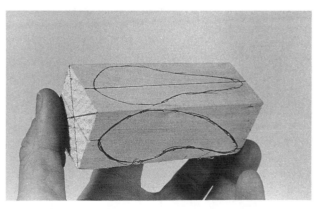

Plug with design roughly drawn on the wood stock, rather than using a template. Such free-hand plug designs are fun to experiment with.

Use a square to draw a straight line through the center mark, which falls at the point the diagonal lines intersect. Continue this straight line along all four sides of the wood block. Place the template on this continuous line, lining up the center lines of the template with the center line of the wood block. Trace the plug outline on all four sides of the block for ready reference while you are carving.

Once the pattern is traced on the wood, begin carving. Use safe carving technique and carve away a little at a time, being careful to cut away from you. First, cut away those parts of the plug pattern that are noticeably thinner than the wood block. For example, in a stickbait both ends will be thinner than the center, while in a chugger only the tail end will be thinner. Carve these portions before you round off the plug. In other words, in the first phase of carving the wood should still be blocky and square but formed in the general shape or silhouette of the plug. Once this is accomplished, begin to round off the plug, working a little at a time so as not to take away too much wood.

Carving the block of wood with a carving pocket knife, following the template lines.

When the plug is completely roughed out, start the final rounding with a wood rasp. Remember that the final finishing with sandpaper will also remove some wood, so don't try to rasp the block down to the final, finished dimensions. I prefer to leave the plug about 1/16-inch larger than the final dimensions after it is rasped to shape, then I remove the remaining 1/16-inch with sandpaper. (If that 1/16-inch dimension sounds like too much wood to leave on, remember that it translates to only 1/32-inch per side.) This is a good time to

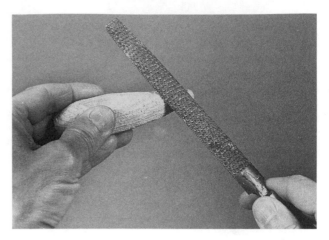

After the plug is roughed out with a knife, use a rasp to round off the edges and prepare the plug for sanding.

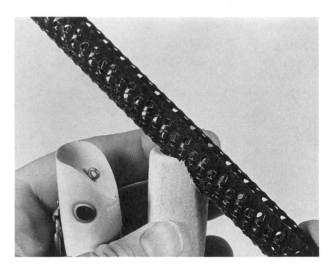

Round rasps or wood working tools can be used to shape lips such as this sloping lip in a plug, similar to the commercial plug shown to the left.

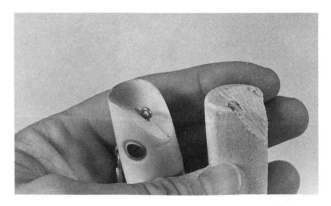

Wood plug body (right) with shaped lip similar to that of a commercial plug (left).

check all dimensions with an outside caliper or vernier caliper for accuracy against the plug model or drawn template.

Now start sanding with grade 1 sandpaper, progressing to finer grades until you are using grades 6/0 or 8/0. You do not have to use each and every grade along the way but can jump several stages, since there are eight different grades between 1 and 6/0. You can buy sandpaper in coarse, medium, and fine grades, or by the grit, which indicates the number of grains that would equal 1 inch if they were laid on top of one another.

A rough comparative chart of sandpapers is as follows:

GRIT	"O" SYMBOLS	BASIC MARKINGS	USE
220	6/0	Very Fine	Final Sanding
180	5/0	Fine	Final sanding
150	4/0	Fine	Final sanding
120	3/0	Medium	General sanding, light wood removal
100	2/0	Medium	General sanding, light wood removal
80	1/0	Medium	General sanding, light wood removal
60	1/2	Coarse	Rough wood removal, shaping, rounding the plug shape
50	1	Coarse	Rough wood removal, shaping, rounding the plug shape

There are other grits and grades than those above, both coarser and finer. Also, various abrasives are used in all of these grades, including flint, garnet, and aluminum oxide. Abrasives such as silicon carbide are usually used for wet work, while emery cloth and crocus cloth are used on metal.

For a final smooth finish, take a tip from cabinetmakers. Save some fine sawdust, sprinkle it on the backing of the sandpaper and on the plug, then use the back of the sandpaper to polish the wood. At this stage the shaping of the plug is complete.

At this point the plug may still not be complete and ready to seal for painting. For example, if you wish to carve out special sockets for eyes, make gill plates behind the head, carve a dorsal fin, or make other additions, do it now. This can be done by hand or by using small power tools such as

the Dremel Moto-Tool. The small cutters and grinders on such tools make quick work of modifications and additions.

Balsa requires special treatment because it is a very soft wood, and screw eyes, even long screw eyes, might pull out of it in time. Some commercial plug manufacturers use through-wire construction (which I recommend, although mono can be used just as well on most freshwater plugs) or insert a dowel or plug of hard wood into the center of the long axis of the lure to hold the screw eyes. This works great but is a lot of added trouble for amateur plug-building. If you use balsa, be sure to use some method to insure the integrity of the hooks and line-tie.

If you make a plug with through-wire or plate construction, it is necessary to use a power tool to drill holes or a hand or power tool to make the slot for a plate. The methods and techniques for doing this will be discussed later in this chapter.

Once the carving of the plug is complete, it is still possible to make additions by adding metal or plastic parts. For example, dorsal fins of metal or plastic can be fitted to a slot cut into the back of the wood lure and glued in place using a good twenty-four-hour epoxy. Any sheet metal will work, as will durable plastic fins cut from coffee-can lids, plastic bottles and containers, or from scraps of acrylic plastic such as is used for some storm windows and hobby parts. If you use the flexible plastic from coffee cans, cut the fin with extensions or "wings" at the base so the glue will completely cover them when the fin is glued in place. Glues do not stick well to these plastics, and if you omit this step the fins will come out easily.

USING POWER TOOLS TO MAKE WOOD BODIES

First and foremost in the use of any and all power tools for making plugs or other tackle operations, make sure you completely understand the tool, have read the complete operations manual, and follow established shop-safety procedures. This is mandatory.

Generally, safety means using goggles for eye protection, rolling up your sleeves to prevent them from catching in power tools (remove your tie for the same reason), and taking off all jewelry (chains, bracelets, watches, rings).

A number of power tools can be used in the construction of wood plugs.

LATHE

Any wood lathe can quickly turn out a number of plug bodies. The possibilities include working with a standard lathe with a spur center on the head stock and dead center on the tail stock, using a through-head lathe (the stock will go through the head of the lathe and chuck) and chuck to hold the stock in conjunction with a dead center on the tail stock for quick turning. If you work with round stock, such as a dowel, you can use a three-jaw chuck. If you work with square stock you can only use a four-jaw chuck, in which each jaw must be adjusted independently. In all cases, you must use a live (moving) or dead (stationary) center or taper on the tail stock to hold and support the wood while working it.

Practice good lathe operation and begin with a gouge to rough the wood to shape and to remove all corners from square stock. Shape with the appropriate round-nose, skew, or spear-point tool. Sand with strips of sandpaper, either cut for the purpose from sheets or from the coils of special lathe sandpaper. Use the finer grades until the plug is completely polished. Use calipers or a template (cardboard, sheet metal, or sheet plastic) to check the work for shape and dimension but do this *only* when the lathe is turned off and has *completely* stopped. Do not attempt to check when the work is turning.

Lathes are ideal for turning out rough cross-section plugs such as can be used for top-water lures (propeller baits, stickbaits, chuggers, poppers) or underwater diving lures to which a lip or bill is attached. They can even be used to make thin-sided lures: Turn the plug to shape, then use sandpaper or a belt or disc sander to remove material from both sides to make it slimmer from side to side than from top to bottom. Because of the way in which stock is held in a wood lathe, it is often necessary to sand down both ends once the finished piece is removed from the lathe with a parting tool.

BAND SAW

A band saw can be used to rough out wood plugs for final shaping with a knife, sander, rasp, or router. To do this, first outline the shape of the plug on a square wood block, marking the outline on all four sides. If possible, install the narrowest possible blade in the band saw. Some better band saws have the capability of using saw blades as narrow as 1/16-inch, enabling them to cut in the smallest radius possible. Otherwise, 1/4-inch

A Dremel Moto-Lathe and small lathe chisels are ideal for turning plug bodies. This particular lathe has been discontinued by Dremel, but some are still available through used tool outlets.

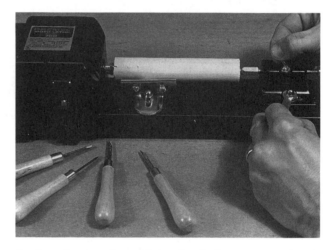

Setting the wood stock in the lathe. Here, a hardwood dowel is being used.

Using the small lathe chisels for turning the dowel into the plug shape for a surface lure.

Checking a wood surface plug shaped on a lathe.

Using an X-Acto saw to remove the excess wood at each end.

Using strips of sandpaper to smooth the lure body.

Wood plug shapes can be checked with a cardboard template. The lathe must be stopped for this or any other checking or adjustment.

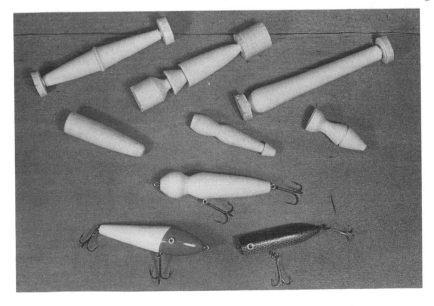

Examples of various symmetrical surface-lure shapes that can be made on a lathe, along with some finished wood lures made this way.

Using a small band saw to saw out the plug after the first saw cuts have been made in the opposite plane.

The sawed out plug with the scrap wood that results. Tape can still be seen on the wood parts.

blades are often the smallest possible. Set the sawblade guide for the height of the wood block to minimize any bowing or twisting of the blade.

With the blade guide set and the saw on, run the block carefully through the saw, following the entire pattern outline on one side. If it proves difficult to go all the way around the outline, first saw one half of the outline, then the second half, working always with the same side up. Save both of these scrap pieces. Then turn the wood block 90 degrees to the side, keeping all of the wood pieces (plug, block, and scrap) together. This way, you will have a square block of wood to saw the second time, even though the plug blank has already been shaped by the saw. In essence, you are using the scrap piece of wood as a base, or cradle, with which to hold the plug body as you make the second set of cuts. Often it helps to tape these sections together before making the second set of cuts.

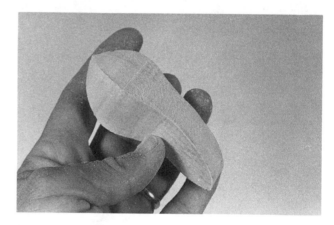

Rough plug body after being sawed out in both planes.

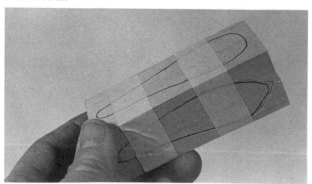

Once the plug body is sawed in one plane, it is easy to reassemble these parts and tape them with masking tape for easy, safe sawing in the other plane. The excess wood here serves as a base to hold the plug body.

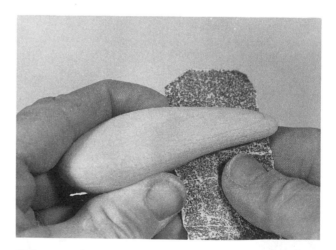

Using sandpaper to smooth a plug body. Rough shaping can be done with a rasp, as shown in the hand carved plug bodies.

If you saw out the two sides with the first cut, the 90-degree turn allows you to cut the back and belly of the plug. The result will be a silhouette of the plug from the top, bottom, or sides. By rounding off the corners and angles with a knife or rasp, you will begin to come close to the final shape of the plug. The rest of the shaping and finishing is just like that for carving a plug: Use the rasp or knife to shape, and the successively finer grades of sandpaper to bring out the finished form.

SCROLL SAW

Although roughing out can be done with a scroll saw, this is not recommended. Scroll saws have a reciprocating action with their short blades (as opposed to the continuous action and blade of a band saw) and thus are designed for cutting thinner material, primarily sheets of wood and plastic. They are not designed for, nor do they work well with, wood in the 3/4- to 1 1/2-inch thicknesses used to make plugs. If you must use a scroll saw, be sure to use it slowly and carefully, and use blades with the least number of teeth per inch for the fastest cutting. The resultant plug bodies will require final shaping and polishing as previously described.

DREMEL MOTO-TOOL

Dremel makes a number of different models of their Moto-Tool, a high-speed specialty drilling and grinding tool. These are versatile tools; the special collets will hold not only small drill bits, but also cut-off wheels, routers, grinders, cutters, diamond wheel points, wire brushes, sanding discs, sanding drums, and polishing wheels. All of these accessories come in a variety of shapes and sizes. Close to 150 of these bits and accessories are listed in the current Dremel catalog. The Moto-Tool itself is available in single-speed, two-speed, or variable-speed models; the variable-speed models have settings from 5,000 to 30,000 rpm. There are cordless models, although this feature would probably not be important to the tackle-crafter. A flexible-shaft attachment allows you to hang up the Moto-Tool and use its 36-inch-long cable for precise working control. Other attachments allow you to convert the Moto-Tool to a router, shaper/router, and mini drill press, while a holder and base allow you to secure the Moto-Tool so that you can work the wood plug against the stationary tool.

The best bits for making plugs seem to be the 1/2-inch-diameter sanding drum, which makes it easy to sand and shape plugs; the cylindrical tungsten carbide cutters, for fast removal of excess material; the high-speed steel cutters; and the cut-off wheels. Although you cannot easily work a plug from start to finish with these tools (though it *is* possible—decoy carvers use these and similar flexible-shaft tools in their work), they are ideal for shaping and finishing after the plug is roughly blocked out or sized to a general shape.

ELECTRIC DRILL

An electric drill is a versatile tool for drilling and similar operations, but clamped down or with the addition of a flexible shaft like the one mentioned for the Dremel Moto-Tool, it is also handy for shaping and carving. Special router, grinder, and polishing bits, along with sanding drums larger than 1/2-inch (1- and 2-inch sizes are readily available) allow easy shaping and polishing of plug bodies. Even the smallest sizes are too awkward to hold by hand for this work, so the flexible shaft or a permanent holder for the drill are best, allowing you to use both hands to hold and work the plug with a foot-control switch or locked "on" setting for the drill. It is easier to work the wood block against a stationary tool than it is to work the tool against a stationary wood block.

BELT OR DISC SANDER

Sanders are ideal for the final polishing of plugs. I find the belt sanders most useful; the disc sanders will only sand on a flat plane and thus have limited use for the curved surfaces of plugs. Bench-type belt sanders usually have a backing plate, but most also have an area with no backing where the curves of the plug are more easily shaped because the sandpaper there will flex and give to match the plug curvatures. Fine sandpaper is best. Usually, however, some final hand-sanding is also required because these tools will not always allow a final, complete sanding.

Any of these tools would be handy to have for the purposes just outlined, but it is not necessary that you buy them solely for tackle-building. Naturally, these tools can be used for other tackle-crafting purposes: drills and Dremel Moto-Tools with router bits can clean flash from bucktails; a drill mounted as a lathe can turn rod handles and wood reel-seat inserts; a grinder can carve sprue holes in aluminum block molds for soft-plastic or lead lures. Such tools also have many other general workshop purposes, which would help amortize their cost.

THROUGH-WIRE
AND PLATE CONSTRUCTION

Through-wire or plate construction is possible on any wood lure for fresh or salt water. It can be done with homemade and preshaped, purchased wood bodies. Through-wire and plate construction are the means by which a plug's line-tie and hooks are connected, by a wire or metal plate, so as to absolutely exclude the possibility of losing a fish to a pulled screw eye or a ripped-out line-tie, or a plug to the forceful strike of a particularly vicious fish. This reinforcement is done on most saltwater plugs; it is better to have a shattered plug but land the fish than to lose both the plug and the fish. (You might lose the fish some other way, but it should not happen because of the plug or hardware.)

There are several methods for through-wire or plate reinforcement, most of which involve drilling a long hole through the plug or cutting a slot into its back or belly. Neither is done on plastic plugs, since forming the slot or hole for the wire or metal plate and sealing the plug up again is either next to impossible or not worth the extra effort.

Although this section might seem a little out of order here because it includes information on the assembly of plugs, it is necessary because you first have to know how you are going to make and assemble the parts before knowing what, where, and how to cut or drill.

There are several ways to rig through-wire or plate construction. The first, and simplest — and one that can be done with any plug, commercial or homemade, wood or plastic — involves using twisted-wire cable appropriate in size to the plug and the fish sought. Use leader sleeves to connect the line-tie to the cable with a simple crimped-loop connection. Then bring the wire through the eye of the belly hook or hooks and repeat the sleeve and crimped-loop connection to the eye of the tail hook. The result is one that will obviously show but that will also guarantee you won't lose a fish to a shattered plug.

You can drill a hole through the center of the long axis of a shaped and finished plug (before painting) and thread wire through the plug. In this method you must also drill a larger, short hole through the belly of the plug for each belly hook

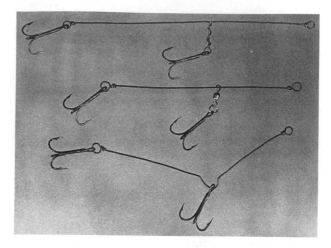

Through-wire construction involves using wire or plates through the body of a plug to prevent loosing the fish should the plug shatter on the strike or break during the fight. These are some examples of wire rigs used.

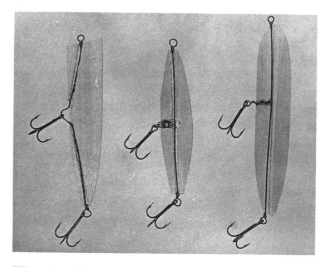

Wire rigs shown in cross sections of wood lures, showing the drilling directions and types of hook-hanger rigs used.

used (usually only one treble). Construction involves using heavy (about 1/16-inch) wire, twisted into a loop eye at one end and threaded through the plug. A short connector link or barrel swivel is placed in the center of the belly hole (one for each hole) so that the wire passes through the eye of the connector link or barrel swivel. (Brass swivels are the best and strongest.) Use one of a size that will allow the eye on the opposite to remain clear of the belly surface of the plug.

Continue threading the wire through to the end, cinch it up tight, make a loop, add the rear treble or hook (this is just like adding a hook to a

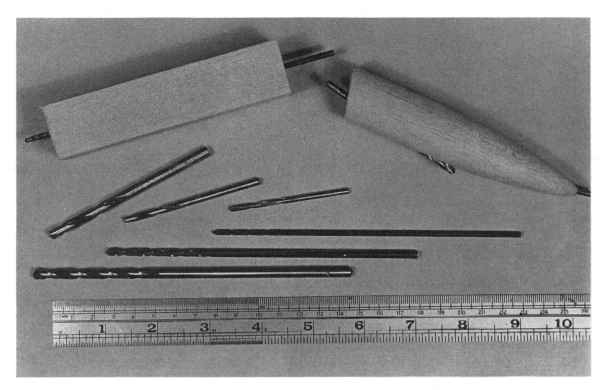

Long bits, sometimes called aircraft or electrician's bits, are best for drilling straight through wood plugs. Standard and long bits are shown here

spinner wire), and wrap the standard part of the wire to secure it. Finish by adding the belly hook to the swivel with a split right or by using an open-eye or split-shank hook. Single hooks, doubles, and trebles can all be added this way.

This method of making wired plugs is most suited to small (or at least short) plugs. Most 1/16- or 1/8-inch drills are not long enough to drill all the way through long plugs. And the longer a plug, the easier it is to drill off-center and end up with an eccentric hole in the plug, ruining it for all practical purposes. Even with short plugs this is a problem, because most 1/16- or 1/8-inch-diameter drill bits are no more than 1 to 2 inches long—hardly long enough for any but ultralight spinning plugs, where this construction is seldom necessary.

To use this method and drill longer holes, use the so-called aircraft, electricians', or extra-long bits. These are available in both 6- and 12-inch lengths, with the 6-inch the most practical for making plugs. They are more readily available now than when the first edition of *Tackle Craft* came out and should be available at many good hardware stores and through specialty mail-order hardware houses. The best sizes are those that are 1/16-, 3/32-, and 1/8-inch in diameter.

Drill the plug from either end, preferably with a drill press for accuracy. If you don't have a drill press, you can get a small inexpensive drill press holder for most electric drills. Use a bench vise or some other support to hold the plug absolutely

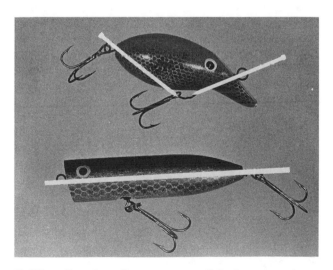

Drilling directions for two types of rigging operations. The top involves two separate drilling operations and can sometimes be done with standard drill bits. The bottom plug requires a longer bit and accurate, straight-through drilling.

vertical. If you don't have a special vise, you can make a three-board corner that can be clamped to the drill press table, and the plug body may be clamped or held in place in this corner. Naturally, when you make such a corner from scrap shelving, make sure all the pieces are square and straight and that the jig forms an accurate right angle.

You also may wish to do this before the plug is completely finished, since a plug roughed out on a band saw will have the scrap that can serve as a "cradle" to hold the plug, with the flat side of the scrap resting against a vertical support. If you work with completely finished plugs, you may wish to make such a support so that the two ends are in a perfectly vertical plane.

Another way to make longer holes is to cut blocks of wood in the correct sizes, drill the center holes, and then carve or saw the plug around these holes. In this case, you would use the holes as the axis of the plug, the centerline if you will, on which the rest of the plug shape and design will be based. The advantage of this is that even if the holes are drilled slightly off-center, the plug can be carved accordingly and will end with an accurate, on-center hole at each end.

The same methods can be used to make plugs with twisted cable in place of single-strand wire. The advantage to the cable is that it will be thinner and slightly easier to handle in making loops with leader sleeves in place of wrapped eyes, but it will have a tendency to slip out of the plug or to have more "slop" when the plug is worked. It is simpler, too, in that a loop with leader sleeves can be formed in one end, and the other end of the wire slipped through the long axis hole, run out the belly hole, through a leader sleeve, through the eye of the center hook and back through the same leader sleeve, up into the belly hole, and down to the tail. The wire is pulled snug, the leader sleeve is crimped to hold the belly hook in place, and the tail hook is added with a leader sleeve in the same way. To keep this light-wire arrangement from sliding around, it helps to use some epoxy glue or gel in the hole to hold the wire in place.

You can use heavy mono in the same way, tying secure knots or using mono-safe leader sleeves. In most cases single-strand wire or cable is better, because most fish that can shatter a plug can also bite through mono.

You can use short or long (6-inch) drill bits in another procedure, drilling a hole in each end, but not going through to the other end of the plug. The hope here is that both holes will be close to if not exactly on center all the way through, and by drilling a belly hole for the swivel, you can connect all the parts with the straight wire or cable. The advantage is that you definitely get on-center holes on the axis at both ends. If the wire goes in a slight angle or dogleg through the center, it will not affect performance.

Although these methods work well for all plugs and especially for slim plug bodies, there is another method that can be used with fat-bodied lures such as the so-called pregnant minnow or Big O styles. This method involves first drilling a hole straight through the plug body from nose to tail and then making a second hole from the opening through the nose, angled down to exit at the belly. Bend the wire with round-nose pliers into the shape of a V and insert the cut ends so that one end of the wire goes through the straight nose-to-tail hole and the other angles down to exit at the belly. Slide the wire into place and leave enough exposed for the line-tie (thus the need for the round-nose pliers in forming the V). Use pliers to make loops at the belly and tail, add the hooks, and finish the eye by wrapping around the standing part of the wire.

This method can also be used with heavy twisted cable and leader sleeves to close the wire loops holding the hooks. Add a split ring to the nose wire for a line-tie.

A method that avoids the belly-drilling for the swivel and belly hook is to drill a hole from each end that angles in such a way that the drill exits through the center belly of the plug. Drill from each end, making sure the belly exit holes are as close together as possible. This will assure that the end holes are exactly on center. The one disadvantage here is that it is often difficult to place the belly holes precisely. Once drilled, the lure is assembled by making a wrapped eye with single-strand wire, running it through the plug, then through the hook eye as it comes out one hole. Bend the wire slightly to guide it into the other belly hole and help push it through the tail hole, where a tail hook can be added and the wire twisted securely. The same technique can be used with flexible cable or heavy mono. It will be easier with the cable or mono to make the change of direction at the center of the plug.

A similar result is possible by cutting a slot into the plug and adding a completed wire assembly or a precut metal plate. If you use single-strand wire you will not need the swivel because the two (or more) hooks can be added to the tail and center of the plug at the right positions by

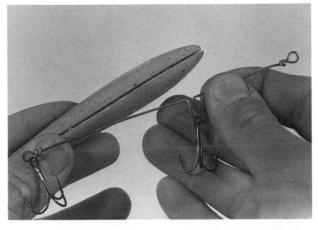

Slots can also be cut into the belly of a plug for through-wire or plate hook hangers. This slot would hold a plate, but would have to be widened for a wire rig.

Wire hook hangers being made for insertion into a slot in a wood plug body.

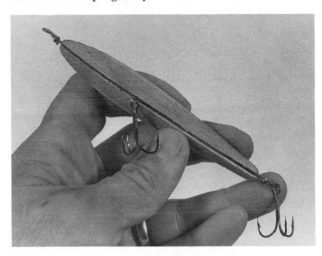

Wire rig inserted into the plug body. The wire rig must be glued to the glue body.

using a wrapped eye for the tail hook and a slightly twisted wire (like a haywire twist) for the belly hook or hooks. With this arrangement you can preassemble the wire assemblies so that they are ready to go into the slot.

Once the plug shape is complete and sanded, you can only cut the slot with a hand saw. To try to use a power saw is definitely too dangerous! Cut the slot by holding the plug body in a vise, using soft wood on the jaws to protect the plug. Cut down to and slightly past the center axis line so that there is room for the wire assembly. Make sure you use a saw that will cut a wide-enough slot, or "kerf," into the wood for the wire, including any wire wraps. Once you have a proper fit, place the complete assembly in place and use epoxy glue or gel to fill up the hole.

If the plug is not painted when you install the assembly, you will have to mask the wire eyes and hooks during the painting process. Another possibility is to wrap only the line-tie eye and twist the center hook eye, but do not add the center hook or tail hook. Place the assembly into the slot, add the glue or gel, and then paint. Once the plug is completely painted and finished, use an open-eye hook to add to the belly and finish twisting the wire eye for the tail hook, also to be added at this time. Another alternative is to make all of the eyes — line-tie, belly hook, and tail hook — and add the hooks later, using the open-eye hook style or split rings.

Naturally, the same techniques can be used for flexible cable; use leader sleeves to make the loops for the line-tie and hooks. To use mono, tie the mono or use mono-safe leader sleeves.

The slotting method is ideal for working with plates. A plate accomplishes the same thing as does wire, but a single sheet-metal plate is used. For this, any tough metal plate of aluminum, sheet steel, copper, or brass will work. It must be thick enough so that the hooks or line-tie split ring will not pull out of it under severe stress.

Cut the slot as before and make a cardboard template of the plate you wish to make. Usually this plate need be nothing more than a very slim triangle with drilled or punched holes at each corner. Each of these corners will protrude from the body of the plug when it is complete, with the rest of the plate hidden and glued in place. Similar plates can be made in the shape of a very low, wide T, but any shape used for this purpose will require that the drilled, eyed ends for line-tie and hooks protrude.

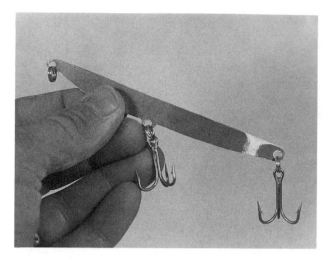

A typical plate cut from sheet metal and shaped and drilled to hold hooks and line ties using split rings. The plate is glued into a slot in the plug.

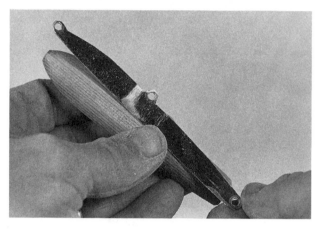

Plate being checked against the plug body for length and position of hooks.

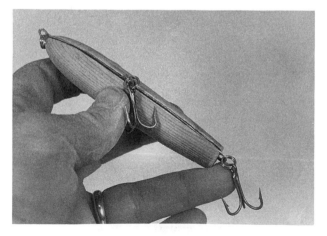

Plate hook hanger in position in plug showing hooks and line tie in place. The plate must be glued in the slot.

Fill the slot with glue, add the plate, and fill up the slot with glue or epoxy gel. Remove any excess glue. Finish painting the plug and then complete the assembly by adding a split ring for the line-tie and split rings or open-eye hooks for the belly and tail hooks. In this construction, *always* use a split ring or strong snap on the end, because line tied to any drilled or punched hole will wear through in time.

One additional way to prevent the plate from coming out of the slot is to drill several large holes in the plate's center. Glue will fill these holes and help to cement the plate to the slot in the wood body.

A variation involves cutting the slot before the plug is carved or shaped. For this, you can use a power table saw provided you cut an entire length of wood and only afterward cut it into the short lengths that will be used for each plug. To try to cut the short lengths that are used for plug construction is too dangerous with a power table saw.

Using a billet measuring 1 1/4 × 1 1/4 × 4 feet long, first set the power table saw blade for just slightly more than half the depth of the wood, a little more than 5/8-inch. Then set a table guide (a rip fence, to guide the wood through the saw blade at a specific measurement) to cut the wood strip in the center, exactly 5/8-inch.

Make a test cut, then cut all the wood for this series of plugs. Remove the rip fence from the saw, replace with a miter gauge to cut cross-grain, and cut the wood into the lengths required for each plug. Carve or shape the plug around the slot and finish, paint, and assemble as described.

The sizes of wire and plate to use in these assemblies are not precise, but as a general rule, single-strand brass or copper wire of .060 diameter is good, and brass wire of this size is used on many commercial through-wire plugs. South Florida anglers who make their own plugs are using stainless steel no. 15 leader wire with equally good results.

Any relatively thick scrap sheet metal can be used; stainless steel, copper, brass, and aluminum are better than sheet steel, which will rust. Stainless steel is the hardest to work, although it's tougher than brass, copper, or aluminum. In most cases, sheet metal of about .030 thickness is fine, but other sizes will work provided they are thick enough to hold the fish but not too thick to fit into the sawn slot.

SEALING AND PAINTING

Once the shaping of the plug blank is complete, it should be sealed with a clear lacquer, base paint, or special wood sealer before any further work is done. Before doing this, make sure you have completed all possible carving or shaping operations. For example, make sure you have drilled any necessary pilot holes for screw eyes, drilled holes or slots for through-wire/plate construction of saltwater plugs, countersunk the screw-eye holes for the cup washers, and made any carving for eyes or gills. Only when all such operations are done should the plug body be sealed.

Commonly, sealers are slightly thinner than paints, because they are designed to penetrate the wood. Permeation will vary with the wood; soft woods are penetrated more thoroughly than are hard woods. Sealing also helps to waterproof the plug, which is why it is done only after all other carving, drilling, and cutting operations are complete. Several coats of sealer are best. Add one coat, allow it to dry, and then light-sand with fine sandpaper or steel wool to bring down any grain that might have been raised. This action will also vary with the wood and is more common in soft woods. Sealing prevents the final coats of paint from being absorbed, sometimes unevenly, into the wood, and provides for a good finishing coat.

After this point the plug is painted or finished in some other way. A variety of finishes are available, including paints and lacquers, scale finishes, glitter, masked patterns, prism tapes, fluorescent paints, phosphorescent paints, metallic dust finishes, and so forth. (Since finishing methods for plugs, spoons, jigs, and other lures are similar, Chapter 15 has been devoted to this subject).

After the plug is painted or otherwise finished, it is completed by the addition of the necessary hardware: through-wire hook hangers, hooks, hook hangers, screw eyes, lips, cup washers, and so on.

ADDING PLUG HARDWARE

There is no particular order in which the hardware must be added to plugs, top-water lures, or crankbaits. I prefer to start at the front end and add the closed screw eye to which the line or leader is tied. Use a closed screw eye, preferably one as long as possible for added "bite" in the wood to keep it from pulling out. Some of those supplied in kits and even some found in commercial plugs are a bit too short for my taste. I

particularly like a long screw for the nose and tail because these are usually screwed in parallel to the grain of wood rather than across the grain as in a belly hook, which holds better for a given length of screw thread.

I may be slightly overcautious on this. As a test, I once screwed a 1/4-inch-long screw eye into the end grain of a 1-inch-thick block of basswood used for making plugs and pulled it against an industrial-grade tension tester accurate to plus or minus 0.5 percent. It did not pull out and finally deformed at 24 pounds pull. This is far more tension than would ever be exerted on a small plug with such a screw eye in landing a fish.

On the other hand, I have heard too many tales of screw eyes coming out of homemade plugs to be complacent about them. Plugs are not just thrown into the water to occasionally retrieve a fish. They get hooked on snags and stumps and knocked about in tackle boxes and boats. Lines are snapped off sharply to the side to change lures, and plugs are cast into rocks and rubble, brush and boat docks. All this can weaken and loosen the hold of screw eyes in plugs — especially over a period of time.

Using a long screw eye does create some other problems, however. I have occasionally had the eye part of the screw eye twist off while I was still turning the thread into the wood. This will happen with hard woods or with long screw eyes; thus the suggestions made previously to drill pilot holes for all long screw eyes used in hard woods. Some suggestions for pilot-hole sizes were made, but it is always best to experiment and determine what is best for you, since there are too many variables in screw-eye size and wood density. Another tip is to use a bit of soap on the threads to lubricate them for easier turning.

Cup washers through which the screw eyes are fastened into the plug are not absolutely necessary, but they do help to limit any swinging of the treble-hook points, and thus help to prevent damage to the plug finish. They also add a professional touch. Deeper cup washers, called disc washers or derby washers, serve the same purpose as cup washers, but even further limit hook movement and reduce or eliminate the possibility of hooks tangling on short or small plugs. Often the deeper disc washers are used at the belly of the plug, and cup washers at the nose and tail.

Countersink the area for the cup washers, and drill a small depression for the disc washer. Do this before painting.

If wiggle plates on surface plugs are to be

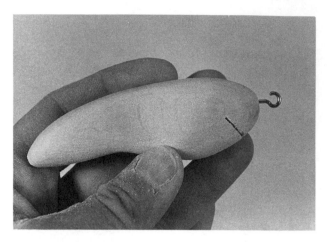

Small slots like this can be cut into the front of wood plugs for the addition of plastic or metal lips. Some lips are available through mail-order companies, or they can be made from scrap metal.

Open screw eyes in the plug body to check for position before painting and assembling. The belly screw eye uses a cup washer, fitted into a hole countersunk into the wood body.

added, they must be lined up properly and attached with the small 1/4- to 3/8-inch screws used for the purpose. Metal lips are added the same way, using small screws to hole them in place. Some of these have a built-in hook hanger for holding the belly or center hook, which must be added before the lip is secured.

Plastic lips are usually inserted into the plug, and for this a slot must be cut into the wood either before or after painting. If the slot is cut before painting, you may have to cut or resize it again, because some paint will have soaked into it. To fasten the lip, use a good grade, long-setting twenty-four-hour type, not the weaker (five-minute kind) epoxy. For best results, drill a pilot hole before gluing so that you can insert a small screw for additional strength and security. When gluing, make sure that the lip is perfectly lined up with the body, and mop up any excess glue. One way to prevent glue smearing onto the plug finish is to use masking tape around the edge of the lip, insert the lip, then remove the masking tape with the excess glue on it. Then do any final cleanup.

When using metal and plastic lips, be sure the line-tie is rounded, i.e., a round wire in the case of some plastic lips. If it is not, then be sure to add a split ring, Duo-Lock snap, or connector link for the line attachment.

Add the tail screw and cup washer to complete the lure. In adding all treble hooks and screw eyes, use open screw eyes. Insert the screw eye into the wood until about three turns from the end, then add the hook, close the screw eye with pliers, and finish turning the screw eye into the

plug. Line up the plane of the screw eye with the axis of the plug. Both the belly and tail hooks can be fastened with hook hangers and the small screws used to hold them. With these, the "trowel" blade part of the hanger is always faced forward so as to limit the forward swing of the hook.

Some surface plugs have propellers for added flash, noise, and splash. On some plugs they are on the tail, on others they are on both ends. Add these to the shaft of the nose and tail screw eye before inserting into the wood. Also, since part of these screw eyes will protrude from the lure, you will need screw eyes about 1/4-inch longer than you would otherwise use. Use small cup washers both fore and aft of the prop for bearing surfaces. Also, take care not to draw the screw up tight, because this will prevent the prop from turning.

Another tip, if you make plugs with props both fore and aft: Get counter-rotating blades or twist the blades of one prop to spin in the opposite direction of the second to eliminate any torque that might otherwise tend to spin or rotate the lure and cause line twist. This is particularly a problem with small lightweight lures, but it can happen with large saltwater lures as well.

VARIATIONS IN MAKING WOOD PLUGS

Variations in shape, style, running depth, and design of wood plugs are unlimited. Anything that is similar to commercial designs, or anything that you imagine can be carved on wood and rigged for fishing. Some simple variations on the basic

Using a hobby tool with a cutting disc to cut a slot in the top of a wood plug body for addition of a plastic or metal dorsal fin.

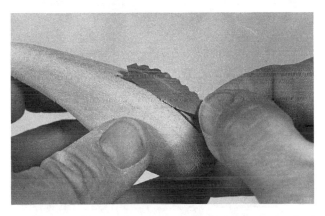

Dorsal fin, cut from scrap metal, being checked against the slot.

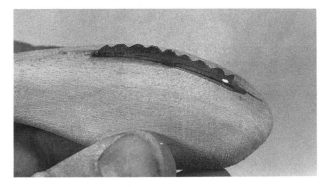

Metal dorsal fin glued in place on top of plug body.

construction of a basic plug include:

Jointed plug. These are easy to make because they are really nothing more than a plug cut into two or more parts, and the parts joined by connectors. In most cases, jointed plugs consist of only two parts. In some, three or even more are used, although these usually make for excessively

Jointed plugs are easily made by cutting plug bodies in half or thirds, tapering the facing ends to allow for the jointed action, and using screw eyes for the hinge.

long plugs that have limited use or are little better, if at all, than single or two-part plugs.

A simple way to make jointed plugs is to plan for this in the design, carve or shape the plug, and then cut it in half at the desired spot to make the two parts. Whether carved by hand, shaped with a band saw, or turned on a lathe, this is far easier than making each part separately.

Once the parts are cut, use a rasp, knife, or sander to slightly round or angle the sides of the connecting surfaces. This will allow the side-to-side movement of the two parts, giving them clearance.

There are several ways to connect the parts. The easiest way is to use long screw eyes centered in the two parts, with one eye arranged vertically, the other horizontally. Another method is to use a short connector link or to make a similar thin connector plate with holes at each end. Cut a horizontal slot into the center of the connecting surfaces, insert the connector link or plate, and secure it with a thin, long screw fastened vertically through the plug and the holes in the link or plate. A large split ring could be used as a connector in the same way.

Naturally, both parts must be painted before the assembly, and the proper connections are part of the final assembly process, along with the addition of line-ties, hooks, and any finishing parts.

Rotating tail section. This is similar to the two-part lure, but instead of a wiggling jointed lure, the second part rotates on a shaft for a different action or more flash. This is not often seen on commercial lures, and when it is used is primarily for muskie and saltwater lures.

For this variation, make the lure as previously

Another way of making a jointed body is to place a small plate, cut from sheet metal and drilled at both ends, in a slot cut into the plug body and then pin it to each part of the plug body.

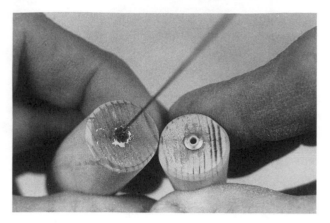

Rotating tail section on two-part plug bodies are possible by through wiring and then making fins for the tail section to rotate. Here, the wire is glued into the front body and a collar (pop rivet head) is placed on the tail as a bearing.

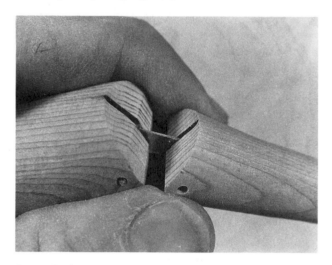

Jointed plug body showing the taper on the facing ends of the jointed parts and the plate pinned in place. Pins are easily glued in place.

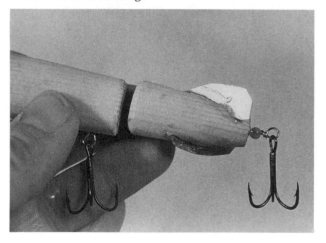

Fins glued into place on the tail section to cause this tail section to rotate. Note the bearing bead between the tail section and wrapped wire eye for easy rotation.

described, and cut it in half. Drill a center hole through both parts, but make the hole in the forward section just barely large enough for brass wire, and make a larger-diameter hole through the rotating rear section.

Rig as with through-wire construction, but make sure that the hole in the rear section is large enough for it to rotate easily on the wire. Glue the wire in place in the forward section to prevent it from sliding back and binding against the rear rotating part. Use a small plastic bead as a rear bearing on the wire for the rear section and finish with looped eyes to hold the hooks.

Naturally, to make the rear section rotate you will have to add metal or plastic fins or cut planes into the section that will make it like a propeller.

One other way to get good rotation to the lure is to drill slightly larger holes in each end of the rear section and insert glass or plastic beads or derby washers that will serve as bearings for the lure tail, preventing the lure from binding on the wire.

One easy method of construction in making some lures involves making two of them at one time by carving or on a lathe, and then cutting them apart. That way you can get the same taper on each end and save time and effort. This is best when making chuggers, since the two lures will be fat in the middle (where the two faces are) and tapered at the ends. These lures can be cut apart square, or at an angle to make an angled face.

Adding Weight. Many lures can be completed without any addition of weight. In some cases, weight helps to get the lure deep or to give it a certain action. Even surface lures can benefit by the addition of weight, because many surface lures, stickbaits, chuggers, and the like will work differently when they float flat on the surface than when they float vertically, tail under and head above the water.

Deep-diving lures, even floater-divers, often need weight to work properly or to make them into a "neutral buoyancy" lure, in which they will neither rise nor sink, but will remain suspended at rest at a given depth. One point about these lures —whether homemade or commercial: Neutral buoyancy is a goal, one that can be approximated but seldom exactly achieved. Water temperature and salinity, along with other properties, will affect suspension of a lure. Thus, a lure that will suspend perfectly at one water temperature and salinity (or lack of it) will rise or fall under slightly different conditions.

Usually, lead is used as weight, and it is almost always added to the belly of the lure, although for surface lures the tail is favored. Be sure to experiment with other locations when adding lead, but realize that the lower part of a plug body is best in order to prevent the lure from turning over and losing stability.

To add weight, drill a hole in the belly of the lure and add the chosen amount of lead. A good way to add lead is to use split shot glued into place in the hole or to use short, cut lengths of the pencil type of lead used in T-type rubber tubing holders for West Coast drift fishing. This lead is readily available in the Northwest, but it can be bought through catalogs as well. The lead comes in 1/8-, 3/16-, 1/4-, and 3/8-inch diameters, in

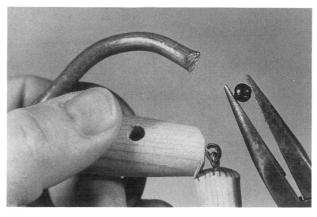

Plugs can be weighted for balance by adding pencil lead (left) or split shot to holes drilled into the belly. Molten lead can also be poured into drilled holes.

coils, and can be easily cut to size and glued into drilled holes in plugs. For added security, the pencil lead with a hole through the center can be used; a screw should be run through the hole and into the body of the plug to secure it. It should also be glued, if for no other reason than to smooth the surface of the lure prior to painting. If you do this, be sure to measure and/or weigh the lead used in a given lure so you will later be able to duplicate it exactly.

In all cases, be sure to use a good epoxy glue to hold the lead, and smooth the glue surface once it's cured and before painting.

Another way to add lead to a lure is to drill the hole for the lead weight, then use a smaller drill to poke holes in the side of this larger hole and rough up the inside surface. Then, with a batch of these lures, use lead-molding techniques to melt lead and pour a little into the belly hole of each lure. The roughening of the inside of the hole is necessary to keep the lead from slipping out later.

Adding rattles. Rattles will always contribute weight to a lure, but because the rattles must be in a loose chamber, the added air pocket helps to overcome this. Rattles can be lead shot, copper BB's, or tiny 2-mm glass or plastic beads. Rattles are often found in hollow plastic lures and less so in wood lures because of the added manufacturing cost. Basically, you must drill a relatively large hole into the plug, into which rattles can be added and the hole plugged or sealed. The best way to do this is to drill the hole, clean it, and add enough rattles to make a noise (check this by placing your thumb over the hole and shaking the plug).

Wood will tend to deaden the sound of the rattles somewhat, but there are ways to increase the noise. One way is to make a "liner" from a sleeve cut from a discarded ballpoint pen and placed in a drilled hole. This will help the rattles make a sharper clicking noise.

Another way to add rattles is to obtain some of the new rattling worm weights, drill an appropriate-sized hole, and glue one of the worm weights into the lure. Coat the hole with glue and smooth it off after the glue has cured and before painting.

Adding spinner tails. Spinner-blade tails will add some flash to a lure and are easy to add by using a Duo-Lock snap to attach the spinner blade to the rear hook hanger or screw eye in the plug.

Changing hooks. Hooks are easily changed by using split rings or the open-eye style of hook, available in single, double, and treble styles. If you don't have these, the split ring can be opened and the old hook taken off and the new added at the same time. Single hooks are often used for some fishing, because a hook size larger than that used for a treble is then possible. This means a larger gap for better hooking, more strength in the wire for big fish, and easier unhooking of toothy fish such as bluefish, mackerel, and barracuda. The use of double hooks instead of trebles is often best for fishing in weeds. Arrange the hooks with the points up to minimize snagging.

Adding soft-plastic tails. Soft-plastic tails, including grubs, spinnerbait tails, and short worms, add attraction to plugs. The one problem with this is that the soft plastic will often react adversely to the paint used for wood lures (or with the plastic used in plastic lures), so the paint surface and plastic tail should be kept separate in storage.

There are several ways to add soft-plastic tails to plugs. One is to add a lure corkscrew to the rear screw eye of the lure and twist the worm or grub onto this screw eye. To make your own, use small 1/8- to 3/16-inch-diameter compression spring (the type with each coil separated by a space), bend one end to fit onto the screw eye, and twist the worm into the open wire of the other end. If the free end is not open, use wire cutters to remove some of the spring, or pliers to bend out a free point of wire. You don't need a long spring for this — about six full coils will do fine.

Another way to do this is to replace the standard treble hook on the tail with a bent-shank worm hook, designed specifically for Texas-rigging worms. Then add the worm or grub tail to the worm and Texas-rig it to make it weedless. To help prevent the worm from sliding down on the hook shank, use the bass fisherman's trick and peg the worm to the eye of the hook with a toothpick. Break off the excess toothpick. A variety of hooks are available for this, but I like the large Tru-Turn hooks, the Eagle Claw 44, 45, 95JB, and the Mister Twister Keeper Worm hook.

PLUG-MAKING KITS

Plug-making kits are available from a number of catalog companies, including Cabela's and Netcraft, although kits for plastic lures are more common. Most come with the unfinished but shaped wood lures and include the lips, bibs, hooks, screw eyes, or hook hangers necessary to complete the lure. Some include paints; others are already painted.

COSTS

Costs for wood plugs can range from only a few cents each to several dollars for commercial shaped wood bodies in large sizes. If you carve or shape them yourself from raw wood stock, the cost is only pennies each — mainly the cost of hardware, hooks, and paint. Kits and preshaped and prepainted wood plugs add to the cost.

10

Plastic Plugs

INTRODUCTION ▪ TOOLS AND MATERIALS ▪ PLUG HARDWARE ▪ PLASTIC PLUG BODIES ▪ ASSEMBLY OF PLUG PARTS, GLUING, AND SEALING ▪ PLUG BODIES FROM SOLID PLASTIC ▪ MOLDING OR CASTING PLASTIC LURES ▪ ADDING PLUG HARDWARE ▪ PAINTING AND FINISHING ▪ VARIATIONS IN MAKING PLASTIC PLUGS ▪ PLUG-MAKING KITS

Basic Safety Requirements
Safety goggles
Carpenters' apron
Gloves

Basic Tools
Pocket knife
Sandpaper

Basic Tools For Assembly
Small screwdriver
Pliers
Split-ring pliers

Helpful Tools
Electric drill

Long-shank, electricians', or aircraft drill bits
Lathe
Lathe chisels
Dremel Moto-Tool
Band saw
Carpenters' saw
Knife
File set
Sandpaper, assorted grades
Glue
Contour gauge
Calipers
Rule
Awl
Saw
Polyethylene lure molds

INTRODUCTION

There are pros and cons to the issue of plastic plugs versus wood plugs. First, there is no way a hobbyist can make injection-molded plugs such as the floater/divers or top-water models that are made by today's lure manufacturers. They can't be "poured" as plastic worms can, and the equipment for making them runs into tens of thousands of dol-

lars, perhaps ten to twenty thousand for the mold alone. You *can* cast plugs and poppers using a polyurethane foam developed by Roy Hilts of Hilts Molds. This is different from injection molding in that the material used will expand to twenty times its liquid volume, in the process becoming very light, to make surface lures or floater/divers.

You can turn plastic plugs on a lathe with clear acrylic plastic rods, but these end up as solid plugs that will sink and are thus limited in their usefulness when compared to modern commercial lures.

Plastic plug bodies are available in two parts, which must be glued together. They are also available in finished but unpainted lures, and in finished painted lures that require only the addition of hooks for completion. As a result, they are generally a lot easier to make and also have somewhat of a "guaranteed" action in the water. These plastic lure bodies sometimes come from the same molds in which commercial lures are made.

Plastic lures do not have the versatility of wood lures. You can't easily change their length, shape, or action. What you buy is what you fish with, unless you make the lures from plastic rods. With wood, you can make up any shape or design you wish, including the standard proven designs available in commercial wood lures, or some offbeat experimental model that may work great—or not at all.

TOOLS AND MATERIALS

The tools and materials for making plastic lures are usually far simpler than are those needed or often used for making wood lures. For example, if you purchase finished, painted plastic plugs, you don't need much of anything at all—just pliers or split-ring pliers to insert the hook-hanging screw eyes into the lure.

The list of tools at the beginning of this chapter does, however, indicate the extent to which you can go in making plastic plugs if you work from raw plastic such as a plastic rod. For example, you can use a lathe to turn a plastic rod to shape the plug, use an electric drill to drill pilot holes for the screw eyes, and a Dremel Moto-Tool for final carving and making eye sockets for solid-plastic plugs. The basic operations of these tools on plastic plugs are no different from that mentioned in Chapter 10 on wood plugs, and the approriate sections there should be reviewed before you work on plastic.

One basic suggestion in working plastic is to use far lower, slower speeds than you would for metal or wood. Wood can take high speeds, but the use of high speeds in cutting or drilling plastic will only result in melted plastic, often deforming the plug. Check your tool's owner's manual for suggested speeds for drilling, turning, or working acrylic plastic.

Acrylic plastic rod is available in several diameters, with the most useful those of about 1-inch to 1 1/2-inch diameter. Popular sizes include 1/4-, 1/2-, 3/4-, and 1-inch diameters. The cost varies with the diameter, and the material is priced by the foot. Six-foot lengths are standard. Clear is probably the best choice, but colors are sometimes available. Look for this material under "Plastics" in your phone book.

Acrylic rod is ideal for working in a lathe, using a universal three-jaw chuck and a through-hole head: The rod can be run through the head, shaped, cut off, the next section run out of the lathe chuck for shaping.

Other tools and materials include only a few hand tools. For example, you might want a knife to gently scrape away any flash or excess glue that forms along the seam lines of preassembled plugs. If you glue the parts together, you will need the same tool for the same purpose. If you work with solid plastic (acrylic rods shaped into plugs), you will find final-shaping uses for a wood rasp, sandpaper, and countersink to make a recess for the screw eyes.

If you make plugs from solid plastic rod, you may also want to drill it for through-wire construction; thus the need for long 6-inch aircraft/electricians' bits for the drill.

Glues for assembling the two halves of a plastic body must be chosen carefully. Special glues that will glue the butyrate or PVC plastics used in most plug bodies are a must. Check the labels to determine the best choice. The regular hobby-style Duco glue is fine, along with the vinyl glues designed to "hold everything," the so-called super glues of cyanoacrylate. It is also often possible to use some special solvents of these plastics that will in essence "weld" the two halves together. Often, ketones work for this, and acetone is the most common and is sometimes available from pharmacies or hardware stores. Acetone is also the major component of some, though not all, finger-nail-polish removers. You can try some, but experiment first on this or any other similar solvents not specifically designed for plug "welding."

Molds for casting poly-foam plastic plugs are made of polyethylene. You can't make your own molds, because at the present polyurethane foam will stick to most of the substances used for molds. Thus, aluminum and plaster molds are out. Some rubber molds might be worth a try, but the release agents required to get the lure out of the mold apparently sometimes cause a reaction that results in holes, bubbles, or "voids" in the lures, making them unusable.

Pliers are handy for inserting screw eyes into the plug, and also for closing the open eyes to hold hooks or to make the closed-eye line-ties for the front of the plug.

Again, review the more extensive discussion of tools in Chapter 10, or refer to the section on tools in Chapters 1 and 2.

PLUG HARDWARE

Plug hardware for plastic plugs is no different from that used for wood plugs. Lips are separate in wood lures but are generally molded into shallow or deep-diving plastic lures. So while lips are seldom used for plastic plugs, you will need the same screw eyes, hook hangers, propellers for surface lures, hooks, and the like used in wood plugs. The one difference is that for most wood lures long screw eyes are best, and lengths can vary depending upon the type of wood (its hardness) used and the presence or absence of a pilot hole. Injection-molded plastic plugs usually require a specific length of screw eye, since most have molded-in sockets or recesses for this specific length. Shorter screw eyes will only make for a weaker hook attachment; longer screw eyes will go through the bottom of this molded-in recess and penetrate the hollow interior of the lure, perhaps weakening it or allowing water to enter. I've even seen cases where long screw eyes have split these plugs.

As with wood plugs, you may want split rings, connector links, or Duo-Lock snaps to serve as a

Some ultralight plugs are available in two parts and must be glued together before adding line-ties and hooks. Since they are available with red heads and white bodies, no finishing is required.

line-tie for the plug and to give the plug additional action. This is particularly important when using heavy line, since a tight knot to an immobile line-tie will impede lure action.

For making plugs of acrylic rod, you can use any length of screw eye but must drill pilot holes appropriate to the diameter of the screw eye. The hard acrylic plastic will not yield as will wood, and thus the pilot hole is mandatory to insure proper holding without the hole stripping or twisting off the screw eye from too tight a fit.

You can also through-wire acrylic rod plugs by straight-drilling a hole through the plug body, through which a wire can be run to connect hooks and line-tie. (The techniques are the same as for wood plugs but will be briefly discussed later in this chapter.) Either stiff wire or twisted cable can be used. Heavy wire should be chosen, and braided wire is best, in thirty- through fifty-pound test sizes for most plugs. Either bright or black wire can be used. Leader sleeves for making the necessary loops for line-tie and hook attachment are also necessary. If using stiff wire, you only need to form eyes and wrap them as is done when making spinners or wood plugs.

It is possible to cut a slot along the long axis of the plug to insert a metal plate for the line-tie and hook attachment, but this is only done infrequently.

Eyes for plastic plugs are similar to those for wood plugs, except that wire-mounted glass eyes can only be used on acrylic-rod plugs or plugs that are solid in that area, because holes must be drilled to hold the glued-in wire. Eyes can also be painted, decals, wiggle craft-type eyes (doll eyes), or self-adhesive reflective tape.

PLASTIC PLUG BODIES

Most molded plug bodies available from tackle shops or mail-order catalogs today are composed of butyrate or ABS. Both are hard, tough plastics; the butyrate is clear and the ABS is opaque. The choice of plastic by commercial lure manufacturers is often based on whether the final lure will be completely opaque, clear, or with a translucent, see-through finish.

As previously stated, plastic plug bodies come several ways. Some are available complete—molded, sealed together, with molded-in hook hangers, and painted with a professional finish. Others are available just as complete but unpainted. Others are available painted or unpainted and without hook hangers or line-ties: These are add-

ed by installing screw eyes of the correct length and size. Some plugs are available in two parts, right and left, which are then glued together or sealed with a supplied or separately purchased sealer.

The shapes available include most of the basics, such as top-water stick baits, top-water propeller lures, shallow-running minnow imitations, deep-diving plugs, banana-shaped plugs, surface poppers, and salmon-trolling plugs.

Some plugs have separate bodies and bills or lips: The lips are of clear butyrate, the bodies are of an opaque plastic, probably ABS. These are easily glued in place. Those plugs that are in two parts have molded-in registration pins along the sides so that the two parts will be in perfect align-

Examples of commercially available plastic plug bodies. Such bodies are molded and completely assembled and ready for painting and adding hooks and line ties.

Examples of commercially available plug bodies that come finished, requiring only addition of hooks using split rings.

ment when glued together. Some that are available in two parts also include a small weight of molded lead, to be glued inside the plug in a special cavity so as to properly weight and balance the lure in the water. Plugs of the several types listed are currently available from Hille, Netcraft, Jann's, and Cabela's.

Most companies that sell the two-part plastic plug bodies also sell the solvent or glue for affixing these two parts to each other. Incidentally, solvent and glue are different. Glue binds to each of the two parts and holds them tightly together. Solvent softens the two parts, or seam lines in this case, so that when properly softened and then joined, the two parts are in effect welded together. The solvent eventually evaporates to leave the two parts joined permanently.

Commercial plugs are usually made in one of two ways. One is to use a solvent as described above, allowing the joining edges to sit for a specified time on a pad soaked with solvent, then joining and clamping the parts together for the few minutes necessary to achieve a good bond. The other method can't be done by the home tackle-maker, because it involves expensive ultrasonic equipment to produce vibrations (15,000 to 20,000 cycles per second) that create friction, which in turn creates heat, which in turn welds the two parts. Lures to be sealed this way are made slightly differently, with a small triangular ridge molded on the edge of both halves. This ridge serves as an "energy director" to "aim" the ultrasonic energy. The ridges are small—about 12/1,000 of an inch wide and 8/1,000 of an inch high—but will melt under the ultrasound cycles to form a solid welded unit.

If you can't find solvent to weld lure bodies, special plastic cements are available (often from hobby shops) that will work best with these plastic parts.

ASSEMBLY OF PLUG PARTS, GLUING, AND SEALING

Plugs that come in parts must be assembled. Most of these are lures in two halves. Some require only the addition of a clear lip to an opaque body. For this, you must use glue or a solvent, the solvent often one of the ketones, such as acetone. Be sure to follow the plug manufacturer's or seller's instructions, and use only the glue or solvent recommended. Plastics differ, and the glue or solvent required for one type of plastic may not work on another type, or may even react

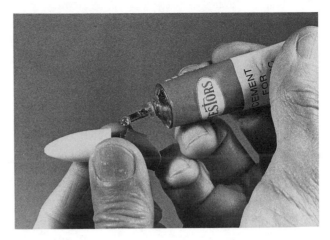

Gluing the two parts of an ultralight plug.

adversely to it and ruin the plug. Failure to use the right glue might cause the lure to pull apart later.

In most cases the solvents used are very liquid, while glues are usually a little more viscous. In both cases, use a small brush to coat the adjoining lure surfaces with the glue or solvent. If using a solvent, you must do this rapidly and press the parts together immediately, because solvents evaporate fast. Failure to work quickly can cause the future failure of this joint. You do have a little more time with glues, since they will not set up as quickly. Many glues come with a small brush in the container lid for easy and quick application. Don't get solvent on your hands during this operation; solvents are harmful, and in addition, any transferred from your hand to the plug body will leave a distinct mark.

If you work on a larger scale and make a lot of plastic plugs at once, you can use the technique of the lure manufacturers and prepare a small metal pan with a thin sheet of foam or sponge, pour solvent in the pan, and set the two plug parts on the foam or sponge pad to soften or soak up the solvent for the welding. Do not use a plastic pan for this—the solvent might react with it. Also, some plastic foams and sponges will react. If you're unsure of your material, use a felt pad to soak up the solvent.

Use solvent safely, with adequate ventilation and under controlled conditions. This should not be done just anywhere, anytime. Lure manufacturers using this technique keep pans under large vacuum-ventilation hoods to vent fumes from the shop and protect their workers. You won't have access to equipment like this, so work with solvents outside only, on a patio, in a carport or

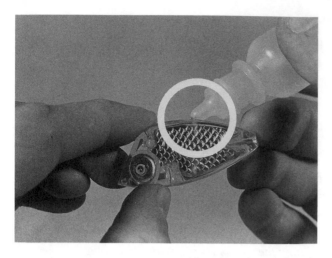

Gluing together two halves of a plastic plug after foil insert sheets have been added. The foil sheets show through the clear sides, eliminating painting or other finishing.

similar shaded but open area. It does help to place a small cover over the pan to prevent excess evaporation of the solvent. For this, consider cutting down one side of a large cardboard box and inverting it over the pan. The open side will allow you room to work.

Whether using the pad or brush technique, try to avoid getting too much solvent or glue anywhere on the plug except the fine seam lines where the plug snaps together. Although glue can be wiped off and solvent will evaporate, both will leave a mark. The fish won't notice, of course, but it's best to try to do the best job you can in every stage of tackle-crafting.

PLUG BODIES FROM SOLID PLASTIC

Plug bodies can be made from solid plastic such as acrylic rod or acrylic block. Rod is easier to work with because you do not have to round off the corners before shaping. Block or square stock can be used; use care in rounding off the corners to get the block to a round shape. The best way to do this is with a lathe, using safe and standard lathe practices to place the rod in the lathe and shape it. Use a three-jawed or four-jawed chuck, with a live or dead center tail stock. (A live center will turn, a dead center does not turn.) Both types come to a point to hold the plastic rod at a small hole punched or drilled into the center of the stock. A live (turning) center is much preferred, because most plastics of this type will expand when heated and can cause binding with a dead center, which will heat up and create more friction.

Optimal turning speeds for plastic will vary, and you should consult a good lathe operation book for advice here. This book covers making lures in a variety of ways, including lathe operations with plastics, but it is not intended as a complete guide to working all types of materials with all types of machine tools. However, a good starting point with most acrylic and acrylic-type plastics is to run the lathe at a speed that will turn the material at about 200 feet per minute. Thus, with a 1-inch stock, one turn will equal 3 inches. Three inches into 200 feet would be a rotation of about 800 rpm. Too slow a speed may not cut properly, but too fast a speed will melt or burn the plastic. Also, if you use a dead center be sure to check the material periodically (with the lathe off) to see if binding between centers is occurring from plastic expansion due to heat.

Once you are set up for the lathe operation, cut the plug to shape using standard cutting tools, but cut with a thin bite to prevent the tool from digging in — a potential problem with plastic.

If you make cupped faces for chuggers, consider mounting the plastic rod into a three-jawed chuck with no tail center and working on the face to cup it. Then the stock can be placed between centers to finish the shape of the rest of the plug.

Once the plug body is finished, use a drill (again at a slow or medium speed to prevent burning or melting) to make the holes for the screw eyes for the line-tie and all hooks. If you desire through-wire construction, use a drill press and vertical support (see Chapter 9 for details) to drill through the long axis, using long 6-inch aircraft or electricians' bits. Note that it is important *before* drilling to decide the size of the screw eye you will be using and to drill an appropriatesized pilot hole. If you are unsure of the propersized pilot hole, drill a few different-sized holes in scrap plastic and test them with the screw eyes you intend to use. The screw eye should go in firmly, without any looseness and without twisting or weakening the screw eye itself. Plug hangers using the small screws can also be used, again with tiny pilot holes. All holes to be drilled should be marked first with a fine-tip felt-tip marker or can bc marked with an awl or punch. The latter will also provide a guide for the drill bit, preventing slipping.

MOLDING OR CASTING PLASTIC LURES

Recently, techniques have been developed by which anglers can mold — or more accurately, cast

—their own fly-rod poppers and plugs. The plugs possible include surface stickbaits, shallow-running minnow imitations, and deep-running lures.

These techniques, plastics, and molds were developed by Roy Hilts of Hilts Molds, and use a special plastic that, when added to a catalyst, foams, expands, and becomes very lightweight. The plastic is a polyurethane that when mixed with the catalyst will expand to twenty times that of its liquid form and weigh only 2 1/2 pounds per cubic foot.

Unfortunately, this plastic does not allow the use of molds other than those specifically manufactured for this process. The manufactured molds are polyethylene. Using other plastics, plaster, aluminum, or any other material results either in the plastic bonding to the mold cavity or forming voids and bubbles (sometimes as a result of mold release compounds that must be used).

The steps for making popping bugs or lures this way are:

1. Make sure you have an adequate work space with adequate ventilation. Because the plastic starts to foam very rapidly after mixing, you must have everything arranged properly and ready to use.

2. The two-part molds must be sprayed with a mold release (available from Hilts, or use a cooking spray such as Pam: Pam works fine to help release the bodies from the mold).

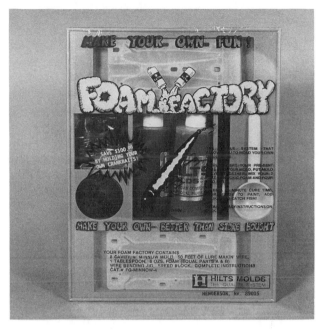

The Foam Factory from Hilts Molds allows molding your own plug bodies by using fast-acting foam and plastic molds.

3. The two-part molds must be fitted with hooks (for popping bugs) or wire hook hanger forms (for plugs) before molding. Lay one half of the mold down, fill it with the hooks or hook harnesses, and place the other mold half over it. Close with the special spring locks provided.

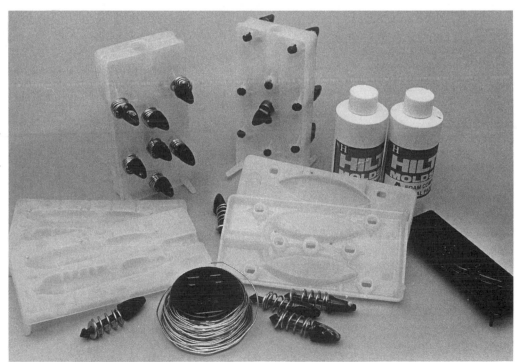

Foam, molds, wire rig forms, and wire needed for making foam plastic plugs.

4.   The plastic comes in two components, to be mixed in equal amounts. Since the foam expands, mix at one time only enough liquid to fill each of the available molds two-thirds full. Use paper or polyethylene cups (such as those 1-ounce medical cups used for mixing rod-wrap finishes) when mixing to prevent reaction.

5.   If you wish to add color, you can do so by adding powdered or liquid color to the liquid plastic before mixing it with the catalyst. Mix the color thoroughly, then mix the plastic and the catalyst. Note that because the foam expands, you will need a lot of color. The expansion will dilute the shade you achieved in the liquid plastic. Don't add too much color however, since this will inhibit the blowing agent—the ingredient in the catalyst that causes the liquid to expand and foam.

6.   Since the liquid plastic and the catalyst are of two different colors, a uniform color will indicate you've achieved a thorough mix. Pour the proper amount of the two parts together and mix them, stirring rapidly. Don't worry about bubbles in the liquid, because it will foam and expand anyway. *Speed is mandatory.* You have only 35 seconds from the time you pour the two parts together until the time the mix starts to expand and foam. Mixing should take no more than about 10 to 15 seconds—use the rest of the time for rapid pouring into the molds.

7.   Once the plastic is thoroughly mixed, pour the foam rapidly into the sprue hole of each of the prepared molds. The plastic is slightly viscous, much like the molten plastic used for making soft-plastic lures, so pour rapidly but carefully, preferably down one side of the sprue hole for rapid filling while allowing air to escape.

8.   Once the molds are filled to about a third of the cavity depth (you can see this through the translucent sides of the plastic mold), the plastic will expand almost immediately to fill the mold, and often to slightly overfill it and emerge from the sprue hole.

9.   Wait 30 minutes before removing the bodies from the mold. Do this too soon and the bodies may not be completely cured. Wait too long and it may be more difficult to separate the bodies from the mold cavities. Some bodies will have undercut parts—such as the faces on poppers. To avoid breaking these when you open the mold, open the mold like a book, treating the sprue-hole side as the spine area. Gently pry the bodies out.

10.   The completed lure will be a beige or tan color if color was not added. Some flash will likely

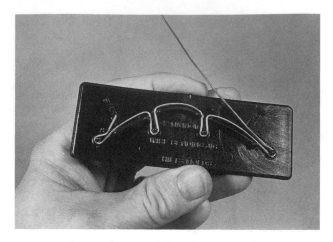

Plastic jig forms, from Hilts Molds, make it possible to easily make rigs that will fit into the company's molds. These forms make the hook hangers and line-ties for plugs. The wire would be clipped off before removing the jig from the form.

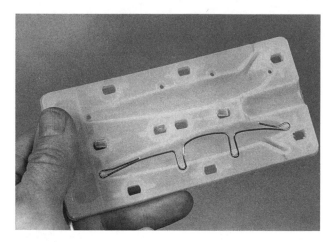

Wire form placed into the mold—this for making a shallow-running crankbait.

Mixing the foam involves adding equal parts of two foaming liquids. Begin by placing equal amounts of both parts into separate cups.

Mixing the two liquids of the foaming plastic. From this stage the foam must be mixed and poured into the molds in 35 seconds.

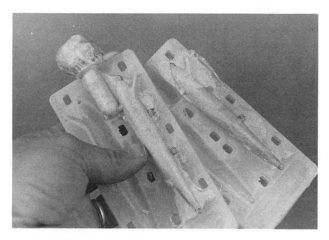

The locking pins have been removed to show the two molds and the two lures that resulted. Some flash formed along the seam line of the lures.

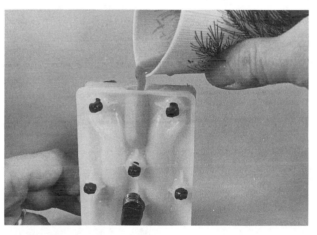

Pouring the foaming liquid into the mold. Note the spring-operated locking pins that hold the two plastic mold halves together.

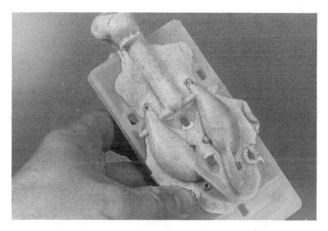

Another plug mold showing some foaming that resulted from using too much liquid foaming agent. Practice eliminates this. The plugs are still quite useable by simply cutting off the excess plastic.

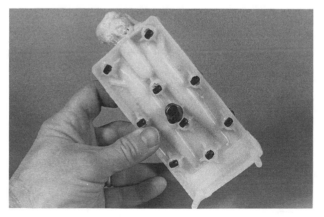

The mold after foaming and curing. Complete curing takes about 24 hours, but the lures can be removed after about an hour. Here, excess foaming liquid has foamed out through the sprue hole.

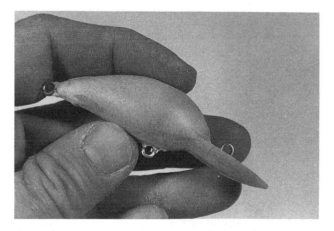

Completed lure, ready for painting and assembly. Color can also be added to the plastic to make solid-color lures, eliminating painting.

be on the mold, but this is easily cleaned up with a raxor blade, scalpel, or X-Acto knife. Final cleaning is best done with an emery board to sand along the seam lines.

11.   The lures or poppers can be painted if color was not added to the foaming plastic. Allow the completed bodies to cure 24 hours before painting. Any paint that will not react with the polyurethane foam will work, although Roy Hilts recommends his own Roy's Benchmark Paint, described further in Chapter 15.

12.   Once the lure is painted and finished, the lure hardware, consisting of hooks on split rings, split rings for the line-tie, and so on, are added, as is done with any lure.

13.   Clean up the mold, tools, and your hands with soap and water.

ADDING PLUG HARDWARE

In general, plug hardware is added after painting and finishing, but there is no particular order in which various pieces of hardware must be added to the lure. With plastic lures it is important to pick the right hardware. Most injection-molded plastic plugs have specific diameter and depth recesses to hold screws or screw eyes. Shorter or thinner screw eyes or fasteners will not hold securely, while longer or thicker (or both) screw eyes may split the plug, cause it to crack, cause it to leak, or cause the screw eye to twist off or weaken as it is added.

Cup washers, although generally used with wood lures, are not used much with plastic lures. There is nothing wrong with adding them, but they do not help to seal the lure, protect the countersunk area, or otherwise add to lure appearance or function. Cup washers are used in plastic plugs with propellers, for instance top-water lures that require props. Here the cup washers are used as bearings to help the propellers turn, just as they are in wood plugs. A cup washer both in front of and behind the propeller is required, the convex sides facing the propeller. If you use two props, consider turning the pitch of one counter to the other to reduce the possibility of the lure spinning.

In making cast-plastic plugs or when using unfinished or finished assembled plug bodies, the hook hangers are usually molded in place. For these, only need split rings and the hooks (usually treble hooks) to finish the lure. Use split-ring pliers to open the split ring and start it on the wire hook hanger. As soon as it is started on this wire

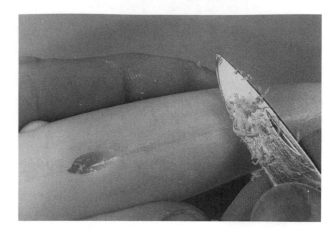

Some plastic plug bodies might need some work before painting and finishing. There may be some flash along the seam lines, easily removed by scraping with a knife.

form, add the treble hook eye and continue to turn the ring until the hook is loose on the ring and plug. It is also helps to add a split ring to the line-tie wire to add action to the lure.

Solid-acrylic plastic plug bodies are generally sinking lures and made with sloping faces to help them dive and run deep. Metal or plastic lips are available but are often too difficult to attach to be worth it. Some saltwater top-water plugs can be made of acrylic plastic, even though this plastic sinks. This seeming incongruity is a result of the different way in which saltwater surface chuggers are worked. They are worked fast, and a heavy lure actually helps to hold the plug in the water, making it splash through the surface. A hollow lightweight plug will often bounce around, sometimes hanging the line on the hooks and causing missed fish. The sinking top-water plug has enough weight to hold position, while the sloping chugger face keeps the plug on the surface with rapid jerky retrieves.

If you make through-wire construction acrylic plastic plugs, the best method to follow is that for wood plugs in which a straight, thin hole is drilled through the body, front to rear, and a larger hole drilled in from the belly. The size of this second hole should be just large enough to contain the barrel swivel used to hold the belly hook. Cable or single-strand wire is formed into a line-tie (often a split ring is added to the loop with cable), the wire is run through the body to engage one eye of the swivel, then out the back where a second loop or twisted eye is formed to hold the tail hook. The hook can be attached to the belly swivel using a

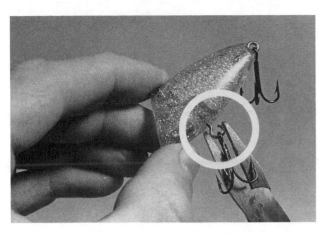

Assembly of plastic plugs is really no different from that of wood plugs. Here an open screw eye and hook (circled) are being added to a plastic sonic-style plug body. The pliers will close the screw eye before it is completely screwed into the lure.

split ring or an open-eye hook that can be closed with pliers once on the swivel eye.

PAINTING AND FINISHING

Painting and finishing with tape, eyes, and so on, is covered in Chapter 15. Generally speaking, painting and finishing is done before adding the plug hardware and hooks to the lure in order to prevent painting and masking difficulties.

VARIATIONS IN MAKING PLASTIC PLUGS

Many of the variations outlined for wood plugs can also be accomplished with plastic plugs. Refer to those sections in Chapter 9 for details. Some of these variations include adding spinner blades to the tail, adding soft plastics (though the soft plastic will react to the lure plastic just as it will react to the paint on wood lures), changing hooks, and so on.

PLUG-MAKING KITS

As with spinners and spoons, kits for plastic plugs are available and contain complete plug bodies and hardware for a number of lures. Netcraft has several such kits, most of them assembled but unpainted lures. One kit includes parts to make nine finished lures. Cabela's does not have a kit but sells its plastic plug bodies individually, though complete with all hardware and hooks — so the result is the same. At this writing, these plugs are sold in groups of three in the same size and style. Kits range in price, based on size and type. Jann's has a good assortment of professionally painted plastic crankbait bodies.

11

Offshore Lures

INTRODUCTION ▪ TOOLS ▪ MATERIALS ▪ STEP-BY-STEP ASSEMBLY OF BEAD LURES ▪ BEAD-LURE VARIATIONS ▪ MOLDED-PLASTIC LURES ▪ PLASTIC LURE MOLDING STEPS ▪ STEP-BY-STEP CONSTRUCTION OF WOOD LURES ▪ SOFT-BODIED LURES ▪ ADDING SKIRTS ▪ RIGGING HOOKS ▪ VARIATIONS

Basic Safety Requirments
Goggles
Respirator mask suitable for protection from casting resins
Apron
A clean, clear place with a heavy countertop on which to work

Basic Tools
Waxed cups for mixing plastic
Stirring sticks (popsicle sticks or craft sticks)
Electric drill and long-shank drill bits
Machinists' vise or Vise-Grip pliers for hook-rigging
File
Leader-crimping pliers
Wire cutters
Pliers
Carving knives for making wood lures (see tools in Chapter 9)

Helpful Tools
Drill press
Lathe (for making wood lures)
Scissors (for cutting, preparing skirts)

INTRODUCTION

Offshore lures were not included in the first edition of *Tackle Craft*, an unintentional but definite omission. Offshore lures can be made with ease by any tackle-tinkerer. In fact, with the existing diversity of offshore lures, there are several ways they can be made, and made radically different in construction, even if the end result is for skipping or trolling lures for inshore and offshore species.

Offshore lures by definition are those lures that are used primarily (but not always) offshore for ocean species such as dolphin, wahoo, billfish, shark, tuna, and mackerel. Although they are often referred to generically as "offshore lures," in smaller sizes they are equally useful when trolling inshore for species such as bluefish, barracuda, false albacore, mackerel, bonito, and roosterfish.

While smaller sizes can be cast, these lures are really designed to be trolled. Some are skipped on the surface in the wake of a fishing boat, either chugging along on the surface or alternately diving and skipping, with the action determined by the basic design, the shape of the head, and the cut of the face. Others, in a size and construction to take heavy saltwater fish, are fished deep and are more like large wood or plastic bass lures.

One of the simplest ways to make offshore lures is to thread a series of large plastic beads on a leader/hook rig and add an egg sinker, which is turn is covered and hidden by a vinyl or similar skirt. Wood lures like the offshore billfish heads and skirts can be made by carving, turning on a lathe, or cutting out of a large-diameter dowel or closet rod, painting and finishing, and finally wrapping with a skirt. The same applies to the offshore cedar plugs favored for early-season tuna fishing. Molded hard-plastic heads of clear casting resin molded with eye inserts, prism reflectors, glitter, and other materials for flash and color are also easily made in one- or two-step molding processes.

While the creation of any lure requires care (as continually emphasized in this book), there is an additional concern with using casting resin: It is highly volatile and gives off noxious and dangerous fumes. When I bought some at a hobby shop recently, the owner related to me tales of the liver damage and near-death of a hobby magazine editor who was using a similar compound under confined conditions. Only a casual comment made in the hospital about the hobby led his doctors to the true nature of his condition and thus the cure. As with any material, but especially with these

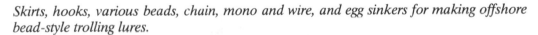

Skirts, hooks, various beads, chain, mono and wire, and egg sinkers for making offshore bead-style trolling lures.

casting resins, use extreme care and follow all manufacturer's directions and safety instructions *exactly*.

TOOLS

Tools for making offshore lures will vary with the type of lure and its construction. In most cases only a few tools are needed, although some helpful tools will allow you to make the lures quicker or easier.

The tools and their uses in making the lures in this chapter include:

Crimping pliers. These are used to make crimps in the leader sleeves used in wire and mono riggings. They are useful for virtually every single style of offshore lure, unless, of course, you are buying prerigged hooks and adding them to your homemade lures. Although knots and snells can be and sometimes are used for rigging smaller lures for smaller species, leader sleeves are typically used for most connections when attaching hooks and making leader end loops.

Leaders-crimping pliers come in several styles and sizes. It is important, as noted by outdoor writer Mark Sosin in an October 1989 column in *Salt Water Sportsman*, to choose the right kind of crimping pliers for the sleeve to be used. Sleeves are made in two styles: one a round cross section, the second shaped like an elongated 0, an open 8, or hourglass. The pliers designed for the open 8 or hourglass are a cup-opposing-cup style and are usually compound action for greater leverage and swaging force, with the rounded sides of the sleeve fitting into the matching cups of the pliers jaws. Pliers for the round sleeves are the point-opposing-cup style in which the sharp ridge of one jaw pushes the sleeve into the cup on the other jaw. Be sure to match pliers and sleeve-type properly. Popular crimping pliers are the Nicopress and Hi Seas brands (these two are often rated the best by many serious captains, mates, and anglers). Smaller but also excellent pliers for most applications are made by the Mason, Sevenstrand, Berkley, and other companies. For more information, see Chapter 13.

Wire cutters. Often, compound-action fishing pliers or crimping pliers will have wire cutters built into the side or end. If not, a good pair of compound wire cutters is necessary for finishing offshore-lure riggings. Be sure to get wire cutters that will cut the tough braided or twisted wire used in leader riggings and not just soft copper electric wire. A good cable cutter is the Felco model C-7.

Snap-ring pliers. These are required for slipping short sections of surgical tubing over the leader and down onto the hook and tag-line (the cable running from the eye of the forward hook to the eye of the trailing, or gaffer, hook). Long straight-jaw pliers are best for this.

File. A file or two is handy for a variety of tasks, including coarse cuts for roughing and finishing. They are good for smoothing the edges of a molded-plastic lure and roughing out wood plugs and trolling heads. An 8- to 12- inch file is a good length for most tackle tasks.

Vise. A good vise is necessary for many tasks, including tightening mono knots and wire connections, sharpening large offshore hooks, and holding molds for pouring plastic.

Drill. A good electric drill with a 3/8-inch or larger chuck, variable speed and reversible, is ideal for drilling the long holes necessary for rigging offshore lures or constructing the molds and jigs necessary to make them. Both standard bits and longer six-inch-shank aircraft bits are best.

Drill press. A small drill press is ideal for many drilling operations, though it is not mandatory. The best are those that are fitted with a sturdy drill press vise to hold materials for accurate drilling.

Lathe. A small lathe for turning cedar or hardwood dowels into offshore trolling heads or cedar tuna plugs is handy but certainly not necessary. A lathe makes it easy to turn out identical plugs and heads quickly and easily.

Scissors. Necessary for cutting skirt material to finish the trolling lures.

Knife. A whittling knife is a must (unless you have a lathe) for carving out wood heads and plugs. The techniques are similar to those used in making freshwater plugs, as outlined in Chapter 9.

Stirring sticks. Popsicle sticks, also called craft sticks when sold in boundles in craft and hobby shops, are disposable and ideal for stirring glue and the two-part molding plastic used for making offshore trolling heads.

MATERIALS

Materials for making offshore lures vary widely depending upon the type of lure to be made. Although some materials are basic to all lures (skirts, wire or mono rigging and leader material, hooks), others vary according to the type of lure.

Beads. Beads vary widely and are available from tackle shops, mail-order component houses, and craft/hobby shops. Although any type of bead can be used for these or other lures, the most popular are the nesting tri-beads. These are small triangular beads that, when threaded on mono or wire, match the angles to the flat edges in order to nest. Two sizes and many colors are available. In addition, round, oval, square, and many other types of beads can be used, although for offshore use they should be of a large diameter: 10 to 12 mm or even larger is not too large for these lures. They are strung on the wire or mono under the skirt. In addition to the color they give a lure, they also serve as spacers to properly position the hook and lure head.

Monofilament and wire leader material. Leaders for offshore lures can include single-strand wire, braided or twisted cable, and nylon-coated cable. Each has its enthusiasts and critics, often reflections of the type of fishing, species sought, or lure used. Mono or single-strand wire is often used with cedar plugs for early-season tuna. Mono is often used for marlin, tuna, sailfish, and dolphin, along with smaller inshore species, but certainly is not good for toothy critters such as king mackerel or sharks. Nylon-coated cable is favored in some ports but becomes unusable if and when the nylon coating becomes frayed. Cable is fine for big game but is often a disadvantage for leader-shy fish such as marlin. Single-strand wire is thin and almost invisible, but if kinked it will break readily and then becomes completely unusable.

The leader material must match up with the size of the lure and the fish sought. Thus, there is no need for two hundred pound or heavier mono for inshore trolling. Generally, leaders will range from about fifty to four hundred pounds, although there are no minimum or maximum limits. Often, commercial prerigged mono leaders are 125-, 200-, or 250-pound test. Most mono specifically for leaders is tough and stiff with high abrasion resistance. The stiffness is especially required for big-game offshore trolling by those anglers who use a two-hook rig, with the trailer hook at 90 or 180 degress to the main hook. The stiff mono prevents the hook from changing position when properly snelled in place. Clear, mist-colored, and black mono is available for leaders.

Single-strand wire such as monel or stainless steel ranges from as light as size 2 — 29-pound test — to as heavy as size 19 — 400 pound test. It usually comes in large coils that are restraightened, which means that when uncoiled the leader will be straight. Stainless steel comes in bright silver, black, or coffee (bronze) color, in lengths ranging from twenty-five feet to quantities sold in one-quarter- or one-pound bulk spools.

Cable is available in stainless steel in silver or coffee (bronze) color in various pound-tests and configurations. Although it's often called "braided," cable is really a twisted wire, and saltwater leaders range from 1 x 7 (one cable formed by twisting seven separate strands together), to 3 x 7 (three of the 1 x 7 cables twisted together to make a single cable of twenty-one strands of wire), and 7 x 7 or 49-strand wire (seven strands of the 1 x 7 cable twisted to make one heavy cable of forty-nine strands).

The 1 x 7 wire can test as high as 250-pound, while the 7 x 7 will range from as light as 175- to as high as 920-pound test, all depending upon the size of the wire used.

Nylon-coated cable is identical to wire and cable, expect that it has a thin nylon coating. It comes in bright or camouflaged (bronze, or coffee) wire with a clear or black nylon coating. Coils of cable are available in lengths including 30 feet, 100 feet, 150 feet, 200 feet, 300 feet, and up. Not all manufacturers will make all types of cable or offer it in coils of every size.

Leader sleeves. Leader sleeves are used to make eyes in leader material to which are attached hooks and to make the eyes for double-line or snap attachments. Leader sleeves are used with all cable, nylon-coated cable, and mono, although knots and snells can be used in mono provided it is not too heavy. Single-strand wire requires only a haywire twist to make a strong and effective eye or loop, something far simpler and often quicker than working with sleeves.

Different companies label sleeves differently, although it is mandatory to have a sleeve that matches the size of the mono. Thus, with Sevenstrand, a size A3 sleeve would fit ninety pound test Sevenstrand cable, forty-pound test Sevalon (nylon-coated cable), and fifteen- and twenty-pound test monofilament. A size A7 would fit 90-pound test Sevalon, 275-pound test Duratest (forty-nine-strand cable), and one hundred- and one hundred and twenty-five-pound test monofilament. Similar ranges will be found with other manufacturers. Note that in all cases, these sizes are based on two strands (to form an eye or loop) fitting through the sleeve. If you use a sleeve as a spacer only on a single strand of leader, often a smaller size will work. In addition, some companies make special sleeves for monofilament leader, with sizes for one hundred- to five hundred-pound test mono. The sleeves for wire and mono range from small freshwater sizes to heavy saltwater varieties. From Sevenstrand, they range from an A1 sleeves for cable to twenty-seven-pound test, to A12 for eight hundred-pound test Duratest (forty-nine-strand), to A14 for two hundred and fifty-pound test mono.

Sinkers. Egg sinkers are best for use as weights in beaded, vinyl-skirted trolling lures, because they have a center hole, fit easily under the molded vinyl skirt, and will weight the lure properly. Egg sinkers from those too small to use in trolling up to those several ounces in weight are readily available at most tackle shops or can be molded easily (see Chapter 5).

Hooks. Hooks for salt water must be strong and corrosion-resistant, with sturdy, often welded, eyes. All the hook companies make hooks in styles, materials, designs, and sizes specifically for heavy-duty saltwater fishing. Favored hooks include the model 254SS and L9021 from Eagle Claw, and the Perma Steel no. 9729 and 9730 from VMC, and the 7732 and 7754 from Mustad.

Molded vinyl skirts. These skirts are molded to slip on the lure. In essence, they look like brightly colored long, tough glove fingers, with the tail section sliced into individual skirt strands. Weber, Sevenstrand, and other companies make these, and they are often sold as replacement skirts for commercial lures . They can, however, be used for homemade lures.

Sizes generally range from about 4 to 16 inches long, with proportioned diameters. Colors are usually bright with a high preponderance of red, pink, orange, blue, bright green, yellow, and purple, although black and white are standard. Solid colors, multiple colors, two-skirt multiple colors, and skirts with molded-in glitter are all readily available. In use, the skirt head is cut or punched with a small hole to take a leader, as for a bead lure, or a larger hole, to be fitted and tied onto a separate lure head. The shape of the head end of these skirts will vary with the manufacturer: some are pointed, others rounded, and still others rounded but with a narrow waist or bell shape.

Wrap skirts. Some companies also make wrap skirts: skirt material that looks like a frayed strip of sheeting. The unfrayed or head end is tied or wrapped to the rear of the trolling head. Often several of these skirts are used for a multiple-color look, for more bulk in the skirt, and to completely fill in large heads that might not be covered with just one wrap. Excellent skirts are available from Model Craft.

Molding plastic. This is a liquid plastic that when combined with the right amount of catalyst produces a hard, clear casting. The polyester resin is available in 16-ounce, 32-ounce, 1-gallon, and 50-gallon drum containers—the latter primarily for commercial users. It does require a small amount of catalyst, available in 1/2-ounce, 1-ounce, and 1-gallon sizes. The 16-ounce container of resin and 1/2-ounce of catalyst will make several lures, depending upon their size. Although there are no standards as to offshore or inshore trolling lure head sizes, small lures will require about 2 to 3 ounces, medium lures about 5 to 6 ounces, and larges lures for big game about 8 to 10 ounces of resin. Since the catalyst is measured in drops per ounce to the resin, it is easy to measure the volume of resin required and mix it to the catalyst for precise results with no waste.

The resin must be stored properly, according to Environmental Technology, Inc. (ETI), its manufacturer. High heat will cause the resin to soldify even without the addition of the catalyst. "If you take the sixteen-ounce can and place it in a window where it will get the sun every day, in a couple of weeks it can set up," says Ed LaFley, national sales manager for ETI. Normally, the casting resin will have a useful shelf life of about nine months. A dating code on the bottom of each can from ETI indicates both the manufacturing date and control number. The code consists of a letter followed by a series of numbers with no spaces or dashes. For example, a code of K08310 indicates manufacture in 1990 (the first 0), the month of August (the 8), the third day of the month (the 3), and the last two numbers (10) are the batch number. By understanding the code you will know if you are getting fresh casting resin and how long the container can sit on your shelf.

Mold Builder. This product is also manufactured by ETI and consists of a pure latex compound that can be used to make molds for casting resin lures. Thin coats of it are brushed on a model lure or prototype in many layers to build up a mold. The latex mold is then pulled off the model and filled with casting resin to produce a copy exactly like the original. (For more details on making molds this way, see Chapter 16.)

Other additions for lures. Molded lures can include prism or mirrored inserts, glitter, eyes, scalelike tape patterns, and so on. Eyes for big-games lures can be found in component-parts catalogs, some tackle shops, and most craft shops, where they are sold for dolls and other art/craft items. Eyes can be molded into clear-plastic heads or glued onto wood bodies. Self-adhesive or glue-on tape eyes can be added to vinyl skirts or soft-head lures. Molded-in eyes that are commonly used are the craft-style "wiggle eyes," in which the black pupil is loose inside a clear bubblelike case. These eyes comes in many sizes, from 2 or 3 mm on up to 1-inch-diameter sizes ideal for big-game lures. There are also plastic "crystal eyes" in similar sizes that are solid and feature a post (for attachment to stuffed animals through a backing plate) that can be glued onto the outside of a molded-plastic lure for a pop-eyed look or molded into the clear head. Round acrylic stones on a metal base are also available from craft stores in a variety of sizes and are usually sold in multicolor packs. With a contrasting head color, they can be used as "eyes" when molded into a lure. Most of these items are available at craft stores or from craft catalogs.

Tape eyes, available from craft and tackle stores and catalogs, are thin self-adhesive strips that can be stuck onto the outside of a lure or molded into its center. Since water pressure will tend to strip off anything on the outside of a lure, these are best used in the center of a clear-plastic lure. Many sizes are available.

Prism tape is available in dozens of different colors and patterns. This tape, available through tackle shops and made by companies like Witchcraft Tape Products and Phantom Tape Products, is easily cut to size and placed on a center insert for molding into a plastic head.

Craft shops sell packets of small mirrors in various shapes, including round, square, rectangular, and diamond. These can be glued to an insert placed into the mold for additional flash. Small metallized plastic sequins, often labeled "palettes," are available in many colors and can be molded into a lure. Sequins are another possibility, either loose and mixed with the resin, or on a string (they are sold this way) and glued into place to resemble cheek or head scales. For this, they must be glued to the insert brass rod (through which the leader will run) or to an insert plug or plate placed in the mold for this purpose. Buttons have also been used as eyes or decorative inserts, as has aluminum foil crinkled and glued to insert plates: the crinkling adds to the flash produced by the lure in the water.

Glitter, available in many colors and occasionally different particle sizes, can be added to casting resin when it is mixed with the catalyst for random flash in an otherwise clear lure. Resin may also be colored with transparent dyes available from craft stores or the shop where the casting resin and catalyst are purchased. If these dyes are used properly, prism, mirrored, eyed, or other molded-in inserts will still show through readily, even though the head has a definite color.

Tubing. To run the leader through the lure, a hole is necessary. For this, brass tubing is most often used: the tube is placed in the mold used to make the lure. Brass tubing of about 1/8- to 1/4-inch in diameter is good, and 3/16-inch is a good compromise. In any case, make sure the tubing is large enough to accommodate the diameter of the leader you plan to use. A little play to get the leader through the tubing is fine, but avoid too much play or looseness. Although other tubing could be used, brass tubing is best; (copper or aluminum would be close second choices) because they will deburr easily to prevent leader abrasion and cutting, and are easy to cut and shape in the home workshop. Brass tubing is available at hobby shops, copper tubing at hobby and automative shops.

Wood. Cedar is the most commonly used wood for making offshore wood plugs, which is why they are usually called cedar plugs. Other wood can be used, including basswood, fine-grain pine, oak, and poplar. These woods are different in quality from one another, and some require more care in drilling and shaping. Others, like oak, are tough but prone to split if not worked carefully. In all cases, wood choices and construction methods are identical to those covered in Chapter 9.

STEP-BY-STEP ASSEMBLY OF BEAD LURES

Trolling skirts of bead lures, often called "hoochies," "hoochy trolls," or just plain "vinyl-skirt" lures are effective and have lots of action. They come in a wide variety of sizes and colors and will take anything from inshore bluefish to offshore tuna, wahoo, and marlin.

To make these lures, you need only the skirts, egg sinkers, single saltwater hooks, beads (usually tri-beads), and wire, mono, or chain for the rigging. Crimping pliers are necessary if you work with wire and leader sleeves.

Hooks will range from 4/0 to 10/0 in size, although smaller or larger hooks are possible. Make sure they are saltwater style, stainless, tinned, or cadmium-plated, and with a welded eye in the larger sizes.

Mono and cable can vary from as light as forty-pound to as heavy as two hundred-pound test, depending upon the size of the fish sought and the size of the lure.

Beads come in a number of styles and sizes. Those chosen for these lures are the tri-bead style, which stacks up easily and gives the appearance of a segmented, scaled body. The similar "snowflake" beads also stack up and create a lifelike, flashy, and scaled appearance, though they are more fragile than the tri-beads. Beads come in many colors. Various-size bags, both of mixed- and same-color beads, are available. All are available at craft and hobby shops and through some tackle shops.

The advantage of tri-beads or snowflake beads on these lures is that they will stack up almost like bricks or building blocks, to give the lure body some bulk and "life." Regular round, tapered "spaghetti," or other beads will not do this and will create only a thin line of color in the lure. T style beads will work, but are not generally used. The stacking beads, as a result of the way they lock together, give a segmented or scaled appearance. As the sun strikes the surface of the stacked beads, it creates flash and spectacular highlights, similar to the flash that would occur with a live baitfish. In addition, the snowflake beads in particular will catch the water as they skip on the surface and will leave a trail of bubbles —"smoke" in the parlance of the big-game angler. This trail of bubbles or smoke is particularly good for attracting gamefish.

The beads serve several purposes. First, they make an easy-to-construct spacer on the leader to separate the hook from the egg sinker. This sinker gives the lure some trolling weight and also fills out the head of the skirt. Second, the beads provide lifelike flash and color that resemble ocean baitfish. Naturally, you can build this up with colors that are attractive to a particular species or effective in a particular geographic area. Third, they give the leader between the egg sinker and the hook some stiffness or body.

Vinyl skirts come in lengths ranging from about 3 to 16 inches, and in single or double style. The single style are of a single color; those that are double are in essence two skirts "welded" together. Often these contain a single color underskirt with a slightly shorter overskirt in flake or glitter colors.

The egg sinkers that fill up the head of the vinyl skirts and give the lure trolling weight and bulk range from small 3/4-ounce sizes for small, thin skirts to 3- and 4-ounce sinkers for large skirts.

We'll work with mono to make a basic lure, although there are variations to be covered later. Begin by choosing the right size mono for your quarry. This might be fifty-to eighty-pound mono for inshore species, to one hundred- or two hundred-pound mono for offshore species.

Tie or snell one end of the mono to an offshore hook, again picking a size consistent with the size of the fish sought and the finished lure. Use a secure knot such as a clinch, Palomar, or improved clinch, or use crimped leader sleeves to fasten the loop. Another excellent alternative is to use a hook snell (see the section on rigging hooks in this chapter, as well as the drawings in Appendix E); this will provide a straighter connection between the hook and the leader. A third alternative is to use a double overhand knot pulled down tight and two leader sleeves crimped in place to make a strong, secure loop.

At this point, decide if you want the lure with or without a leader. Many offshore lures come built on the leader, so that you have a coil of mono or wire ranging from 10 to 20 feet long. This is probably the best way to make lures, since by means of a loop tied in the end, the leader can be snapped directly and quickly onto a heavy snap at the end of the double line of any offshore outfit. An alternative is to make the lure with a short leader of only a foot or two, this to be tied to a heavy shock leader. The advantage here is in lure storage, either in tackle drawers on the boat, in a large saltwater tackle box, or in a soft roll-up lure pouch.

Once you make this decision, cut off the appropriate length of mono and begin by threading the beads one at a time onto the mono leader. The

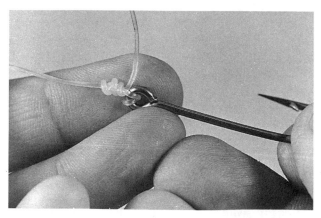

The first step in making any bead-style trolling lure is to use a good knot or snell to attach the hook.

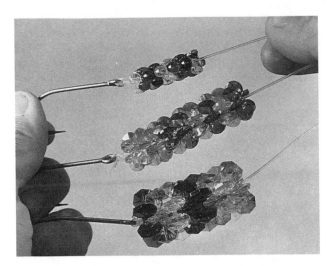

Various sizes and colors of beads can be used, but most are the tri-beads or snowflake beads that nest together when stacked. Different colors are shown here, although beads can be single- or multi-color.

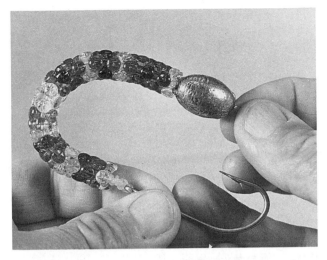

Completed bead body with nesting tri-beads and egg sinker for weight and to hold the skirt.

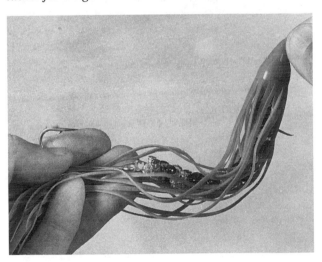

Completed lure with vinyl skirt added to the lure. The egg sinker is hidden under the skirt head.

beads can be mixed in color, of one single color, or in segments of several beads each of a particular color, the segments separated by other color segments and repeated as desired.

There is no rule for the number of beads that go onto the leader, but because beads serve as spacers, check length frequently. For most lures, you will want the end of the skirt to hit at just about the end of the bend of the hook, although each angler has a preference for this. Add beads until you get to the point where the adition of the egg sinker will allow the skirt to fall at this point.

Add the egg sinker, checking to make sure that there are no burrs that might interfere with the straight axis of the lure. Then add the skirt. Because most vinyl skirts are made by dipping forms into liquid vinyl, you will have to punch a hole through the end of the point in the head of the skirt or use scissors or cutters to cut off the tip end to make a hole.

Check again to make sure that the skirt length is appropriate for the lure and make adjustments as necessary. Adjustments can include adding or removing beads or slightly trimming the skirt. Cut the end of the mono or wire (if this was not done before) to the length required. Make this long for a leader attachment, short — 1 foot at most — to use as a lure separate from the leader.

To finish, make a loop in the end using a perfection loop knot, surgeon's loop knot, or figure-eight loop knot. Another alternative is to use a double overhand knot pulled into a tight loop and secured with two leader sleeves.

BEAD-LURE VARIATIONS

There are variations to the above. One is to use two or more skirts in line with bead spacers between them to create a longer lure or one with more bead and skirt colors. To do this, proceed as before. In place of one large egg sinker, add a small one that, together with all the egg sinkers under the skirts, will total the desired weight and balance of the lure. Once the first skirt is added, add more beads, then add a second sinker and second skirt. Continue with more beads, an egg sinker, and another skirt if you wish to add a third skirt for a longer lure. For this, fewer beads are usually used ahead of the main skirt, as well as a shorter skirt.

If you do not wish to add additional weight to the lure, you can use a large bead or poly-foam ball (available from craft shops) as a "stop" to make up some bulk on which the head of the skirt can rest. In this case, be sure to use a large egg sinker at the head of the forward skirt. Although the poly-foam balls are worth a try, often it is best to use sinkers to give the middle and tail of the lure some bulk and weight to prevent it from flopping and possibly tangling when trolled.

Another variation is to use a few beads and a tubing spacer to separate the beads from the egg sinker and keep the skirt in the right position. For this, any type of flexible plastic tubing can be used, provided it is stiff enought to prevent the lure from collapsing under the pressures of all-day trolling. Plastic tubing from craft stores, from tackle shops, off the handles of shopping bags (these are vinyl tubes of varying colors), and even thin clear-plastic tubing from hardware, hobby, and pet shops will all work well. Thick tubing of 1/4-inch or larger diameter is often available from hardware stores; thin tubing is available from pet stores (as aquarium air hose), or hobby shops (as model airplane fuel line).

To use tubing, begin as before to tie or snell the hook, and add several beads. Then cut a length of tubing that will serve as a spacer between the beads and the egg sinker. Add the tubing, then the egg sinker and skirt, as before. Check for proper length and adjust where necessary by cutting the tubing, adding or removing beads, or trimming the skirt as desired. A variation of this is to use clear-plastic polyethylene tubing, threaded with an inner core of braided mylar as is used for saltwater fly tying. Remove the cord core of the braided mylar and then thread the mylar through the plastic tubing. Thread the mono leader through the center of the mylar. You may wish to add some waterproof glue to the plastic tubing to prevent the mylar core from sliding out.

It is also possible to use mono with a section of chain as a spacer. This will lack beads but is an advantage if trolling for toothy fish such as bluefish, king mackerel, or wahoo.

If you build a lure this way, first choose chain that will hold up in salt water. Interlocking copper or brass safety chain works well. Also be sure to check the pound test of this chain to make sure it is the strongest part of the lure. Add the hook to the chain by using a large split ring, preferably in brass for long life in salt water. If possible, weld it shut to prevent its opening during the hard fight of a big fish. Measure the chain for the right

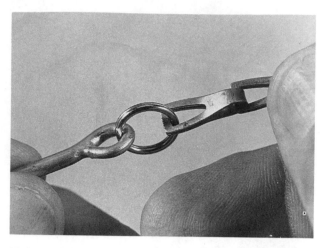

For toothy fish or more durability and strength, chain can be used in place of mono. For this, use welded jump rings or heavy-duty split rings (shown) to attach the chain to the hook eye.

length as a spacer between the hook and the egg sinker. Cut the chain, add a welded split ring and tie in mono, or use leader sleeves on heavy mono or braided wire. If you use safety chain or some other type of interlocking chain links, a split ring is a must because the sharp chain surfaces can cut mono and even abrade wire. Tie the mono or sleeve the mono or wire (using a double overhand knot and two crimping sleeves) to the split ring, add the egg sinker, and finish with the skirt. An alternative is to use heavy single-strand wire as a connector link on which the egg sinker, beads, and skirt are placed; the wire is secured to the hook with a wrapped eye, and a second eye at the forward end is used as a line- or leader-tie.

Using any of these methods, it is possible to make a complete assortment of offshore lures in one evening. This simplicity even makes it possible to thread or assemble the lures while watching television, and their effectiveness makes them well worth the little bit of time it takes to put some together.

Best of all, these lures can easily be changed or repaired. If some snowflake beads become broken from a hard strike, or a skirt becomes damaged or torn or a hook becomes rusted or bent, it is easy to cut either end of the wire or mono, remove the damaged parts, and replace with new beads, skirts, or hooks. Thus, there is no such thing as a lure that is "bad" and has to be thrown out. Any lure can have parts added to it to make it completely new, or if in really bad shape, stripped and used for parts for other new lures or lures needing repairs.

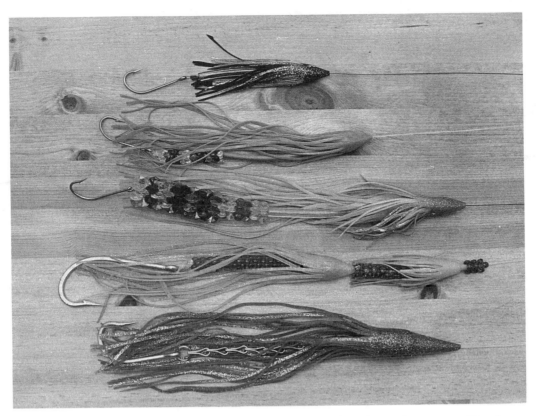

Various sizes and styles of single- and double-skirt bead and chain-spacer trolling lures. All are easy and quick to make.

MOLDED-PLASTIC LURES

While casting resin could be used for making almost any type of solid lure, it is usually reserved for offshore trolling lures. Casting resin is heavier than water and thus will sink, while most bass, walleye, and other freshwater and saltwater lures are floating/diving styles, in that they will float at rest and dive as a result of a bill or lip built into the front of the lure. Conceivably, casting resin could be used to make clear, glitter-filled, or colored (opaque or translucent) jig heads, sinking plugs or crankbaits, saltwater surface lures (these are worked rapidly, usually have a sloping face, and thus will not sink when fished), spinner bodies, spinnerbait and buzzbait heads, some "spoons," and various miscellaneous lures. In most cases, there are easier, quicker, better, and cheaper ways to make these lures or parts. But there are no alternatives for offshore lures, however, other than in the wood bodies that are occasionally used (and discussed later in this chapter).

Molded offshore lures are typically short, stubby cylinders of casting resin with molded-in tubes for leaders and rigging, and cast-in color, prism tape, glitter, eyes, or other attractors. As heads, they are finished into lures with the addition of a slip-on or wrap-on skirt, usually of vinyl material.

ETI, the major manufacturer of casting resin for hobby and fishing use, suggests that any number of materials can be used for molds for such lures (in addition to their Mold Builder latex material). They do suggest that, if possible, it is best to stay with polypropylene materials for molds, to avoid plastic foams (such as foam coffee cups or similar containers), and also to avoid any plastic that might be harmed by the high heat generated by the curing resin-and-catalyst mix. The problem here is not so much with the mold, which is usually disposable, and which in any case can be replaced, but with the finish on the completed lure, which can made rough or pitted as the resin attacks the mold container.

PLASTIC LURE MOLDING STEPS

A good workplace for molding is a must. You will need a bench or bench-type work space in an area with adequate ventilation. Casting resin is highly volatile and does emit a harmful vapor.

Materials needed for molding cast plastic offshore lures. The mold builder to the right allows making a mold from an existing lure, discussed in Chapter 16 — Making Lead and Soft Plastic Lure Molds.

Without proper ventilation, severe headaches and possibly other medical problems from prolonged and continued inhalation could result. Since the product is combustible, do not use it near an open flame. A kitchen countertop completely covered with heavy cardboard or scrap plywood will work well, *PROVIDED THAT THE STOVE OR OVEN DOES NOT HAVE A FLAME PILOT LIGHT*. Do not use casting resin around any gas stoves or ovens, or even near a gas clothes dryer. If you work in the kitchen, be sure to use the stove's exhaust fan and avoid using the kitchen for food preparation until all resin fumes are completely removed. Make sure there is no food open or improperly stored. As with lead-molding in the kitchen (see Chapter 4) make sure others are not or will not be using the kitchen at the same time. To avoid possible accidents and spills, make sure children and pets are kept from the work area at all times.

If your kitchen is not suitable as a work space, consider other well-ventilated areas, such as a garage (with open doors), carport, deck, patio, or porch. If you work in a basement or any other room in the house, make sure several windows are open and that there is plenty of cross ventilation. Ed LaFley of ETI states there should be no problem for any hobbyist using casting resin for a half-hour or so at a time, but those working with the resin repeatedly or for long hours at a time

should consider getting a good mask. This does *not* mean a simple filter-type painters' mask but instead a good laboratory/industrial-style mask.

Before beginning the casting, have a definite plan for the lure you will make, the number to be cast, and the steps involved. In addition, you must have sufficient molds for the number of lures you plan to make in one session. Molds can be disposable — destroyed when removing the lure — or reusable, in which case the lure must slip or pop out of the mold. Mold possibilities include the plastic bottles and jars that contain spices, herbs, decorative cake granules, bouillon, film, and so on. The best are those in the range of about 1 to 2 inches in diameter and about 2 1/2 to 4 inches long. In some cases — particularly with the spice containers — the bottles will have varying constrictions, such as necks and decorative indentations, that require them to be destroyed in order to remove the lure, but they do make workable molds. For example, a plastic bottle currently used by McCormick for spices is a little over 4 inches long, 1 3/4 inches in diameter, and has a long constricted neck. That neck is ideal for attaching a wrapped skirt. Since these bottles are completely clear, it is also possible fill them with the casting resin (colored or with additives as desired) and leave them on as a "skin" over the body of the lure. Naturally, with colored or frosted containers you will want to remove the mold. Several other spice companies have similar small clear-plastic bottles that have constricted necks for easy skirt attachment.

You will need to plan how to make the lure. Jim Rizzuto, in an article in the February 1986 *Salt Water Sportsman*, outlines a method of first molding inserts to hold eyes and prism tape from Tic Tac breath-mint boxes, using 35-mm plastic film cans to mold a tail piece (to hold the skirt), and inserting the cast results into a larger bouillon container to make the finished lure, with a large prism-and-eye-insert and smaller round tail stock for the skirt. In essence, this molding process becomes a two-step operation, first in molding the rectangular Tic Tac and round 35-mm can inserts, then in completing the lure in the bouillon container. Jim suggests drilling the completed lure in order to glue in a brass- or copper-tubing leader hole.

Others suggest carefully drilling the mold to hold the 3/16-inch (the typical size used) brass or copper tubing for the leader-fastening insert eyes and prism tape to this tubing, then molding the lure in one shot. Naturally, there are endless variations of these two basic methods. Let's take each of them step by step and cover all the procedures.

ONE-STEP LURE MOLDING

1. You will need the following: A short length of brass or copper tubing about 3/16-inch in diameter, a mold of the proper shape and size for the lure you wish to make (this could be a spice jar, silastic rubber mold, or latex mold), casting resin, casting catalyst, mixing cup (usually a paper-type cup—not a poly-foam cup), stirring stick (such as a craft or popsicle stick), any insert materials (such as plastic eyes, prism tape, mirrors, glitter, dyes or opaque pigments for the casting resin, sequins). You will also need a vinyl skirt or skirt wrap material, hooks, leader material (cable, single-strand wire or mono), leader sleeves, crimping pliers, and bead spacers, if necessary, for positioning the hook.

2. Gauge the amount of plastic needed by filling the mold with water and measuring the water. This will give you the volume of plastic needed, less, of course, any inserts. If the inserts are large, you may wish to add them to the mold before adding the water (they do not have to be glued onto the brass tubing at this time) to more accurately determine the volume required. Dry the mold and any insert materials completely before casting.

3. Most plastic bottles or jars of the type we will use have a small mold mark in the bottom center. Some jar tops (used to help center the inserted metal tubing) have a similar mark. Drill through both the bottom and the top with the exact drill size required to insert the brass or copper tubing. Carefully measure the tubing diameter first.

4. Add the insert materials to the brass tubing. You can do this by using double-sided tape (carpet tape), craft adhesives or glues, airplane glues, or epoxy. If you use tape, be sure the insert materials will stay in place in the mold and will not loosen while the plastic is curing. Heavy items such as large plastic eyes and mirrors are best glued in place using a five-minute epoxy.

Glue the inserts onto the brass rod, making sure that inserts on both sides of the tube are in the same position and parallel. Carefully insert the brass tube into the mold through the hole in the bottom. If there is play in the hole, use masking tape to stop leaks. In any case, use masking tape to secure the tubing in the proper position in the mold so that the inserts are accurately placed. Do this with all the molds you will fill at one time.

5. Using the measurements you previously determined with water, pour casting resin into the waxed-paper-style cup, which you have marked at the precise level where the correct volume is reached. Add the catalyst: Follow the manufacturer's instructions for the proper amount. For ETI products, this will be about two to five drops of catalyst per ounce of resin, based on a resin and room temperature of 70°F. Do *not* add excessive catalyst, because this can cause the completed lure to fracture. In this case less is better than more: Too little catalyst will only prolong the curing process, it will not ruin the lure.

Use a stirring stick to carefully and thoroughly fold the catalyst into the casting resin. Be sure to scrape along the sides and bottom for a thorough mix, stirring for about one minute. Do not beat the resin to a lather, since this will add bubbles that are unattractive and difficult to remove. At this time, and according to the manufacturer's directions, add any dyes or pigments to the liquid plastic. Dyes are usually used because they will make for a translucent lure in which the inserts and eyes will show. Pigments make for an opaque lure, eliminating the need for inserts.

If you use a release agent to ease removal of

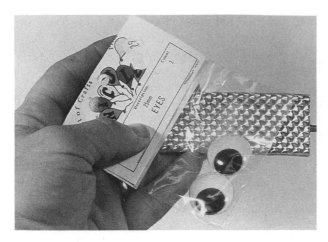

Eyes from craft stores, such as these large 1-inch craft eyes, are often used on foil and other inserts that go into the offshore cast plastic lures.

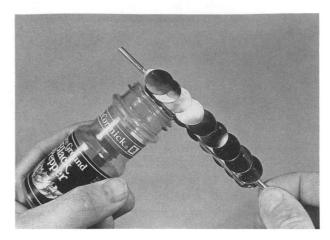

Insert in which shiny sequins are glued to a small strip of wood, through-drilled to receive the tubing shown.

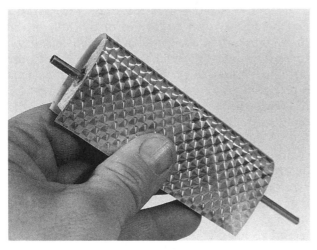

Checking a strip of self adhesive foil to see if it will go around a wood insert body made for insertion into a cast plastic body.

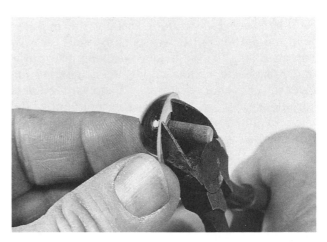

Adding solid eyes from craft supplies often requires cutting off the stem to glue the eye onto the flat insert sheet.

Insert sheet made from several layers of wood, built up and glued together around the central tubing sleeve.

Eyes glued to a flat insert sheet, covered first with self-adhesive foil and designed to fit into a discarded spice bottle for molding the lure.

Insert sheet and tubing in the spice bottle ready for molding.

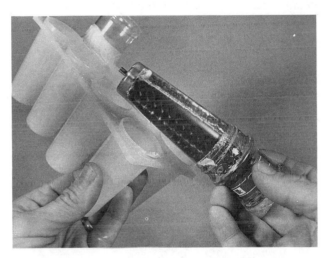

Other plastic containers can also be used for molding. Here, a popsicle tray makes tapered lures. The collar around the back, not yet removed, is from a spice bottle.

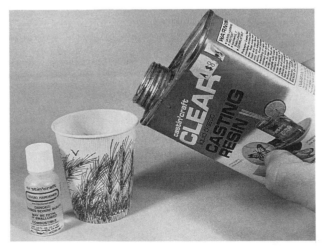

To mold, first pour out a measured amount of casting resin sufficient for the mold or molds to be filled.

Add hardener or catalyst, using only a few drops per ounce. Too much catalyst will cause the lure to cure too rapidly and crack. Experimentation is a must here to develop the right proportions for the molds and conditions.

the lure from the mold, add it now. Once it is properly mixed, pour the resin slowly and carefully into the mold. For this you may wish to tilt the tubing holding the inserts to one side for easier pouring and to lessen the possibility of spills. Once the mold is filled, slowly return the tubing to a straight upright position. Place the drilled cap over the tubing and rest it on the bottle to hold the tubing in a straight vertical position. If there is no cap, use masking tape to support the tubing.

In all of the above, work at your arms' length to keep from inhaling fumes from the casting resin. Curing time will be at least a few hours and will depend upon the amount of catalyst used, the volume and size of the casting, room temperature, the resin temperature when it was poured, the color additives used, and humidity.

6.   Once it has cured, remove the lure from the mold. In some cases, for instance as with using spice bottles, the mold will have to be broken off the lure. Do this with care, using pliers to peel the mold off of the lure, or use a knife or razor blade to partially score the mold lengthwise (carefully!) on both sides before you peel it off. Do not cut all the way through the mold, because this will score the lure — the fish won't mind, but it will make for a less-attractive lure.

If the mold does not have constrictions that require you to break it, it can usually be separated from the lure and the lure worked free. Often, you can roll the mold between your hands to separate it from the lure, gradually working the lure out. Once the mold and lure are loose, you

Completed head with foil insert and eyes, still in the spice bottle and with the tubing not yet trimmed.

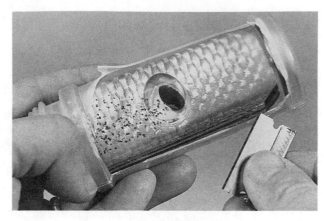

Mold partially removed, using care and a razor blade to cut away a little of the mold at a time.

To remove the lure from the spice bottle, use a sharp utility knife to cut carefully along the sides to pry out the lure. Do not cut deeply as this will scar the lure.

Cracks in a lure, often a result of too much catalyst. This may or may not harm the effectiveness of the lure, depending upon the extent and location of the cracks.

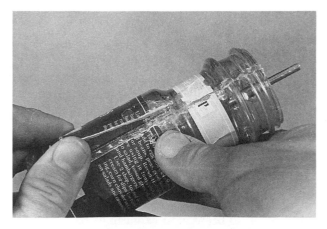

Beginning to remove the cut spice bottle by prying it off the lure. Often rolling the mold between your hands first will ease separation of the mold from the lure.

One way to smooth the area where the skirt will be attached is to turn the lure on a lathe.

can also pull on the leader tubing to force the lure out of the mold.

7. Once the lure is out of the mold, examine it and make sure that it is completely dry and hard. If not, set it aside to cure completely, and do not handle it. If it is completely dry, shiny, and hard, wrap it in rags, clamp it lightly in a vise, and cut off both ends of the leader tubing flush with the ends of the lure. If necessary, polish the ends of the tubing with a file and then use a countersink to polish the hole in the tubing and remove any burrs.

There are variations of this basic method. For example, you can mold the lure without tubing and later drill a hole through the lure. This does have some disadvantages, though. First, it is not always possible to drill straight through the lure unless you have a drill press, something not every angler has. And even this requires the construction of a rig to hold the lure absolutely vertical while drilling. Second, most lures use inserted flash materials and eyes, so that these still have to be placed in the lure in some way. These can be built or assembled on wood or plastic sheets and inserted into the mold before pouring but must be kept in the center for best results. And there still must be enough space in the middle to drill the leader-tubing hole. Third, once the lure is molded and drilled, the tubing must be added and glued into place.

MULTIPLE-STEP LURE MOLDING

The second method of making offshore cast-resin lures involves several steps, such as those mentioned in Jim Rizzuto's article. In this method the basics are the same, it is just that there are two or more extra steps to complete the lure.

1. Use small Tic Tac breath-mint container and film-can molds to fill with resin. If desired, these can be filled with colored resin, which will make for a contrasting inner color to the clear-resin outer lure coat.

2. Once these lure components are cured, remove the mold from them.

3. Glue the Tic-Tac-mold component to the film-can component end to end.

4. Glue any eyes, prism tape, or similar additions to the sides of the flat Tic-Tac component.

5. Place these glued inserts into a larger mold (usually a round bouillon jar), with the tail stock (film-can component) up. Add clear casting resin to fill this mold and allow it to cure.

6. Once it has cured, pop the lure out of the

Drilling a cast plastic insert piece for the brass or copper tubing that will serve as a leader guide and sleeve. This cast piece was molded from a Tic-Tac box.

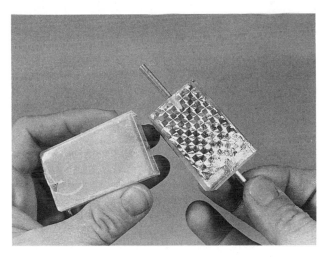

Molding insert piece, with tubing inserted, removed from a Tic-Tac box. The box is cracked, as they often are, as a result of hammering on the mold to remove the insert.

mold, drill straight through it (preferably with a drill press), and glue a brass or copper leader tube into place.

7. Cut the ends of the leader tubing, file to smooth them, polish with a countersink, and the lure is ready to have the skirt added.

Variations of this method are to use shaped wood slats, available in various widths at any good lumberyard, cut to the appropriate length with one end cut down to fit into a film can or similar mold used for the tail stock. This eliminates the need to cast the first component, reducing the amount of casting resin needed for any one lure.

The insert-eyes and any prism or tape can be glued to the wood's sides and the cured insert placed tail-stock-up into the round bouillon-jar (or similar) mold.

Another alternative is to use this method and to drill the wood and tail stock, insert leader tubing, then complete the casting in the larger mold. Other possibilities are bound to occur to you. Some anglers, to avoid the use of constructed molds that must be destroyed and the several steps involved in the second method, will mold a single cylinder with inserts and tubing, then use a coarse sander or grinder to shape a thinner neck or flange, to which the skirt is attached. Finally, polish the lure with boat or car polish to shine the plastic.

The main thing is to consider all the steps and requirements first, plan completely, and try one lure before committing to many lures in one pouring.

STEP-BY-STEP
CONSTRUCTION OF WOOD LURES

Several types of offshore lures can be made from wood. Though they will lack the visual appeal of the clear-resin cast offshore lures, wood heads can be carved or turned on a lathe and painted. The lathe is the best way to go, using the techniques outlined in Chapter 9. With a wood lathe and using closet rods, hardwood dowels, or blocks or poplar and oak sold specifically for lathe work, such lures are easy. In fact, although the shapes are different, they aren't much longer or more difficult to make than a big freshwater plug is. Most offshore lures will vary from as small as about 3/4-inch diameter to as large as 2 inches in diameter and range from about 2 1/2 inches to about 6 inches long. Some teasers—lures used to attract fish to the baits but that lack hooks—are larger.

Using standard lathe practices, you can make blunt-nose lures, round-head lures, or cup-faced lures, all with necks or flanges for adding skirts. Cutting the completed lure face at an angle once it is out of the lathe will make slant-headed lures that alternately skip, bounce, and dive.

In addition, it is possible to drill a number of holes straight through the heads or at an angle, using a hand drill, although a drill press is better, to make lures that smoke (the multiple holes cause bubbles). If you're not accurate with a hand drill and you lack a drill press, one way around this is to take a square-cross-section block, run a

centerline down each face, and carefully cut wide slots (about 1/4" wide, 1/4" deep) with a hand saw. Make four 1/4" slots, one on each face. Then place the block in a lathe and turn it to size and shape. Cut it to a size that will just fit into a piece of PVC, CPVC, or ABS pipe of about 1 to 1 1/2 inches in diameter. Make sure that the slots in the side of the block remain so that you will have straight-through holes in between the wood block and the wall of the pipe. The result will be smoke holes that will create bubbles. The outside of the lure will be the plastic pipe, painted, while the inside will be the wood core. The wood is glued into the plastic pipe and then the whole lure is painted with several base coats of white followed by a finish color.

In addition to offshore trolling lures, cedar plugs are also easy to make. These are popular for early-season trolling for tuna on the Northeast coast and are just what they sound like: cedar-wood plugs, usually in a chunky cigar shape, with multiple hooks or a single hook.

These can be made by using the same methods outlined in Chapter 9. Typically, they have a metal or lead head and cedar body with a line-tie in the head for the line and one single hook in the tail. The cedar body can be turned on a lathe, the head molded in a plaster or Silastic rubber mold (using the type required for high-heat lead molding), and the two parts glued and fitted together. For saltwater fishing, the completed lure should be through-drilled with a wire leader run through the lure for a solid line-to hook connection.

Making a bubbler for a lure by cutting four grooves around the perimeter of a dowel for passage of air and water through the lure.

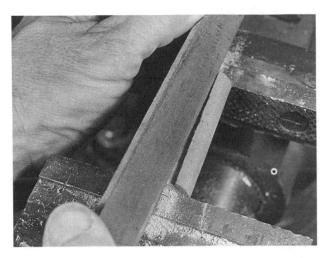

Using a file to smooth the cut grooves for the bubbler.

Completed bubbler insert, here ready to be glued into a piece of PVC pipe section to make a bubbler that is part of a lure, or can be threaded onto the leader ahead of the lure for added froth — "smoke" in the parlance of the offshore angler.

SOFT-BODIED LURES

You can make soft-bodied lures using plastic bottles and jars, aluminum, wood, or Silastic rubber RTV molds. For this, the methods of molding are almost the same as outlined in Chapter 7. The differences are as follows:

Because you will be making saltwater lures, you must add a considerable amount of hardener to the plastic to make for a tougher lure. You will have to experiment with this, but remember that commercial soft-vinyl lures are very tough for the severe trolling conditions under which they are used.

You will be making far larger lures than the soft-plastic worms used for freshwater fishing, so use a sufficiently large pot and plastic to melt enough to fill the mold.

Molds for these lures are basically cylinders that are similar in size to molds for trolling lures. You can use bouillon jars, other small jars, 35-mm films cans, or spice bottles, as previously outlined. You can also make your own molds, using wood, Silastic rubber, or small aluminum juice cans. If you use Silastic rubber, you will have to make the mold using a model of the lure you wish to duplicate.

You will not be able to mold the skirts that are a part of commercial lures. All you can effectively make is the cylindrical head — the skirt must still be added or wrapped on.

You can use inserts such as plastic or wood slats, to which eyes, mirrors, prism tape, sequins, or other additions are attached. These will not show nearly as well as they will through the clear, hard-plastic casting resin.

ADDING SKIRTS

Once the molded parts of the lures are complete and polished (they can be polished), skirts are added. There are two basic ways to do this. One involves using a ready-molded skirt, such as those used on bead-chain lures and resembling a large, thick, shredded glove finger. The second involves using strips of skirting material wrapped and sometimes glued in place.

For the first method, buy ready-made vinyl skirts such as Psychotail replacement skirts or similar brands. Cut the head off so that you get a tight fit onto the tail or lure or tail stock, whichever method you use. For one method, use a good vinyl glue on the flange or neck and slide the skirt onto this area. If the glue is not holding securely, or if there is not a neck or step-down to the skirt area to prevent water pressure from ripping the skirt off, you may wish to use wire, cord, dental floss, or braided-nylon fishing line to tie the skirt in place and secure it. Use many wraps, but do not wrap too tightly because this will tend to cut the skirt.

Another method is to cut the head off the skirt, reverse it, and glue the reversed side (the outside) to the neck or head flange. In this, the head end will be pointed toward the tail, the skirt end will be up over the forward part of the plastic head. Secure with a wrapping of cord, nylon fishing line,

Usually several skirts are combined, using flexible glues to cement one skirt inside of another.

Here a silver skirt is being glued inside of a black skirt.

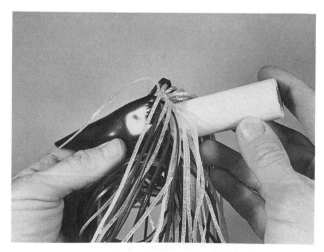

A dowel placed inside of the head allows cutting the skirt at the right position for stretching and gluing onto the head.

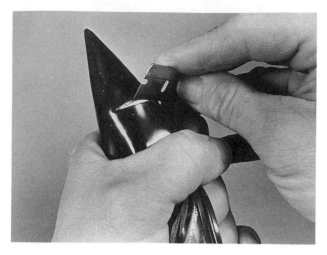

Using a razor blade to cut around the perimeter of the head of the skirt for attaching to the cast plastic head.

or wire. Many of the commercial lure manufacturers use fifty-pound test Dacron line.

If you use wire, twist the ends to secure them, and lay them flat against the body. Then, slowly and carefully roll the skirt (almost as if you were pulling or rolling off a pair of surgical or rubber kitchen gloves) to pull the outside down over the neck and to hide the wrapping holding the skirt in place.

It is possible to use both methods with two or more skirts, making the inner skirts of different colors than the outer skirt. Although three skirts are sometimes used, two skirts are more common. It is also possible to find single skirts in which the underside is a completely different color (usually

Using automobile polish to clean and polish the head after the skirt is glued in place.

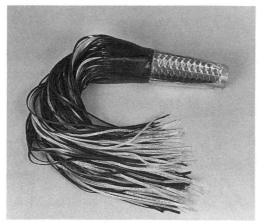

Completed lure, unrigged but otherwise ready to fish.

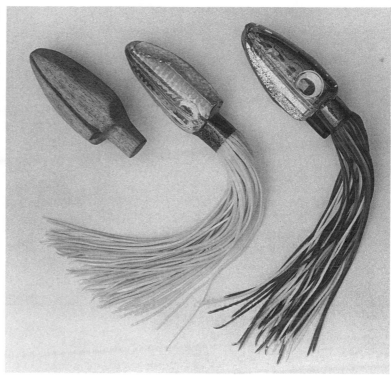

Example of steps in making a lure from a wood prototype. The wood prototype serves as a model for using Mold Builder (see Chapter 16— Making Lead and Soft Plastic Lure Molds), with examples of completed lures to the right.

white or light) than the upper side, giving the appearance of two colors in one skirt.

Yet another method involves using strips of skirts and wrapping them around the neck or flange of the lure head. These strips are available from Mold Craft in an 11 1/2-inch by 3 1/2-inch size, in twenty colors. In use, the strips are tied in place after being glued to the neck. Most of the commercial lure manufacturers use Zap glue. Similar to the various "crazy" glues, Zap glue (originally the highly expensive Eastman 910) is not completely waterproof but is highly water-resistant and has proven the best so far in gluing the soft vinyl skirts to the hard casting-resin heads.

One skirt of about 3 1/2-inches width will wrap one lure with a neck of about 1 inch in diameter. If you work with larger lures, the skirts can be cut with a razor blade, glued, and wrapped in place. In both methods, some anglers use a foil tape wrapped around the head of the skirt to cover the cord wrappings. The tape can be glued in place with the Zap glue or with a PVC glue that serves as a good "weld" to the soft-vinyl skirts.

RIGGING HOOKS

Rigging is done with single-strand wire, mono, or twisted-wire cable: Twisted-wire cable and heavy mono are most commonly used. You will need an offshore hook appropriate to the size of the lure and the fish sought. Leader sleeves are a must with wire, and usually with mono also. Be sure to use the right leader sleeves with the right tool (point-opposing-cup with the round sleeves, cup-opposing-cup with the oval or figure-eight sleeves). Be sure also to use the right-size sleeve to hold the wire or mono securely. Heavy mono can be snelled to the hook to make single or tandem rigs.

To make single-hook rigs, first decide on the test and type or leader to be used. Then snell, tie, or secure with leader sleeves the hook to the leader. If you work with mono, you have all three choices; if you work with cable, you can only use leader sleeves.

To use leader sleeves to attach the hook, make a double overhand knot around the hook eye. The easy way to do this is to first place two leader sleeves on the leader. Run the leader through the hook eye twice, then wrap the end of the wire twice around the resulting loop. Pull the cable into a small loop and adjust the length of the end to fit the two leader sleeves a few inches apart. Run the end of the leader through the first sleeve and slide the sleeve close to the loop. Crimp tight with crimping pliers. Twist the end of the leader about 180 degrees around the standing wire and slip the second leader sleeve in place. Make sure the end of the wire is not exposed through the leader sleeve. Crimp to secure.

The method just described will make a free-swinging hook, and there is a method to make the hook straight and stiff with the wire cable. Often this or a variation is called a "pro rig," in reference to the number of serious anglers who use it. For this rig, first place two sleeves on the leader, then run the leader through the eye of the hook toward the gap or hook point. Then wrap the cable up, over, and around the hook shank in back of the hook eye and back out the eye down toward the point. Makes these wraps as tight as possible. Secure with the leader sleeves as before. The result is a hook that remains stiff and in line with the leader cable.

If you use mono, it is sometimes possible to tie knots, such as the clinch, improved clinch, and palomar knots, although these become more difficult with large-size mono. Tie these knots carefully and tightly, and use pliers to pull up the ends. It is also possible to use leader sleeves (some special leader sleeves are made just for mono) using the same connections (double over-hand knot and figure-eight wrap) previously mentioned for cable.

Snelling hooks is often the preferred way to rig hooks on heavy mono. In this, the mono is not run through the eye of the hook. Rather, the eye is used as a "stop" to prevent the snell from sliding off. To make a snell, hold the mono on and parallel to the hook shank, and allow it to extend past the bend of the hook. Loop the mono in a circle so that the end lies next to the first part of the loop of mono on the hook shank. Hold the mono securely and use the resulting loop to wrap around the two overlapping strands of mono and hook shank. The wrap is from the bend toward the eye, with the first wrap crossing over the mono and subsequent wraps evenly made around the two pieces of mono and the hook shank. Make at least five turns, then finish by holding the shank and mono loops securely while pulling the end strand of mono. This will gradually decrease the size of the loop until there is no loop and the mono ends are completely under the wrap. Position this so that the snell is up against the eye of the hook and the leader runs from under the eye. Finish by grasping the tag end with pliers, holding the leader end securely, and pulling both simultaneously to tighten the knot.

Tandem hooks are common in offshore lures; the second hook is on the same leader or is attached by a second short section of cable. With cable, you will need a short length of cable and the appropriate sleeves, along with some straight-jawed snap-ring pliers and some short lengths of surgical tubing of a size that will hold the leader on the hook securely. An alternative to the surgical hose method is to use shrink tubing, which will tighten with heat, or to tie the rig in place with braided fishing line or cord.

Note: Although this description comes after the description for making a single-hook cable rig, in actuality you would make the second rig first, then attach it to the forward hook. This reduces cable waste and also makes it far easier to slip the one or two pieces of surgical hose onto the forward hook. Otherwise, you would have to run the surgical tubing down over the complete cable leader.

Begin by securing the hook with the tight figure-eight pro-rig wrap. Then run the cable forward and through the eye of the forward hook. Slip a sleeve or two onto the cable. Position the cable through the eye at the exact position desired for the two hooks. How you hold the cable and hooks now is critical to the resulting rig. Most anglers like a rig in which the two hooks are at 90 degrees or 180 degrees to each other. To do this, you must position the hooks this way before making any bends, since any changes will be impossible later.

Remember that if you fish by the International Game Fish Association (IGFA) rules for tournaments or records, you cannot have the eyes of the hooks less than a hook's length apart, and no more than 12 inches apart (eye to eye) in lures (18 inches in baits).

At the chosen position for the hooks, bend the cable into a loop and slip the end through the leader sleeve and crimp. Repeat with the second sleeve (if one is used) and crimp. Place a small piece of the surgical hose onto the snap-ring pliers and slip this over the forward hook eye, leader, and crimped sleeve (moisten with saliva or suds for easy application). Slide the tubing down on the hook close to the bend, where it will hold the hook shank and cable in alignment. Add a second piece of surgical tubing the same way, placing it directly over the hook shank and crimped leader.

Other alternatives for securing the cable to the first hook are to use shrink tubing, which can be slid in place and then shrunk by applying heat or attached by wrapping with self-adhesive tape or tying with dental floss or cord. Once this is done, the leader can be added to the forward hook as per the original description.

It is also possible to make a free-swinging hook rig, using the previous method of using a double overhand knot and two leader sleeves for a free leader/hook eye connection. Usually the short length of cable is still firmly attached by surgical hose or shrink tubing to the hook shank of the forward hook.

To add a second hook using snelled mono, the second hook is attached after the first, opposite the method for making the two-hook cable rig. In this, you use the same method described for snelling a hook, beginning with the eye of the second hook held in position at the bend of the forward hook. Since the excess line is pulled through the wraps to the rear, the position will only change slightly as any slack is taken out of the snell upon tightening.

Single-strand wire can also be used for big-game offshore lure riggings, with a simple haywire twist typical of connections to the hook. Because of the tendency of single-strand wire to kink and the frantic antics of a hooked fish, cable is typically used for two-hook rigs even when the rest of the leader is single-strand wire.

Note that in making any of the two-hook rigs, there is plenty of room for experimentation. As this is written, serious offshore anglers are experimenting with two-hook rigs by varying the angles of the planes of the hooks, using a larger hook for the tail hook, using a smaller hook for the tail hook, and using different hooks styles. The goal of all these experiments is to achieve better and more secure hooking, though the ultimate, perfect rig is still elusive.

VARIATIONS

Given the nature of offshore lures and offshore fishing, there are almost endless variations in lures. not to mention the constant arguments that go on as to speed, action, and the best color head and skirt for a given game species. Some possible variations to consider include:

1. Casting a basic clear or dyed resin cylinder-lure head, with eyes and molded-insert prism material, then turning it on a lathe to the desired shape and size, and finally polishing it with a polishing or rubbing compound. Doing this results in an absolutely accurate round lure, with the center hole dead-on center as a result of the live centers used on the lathe. It is possible to exactly duplicate a commercial or homemade lure using a template or contour gauge, or to experiment with different shapes for different action, bubbling, or flash when trolled. It is also possible to cut a lure flange or neck to the exact size needed for a given vinyl skirt. For the groups of plastics that include cast resins, cutting speeds of about 200 to 300 feet per minute are rated best, with cuts and feed no more than 0.010. No lubrication is required, but it is important to check the tightness between centers because these plastics often expand with heat and may have to be adjusted.

2. Clear- or colored-plastic acrylic rods (such as Plexiglass, a trade name for acrylic plastic) can be similarly turned on a lathe to make lures. As with the cast lures, the result is a perfect cylinder in relation to the lure center, and any shape can be cut. Finish with a polishing or rubbing compound. These lures have to be drilled, which is best done on a drill press, following the marks made by the lathe centers while turning. Since these begin as solid-plastic rods, any eyes or other attractions must be added to the outside of the lure, using a Zap glue or similar glue designed to work with acrylic plastics.

3. Soft-style offshore trolling lures can be made from large diameters (1 1/4 to 1 1/2 inches are usually the largest sizes available) of foam rod-handle material, commonly called EVA or Hypalon. Often these will be available with a small hole of about 1/4-inch through the center, but are more commonly available with larger holes up to about 3/4-inch. This material is available in up to 18-inch lengths, often in various colors. To make a lure with this material, use a core tube of copper, brass, or polyethylene plastic, and glue it into the hole in the foam rubber. If the hole is larger than 1/4-inch diameter (the right size for 3/16-inch or 1/4-inch tubing), you must build up the difference. One way to do this is with inner-tube rubber or rubber gasket material, cut to the right length for the lure and wrapped tightly around the tubing using rubber cement while wrapping to secure the material. To do this properly, measure first the amount of flat rubber materials required, coat both sides with the rubber cement, allow the cement to become tacky, and then tightly roll the rubber material around the tubing. Add rubber cement on the inside of the rubber foam and around the rubber core and insert the core into the foam body. Wait until the cement has cured, then use a lathe or work a rasp manually to shape a neck or flange on which to add the skirt. The skirt can be made with flat strip material such as Moldcraft Tuff Tails or by using a vinyl skirt such as the Sevenstrand Psychotail replacement skirts.

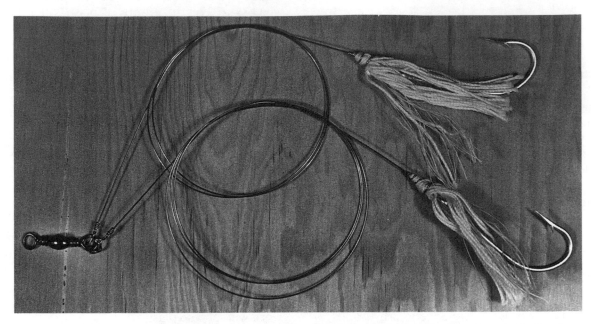

Simple lures can be made by wiring cord or nylon strands onto the wire leader ahead of a hook as shown. These are trolled together as a unit, so both are attached to the same swivel.

Glue the skirts with a PVC glue or rubber cement, and/or wrap with floss or cord.

The wide range of and uses for offshore lures still leave plenty of room for experimentation and testing. This chapter outlined only a few of the methods that can be used to construct what are today considered standard lures. Tomorrow new techniques and methods will no doubt be discovered and tested.

12

Miscellaneous Lures

INTRODUCTION ▪ PLASTIC-PIPE LURES ▪ METAL-TUBING LURES ▪ SWAGED-PIPE LURES ▪ METAL-BAR LURES ▪ PIPE-SLAB LURES ▪ SURGICAL-HOSE LURES ▪ SPLIT-SHOT JIGS ▪ EGG-SINKER JIGS ▪ ROPE JIGS, FLIES, AND LURES ▪ ICE "FLIES" ▪ TROLLING RIGS ▪ OTHER LURES ▪ BIRDS

INTRODUCTION

For this chapter we will abandon the listing of tools and materials, although step-by-step instructions will be included with each lure example. That's because these lures are unusual and defy categorization as in previous chapters and lure types.

In most cases the lures here are simple to make or involve methods that have been discussed in previous chapters. In some cases they require experimentation to perfect the best action. They are not "miracle lures" — there is no such thing — but they are fun to make and fish and will often take as many fish as other lures. Sometimes they will take fish when nothing else works. In any case, most are easy to make, very inexpensive, and well worth a try.

PLASTIC-PIPE LURES

Plastic pipe can be used for an unusual type of tube lure. Many types of plastic pipe are available, including pipe of PVC, CPVC, ABS, and similar plastics. Some are available only in large sizes. Those that you will want for this lure range from 1/2-inch through about 1 1/2 inches in diamter and are usually PVC or CPVC. The lure is simplicity itself to make.

To make a plastic-pipe lure, choose the

diameter of pipe best for your fishing. Generally this will be a diameter about the same as that of a plug or crankbait you would use. Use a saw to cut the pipe into lengths, again choosing a length about the same as for a crankbait you'd fish. Suggested diameters and lengths would be: 1/2-inch-diameter pipe in a 3-inch length for bass and pike; 3/4-inch-diameter pipe in a 4-inch length for light-tackle saltwater trolling; 1-inch-diameter by 5 or 6 inches in length for saltwater trolling and light surf casting; and 1 1/2-inches-diameter by 6 to 8 inches in length for offshore trolling, heavy surf casting, and heavy saltwater fishing.

You can cut the pipe square at both ends or cut one end at an angle or cut both ends at an angle. The degree of cut will affect the action in the water, although at any angle the lure will have an erratic action in the water or when trolled on the surface. The angle does help in attaching the hooks, through-wire leader, and line-tie, though. After cutting the pipe, smooth it. You can do this by using a large reamer, sanding lightly, or scraping with a knife blade on both the inside and outside of the cut.

Once the edges are smooth, drill a 1/8-inch to 3/16-inch hole through each projecting end of the tubing. Smooth these holes with a countersink. Next, prepare a through-wire leader of cable, single-strand wire, or heavy utility wire (the kind available in small coils at any hardware store). The leader, with formed or sleeve-crimped eyes, must measure the same as the distance between the two drilled holes. Also, if you wish to weight the lure for casting, deep-jigging (requiring lots of weight), or a special action while trolling, add it to the leader at this point. The easiest way to do this is to use a series of egg sinkers or one large egg sinker on the leader. These must be small enough to fit into the plastic pipe. Use a leader sleeve to hold the sinkers in place on the leader. The position of the weight on the leader—essentially at the head or tail of this tube lure—will change the action and retrieve or trolling depth somewhat.

In place of the egg sinker, you can mold small "ingots" of lead in a homemade mold of wood or plaster of paris (quality won't matter here); use a small pan-head sheet-metal screw to hold this lead weight inside the tube.

Once the through-wire leader is prepared, the last step in construction is to slip the leader into the tubing and secure it in place by using large split rings at each end—the split rings go through the leader eye and the tube hole. At the tail end use the same step to add the hook—treble,

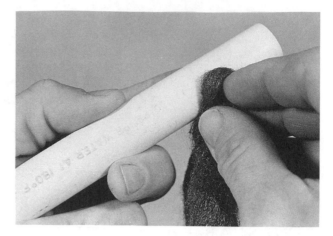

Making a plastic PVC-pipe lure first requires removing the printed markings on the side of the pipe. Steel wool is ideal for this.

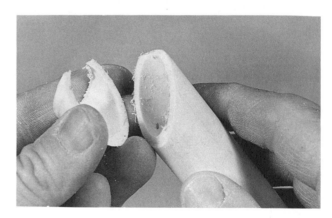

To making a sloping-face lure, use a saw to cut one end at a sloping angle.

Rigged wire forms that serve as a connection between the line-tie and rear and belly hooks. This is necessary for strong fish.

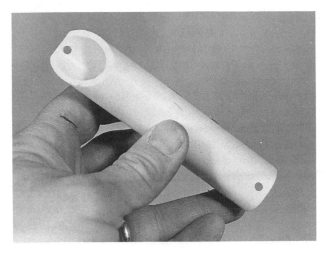

Pipe lure with sloping face and holes drilled for line-tie and hook attachment.

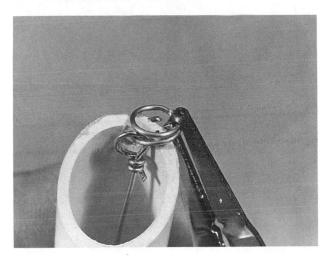

Adding the internal wire rigging to the pipe form with split-ring pliers. On the tail and belly attachment, the hooks would be added at the same time.

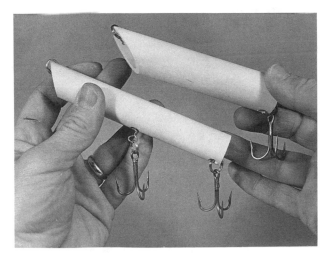

Examples of finished lures.

double, or single — at the same time. If desired, you can also add a belly hook by drilling a hole through the PVC tubing and using a hook on a barrel swivel (connected with a split ring), with the swivel placed inside the lure where the leader wire will run through it. This secures all the hooks — tail and belly — to the wire leader.

To run the split ring through the hook eye, tube eye, and leader eye all at the same time saves time and also prevents excessive spreading of the split ring. The addition of the egg sinker(s) gives the lure some weight for casting, and the leader prevents the loss of a fish should the eye in the plastic tubing pull out in a fight. Ideally, it is best to rig the lure so that the stress of fighting the fish is on the leader — not on the drilled holes in the plastic pipe.

One added touch to increase action is to make a saw cut or slot partway through the lure at right angles to the tube's length. This can be at different angles in different lures to hold a glued-in "lip" of plastic or metal. Sturdy scraps of metal or plastic, cut into shape and glued in place with epoxy, will work well and give the lure added action. Experiment with different lip materials, lengths, and angles to find the best action for your lures. The best and toughest material for lure lips is clear Lexan, often available at plastic-supply houses (check your Yellow Pages) as scrap and sold by the square foot in 1/8- and 1/4-inch thicknesses.

Final finishing (discussed for all lures in Chapter 15), can include painting, coloring with felt-tip markers, adding of prismatic tape, and so on.

METAL-TUBING LURES

The same techniques described above can be used with metal tubing such as copper, brass, and aluminum pipe. In fact, any pipe can be used. For a very bright lure, try using sections of chrome-plated bathroom pipe such as is used for drain pipes (though this is large — about 1 1/4-inches diameter) and inlet water pipes (about 1/2-inch diameter). Cut the pipe at an angle for the split-ring attachment, smooth the cut with sand-paper or a file, and drill a hole in each projecting end. Since this pipe is metal and can't possibly crack as could the plastic pipe, you will not need the leader wire for protection against loss. Also because it is metal, you can add weight by plugging one end and pouring a given weight of lead into the lure and allowing to cool. (Be careful in doing this and

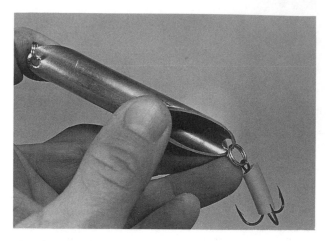

Finished metal-tubing lure, this made from copper water pipe. The metal is strong, so no internal wire rigging is required.

be sure to read all safety precautions in Chapters 4 and 5.)

Use a section of dowel, a cork stopper, or similar plug to stop up one end of the tubing. Since the lead may eventually slide out if it's not secured, drill a hole through the side wall of the tubing where the lead is located and insert a short stainless steel or brass sheet-metal screw to hold the lead in place. Add a split ring to one end for a line-tie and a split ring and hook to the tail end. In addition, you can add a belly hook (as described with the PVC lures) by drilling a hole in the body and adding a hook on a swivel, using a leader wire to run through the swivel eye as it runs from the tail hook to the line-tie. Another method of attachment is to drill a hole to take the swivel, run a large split ring through the eye of the swivel, and slip the swivel through the hole in the pipe from the inside. The large split ring will prevent the swivel from pulling through. Then use a split ring to attach the hook to the external swivel eye.

Finish by polishing the lure and coating it with a clear lacquer, paint, a clear prism tape cover, plastic tape, or whatever suits your design.

Swaged-Pipe Lures

Metal pipe is used for these lures also, which consist of a short length of pipe completely swaged into a flat lure, or left round but swaged at each end for the hook and line-tie attachment. If you make a lure that will be completely flattened, remember this when choosing the diameter of the pipe: Any round tubing will flatten out to about 1 1/2 times the round diameter. Thus, a pipe of

1-inch diameter will make a flattened swaged lure that is about 1 1/2 inches wide.

You can flatten copper, brass, or aluminum pipe or tubing in one of two ways. One is to squeeze the pipe in a large vise, preferably one that has jaws as wide as the tubing lure is long. If not, squeeze gently in several steps. The second way is to place the tube on an anvil or suitable substitute and hammer the tubing flat. Do this also a little at a time, turning the tubing over often for an even result.

Once the tubing is flattened to your satisfaction, make sure that the ends are completely flat, then round the end slightly with a file or grindstone. Drill a hole straight through each end,

An anvil and heavy hammer are necessary for swaging flat lures from pipe. Either one or both ends can be swaged, or the entire lure can be flattened.

Flattened pipe lure, with hammer marks made with ball-peen hammer.

smooth with a countersink, and add a split ring at one end for a line-tie, and a split ring and hook to the other end.

To make a round lure with swaged ends, use the same techniques above, only use the vise or anvil and hammer to flatten the very ends only—not the middle. Hammer alternately from both sides to make them even. Drill a hole through the ends and finish as above.

This method also allows the easy addition of lead to make a heavier lure, a specialized jig, or to change the running depth or action of a trolling or casting lure. To do this, crimp one end shut and make sure that it is *completely sealed* to prevent any leakage of molten lead. Secure the lure with the open end up (you can make a special rack for this or just stick it in a bucket of sand) and add the desired quantity of lead. Once the lead is cool, crimp the open end and continue as above. A simpler alternative is to crimp one end; add sufficient scrap-lead pieces, bird shot, old lead sinkers, or split shot; pour in some glue to hold the scrap securely; allow the glue to cure; and hammer the open end shut. Finish by drilling and adding the hooks and line-tie split rings. The same method can be used to add BB's shot, and other rattles, which can be particularly effective in these lures when they are used for vertical jigging.

METAL-BAR LURES

Metal bars and rods of any type can be used for casting, trolling, and jigging lures. Scrap bars, metal rods, and bars available from hardware stores, the handles of old discarded kitchen utensils, even threaded rod can all be used for making metal-bar lures. In the case of flat metal bars, such as the do-it-yourself materials available at hardware stores that average about 1/8- or 1/4-inch thick, this involves nothing more than cutting the bar to length, grinding or filing the ends to smooth them, drilling a hole in each end, and adding a line-tie and hook with split rings.

If you use round stock such as threaded or smooth rods (both available at hardware stores) you will have to grind or file the end flat—to a thinner diameter—to make it possible to add the split ring and hook easily. The handles of old kitchen knives, spoons, and forks are ideal because they are usually stainless, heavy enough for casting, with a slight bend for some action, and flat enough to drill easily for hook and line-tie attachment.

Any of these lures can be bent slightly to give them more action in the water. Such lures, in large sizes to cast easily (several ounces), are ideal for surf fishing and often resemble the best tin squids or metal surf spoons you can buy.

PIPE-SLAB LURES

Pipe-slab lures can be made of lead-filled metal or resin-filled plastic pipe. The metal lures are filled with lead but are not used or made as are the ones above. They end up like an angled slab of metal—not round but oblong, the degree of oblong dependent upon the angle at which the pipe is cut. To make them, first plug one end of a pipe that has the diameter you want in the finished lures. Then fill to the top with molten lead or tin. (Tin will be lighter in weight but also shinier.) Allow the lure to cool and cut the pipe at an angle and into very thin sections. The angle of the cut will determine the length of the lure, the thickness of the cut the resulting action and weight of the lure. Once the slabs are cut out (using a hacksaw or working carefully with a power saw or band saw), smooth the cut sides with a file, grinder, or belt sander. Once the sides are smooth, you might find that the lead or tin center is loose in the outer ring of metal. If necessary, you can pull this out and glue it in place with epoxy glue, or you can just drill the holes on each end through the lead and the metal rim to secure the center in place with the split ring. Add split rings at each end for the line-tie and the hook.

A variation of this is to use the metal pipe but fill the center with casting resin, the same material used to make offshore trolling lures (see Chapter 11). You must plug the end of the metal pipe, just as when filling with molten lead. Follow the directions in Chapter 11 for care, handling, and safety in working with the plastic, and also for suggestions as to the proper amount of catalyst to use for a large mass of casting resin. For colorful lures, add color dye (for translucent lures) or color pigment (for opaque lures) to the casting resin before pouring.

Once the plastic is poured in the metal tube, allow it to cure and then carefully cut at sharp angles to make the slablike lures. These will differ from those with the lead in that they will be lighter and also transparent or translucent, giving a completely different effect. In addition, while the metal pipe adds weight and a shiny surface to these lures, you can also make them using PVC, CPVC, ABS, or similar plastic pipe, leaving the pipe bare or painting it after pouring but before

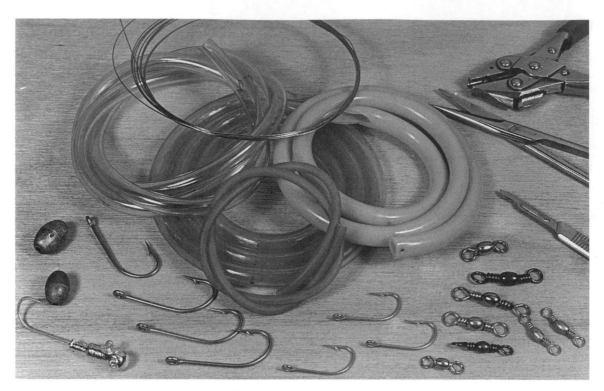

Materials needed for making surgical-hose lures.

cutting into the oblong slabs. And, since you are working with clear casting resin, variations of color in the plastic can be created by adding opaque or translucent coloring to the plastic, or by adding glitter, small aluminum or mylar craft mirrors, or colored or shiny sequins to the mix. When adding particles like this, you must rotate the tubing periodically to prevent settling of added materials.

SURGICAL-HOSE LURES

Surgical-hose lures go by a lot of names and are readily available commercially. They are called hose lures, surgical hose, and surgical eels. Although the basic concept behind these lures is an old one, they have only recently gained widespread popularity. They are good for striped bass, bluefish, and other saltwater species when trolled, and for barracuda when rigged straight and cast on tropical flats. Basically nothing more than a length of rubber or plastic tubing over a hook and short leader attached to a barrel swivel, such "surge" lures are extremely simple to make.

The tubing comes in a variety of sizes and colors, including the natural amber color, as well as red, yellow, black, blue, green, pink, and others. Fluorescent colors are also sometimes available.

Similar hose is also available in clear plastic, which can be used with insert materials such as colored or shiny tinsel, mylar tubing, and so on. Some anglers even use the very thin catheter tubing for special fishing applications. Diameters range from as thin as 1/8-inch to larger than you would want to use. You can get the tubing today at most mail-order houses and many tackle shops. Hooks should be strong saltwater single hooks. Either wire or heavy mono can be used for the leader, with wire usually getting the nod in case of hits from toothy critters such as bluefish.

Determine the length you desire for a given lure. Most of these lures will vary between about 6 to 24 inches, with 14 to 18 inches being a good average for saltwater striper and bluefish use. For the hook connection, use forty- to fifty-pound mono, and similar sizes of braided wire or single-strand wire. Use a haywire twist (single-strand) or leader sleeve (mono or braided wire) to fasten the hook to the leader. The size of the barrel swivel will be determined by the inside diameter of the tubing. The tubing should fit snugly around the center barrel of the swivel. Cut one end of the tubing on a sharp angle, using sharp scissors, so that this short "tail" will extend beyond the hook bend. Lay the tubing alongside the partially prepared hook and leader, placing

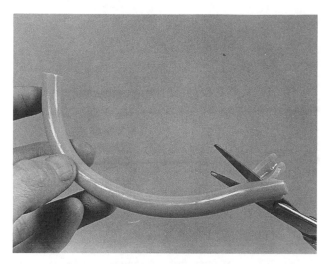

Cutting the end of the surgical hose on a slant to make a tapered tail for the lure.

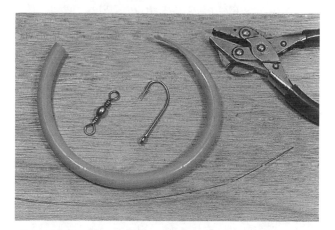

Wire, swivel, hook, hose, and pliers are all that are needed for making simple "surge" lure.

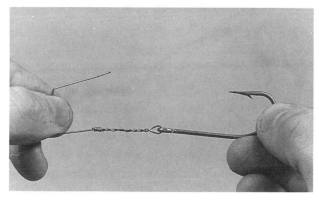

Hook is attached to wire with a haywire twist. Here the excess wire has been broken off to leave a tight wrap.

the forward part of the slanted cut at the bend of the hook. Cut the leader, leaving enough wire or mono to finish the eye for the barrel swivel.

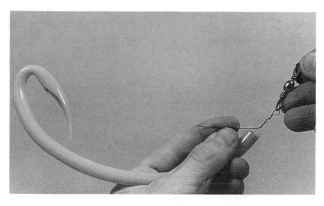

Hose being threaded onto the completed wire/hook rig. The excess wire at the head end can be used to wire the hose to the swivel, or can be clipped off and then a separate wire used to secure the hose to the swivel.

Run the leader through the tubing, allowing enough wire or mono to form the eye at the end. Grasp the leader with pliers and roll the tubing back onto the leader wire and up onto the bend of the hook. This is to allow room for making the eye in the leader and to attach the barrel swivel. While holding the tubing back in this position, run a leader sleeve onto the wire or mono, run the wire or mono through one eye of the barrel swivel, form the loop or eye, and run the leader back through the leader sleeve. Position and crimp the leader sleeve. Slide the tubing back up onto the wire, placing the end of the tubing over the center part of the barrel swivel.

It is also possible to premeasure the tubing against the complete wire-leader rig (complete with hook and swivel). Slip the swivel eye of the completed leader rig over a strong doubled wire (straightened coat hanger will do fine), and thread the surgical eel over the double wire, pulling it

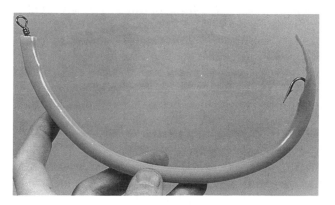

Completed hose lure.

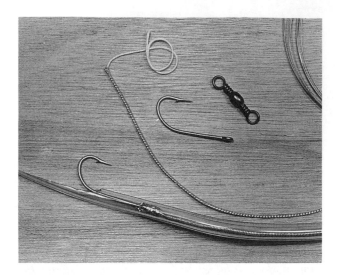

Using clear, or translucent, colored plastic tubing allows using Mylar or other braided tubing over the wire and in the plastic tubing for added flash.

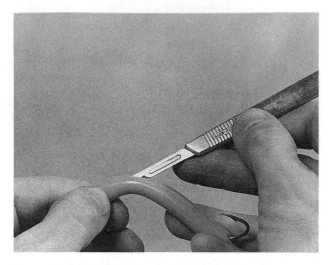

To add additional hooks without using wire, use long-shank hooks and thread the rear hook in the tubing first, making a cut at the point where the hook eye is located.

down (carefully!—watch the hook!) onto the leader and the hook. Once the eye of the swivel is clear of the end of the tubing, remove the doubled wire.

Since the tubing will fit tightly around the barrel swivel, be especially careful not to slip and run the hook into your hand. A little warm soap solution, Teflon spray, or similar lubricant rubbed on the barrel swivel, or soaking the tubing briefly in a soapy solution, helps greatly. The lubricant or soap is easily washed off.

To secure the swivel to the tubing, some anglers use several wraps of single-strand wire around the tubing and the swivel to hold it in place, or through the tubing and the lower eye of the swivel.

By using extra-long-shank hooks it is also possible to rig surgical hose without a wire leader. For this, get hooks as long as possible and make the surgical-hose lure the length of two or three hook shanks, depending upon how many hooks you wish to use and the length of the surgical hose desired. Hooks with turned-down eyes are best. Also, you must be able to run the point and shank of one hook through the eye of the second hook. You can slightly open the eye or bend down or file the barb of the hook point to make this possible.

To rig, hold the tail hook alongside the surgical hose and make a small cut in the hose at the point where the hook eye lies. Next, run the hook up the hose and the eye of the hook out through the small cut. Run the second hook through the eye of the tail hook, slide it all the way on so that you can

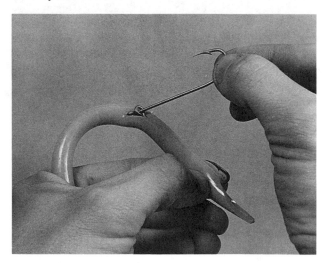

At this point, force the hook eye out of the hose, thread a second hook through this hook eye, and then force the second (forward) hook up through the tubing.

force the eye of the front hook through the hole in the hose and slide the hook forward. This will place only the point and bend of the forward hook through the hose but will hide the rest of the hook in the hose. Once all the hooks are attached this way (three is about the maximum you will want), attach the forward hook eye to a hookless jig head, jap feather-style of jig head, and similar setups. To finish the hose lure without adding weight (as in the originals), use a split ring to attach the forward hook eye to a barrel swivel and wire the hose to the swivel to prevent slippage.

It is also possible to rig a surgical hose to a

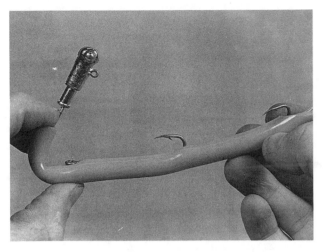

Repeat the above as required, finally forcing the hook eye onto a jig hook or attaching to a swivel with a split ring.

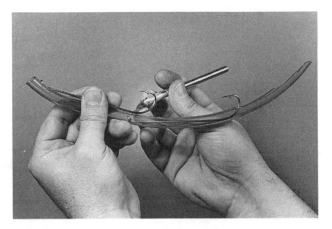

Details of the above in transparent plastic tubing, showing the cut in the tubing.

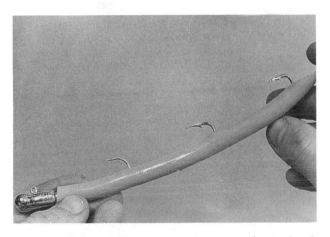

Completed lure with three hooks — one the jig hook and two connected to each other through the hook eyes.

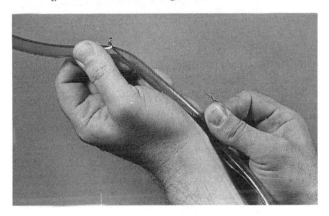

Forcing the eye of the hook through the cut in the tubing.

heavy tin squid, jig head, or fixed-hook swimming spoon. To do this with a hook at the end, the same procedure is necessary to use a wire or mono leader to fasten the tail hook to the head. For this, the leader eye can be used to fasten to the forward hook in the lure. Sometimes some imagination and ingenuity is required here, depending upon the type of lure desired and the fastening that will be necessary. Jap-feather-style hole-through-the-center jig heads can be used also, the surgical hose wire-wrapped around the collar on the head to hold it in place, the leader wire through the hose and the lead head.

Another possibility with surgical hose is to use bead chain in place of the mono or wire. This will definitely allow twisting of the hose portion of the lure without affecting the jig head or twisting line. The method is to use a bead-chain rig of the right length for the lure you are making, adding a hook to one end with a split ring. Cut the tubing about 1 to 1 1/2 inches short of the length of the bead chain, depending upon the lure you are making. Run the bead-chain hook rig through the hose, beginning at the sloping-cut tail end. At the upper or forward end, use a short section (about 1 to 1 1/2 inches long), run the bead chain through this short length of hose, and then hook the eye of the bead chain to the lure. For a jig, this can be to the forward eye of the jig. Use the short length of surgical tubing to hold the bead chain in place on the lure. If you're making a hose with a jig head, you can run this over the molded-in jig hook. With a spoon, this can replace the standard tail hook or be added in addition to that hook.

Small "banana" type hose lures are made using a short length of hose cut at the rear at an angle and threaded onto a long-shank saltwater hook.

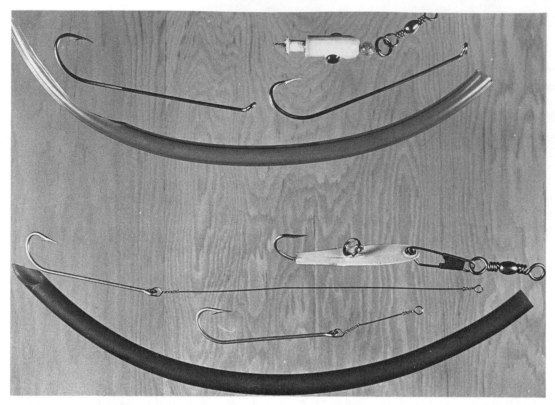

Parts required for making various types of multiple-hook surgical-hose rigs. Top, a two-hook through-rigged surgical hose with a lead head. Bottom, a three-hook rig, each of the hooks attached to the main jig head with separate leader wires of the appropriate length.

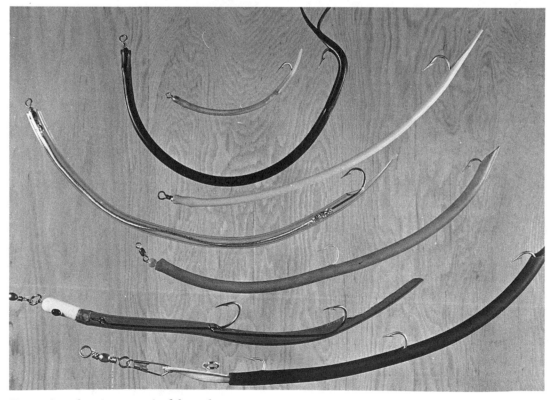

Examples of various surgical-hose lures.

The secret here is to use a tubing and hook combination in which the hole in the hose is just slightly smaller than the diameter of the hook eye. That way, you can slip the tube onto the hook and it will not slide and slip off.

Other alternatives, if you use mono in place of wire for any of the previously mentioned tasks, is to use knots to attach the leader to the hook and barrel swivel, or to snell the hook with the mono (see Chapter 13).

SPLIT-SHOT JIGS

A standard saltwater hook, fixed with one or two large split-shot jigs securely crimped on and with a tail of tied-down feathers, fur, or nylon, will make a passable jig. The jig head can be painted but does not have to be. And you do not have to have a tied-on tail but can instead use a slip-on piece of surgical hose, soft-plastic grub, or similar tail. These jigs are simple, effective, and, best of all, can be made in the field in only a few seconds with a pair of strong pliers for crimping the sinker in place. The sinker might become loose in time, but for something this effective and easy, who cares?

EGG-SINKER JIGS

These are nothing more than a variation of the split-shot jig in which an egg sinker or two is threaded onto a wire, and eyes are formed in the ends of the wire with one eye used as a line-tie and the other attached to a straight-eye hook. The hook can have a tied-on tail, slip-on soft-plastic tail, or short length of surgical hose for a tail. As with the split-shot jigs, the egg-sinker body can be painted or left unpainted.

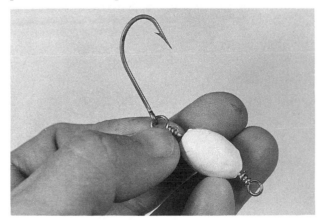

A simple swinging hook jig made from a lead egg sinker (here painted white) and stiff utility wire.

ROPE JIGS, FLIES, AND LURES

One type of rope lure consists of nothing more than multiple strands of soft cotton or nylon rope with the strands tied in the middle to the line or lure with a wire wrapping and the strands frayed out. Usually these are made so that they are about 12 inches long and are used primarily for billfish or gar. No hook is used, since when the fish hits, the rope strands get tangled in the rough bill or teeth, holding the fish as securely—probably even more securely—than would a heavy hook. While these lures might work for other fish where teeth or bills could get tangled, this is the only use I have heard of for them. There are disadvantages in that this lure may be illegal in some states or areas because it is an entangling device. It is prohibited under IGFA rules, and fish caught by these lures cannot be entered in IGFA events. Also, since the "mop lure," as it is sometimes called, will become entangled with a billfish bill, it must be cut free to release the fish. This can injure the fish by keeping it stationary and with the head out of the water for the time required to free it. With billfish becoming increasingly rare, it is often not worth it, unless you begin fishing with plans to keep the catch for a wall mount. And since you must cut out the lure to free the fish, you tend to destroy the lure.

My fishing buddy Norm Bartlett was the first angler I know of to use rope for lures and flies (with a hook), though I am sure many have tried it. Norm uses several methods of making these, depending upon whether he is making flies or lures. He used a heat glue gun for attaching the rope to the hook but more recently has gone to jig hooks—the type with a bend in the shank—and using a cigarette lighter to seal the rope on the hook. To do this, cut a length of rope appropriate to the jig hook being used. Both braided nylon and polypropylene rope will work well, although with poly rope you may wish to remove several straight core strands for easy threading on the hook. Run the hook through the rope and position the rope's end near the bend in the hook shank. Use the lighter to melt and seal the rope around the bend to prevent it from slipping. Then use the lighter lightly on the body of the shank to slightly melt the rope and give it some body. For that part of the rope that extends beyond the hook bend, use a pick or comb to fray the strands to make a "tail." A tip: Use the side of the flame against the rope to heat and melt it and to prevent it from becoming dirty from any smoke or residue from the flame.

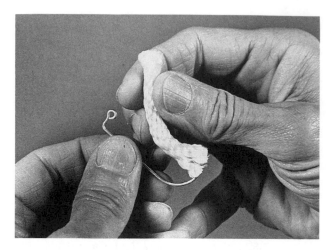

Rope jigs, here made by threading braided rope onto a jig hook.

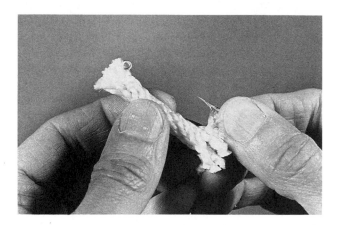

Rope in place on the jig hook.

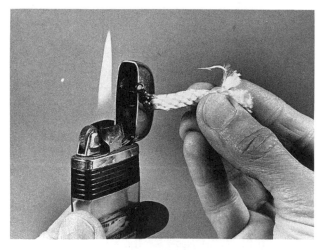

Using a lighter to melt and fuse the nylon rope to the bend in the jig hook. The jig hook, and this bend, help prevent the rope from sliding back.

It is possible to use these same techniques with a long strand of rope for a needlefish imitation or barracuda lure. Although white rope is often used, you can buy colored rope (poly rope often comes in white, yellow, red, blue, and other colors) or dye the rope (braided nylon rope) with household dyes such as Rit or Tintex.

ICE "FLIES"

Ice flies are really small lures for jigging with ice-fishing tackle and are sometimes used for panfish and crappie the rest of the year with ultralight spinning tackle. Most are made on hooks no larger than 10; sizes 12, 14, and 16 are common.

Ice flies are tiny weighted jigs or spoon-jig combinations that you can easily make yourself. There are lots of ways to make them. One is to use small spinner blades and solder a small hook to the blade, adding enough solder to fill the spinner concavity and add some weight. You will have to flux the spinner blade first for a good bond or use a solder with a built-in (core type) flux. The resultant ice-fishing fly can be left bright or painted, or even have some tail material (marabou, fur, feathers, or artificial fur) affixed to the bend of the hook for added attraction.)

You can also make tiny versions of split-shot jigs, again painting and tying in tails if desired. You can mold your own of lead, using an open-face mold (see Chapter 16) of plaster of paris, wood, or RTV Silastic rubber.

Another method is to cut out small circles or strips of aluminum from cans with scissors, or punch them out with a paper or leather punch, then fold the circles over and glue them onto a small hook. Folding and crimping, with a little bit of epoxy glue applied to the hook first, will hold these small bits of metal. These jigs can be left bare, painted, or have a tail tied on.

TROLLING RIGS

Trolling rigs are long wire leaders with a series of trolling blades ending with a snap by which lures or a baited hook can be added, or ending with a spoon or spinner lure. They are primarily used for slow, deep trolling to take trout and salmon in the Upper Midwest, but can be fished anywhere. I've used them to take trout on large ponds in Maryland.

The blades used are similar to those used for making spinners but are more often larger and sometimes fluted. The distinction between special blades for trolling rigs and those for spinners is blurring though, and any blades that work can be used. This includes all the standard spinner blades, such as Colorado, Indiana, willowleaf, and other styles. Often several sizes are used in a trolling rig, starting with a larger blade and gradually working to smaller ones toward the rear of the rig.

In addition to the spinner blades, the only other parts needed are appropriate-sized clevises, twisted-wire leader material, leader sleeves, snaps, and swivels. Begin by deciding on the length of the rig desired, and then cut a length of thirty- to fifty-pound test twisted-wire leader to that length (most are about 3 to 5 feet long). Slide a leader sleeve onto one end, add a swivel, and then reverse the leader wire through the sleeve to make a tight loop holding the swivel. Crimp the leader sleeve. From the other end, slide on a clevis and spinner blade with the concave side of the blade against the wire when facing the rear, and position the clevis just behind the swivel. Add a bearing bead or two, and then a leader sleeve. Crimp the leader sleeve where you want the blade, usually a few inches from the swivel. Continue this process, adding successively more spinner blades on clevises and bearing beads and leader sleeves in the same way, using several of one size smaller than the first, then a few more one size smaller still. All should be arranged a few

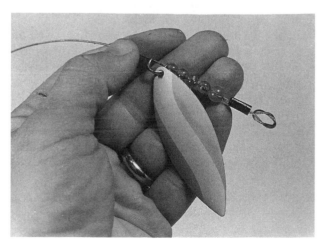

Typical arrangement for making a trout or salmon trolling rig in which spinner blades are attached separately and in series along a several-foot-long leader wire. Leader sleeves are used here to form the rear loop. Leader sleeves are also used on the single leader wire to position the beads and spinner blades on clevises.

inches or more apart, so that a six-blade rig will be about 2 to 3 feet long. You can use as many blades as you wish and as many beads, and then end the rig with another sleeve, run the leader through the sleeve, then through a snap (to attach a lure or bait), and then back through the sleeve to crimp it.

Variations of this include using different sizes, colors, styles, and numbers of blades. In addition, you can rig a keel-type sinker to the front of the lure either in the rigging or by crimping the leader wire onto the eye of the sinker, then adding a split ring and swivel to the front of the keel sinker. This will help to get the rig down deep and also prevent line twist from the many blades.

OTHER LURES

Although the foregoing covers some of the more typical variations of lures that can be and are made by tackle-tinkerers, lures can be made from virtually anything, as witness the occasional bass angler who fashions a hook to a clothespin and catches a bass just to prove it can be done. Some other possibilities we hear about, or that occasionally show up in a magazine article, include:

CO_2 jigs. Old CO_2 cartridges can be made into shiny, smooth, oblong, albeit somewhat large, "jigs" by taking the old cartridge (make sure it is empty), drilling it at both ends, running an eyed spinner wire through it (such as the 0.030 wire used for making spinners and small spinnerbaits), and fixing a hook to the end. To drill these hard-metal containers you generally have to use a drill press and vise with a punch to slightly indent the end of the cartridge to prevent the drill bit from sliding across it. Drill straight through both ends with a 1/16-inch bit and enlarge one end with a larger bit so that you can pour molten lead or tin into the cartridge to weight it. Run the wire through the lure and tape one end to prevent leakage, then add the molten metal. Single, double, or treble hooks can be attached with a formed eye to the end of the wire. The completed lure can be left as is, covered with shiny lure tape, painted, or coated with glitter.

An alternative is to drill a hole in one end large enough to pass the eye of a single hook through, place a long-shank hook into the cartridge through this hole, tape the end closed, and then pour molten metal to lock the hook eye into the lure. This style, or the swinging-hook style, can be left bare or dressed with fur, artificial or craft fur, or feathers.

Shell-casing lures. Casings from small-caliber bullets can be made into simple jiglike lures. Any size can be used, but those in calibers of .22, .25, or .32 are best for most freshwater fishing; larger sizes can be used for saltwater fishing. Remember, we are talking about casings—spent from shooting—not live ammunition!

To make these lures, clean the casings and drill a hole at one end large enough to pass a hook eye through. Using fly-tying methods, tie a tail or feathers, fur, or artificial fur to the hook, making sure that the wrap is a little back from the hook eye to give it clearance through the casing hole. Place the hook into the casing and position it so that the casing completely covers the thread wrap over the tail. Tape the hole and eye to prevent leakage, turn the casing up on end, and fill it with thick waterproof glue. (Thick glue will not run out of the hole at the end.) Make sure the glue completely covers the tail wrapping to seal it in place. Allow the glue to cure, remove the tape from the front end, and the lure is ready to fish.

Lures in different lengths and weights can be made by using different shell casings. Shell casings of .22 caliber, for example, come in short, long, and long-rifle lengths.

Ballpoint pen lures. The two-part click-on-and-off pens can sometimes be fitted with replaceable ink cartridges, but often are thrown away. The front ends of these pens can be used to make a small squidlike lure for trolling or casting. Since these already have a small hole in one end and are of colored plastic (pick your pens by the color you like to fish), an easy way to rig them is to attach a small trolling skirt to a mono or wire leader and use the pen half slipped over the wire as a head. An easy way to weight the lure for casting or deeper trolling is to pinch split shot onto the wire leader just above the trolling skirt. The split shot will be covered by the pen half. Just make sure the split shot is smaller than the inside diameter of the pen so that it can be completely covered.

Another method is to use a large, very-long-shank hook, and at the rear of the hook shank use fly-tying methods to tie on a tail or fur or feathers. Coat the wrap with waterproof glue, fly-tying head cement, or fingernail polish to seal it, then slide the pen half over the hook. If the hook is large and long enough, use an ice pick to enlarge the hole in the end of the pen through which to fit the hook eye. An alternative is to use a wire or mono leader on the hook and to run the pen half over the leader to butt up against the hook eye. Make a loop in the end of the leader.

Natural shell lures. Natural shells are available throughout the country. In saltwater areas, the shells of clams, oysters, mussels, and similar shellfish are readily available for making lures. In freshwater areas, freshwater clams and mussels can be found in most river systems. In fact, the thinner-shelled freshwater clams and the thin-shelled saltwater mussels are better than the larger clams and thick-shelled oysters. And, the natural curve in the shells of these shellfish makes for a natural curve in the lure, which will cause it to wooble, as will any commercial spoon. To make this task easier and to prevent needlessly killing live shellfish, you can often find empty shells that are completely cleaned naturally and are ready for the workshop. Such shells are ideal for spoons and spinner blades. In fact, back in the 1930s and through the 1950s such commercial spoons and spinners were in high demand and highly effective. Today they are probably too labor-intensive for commercial concern.

To make these spoons and spinners, use a template of the size and shape you want, trace it onto a shell with a felt-tip marker, soft, heavy pencil, or grease pencil. Using proper safety procedures, first drill the hole or holes for the hook and line-eye (or clevis in the case of a spinner blade) attachment. The reason for doing this now is that shell does have a tendency to splinter and split, and drilling before shaping the shell provides a thick-edged wall to reduce such problems. Use a sharp bit, slow speed, and very light pressure to drill through the shell. Then use a bench grinder or bench sander to remove the excess shell and shape it into the spoon or spinner blade. Hand-sand to round and smooth the edges.

Since shell blades are subject to breakage, rig the spoons by running a wire through the holes at each end for line-tie and hook attachment. That way, should the spoon shatter on a strike or during a fight, you won't lose the fish. The best way to do this is to make a wire form with eyes at both ends of the proper length to absorb the strain of the fight when split rings are run through the eyes in the wire and the holes in the shell. Another way is to run the wire through the holes at each end and make a slight bend or kink in the wire. Although this works fine in most cases, the strain of the fight could straighten the wire and break the hole in the shell spoon. This is not a problem with spinner blades, because the blade is attached only at one end to a clevis (usually) and there is no stress on the blade.

BIRDS

Birds are not lures but do deserve a place here because they are used with lures to attract fish to the lures when trolled. They are primarily used offshore but can be used inshore and even for some forms of big-water freshwater trolling.

Birds have been popular for about ten years now. Their precursors were first the cola bottles and similar devices that were trolled for the bubbles and smoke they created, and then the large trolling birds used in the Asian and Pacific fishing methods.

Birds are basically nothing more than a long strip of wood with some angled crosspieces that create bubbles and surface disturbance, and may cause the bird to rock or wobble when trolled. They are all made and rigged to troll on the surface, and behind them a lure is trailed to hook the fish. Birds can be any length, and some as small as several inches long have been used. Others are as long as 3 or 4 feet. Most would average about 10 to 18 inches.

Birds can be made of any type of scrap wood of almost any reasonable thickness. They can be drilled with holes to make them lighter, can have rattles added (either commercial or homemade with ball bearings and 35-mm film cans), can have lead poured into cavities for greater weight and more water disturbance, and can have more than one wing for additional surface splashing. From the top, a typical one would look like nothing more than **X** or a cross, the features created from the long body and the right-angle wing.

Good stock to use is 1-inch shelving (actual size about 3/4-inch) or similar wood that is about 3/4 to 2 inches thick. A two-by-four works well for the body. The wing can be 1-inch shelving on the large birds made on two-by-fours, or lathing or furring strips for the smaller sizes.

There are only a few critical factors to consider in making a bird. The wing is placed from the top by cutting a slot in the body. While there are no absolutes, the angle of the wing should be about 30 degrees from vertical and about 60 degrees from horizontal. The width of the wing should be about a third to a half of the length of the body. Generally, the front and tail of the body are tapered to allow the bird to skip easily and not plow into the water. The farther the wing is placed to the rear of the bird, the better it will track; too close to the front and the bird may dip and dive. A wing placed deep or low in the body will cause the bird to roll and woble more than will one

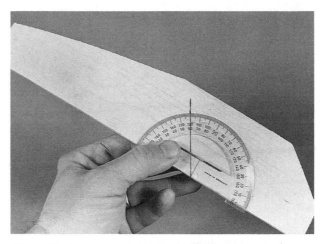

Most birds—attractors for offshore fishing—are made with the short wings at about a 60-degree angle, as shown and drawn on this bird body.

placed higher up.

Cuts to hold the wing do not have to be very accurate, since the fish won't care and a good epoxy will hold the wing in place. You can cut out the parts in minutes with a hand saw or on a band saw, scroll saw, saber saw, or other power saw. When using any power tool or saw, be sure to practice proper safety procedures. Small items like this should be cut out with a table or radial saw.

Once the parts are cut out, round off the edges, soak the slot for the wing with glue, and set the wing in place. You can paint it bright colors to add to its attractiveness.

There are several ways to rig birds. One is to cut a slot longitudinally through the body during construction, epoxy a heavy wire into place, and form wrapped eyes on both ends once the lure is complete and painted.

Completed bird with wing glued in place, before painting and rigging.

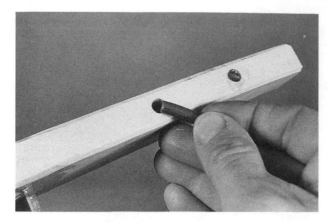

Weight can be added to a bird using pencil weights glued into holes drilled into the bottom of the bird.

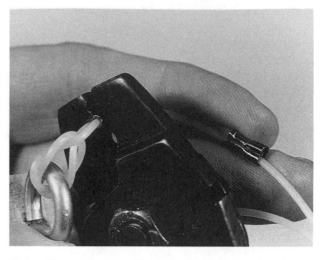

Using Mason leader pliers to crimp the leader sleeves to hold the heavy mono on the bird.

Another method is to use a separate short length of leader from which the bird will hang at both ends. This places the strain from the lure on the leader and allows the bird more movement and action. Use heavy wire or mono, about two hundred-pound test and about one and a half times the length of the bird when loops are added at each end using leader sleeves. When making these loops, add a good swivel to the front end of the leader, and a snap or snap swivel to the rear. It is this leader that will take the strain of trolling, with the line fastened to the front swivel, the leader and lure fastened to the rear snap. To attach the bird to this separate short leader, use short lengths of mono or Dacron for flexibility. You will need two of these lengths of line, and when it's complete the bird should hang down from the taut leader no more than several inches. Tie each length of material to the swivel eye and then fasten it to the other end of the bird. (An alternative to this is to use a longer length for the suspension leader, make a loop at each end using a leader sleeve, and use the ends of the mono as the attachment from the leader to the front or back of the bird.)

Attachment can be made four ways: through a screw eye fastened at each end; a heavy wire with an eye formed at one end, run through a hole drilled through the wood; the line directly through a hole in the wood and knotted in place; or a small eye bolt run through the bird with the nut secured with Loctite or glue.

Variations may be made in size or general shape (consistent with the basics of bird con-

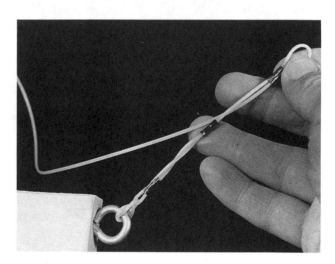

Close-up showing the rigging for one end of the bird. The line is tied to the loop held by the thumb and index finger.

struction), with holes in the side to reduce weight, with lead poured into the body for added weight, with holes in the wing for added surface disturbance, and by the addtion of rattles and bright finishes, including glitter, mirrors, and prism tape. Rattles are best added by drilling holes through the main body of the bird and inserting canisters holding ball bearings or BB's. Film canisters are good for this, as are any small metal cans. Ideally, these should be shorter than the width of the bird so that you can use an epoxy gel to cover the rattle and make the outside finish smooth.

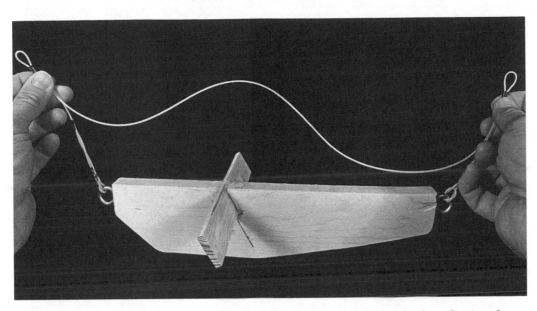

Complete rigged bird with heavy, offshore mono leader attached to both ends, rigged as a "trolley" from this leader section. As a result, the stress of trolling this bird when rigged with an additional teaser behind it will be on the leader.

13

Wire Leaders And Rigging

INTRODUCTION ▪ TOOLS ▪ SAFETY EQUIPMENT AND
PROCEDURES ▪ MATERIALS ▪ USING LEADER SLEEVES ▪
WORKING WITH SINGLE-STRAND WIRE ▪ BAIT AND LURE
RIGGINGS ▪ SINKER RIGGINGS ▪ KNOTS, SPLICES, AND
SNELLS

Basic Safety Requirements
   Safety goggles
   Work gloves
   Work apron

Basic Tools
   Pliers
   Round-nose pliers
   Wire cutters

Helpful Tools
   Wire former (various ones are available from
      Worth, Netcraft, and others)
   Bench-style professional-type wire former (i.e.
      Cabela's)
   Leader-sleeve crimping pliers
   Homemade wire-eye former and bender

INTRODUCTION

Even though rods and many lures have been considered the proper domain of the tackle craftsman for years, wire rigging and such are equally easy to accomplish and just as important. Fortunately, there have been some booklets in-recent years that have been devoted to wire-riggings work, and several excellent books by Vlad Evanoff on dozens of bait and lure-rigging arrangements for fresh and saltwater fishing.

Wire leaders and terminal tackle rigs of all types are among the easiest of all tackle items to make, requiring only the simplest tools and no expensive materials. There are special wire-forming tools on the market that cost several dollars or more, but they are not required except

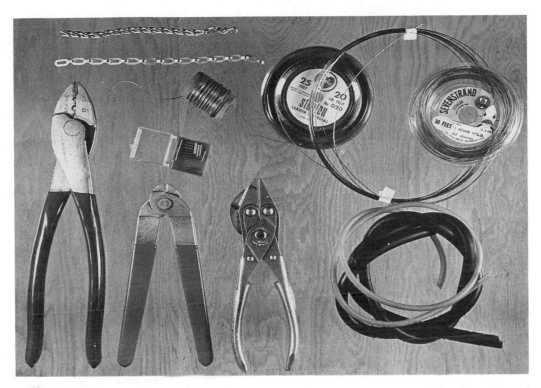

Crimping pliers, compound action pliers, leaders sleeves, various type of leader wire and chain used for making wire riggings, hook lears, and leaders.

by the angler whose hobby might turn into a part-time business, or by a fishing club for community use, or by anyone fishing extensively (perhaps a guide or charter-boat captain) who must constantly replace a lot of terminal tackle and riggings.

Trying to definite this chapter is somewhat difficult, like trying to wrestle with a bag full of basketballs. Wire leaders, rigs, terminal-tackle items, and rigged lures can encompass a wide range of tackle ideas often diverse in both use and construction. Simple wire leaders, bottom-fishing spreaders, surf-fishing bottom rigs, spinner shafts for making spinners, hook lears for bottom rigs, drop-sinker trolling rigs, sinker releases, spinner-bait rigs, wire weed-guards for weedless hooks, and a host of other small items all fall into this broad category. To further confound things, there are often several ways in which each of these items can be made.

TOOLS

The tools required will vary widely with the tackle to be made. Let's look at some possibilities and their uses.

Needle-nose pliers. Needle-nose pliers are handy for general bending operations, making eyes in wire, making hook lears, and so on. They do have a disadvantage in that the contact surfaces of the jaws are flat, not round, and thus make it difficult to make a neat rounded eye. Many have side cutters that work well for cutting wire and heavy mono.

Round-nose pliers. These are often long or with tapered or step-type jaws that are completely round (or round on one side and flat on the other; these also work well). They are best for making precisely round eyes.

Worth wire former. This is a small hand tool that allows the tackle-crafter to make several types of eyes for spinners, spinnerbait rigs, wire rigs, spreaders, and so on. It comes with instructions and is easy to use.

Netcraft wire former. This wire former, or wire winder, as Netcraft prefers to call their Model 20 Tack-L-Tool, works on a slightly different principle than the one above, and can be hand-held or mounted on a workbench. The supplied instructions described how to make a number of eye types along with springs, coil fasteners, and various other wire bends.

Professional-style wire formers. These are available from several outfits. A typical one from

Cabela's is not unlike one Herter's used to carry years ago. It clamps to a workbench (up to 1 3/4 inches thick), and has two separate handles by which all types of wire forms can be made. It is primarily designed for making various spinner, spinnerbait, bait, and similar rigs, not for working with long fishing wire or leaders. It is far heavier and also far more expensive than the smaller hand-held wire formers listed previously. It will handle a variety of wire sizes, but different heads are required for the various ranges of wire sizes. Heads are available for wire sizes 0.018 through 0.025, 0.026 through 0.029, and 0.030 through 0.035. The tool is made of cast iron.

Single-strand wire benders. These are small devices for easily making haywire twists or barrel twists in single-strand wire. Three sizes are available, each for a different wire size range. There is a small size for wire sized from 0.012 through 0.020, a medium size for 0.022 through 0.031, and a large size for 0.033 through 0.045.

Compound-action fishing pliers. These fishing pliers are made by a number of companies—Berkley, Manley, and others—in several sizes. As on-the-water fishing pliers stored in a belt holster they are ideal. Since the jaws remain parallel when opened and closed (unlike regular pliers, in which the angle of the jaws changes), they are also ideal for tackle work. They all have side-action cutters for mono and light wire and hooks, and most have a small hole drilled into the jaw with which wire can be bent and formed.

Crimping pliers. These vary widely by type, size, the force they bring to crimp a leader sleeve, and even by the type of leader sleeve used. They are made by Berkley, Sevenstrand, Mason, C and H, PFC, Felco, and other companies. Some of these are small hand tools that are ideal for crimping leader sleeves for light-tackle fishing. Big-game anglers generally do not like these, however, and opt for the Felco model or similar large long-handled pliers with a stop that predetermines the exact amount of pressure needed for a given leader sleeve.

One of the most important aspects of choosing crimping pliers is not only the size and usage of the pliers, but the type of leaders sleeve on which it will be used. Often, problems result from mismatched sleeves and pliers. There are two types of jaws on crimping pliers. One, with two cups or sockets opposing each other, or the cup-opposing-cup style, is designed specifically for single and double oval sleeves. The other type of crimping pliers, in which a point is opposite a socket, or the

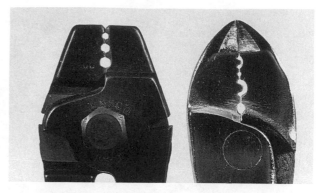

Examples of cup-opposing-cup pliers (left) and point-opposing-cup pliers (right) for crimping leader sleeves.

Leader sleeves (oval, left and round, right) held in place in their respective crimping pliers.

point-opposing-cup style, is designed only for round sleeves. Mixing sleeve and pliers styles can result in inadequate force in crimping the sleeve, and thus early failure of the crimp. In addition, it is vital that you match the size of the crimping pliers jaws to the crimping sleeves. Most pliers will have several positions at which sleeves can be set. More expensive ones will have an adjustable stop that can be changed to adjust the degree of pressure on the sleeve.

SAFETY EQUIPMENT AND PROCEDURES

As with any tackle-building task, some safety equipment is required. These requirements are minimal and include:

Goggles. These are the main requirement, since cutting wire often causes pieces to fly off. Safety goggles protect the eyes and should be worn during all wire-working operations and especially when cutting wire with wire cutters or side cutters on pliers.

Work gloves. These are suggested but not absolutely required. The advantage is that they will protect your hands from scrapes and possible puncture wounds. The disadvantage is that they make it more difficult to work with the wire, since with them you lose a sure sense of feel and the ability to pick up strands of wire easily.

Work apron. This is handy to keep from soiling your clothes. Some wire has a slight oil residue from the manufacturing processes or to keep it from rusting or corroding; cutters and crimping pliers can also leak oil. A work apron for *all* tackle-making tasks is just a good idea.

MATERIALS

Materials for making wire rigs can encompass a wide range, including surgical hose used to stabilize hooks in some double-hook offshore rigs, electricians' tape used for the same purpose, and so on.

Some typical materials for most leader and wire rigs include:

Twisted wire. Braided wire or cable is really twisted and has a lot of advantages for anglers. First, it is very strong. Second, it is very flexible, far more so than single-strand wire. Third, although it will kink, this is not as much of a problem as with single-strand wire, where a kink means that the wire is markedly weakened and must be cut and thrown away and new wire spooled onto a reel or rig. Twisted wire comes in a number of configurations, depending upon the manufacturer and strength. Sevenstrand, Mason, and PFC are among the large manufacturers of this wire for the tackle industry.

This wire is often listed as to its fabrication, using symbols such as 1X3, 1X7, 3X7, and 7X7. The figures indicate how the wire was made. For example, a 1X3 is three separate strands of wire wound or twisted into one wire. 1X7 indicates seven strands around one. In 3X7 wire, seven strands of wire are twisted into one strand, then three of the resulting strands are twisted into the final wire. In 7X7, several strands are twisted into one strand, then seven of these are twisted together. Often the lighter fabrications are considered wire; the heavier 7X7 is considered cable. The type of fabrication varies with the test of the wire. 1X3 is often light eight- to twelve-pound test. 1X7 will range from 18- to 250-pound test. 7X7 can range from 175- to 920-pound test

and is primarily used for big-game leaders. Naturally, the single-strand wire size of each varies with the pound test also.

Wire is available plain in bright, bronze, coffee, or dull black finishes; nylon coated; or black-nylon coated. It is sold in both spools and coils: The heavier pound-test sizes used for leaders are often sold in coils, the ligher tests in spools. Coils of 30 feet are standard for most wire, with large spools ranging in capacity from 100- to 5,000-foot spools. Note that while most mono line is measured by the yard, wire is generally measured by the spool. Although it is widely used for fishing line and big-game leaders, twisted wire can be used effectively for various riggings also.

Single-strand wire. This is used for some trolling but can also be used for riggings. Sizes vary from 2 through 19, with size two of about twenty-nine-pound test and size 19 of about four hundred-pound test. Most is of stainless steel in coffee, black, or bright silver, and sold in 25- or 30-foot coils and larger-bulk spools.

Monofilament line. The mono used for riggings is no different from the mono used for line. Naturally, depending upon the rigging, you might pick a line known for abrasion resistance, thin diameter, or other qualities, but these are also available in standard fishing line through many manufacturers.

Single-strand spinner and spinnerbait wire. This wire is of the type that was used in Chapter 3 to make spinners. It can be tinned or stainless steel (both are about the same price, so it makes sense to buy the stainless steel type), in various short lengths and also prestraightened coils. It is sold in coils, but when uncoiled becomes a straight-shaft wire.)

Sizes range from about .024 to about .040, with the .024 and .030 sizes used most for making spinners, as in Chapter 3.

Single-strand weed-guard wire. This is a lightweight wire of about .009 to .012 in size for most lures. It is no different from size 2 single-strand leader wire (measuring usually about .011).

Utility wire. Utility wire in brass, copper, steel, aluminum, and other metals is available from hobby and hardware shops and is often ideal for tackle riggings, hook lears, bottom rigs, spreaders, keel sinkers, sinker releases, and other tackle riggings. It is available in various diameters ranging up to about 1/8-inch thick, the largest suitable for most tackle rigs, Regular 14-gauge electrical wire can be used (it measures about .065—the same as for some bottom spreaders I have checked with a micrometer). Some companies (Netcraft, for example) sell straightened 14-gauge spring-brass wire, which would be better for most spreaders and hook lears.

Some wire is very flexible and thus ideally suited for the twisting and turning in making hook lears and keel sinker rigs. Other wire is springier and thus better suited for making spreaders and long, extended hook lears. Although not designed specifically for fishing, this wire is handy to have around and ideally suited for many rigging operations and much experimentation.

Leader sleeves. Leader sleeves are available in many sizes, materials, and styles and are usually made by the same manufacturers who make and sell wire. They are available in round, oval, and double oval styles, and each style must be matched to the proper crimping pliers.

Different manufacturers rate sleeves in different ways. Sevenstrand uses a letter and number system: from size A1 through A14 for wire, cable, nylon-coated wire, and cable and mono. Their AM9 through AM14 sizes are made for mono. Mason uses a number system of from 1 through 14 in the round sizes and 11 through 71 in the double oval or double connector sleeves. PFC labels their

sleeves in inch diameters—1/32-inch through 5/32-inch, with extra long (1 1/2 times the standard length and designed for mono sleeves) in the same sizes. Berkley uses a letter and number system that ranges from B2 to B6 for general sleeves and MS1 to MS4 for monofilament sleeves.

Sleeves are often available unplated in zinc finish or black oxide in small packs of fifteen to forty (depending upon size) or in bulk one-hundred-count packs. Copper and brass are the two most commonly used materials for making leader sleeves, with copper getting the nod for saltwater fishing because it is more resistant to corrosion.

Terminal fasteners. Terminal fasteners or tackle include the variety of snaps, swivels, and other devices used in making up rigs. Two excellent references on terminal fasteners are *Hook, Line and Sinker*, and *Soucie's Fishing Databook*, both by Gary Soucie. Some of the more important terminal tackle parts include:

• Safety snap. This can be of steel or stainless steel and is sold everywhere. The big disadvantage with safety snaps is that they can be pulled open under heavy stress, unlike the interlock snap. A range of small to large sizes is available.

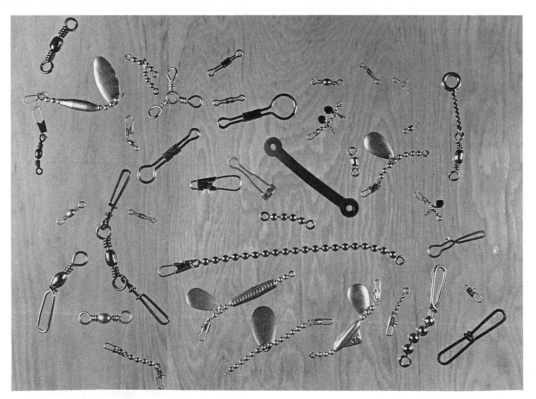

Some of the many types of terminal fasteners available for making leaders and wire riggings. These include swivels, three-way swivels, bead-chain snaps and swivels, keel trolling sinkers, fish-finder rigs, etc.

- Interlock snap. Also called the lock snap, this is similar to the safety snap with the addition of a small bend at the end of the snap wire that fits into a hole in the lock mechanism. This makes it far stronger and harder to pull open under stress. Small to large sizes are available.
- Duo-Lock snap. This is a simple wire snap that does not have a metal plate, as do the safety and interlock styles. It is strong and can be opened from either end, which has many advantages in the construction of much fishing tackle. It is usually stainless, and so is good in fresh or salt water. Sizes are more limited than for safety and interlock snaps.
- Cross-Lok snap. This was developed by Berkley and is similar in some ways to the Duo-Lock snap in that it consists only of wire and can be opened from either end. It differs in that the locking tangs are both on the same side rather than opposite sides of the snap, and that the locking pieces overlap each other to make this very strong for its size.
- Coastlock snap. This is a long snap with a wire wrapped eye and locking tang that fastens over the wire of the snap. It is popular for saltwater fishing and comes in large sizes.
- Pompanette snap. This is almost identical to the coastlock but with a tighter bend in the end. It is popular for saltwater fishing. Under high stress, this and the other four snaps will deform slightly before opening.
- Lockfast snap. This is a snap similar to the coastlock snap but with a bend that is in line with the snap eye, rather than slightly off to the side, as with the others. It is most useful for saltwater fishing.
- McMahon snap. This resembles a pair of closed ice tongs, is made of wire, and because the overlapping ends are tight requires snapping onto whatever is being fastened to it.
- Pigtail or corkscrew snap. This is not really a snap but a type of end-fastener with a spiral or corkscrew design that allows a loop of line, swivel, split ring, or other device to be threaded onto it quickly . It is not as readily available as the other snaps but can be made using spring wire and a small homemade tool (the tool construction is described in Chapter 2).
- Barrel swivel. This is a simple swivel with a twisted eye on each end. The shaft of the eye is inside the central barrel. Available in black, brass, and nickel plate, it comes in a range of sizes.
- Box swivel. This works like the barrel swivel but has an open box into which the shafts of the two eyes fit. It was once popular but is seldom seen today.
- Three-way swivel. This is nothing more than three eyes, all swaged and held in place in a small flat ring. It is used for many bait and bottom-rigging situations.
- Cross-line swivel. This has three eyes, but unlike the three-way swivel, in which the eyes are all at an identical angle to one another (120 degrees), this swivel has two eyes in line with each other (at 180 degrees) and one eye at right angles (90 degrees) to these. If the swivel is to be stressed in a straight line, this one is far better than the standard three-way swivel but is much harder to find. It is made in barrel, box, and bead-chain styles.
- Ball-bearing swivel. Made by several companies (Sampo, Berkley, Rome, South Bend, and others) this swivel incorporates small ball bearings in the barrel for easy turning, even when under stress. Many sizes are available, most with split rings for line and lure attachment. In larger sizes for offshore trolling, larger welded rings are used
- Snap swivel. This incorporates a snap and a swivel. In almost all cases it can be found in a variety of styles, including those with standard or ball-bearing swivels; with safety, interlock, Duo-Lock, Cross-Lok, coastlock, pompanette, and pigtail fasteners or snaps; and in bright, brass, and black finishes.
- Bead-chain fastener. Many snaps and snap swivels are made by the Bead Chain Company in many styles and lengths, and all incorporate the unique series of multiple beads, as is used in some electric-light pull-cords.
- S connector. This looks like an S and is designed for fastening, but not for anything that might come under great stress. It is not commonly seen in most tackle shops.
- Solid connector. This is used mostly as a permanent addition to a lure or plug line-tie and resembles various lengths of open figure-eight wire shapes. It is strong when closed with pliers.
- Slide-link connector. This is used on some lures and saltwater bottom rigs, and consists of a single length of wire, bent, with an eye at each end and with the two ends turned to the middle, where they are secured with a sliding link, thus the name. It is secure and strong but somewhat unwieldy.

USING LEADER SLEEVES

To construct a basic leader using leader sleeves, you must have the right-size sleeve for the wire, nylon-covered wire, or mono used. (A listing of these sizes may be found in Appendix D.) You must also have the right type of crimping pliers for the type of sleeve being used (cup-opposing-cup for the oval or double-connector sleeves; point-opposing-cup for the round sleeves).

Run the leader through the sleeve and any additional part that is being permanently attached to the leader, then back down through the sleeve. Position the end of the wire so that it is slightly hidden in the body of the sleeve, place the crimping jaws of the pliers over the center (not the ends) of the sleeve, and crimp hard *once*. Do not try to make several crimps or repeatedly crimp the sleeve because this will weaken it.

Crimped leader sleeve making a double loop in the end of a wire leader.

For an even stronger crimp, use two leader sleeves (take the leader through the two sleeves first, make the loop, then run it back through the sleeves). Crimp the first sleeve (the one adjacent to the leader loop) and then twist the wire end several turns around the standing wire, place the second sleeve so that the end of the wire does not protrude from it, and crimp. These sleeves should be about 1 to 2 inches apart.

For a variation of making a loop, run the leader through a sleeve, make a double overhand knot by passing the mono twice through the loop (this is almost like a surgeon's knot), pull it up into a small loop, and then run the end of the wire back through the sleeve or sleeves and crimp. This additional step is best with heavy wire or cable, such as the 7X7 fabrications.

When using leader sleeves this way, it is a simple matter to make loops, connect two lengths

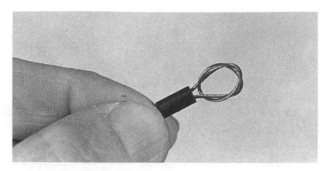

Completed end of the wire leader loop formed in the above photo.

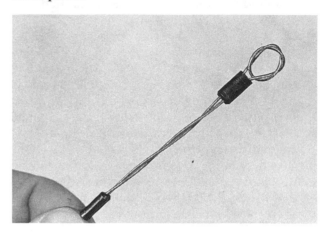

For added insurance, many leader connections use a second leader sleeve several inches above the first.

of leader wire together, attach hooks to leaders, make short leaders with snap-and-swivel ends (as for pike or bluefish), construct one- and two-hook bottom rigs for surf fishing, and accomplish similar tackle functions.

WORKING WITH SINGLE-STRAND WIRE

Single-strand wire is also easy to work with, although different methods are used depending upon the size of the wire and the intended fishing purpose. Light wire such as is used for trolling, for big-game leaders, and such does not require (in fact can't use) leader sleeves. The proper connection here between two lengths of wire or to make a loop is the haywire twist. To make this twist, first fold the wire over to make a loop; lay the two lengths parallel. Overlap the wires and gently twist them together repeatedly. The key is to make a gentle twist, not a hard wrapping twist, and to make sure that the two wires are twisted *together* not one twisted around the other. If that happens, cut off and start again, since it will not work. After about four turns of twist, bend the tag end of the wire at right angles to the standing wire and make several wrapping turns that are *tight* against one another and around the standing part of the wire. After several turns, bend the end of the wire into a right angle to make a "handle" by which to break off the end of the wire. Use this handle to bend this tag end back and forth against the shoulder of the last wrap. After several back-and-forth bends, metal fatigue will snap the wire close to the wrap. *Never* use pliers or cutters to cut the wire, since this will leave a protruding burr that could injure you when you are handling the wire or landing or unhooking a fish.

Although this connection works well for lighter wire and terminal-tackle rigs using this wire, probably the most important single-strand wire techniques involve heavier spring wire in sizes from .024 to .040, and averaging .030, for making spinner shafts and forming different eyes for spinners and similar lures.

For these eyes with this heavier wire you can use round-nose pliers, needle-nose pliers (though they will not make a neat rounded eye), the Worth wire former, Netcraft wire former, and other wire formers on the market. One advantage of working with the wire formers is that you will waste for less wire than you will by working with pliers, since the wire former can work and bend wire right up to the tag end. Thus, while you need extra wire for the wraps and eye, you will not need it for the leverage of finishing the wrap.

The basics can be done with round-nose pliers. Wire formers all include directions for making specific eye types. First, select a piece of wire, leaving about 1 1/2 to 2 inches extra length on the end or ends on which you wish to form an eye. (Thus, if you are making eyes on both ends, you will need a wire about 3 to 4 inches longer than the rig or lure.) The eye will not take up this much wire, but you will need it for leverage in working the wire with pliers and to make a neat, tight eye.

To make a wrapped eye, grasp the wire 1 1/2 to 2 inches from the end with the pliers and bend the main end (the longer or lure end) at a slight angle. An angle about 30 to 45 degrees off the straight wire is about right; after a wrap or two, experience will dictate the right bend to you. Continue to hold the wire in the same spot with the round-nose pliers and bend the short end tightly around one jaw of the pliers. You will only be able to go about two-thirds of the way around because the other jaw will block continued movement. Shift the jaws of the pliers on this eye until

you can make a complete 360-degree turn around the one jaw with the wire to form a complete circle. Now the reason for the first bend becomes obvious — making that bend places the wire shaft in line with the center of the eye. At this point, you will have a complete wire circle and the tag end of the wire will be at right angles to the main wire shaft. Remove the pliers jaw from the eye and hold the eye between the two jaws, allowing clearance of the tag end. Using your fingers, or another pair of pliers, wrap the tag end of the wire twice, tightly, around the main shaft. At this point, use cutters on your pliers or wire cutters to cut the tag end of the wire close to the wrap. (This wire is usually too heavy to make a handle and snap the wire through the metal fatigue of back-and-forth bending.)

To make a self-lock snap eye, begin with the steps just outlined and make the sharp bend and then the bend around the one jaw to form about two-thirds of a circle. At his point, shift the jaw of the pliers so that you can make a second sharp bend, like the first, in the tag end of the wire. You should have about 1 to 1 1/4 inches of tag-end wire remaining. About 3/8-inch from the end, make a sharp right-angle bend toward the main wire shaft. Hold this section of the shaft, and using the fine ends of tapered round-nose pliers, make a small (as small as possible) U-shaped bend in the very end of the wire, positioned to catch on the main shaft. If there is excess wire, clip it. At this point, the bend and eye are complete and in an open position for addition of a hook or lure. To close, spring the end of the wire close to the main shaft and catch the small U on the main shaft.

Making a coil-lock snap is identical to this except that there is no final bend to hook the main wire shaft. Begin by sliding a proper-sized coil spring onto the wire shafts. Thus, the coil spring, usually about 1/2-inch long, must have an inside diameter that is slightly larger than the diameter of the two wires. Several different sizes are available in both tinned and stainless steel. After the coil spring is slid into place, make the sharp bend with the pliers, bend the wire about two-thirds of the way around one of the jaws, and make a second bend. The result will look like the Greek letter omega, or like the outline of a keyhole. A coil spring is used to close this eye: hold the main shaft and the end parallel and slide the coil spring over the open end.

BAIT AND LURE RIGGINGS

Wire can be used for a wide variety of bait and lure riggings, including spreaders, hook lears for single- and two-hook bottom rigs, umbrella trolling rigs, and so on. Some of these, and some options in making them, include:

Spreaders. Bottom spreaders consist of a long flexible wire fitted with snelled hooks on each end; the line is fastened to the middle of the wire and a sinker is added to this middle area to hold the rig on the bottom. Heavy brass wire, copper wire, and light but bendable stainless wire are all used to make spreaders. To build these simple rigs you can use either round-nose pliers or a homemade wire former consisting of a nail or two hammered into a block of wood with the heads cut off the nails and the block of wood held in a vise. The wire is wrapped around the nails to form the eyes and loops needed, and then is slipped off.

One easy way to make a drift spreader that does not include a sinker is to take a long section of wire, make a simple twist for a line-tie in the center, then make several circular wraps on each end to attach the snelled hooks. These end wraps are similar to a spring or the coils found on most key rings. Thus, the loop of the snelled hook can be threaded onto and around this spiral. Any length of wire can be used to make this type of

Another wire former, this to form the brass wire eyes used in tin squids and some saltwater sinkers.

spreader, and most spreaders are about 18 to 24 inches wide. Thus, allowing for the extra wire needed for the central line-tie and the end twists, you will need wire about 4 to 6 inches longer than the desired result.

To make a spreader with a sinker snap, first use a short length of wire to form a large open eye and a loop to hold the sinker. Then make a second smaller eye, the function of which is to hold the beads in place that will allow the rotation of the spreader on the central shaft. Once this part is made, use round-nose pliers or the nail wire former to make a double wrap in the center of a long length of wire. This bend should be at right angles to the plane of natural bend in the wire. Finish the two ends with spiral loops or snaps or snap swivels to attach the snelled hooks. Once this is complete, add a bead to the partially completed central shaft. Usually the small hole-diameter beads used for making spinners will not work on this heavy wire, but pony beads available from craft and hobby shops have a larger-diameter hole and will work fine. Slip the round eye over the central shaft, add a second bead, and finish the central shaft with a wrapped eye for the line-tie. If it is not necessary that the spreader rotate on the central shaft, the beads are not needed.

Hook Lears. Hook lears are those devices that hold a snelled hook out and away from the main line to prevent tangles. They are used on single-hook, two-hook, and multiple-hook bottom rigs. In essence, a hook lear is a short length of wire that works as an arm to hold the snelled hook. As

Using a homemade wire former to make a hook lear. For this, the first bend is made by twisting heavy utility wire around the two adjacent posts. This homemade wire former, previously described, is made by hammering nails into end-grain wood blocks and then sawing off the heads.

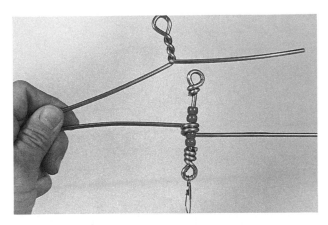

Bottom spreader rig bends. These are made with long side arms for holding snelled hooks, the line attached to the eye. The bottom one includes a snap for holding a bank or pyramid sinker.

After the first bend is made a second and then third bend is made.

Completed example of hook lear made from heavy utility wire on homemade wire former. Each such wire former must be set up for making a specific type of bend.

such, it can be incorporated into the bottom rig or added to a leader or line as an addition to extend the snelled hook.

One easy way to make a hook lear is to take a length of wire 8 to 12 inches long, fold it in the middle, and wrap it like a loose haywire twist. At the ends make two tight wraps, these at right angles to the plane of the eye at the middle of the wire. These eyes will then ride and rotate on a leader wire used for the main bottom rig. Thus, the rig can rotate without twisting line.

Another way to make a hook lear is to use a slightly longer length of wire, fold it in the middle and twist as above, but about 2 inches from the end make a right-angle bend so that the two ends are angled 180 degrees to each other. Form an eye in the end of each wire and attach the bottom leader to these eyes with knots or leader sleeves,

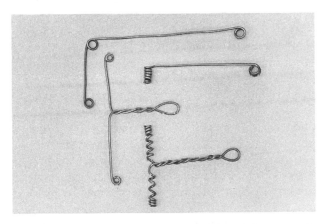

Examples of wire hook lears formed with homemade wire formers. Any type of bend or wire rig can be made this way.

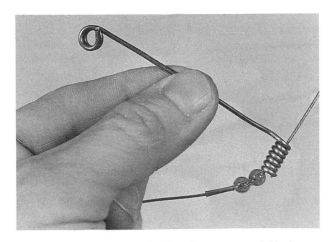

A hook lear in use. The beads serve as 360-degree rotation bearings above a leader sleeve crimped onto the wire bottom rig.

or run the leader through the two eyes using a leader sleeve and bead on the leader to hold the hook lear up in place.

Yet another method is to take a length of wire and make an eye at each end and one on the shaft, with the shaft bent at right angles at the central eye. The eye on the shaft should be offset to one end so that there is a long arm to extend the snelled hook and a shorter arm for tying into the leader. Usually these ends will be about 2 inches and 4 inches, respectively, although other lengths can be used.

Umbrella Rig. These are used for trolling and consist of several arms—similar to the ribs of an umbrella—extending out from a central eye or line-tie with various lightweight trolling lures on long snells attached to the end of each arm. In essence, these arms are similar to spreaders but with two or three spreaders attached at a central point to make a rig with four or six arms.

One easy way to do this is to use a small stainless steel screw-eye bolt (they are available at hardware stores) and two larger washers (usually called fender washers) to fit it. Make up long arms like spreader arms but with a central eye large enough for the eye bolt (usually 1/8- to 1/4-inch diameter). The bolt should be about 1 1/2 inches long. Slip a nut onto the threaded part of the bolt, add one fender washer, then, in order, the two or three spreader arms. Finish with the second fender washer and finally a wing nut. To prevent loss of the spreader arms (and the attached lures) while trolling, bend or deform the last threads on the bolt to prevent the wing nut from coming off. The wing nut then allows you to adjust the umbrella from a spread (fishing) to folded (stored) position. Since the lures used for this fishing will often twist, be sure to use snap swivels on the end of the spreader arms for the snell or mono attachment.

To prevent the arms from tangling together while fishing, you can make a small separator out of a film can. To do this, drill a hole large enough for the bolt through the bottom of the can. Then, using scissors, carefully cut six slots evenly around the perimeter of the can's top. The result should be like the battlemcnts on a castle's walls. Slide the arms onto the bolt, followed by the separator. Position the slots on the separator under the arms to hold them in position.

Weed-Guards. Weed-guards to protect the point of a hook from snagging are easy to make. Size .009 or .012 spring wire should be used for most fishing and most fishing conditions. Cut a

"Umbrella" rig made from spring utility wire, an eye bolt, and a plastic film can. Bends in each of the three arms fit onto the eye bolt and slots in the film can hold the arms in a spread position for trailing lures while trolling.

Underside of the above rig, showing the washers that fit between each of the wires.

piece of wire about one inch longer than twice the distance from the eye of the hook to the barb. Double the wire in the center, hold this bend with pliers, and bend slightly about 1/8-inch from the doubled end. This will form the "loop" that fits at the hook point. Hold the wire bend at the hook point, with the end positioned between the point and the barb, and measure to the eye of the hook. Bend the wire again at this point so that the two ends of the wire can be slipped through the hook eye and fastened to the shank of the hook.

Obviously, the length of wire needed for each

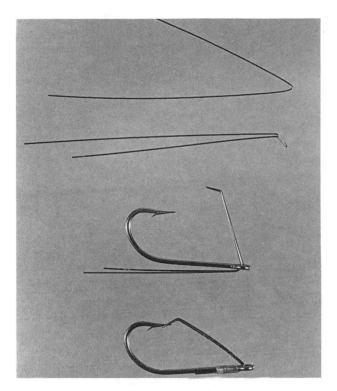

Making a wire weed-guard from light wire. Steps, from top to bottom, show bending the wire in half, forming the kink that fits over the hook point, fitting and bending the wire into the hook eye, and wrapping the weed-guard in place on the hook shank.

size and style of hook will differ slightly, so if any number of weedless wires for specific hooks are to be made, keep a record of the length of wire needed for each hook size.

There are several ways to fasten the weed-guard in place. The two ends of the wire can be wrapped onto the hook shank using mono or size A, D, or E thread. The technique used here is the same as in fly tying, wrapping a guide on a rod, or snelling a hook. (See Chapter 22 for this method.) However, instead of tying off the wrap by pulling the end of the thread under the last wraps, finish with a series of half-hitches, commonly used in finishing a fly in fly-tying.

Other techniques to fasten the weed-guard to the hook are to solder the wire in place, wrap the ends with wire, wrap with wire and solder to the hook, use thin-diameter shrink tape or tubing (the kind that shrinks with the application of heat — usually from a cigarette lighter). Incidentally, clear shrink tape and tubing is now available — you don't have to use black exclusively anymore.

There are other methods of construction. One is to cut the wire and make the first center bend

exactly as above but then position the two ends of the wire over the point of the hook. Then bend the remaining wire to fit through the hook eye, and fasten in place. Once the wire is wrapped or soldered in place, spread the two wires and, if desired, slightly bend the ends to make a spread-V weed-guard.

It is also possible to use just one length of wire, wrapping one end around the shank of the hook with the wire going through the hook eye and extending over the hook point. The result will be the wire bent on an acute angle — one leg wrapped to the hook shank, one extending down and in front of the hook point.

SINKER RIGGINGS

Sinker riggings from heavy brass or copper wire are easy to make; follow the techniques for making eyes with the homemade wire former.

Keel Sinkers. These are easy to make from simple egg sinkers: Form wire into a large D shape with an eye at each end and thread egg sinkers onto the bend in the D. To do this, use a length of wire, form an eye at one end, and then add a second eye about a third of the way up the shaft. Add egg sinkers to the shaft, bend this wire into an arc, and wrap end of the wire close to the first wrapped eye. The result is a large D with an eye at each end for placing in-line on a line/leader trolling rig.

It is also possible to make a keel trolling sinker that is adjustable for weight by making the D-shaped wire like a large safety pin so that egg sinkers can be added or subtracted at will. The end of the wire is held in place with a wire catch.

Trolling sinkers can be made by forming an eye on each end of wire that holds one or more egg sinkers, but these sinkers do not have a keel and will tend to rotate if there is any lure or bait twist.

You can make a triangular-shaped wire with eyes at each corner, an eye for the line-tie, leader-tie (to lure or bait), and drop-sinker tie for hanging a weight (for a trolling sinker). It is not necessary to make these in a triangle shape though, and a similar effect can be achieved with three eyes on the ends and bends of L- or T-shaped wire.

Eyes for molding sinkers and tin squids are easily made from heavy brass or copper wire using the nail wire former to make eye forms in the shape of a keyhole or figure eight.

Rigs for using pencil lead as West Coast steelhead fishing are possible with a crossline

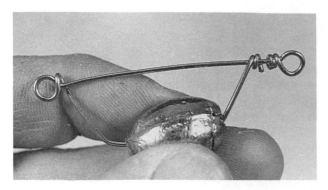

Brass or copper utility wire can be used to make sinker rigs, such as this keel-style rig made with an egg sinker. Line is tied to one eye of this rig, the leader to the other; the sinker prevents line twist.

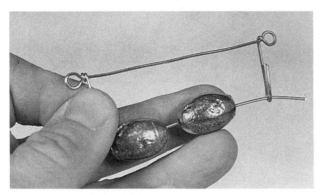

Another example of a keel sinker rig, this with a clip fastener for removing and adjusting the number and weight of sinkers used.

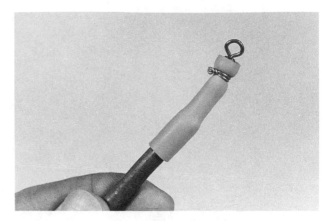

Making a sinker rig using a swivel, a short length of wire, and a short length of surgical hose. The surgical hose is slipped and wired onto the swivel and then holds any size and length of pencil lead for river fishing and drifting.

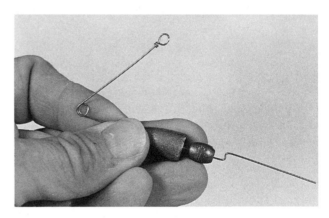

"Bait walking" type of sinker rig. The sinkers added to the lower wire (these can be changed and adjusted) allow the lure (tied to a leader at the top eye) to swim close to the bottom. The line is tied to the eye in the center of the rig.

swivel (three eyes in the shape of a T) and a short length of surgical hose. Use surgical hose slightly smaller than the diameter of the swivel eye, run the hose onto the 90-degree angle swivel eye, and secure it in place with a wrapping of thread, cord, or wire through the eye and the end of the hose. It is then easy to tie the line and leader to the other two eyes. The pencil lead is easily cut to the length (weight) required and slipped into the surgical hose.

Another way to make a river type of drift sinker is to use utility wire, preferably with a slight curve in it, and form an eye at one end. Then thread egg sinkers on to obtain the weight you need. After these are added, make a very *slight* bend in the end of the wire to just barely keep the sinkers in place. That way, if they get hung up, a strong continued pull on the line will pull the sinkers off

the wire and free the rig. Naturally, this sinker has to be adjusted each time you change the weight being fished.

KNOTS, SPLICES, AND SNELLS

Proper knots, splices, and snells are vital for any good rig. Knots are listed in Appendix E with drawings and text. It is important to use a knot for its stated purpose, since not all connections will work with all materials or at all tests.

14

Tackle Accessories

INTRODUCTION · TACKLE BOXES · BAIT BOX · CHUM
POTS · FLOATS · NETS · NET FRAMES · SAND SPIKES,
ROD HOLDERS, ROD RACKS, ROD CASES · SURF BELTS ·
SURF GAFFS · GAFFS · TAILERS · PRIESTS · WADING
STAFFS · DEHOOKERS · SNUBBERS · LEADER
STRAIGHTENERS · FISHING MARKERS · LURE RETRIEVERS

INTRODUCTION

There is no listing of tools, basic materials, or safety equipment in this chapter. That doesn't mean that tools and materials and safety equipment are not used, but only that this chapter is a "catchall" that includes those items that do not fit well into other chapters but that are easy to make.

Tools and methods are suggested where practical, and safety must be paramount, as in any tackle-making operation. Use a safe workplace, goggles, and any special safety equipment or protective clothing or gloves. Be sure you know how to use the tools needed before attempting any task.

TACKLE BOXES

It is possible to make tackle boxes—I've done it—though to be perfectly honest it is usually not practical. Today there are plenty of options in tackle containers from the major tackle-box companies such as Plano, Flambeau, and Woodstream, as well as special boxes designed to be built into boats and often seen advertised in boat and saltwater magazines. Some box styles are just plain impractical to build. Single- or double-side satchel boxes would be difficult at best and too heavy for practical use.

You can build drawer-type boxes—I built these long before the tackle-box companies came out

A homemade tackle box using thin shelving and dovetailed compartment dividers.

with their models — but they are still heavy and best when designed for semipermanent use in a boat or as a basic box to be kept in a beach buggy or fishing vehicle.

In building this type of box, I did not use a hinged front-lid cover, but instead opted for magnetic strips in the back of each drawer to hold them in place in a closed position. They worked well, although I did use a pin-type catch mechanism to hold the drawers for extra security.

Basic for any boxes are to use the lightest wood possible and to design drawers for the size of the lures you plan to carry or the type of tackle to be stored in the box. For fasteners, use a good grade of carpenter's glue, and brass or stainless steel screws.

BAIT BOX

Bait containers or boxes are preferred by some boat and bank fishermen for minnows and other aquatic bait. They are available commercially but can also be made. In fact, a floating bait box can be constructed in any size and will keep minnows in the water where they are to be fished — reduc-

ing loss through changes in pH, temperature, or salinity. There is no need to use battery-operated air pumps or to change the water at regular intervals. Basically, a floating wooden bait box is like a small boat, except that the bottom is made of hardware cloth (wire-mesh screening) to facilitate the free flow of water.

General dimensions of an average bait box are about 10 inches wide, 18 inches long, and 6 inches deep. Scrap wood can be used for the sides, end, and top, with standard shelving or plywood most popular. If you do use plywood, it should be the marine type to resist delaminating. Any wood box should be coated with a good water sealer and painted. The bottom of hardware cloth is simply stapled or nailed into place and the lid is cut from the top, hinged, and closed with a simple toggle latch. Stainless steel toggles and hinges are best, although brass and sometimes plastic are available. Screw the box together with brass screws to prevent rusting. Fasten a large screw eye or through-eye bolt to one end of the bait box to use to tie it to the boat or stake it to the bank. Varnish or paint it, and it is ready for use — just be sure to allow several days curing to prevent the paint from harming bait.

Parts necessary for making a floating bait box. This bait box is easily made from scrap lumber and hardware cloth (metal screening).

Completed box top with hinges and lock on lid.

Simple tools are all that are necessary to complete the box. The bottom will be completed with hardware cloth.

Floating box. This bait box is ideal for use at docks or attached to a boat for still fishing or drift fishing.

CHUM POTS

There are several ways to make chum pots. These useful pieces of tackle have their place in freshwater fishing for carp and catfish as well as in much saltwater fishing. Flounder, bluefish, striped bass, white perch, and other species are readily attracted to a chum line. Sometimes chum is broadcast behind an anchored boat, but a chum pot is preferable for most fishing because it concentrates the chum in a specific area and thus concentrates fish attracted to the chum.

One easy way to make a chum pot is to use a large, wide-mouthed plastic jar. Gallon sizes for mayonnaise or mustard used by restaurants are ideal for this. (Check with a restaurant, school, church, or other large user for these.)

Wash the jar thoroughly and drill or punch a

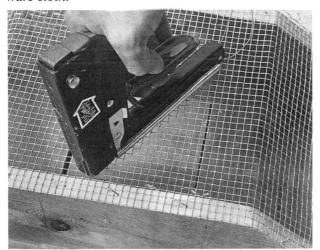

Using a stapler to staple the hardware cloth to the frame of the box.

Another way to make a chum pot is with a gallon-size plastic container. Use a drill or reamer to punch holes throughout the side of the container.

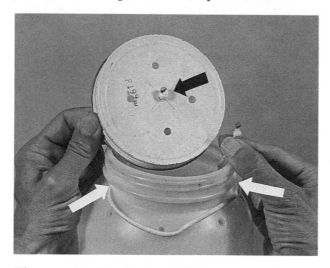

The top should also be drilled; a rope threaded through the side and knotted to the top prevents loss of the top. Arrows point to the attachments in the lid and through the sides of the container.

hole in the center of the cap. Punch more holes, all in the size preferred for the chum used, in the sides and lid. Use a drill, awl, reamer, red-hot nail, or hot soldering iron (though heated tools will make the plastic smell!). Make two more holes, one on each side at the jar's top and just below the lid. Weight the pot with several ounces of lead bars or sinkers screwed to the bottom. Knot a rope handle to run from the top center hole in the lid down through one hole in the top side and around the outside to the other top-side hole.

This will serve as a handle and a tie point for the pot, and will prevent the loss of the lid.

Another way to make a good chum pot is to use hardware cloth (wire mesh) available from hardware and building-supply stores. Hardware cloth comes in different mesh sizes, from about 1/4- to one inch—choose the mesh size best suited to the chum you plan to use. With pliers, join the mesh edges to make a container of any shape desired. Square (like a crab trap), rectangular, and cylindrical are typically good shapes. Making such a container is easy, since with wire cutters you can cut the mesh so that you have wire "fingers" along each edge to be wrapped around the edge to be joined. In all cases, make the container with the

Various sizes of hardware cloth (metal screening) can be used for chum baskets, based on the size of the chum particles.

Use pliers to crimp the edges of the hardware cloth into a circular container to make a chum pot.

top open. Use more hardware cloth for the top, making hinges of heavy wire (copper or brass is good and easily worked) so that you can open the top to add chum. A simple large snap or large safety pin will secure the lid. Attach a rope to the chum pot and add several large sinkers to it to weight it.

An alternative is to mold the weight into the pot. One easy way to do this is to use a disposable mold, such as an old metal pie tin, for the bottom weight. Make a cylindrical wire-mesh pot that will just fit into the pie tin. Melt lead (see the proper procedures and safety rules listed in Chapter 4). Pour the molten lead into the pie tin and immediately immerse the wire mesh cylinder in it. The lead will cool around the bottom of the wire to create a solid lead-weighted bottom. Make a top of mesh for the pot.

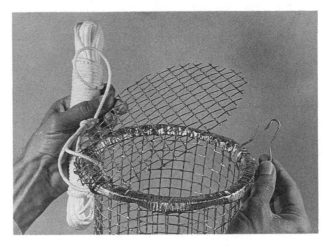

The simple top with a rim of lead and screen top secured with a shower-curtain clip.

A simple way to weight the chum pot is to set the tubular screening into a metal pie plate and fill it with lead so the screening is imbeded in the bottom.

A third possibility is to use PVC tubing, 4- or 4-inch-diameter pipe. Make it as long as you wish, but about 12 to 18 inches is best. Use one solid end or cap and a threaded clean-out flange and clean-out plug. Use the proper glue (special glues for these plastics are available at hardware stores) to attach the solid cap to one end and the threaded clean-out flange to the other. The clean-out plugs usually have square ends so they may be opened with a wrench, but you will not have to secure the end tight enough to require this. To prevent loss of the plug, drill a hole in the top center of the square end, run a knotted rope through this (with the knot on the outside), and secure the rope (again knotted on the outside)

through a hole drilled into the side of the pipe. Make sure you have enough clearance in the rope to remove and replace the plug. Drill holes throughout the rest of the pipe, using a drill size that suits the type of chum you will be using. Holes of about 1/4- to 3/4-inch are best.

In use, fill the pot with chum of your choice and lower it over the side of the boat by a short rope. The weights in the pot will sink it and the holes will allow the chum to dissipate slowly. Periodically jiggling the chum-pot rope helps to spread the chum. Another technique is to rope the chum pot on the boat just at water level where the waves and rocking of the boat will regularly wash over the pot to maintain a continual chum stream.

Two types of chum pots, with lead for weighting and rope.

FLOATS

Floats can be made in a number of different ways. The simplest version is to get a cork ball, drill it (if it does not come with a through-drilled hole), glue a length of dowel of the right diameter into the hole, and wrap several turns of wire around one or both ends of the dowel for line attachment. Naturally, most such floats are painted, and if this is desired, do so before adding the wire. In addition to cork, balsa is also a good high-floating wood, and craft stores sometimes have small plastic-foam balls that can be used as floats. If you use plastic foam, use only epoxy glue for any attachments, since other glues may attack some foams.

Refinements can include using floats of various shapes: round, oblong, tapered, football-shaped, cone-shaped, and so on. You can weight the finished product with lead so that the float is more sensitive to light nibbles, and thus better for fishing. In some cases, you might want to make floats of different sensitivities for different fish species and fishing situations. If you add lead, do so symmetrically around the bottom, adding it little by little until the desired sensitivity is reached. Epoxy the lead in place and paint the resulting float. A good way to add lead is with small split shot, lead bird shot, lead wire, or BB's.

Porcupine quills are often used for delicate floats: They can be bought from some tackle dealers and most fly-tying outlets. A loop of mono or wire wrapped to the lower end of the quill, and a small twist of spring wire or a small rubber band (such as those used for orthodontic braces, or you can make your own by cutting thin sections of rubber surgical-hose tubing left over from making hose lures) placed around the center completes the quill float. To use, run the line through the loop and then clip it in place in the center of the float with the spring wire. If a rubber-band fastener is used, the line must be run under the rubber band and through the loop at the bottom.

NETS

As inexpensive as are both original landing nets and replacement bags, it might seem foolish to even consider making one. However, there are several advantages to doing just that. First, the net can be made in any size or dimension desired. It

Tools required for making and repairing nets. The shuttles and mesh gauges at the top are from Netcraft, those on the bottom are homemade from stiff cardboard.

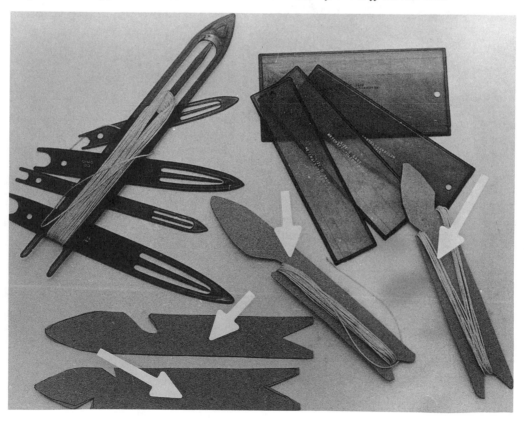

can be made of any thickness of cord, with any size mesh, of either cotton or nylon. And once the basic net knot is learned, you can make any style of net you wish. Usually, a medium-sized net bag can be completed in one evening.

Several tools are required, but all are inexpensive. You will need shuttles to hold the netting cord and mesh gauges to keep the net mesh (openings) even and uniform. Both individual and sets of these items are readily available from Netcraft.

Either nylon or cotton cord can be used for nets Nylon is more expensive but also longer-lasting and stronger for any given size. One consideration in this age of awareness of conservation and catch-and-release is that cotton nets are less damaging to fish than are those made of harder nylon. Polypropylene nets are even more damaging, though polypropylene cord is not used for hobby-net construction.

Bonded nylon, such as is available from Netcraft, is the easiest material to use because it has a slight "tackiness" that helps to "lock" the knots securely and prevent them from slipping. It is not sticky or difficult to work with. Regular nylon can be used, but it is more difficult to work with and more likely to slip, both in construction and while landing fish.

Cord for making nets comes in different sizes, but these sizes differ with each type of cord. Bonded nylon ranges from size 5, testing forty-two pounds with 4,200 feet per pound, to size 48, testing four hundred pounds with 348 feet per pound. The smaller sizes are sold in 1/4-, 1/2-, and 1-pound sizes, the larger sizes in 1/2- and 1-pound sizes. Sizes include 5, 7, 9, 12, 18, 24, 30, and 48. Generally, sizes 9 or 12 are best for landing nets, size 18 for turtle traps, and size 5 for cast nets, according to Netcraft, specialists in these supplies.

In addition to the cord, you will need some tools. These include a shuttle or two. Plastic shuttles vary by length and thickness, the thickness determined by the mesh size to be made. A small size for minnow nets is 6 inches by 3/8-inch, and the largest measures 13 1/2 inches by 1 5/8 inches. They are inexpensive and a set of eight shuttles of all sizes costs only a few dollars.

Mesh gauges are required to measure and check the size of the mesh while working. These are also made of plastic, and a set of eight costs only a few dollars. Mesh sizes include 3/4-, 1, 1 1/4, 1 1/2, 1 3/4, 2, 2 1/2, and 3 inches. These are for *square measure*, one of two methods of measuring net mesh size.

Parts available for net-making include wire frames for making landing nets, net weights for minnow seines, live-bag rings (for making the live bags to hold catches and to keep the net expanded), floats for seines, "swivels", and thimbles for cast nets.

Before beginning, the cord must be transferred from the spool or skein to the proper size shuttle, which is determined by the size of the net. Most nets have a large mesh at the upper end and gradually progress to a smaller mesh at the bottom. The plastic shuttles are flexible and the cord should be placed with as little tension as possible to avoid building tension and twisting the shuttle. Begin by locking the cord over the center "tongue" on one side of the shuttle, then alternate the cord back and forth around the end (foot) and up over the tongue each time. Quite a lot of cord can be placed on a shuttle this way. In practice, I find it easiest to hold the shuttle by one edge in my left hand, pushing the tongue out from the

The netting cord is locked in place on the shuttle to fill the shuttle.

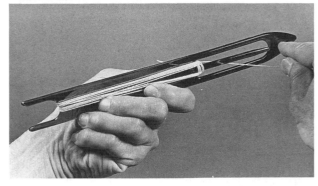

The shuttle is filled with net cord by wrapping alternately from side to side, wrapping the cord around the tongue of the shuttle each time.

main body of the shuttle to slip the cord over it. You can push the tongue back and forth this way with your finger and thumb to fill the shuttle.

Once the shuttle is loaded, you can begin in one of several ways. One is to make a short square net (a little like a short commercial gill or minnow net). Once the square net is finished, join the edges with net knots to make a completed round landing net. The Twin Bar Loop tool and the Ringway Fixture, both available from Netcraft, allow you to make nets in the round, completing one row of meshes at a time working from the frame end down to a brass ring, or from the brass ring up to the frame. Netcraft used to make a net wheel that held cord in place at the frame position, allowing the net to be constructed from the frame position to the bottom. Some of these tools are still in use and allow the making of round nets also.

Net meshes are measured in two different ways —stretched and square. Square measurement is the size of each square of mesh from one side of the square opening to the other (from one knot to the next knot). A net measuring 1 inch from one knot to the next would have 1-inch-square mesh. The same mesh would be 2-inch *stretched* mesh, since this type of measurement is taken with the mesh stretched, and the length of the slit of mesh thus formed measured.

The mesh gauge you use determines the square-mesh measurement. Thus, a 1-inch-thick mesh gauge would form a 1-inch-square mesh netting, or 2-inch stretched netting.

To begin any net, the cord must be held, secured, or clipped in place, with enough loops for the net desired. If you make a flat net, you will need a metal or wood rod on which to lay the first row of loops. Metal rods are probably best, and plain metal rods of about 1/4-, 3/8-, and 1/2-inch diameters, usually about three feet long, are available at most hardware stores. At the same time, buy two screw eyes or screw hooks with eyes larger than the rod. These are screwed into the edge of the workbench to hold the rod. The screw hooks are better because they make it easier to attach and remove the rod and working net.

Although you can make a series of open meshes that can then be transferred to the rod for making the net, you can also use a small home-made tool that will help. The tool is the mesh-net starter, and it consists of a series of screws or nails secured about 1 inch apart in a straight line onto a block of wood. Each nail or screw holds a compression spring and washer. With this tool, each

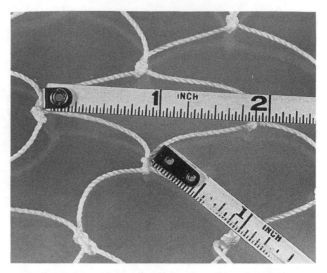

Measuring net mesh size; top, measuring the meshes stretched into a slit; bottom, measuring the sides of the square mesh opening from one knot to the next.

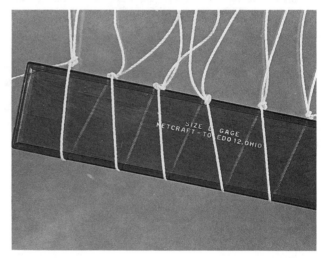

A mesh gauge is used to assure even mesh sizes while working.

Simple homemade tool for beginning net-making consists of a strip of wood with a series of fasteners one inch apart. The fasteners for fastening net cord, consist of a spring-loaded washer held in place with a screw.

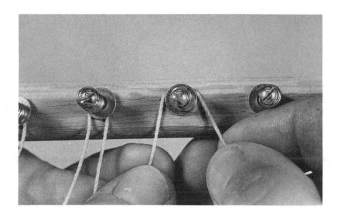

Detail of slipping the net cord onto the spring fastener of homemade net starter. Loops have to be adjusted for length with rod or mesh gauge.

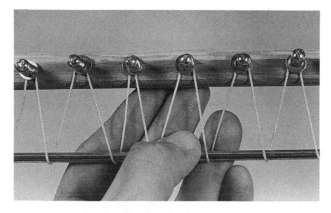

Adjusting and checking the loop length of the initial row of loops, using a rod.

loop of cord can be held in place between the wood and the spring-loaded washer: the tension keeps it from slipping as you adjust the mesh size. This also allows the use of double cord, or double selvage, to combat the added wear of the meshes on the frame or top row.

You can get by with as little as three of these spring-loaded holders, but the more you have the easier the job will be. I like at least ten. In using this tool, you will have one cord attached and spaced to these holders, and you'll begin the meshes with a second cord wrapped on the shuttle. Make sure you have enough cord for the top row to complete the length you want. If you run short it won't be a disaster, but it will require a knot.

Begin by wrapping the cord around each nail or screw under the washer to hold it in place. Use the chosen mesh gauge to check for the proper size loop. (*Note.* If you place this net on a larger-size frame, you may wish to begin with a larger mesh size that will slip easily onto the aluminum or metal frame. If so, adjust for that size and then switch to a smaller mesh gauge for the remainder of the net.)

Once you have the holders filled, use the shuttle to add meshes to begin making the net. But remember that you only have loops prepared for as many holders as you have. Thus, for this first row, you will be making a mesh row attached to the top loops for the length of the holders, then you will be removing the loops from the holders and rerigging the holders with the remaining cord, making more meshes, and repeating these steps until the first two rows (the row of loops on the holders and the first row of "real" meshes) are complete. At this point, transfer the top loops to

the rod held with the screw eyes for working the rest of the net. Naturally, if the net is long, you may have to do this in stages or get a longer rod to hold the meshes.

To make the meshes, knot the shuttle cord to the bottom of the end loop, taking care that this knot does not slip. Then hold the mesh gauge so that its top edge hits this knot, take the cord around the mesh gauge from front to back, and bring the shuttle up through the second loop, back to front. Pinch the cord at this point while holding the mesh gauge with the cord tight around it. Take the shuttle around in back of the upper loop (now pulled into a V) and around in front of the loop just formed. Pull the knot tight to make a knot on the V of the upper loop.

Let's consider the steps. I find it easiest to work from left to right, bringing the shuttle up under

Beginning the second row of mesh loops using the mesh gauge and shuttle.

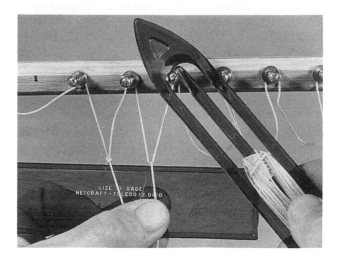

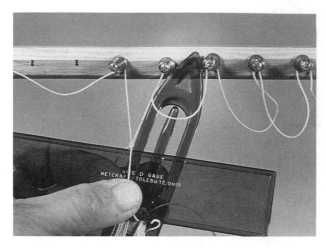

The shuttle is passed through the upper loop from behind and pulled tight to form the loop.

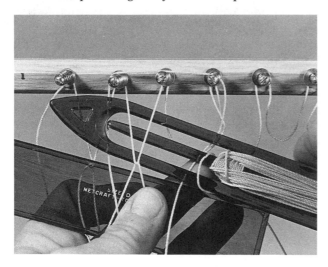

Once the loop is formed, the excess cord is held up and the shuttle passed in back of the upper loop, as shown, but in front of the loose cord.

the mesh gauge with my right hand, taking it through the upper loop with my right hand and crossing that hand over my left, pulling tight, and holding the taut cord with my left thumb. I then flip the loose cord above the mesh row, take the shuttle right to left behind the two cords forming the upper loop and through the loose cord loop just thrown up by my shuttle hand. Pull the shuttle down and to the right and tight to make a knot on the upper loop. If the knot is going to slip, it will be at this point: The just-formed knot may slip below and off of the loop. Correct this when it happens, because the slipped knot will make for uneven meshes.

Repeat this procedure with the adjoining loops all the way to the end of the net. Once at the end of the row, reverse the rod position so that you

can continue working from left to right. Naturally, if you are left-handed you may wish to completely reverse these instructions.

If you make a minnow seine or square drop net, these step are all that is required, although you may wish to add a perimeter row of double selvage or heavier cord to guard against wear. In addition, if you make a minnow net you will need a heavier cord at the top and bottom for the floats and weights. For this, string the proper number of floats or weights onto a cord of the proper length. Use the standard netting knot to attach the cord to the top or bottom of the net and use half-hitches on either side of the float or weight, around the cord on which they are strung, to hold them in place on the net. Plan equal distribution of the floats and weights along the net perimeter.

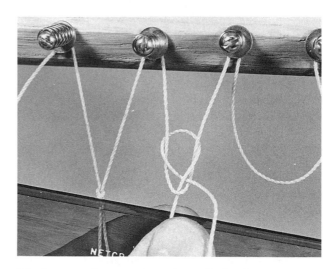

The loop net knot ready to be pulled tight.

Another view of a net knot being pulled tight correctly.

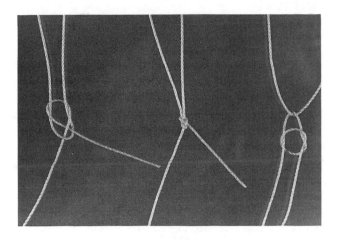

Good and bad net knots: left, open view of proper knot; center, proper knot pulled tight; right, knot that has slipped and must be corrected.

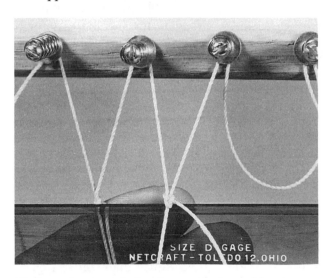

Tight net knot ready for the next loop and knot.

If you make a landing net, you may wish to decrease the size of the mesh as you proceed toward the bottom. This is simple to do by beginning a new row with a smaller mesh gauge. Continue for several rows, decreasing mesh size as desired.

If you make a square or rectangular net and convert it to a circular landing net or live net, bring the two edges together and run a row of netting knots to join the two edges. To close the bottom, use a brass or heavy-plastic ring and with a length of cord form a series of half-hitches around each loop and the ring to secure it in place. Half-hitch all the way around the ring, including all the loops, and then tie off with a square knot.

To attach the completed net to the frame, you must remove the hoop portion of the frame from the handle and thread the top row of loops or meshes onto the frame, then reassemble the net. An alternative method is to use a heavy cord to loop through each top mesh and around the frame, going completely around the frame and tying off at the yoke (where the hoop meets the handle). Wood net frames, whether for long-handled boat nets or short trout nets, require a different technique. Most have small holes through which the top loop (mesh) is threaded: the loop is prevented from coming out by means of a cord that runs the outside perimeter of the net hoop frame in a slot cut into the wood. To make a bag for these frames you *must* make the replacement bag with the exact same number of loops as the number of holes in the frame because each loop must be threaded through one of these holes.

To make a landing net, beginning on a circular frame is easier. For this, you will want a frame to make the first row of meshes and to hold the net bag while you work on it.

If you work on a circular frame to make a circular or landing net, you will want to decrease the number of loops to form a tapered shape as you work toward the bottom. This is easy to do. Run the shuttle through two loops of the upper row and then form the net knot. Do this systematically around the net, perhaps at three, four, or five equidistant points around the perimeter, depending upon the total number of meshes in the existing row. Thus, if you start with a series or forty meshes, you could decrease to thirty-six by

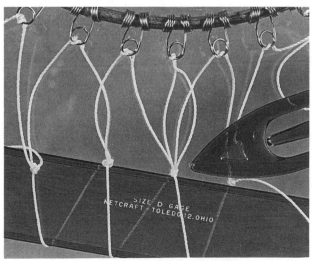

Net size can be decreased by knotting the two upper loops as shown. This is usually done several times in a single row, evenly spaced around the net.

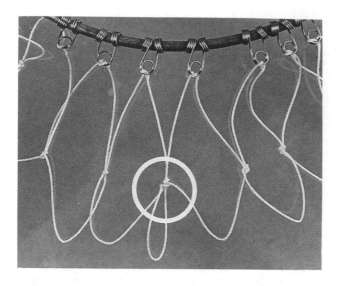

Nets can be expanded (as when making a live-bag net) by adding a second loop to the same upper loop as shown. Additional loops like this are spaced evenly around the net perimeter.

picking up two loops at four equidistant points around the bag (every ninth loop), or decrease to thirty-five by picking up two loops at five points (every seventh loop), and so on.

It is also possible to widen a net by adding extra loops. To do this, tie in an extra loop in between the regular loops. Make these equidistant around the net also. Thus, you could go from forty to forty-four or forty-five or forty-eight, if desired. Although it is not mandatory to have these additions or deletions of loops exactly equidistant, doing so will make the bag more uniform and professional-looking.

One final type of net is the bridge net. This is simply a net in a circular frame, which is suspended by three lines running to a main line. The net is used to drop to fish when fishing from high places such as bridges (thus the name), piers, bulkheads, and jetties. The best frame here is not aluminum but heavy steel rod, since you want the net to sink rapidly so that the fish can be led to it for landing. Often, it helps to place pinch-on sinkers around the bottom of the bag to sink it and prevent it from ballooning in the water.

NET FRAMES

Woven nets can be used in several different ways. First, they can be used for replacing rotted nets in standard landing-net frames. Alternately, they can be placed in discarded tennis-, squash-, and badminton-racket frames. Almost every house has in it somewhere an old racket or two that may be easily converted into a landing net.

Frame sizes of the three types of rackets will vary, and some odd sizes, such as in oversize tennis rackets, are also available. Of the three, the badminton racket is perhaps the most useful, since a tennis-racket frame is a bit heavy and the squash-racket frame is a bit on the small side.

First remove the webbing from the frame, then cut the handle to the length desired. This will be necessary on any of the frames if you are making a short-handled landing net; it will not be necessary if you are making longer-handled nets.

A cork fishing-rod grip (preformed, or built up as described in Chapter 20), a plastic or rubber-foam fishing rod grip, or a plastic bicycle grip can be used as a new handle over the racket shaft.

Once it is finished, attach the new landing net to the frame by threading the net loops through the holes in the net frame (just as described for wood-frame landing nets) or by looping the net to the frame with lacing cord spiraled around the net frame.

It's also possible to construct the rim and handle of your net. Netcraft supplies net hoops in several sizes; these are of metal rod with lugs for attaching to a wood handle. Using these, the bag is slipped over the frame or hoop and the net is attached to the wood handle in a manner to be described shortly.

It is also possible to make your own wire rims or hoop frames. Use heavy steel or aluminum rod or wire. Steel rod comes in 3/16-, 1/4-, 5/16-, 3/8-, 7/16-, 1/2-, 5/8-, and 3/4-inch diameters, often in 36-inch lengths (limiting you to a net diameter less than 12 inches), but with longer lengths available. A hoop of this wire attached to a wood handle makes a fine frame. Or the entire net may be made with aluminum tubing.

The net frame must be bent into a circle, a job best accomplished with tube benders or a wood jig that can be made to bend tubing or steel wire to different radii. Tube benders for bending conduit for electrical work are available for 1/2-inch and 3/4-inch tubing, but these are really designed for the tightest possible radii for making sharp turns and bends. Although it can be accomplished, it would be difficult to make an even circle or a larger diameter with these tools.

Steel or aluminum frames should be sized to the strength you feel is needed for the size of the net and the weight of fish to be landed. The larger and heavier the fish, the stronger the hoop frame must be. The length can be determined by multiplying 3 1/2 to 3 3/4 times the chosen rim diameter. (The circumference of a circle is 3.1416 times the diameter — the additional length is used for the lugs that will bind the net-hoop frame to the wood or aluminum handle.)

The wood jig for bending net frames is not really worth making unless you will be constructing a large number of net frames, or if you're making it for a fishing-club project to be loaned to members for their tackle-making needs. The jig consists of wood cut into a curve; the radius of the curve is determined by the size of the net you wish to make. You can use thick plywood (or several sheets of plywood); several layers, sandwiched, of wide shelving; a 2 × 6 or 2 × 8 (or larger) piece of lumber; or similar scraps. Use a saber saw or band saw to cut the wood into a even curve. To bend the aluminum or steel wire or rod, clamp the jig into a vise and clamp one end of the hoop material to one end of the jig. A good way to do this is with a C-clamp. Bend the rod gently. Once it is bent sufficiently, remove the C-clamp, shift the rod, and bend a new section. Repeat these steps until the frame is bent into a circle.

Once the frame is bent into a full circle, bend the two ends at right angles to and away from the frame rim, making each straight piece 3 to 4 inches long. At each end of these pieces, bend short lugs inward to fasten into the wood frame or into a wood plug if the net is used with an aluminum handle. This will keep the net from canting sideways when you are landing a big fish. To make these final bends, it might be necessary to clamp the wire ends in a vise, hammering over the short lug. It is also possible to use a longer length of wire, bending it over the lugs and then cutting to length; this is an easier but more wasteful method.

The same jig can be used to make hoop frames from aluminum or other tubing. The Reynolds Metal Company, and more recently other companies, for some years has marketed do-it-yourself aluminum materials, including tubing, strap, rods, bars, channel, and sheets. The tubing comes in 6-foot or 8-foot lengths in 3/4-inch, 1-inch, and 1 1/4-inch diameters. Before choosing it for your hoop frame, make sure that the tubing will not create too much resistance when you swing the net under a fish for landing. Some specially shops sometimes carry 1/2-inch-diameter aluminum tubing.

As with wire, choose the framing length by multiplying the diameter of the net by 3 1/2 or

3 3/4 times to determine the length of the rim material required. Take care not to bend the tubing into too sharp a bend. Tubing bent at too sharp an angle will deform or crack — examples of which can be readily found in old and abused aluminum lawn furniture.

The smallest bending radii recommended for the three diameters of aluminum tubing are as follows: 3/4-inch tubing, 6-inch radius; 1-inch tubing, 11 1/2-inch radius; 1 1/4-inch tubing, 13-inch radius. If required, these radii can be cut in half by tamping damp sand into the tubing before it is bent.

Once the tubing is bent in a full circle, remove it from the jig, tamp damp sand into both ends, and place the tubing on a jig with a smaller 3-inch-radius circle (or bend around a large pipe or similar object of this size). *Note.* The sand should be damp; not so dry that it falls apart when cupped in the hand, but not so wet that water can be squeezed from it.

Plug the end and then bend the end of the tube in the jig, making the bend opposite the curve of the frame. Repeat with the other end. The two ends of the hoop frame will now be parallel so that they can be slipped into an aluminum handle. Knock out, and then wash out, the sand.

Flatten the inside edges of the frames ends until they slip inside the 1-inch or 1 1/4-inch aluminum handle. In doing this, take care that you do not completely flatten and thus weaken the sharp bend you've just made. Once the ends of the frame hoop are securely in the handle, drill two 1/8-inch holes; each hole goes through the handle and one of the frame ends. Add self-tapping sheet-metal screws to the handle through these holes and the frame is finished. (Unless you spiral cord around the net frame to hold the bag on the frame, add the bag before completing this step of fastening the hoop to the handle.) The screws make it possible to remove the hoop frame and add the net or replacement bags.

Cut the handle to the desired length. Nine-inch handles are standard for stream nets; 24-inch to 48-inch handles are standard for boats and canoes, the exact length to be determined by the fish sought, water, and conditions. The handle can be finished with an aluminum spring snap cap (designed for this in do-it-yourself aluminum) but I prefer a crutch tip, chair tip, or, best, a bicycle handlebar grip of the proper size. In addition to smooth aluminum tubing, there are also oval-embossed, hexagonal-embossed, and rib-embossed patterns. These patterns make a more attractive net handle, one that will less readily show scratches, and what is more important, will provide a better grip than the smooth tubing.

Frames of wire or rod can be finished the same way, but you might have a problem in securing smaller-diameter rod into a relatively large-diameter tubing. One solution to this is to use a short section of dowel as a spacer between the rod lugs and the internal diameter of the handle.

For this, first select a short length of dowel that will fit snugly into the aluminum-handle tubing, or cut a dowel down to size. The dowel should be about 6 inches long for most nets. To fit the hoop frame to this plug, cut, saw, or rasp grooves along two sides of the handle the diameter and length of the net wire or rod. Cut an additional hole or depression (it can be drilled straight through the plug) at one end of the dowel to hold the short inward-bending lugs that will keep the frame from twisting. This hole must be the diameter of the net rod or wire.

Place the net frame into the plug (add the net bag first unless you intend to tie it on with cord), and slip the plug with the lugs in place into the end of the aluminum handle. This should be a snug fit, and you may have to hammer it a little to get it into place. Once the end of the plug is flush with the end of the handle, drill two 1/8-inch holes on each side of the handle over the plug area. Use four pan-head sheet-metal screws to hold the plug in place. By removing these screws you can remove the hoop frame for bag replacement.

The same technique for making the wood plug can also be used to attach the hoop frame to a wood handle. In this case, however, you will have to use a sleeve of aluminum to hold the lugs in place in the wood-handle grooves, or you will have to wrap the handle/lug area to secure it. If the wood handle is the right size, you can use a sleeve of aluminum tubing left over from other projects or perhaps salvaged from old discarded lawn furniture. If you wrap, use light wire of brass, aluminum, or stainless steel and the same method as for wrapping a rod (see Chapter 22) or whipping a rope.

Because the wire is stiff and harder to work than thread, it may be necessary to wrap the wire by securing the end in a vise and rotating the handle under tension to maintain pressure on the wrap. To begin the wrap, you may wish to use a small nail, wrapping the wire one or two turns around the nail before beginning to wrap around the wood handle and the frame lugs. Also, you usually cannot finish by pulling the wire under the previous wraps, as with rod wrapping, but must use a long staple or another nail or wood screw to hold the end securely.

SAND SPIKES, ROD HOLDERS, ROD RACKS, ROD CASES

ABS, RS, PVC, and CPVC plastic pipe, along with plastic conduit used in electrical work, can be used for a number of fishing-tackle items. You are not limited to the four plastics listed, but they will illustrate uses and applications in tackle-making.

CPVC is chlorinated polyvinyl chloride pipe, PVC is a similar polyvinyl chloride pipe, RS is rubber styrene plastic, and ABS is acrylonitrile butadiene styrene. These materials are all rigid and will not rust, rot, or corrode. They are lightweight, easy to cut and work with hand tools, and are readily available at hardware and plumbing-supply houses.

Plastic pipe comes in different wall thicknesses. PVC, for example, comes in different "schedules" of 80 (very thick and strong), 40 (medium strength and thickness—ideal for rod cases), and a light-wall 120 (thinner and ideal for lightweight rod cases and rod racks in boats). (There are also "SDR" sizes of PVC pipe, which are not generally found on the homeowner market, but which include SDR 13.5, SDR 21, and SDR 26.) I like the schedule 120 for lightweight projects (rod cases, rod racks, tubes to hold lures in surf bags) and the heavier schedule 40 only for large-diameter rod cases for airline travel, and sand spikes.

Diameters of plastic pipe range to 10 inches or larger, but the most useful for tackle-building are the 1/2-inch to 6-inch sizes, usually available at hardware, plumbing-supply, and lumber-supply houses. Both PVC and CPVC pipe come in these size ranges, including 1/2-, 3/4-, 1, 1 1/4-, 1 1/2, 2, 2 1/2, 3-, 4-, 5-, and 6-inch in both schedule 40 and 80. The lighter-wall schedule 120 comes in all these but the 5-inch size. ABS, a black plastic pipe, is useful in sizes of 1 1/2-, 2-, and 3-inch diameters.

Most of the pipes come in different wall thicknesses made for specific purposes, such as meeting health standards for piping drinking water, or burial underground, or high temperature. For example, a 6-inch pipe that you might want for a large travel rod case will come in eight different types of pipe, each with a different wall thickness and each requiring different end fittings and caps.

The size of pipe needed will vary with the project. In all cases, you need the pipe large enough to hold the rod. For example, with most sand spikes or rod racks, you will want 1 1/2- or 2-inch-diameter pipe, but with some rods with large butt caps or large grip diameters you may need 2 1/2-inch diameter. For the sand spikes, the larger, heavier, schedule 40 pipe is best; for rod racks that just support rods, the lighter schedule 120 is fine.

Pipe is generally available in 10- or 20-foot lengths, but often hardware stores will sell you exactly the length you need. In addition, you might check the trash bins of plastic-pipe distributors or construction contractors (ask at the front desk first and explain your interest—many companies are understandably opposed to people just randomly rooting through their trash bins.)

WORKING WITH PLASTIC PIPE

The basics for working with this material are simple. The pipe is easily cut with any type of saw, including wood or hand saws. While these will leave some rough edges (the coarser the saw the rougher the edges), these can be smoothed with a wood rasp or half-round coarse file. Often it is

best to flare the pipe for easier insertion of the rod butt into the sand spike or rod rack. To do this, it is necessary to heat the pipe. Heat it over a stove or propane-torch flame, taking care to keep the pipe away from the flame, which could scorch it. One way to do this is to hold the pipe to the *side* of the flame, not over the top of it. This will provide heat to soften the pipe without the flame that could char it. Rotate the pipe slowly to heat evenly. Be sure to heat only the end of the pipe

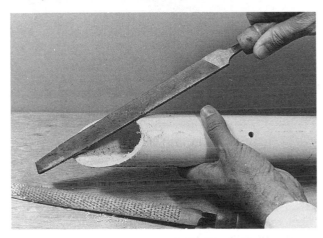

Rasps and files can be used for smoothing cut ends of pipe after sawing with a wood or hacksaw. Here, a tapered cut has been made for the end of a sand spike.

Tools and materials for making sand spikes, rod holders, rod cases and similar items from plastic pipe include the pipe, some hardware and simple saws and drills. A bottle is necessary for flaring the pipe for some uses and PVC cement allows welding parts together.

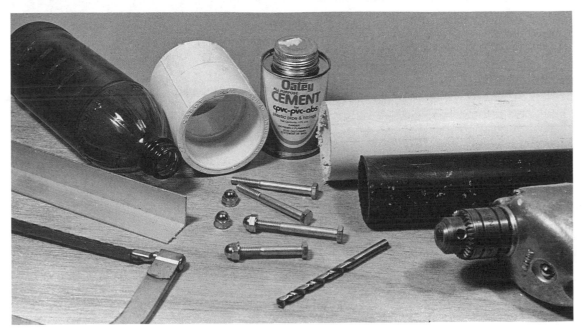

Heat applied to the end of the plastic pipe allows flaring the pipe with a bottle. Use sufficient heat to flare the pipe—pressure is not necessary and should not be used. The towel is used for safety should the bottle break.

you wish to flare. Heating the pipe over too large an area will lead to bulging and deformations when you try to flare it.

When the pipe is hot (hot enough to flex very easily), quickly press the end firmly onto the neck of a glass soda bottle you've chosen for its taper. Take care when doing this to hold the pipe well up and away from the bottle and to wrap your hand with a towel for protection in case the bottle should break. Also, make *sure* that the pipe is hot enough to flare evenly and with little pressure. While I have never had this happen, it is always possible that the bottle could break. Be prepared and protected for this possibility, even if it is a remote one. Once the pipe end is flared properly, hold it in place on the bottle until it cools sufficiently to hold the flare. Plastic pipe has a memory and will return to its original shape and diameter if it's removed from the bottle neck while still hot. If necessary, repeat this process with more heat until the pipe is properly flared for your purposes.

SAND SPIKES

Sand spikes are nothing more than tubular rod holders most often used for surf fishing but also suitable for other shore and bank fishing. Use 1 1/2-, 2-, or rarely, 2 1/2-inch plastic pipe to make them. Generally, 2 feet is a serviceable length for sand spikes, although commercial ones range from 20 inches to 36 inches. Five 24-inch-long sand spikes, or four 30-inch sand spikes, can be made from one 10-foot length of pipe. Actually, if you cut the pipe end (the bottom end) at a 30-degree angle, you will end up with sand spikes slightly longer than the above dimensions. For this, do not cut the pipe into four or five equal lengths, but alternate the angled (30-degree) and squared (90-degree) cuts so that there is no waste, except perhaps for one small section at the end. To get the sand spikes of identical lengths, measure and mark the pipe, but when making the angled cuts (30-degree), use these marks for the *center* of the cut and cut at an angle across it.

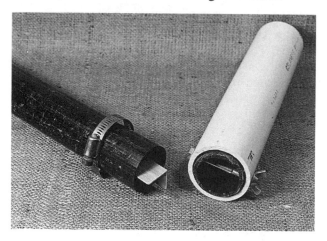

Examples of collapsible sand spikes made in two parts for easy storage in a surf bag. The parts are reversed and clamped in place to use.

Now flare the upper end of the pipe using the bottle technique. To complete the sand spike, drill a 1/4-inch hole straight through the pipe about 12 to 15 inches down from the upper end. (You can make this hole higher or lower if desired—check your rods before drilling.) Insert a 1/4-inch stainless steel or brass bolt through the hole. If possible, make the bolt exactly the right length to just slightly protrude through the far side of the pipe and use a cap nut (blind nut) with some glue or Loctite. The bolt keeps the rod from falling into the sand spike.

Naturally, you can also make a longer sand

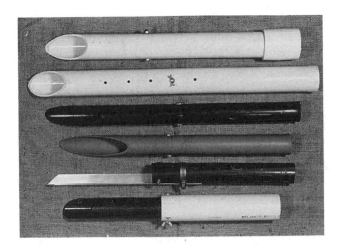

Different types of sand spikes using different kinds and diameters of plastic pipe with flared, straight and collared ends. The second from the top uses a series of holes and a bolt and wing nut as an adjustable rod stop for different length rod handles.

spike of longer plastic pipe to place the rod higher, an advantage when fishing heavy surf where raising the line will help prevent the waves from dragging the line, and thus the bait.

While it gets off of the subject of plastic pipe a little, there are other ways of making sand spikes. Aluminum tubing of the right diameter (perhaps an old but damaged aluminum rod case?) can be cut at an angle, drilled for bolt placement, and used as a sand spike. Similarly, a 2-foot length of plastic tubing can be fastened to a 3- or 4-foot length of 1- or 1 1/4-inch aluminum angle using two hose clamps. (An alternative is to use a hose clamp on the upper part of the pipe and run the bolt through the pipe and the aluminum angle to secure the lower end.) Cut the aluminum angle at a sharp angle at the end to make a spike or point that can be sunk deeply into the sand. Such a sand spike will provide a high "reach" for the rod, as will long plastic-pipe tubing.

ROD HOLDERS FOR BOATS

Use the same techniques to make vertical rod holders for boats. Cut a 12-inch-long section of pipe and insert a bolt, long rivet, or similar pin to prevent the end of the rod from dropping below the holder. Because of the variety of boat materials available and boat construction methods, no exact mounting method can be described. In some cases, you may be able to run the bottom bolt through the aluminum or a fiberglass gunnel overhang. Other usual methods for the top of the

rod holder, or for both ends, are to use pipe strap (available in metal or plastic—plastic is better to eliminate corrosion) or short lengths of aluminum strap or U bolts around the sides of the rod holder at two points. Drilling two holes through the sides of the rod holder (straight through both sides), enlarging the hole on one side to take a screwdriver, and screwing the holder to the boat (be sure you have a solid base for this) also works. Another good method for mounting such rod holders on vertical aluminum tubing in boats (grab rails, bimini tops, and so on) is to use two hose clamps, each large enough to fit around both the rod holder and the aluminum tubing.

If you are going to use spinning tackle, cut and file a notch in the upper part of the holder for the foot of the reel to prevent it from swinging around in a bouncing boat. This will not interfere with carrying conventional or trolling rods.

ROD HOLDERS FOR BEACH BUGGIES

Surf anglers always like to have rods at the ready, but the 8- to 14-foot length of some surf sticks makes it hard to carry them in a beach buggy while roaming the beach in search of fish or birds working over bait.

Rod holders fixed to the front bumper of a beach buggy hold rods vertically and ready for instant use. ABS, PVC, or CPVC plastic pipe is ideal for this; choose a diameter (1 1/2 to 2 1/2 inches) suitable for the grips and butt caps on your rods. Lengths can be cut, flared, and drilled as above and attached to the front bumper or a

Rod holders on the front of a beach buggy. Such rod holders are typically made of plastic pipe, clamped to a board that is then fastened to the front bumper.

removable board to make an excellent surf-rod holder. Up to ten rod holders can be rigged together. Leave several inches between each holder so that the rods and reels do not rub together while you are traveling the beaches.

There are several tips for making these. First, you can make them long enough to hit the reel at the upper end of the pipe to prevent the reel from swinging and hitting other tackle. You can cut a notch, as described above for boat rod holders for spinning outfits, or you can just cut a wide, deep V into the upper flared pipe to stabilize any rod and reel combination. Second, although you might be carrying rods on long pipes, run a 1/4-inch bolt through the bottom end anyway. There might be a time when you wish to carry a reelless spare rod in the rack that would otherwise drop straight through. Third, make sure that the pipes and the basic rack are no lower than the lowest part of the bumper on the beach buggy. A lower board or pipes invite trouble with reduced clearance under the vehicle.

A fourth tip, one that I picked up years ago from Ken Lauer, then a guide on the Outer Banks of North Carolina at Cape Hatteras, will prevent

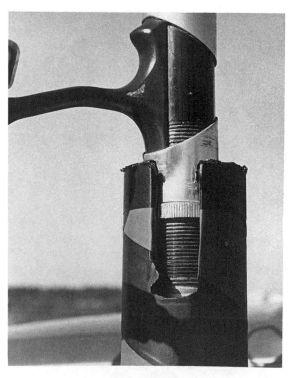

Slot cut into the upper end of a beach-buggy rod holder to receive the shaft of a spinning reel. This will prevent it from rotating and knocking into other reels.

tangles of the bottom rigs and sinkers often used in the surf. Mount a small length (6 inches) of pipe, capped with a plastic pipe cap or drilled to take a through-bolt, to the base of the rod holder in between each pipe holder. Use this to hold the heavy sinkers used in surf fishing and prevent them from swinging around.

One easy way to mount the pipe and rod holders to the vehicle is to use a large 2 × 10 or 2 × 12 board, through-bolt the pipes to the board, and use similar J-bolts or strapping to bolt the board to the vehicle bumper.

ROD RACKS FOR BOATS

Rod racks in boats may be constructed using plastic pipe. The design is for horizontal racks on the sides of small boats, usually just below the gunwale or under an overhanging walk-around gunwale. For this, use light schedule-120 plastic pipe as a sheath for the tip section of the rod, much as you would use a sheath for a sword. Cut a length suitable for the rod you plan to carry in the rack, and flare both its ends. (You flare both ends so that in the eventuality of racking a rod longer than the tube you will have a flare to prevent catching the guides or tip-top as you pull the rod from the rack.)

For the handle end, use a wood or metal platform on which the handle can rest at the reel position. To keep the rods from bouncing around in rough water, use bungee cord (braided-cover elastic cord) in a loop will stretch over the platform and secure the handle. Another possibility that I have used is hook-and-loop fastener. The loop side is glued to the underside of the handle platform; the hook side is secured to the back of the platform where it can be secured over all the rod handles.

Use a platform wide enough for the pipe sheaths you plan to use. Most boats will hold quite a few of these to carry rods ready-rigged. Even on my small johnboat I have 6 racks to a side (racks for twelve rods in all), arranged in two layers of three racks each.

ROD CASES

Plastic pipe can be used for rod cases, either individual-rod or large multiple-rod travel cases. The 1 1/2- to 2-inch pipe is best for most individual rod cases (check handle-diameter and guide size on spinning rods). For travel cases, you will want 3-, 4-, 5-, or 6-inch-diameter pipe.

Schedule 40 is probably best, but if you won't be shipping rods by commercial airline, the schedule 120 will be fine and much lighter in weight. For any size rod case, glue-on end caps are available for the closed end. There are several options for the removable end. You can get a threaded adapter, glue it onto the end of the pipe, and then use threaded end caps (sometimes called plugs) to close the rod case. You can also get a slip-on (really glue-on) cap and rout out part of the inside to take a riveted, hinged hasp, then rivet the staple onto the pipe. That way, you can slip the cap on and off and lock it in place when required. This is most feasible with the larger-diameter multiple-rod cases.

Whenever a permanent cap is required, be sure to use the appropriate glue for the plastic pipe you are using. Most often PVC or CPVC is used, and a special glue (really a solvent) is available that will work on both of these plastics. Follow directions, use with plenty of ventilation, swab the pipe with the glue (a swab is provided in the cap of the glue can), and immediately add the cap. Hold for the few seconds it takes to cure.

Rod cases can be made from do-it-yourself aluminum tubing, available in a 1 1/4-inch-diameter and 6- or 8-foot lengths. By choosing the right length for maximum usage of the aluminum, you can get two or three rod cases from each piece. Special aluminum end caps are available, or you can improvise and use the plastic slip-on caps available for plastic tubing (check for the proper size). One easy way to make a permanent bottom-end cap is to cut a small plug of wood sized to fit snugly in the aluminum tubing, secure it in place, and fasten it tight with three small pan-head screws through the aluminum and into the wood. Paint the wood to seal and protect it from moisture. The main disadvantage of the aluminum tubing case is that the largest-diameter tubing generally available—1 1/4-inch—is only large enough for fly rods or ultralight one-piece spinning rods.

Tools and materials needed for making one type of travel rod case.

Sawing large-diameter PVC pipe for a rod case. Cut the pipe several inches longer than the longest rod or rod section you wish to carry.

A slip-on pipe cap provides a removable cap — scrape the side of the pipe for added clearance.

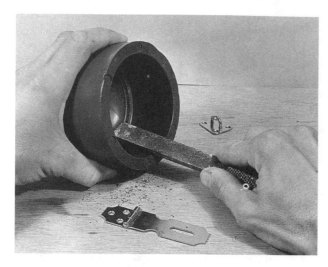

Use a rasp to cut space in the cap for the lock hasp. Hasp can be bolted or riveted into place.

Hasp in place, with foam used as a cushion on the end of the cap.

Completed cap end, with lock hasp parts in place.

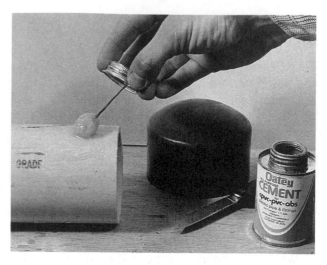

A second slip-on cap can be cemented to the other end using special PVC or other pipe cement.

SURF BELTS

A surf belt is a belt on which is carried all the items needed for surf fishing; these belts are usually worn over waders in high (deep) surf. As a result, there is no standard surf belt or even standard items to carry on it. (some accessories might include a short surf gaff, small bags of plugs and tin squids, a fillet knife, pliers in a holster, and a dehooker.)

Surf belts can be made of almost anything. Often they are assembled from surplus or surplus-style armed-services belts that have quick-lock snaps to fasten in front. Often, small surplus bags can be converted to surf bags for plugs and squids. Since these belts are wide, it is frequently necessary to jury-rig a method of holding pliers holsters on the belt.

A frequently seen possibility is the use of 1 1/2- to 2-inch-wide nylon straps or belting, secured with the quick-lock snaps available in camping, mountaineering, and outdoor-equipment stores. Small belt bags and cases are available at the same stores, and the pliers holsters will usually fit on these narrower belts.

One way to convert a small bag into a plug bag is to use light schedule-120 or lighter PVC or CPVC tubing as vertical compartments for the lures. Alternatives for the PVC tubing are 1 1/4-inch aluminum tubing and the rigid plastic sleeves used over electric candle lights, available from lighting stores.

SURF GAFFS

Surf gaffs are short gaffs used in the surf, and usually carried on a surf belt during wading. The gaff can be made in the same way as other gaffs but has a short handle—usually less than 12 inches long. Too long and it becomes unwieldy. It is best to have a coiled cord to attach the gaff to the surf belt. An old phone cord will work fine for this, but it should have a light breakaway attachment at one of the ends—either the belt or the gaff handle. That way, should the gaffed fish pull the gaff free of your hand, the attachment will break and you won't be pulled into the water.

Make a holster for the gaff by using a base plate of aluminum or plastic with a bolted-on screw eye to hang the gaff. A better alternative is to use hook-and-loop fasteners to secure the gaff hook to the base plate. Instead of hook-and-loop fasteners, you can use snap fasteners, available from sewing and fabric stores. In all cases, the point should be sheathed to avoid accidents.

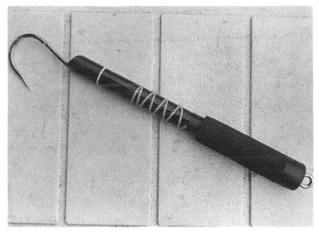

Gaff made by outdoor writer Charlie Most using a length of discarded rod blank, foam grip and a gaff hook cemented into the end of the rod. Decorative wraps match his rods.

GAFFS

It is possible to buy steel or stainless steel rods and wood handles and make a gaff from scratch, but I can't recommend it. Proper construction of such a gaff would require equipment for bending 1/4- or 3/8-inch rod and for tempering it —processes generally not done by the home craftsman.

The best way to make a gaff is to buy a ready-made gaff hook and secure it to a wood or aluminum handle. Gaff hooks are made from both

Making a long-handled gaff using regular gaff hook placed in a dowel. Here the wood dowel has been marked for routing to hold the tang of the gaff hook; the dowel will then be inserted in an aluminum handle.

1/4- and 5/16-inch stock, are properly tempered, and have a built-in tang for attaching to the handle. Gap sizes from 1 1/2 to 2 1/2 inches are commonly available from tackle stores and mail-order outlets.

Wood handles can be made from 1-inch or larger stock dowels, replacement shovel or hoe handles (hickory and very sturdy), or similar wood stock. Wood handles made and sold specifically for gaffs are also available. To make a wood-handle gaff, groove the gaff end of the handle, sizing the groove to fit the tang of the gaff. Notch or drill the end of the groove to fit the right-angle bend at the end of the tang. Then place the gaff hook into the groove to check for fit, add 24-hour

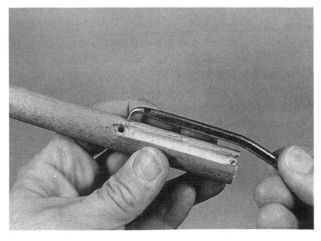

Routed and drilled wood dowel reach to receive the gaff-hook tang.

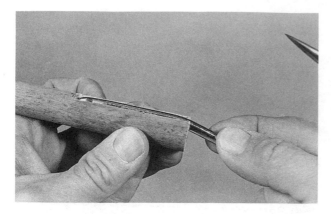

Gaff-hook tang in place in the dowel. The tang should be almost flush with the surface of the dowel, as shown.

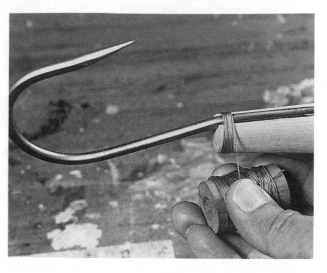

An alternative in building gaffs is to use a wood handle and wrap the end of the handle and gaff-hook tang with wire, as shown.

After completely wrapping the tang, the wire can be held in place using a small screw, as shown.

epoxy glue to the groove and hole, and cement the gaff hook in place. Once it has cured, use a file to remove any excess glue from the surface of the handle. Wrap the tang area with stainless steel or brass wire, using a small screw or nail on which to wrap the wire as a starting point. Wrap tightly and use a similar nail or staple to hold the wire once the wrap is complete. Often, shovel handles used for gaffs and gaff handles are tapered at the end. If this is the case, begin at the gaff end or lower end and wrap up the handle.

If you wish to begin the wrap by wrapping over the wire (as is done with thread in wrapping a guide in place), use a small nail or staple to hold the wire down as you begin the wrap under pressure. One way to maintain high tension on the wrap is to hold the end of the wire in a vise and wrap with your hands, leaning back against the gripped wire to create tension. One way to finish the wrap is to work with tight tension up to about ten wraps from the end, use Vise-Grips or a C-clamp to hold the wraps in place (so that they do not loosen with the next step), and make ten loose wraps, sliding the end of the wire under these wraps. Then go back to the first of the ten wraps and wrap tightly, using pliers if required, to get maximum tension. Work along all of the wraps until you get to the end, and then use pliers or a vise to pull the wire end tight. Another, easier way is to use a long staple or nail to secure the end of the wire.

Another possibility to secure the tang, provided that the end of the gaff handle is not tapered, is to use a short length (about 6 to 8 inches) of aluminum tubing as a sleeve over the end of the handle to hold the tang in place. For this, glue the

tang into the groove and use a block of wood and hammer to gently force the aluminum sleeve into place. Use one or two pan-head sheet-metal screws or round-head wood screws to secure the sleeve in place on the wood handle. This is sort of a reverse of the method in which a wood plug is used in an aluminum handle.

Gaffs can be made with aluminum handles, using 1- or 1 1/4-inch smooth or embossed aluminum tubing. You will still need a gaff hook with a tang. You will also need a short length (about 6 inches) of dowel or hardwood that will fit snugly into the tubing. Groove and notch the wood to fit the tang, making sure that the tang will fit into the groove so that it is flush with the outer circum-

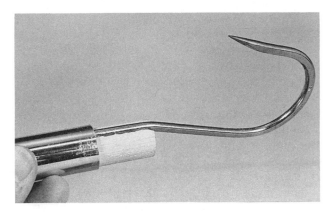

Gaff hook with the tang in a dowel being inserted into an aluminum handle.

One way to hold the dowel in the aluminum handle is to use several pan-head screws, as shown.

ference of the wood plug. Fit the tang into the wood plug and start working the wood plug into the end of the aluminum tubing. It should fit snugly but not be so tight that it will risk splitting or deforming the metal wall of the tube. Now hold the aluminum handle vertically on the floor (with a block of wood under it to prevent scarring the floor) and gently hammer the dowel and gaff hook into the tubing until the dowel is flush with the end of the aluminum handle. Use a block of wood between the hammer and dowel to prevent deforming this plug. Once it is hammered home, drill the tubing and the wood dowel through at two points, with both holes at right angles to the plane of the gaff hook. Secure the gaff hook with long solid-aluminum or brass rivets, sheet-metal screws (four are used — one at each hole on each side, and each no more than half the thickness of the dowel), or wood screws used in the same way as the sheet-metal screws. Use as fasteners as

noncorrosive as possible: stainless steel, brass, aluminum.

Another way to make a gaff is to get a large hook and use this for the gaff hook. There are two possibilities for this. One is to get a needle-eye hook (commonly used in saltwater fishing), file the barb off, and use a wood plug as above. But in this case, drill a hole the diameter of the hook shank through the center of the wood plug and hammer the hook shank into place. Before beginning, measure the length of the hook shank so that you know where to drill to secure the hook. If possible, seat the hook so that the drilled hole that secures the hook will go across the grain to prevent the possibility of splitting the wood. Then gently hammer the wood plug and hook into the aluminum handle. Measure and drill a small hole to go through aluminum, wood plug, and hook eye. Insert a thin bolt or pin through the hole and hook eye to prevent the hook from pulling out, and the gaff is finished. (Naturally, the same technique can be used to place this hook into a wood handle with an aluminum sleeve.)

The second possibility is to use a large-size standard hook with a standard ringed eye. File off the barb. For an aluminum handle, groove a wood plug to fit the hook shank. Use a larger drill to drill a hole at the end of the groove large enough to receive the hook eye. Unlike the previous procedure, make sure the groove and the hole for the eye are deep enough to receive the hook and a pan-head screw that will secure the hook into the wood plug. Place the hook in the groove and secure it with the right size screw. Then gently

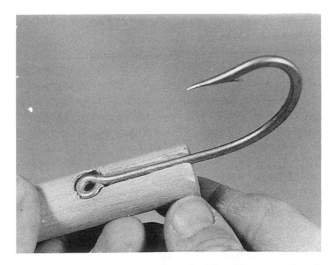

Dowel drilled and routed to hold a big-game hook as a gaff hook. Later the barb will be removed.

Another way to make a gaff using a hook is to drill a hole in the end of a dowel, insert the gaff hook and drill a hole through the dowel to hold a pin through the eye of the hook.

hammer the plug into the aluminum handle and secure the handle with four wood screws or pan-head screws through four pilot holes drilled through the aluminum into the wood plug. This can also be done in a wood handle, but you will have to slip the aluminum sleeve over the hook shank first and then work the hook shank into the previously made groove. As a result, this type of sleeve is often shorter than normal.

The best handles for most gaffs are bike handle-bar grips, available from bike shops and variety stores. These are best glued onto the handle using a vinyl glue. For long gaffs—those usually 4 feet long and longer—two grips are often used, one at the end, and the other a foot or two down the handle. For this second handle you can also use a bicycle grip. Use a razor blade to cleanly cut the closed butt end of the grip off and use vinyl glue to secure the handle where you wish. Then add the end grip.

You can also use the foam grips (EVA or Hypalon) used for rod grips. These provide a good grasp, especially if they are glued in place, but they are more difficult to slide in place on the blunt tubing end. Details can be found in Chapter 20, but basically consist of using an appropriate-sized dowel, tapered and lubricated, as a guide to open the tubing and slide the grip in place. Another alternative is to use a longer aluminum handle than is needed, taper it with a long angled cut, slide the grip in place, then cut the aluminum flush and cap it.

Another handle alternative is to wrap heavy braided nylon cord securely around the handle to form a grip where you wish and of the length you wish. To do this, wrap just as you would wrap a rod guide, beginning under high pressure to over-wrap the end of the cord, then wrapping securely and tightly along the handle. Finish by wrapping over a separate loop of cord six or eight times, cut the end of the wrapping cord, tuck the end through the loop, and pull through. Since this will by necessity be a tight wrap, you may need to use pliers on the cord loop or fasten it in a vise to pull it and the cord under the previous wraps.

There are many variations to these methods, and to gaff styles and sizes. For example, some anglers use heavy-wall rod blanks for handles, choosing blanks that have a butt diameter similar to that of a gaff handle—about 1 inch. The gaff hook is placed in a wood plug, grooved for the tang, and the plug is glued into the small end of the rod blank. A lot of glue is necessary because rod blanks are tapered and the plug can only be as large as the hole in the tip end. The plug should be pinned with a rivet, fastened with small flat-head screws (so as not to impede the subsequent thread wraps), and then the tip end of the rod should be double- or triple-wrapped with heavy rod-wrapping thread (size E or EE) for hoop strength.

Gaff lengths are usually in even feet, but you can make them any length you wish. Short hand gaffs, sometimes called "release gaffs" for their purpose in some fishing, have virtually no handle at all and consist of only a hook in a short handle, most of which is covered by a bike handlebar grip. Longer surf gaffs are about 12 to 18 inches in length, while boat gaffs will vary with the type of boat, the height of the gunwale, and the size and type of fish being landed. Typical lengths are 2, 3, 4, 6, and, rarely, 8 feet long.

It is also possible to make a hand gaff or release gaff that does not have a handle. It is nothing more than a large hook fastened to a braided rope loop through the hook eye. To make one, file or grind off the hook barb and sharpen the point. Run the rope loop through the eye of the hook. Knot the ends or secure it by wrapping it down along the hook shank with lighter cord. The important dimension in this hand gaff is the size of the rope loop. It is *not* used to put your hand through—if you use it to unhook a tarpon, this could result in your being pulled into the water, an unpleasant experience at best and highly dangerous at worst. It is used to loop around

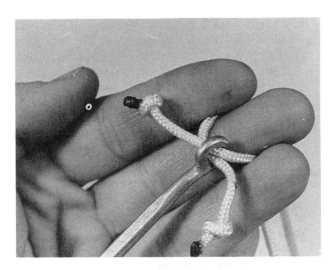

A simple hand gaff made with a loop of cord knotted through the eye of a big-game hook (note the barb has been removed). The loop must be the right length, as described in the text.

your thumb: the rest of the loop goes around the back of your hand and the loop and hook shank are held in your hand. That way, should a fish threaten to pull you out of the boat, simply opening your hand will pull the gaff off your thumb without risk or danger. Naturally, such a gaff, or any short gaff, should *never* be used to land or unhook any toothy critter such as a shark, bluefish, pike, muskie, or barracuda.

Sharks often will roll when gaffed in the body (if you plan to release your shark, cut the leader). Some commercial gaffs are made with additional grips that rotate. Holding these grips allows the shark to twist, and the gaff will rotate without danger of ripping out of your hands. To make a gaff that will accomplish this purpose, use a long-handled gaff, preferably of large-diameter (1 1/4-inch) aluminum tubing. If you can get heavy-wall aluminum tubing for these big-fish applications, so much the better. Add the regular grips, but immediately adjacent to them add two additional grips. These are made by using PVC or CPVC pipe just large enough to rotate on the aluminum tubing. (Remember, these plastic pipes will vary in type and thus wall thickness and inside tube diameter.) An ideal inside diameter for the plastic pipe used on 1 1/4-inch aluminum tubing would be about 1 3/8 inches. For better gripping, it is best to make these grips a little longer than the average 6-inch-long bike grip—a length of 8 to 10 inches is best. In addition, cut two small sleeves from the plastic pipe, each about 2 inches long for each grip. Cut lengthwise through the wall of

these short sleeves to remove just enough material so that the sleeve will fit tightly on the aluminum tubing when screwed in place. (Another alternative is to cut sleeves from the next size smaller plastic tubing, cut the wall lengthwise, and expand the pipe to fit onto the aluminum tubing. Any slight gap that results will not affect performance.)

Make sure that the end cuts on these sleeves and on the rotating grip sections are completely smooth and clean. Assemble by adding one sleeve and screwing it in place with two or three small pan-head sheet-metal screws. Add the rotating grip and then add and fasten the second sleeve. Be sure to leave about 1/8- to 3/16-inch clearance for easy rotation. Add the regular bike grip (with the closed end cut off) above this, and then at the end of the handle add one more rotating grip and one more stationary bike grip. The result is a long gaff (usually about 6 feet) that you can hold with the firm bike grips when sinking the hook into the fish, immediately grabbing the adjacent rotating grips should the fish start to spin. Often it helps to add nonskid materials (available in strips for bathtubs and for boat steps and ladders) to the smooth plastic grip for better grasping.

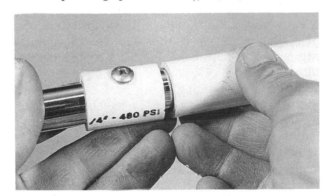

For shark gaffs, rotating handles prevent a spinning shark from twisting the gaff from your hands. One way to make these is to use a loose-fitting plastic pipe for the handles, using short lengths fastened to the aluminum handle as stops at each end.

A completely different form of gaff, but one with the same purpose and function, is the "bridge gaff." While often called bridge gaffs, these tools are ideal for fishing from any high place where it is impossible to pull a fish up with the rod or to get a regular gaff to the water. Bridges, piers, some jetties, and bulkheads are all ideal spots for such a gaff.

A bridge gaff is nothing more than a series of gaff hooks connected to a snap that can be attached to the fishing line: the gaff hooks are connected to a rope to pull up the catch. There are endless varieties of these. Some consist of two or more hooks placed to face in opposite directions and attached to a snap link (available at hardware stores in different sizes); the snap link is also attached to a large fishing snap, shower-curtain clip, or spiral loop of wire that allows quick attachment to the fishing line. The gaff is lowered to the hooked and spent fish on a rope. The snap on the fishing line keeps the gaff hooks close to the fish. Once at the water level, the rope can be mainpulated to get the hooks under the fish, upon which a quick jerk hooks the fish that is then pulled up to the angler. Some anglers leave the barbs on these hooks for a more secure hold; most file or grind them off (see also bridge nets).

TAILERS

Tailers are also used to land fish, but by catching the tail of the fish in a noose rather than gaffing it with a hook. Although this might initially seem less damaging to the fish than even lip-gaffing (if you plan to release it), a tailer can damage the tail of the fish, and the fish's muscles and ligaments if it is lifted out of the water. To help stabilize a fish in the water in combination with a lip gaff to remove a hook, a tailer is usually safe for the fish.

A tailer is nothing more than a noose on the end of a handle (such as a lightweight gaff handle); the noose is held open so that it can be quickly slipped over the tail of a fish. The noose is held open by means of a short length of light flexible cable or braided rope with a ring at the end and a longer length of stiffer springlike cable or spring steel that will bend into a U shape. This, however, requires smooth attachment of the short length of flexible cable or rope to the end of the larger, stiffer cable or spring steel, something usually difficult for the home craftsman to accomplish. (The problem is with the *smooth* attachment of the two parts.)

An alternate and good way to make a tailer is to bind the two cables together, allowing the lighter, more flexible one to extend well beyond the stiffer cable. Thus, for an average salmon tailer, you would want a length of lightweight cable about 3 1/2 feet long, and stiff cable or spring steel about 2 1/2 feet long. Using the plug method described for gaffs, cut a piece of wood 6 inches long with a diameter equal to the internal diameter of the handle. For this landing device,

you can use lighter aluminum tubing: 3/4-inch is fine. Most tailer handles are about 3 to 4 feet long, but you can customize to any length. Groove the plug for the two cables, running the groove along opposite sides of the plug. Butt the two cables and run them along the groove, around the end of the plug, and down the groove on the other side. This wrap-around will hold the cables in the handle securely. Drive the plug into the end of the handle and secure with four pan-head sheet-metal screws. It is also possible to cement these parts into the end of a short length of strong rod blank scrap. Use heavy cord to wrap a "bump" of cord at the very end of any handle used. This "bump" will hold the ring in place when the tailer is in an open, ready-to-use position.

For the other end, attach a bike grip, cord wrapping, or EVA or Hypalon foam rod grip material (see Chapter 20 for details on getting the foam in place on the handle). At the point where the cables exit the handle, wrap to the end of the two cables with cord or plastic (electricians') tape, or secure with a clear plastic polyethylene tubing sleeve. Choose tubing that will fit over the two cables smoothly. (To slide the sleeve in place if

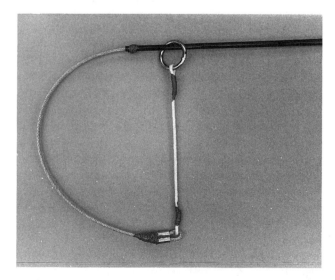

Tailers to land fish by the tail can be made in several ways. This one is made using an old hollow rod blank through which is run some cable, which is then secured to rope or lighter cable. Braided rope is used here; light cable would be used for sharks and large fish. The ring along the rope or cable slide tight and tighten around the fish's tail. The small built-up ball of thread on the end of the tailer rod serves as a stop to prevent the ring from prematurely sliding off of the rod.

the tubing is a close fit, you may have a tie a cord to the end of the long, lighter cable, run it through the tubing first, fasten it in a vise, and then pull the tubing against tension to slide it up to the end of the handle. Lubricating it with an antimoisturizer such as WD-40 will also help.)

Once the two cables are secured you will have about 12 inches of light, thinner cable extending from the end. Get a welded ring, and attach it to the light cable by looping the cable around it and wrapping with wire, or use a sleeve (like an oversized leader sleeve for wire fishing-leader construction) hammered into place to hold it.

To use the tailer, slip the light cable through the ring to form a loop, and slide the ring up over the doubled cables and the end of the handle and over the wrapped thread "bump." Doing so will cause the cables to form a rough D-shaped opening that may be slipped over the tail and body of the fish. To trigger the tailer, pull it quickly against the side of the fish, which will cause the ring to slip off the handle and slide down, closing the open loop as you pull on the tailer to catch the tail of the fish. If the loop slips too easily, you may wish to add a round-head screw to the end of the handle as a stop or detent to hold the ring in place until the tension against the fish pulls it free.

Alternate methods of making a tailor can include using spring steel in place of the heavier cable to trigger the tailer and telescoping the spring steel (or heavy cable) into the body of the handle for travel and storage. The basics of this telescoping method are to use two wood plugs. One wood plug is made small enough in diameter to slide along the internal diameter of the handle, with the spring steel and/or cables securely fastened to (not just looped over) the plug. The second, shorter plug has a hole through its center loose enough for the cables to run through, and is fastened with screws to the handle. It serves as a "stop" for the sliding plug to keep the cables from coming out and to hold the tailer in an open position.

PRIESTS

A priest is nothing more than a club to kill a fish. While perhaps seeming and sounding brutal, this tool is actually humane. If you plan to release a fish, it should not be harmed and should be released immediately—preferably by unhooking it without taking it out of the water. If you plan to keep a fish, it is far kinder to kill it immediately

and get it on ice (or gut or fillet it and place on ice) than to allow it to suffocate in the water on a stringer or out of the water in a cooler, fish box, or on the deck. (Some regulations prohibit filleting fish on the water, so check local rules before doing this.)

To make a club, there are a number of possibilities, all easy to accomplish. Hard wood turned on a lathe to your personal design is one possibility. Other, simpler, ones include using a broken tool handle (shovel, rake, hoe) cut to length, smoothed, and sanded. For added weight, drill a cavity in the end of the priest, run a pin, nail, or screw or two into this open cavity from the outside, and then fill it with molten lead. A few ounces are generally plenty, and the screws or pins will hold the lead in place. Do *not*—repeat *not*—hold the priest while filling it with molten lead. Instead, place it in a hole in the backyard, in a sand pile, or in something equally sturdy. Then pour. (Be sure to read first and follow all the safety tips and instructions for melting lead in Chapter 4.)

Another, similar, alternative is to use a short length of pipe or aluminum tubing, plug all but a few inches at one end (with sand or a cork or wood plug), add a screw or two to keep the lead from sliding, and fill the space with lead. Add a bike handlebar grip to the other end for a handle.

WADING STAFFS

A handy item for any river angler, a wading staff is easy to make the same do-it-yourself aluminum tubing previously mentioned. One-inch tubing is best; the length is dependent upon your individual preference and height. I am six-one and find 55 inches a good length. Parts needed for a wading staff include 1-inch aluminum tubing, a heavy-duty crutch tip, a bicycle handlebar grip, 30 inches of plastic or nylon strap, short wood plugs or dowels to fit the aluminum tubing, screw eyes, 4 feet of light braided rope (about 1/8-inch diameter), and a dog leash or French-style snap.

Use a hacksaw to cut the aluminum tubing to length. If you have any doubt about the proper length, cut it long—it can always be shortened later. Add the crutch tip to one end. (The best type of crutch tip, with a metal plate molded in place to prevent the aluminum tubing from cutting through, is available from some medical-supply houses and better professional drugstores.) Cut a 4-inch length of wood dowel to fit snugly into the other end of the tubing and plane one

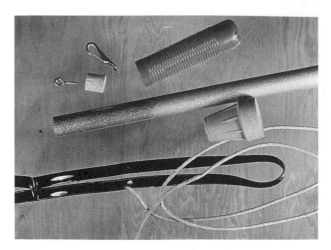

Materials required for making one type of wading staff.

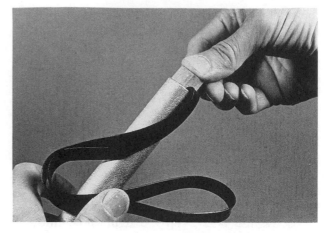

To add a strap handle to the wading staff, use a cork or small wood dowel that has been cut along one side for the strap, pushed into the end of the aluminum shaft.

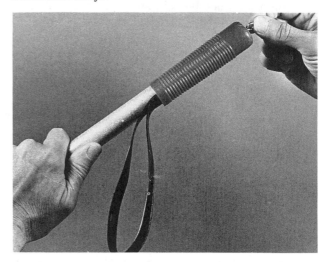

Add a bicycle-type grip as a handle on the wading staff. A screw eye added to the top will allow attaching a tether to prevent loss. A crutch tip goes on the other end.

side to wedge the strap into place. Take 2 1/2 feet of strap, fold it in half, and place it along the flat side of the dowel as the dowel is tapped into place in the tubing. Inserting three inches of the strap ends into the tubing will leave enough strap for a serviceable loop extending out from the handle.

Tap the wood dowel home and fit the 1-inch diameter handlebar grip. Since the grip will have to fit over both the aluminum tubing and the plastic strap, soak it first in hot soapy water to soften and lubricate it for an easier fit. Glycerine and special aerosol-spray lubricants will also help to slide the grip onto the tubing.

Add a screw eye to the top of the staff through the hole in the plastic bike grip and into the wood plug.

Attach one end of the 4-foot cord (1/8-inch parachute cord, available from surplus stores, works well—polypropylene rope will float and is good for this reason) to the screw eye or to the plastic-strap handle, if you desire. Tie the other end of the cord to the snap. A dog-leash snap is okay, but a French snap, which opens at the center, is far easier to use when fishing. The cord will prevent the wading staff from floating away while you're fishing, and the snap makes it easy to secure the staff to clothing such as a fishing vest.

An alternative is a modified ski pole with the ring and webbing removed from the bottom. For certain river bottoms, the sharp pointed end holds better, and some anglers like the molded handles with which most ski poles are equipped. Ski poles comes in different lengths and often can be found in secondhand thrift stores like those of the Salvation Army and Goodwill. As with any wading

staff, use a cord and snap to attach it to your clothing.

DEHOOKERS

Several types of dehookers may be made. They can be nothing more than a stick, forked at the end, by which to catch the bend of the hook and lever it backward out of the fish's mouth for removal. Such dehookers (often called disgorgers) can be made by notching the end of an old toothbrush handle (for small fish), notching a 1/4- or 3/8-inch dowel for larger fish, or notching the end of a thin strip of any metal.

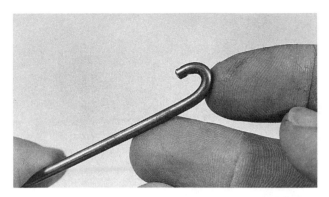

Make a dehooker by using steel or brass rod and bending one end into a tight "J" shape.

A better disgorger for quick hook removal, provided that the hook is not too deep, is to use a length of round-stock steel or brass rod, bent into a J shape. For this, obtain a foot or two of steel or brass rod 1/8- to 3/16-inch in diameter. (Base the diameter on the rod material and size of fish to be caught.) Use a vise and pliers to bend a sharp J shape in one end of the rod. This should be very sharp and small, with a gap no larger than about 3/8- to 1/2-inch at most or large enough to allow passage of the hook eye.

Secure the other end of the disgorger into a handle. There are several ways to do this. One method is to drill straight through the side of a 1- to 1 1/4-inch dowel, 6 to 8 inches long, using a long aircraft or electricians' bit. Run the straight length of rod through the dowel and make a bend in the rod at the end.

Another method is to use a similar dowel 4 to 5 inches long and drill straight through the center of one side. Drill a second blind hole alongside the first hole. Insert the rod through the first hole and make two right-angle bends to fit the end of the

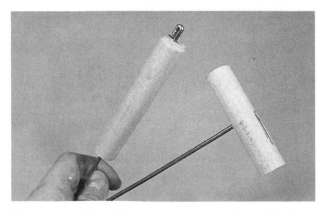

Two types of handles on dehookers. The "T" shape gives a better grip for use with big fish.

rod into the blind hole. Add glue and seat the rod in place.

You can also bend the rod into an elongated D-shaped handle by bending the rod back on itself with three right-angle bends. Wrap the end once around the main shaft of the dehooker, or weld or solder the end to the main shaft.

The dehookers with wood handles are easier to hold and use, particularly with heavy fish. However, the flat all-metal rod model takes up less space in a tackle box or gear bag.

To use the dehooker, lift the hooked fish into the air, slide the J-shaped hook down the line to the bend of the hook (or grab the bend of the hook with the dehooker), and hold the hook while you pull the line and hook down. Often the weight of the fish will pull the hook free. If not, a sharp jerk will snap the fish free of the barb and you can drop the fish into a fish box or back into the water.

SNUBBERS

Used when trolling for trout and salmon with long lake trolls, snubbers are nothing more than surgical latex tubing secured with braided line running through the center and a swivel or snap swivel on each end. The line is connected to the swivels at the ends. In use, snubbers are placed between the long lake-trolling rig and the short leader/lure to take up some of the shock of the strike of a strong fish.

To make a snubber, first gather the parts: two swivels or snap swivels, a 6-inch length of light surgical tubing, 15 to 20 inches of heavy (fifty- to hundred-pound test) braided fishing line, and some light copper or brass wire. Any size surgical tubing can be used; thicker tubing will require a stronger pull (strike) to reach full stretch.

First, tie the braided line to the eye of one swivel or snap swivel using a clinch, improved clinch, or a similar knot. Use a long upholstery needle or fine doubled wire to run the end of the braided line through the 6-inch length of tubing. Pull the tubing up close to the eye of the swivel, slip it over the swivel, and wrap and twist light copper or brass wire around the tubing and the covered swivel eye to hold it in place. Now pull the tubing out to a full stretch, allowing the braided line to run freely in the center of the tubing while doing so. Now pinch the end of the tubing to hold the line and release the tubing.

Tie the loose end of the braided line to the eye of the second swivel. If some slack occurs while

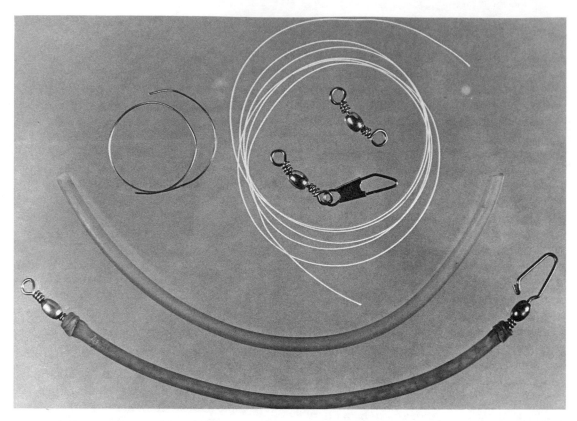

Materials for making snubbers include surgical hose, Dacron line, snaps, swivels, and wire. The line is threaded into the surgical hose and tied to the snaps and swivels, which are fastened to the hose with wire.

you pull the knot tight, adjust for this before tying the knot by pulling some of the braided line out of the tubing. Trim any excess. Pull the rubber tubing out to full stretch again and slip it over the second swivel eye. Secure the tubing around the eye with copper wire. Fold the ends (about 1/4-inch) of the tubing back over the wire wrappings to protect them, and the snubber is ready for use.

LEADER STRAIGHTENERS

With a patch of leather and a small sheet of rubber, it is possible to make a simple and effective fly-fishing leader straightener that can be clipped to your fishing vest or other clothing.

Natural rubber, such as used to be found in automobile tires, is an excellent leader straightener. Pinch the leader between the flaps of a folded-over rubber patch, pull under tension, and the leader is straightened by the heat that is caused by friction.

For a better grip, add a leather backing to the rubber patch. A small square of natural rubber

about 2 × 2 inches, a patch of leather the same size, and some eyelets are all that is needed.

Experiment with rubber before making your leader straightener. The best I have found are the large squares of red-rubber patches found in auto-tire patch kits. The backing can be peeled off and the patches attached to the leather. Eyelets, or do-it-yourself pop rivets, in each corner will secure the two patches together. Eyelets are perhaps best, because a light cord can be run through them to secure the leader straightener to your vest or to a retractable pin on the vest.

FISHING MARKERS

Fishing markers have a number of uses in both freshwater and saltwater fishing. Essentially, a marker is a float with a line and sinker or weight attached. Admittedly, some types can be bought cheaply enough, but you can make your own if you so desire. Markers serve to mark channels, fishing reefs, stream bottoms in man-made lakes, dropoffs, points, breaklines, FADs (Fish Attractor Devices), and other fishing spots—most located first with a depth-finder.

Carried on a boat, markers make it easy to mark a fishing spot temporarily because they can be thrown out immediately to mark the chosen spot and will unwind. Once you are through fishing, they are picked up, rewound, and saved for the next trip.

Freshwater markers are smaller and lighter than those used in saltwater because the area covered is usually smaller and the chop on the water usually less. The buoy or marker for saltwater fishing must usually be larger, both for buoyancy and easy visibility.

There are many ways to make markers. For a freshwater marker, cut a 1 × 4 × 5-inch board or similar-sized plank into an H pattern. The center of the H is used to wind the cord, and the "wings" prevent the marker from unwinding further once the sinker hits the bottom.

The dimensions of the H depend upon individual preference. However, if the H is made too big, or if the center core is cut too narrow, it will take a heavier sinker to unwind the board.

Once the board is cut out, paint it white, fluorescent orange (over a white base coat), or a similar bright color that will contrast with the water. Tie on and wrap light nylon cord on the center bar of the H, wrapping on enough to allow the sinker to hit the bottom of the deepest hole of any fishing water. For freshwater fishing, this is usually 25 feet for ponds and shallow rivers; 50 feet in deeper ponds, rivers, and shallow lakes; and 100 feet in the deepest lakes. A sinker of several ounces tied to the end of the cord completes the outfit. Since these are simple to make, it is best to cut out several at once, in case you find it necessary to mark several fishing spots in one area, or to mark the border of a breakline, channel, or streambed.

For saltwater markers, a larger, more visible buoy is desirable. One-half to 1-gallon bleach or similar household-product bottles serve well as buoys. Clean off the labels, rinse the bottle out, and glue the cap in place. If the bottle has a handle, tie the nylon cord to it and then wrap the cord around the middle of the bottle. (Otherwise, fasten the cord securely around the middle of the bottle.) Depending upon the depth of water you fish, this line may be from 50 to 200 feet in length.

The one disadvantage of this method is that, because the bottle is not flat, the entire cord will unwind once the bottle is thrown out of the boat. For this reason, do not make the cord any longer than necessary. However, even with the entire

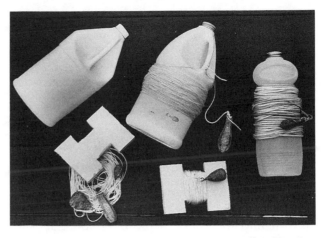

Examples of various types of fishing markers made from bottles and scraps of wood cut into "H" shapes.

cord unwound, the cord angle that is caused by tides and winds will not be enough to misrepresent the marked location significantly. Because of the larger size and more rugged intended use of saltwater markers, a heavier sinker might be necessary to hold bottom.

One solution to the problem of the cord completely unwinding is to use a flat bottle that will have less of a tendency to turn over once the sinker hits bottom. These flat bottles are usually smaller than round ones—about 1 quart is a common size—but white ones will still be readily visible and will float high enough to be seen.

An alternative is to take one of the 1/2- to 1-gallon round bottles and partially fill it with wet plaster, concrete, or gravel mixed with glue. Run a couple of large screws through the side of the bottle, fill it about 1/5 to 1/4 full with the material you've chosen, and turn it on its side with the screws down, to be covered by the plaster or concrete. Allow the mixture to cure. The screws will prevent the weight—which serves as a keel—from rolling. Coat the screws on the outside with silicone sealant to prevent leaking.

You can also make markers from the dense closed-cell foam used for packing delicate instruments. The brittle type of foam will break with time, but the flexible rubbery type (such as Dow Ethafoam) will last forever. It can be found as supports and packing shims for TV sets, VCRs, and other electronics, and is easily cut to shape with a sharp knife.

Still another method is to buy two polystyrene 3-inch-diameter balls (though other sizes can be used also) and drill a blind hole in each to accommodate a short length (4 to 6 inches) of dowel or broom handle. Use epoxy glue (other glues might "melt" the plastic) and glue one ball onto each end of the wood dowel. To give the marker an off-center weight to keep it from unrolling cord completely, drill two additional holes in the foam balls (both holes at the same relative position on the balls) and glue in 1/2- to 1-ounce lead weights. Drill a small hole through the center of the wood dowel and insert nylon cord, wrapping it around the wood dowel. Add a sinker or lead weight at the end of the cord that is sufficient to cause the marker to roll when it is thrown into the water. If desired, you can paint the marker, but use caution because some paints will dissolve some foam plastics. If possible, use an epoxy paint.

An important tip on weights for any markers: Although you can use lead sinkers, old spark plugs, or other such weights for markers, the best method is to use a weight that can be attached or wrapped onto the marker to prevent the cord from becoming loose while the marker is stored. You can use pure lead and pour out a thin layer of it, or fill a small discarded cookie sheet to a depth of 1/8-inch. Allow the lead to cool and cut

the lead into stripe about 1 inch wide by 4 to 6 inches long. These will be similar to the strips used in some commercial markers and will wrap around the center core. A second method is to obtain (or mold) hollow pencil lead, such as is used for West Coast steelhead and salmon fishing. Run a screw eye into the hollow core and cut off the length you need for the marker weight desired. Since this material comes in several diameters, you can adjust weight by varying its size. (In cases of molding lead strips or pencil-lead weights, be sure to check the instructions, general tips, and safety rules in Chapters 4 and 5.)

LURE RETRIEVERS

Lure retrievers, used to retrieve lures caught on the bottom, can be made in a variety of ways. All involve a weight to get down to the bottom, some way to temporarily attach the retriever to the fishing line to act as a "trolley," and a heavy line to pull up the lure.

One of the best retrievers is one that I designed years ago and that consists of the attributes just listed, with some chains on the weight to help catch and pull free the lure; the heavy line is

Tools and materials needed to make plug retriever.

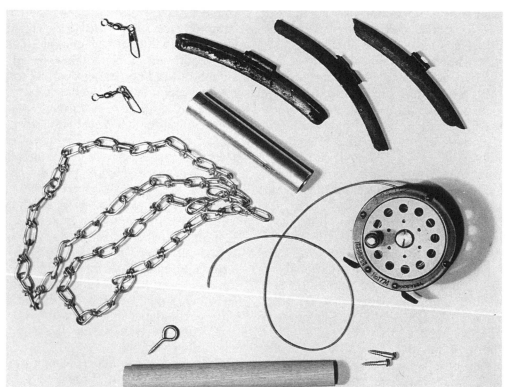

spooled on an old fly reel for storage.

To make this retriever, you will need 4 feet of light chain, a short length of aluminum tubing, a little lead, some heavy nylon cord, part of a broom handle, and a cheap or discarded reel. Construction is simple. Take a 4-inch length of 3/4- or 1-inch aluminum tubing and drill two holes completely through the sides. Make each hole large enough to thread the chain through (I like no. 3 Inco Coil chain, a double-loop weldless wire chain, but similar-size jack chain or other types will also do. For this chain, a 3/8-inch hole is just about right.) Make the holes at right angles to each other and separated so that the chains threaded through the tubing will clear each other.

Slipping the chains into place in the drilled holes.

Drilling the aluminum tubing to accommodate the chain.

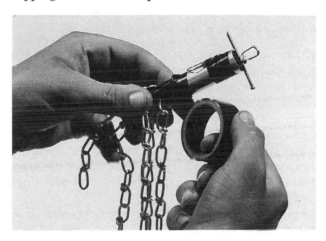

Wrapping the hole openings with tape.

Drill two smaller holes in line through one wall of the tubing. Cut the chain into three equal 12- to 14-inch lengths. Run one length of chain through the center of the tubing, leaving one link exposed at the upper end. Then run the other lengths through the larger holes so that you have a total of five chains hanging down from the lure retriever (one from the center tube and one from each hole). Make sure you have equal lengths of chain hanging from each hole. Getting the last length of chain into position might be a little difficult, but if you twist the chain it can be worked through.

To make a hanger that can be attached to the fishing line, use stiff wire, preferably stainless steel, about 15 inches long. Bend a curve in the middle. Then, holding it in a vise or with pliers at this bend, make several complete spiral turns with each end. Position the ends of the wire into the smaller holes in the tubing and use needle-nose pliers to bend these at right angles once they're inside the tubing. This special twist of wire allows

you to place the lure retriever onto the fishing line with ease at any point on the line.

At this point, wrap the lure retriever with masking or electricians' tape to hold the chain and the wire in place and to prevent lead leakage around the holes. Paper tape, such as masking tape, works better than plastic tape, which has a tendency to burn when lead is poured. Wrap as securely as possible around all of the holes, and completely cover the bottom of the tube through which the chain hangs. Place the lure retriever into a container of sand, leaving only the top opening exposed. The sand will prevent additional leakage of the lead, will absorb the heat of the lead, and will safely hold the tube upright during the pouring. If the top link of the chain slides down inside the tube, hold it in place with a nail run through the link and laid across the top of the tube.

If you have a ladle for pouring, so much the better. If not, an old discarded pot or coffee can

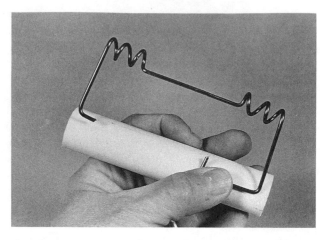

Pouring the plug retriever full of lead. Note that the plug retriever is placed in a can of sand and that the top link of chain is held in place with a nail.

(held with a pair of pliers) will do. Junk lead is fine for this, including lead wheel weights from service stations, printers' lead, and other lead alloys. *Before you go further, be sure to read all the pouring instructions and follow the safety directions found in Chapters 4 and 5.*

Melt and pour the lead outside the house — lead fumes are dangerous. When pouring the lead, make sure it is hot and completely molten — not just slushy.

Pour the lead rapidly into the tube until it is filled. Make sure that the top link of the chain is centered in the lead. It can be positioned in the liquid lead with a pair of pliers if necessary. Allow the lead time to cool and then remove the retriever from the sand and unwrap the tape. If all has gone well, the tube will be completely filled with lead and no lead will have leaked through the wrapped openings. Remove any such excess lead with wire cutters, pliers, or a file.

While the above describes the original lure retriever as noted in *Tackle Craft* (with the variation of the bent wire in place of snaps for adding the fishing line), there is an easier way to make the same tool. For this, use aluminum or PVC tubing for the retriever, run the chain through the tubing, and add additional chains at the end using large split rings or chain repair links. Make sure that the chain goes all the way through the tubing so that the upper link is the tie for the heavy cord. Add the bent wire used for placing the lure retriever onto the fishing line.

Then tightly wrap masking tape around the bottom of the tubing to seal off the area where the chain links exit. An alternative that works better is to use some flexible kids' clay (the kind

Another way to make a plug retriever with an improved line attachment is to use PVC pipe, filling the pipe with lead bits or sinkers glued in place with casting resin or glue. The twisted rod that will be inserted into the pipe makes it easy to add or remove fishing line.

that does not harden) and pack it around the end of the tube and chain. Use a nail across the tubing to hold the upper link out of the tube and then alternately add a little resin, then some lead, then some resin, then some lead, until the tube is completely filled. For this you can use regular or five-minute epoxy glue or casting resin (the same kind used for offshore lures, which see). For the

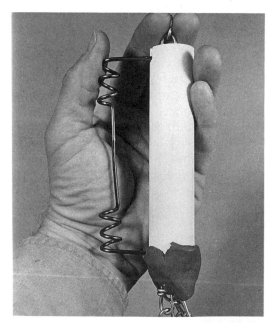

Plug retriever ready to pour. The clay at the bottom prevents leakage of the resin or glue where the chains are attached. One chain goes all the way through the pipe.

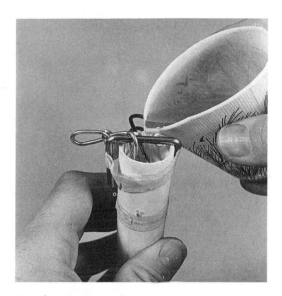

Pouring the casting resin.

lead, you can use old sinkers, scraps of lead from the molding operation, old solder, or other heavy materials. Allow the resin or glue to cure and then remove the tape or clay.

Another simple version is to buy or mold a very large (several ounces) egg sinker, form an eye in heavy wire, and run the wire through the egg sinker. Then form another eye, but instead of cutting the wire after wrapping this eye, extend the wire at right angles to the main wire, make a second 90-degree bend, and then bend into loose coils. These loose coils make it easy to add the fishing line to track the lure retriever down to the hung lure.

The heavy cord holding the lure retriever is tied to one of the eyes. If desired, chains can be added to the other eye to catch the hooks of a lure.

To make it easy to use the lure retriever, I mounted a cheap reel (fly reel) onto a 6-inch length of broom handle (1-inch dowel will do fine also), using a screw to attach each end of the reel foot to the wood handle. At the end of the dowel, I attached a screw eye through which to run the heavy cord. Fill the reel with heavy nylon cord, or at least enough cord to reach the bottom of your fishing waters.

To protect the end of the cord from rocky ledges, stumps, and rocks, cover it with plastic tubing. To do this, use an 18-inch length of thin

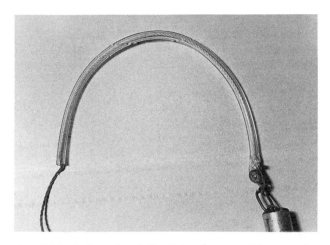

An 18-inch length of flexible plastic tubing at the terminal end of the cord prevents the cord's fraying on rocks while retrieving lures.

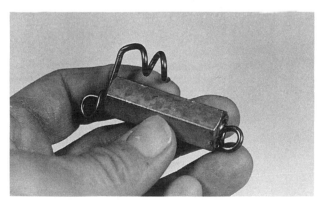

Another type of plug retriever can be made with an egg sinker or large bolt link as shown. The wire goes through the bolt link or egg sinker with the twisted rod used as a guide on the fishing line. Heavy cord can be attached to either end.

Completed plug retriever.

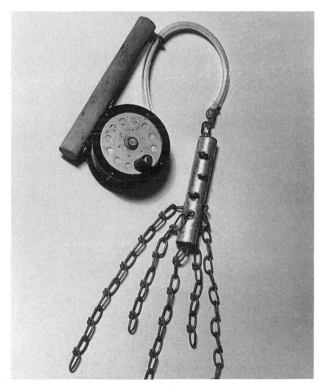

vinyl tubing over the end of the cord. To get the tubing over the cord, run a thin doubled length of wire through the tubing, catch the end of the cord with the doubled wire, and pull the cord through. Knot the heavy cord securely to the top link in the lure retriever and slide the clear tubing down over the end of the cord. To prevent the tubing from slipping up and exposing the cord to damage, rivet or wire the tubing to the top chain link.

Using the lure retriever is simplicity itself. Once you are hung up on the bottom, wrap the fishing line through the spiraled wire holder on the lure retriever and drop the retriever to the bottom, spooling line off the reel. Often, just the heavy lure retriever knocking against the lure will be sufficient to jog it free. If the lure remains snagged, jig or bounce the retriever up and down a few times to knock it free. If this does not work, continue jigging the lure retriever until the chains catch on a hook or some other part of the lure. Wrap the heavy cord several times around the wood-dowel reel handle to prevent line cuts to your hands. Pull the lure up. Usually you can pull the lure to the surface easily, although you may bend or break one of the hooks on a treble-hook crankbait. Once, while using this retriever, I pulled up my plug but left one of the treble hooks in a log. This was a minor loss when compared with the cost of a new lure.

15

Painting and Finishing

TOOLS ∎ TYPES OF PAINT ∎ OTHER FINISHING
MATERIALS ∎ PAINTING METHODS: DIPPING ∎ PAINTING
METHODS: SPRAYING ∎ PAINTING METHODS: BRUSHING ∎
PAINTING WOOD LURES ∎ PAINTING PLASTIC LURES ∎
PREPARATION OF METAL LURES FOR PAINTING ∎
PAINTING METAL SPOONS AND SPINNER BLADES ∎
PAINTING LEAD BUCKTAILS AND LURES ∎ PAINTING
PATTERNS AND USING STENCILS ∎ PAINTING SCALE
FINISHES ∎ ADDING AND PAINTING EYES ∎ BAKING
PAINTS ∎ ADDING GLITTER TO LURES ∎ ADDING FLOCKED
MATERIALS ∎ ADDING TAPES ∎ COLORING PLASTIC
WORMS AND LURES WITH FELT-TIP MARKERS ∎ FIELD
PAINTING AND DYEING ∎ FINAL LURE FINISHING ∎ KITS

Basic Safety Requirements
Goggles
Painting face mask
Rubber or plastic gloves
Apron or protective smock

Basic Tools
Paint brushes
Scale netting
Finishing nails and pins

Helpful Tools
Air brush
Masking tape
Embroidery hoops

Felt-tip markers
Various stencils
Disposable brushes
Sponge makeup applicators

It is not enough to turn out fine wood plugs, assemble a series of plastic lures, cut, bend, and finish spoons, or mold bucktails by the hundred. Before any of these can be fished, they must be painted or finished in some way. (Admittedly, lures can be fished unfinished and will still catch fish. But these cases are more the exception than the rule. Day in and day out, well-finished lures will catch more fish than those left unfinished.)

There are numerous ways to finish lures, depending upon the lure material, the method used, your choice of colors and patterns, scale finishes, and the use of tape, glitter, and reflective materials.

TOOLS

Very few tools are needed for finishing lures. The best methods involve dipping or spraying the paint to prevent paint buildup or brush marks on the finished lure. If brushes are used, they should be the best obtainable. Having said that, there are small packs of inexpensive brushes available from craft and hobby shops, some tackle-component supply houses, and other outlets that are ideal for small items or for use with thicker paints, in which the brush marks will disappear before the paint cures. They are also ideal for touching up paints on lures, painting some eyes and patterns, and similar tasks. The one big advantage of such brushes is that they can be thrown out after one use without pangs of economic conscience. Packets of sponge-tip makeup applicators are also fine for quick touch-ups and for painting a few lures. They are disposable and work well with most paints used for lures.

If brushes are to be reused, and if the highest quality job is desired, the best brushes are flat brushes of 1/4- to 1/2-inch width available from artists' supply stores.

You can use aerosol sprays, but there are more and more environmental concerns about such products. Airbrush guns can be used, but simpler, cheaper air-gun sprays that are operated with a can of air or propellent are available. Kits that include a spray gun, hose, and can of air are available for about one-half to one-quarter the price of a complete system that also includes a compressor. The disadvantage of these systems is that you must constantly buy the cans of propellent. Currently, a large can is good for about 1 to 2 hours. The cost of ten cans, or about 20 hours' use, comes close to the current cost of a low-priced compressor system. Another disadvantage is that using the propellent chills the can, so that you usually can work for only about one-half hour before having to stop to allow the can to warm up.

The compressor systems work with an AC motor and air compressor to provide a constant source of air pressure for the gun. The lower-priced compressors require rests, since too much continuous work will accelerate motor wear. The most expensive are those that have an automatic cut-off—when you release pressure on the gun

trigger, the compressor stops. Others are stopped by a separate on/off switch or by removing the plug from the wall outlet. Also, the less-expensive models have a control that, when opened, releases air and paint at the same time (called "single action"). In short, open the control and you are painting.

The more expensive models have a control that when pushed down releases the air from the nozzle, and a separate pull-back switch (like a small trigger, but operated by the thumb) releases the paint (called "double action"). Thus, these models have finer control.

There are a half-dozen manufacturers of such air-compressor equipment, including Paache, Thayer/Chandler, Badger, Iwata, and Devilbiss.

The big advantage of this relatively expensive type of spray system is in the versatility of the spraying operation. Unlike a can of spray paint, the guns allow adjustment of the spray area. Some are capable of spraying a line no wider than that made with a standard pencil. Others have minimum spray areas of 1/16- or 1/8-inch. Most also have maximum widths, ranging with the gun model from about 1 to 2 inches. Thus, choice of a nozzle or gun, based on the type of spraying you plan to do, is important. If you will be spraying entire lure bodies, spoon blades, spinner blades, and larger jig heads, choose a spray gun that will cover an area the size of the lure. If you plan to paint fine designs on the lure body, spray patterns, or "draw" gill plates, fins, and so on, then choose one with a head that will make fine lines.

One other thought. These air brushes are designed for using water-based paints, primarily for artwork and retouching. This does not allow for the use of enamels or lacquers, but does allow acrylics, which do wash up with water (actually a water/vinegar or water/window cleaner mix is used), but which are waterproof when dry. Many use these paints for decorative work on motorcycles, autos, and trucks. One machine, which holds the paint externally in a small pan, would probably allow use of solvent-based enamels and lacquers.

In any case, such equipment—cans or compressors—is a must for serious finishing of large numbers of lures. Initial setup costs are high, however, so consider the depth of your involvement in making lures and painting before investing.

Standard aerosol-paint cans are also good for painting lures, and some of them have a nozzle that can be adjusted to a thin or broad spray pattern. If you are planning on more than a solid coat of color on your lures, you will need masking tape. You can also use other patterns, scale finish nets, templates such as broad-tooth combs, and other such devices to make patterns on lures. It is possible to cut patterns in masking tape, tape the pattern on the lure, spray, and remove the tape. Tape is also necessary when you spray-paint the head of a lure a different color than the body of the lure, as in the popular red-head, white-body topwater lures and crankbaits. Masking tape is readily available in the standard widths of 3/4-, 1, 2, and 3 inches. Thinner masking tape is available from art-supply stores in 1/4-, 3/8-, and 1/2-inch widths.

To add a scale finish to a crankbait, top-water plug, spoon, or spinner blade, a special netting pattern will be needed. This netting is available from most component suppliers and from some tackle shops. The pattern from the hexagonal mesh will simulate the scales of a fish. The cost is low, the material is usually sold by the yard, and different sizes are available for different lure patterns. In addition, other types of netting can be obtained from craft stores. Just check the mesh closely to determine the size and type of pattern that will result.

There are several ways to use the finishing netting, the handiest of which involves stretching it over an embroidery hoop so that the lure can be held against the netting and sprayed with the scale color. Embroidery hoops consist of two rings, one fitted inside the other; material is stretched tightly between them. They come in both oval and round styles, either spring-loaded or with a small screw to tighten the outer rim against the inner hoop. Sizes suitable for spraying lures range from about 4 to 12 inches in diameter. Embroidery hoops are very inexpensive and available from sewing, notion, and department stores.

Eyes can be painted on lures using simply made tools. These tools are nothing more than several sizes of finishing nails or straight pins pushed into the ends of short wood dowels, which serve as handles. The different-sized heads on the pins and nails, when dipped into paint and then touched lightly to the lure, make different-sized eyes and/ or pupils.

Since painting can be a messy job, the workbench or work area should be covered with oilcloth, newspapers, or other coverings to make cleanup easier. Spraying is especially messy, since the fine paint mist tends to float in the air. If you use spray paints, use some sort of "trap" to keep the paint in a confined area. One way to make a simple no-cost trap is to place a cardboard box on

Tools for painting eyes in lures. The three sizes of nails in wood handles make it easy to paint eyes and pupils.

its side behind the lures to be painted. A length of bead chain, pipe strap, or small-link chain hung horizontally along the front top edge of the box will serve to hang the lures during spraying. Even a box like this, in which only the front is open, will allow some of the paint spray to bounce back out of the box. One way to lessen this is to line the

Drying rack for holding painted lures. The bead-chain racks prevent lures from sliding together while the spring on each end maintains tension on the bead chain.

back and sides of the box with an old Turkish towel. Better still, hang a second towel, cut into fine strips, in front of the backing towel. The backing and strips will serve to trap much of the excess spray paint and prevent it from filling the room.

When using spray paints, wear goggles to protect your eyes and a small face mask to cover your nose. Both are available at hardware and paint-supply stores and are very inexpensive. If possible, an exhaust fan should be employed during extensive spray painting, or the painting should be done outside on a *calm* day. Another possibility is to use an open garage or protected carport or patio. If you spray lures extensively, consult the book *Ventilation: A Practical Guide for Artists, Craftspeople, and Others in the Arts* (Lyons and Burford, 1984) for ideas on reducing or eliminating any dangers or problems.

TYPES OF PAINT

Paint is supplied in two basic ways: as a liquid in a container and in aerosol sprays. The spray paints are generally more expensive for several reasons. First, packaging the paint with an aerosol propellent adds to the initial cost. A quick look at the net weights and costs of aerosol paints versus liquids paints will show this to be true. Also, because of the spraying technique, much spray paint does not cover the lure but instead is dispersed into the air. This is particularly true when spraying small items such as lures. For this reason, it is best to use some sort of rack to hang the lures close together (but not touching) and spray many lures at once to reduce waste as much as possible.

To its advantage, spray painting gives a very good, smooth finish on a lure if it's done correctly and in several light coats. Too heavy a coat will cause running and dripping and can also cause crackling of the resulting finish. Spray painting is also the only way that scale finishes, "feathering," (blending two coats), and painting through stencils and masks can be effectively accomplished.

Paint sold in a container (usually a can, but sometimes in bottles or jars) can be used with a brush or for dipping lures. If you are dipping, thin the paint to prevent running streaks or the formation of a solidified paint drop at the lower end of the lure. Lure companies using dipping techniques (most do, at least for base coats and clear finish coats) avoid this by employing a mechanized conveyer chain that dips the lure and slowly removes it from the paint trough to pre-

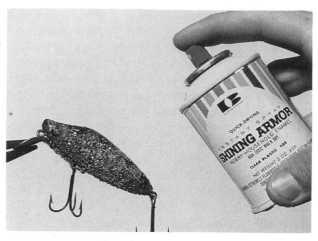

Spray cans of clear finish make it easy to paint and refinish lures. This lure with added glitter is being protected with a clear plastic coating.

vent solidified drops. Usually the rate of withdrawal of the lure from the paint is the critical factor—it must match or be slightly slower than the rate at which excess paint runs off the lure. However, since such a device is generally beyond the scope of the home tackle craftsman, thinner paint is a must.

Since paints of different types and manufacture can vary greatly as to their viscosity, no definite thinning directions can be given. For dipping baits, the best method is to thin the paint slightly and experiment with small quantities of paint (on scrap pieces of wood—not on a completed lure!) and the proper thinner until good results are achieved. For those using air-brush equipment, the basics are to thin paint with thinner in a 50/50 ratio. In all cases, keep records so that your results can be duplicated with other colors and larger quantities.

Another factor to consider when dipping lures is that larger quantities of paint will be needed than for brushing or spraying. Even one-pint cans are seldom deep enough for larger lures. The paint must be transferred to a taller, thinner container to allow the lure to be completely submerged. This is not necessary when using brushes; even the small 1/4-ounce bottles of Testor's Pla enamel, available in hobby shops, can be used with a brush to paint large saltwater lures.

Both types of paint, container or aerosol, vary greatly in their properties. Some are best for wood lures, some for plastic, and some for metal. Mail-order companies specializing in do-it-yourself fishing supplies often offer different paints for different purposes. It is particularly important to choose the appropriate paints for foam lures—

those lures that are like a hard polystyrene foam and found in some bass bug bodies and some bass and saltwater lures. In some cases, standard paints will react with the body and cause it to partially dissolve. (This is also a problem with glues, since standard household waterproof glues will do the same thing. Epoxy glue usually works well, but test on one or two lure bodies before gluing up a gross or two.)

The term "lacquer" can apply to clear finishes and also to a colored nitrocellulose base paint of thin consistency. Sometimes these color lacquers are called "lacquer enamels." They are usually excellent for painting metal (such as spinner blades, spoon blades, and lead bucktails), and are very fast-drying. Often they are not acceptable for plastics, since the solvent in some lacquers may react chemically with the plastic or the plastic solvent (plasticizer). But they vary widely. Check the fine print on the label or the catalog copy. Some companies carry standard, fluorescent, pearlescent, and similar lacquers that can be used on all lure materials. Lacquers can usually be bought in ounce-size bottles and several sizes of larger containers.

Automobile touch-up lacquers are excellent for dipping or spraying, and they come in aerosol and liquid. Hardware and auto-supply stores carry them in the same colors to be found on the late-model cars of most manufacturers. For metal lures and lead jigs, they offer a durable, tough finish.

Enamels are usually heavier, thicker paints, often advertised as "covering in one coat." They can generally be used on any type of lure material but are not available in the same variety of colors as lacquers and auto touch-up paints. They are also slower-drying than lacquers. Prices are about the same as for lacquers, and enamels are available in many container sizes in bottles, cans, and aerosols.

Alkyd and acrylic enamels are more modern enamels. They are available in small cans from lure suppliers as well as department and paint stores. They can be used on metal, wood, and some but not all plastics.

Epoxy paints, like epoxy glue, are separated into two parts that must be mixed together before use. These paints are very tough, but many have the disadvantage of a flat finish rather than the gloss preferred for most lures. This can be overcome by using a finishing gloss coat of clear lacquer over the epoxy, or a finish coat of clear epoxy. One notable exception is the new two-part

The Epoxy Paint Set of 24 colors from Hilts Molds is made specifically for lures.

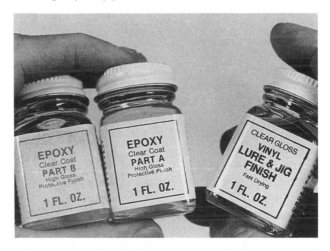

Other paints for finishing lures include epoxy and vinyl clear-coat finishes to protect paints.

epoxy paints in Ray's Benchmark Paint from Hilts Molds. These are a 50/50 mix of the resin and catalyst, which produces a clear finish. The paint is added in paste form from a small jar (twenty-four colors are available). The color is added to the first part before that is mixed with the second part. This allows you to achieve a complete color mix before the two parts are combined and the clock starts ticking on the curing or setup time. These paints will dry to the touch in about 45 minutes at 70° to 75° but can be kept mixed and usable in the refrigerator for about one week, or kept unmixed for years. The advantage of this paint is that it is extremely durable and tough for all lures and especially when used on lead lures, which are often subject to chipping.

Vinyl paints are also good for lead lures because they are slightly rubbery and flexible, and thus will not chip as readily as will many other paints when the lure is knocked against a hard rock or is dented. Unlike epoxies, vinyl paints do not require mixing but are used straight out of the bottle. Vinyl paints in a variety of colors are readily available from mail-order suppliers. Most of these paints are available in basic colors such as yellow, red, orange, blue, green, white, black, and brown, although Do-It sells over twenty different colors of vinyl paint, including a clear gloss. These paints are available in 1-ounce, 4-ounce, and 16-ounce containers. As with painting any lead lures, two base coats of white are suggested to make sure that subsequent colors retain their brightness for a professional-looking lure.

In addition to the standard range of colors in the paints already mentioned, there are also special color and paints that make even more elaborate lures possible. Fluorescent paints in red, orange, pink, yellow, green, blue, and purple are available. Currently, these paints are sometimes referred to as "neon" colors. Many times these colors can be found either in cans or aerosols in drug, hobby, department, and stationery stores. For obvious reasons, avoid buying fluorescent paints that are water-based and designed only for poster work.

For best results, fluorescent colors must be used over a base coat of white. Painting them over any other color or over bare metal or wood will not produce the expected bright color.

Phosphorescent paints, which glow in the dark, are also available for lure-finishing. In some states or areas they might be illegal on lures or when fished in certain waters, so be sure to check local laws and regulations before using them.

Phosphorescents also come in standard colors. The most common are yellow or white, but blue, green, red, and orange are also available. Any lure painted phosphorescent will not glow indefinitely but must be "recharged" with light periodically. Therefore, this paint works best on lures that are frequently cast or exposed to the sun rather than on lures that are used for continual deep-water trolling, such as downrigger fishing. (However, it is not necessary to fish phosphorescent lures

Parts and materials necessary for using the epoxy paint set from Hilts Molds.

Pouring one part of the epoxy into a cup to mix the paint.

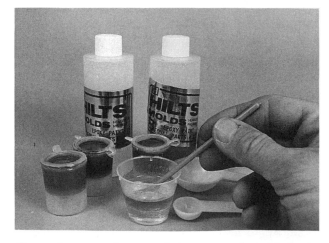

Once the second part of the epoxy is added, the epoxy is mixed.

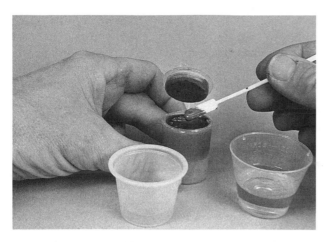

The pigment is added using a spatula, as shown. Coffee stirrers from fast food shops are often ideal for this.

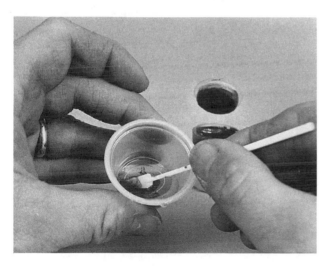

Mixing the pigment in with the epoxy.

Pearl pigments and similar paint additives give lures a shiny mother-of-pearl look. They can be combined with paints and used to paint plugs, spoons, spinner blades, and bucktails. They are most often seen on spoons and bucktails.

Don't neglect other paint possibilities. At Christmas and Halloween I have found special paints, additives, and paint coverings that are designed for holiday decoration but that do well on a lures also. Some of these include colored spray paints that contain fine bits of bright metallics to imbue the base color with a silvery, glittering overcoat. Paints are also available that, when dry, make a crystal pattern on a lure. These are sold at Christmas to simulate the crystal patterns formed by ice on windowpanes. Prices are reasonable, but remember that any of these items are drastically reduced in price immediately after the holiday season.

Another possibility that is particularly good for lead heads, although limited in variety and color patterns, is plastic dips. These are primarily designed for building up a rubberized coating for pliers and other tool handles but will also work well as a tough, durable, thick coating on lead heads (since these are particularly prone to chipping, flaking, and other damage as the lure bounces off rocks). The only disadvantage is that colors are limited — usually only one color coat is possible — though sometimes you can paint over this material with eyes or spray-painted patterns.

only on sunny days and to avoid dawn, dusk, or night fishing. Any light can be used to recharge such lures — flashlights, camp lanterns, cigarette lighters, matches. One great way is to "hit" the lure with a small photographers' electronic flash by using the "open flash" button. If your camera lacks this function, short out the hot shoe with a key or wire to get a flash. To avoid hurting the flash, be sure the flash recharges completely before firing again. A couple of flashes on the lure are as good as ten minutes in bright sun.)

There are also phosphorescent pigments that can be added to regular paints to give an underwater phosphorescence in addition to a daylight color. These are usually sold by the ounce. Any of the phosphorescent paints should be used over a base coat of white for best results.

Various dyes for coloring lures are also available. They can be used on hard baits, but are best used on plastic worms and skirts where the dye can penetrate slightly.

OTHER FINISHING MATERIALS

Other materials for finishing lures can be used in place of paint or in combination with it. Reflective and colored tape can be added to fishing lures, including plastic and wood plugs, spoons, and spinner blades. Some tapes, such as the many types of prism reflective and scale-finish tapes, have shiny mirrorlike finishes in metallic colors (silver, gold, copper, and brass), along with many bright-colored finishes. Most have a self-adhesive backing and are easy to add to any lure. Some come in solid sheets, others in small packs of several sheets, and some are precut into patterns specifically designed for lures.

The red reflective tape designed for use as car-bumper reflectors can be used on lures with the same results. Some supply houses carry other tapes, such as glitter-flake tape that is available in several colors. Similar glitter tape is available from hardware and hobby shops in rolls: usually about 6 feet long and available in several widths of 1/2-inch and wider.

Reflective tape made with microscopic glass beads is available in a variety of colors in both sheets and rolls. Fluorescent tapes are also available in bright colors (many colors are available), along with some phosphorescent tapes.

Pigments and glitter materials also make it possible to add flash to any drab or scarred lure or to design new lures with extra fish-attracting flash. Most popular are the glitter materials in gold, silver, red, green, blue, and some other colors. These are tiny metallic bits, or more frequently today, Mylar that looks metallic. These can be glued in place, sprinkled on a fresh coat of paint or clear finish, or added with a special glitter adhesive. They come in small bottles and tubes and are low in cost. This material is also available in tubes of clear glue that can be squeezed onto a lure or spread over a lure. Once cured, this material won't come off, and it's waterproof.

Fluorescent, phosphorescent, and standard-color pigments can also be added to lures by dipping the lure into a clear lacquer or thin adhesive and rolling or sprinkling the pigments onto the lure where desired (detailed methods follow).

Electroplating spinner and spoon blades is also possible, and some kits are available for this.

Caution. Once you begin to paint any lure, follow through the entire process with paints of the same type, or at least paints that will not react adversely when mixed. This includes base coats, finish coats, scale finishes, masked sprays, eyes, and clear protective coats. Switching from one type of paint to another, even though the underlying coats are dry, may cause a chemical reaction. The result could be that the new coat may never dry, or might wrinkle, crinkle, crack, peel, blister, or bleed. Unless it is clearly stated that a paint (of any type) can be used over other types of paint, try to avoid such a practice. If you must mix paint types, test the combination on one or two lures, or on scrap pieces of wood, to determine results.

PAINTING METHODS: DIPPING

For most lures, dipping is perhaps the best method to get a base coat or single-color coat of paint. Wood and plastic lures, spoon and spinner blades (where it is desirable to cover both sides of the blade with paint), and bucktails can all be dipped.

The paint must be thinned with the proper thinner. It is hard to give exact directions on thinning because of the infinite variety of paints, but a one-to-one mix is a good place to start. If in doubt, experiment with small quantities first, and add minimal amounts of thinner. It is usually easier to add more thinner than it is to double or triple the amount of paint to get the right paint-to-thinner mix.

Since the entire lure must be dipped into the paint, often the paint must be transferred from the original bottle or can into a deep container. This is especially true with long plugs and spoons. Cheap juice glasses, olive jars, and similar tall containers are excellent for this. You can also make your own by using short sections of PVC, CPVC, or ABS plastic pipe fitted with a glued-on, flat end cap. (You need the flat end cap, not the rounded style, so that the container will stand upright. Even so, it is best to support the pipe container in some way to prevent spills. Insert it into a bucket of sand, wedge it upright into the corner of a cardboard box, or tape it to an L-shaped bracket clamped to the workbench or held in a vise.)

Be sure to cover the work area with old newspapers and to have a rack handy on which to hang the lures to dry. A simple length of wood shelving with two end supports (to make a wide U shape) works fine. Use metal L brackets to support the end pieces. At the top, string a length of bead chain, pipe strap, fine-link jack chain, or similar chain from one leg of the U to the other, from which to hang the lures. Bead chain (available

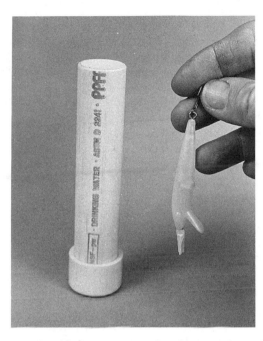

One simple aid for painting slim lures is to make a pipe container with a short length of plastic pipe and a cemented-on end cap. This requires less paint for coverage when dipping. Note that the lure line tie is masked for this.

able in several sizes from any hardware store, where it is sold by the foot for light pulls) is ideal because it separates the lures, does not allow them to slide together, is inexpensive, and will not catch the lure when it is removed as might chain link. Do *not* use wire or cord for a hanger, since the weight of any lure will cause all lures to slide to the center: the lures will stick together, ruining the painted finishes. Make sure that the rack side supports are higher than the length of any lure, including the hook or hanging wires.

Bucktails and spoons can be hung by their hooks. Since plugs must be painted before any hardware is added, it will be necessary to use open-end screw eyes partially turned into the tail or head of the lure, or a straight pin or thin nail pushed into the plug with the shaft of the pin or nail turned in a J shape, for hanging on the rack.

Dip each lure carefully and slowly into the paint. Dipping slowly is necessary to prevent the formation of air bubbles on the lure. Cover the lure completely with paint and withdraw it slowly to minimize running streaks or dipping. Once the lure is completely out of the paint, hold it over the container briefly to allow any excess paint to run back into the container.

It helps to touch the lower part of the lure to

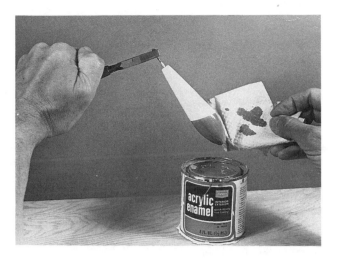

Dipping is one easy way to paint lures. This surface plug has been dipped first in white and then on an angle into red.

the top of the paint surface here to remove the last drop. If the paint is thin enough, or if the lure has been removed slowly enough from the paint, this may be sufficient to prevent a dried droplet of paint on the finished lure. If the paint is not thin enough, it may be necessary to check the drying lures later, touching the lower part of the lure with a rag or absorbent towel to remove any drops of paint. The proper time to do this will depend upon the paint's drying time: With lacquers, it may be necessary in a matter of minutes; with slower-drying enamels, you might have to wait an hour or longer.

Dipping can be used for sealer coats, base coats, and a series of finish coats. Sealer coats are coats of sealer, designed to penetrate wood lures and to allow for a good, even coat of finish paint. Base coats are coats designed to take a finish coat of paint. Base coats are primarily white, and *must* be white when the finish coat is to be a light color or when any of the fluorescent or phosphorescent colors are used. Once a base coat or two is added, you can then add finish coats by dipping, brushing, or spraying.

PAINTING METHODS: SPRAYING

Spraying, provided it is done correctly, has the advantage of covering a lure evenly, without streaks or droplets. Do it incorrectly (too heavy a coat, too light a coat, spraying too soon after a first coat) and you can end up with runs, drops, crackling, crinkles, or gaps in the finish. Spraying

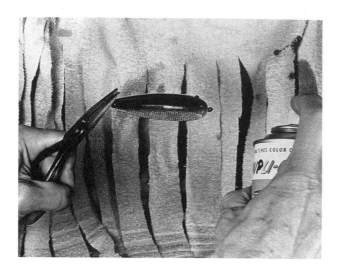

Once the sides are sprayed on a plug, the back is sprayed a dark color. The strips of cloth in the background are part of the spraying box described in the text to contain excess spray.

should be done lightly and evenly, with several light coats sprayed over a sealer or base coat.

Use a spraying box and line up the lures to be sprayed as closely as reasonable to prevent waste of the aerosol paint. Since one spray coat will cover only one side of a lure, the lures must be turned. There are several methods to accomplish this. One is to use a small spraying box and a separate hanging rack: Spray each lure evenly and thoroughly by holding the lure's support pin with pliers and turning the lure to cover all sides with the aerosol spray. Then hang the lure up on the separate rack. If you rack all the lures to be painted in the spraying box, consider using an overhead frame that will hold bead-chain or pipe-strap hanging strips so that you can reverse the lures 180 degrees after the first spraying. Another possibility is to use a spraying box that has a fold-down front and back: Keep the hanging racks stationary but spray from both sides and reverse the positions (up or down) of the front and back flaps when spraying from the opposite side.

Once sufficient finishing coats are on the lure, additional secondary coats can be added by spraying. In each case, each plug or lure will have to be done separately. This is usually the case whether spraying freehand or using a mask or scale-net finish for more lifelike results. This does give good results, since the second coat of color can be "feathered" to blend with the first coat, giving a professional appearance.

If you are spraying with an air-brush gun, you can often add details with the gun adjusted to a fine spray, avoiding the use of masks or stencils. However, most of the lure manufacturers do not do this, but for expediency and consistency use special, precisely cut masks and stencils for spraying details in different colors.

Since lures must be held individually, by hand or with cheap long-nose pliers, wear rubber or plastic painting gloves to keep the spray off your hands. Sometimes medical-type rubber gloves in bulk (100- or gross-count boxes) are available for this and are ideal because they can be worn on either hand. Rubber gloves are available in housewares departments of department or discount stores; plastic painting gloves are available from hardware and paint-supply stores.

Spraying does have some disadvantages. When spraying a base coat on the lead head of a bucktail (before the tail is tied down), you may get paint on the hook point. Unless the paint is removed, hooking a fish will become more difficult. One way to avoid this is to use a bit of petroleum jelly on the hook point (though be careful to avoid getting it on the lead head, because it will not allow paint adhesion, or to use a small bit of masking tape on the hook point. A better way is to use a flat shield behind which the hook point is held, exposing only the lead head to be painted.

Before you put a finishing coat on a bucktail, tie the tail in place. This is done for the specific purposes of covering the thread winding with a protective layer of paint and giving the lure a uniform color. However, paint must be kept off the tail: Cover it with masking tape or use a flat shield.

Spraying produces a smooth finish coat. Note that this lure body has had the hardware and painted head covered with masking tape.

Spraying does not have to be limited to just one color or coat. In fact, it is at its best when several colors are used to blend or feather one color into the next. For example, one way of making an attractive underwater plug or crankbait is to first coat the lure with a base coat of paint, then paint a belly color of white, yellow, ivory, pink, light blue, or some other light color. Then follow with the side color of a darker shade, perhaps dark yellow, orange, light red, medium blue, medium green, or tan. To do this, make a quick swipe or two with the spray can or air gun to hit each side of the lure (turn the lure to do this) without coating the belly. Complete with a quick swipe along the top or back of the lure with black, dark blue, dark green, or a similar dark-color paint. Do this lightly so as to not affect the side colors and shading. The result of this is a very professional-looking lifelike lure with a dark back, medium-color side, and light belly — just like the natural coloring and shading of a live baitfish. Naturally, this can be combined with eyes, scale finishes, vertical bar marks, or other embellishments. Once you know the basics of spraying, the possibilities are limitless.

PAINTING METHODS: BRUSHING

Brushing is not generally advisable for painting lures. It can leave brush marks, and there is a chance that a bristle will come off the brush and stick to the painted lure surface. In reality, this is more an aesthetic than a practical concern, since the fish are not going to examine the degree of expertise of your paint job. The lure will look lifelike to them and they will hit it, or it won't and they will avoid it.

Brushing does have two advantages over dip-

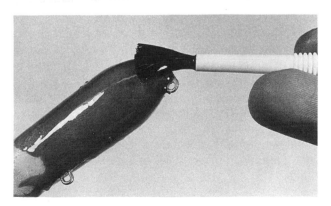

Brushing the mixed epoxy finish onto a lure.

ping and spraying. It requires no special quantities of paint or special containers, as does dipping, nor does it require room for a spraying box or that you waste paint as happens with spraying. That having been said, brush-painting has no other advantages over dipping or spraying. It does not allow professional-looking fine details, even when a fine brush is used. Delicate bars, stripes, spots, and similar markings can be made, but generally not as well as when they are sprayed through masks or stencils.

PAINTING WOOD LURES

Once they are carved or turned, wood plugs should be finished with a fine 7/0- or 8/0-grade sandpaper in order to get good results from painting. Once sanded smooth, the plug should be dipped, sprayed, or brushed with a wood sealer to seal the pores of the wood and prevent subsequent coats of paint from soaking into the wood. If a wood sealer is not used, the paint will soak into the wood in an uneven pattern (soaking more into end grain and summer grain than into the denser winter grain), making several more coats of paint necessary. Usually one coat of wood sealer is sufficient; if not, use a second coat and allow it to dry completely before the next step.

Once the wood sealer is dry, rough the surface with fine sandpaper or steel wool to give the sealer some "tooth," so that the next coat of paint will adhere to it. Each subsequent coat of paint, except for the final coat, should be buffed lightly with steel wool to give it tooth for the next coat. Both spraying and dipping work particularly well on wood lures, and spraying is best for final touches and patterns applied through stencils.

PAINTING PLASTIC LURES

Plastic lures are painted in the same way wood lures are, except that additional care must be taken in the choice of paint. Some plastics will react chemically with some paints, so the paint being used should be clearly marked as suitable for plastic. If it is not so marked, test it first on an old plug or a small corner of one you are painting to be sure that the paint cures properly without softening the lure or otherwise causing a chemical reaction. While softening or dissolving is the most common effect when solvents react, other effects could be a softening of the surface of the lure or a crinkling of the lure surface that will make a smooth final finish difficult or impossible. Ideally, what you want is a paint that will *just slightly* soften or dissolve the surface enough to allow a penetration of the paint into the plastic and a "binding" of the paint with the plastic surface.

Spraying, brushing, or dipping techniques can be used for painting plastics, and spraying is the best method.

PREPARATION OF METAL LURES FOR PAINTING

Preparation for painting bucktails, spoons, spinner blades, and similar metal lures is extremely important. Some paints will be affected by light oils, which will prevent good paint adherence. As a result, all rust, grease, oils, perspiration, and dirt must be removed from metal lures before painting. Use an acid or metal cleaner, dipping the spoon, spinner blade, or bucktail body into the solution according to directions. Several types of acid cleaners are available from mail-order supply houses. Some are used undiluted, others are diluted with water. Most of these cleaners are of an "inhibited" acid type that will prevent any damage to the surface of the metal.

Because of the acid content of these cleaners, they can be used only in plastic (polyethylene), glass, or crockery containers; they will attack metal containers. The solutions are often irritating to the skin and toxic if breathed extensively, and are volatile, with low flash points. Handle them with care, and *use them only with proper ventilation or outdoors.* Don't smoke when using these cleaners, and don't use them around any pilot lights (from hot-water heaters, stoves, gas clothes dryers, or the like) or where a motor is in use (air conditioner or heater) that may spark.

A weak acid, such as white vinegar or acetone, can be used as an alternative to clean and prepare metal lures. These materials are less dangerous to use than the commercial preparations but should still be used with caution. These acids are best only on lead surfaces or those with zinc (some lead alloys); they will have far less effect on the nickel-plated surfaces of most spoons and spinner blades. They will work on copper or copper-plated metals.

One danger, and a concern of painting professionals such as Jeff Janos of Rustoleum, is the possibility of "wiping" the surface with a solvent- or acid-soaked rag and in the process leaving more oils or dirt than are being taken up by the wipe. Then too, enough wipes with the same rag will eventually soil the rag and dirty the surface you think you are cleaning.

Another cleaning alternative, and perhaps the simplest and best one, is a good wash with soapy water, which will remove oils and grease, then thorough drying. When washing, strong dishwasher detergent is better than plain soap. Soap will serve as a solvent for grease and oil, but detergents will actually "encapsulate" the oil to remove it completely without leaving a residue.

Shortly after the metal surface is cleaned, it should be painted. Waiting will only allow additional accumulation of more dirt, oil, grease, and fingerprints, which will prevent a good adhesion of the paint. Lead lures begin to oxidize on the surface shortly after being molded, and this oxidation also interferes with good paint adhesion. To protect lures of lead or other metals, clean and then paint them immediately, using a white paint as a base coat. White paint as a base is good under any additional paints and is required for maximum brightness with fluorescent or phosphorescent paints.

PAINTING METAL SPOONS AND SPINNER BLADES

Painting any metal surface, such as the plated surfaces of spoons and spinner blades, is best only after cleaning. Often, spinners and spoons are painted only with a few stripes, dots, or bars, or with a solid color on one side of the blade only. As a result, dipping is seldom used, except in those rare cases when you want both sides of the spoon or spinner painted the same color.

Spraying is the best method to cover spoons and spinner blades with a single coat or to apply a pattern of stripes or bars. Brushing can be used if aerosols are not available. To spray a solid color on one side of the spoons or spinner blades, lay the blade on old newspapers in front of the spraying box and spray evenly with several light coats. This same technique will work if you use masking tape or stencils to paint stripes, bars, or similar patterns on the blade.

The best paints are those that will provide a hard durable finish; the best start with an epoxy primer—preferably one made specifically for metals—and end with an enamel or lacquer finish coat. Baking the paint also helps to give it a hard finish.

PAINTING LEAD BUCKTAILS AND LURES

Before you apply a base coat to any lead lure, the head should be dipped into a mild acid (acetone or vinegar solution), rinsed with water, and dried thoroughly. Bucktails can be painted either before or after the tail is tied down. The advantage of painting before tying is that the entire paint job can be finished and the tail then tied on with an identical- or contrasting-color thread. The thread is then protected with epoxy finish, fly-head cement, or by painting it after it has been tied off.

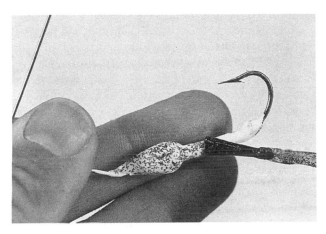

Glitter is available in a clear base for painting on lures. Here, glitter is added to a base coat of white on a spinnerbait body.

It is most important to paint lead heads as soon as possible after molding. This is impossible if you buy your lead heads, but not if you mold your own. Try to paint the heads the same day they are molded. The less time that elapses between molding and painting, the less chance there is of oxidation buildup. Paint a base coat even if you won't finish the lead heads immediately, because once this base coat is on, the lure is protected and can be painted and finished any time in the future.

Generally, the adherence of paint to lead lures is not good, even on most commercial lures. The problem is that pure lead is soft and malleable, and thus deforms when the lure hits any structure. Automobile touch-up paints work well, but paint experts suggest that the best solution is a plasticized epoxy primer followed by a polyurethane finish coat. The polyurethane paints stay flexible and thus will tend to give as the lure hits rocks and such and will not chip off, as will harder, brittle paints. The same flexibility is found in the epoxy paints from Hilts Molds. As a result,

painted lead heads should *not* be baked, since this makes the paint more brittle, even though it does make it more durable. Spraying or brushing will work well, but dipping is ideal because most lead heads are finished in one solid color, perhaps with the later addition of eyes.

PAINTING PATTERNS AND USING STENCILS

It is seldom that a lure is painted one solid color. This is true sometimes with underwater plugs, some bucktails, and some spoons, but most lures are given a scale finish, bars, mottled-pattern markings, fishlike vertical bars, or similar finishes. Stencils and various masks can be used over any base coating on any plug, crankbait, spoon, spinner blade, or even bucktail head.

Stencils and masks are essentially sheets of flat material cut out in various designs. Often, the sheets are of plastic, cardboard, masking tape, or paper that has been cut or punched with a design you want on your lure. Stencils aren't restricted only to flat sheets of cardboard and plastic, though. One of the best ways to make vertical perchlike bars on a lure is to spray through the coarse teeth of a large comb—a method used by at least one major lure manufacturer!

Some typical stencil patterns include bars added to the sides of plugs and spoons in wavy lines (such as in the popular red-and-white casting and

Templates are available from a number of sources to create painted patterns on lures. Here are two examples and the templates used.

trolling spoon), dots, mottled patterns, and stripes. Gill slits can also be masked and painted red.

Some plug and spoon kits come with stencils for painting included, but most do not. You can make your own stencils by a number of simple methods. One is to use a paper punch and punch out holes in paper, cardboard, or lightweight plastic sheets (available at art-supply stores). You can even punch some of these holes off center to make them irregular for a mottled froglike pattern. Irregular patterns can be found almost anywhere. I've found them in fly swatters and various grocery wrappers—you just have to keep your eyes open. In addition, craft shops often sell prepared plastic stencils that will make dots and diamonds. These are sold for tole work and other stencil work on wood and fabric.

Stripes and strips can be created easily by using a razor blade to cut in paper or plastic the shapes to be painted. For example, to make a mask for a wavy line with which to paint a red-and-white spoon, cut out two triangles (one side wavy) large enough to cover any spoon to be painted. The trim area will mask the central wavy strip on the spoon. Thus, you will have two triangle cut-outs with the strip in between. This is best for painting any stripe when spraying a dark color over a light base coat. For the reverse—a dark spoon with a light or white center line—just cut out the center wavy stripe in a separate mask. Paint the spoon white, allow to cure, lay the wavy stripe over the center, and spray again with the darker color paint. Any similar stripes, wavy lines, multiple patterns, etc. can be cut the same way.

The best method of using a stencil is to tape one side of the stencil or mask to a base of cardboard so that the tape acts as a hinge. Lift the free side of the stencil, slip the lure under it, and hold or tape down the other side. Then spray. Lift the stencil and remove the lure. Once the paint is cured, do the lure's other side. Both sides are stenciled on plugs, top-water lures, and bucktails, but usually only one side is stenciled on spoons and spinner blades.

Naturally, this method works best with flat lures, since a fat crankbait will not allow a close contact of the spraying mask. The method will still work, but will be slightly blurred or fuzzy at those areas where the mask is separated from the lure. If you wish, you can adjust the sharpness of the line or border of the painted area by making a "nest" to hold the lure precisely with the masking stencil in a frame an inch or two above it. Spraying this way will give softer lines, but experiment for the effect you want, since the distance of the mask to the lure and the spray gun to the mask will affect results.

This is not as time-consuming as it sounds, but it does point out the necessity of making lures in a mini-mass-production assembly line. If you are painting both sides of a lure, you often need two templates (mirror images) and must allow time for one side of the lure to dry before reversing it and spray-painting the other side. (In

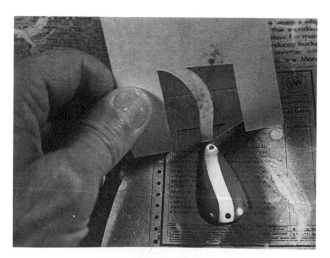

The best way to use templates is to tape them down so the lure body can be placed under them in turn for painting as shown here. This commercial template produces this stripe on spoon blades.

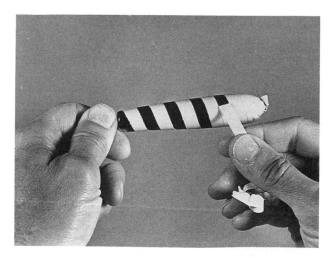

Spiral patterns can be made using thin strips of masking tape. Here a lure has been painted, then masked in a spiral pattern and repainted.

the case of spoons, only one side is painted, usually the convex side.)

Masking tape can also be cut into a stencil and taped onto a lure before spraying. It takes a little more time and the results are not as long-lasting as a flat stencil (the tape will deform or tear after a few uses), but it does work well on small lures or on large round lures where you want sharp lines.

PAINTING SCALE FINISHES

Scale finishes are added over the base coat or over a selected base color on a lure. Where a scale finish is to be added, it is best to use a light color for the base, covering it with a darker or contrasting color for visibility.

The scale netting used for these finishes is available from most mail-order companies and some tackle shops. In addition, you can get this netting, or very similar nettings, from fabric stores. The netting can be used in two different ways. One is to dip it into a paint thinner and wrap it tightly around the lure. The paint thinner in close contact with the net will have a tendency to cut into the base paint of the lure and make a more pronounced scale effect. Once the net is wrapped around the lure, spray the lure with the chosen finish color and allow the lure to dry completely or partially *with the net in place.* With most spray enamels or lacquers, this will only take a few minutes. Remove the netting and wash it in the thinner again for the next lure. Failure to

wash the netting each time will result in smeared lures, since the paint from the spraying operation will get on the next lure. This is a slow operation, and messy, but it produces good results. Naturally, you must use protective gloves (rubber or plastic) to avoid contact with the paint thinner.

A quicker, better method with very similar results is to fasten the scale netting in a frame and hold the lure in place behind and in contact with the netting for spraying. You can build a frame out of wood strips, but an embroidery hoop works just as well. (Embroidery hoops work several different ways, but all have an outer ring clamped around an inner ring. They are available in a variety of sizes in both round and oval shapes. The best for tackle-crafting are those that are about 4 to 12 inches in diameter.) Clamp the netting in the hoop and hold the hoop in a vise or base support to hold it vertically. In any of these frames

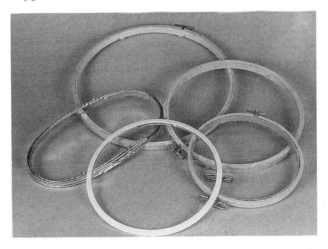

Spring or clamp-style embroidery hoops hold scale netting securely for spray-painting of lures. Different sizes and shapes are available.

or hoops, the netting must be slightly loose, because you want it to fit tightly around the curved side of the plug or lure. The plug can be held by hand (wear gloves) or by a screw eye (even better) screwed into one end of the plug; hold the eye, and thus the plug, with a pair of inexpensive pliers. Remember, when using a vise or pliers, that you will be spraying paint, so buy inexpensive tools or mask them with tape or cardboard shields. Hold the side of the plug or lure tightly against the netting and spray through the netting with one or two passes of the spray gun or aerosol can.

The usual procedure for painting a plug with a scale finish is to spray or brush the entire plug

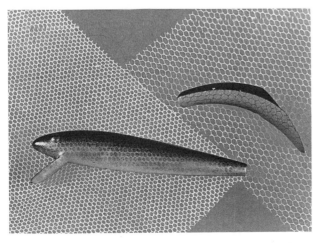

Two different styles of scale netting with the resultant finish on lure bodies.

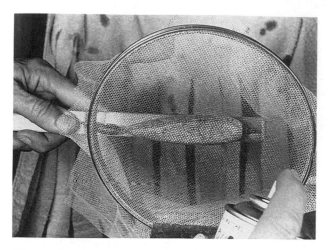

The embroidery hoop with scale netting held in a vise makes it possible to create scale finishes on lures. Hold lures tight against the netting for best results.

with a chosen light-color base coat. Then spray the sides through the netting with a slightly darker shade. Finally, spray the top of the plug (*not* through the netting) with a dark color for contrast. The result is very similar to a baitfish—dark on top, medium on the sides, with a light-colored belly.

Scale finishes can be used on any lure—spinner blades, spoons, bucktail heads, spinnerbait and buzzbait heads and blades, and so on.

Adding and Painting Eyes

Eyes in baitfish have been proven by biologists to be a triggering factor in strikes or attacks by gamefish and other predators. Thus, large, prominent eyes are a must for any lure. They won't ever hurt and might possibly affect how crowded a livewell is at the end of the day. Generally, if there is a question between eyes or no eyes, add eyes. If it is a question between little eyes or big eyes, make them big.

Eyes can be painted on any lure, and there are several techniques for doing this. If you are really expert, you can use the finest spray nozzle of an air brush and spray a small eye, following later with a contrasting color for a smaller pupil. It is also possible to use two different templates or masks, spraying first through the larger of the two for a background eye color, following later (after the first coat has dried) with the smaller template for a dark contrasting-color pupil. The only difficulty with this method is in positioning the second template to center the pupil on the eye

already painted. You can use clear plastic and small punched holes for this so that you can see through the plastic to position the mask. You can also position the pupil at an edge of the background eye to make a forward-, backward-, up-, or down-looking eye. There is nothing wrong with this; in fact some of the lure companies do this as a special design or identifying characteristic on their lures.

You can make simple "tools" for this process, these tools being nothing more than different-sized pins and nails. The best nails and pins for this are those with flat heads, such as regular straight pins and small flat-head brads, common nails, and box nails. Seat them in a small dowel or cork, which acts as a handle.

Dip the head of a larger pin or nail into the background color paint. Make sure you do not submerge the nail or pin head, but only touch the top of the head to the surface of the paint. Then lightly touch the paint-covered head to the lure. Do this on both sides with top-water plugs, crankbaits, and bucktails.

Once the paint is cured, follow with a smaller pin or nail head in a darker contrasting paint to make the pupil. Since you can see the background eye, you will be able to position the pupil exactly where you wish. Even a third color can be added with a still-smaller head.

Eyes are added after all other coats of paint have been applied because they are a finishing touch. The only addition after eyes would be a coat of clear or epoxy finish over the entire lure. For the eyes to show up properly on a lure, it is

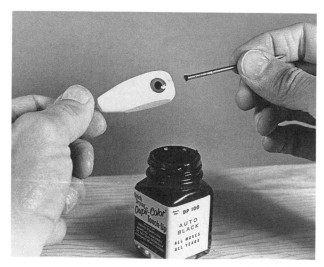

Painting the pupil of an eye using a nail head. A larger nail head was used for the base eye color.

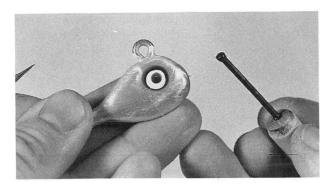

Several sizes of nail heads can be used for making multiple color eyes.

important to use contrasting colors for them. Thus, you would want a color contrasting with the plug for the background eye color and then a color contrasting with that for the pupil. Good background colors include white, yellow, orange, and red. For the pupil, use black or white. Naturally, you can reverse this, using black or red for the background color, then adding a white or yellow pupil.

In addition to painting them, there are a number of other ways eyes can be added to lures. Doll eyes are ideal for this. These come in several styles, including the movable-pupil glue-on styles. The movable-pupil doll eyes come in sizes from 3 millimeters up to about 25 millimeters. Most come with a black pupil and white background eye, although some with pupils of pink, blue, green, and red are starting to become available at this writing. Most have a flat back that is easily glued onto any lure, although some with stems are also useful. With wood plugs you have an added advantage in that you can slightly recess the body with a hole the diameter of the eye and glue the eye into the recessed area. These eyes can be glued onto any lure, though — bucktails, spinner-bait heads, buzzbait blades, plugs, top-water lures, and spoons.

Solid doll eyes on a plastic stem (with a hole in the stem for sewing onto the doll, or with a friction-fit back for fitting through a hole in the doll fabric) or movable plastic eyes on a stem are also good. The solid eyes come in sizes from about 5 millimeters to 25 millimeters, often with a yellow background color and black eye. If they can be found, those with a clear background and black pupil are best, since this allows painting of the back of the eye in any color desired. Since these eyes do have a stem, they must be mounted by drilling a hole into the lure (on lead bucktails or wood plugs only) and gluing the stem in place, or

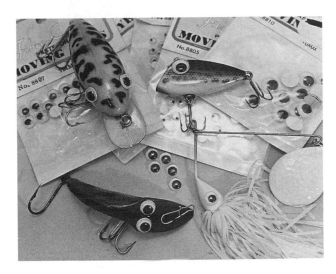

Eyes have proven to be very important on lures. Here, doll eyes have been glued onto several lures. The eyes come in several sizes, shapes, and colors.

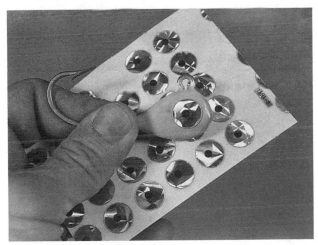

Example of decal eyes available for lures. Many sizes and colors are available. For best results, protect the eyes with a clear finish.

Sew-on doll eyes are also good for lures, but cut off stems before gluing to the lure. An alternative with wood plugs is to drill a hole to receive the stem. These eyes are used on a bucktail.

Examples of solid plastic eyes (top) and rattle doll eyes (bottom) used on spoon blades.

by cutting the stem off to glue the flat back to the lure (on spoons, spinner blades, and plastic plugs).

Another interesting eye material is the half-round beads with no holes that are sold in craft stores and catalogs. These can be painted any color desired and are often best when used in small sizes as pupils against contrasting-color background eyes painted on lures.

Map tacks are another possibility. These are sold in stationery stores and consist of a round head on a pin. They come only in small sizes. They are fine to create a bug-eyed appearance on small lures and especially fly-rod popping bugs. They come in many colors. Because map tacks are completely round, it often helps to countersink a hole in the lure slightly to recess the map tack.

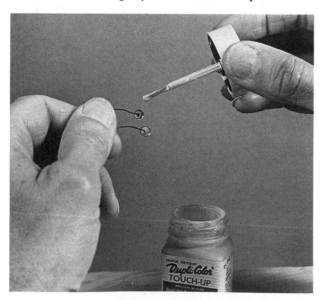

Glass eyes are available for lures, and the backs of the eyes can be painted to make different colored eyes with black pupils.

Glass eyes are available from some craft stores and catalogs, some mail-order-component tackle-supply houses, and some taxidermy shops. They are usually fastened to a wire stem, which can be glued into some lures (wood plugs and bucktails) after you've drilled a small pilot hole, or the stem can be removed and the glass eye glued on the lure surface. They are more expensive than any other type of eye and in small sizes are somewhat limited. Some are colored, but others can be painted on the back to provide a background eye color. To use them, cut the stem of the eye to about 1/2-inch long and glue it in place in a small pilot hole you've drilled.

Another possibility is decal eyes that come in sheets. Cut out the pair of eyes to be used, moisten them, and slide them onto the lure. For permanence, they have to be covered with a coat of clear finish.

BAKING PAINTS

One method of increasing the durability of lure finishes is to bake the painted lures in a kitchen oven. Naturally, this can only be done with metal lures such as spinner blades and spoons. You risk burning wood lures and will definitely melt and destroy plastic lures if you bake them.

However, baking paint does have disadvantages as well as advantages. You will note that in the list of metal lures above, bucktails were left out. This is because baking increases the brittleness of paint as well as the durability. Since bucktails are of a malleable metal (lead) that is often deformed during fishing when it hits rocks, baking would only cause the paint to chip off more readily. Baking is an ideal method for increasing paint durability on hard-metal lures such as spoons and spinner blades.

Baking must be done as the paint is drying. Also, since paints vary widely, baking procedures will vary accordingly. Automotive touch-up paints are especially suitable for baking. Experiment with small quantities of lures, or even with a scrap piece of metal to determine the results with any given paint and color under specific time and temperature conditions. As a starting point, try baking paints in a preheated oven at 175° to 200° Fahrenheit for about 15 to 20 minutes. Some paint experts suggest that baking times can be lengthened and temperatures increased, but do this with caution, experimenting first with painted scraps to check results.

ADDING OF GLITTER TO LURES

Metallic or Mylar glitter flakes can be added to any lure to increase its attractiveness. This glitter, available from tackle, craft, and variety shops, is available in small tubes and shaker bottles. It is also available in a tube of glue that can be squeezed onto lures. Available colors include red, blue, green, silver, gold, copper, and multicolor mixes.

There are several ways to add glitter to lures, depending upon the desired effect. For an overall glitter effect, coat the entire lure with special glitter cement (available separately), or use a clear adhesive coating or a clear finish coat. Then shake the glitter out of the bottle onto the lure, turning the lure if necessary to cover it completely. If the glitter you buy does not come in a shaker bottle, you can transfer it to an empty spice or herb shaker bottle. Salt- or pepper-shaker holes are

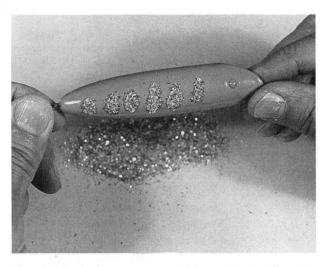

The finished glitter pattern. This method will make for a denser, more compact glitter finish than by sprinkling.

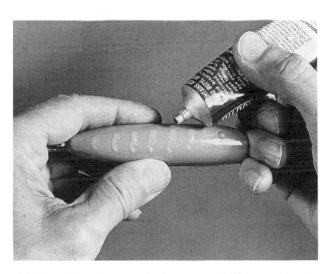

Adding glitter in patterns is easy to do by coating the lure with patterns of glue and then rolling the lure in glitter. Here, the glue is applied to the lure.

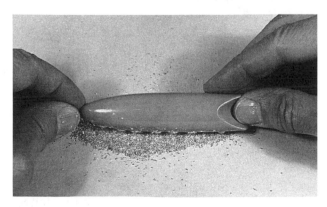

Rolling the lure in glitter.

usually too small to allow passage of the glitter. Also, use a base of newspaper or a large tray under the lure during glitter application. Some of the glitter will not stick to the lure, and any excess that falls to the paper or tray can be funneled back into the shaker bottle.

Another method of adding glitter is to paint the lure with clear cement or adhesive on selected parts and then shake glitter over these parts. The glitter will not stick elsewhere and the result is glitter in a predetermined pattern.

For a denser coat of glitter, paint the lure with adhesive either totally or selectively and roll the lure in a bed of glitter, previously deposited onto a clean surface. Waxed paper is good for this because it will not discolor (as might newsprint) and will allow easy funneling of the glitter back into the bottle. If you cover the entire lure with adhesive, you will need some sort of lure-holder — pins or screw eyes in both ends or split rings in spoon blades.

It helps to add a final coat or two of clear finish to the lure to protect the glitter finish and keep it from flaking off.

ADDING FLOCKED MATERIALS

Some craft stores carry flocking, a loose, furlike material that can be added to a lure using the same methods as for adding glitter. It is most often used on surface lures, where it will help imitate small-mammal lures such as mice, rats, lemmings, and so on.

ADDING TAPES

There are a number of tape products that can be used to dress up lures. Some of these, such as prism and colored tapes, are available from Luhr Jensen, Al's Goldfish, Les Davis, Witchcraft Tape Products, Wapsi Fly and Gator Grip (from J & L Tool & Machine Company), and Flasher Lures (from Five Star Products) are made specifically for lure application. They come in large and small sheets in a variety of different prism patterns and colors. Most have adhesive backs, and some, such as the specific shapes available from Gator Grip, peel off easily for application.

To use tapes that are not precut, cut the tape into the desired shape and size, remove the backing, and position the design over the lure. Since most of these adhesives are permanent

upon contact, take care that the tape is properly positioned before contact is made. In the case of large pieces of tape used on large spoons or plugs (or any lures with severe or complex curves), it may be necessary to cut slits into the tape to help it conform to the shape of the lure. Another alternative is to use several smaller, thinner strips of tape on the lure instead of one large piece of tape. The smaller strips are easier to handle and lessen the problems in placing flat tape on curved lures.

COLORING PLASTIC WORMS AND LURES WITH FELT-TIP MARKERS

Permanent felt-tip markers are good for painting lures. They contain the only type of color (other than dyes) that will affect plastic worms or any soft-plastic lure. Admittedly, plastic worms have color molded into them. However, if you wish to make an on-the-water change of that color to a darker color, you can usually do it with felt-tip markers. The final color may be slightly affected by the base color of the worm or by how dark that base color is, so don't expect perfect colors or perfect results. If you plan on changing colors in the field a great deal, the solution is to buy or mold clear worms, or worms that are very light in color—smoke, yellow, any light-colored shade. That way, you can change color as desired and get as close as possible to the felt-tip-marker color.

Felt-tip markers will also work on other lures. They have the least effect on bare metal, such as on spinner blades and spoons, but will work over painted, finished plugs, top-water plugs, crank-

Many tapes are available for adding to any lure— homemade or commercially available.

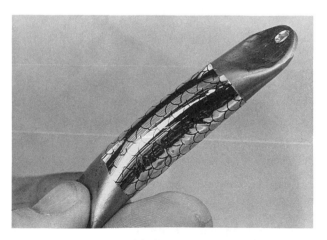

Prism-scale finish added to a structure lure made from copper pipe.

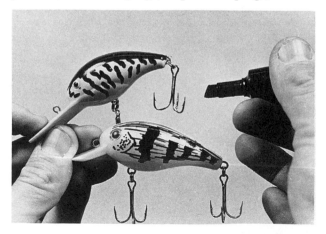

Simple lure finishes on base-painted plugs are easy using different colors and sizes of waterproof felt-tip markers.

baits, and bucktails. They work best if a dark color is used over a light color. However, on both soft-plastic lures and other lures, be forewarned that these colors are difficult to remove later on. In some cases, alcohol or lighter fluid will work, but experiment first before going wholesale with felt-tip color changes. Also, check the felt-tip-marker label, since some of these products contain solvents that will remove color from soft plastic.

FIELD PAINTING AND DYEING

Just as felt-tip markers are ideal for field-coloring lures, so are some dyes and paints made just for the purpose. Companies change in marketing these colors, but The Color Box, Catchin' Colors, and other companies carry quick-dry paints specifically designed for field use.

Most of these paints come in small bottles (1 or 2 ounces) with a lid-attached brush for immediate, no-problem application. Kits of these colors are also available.

For field application, make sure the lure is dry. If you have used it, dry it completely (be careful of the hooks), or allow to lie in the sun for a few minutes to dry after shaking off the excess water. If it's bright, hot, and sunny, use your body to shade the lure as you apply the paint—otherwise it will dry too rapidly. Use rapid brush strokes to cover the whole lure, working first on one side and then on the other. If you are making bars, stripes, or dots, use the brush as evenly as possible. Often it helps to hold the lure on something stationary like a boat deck and support your brushing hand on the same surface to produce even strokes. Although these paints will dry in a few minutes, you can fish almost immediately if you do not touch the painted finish. Just drop the lure in the water and start trolling, casting, or fishing again. After a few minutes in the water, the lure finish will be dry to the touch.

Dyes are available that allow you to dye your lures. These products are best on permeable lures such as rubber skirts, and feather and fur tails. They will lightly color hard lures, though. They are designed for field use and applied the same way as the paints just described.

FINAL LURE FINISHING

All lures, whether plugs, spoons, spinners, or bucktails, will look better and last longer if several final finishing coats of clear lacquer or epoxy finish are added to protect the paints. They will also protect those lures to which eyes (painted or applied), tape, and other final touches have been added. These clear finish coats should be added only after all the base coats, scale finishes, eyes, tapes, glitter, and other finishing procedures have been completed.

Naturally, clear finish coats must be chemically compatible with the previous coats used on the lures to prevent a reaction that might damage all your work. Dipping or spraying is the best method of application for these final coats. The toughest are those finishing coats of two-part clear epoxy.

KITS

Painting and finishing kits are available and provide an easy way to get the proper colors and finishing materials for lures at minimal cost. Cabela's Bass Pro Shops, Jann's, Lure-Craft, Do-It, Hilts Molds, and others listed in the Appendix offer these kits. Kits are a great way to start finishing lures, and you can later add replacement paints or different colors for your specific needs.

16

Making Molds for Lead and Soft-Plastic Lures

INTRODUCTION ▪ ALUMINUM BUCKTAIL MOLDS ▪
SILASTIC RUBBER BUCKTAIL MOLDS ▪ PLASTER
BUCKTAIL MOLDS ▪ MISCELLANEOUS SINKER MOLDS ▪
TIN-SQUID MOLDS ▪ ONE- AND TWO-PIECE
SOFT-PLASTIC-LURE MOLDS ▪ MOLDS FOR OFFSHORE
LURES

INTRODUCTION

The basic tools for making a wide variety of molds are no different from the basics we have already described. You can make many of these molds with no tools at all; others will require only the basics.

To make most molds, you will need odds and ends of scrap aluminum, wood, nails, and other bits and pieces found in most shops. Most of these molds take little time, talent, or materials, and can add greatly to the ease with which tackle can be constructed and to the variety of lures that can be made. While the basics will be discussed here, your imagination will no doubt suggest variations.

As with all lure-making and rod-building tasks, safety procedures must be followed. Thus, be sure you know how to use any tools described in this chapter. Use a work apron, roll up your sleeves, and remove jewelry when using machinery. Use protective clothing and gloves when working with potentially irritating mold-making compounds. Wear safety glasses at all times.

ALUMINUM BUCKTAIL MOLDS

If you have a design for a bucktail and want to make a commercial-type aluminum mold for it, there are ways this can be done. The easiest way is to get a "blank" mold—one with hinges and handles but no cavities. These are available from Do-It, Hilts Molds, and L'il Mac. Do-It makes a standard-size blank mold (4 5/8- × 2 1/8- × 9/16-

inch on each side) that is hinged and handled. You must be able to fit the finished lure into the length, width, and depth of the mold, and you must be able to machine the cavities for the lure yourself, or contract with a small machine or tool-and-die shop for this work. If you do not machine the mold yourself, it may be relatively expensive (maybe four or five times the cost of a standard bucktail mold) to have it done. It is wise to check out this cost before ordering such a mold.

The Perfect Replica Mold from Hilts Molds is a large aluminum mold, hinged and handled, with several gates and a large rectangular cavity (2 × 5 × 1 inches). It comes with two pieces of silicone that are worked like modeling clay to make the mold and then vulcanized in the oven at 375° for 45 minutes, after which the gates are cut with a knife. Extra silicone inserts are available for making molds with several different cavities for use in the accompanying frame.

You can make your own molds from aluminum blocks or by using Do-It or L'il Mac blank mold. You will need block aluminum, special drills,

rotary files, and routers. Do-it-yourself aluminum in the 1/4-inch thickness is okay for small lures; larger blocks of aluminum are available from scrap-metal dealers and some hobby shops. A portable drill on a light drill stand, drill press, or rotary grinder is necessary for machining the cavities in the two aluminum mold halves. A Dremel Moto-Tool also works well, since a number of small routers, sanders, drill bits, and grinding bits are available for these versatile tools.

The basic technique is as follows: First, cut out the two blocks of aluminum to the size needed for the bucktail or bucktails. Allow for at least a 1-inch margin on all sides of the jig. Allow a wall thickness of at least 1/8-inch at the widest (thickest) part of the lure. Clamp the two blocks together and drill a 1/8-inch hole through opposite sides of the two blocks (The sprue holes will be on one of the other sides), drilling the blocks together. Insert a no. 10 finishing nail (or other stiff 1/8-inch wire) through each of the two holes in one block, tapping it firmly in place. Cut the pins flush on the outside of the mold and

Aluminum molds for making lead lures can be made from block aluminum, but require innovative construction methods. To make this mold for shad darts (bottom mold), the builder first drilled angled, tapered holes, then added a separate plate drilled for the sprue hole. The separate plate is permanently screwed in place on the base block. Note the registration pins also placed in each mold.

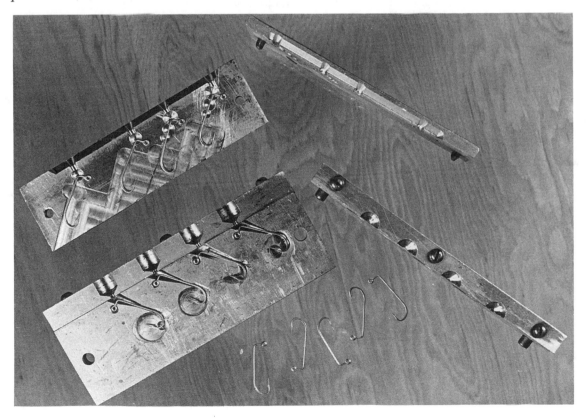

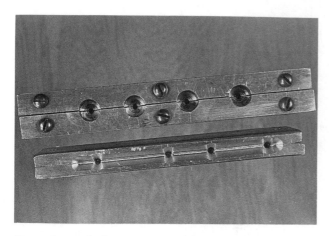

Top view of above two molds showing the sprue holes.

leave about 1/4-inch exposed inside to fit into the holes on the other block. These form registration pins. You may wish to sand the protruding pins a little for a good fit without binding, and you may also wish to tap or swage the pins in place a little to secure them in the one block. This procedure will ensure proper registration of the two mold halves for the rest of the work and for pouring the lead heads once the mold is completed.

You can use the mold as is, or you can finish it with hinges and handles. To do this, drill and tap for the machine bolts to hold the hinges in place. You can also cut the heads off the bolts and glue wood handles in place. Or you can use the Do-It or L'il Mac mold and avoid this step.

Place a sheet of paper between the two mold halves and clamp them together so that the two pins (or nails) cut holes into the paper. (If you use the Do-It or L'il Mac mold, trace the mold outline on both sides because there are no registration pins.) Outline the block on the paper and remove it. Draw an outline of the chosen bucktail shape in the center of the paper square. Cut the bucktail outline out of the paper and retrace it on both sides of the mold halves, taking care that the paper is *exactly* positioned on the pins or on the outline of the mold.

Using rotary files in a rotary grinder (such as the Dremel Moto-Tool), cut out the shape of the bucktail from each half of the mold. Periodically check the shape of the mold by pressing a small piece of beeswax or children's modeling clay between the two mold halves. Continue cutting and shaping until the two cavities are symmetrical, with the edges in perfect alignment.

Similarly, rout out a sprue hole or gate (this is the tapered or funnel-like opening through which

lead is poured into the mold cavities). Mark the proper position for the jig hook, cut slots for the hook shank, holes for the eye, and make any other additions as may be required. These additions could include space for molded-in weed-guards. Once it is completed, the mold can be used in the same ways as any commercial mold would be. Follow the techniques outlined in Chapter 4.

SILASTIC RUBBER BUCKTAIL MOLDS

Silastic RTV mold-making rubber from Dow Corning is an ideal medium from which to make molds of unusual bucktails and other lead lures. (The RTV stands for "room temperature vulcanizing," a method of curing the silicone rubber mold with a catalyst.) There are a number of different Silastic rubber compounds, each of which consists of a liquid that sets up into a solid with the addition of a catalyst. Each of the Silastic compounds would work for making bucktail molds, but some are better suited than others as a result of their viscosities. Some, such as the types C and D, are very thick or viscous and would not pour well. Those most often made available for bucktails molds are the Silastic RTV A and B. These, along with the others, have good temperature stability of up to 500° (600° with the type B), which is suitable for the intermittent heat of molding lead bucktails.

You will also need a catalyst, and the catalyst must match the rubber compound used. Usually for the compound types A or B, the catalyst type #1 is best, since it promotes a standard cure rate and good working time. A #4 catalyst promotes a fast cure rate and should be avoided because it will give you far less time to work.

Note that safety must be paramount when working with these or any mold-making materials. See the safety precautions supplied by the manufacturer.

To make a mold, begin with a bucktail head that is as perfect as possible. If you are working from a finished lure, you must carefully cut off and remove all of the tail materials and wrappings. You can make a model of almost anything —good possibilities for models include wood, modeling clay, and carved plastic. Naturally, the hook for the finished lure must be included, so that cavities for it are left in the finished Silastic mold.

Make sure the model—regardless of what it's made from—is free of grease, oil, fingerprints,

Materials and supplies needed for making molds of Silastic rubber compound. Even though these molds are of rubber, they still allow molding of lead lures.

or anything you don't want reproduced on the molded lures. Select a container to hold the mold material and the bucktail model. If possible, allow for about 1/2-inch all around the sides but no more, since more will just waste the Silastic rubber. Good containers include film canisters, small juice cans, any plastic kitchen container with the top cut off, and plastic disposable bottles with the tops removed. Cut the container to a height that will allow you to hang the bucktail by the hook on a pencil or toothpick laid across the top of the container. Since the bucktail model will hang head-down, this makes it easy to later cut a gate or sprue hole into the tail of the lure, where it will be hidden by the skirt or tail and make a clean, perfect bucktail head.

Mix the Silastic rubber according to directions, using a 10:1 mix (Silastic rubber to catalyst) for best results. More catalyst will decrease working time; less will increase working time. Dow Corning lists working and cure times for various mixes. These are as follows:

The two parts of the Silastic rubber are added and mixed. Different colors make complete mixing easy to determine.

Silastic RTV Type A

Ratio	Working Time	Cure time
20:1	4 hours	48 hours
10:1	2 1/2 hour	24 hours
5:1	1 hour	18 hours

Silastic RTV Type B

Ratio	Working Time	Cure time
20:1	4 hours	36 hours
10:1	2 1/2 hours	24 hours
5:1	1 1/2 hours	12 hours

These cure times are for when Dow Corning catalyst #1 or #116 (used with type A or B rubber only) is used. Dow Corning catalyst #4 is faster-acting, with working times as short at 4 minutes and cure times as short as 15 minutes. (Cure times for other types of RTV rubber are available from Dow Corning.)

Mix thoroughly, using a gentle folding or stirring motion, since beating, whipping, or frothing the mix will increase the possibility of air bubbles —and defects—on the surface of the mold. Mixing to a uniform consistency is easy because the rubber and catalyst are two different colors; a uniform color indicates a complete mix.

One way to prevent air bubbles when pouring the Silastic rubber is to first slowly dip the master lure into the mold compound for complete coverage. Once dipped, it can be hung from a pin in a mold container, in this case a paper cup.

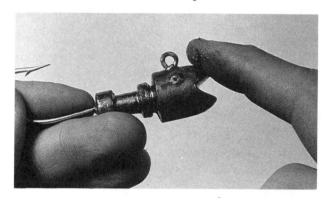

The first step in making Silastic rubber molds is to coat the master lure with a parting compound.

To make sure that the model will separate from the mold, coat the mold with a releasing compound such as Johnson's Paste Wax or with a mix of petroleum jelly to rubbing alcohol in a 1:20 ratio. (Because of its flammability, take care when using alcohol.) To lessen the possibility of air bubbles even further, coat the model lure with Silastic rubber before placing it into the container. Do this by slowly dipping it into the mixed rubber, or better still, by gently and thoroughly brushing the liquid rubber on the model. This latter method is particularly good if the lure has a lot of intricate detail. Then hang the lure into the container by its hook from a rod or pencil and slowly pour the Silastic rubber around it into the mold.

Allow this to cure at least overnight, and preferably for two nights. At this point, you must get the lure model out of the mold by cutting the mold apart. You must do this exactly (or as close as possible) on the same lines or plane of the model so as to free not only the lure but the hook shank and eye as well.

One easy way to do this is to cut down along the plane of the hook with a fillet knife until it hits the rear of the model, then cut along this plane

Once the molding compound is added and allowed to cure, the bucktail mold can be removed.

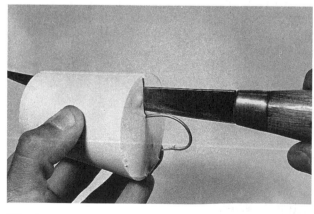

The best way to separate the mold is with a fillet knife, cutting along normal seam lines and in plane with the hook.

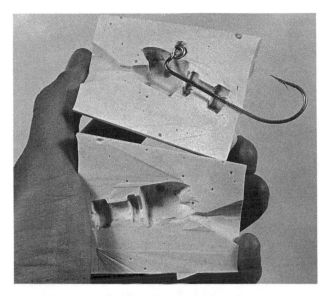

Completed mold in two parts. The sprue hole has been carved into one end for pouring and a hook has been added.

Pouring lead into the Silastic rubber mold. Note the rubber bands used to hold the two mold halves. An alternative method is to mold registration pins into the mold.

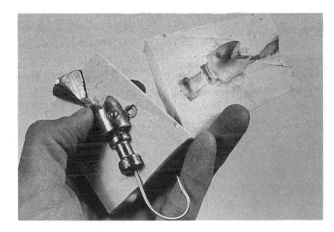

Completed mold with cast lead head.

until you are close to the bottom of the mold. For best results, do not cut the mold completely in half; instead, leave the bottom intact. The model (and later the molded heads) can be popped out of the mold by peeling it back from the top. This also eliminates the necessity of registration pins to line up the mold halves. (However, if you wish to cut the mold completely in half and use registration pins, first position the bucktail in the container and then push finishing nails through the pouring container in at least two points, and preferably four, to properly line up the two mold halves later. Pull the finishing nails completely out when you cut the mold in half, then reinsert them in one side, with about 1/2-inch protruding. When using registration pins or nails, it is best to use a disposable plastic or cardboard drink container for the mold. That way, the nails can be pushed directly and easily through the container to function as registration pins.)

After the model is out of the mold, use a sharp knife to cut a funnel-like gate or sprue hole into the tail of the lure (the top of the mold). Make this funnel about 1/8-inch at the bottom (where it connects with the lure body) and about 1/2- to 3/4-inch at the top.

Once the mold is finished, it can be used just like any other bucktail mold. Place a hook in the mold before pouring, and line up the registration pins or use a rubber band around the top of the mold if it is only split partway through. Follow all of the instructions in Chapters 4 and 5 when

melting and pouring the lead. Pay particular attention to the safety instructions, since these *must* be followed, regardless of the type of mold used.

PLASTER BUCKTAIL MOLDS

Bucktail molds made from plaster require no special tools or skills. Plaster of paris, small boxes or containers for pouring the plaster, a couple of nails for registration pins, petroleum jelly or liquid soap, and a model of a bucktail head are all that is needed. If it is an original design of a bucktail head, make a sample body of wood, plastic wood, modeling clay, liquid steel, liquid aluminum, epoxy, or a similar easy-to-work material. If you are using a standard commercial bucktail, strip off all of the thread and tail material before proceeding. Naturally, although we are describing making a mold for a bucktail here, the same technique can be applied to molds for lead sinkers or tin squids.

Find a suitable small box into which the plaster can be poured. Small plastic boxes, cardboard boxes, even cut-down disposable plastic bottles and jars are ideal. A good size for a single-cavity mold for a 1/2-ounce bucktail would be about 4 × 3 × 1 1/2 or × 2 inches deep. Mix the plaster with water to a consistency resembling thick, smooth pancake batter. (Plastic mixing bowls are ideal for this, since any hardened plaster is easily cracked out by bending or twisting the bowl.) However, the plaster should flow, not drop or "plop" into the mold box. Mix only enough to fill half the box, since the mold must be made in two separate parts. It is important to make the plaster as smooth as possible, without air bubbles that can cause defects in the mold cavity. (To remove air bubbles, rap the mixing bowl sharply with a spoon or tap it on a table.)

At this time it is possible to either lengthen or shorten the curing time of the plaster if it seems to be too thick (setting up too rapidly) or too thin (curing too slowly). Add a little salt to speed up the curing process; add a little vinegar to slow it.

Pour evenly over the bottom of the box, filling half the box with plaster. While the plaster is starting to set, cover the entire bucktail body, hook, and eye with a thin coating of petroleum jelly to prevent it from sticking to the plaster. Place the bucktail on its side in the plaster. There

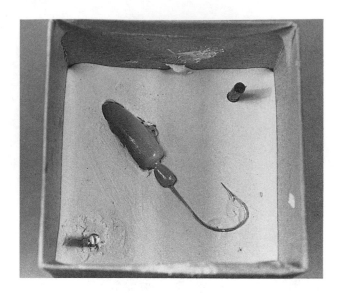

Master lure in mold half, with registration pins (nails with the heads cut off) added.

is a critical time for doing this, since if it is done too early, the bucktail may sink into the still-liquid plaster. If done too late, you may not be able to push it halfway into the plaster. Before the plaster sets, take two thick 1- to 1 1/2-inch nails and sink them vertically—head end first—into the plaster at opposite corners of the mold. Leave about 1/4-inch of the point end extending out of the plaster. These nails will serve to ensure proper registration during casting. Allow the plaster to set for 30 minutes to an hour, then coat the entire exposed surface of the mold with petroleum jelly.

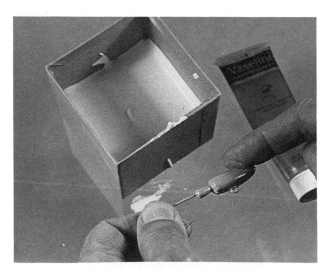

Making a mold from plaster. First half-fill a box with plaster, then coat a master lure with petroleum jelly and lay it on its side in the mold.

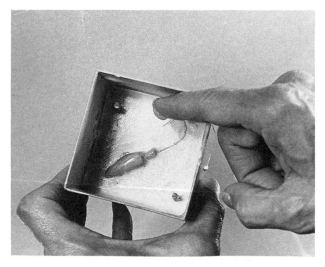

Once the plaster is cured, the rest of the mold is coated with plaster to allow for easy separation.

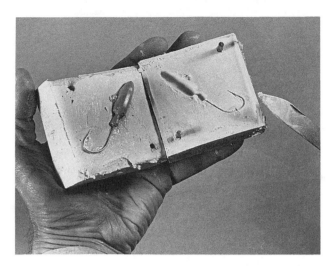

Completed mold after opening by scoring with knife along the seam lines.

As with Silastic molds, a sprue hole must be carved into the end.

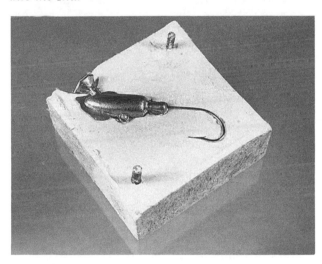

Completed mold with cast lure. Flash is not uncommon with these molds and ultimately the molds must be discarded.

Now mix another batch of plaster and pour it evenly over the bucktail and the first half of the mold. When the second pouring of plaster has set —in about 1 hour—break or cut apart the box used for the mold and remove the solid block of plaster. Carefully separate the two mold halves by running a knife blade along the joint. Remove the bucktail from the mold carefully and allow the mold to cure and dry thoroughly. Plaster holds a great deal of water for a long time, and the curing cannot be hurried. For average-sized molds, allow about two weeks to cure.

Caution Don't ever pour molten lead into a plaster mold that has not been properly cured. The water in the plaster will cause the molten lead to splatter dangerously and the mold will be cracked and ruined.

During the two-week curing time, finish the mold by carving a sprue hole. Sprue holes, or gates, allow the molten lead to reach the bucktail cavity. Usually they are placed at either the head or tail end of the bucktail and between the two halves. (Placing a sprue hole at the tail end is best, since any imperfections caused by cutting off the lead sprue after molding will be covered by the bucktail skirt.) Taper the hole, leaving an opening of no more than 1/4-inch diameter at the entrance to the cavity. You can, if desired, carve slots in the mold for weedless hooking arrangements, spinnerbait wires, or similar additions.

Once the mold is complete and cured, place a hook in it. Clamp the mold together with woodworkers' spring clamps or C-clamps. If you use C-clamps, fasten them very lightly, because excessive pressure will crack the mold. Plaster molds

will not last indefinitely, as will iron or aluminum molds, but with care they are usually good for at least several dozen lures. In time, the mold cavity will start to chip around the edges, causing excessive flash in the castings. If you are making sinkers, this is less of a concern because sinkers do not have to be finely finished or smooth. You can get more from this method by making a multiple-cavity plaster mold that will make several or more bucktails or sinkers at one pouring.

MISCELLANEOUS SINKER MOLDS

While many sinkers are designed and shaped specifically for a special type of fishing, it is possible to mold a common sinker by drilling a hole in a wood block. The result is rough in appearance, but for holding a lake or shore bottom will work as well as a sinker bought in a tackle store or made from a commercial mold.

To make a two-piece wood mold, clamp together two pieces of 1- to 2-inch-thick wood. With a large-diameter drill bit, drill on the center line between the two blocks, so that each block will have a half-hole. Depending upon the size of the wood block, you can drill several or many holes for sinkers. No sprue hole is needed. The drilled hole is filled with molten lead. Hold a brass eye in the center of the sinker with pliers (it will get hot!) until the lead cools. Once the sinker has cooled, separate the two parts of the mold and pry the sinker out with an awl or pliers. The hole in the wood will burn slightly, but many sinkers can be made before the wood is rendered unusable. These cylindrical sinkers in various sizes can be used for many types of fishing.

Similarly, a crude type of egg sinker can be made the same way. Drill a 1/8-inch hole to hold a core rod (usually made from a coat hanger or nail—make this hole deeper than the sinker hole), then drill the larger-diameter hole for the sinker. Place the core rod into the mold cavity and pour the lead around it. Remove the core rod as soon as the sinker cools enough to open the mold.

Carving also allows you to make different sinkers. For example, it is easy to lay out and carve a flat-sided pyramid sinker. With skill, it is also possible to carve out examples of bank sinkers or shallow-sided dollar-style sinkers, or to

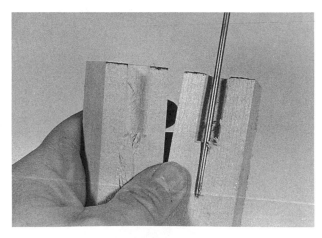

A split block of wood like this, drilled with a larger diameter drill bit and also drilled to take a core rod (shown), will work to make simple egg or net-type sinkers. The split wood allows removal of the sinkers.

carve in sprue holes for more precise molding, and so on. Small routers such as the Dremel Moto-Tool make these tasks easy and quick.

TIN-SQUID MOLDS

Using the techniques for making plaster molds, you can make one-piece (one-sided) tin-squid molds. Tin squids are usually flat on one side and thus lend themselves to one-piece molds, even though molds for them are generally available commercially only in two parts.

Using a tin squid as a model, mix and pour plaster as outlined, placing the tin squid into the mold so that the top flat side is level with the surface of the plaster. If the squid is of the fixed-hook variety, make sure that the hook point is up. If the lure uses a swinging hook, remove the hook and any split or jump rings prior to making the mold.

Since these lures are very simple, another technique is to mold a block of plaster, allow it to cure, and then lay out a design and carve or rout the shape into the hardened plaster. Another technique is to use a tin squid or follow a drawing or design pattern to trace an outline on a block of wood or aluminum, carving it to the shape desired. A small whittling knife can be used for carving wood, while electric tools (such as the Dremel Moto-Tool) are ideal for shaping the cavity in an aluminum block. Take care when using this type of mold, since the mold must be filled completely with tin or lead but without any overflowing. A small ladle for pouring helps in this.

ONE- AND TWO-PIECE SOFT-PLASTIC-LURE MOLDS

Following the directions given for making two-piece plaster bucktail and one-piece tin-squid molds, it is possible to make plaster molds for molding soft-plastic lures.

There are two possible methods of making a one-piece plastic-lure mold from plaster, but both require a good commercial or homemade lure "master" or model. In most cases, these molds are used for making soft-plastic worms, and the model worm, or any lure model, must have one flat side. One method is to lay the model on a flat sheet of glass. This is best when using a lure model that can be glued or stuck to the glass. (Try petroleum jelly for this.) With this method, it is possible to

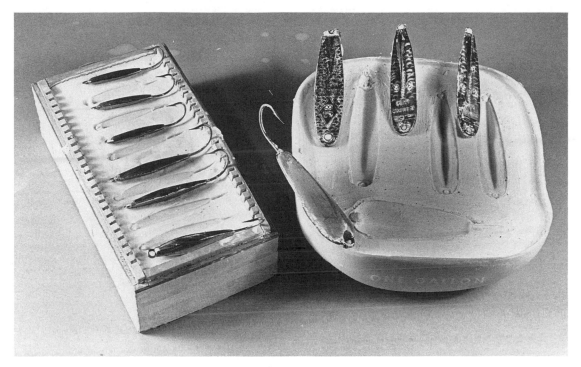

Open-face plaster molds for making jigging spoons and tin squids. Here, master lures have been used to make the mold cavities.

Making plaster molds for molding soft plastic lures. The salt and vinegar can be used to adjust curing times.

get a completely flat mold that is very easy to work with.

Stick the worm or worms or other lures to the glass sheet. An 8 × 10-inch glass sheet is fine for all but extra-large lures. Cover the glass sheet with a thin layer of petroleum jelly. Place a plastic or cardboard box, open at the top and bottom, over the lures and onto the glass to contain the plaster.

Weight the box to prevent plaster leakage, or tape the box in place.

Fill the box with mixed plaster, following previous directions. Allow it to set overnight, then carefully remove the box sides, lift the plaster block from the glass, and carefully remove the model lure or lures. If you have difficulty in removing a worm or lure, stick a pin or nail into one end at an angle and carefully pry the lure out of the mold. Any small pieces of plaster that may

After mixing the plaster, pour into a simple container.

crack off the edges should be shaken or brushed away before using the mold.

In the second method, a box (with bottom intact) is filled with plaster. Place the master lure carefully onto the plaster with the flat side up. Take care to push the worm down into the plaster until the flat surface is flush with the surface of the plaster. Allow the plaster to cure overnight, then remove the model lure and clean as before.

Once the mold is cured and dry, it can be used just as commercial soft-plastic molds are used, as described in Chapter 7. However, if the plaster mold is used without further treatment, the plaster surface will cause the resulting worms or lures to have a dull or matte finish. A shiny lure finish is made possible by first painting the mold cavity with semigloss heat-resistant paint. These paints resist heat up to 400° Fahrenheit (they are often sold for painting auto engine parts) and are readily available in both spray-on and brush-on containers. One important point: These plaster molds can't be slipped into a pan of water to cool, as can plastic molds. As a result, molding will be slower in a plaster mold because it will take more time for the lure to cool enough to remove.

Using these methods, it is possible to make molds for worms, spring lizards, spinnerbait tails, and so on, by *combining* parts of several different soft-plastic lures. One simple example would be to take a standard twin-tail spinnerbait tail and add a worm tail to the fork where the two tails meet to make a three-tail spinnerbait tail. The parts do not have to be welded together. Just placing the parts in proximity in the mold will produce a good

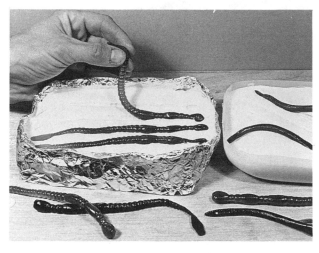

After the plaster is poured, the worms are laid in the liquid plaster. After curing, the worms are removed.

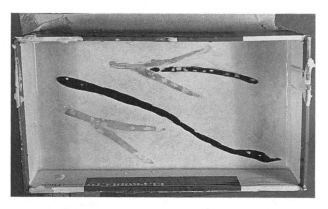

Various worms and soft lures can be combined, as shown, here to make up new designs of soft plastic lures. Here, a worm and twin spinnerbait tail have been combined in an open-face plaster mold.

Completed plaster mold for molding worms.

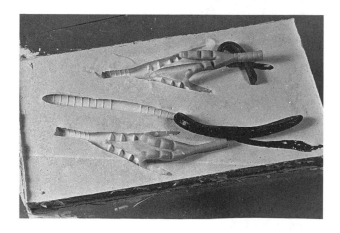

Result of the above molds, with the new triple-tail worm at the top.

To prevent dull matte finishes in soft plastics, the mold cavities must be sprayed with a gloss paint. Any color will work, but heat-resistant engine enamel is best.

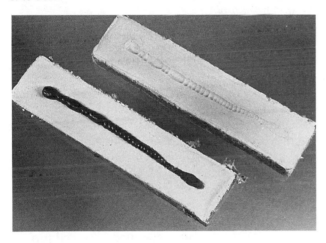

Completed mold showing the worm in place and the mold opened. A sprue hole has not yet been cut in the mold.

connection, although you can use heat or a Wormizer to weld the parts together.

Two-piece plaster molds for soft-plastic lures may be made by following the directions for making two-piece bucktail or sinker molds. The plaster must be poured in two parts, and you should pick a box shape that will match the lure shape. Since worms are made often, this often means a long, thin box for a one-cavity mold. Be sure to pick master or model lures that are completely round; otherwise a simpler one-piece open-face mold will work just as well with less trouble.

When placing a round worm in the bottom part of the two-piece mold, make sure you position it so that the seam line on the worm is level with the

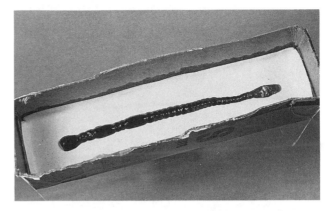

Making two-piece plaster mold for soft plastics. Here, the worm has been laid on the first part of the two piece mold.

surface of the plaster. Otherwise, your molded worms will have two seams—one from the original master worm and the second from the plaster mold. If you mold a curved-tail worm, the curved tail will have to lay out flat on the surface of the mold so that it can be removed easily. Also, as with the bucktail molds, use short nails—at least two of them—to serve as registration pins for the two parts of the mold. These must be placed before the first pouring of the plaster.

Once the first bottom part of the mold is partially cured (in 30 minutes to 1 hour), cover the mold surface and the model lure with petroleum jelly and pour the second portion of plaster. Allow this to cure for about 1 hour and then open or cut apart the box and run a knife around the mold joint to open it up. Carefully open the mold, remove the model, and allow the mold halves to cure overnight.

At one end of the mold, carve a sprue hole through which to pour the molten plastic. If this is a worm mold, place the sprue hole at the head end—for other lures, place the sprue hole at the widest part of the mold cavity. Since the molten plastic is more viscous than is the lead used for molding bucktails, the opening from the sprue to the mold cavity must be relatively large. If the mold does not fill completely, carving the sprue hole larger will usually correct the problem.

Pour the molten plastic in slowly, holding the mold at an angle so that the plastic will flow all the way to the bottom and fill the mold from the bottom up. As with open-face molds, the cavity and sprue hole can be painted with glossy heat-resistant paint to give the molded lures a shiny finish.

Once complete, the two-part mold is secured with rubber bands and filled with liquid plastic.

Completed round worms from the two part mold. The sprue has been cut from one of the worms.

MOLDS FOR OFFSHORE LURES

Molds for offshore trolling lures are easily found: Use plastic spice bottles, film canisters, bouillon jars, and the like, as outlined in Chapter 11. In addition, you can make a mold for your favorite offshore lure by using Mold Builder, a liquid latex-rubber compound manufactured by ETI. Also, you can carve or use modeling clay or plaster to make a master prototype of a lure, using the Mold Builder to make the mold. The compound, available in 16-ounce jars, can be used as is over metal, plastic, or glass. Copper or brass

Making a mold from an offshore lure using Mold Builder is easy, but time consuming. The Mold Builder is brushed onto the master lure. Here a lure molded from a plastic spice bottle is used.

should be shellacked first, while plaster, clay, or similar porous materials should be sealed with a sealer or paste wax.

To use Mold Builder, you must have an exact model of the lure you wish to copy. If you use a commercial lure, first remove all the skirting and rigging. Mount the model tail-down with glue on a level work surface, preferably glass or plastic. Use a brush to coat the lure or model with the Mold Builder. Make sure there are no air bubbles; if any air bubbles form, pop them to prevent flaws from occurring. Also coat the base surface in an area of about 2 inches all around the lure. This will form a flange by which the mold is supported when polyester resins are poured to make the lures.

The Mold Builder, which is white in color when wet, will dry to a translucent tan in time. Allow the material to cure to this tan color before adding second coatings. To prevent damaging the brush, wash it with soapy water between coats. After the first two or three coats, additional coats can be applied more thickly, or strips of gauze can be added to the mold for reinforcement and strength. Usually about six to eight coats are sufficient for a small lure of up to about three inches long; more may be required for larger lures.

After the last coat, allow the mold to cure for 24 hours, and then remove it, first coating the outside with talcum powder to prevent it from sticking to itself. To strengthen the mold, vulcanize it by boiling it in water for 20 minutes.

To make the castings, prepare a cardboard box

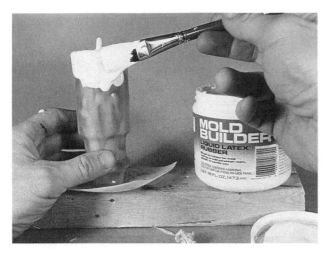

Brushing the Mold Builder in place on the lure. The liquid latex is white, but cures to a tan color.

When lures are poured, this completed mold will be supported on an inverted cardboard box through a hole cut into the box.

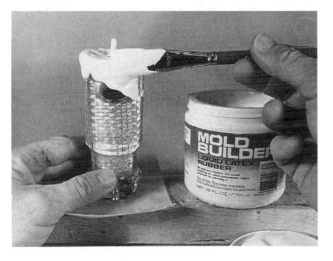

Repeated coatings of the Mold Builder are necessary to give the mold strength.

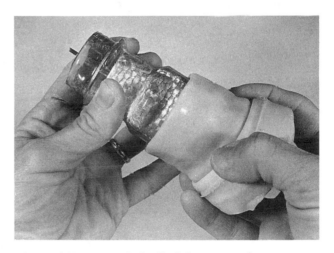

The mold being peeled off of the master lure.

with a hole in the center top, through which the mold can be suspended. Make sure the box is high enough to accommodate the mold. Turn the box over (bottom up), push the mold through the hole, and tape the mold flange to the outside of the box with masking tape. Follow the directions outlined in Chapter 11 for mixing and preparing the plastic resin and adding any previously prepared inserts to the mold. (If you wish to mold in a center hole, you can make the mold with a socket for this. Use an unrigged lure and place a short 1-inch rod into the forward part of the rigging hole. Coat this rod at the same time you are coating the lure. Then, when molding, place thin tubing, which becomes a part of the lure

when it is cut off at both ends, into this socket and tape it to the center of the supported mold when pouring the plastic.)

Naturally, any inserts molded into the lure would have to be drilled for this core tubing (about 3/16-inch in diameter) and placed there at the same time.

Molds can also be made from the latex-rubber material used to make nonslip grips on pliers handles or by using previously described techniques of making molds using the Dow Corning Silastic RTV rubber compounds. This latter, however, will usually produce lures that have a duller finish than those produced with the latex-rubber compounds.

17

Rod Blanks and Rod Parts

INTRODUCTION ▪ BLANKS ▪ GUIDES AND TIP-TOPS ▪ REEL SEATS ▪ GRIPS ▪ HANDLES ▪ BUTT CAPS, GIMBALS ▪ FERRULES, COLLETS, HOSELS, AND WINDING CHECKS ▪ THREAD ▪ FINISHES, COLOR PRESERVERS, SEALERS, AND GLUES ▪ MISCELLANEOUS

INTRODUCTION

Building rods really means assembling rods. Unless you are into splitting your own cane and milling the six strips that go into a split-bamboo rod, you are really combining or assembling parts when you are "building" a rod. This is not to demean the skill required in this hobby, but only to put it into proper perspective. Assuming you follow directions and use proper care, building any type of fishing rod is no more difficult than assembling and gluing a plastic model plane, and is probably less complicated than constructing most home decorations as taught in arts and crafts classes.

All the rod parts are built around the blank, and while the parts might seem to vary widely, all

rods require the basics of a blank, reel seat, grip or handle, guides, and tip-top. What these parts are and how they vary is the subject of this chapter; how these parts are assembled on the blank is the subject of the remaining chapters in this book.

BLANKS

BAMBOO BLANKS

To understand blanks properly, it helps to know a little about how they are made. Six-strip split-bamboo rods were developed by Samuel Phillippe, according to the earliest printed evidence, in 1859; although, according to Martin J. Keane in Classic Rods and Rodmakers, rods with three- and four-strip bamboo tip sections were developed by the British as early as 1801.

Even though entire books are devoted to these rods and their building, repair, and restoration, the basics are relatively simple. Culms of Tonkin cane bamboo, one of the two thousand species of this unique member of the grass family, are seasoned, split into rough strips, and then again into finer strips. These are placed on special V blocks that have tapered Vs cut into the bed at a 60-degree angle. The strips are measured and cut to fit together with five other identical strips. The strips are then glued, crisscross wrapped with heavy cord, and slow-baked to cure. The cord is removed, the resulting blank is cleaned and trimmed, and the appointments are added to the blank to make a fine rod.

Finished bamboo blanks are available for rod-builders through some companies and custom builders.

SYNTHETIC BLANK CONSTRUCTION

Rods from synthetics are made in one of three separate ways: pultrusion, Howald process, and cut-and-roll. Pultrusion is used for making solid glass blanks and results in an inexpensive, heavy, but very strong rod. These blanks are often used for heavy boat rods and shark rods. The process begins with raw glass, which is melted and blown to produce fine glass fibers. The strands of fiberglass are then pulled (thus the name) through a bath of resin adhesive, then through a small die that compresses the fibers into a round rod form. During the assembly-line process, the straight, continuous glass rod goes through an oven to cure; the resin and glass fuse into a single, continuous, and uniform-diameter fiberglass rod. The rod continues through the manufacturing facility, where it is cut into predetermined lengths with a machine. These uniform-diameter rods then go to a second machine that uses abrasive wheels to taper the blank to predetermined butt and tip diameters.

A mandrel design helps to determine the type of rod blank that is made and is required for both the Howald process and cut-and-roll manufacture. Large-diameter steel mandrels, or tapered rods, are used for large blanks such as would be used for heavy fishing or saltwater use. The large diameter helps the blank resist breaking as a result of the hoop strength (just as a large-diameter pipe or

Rod blanks in a factory ready for shipment. Blanks are separated by type and length.

tube resists bending and breaking more than does an otherwise identical small-diameter tube or pipe). Thinner mandrels are used for freshwater blanks and fly rods. Mandrels can also vary with their taper. A straight-taper mandrel will result in a rod (everything else being equal) with an even progressive bend from butt to tip. A mandrel with a nonlinear taper that becomes sharply thinner in the tip end will result in a rod with more tip action. Where this taper begins will determine the degree of tip action—moderate, fast, or extra-fast.

A single mandrel can be used to construct several different styles of rods, making them more cost-effective. Mandrels are often longer than the rod that is made on them, so that the position of the rod material on the mandrel will determine the degree of taper or the action of the blank. For example, an 8-foot-long mandrel with a sharp taper in the middle could be used to make an eight-foot rod with moderately fast action. By placing the rod material on the lower six-foot, or butt end, of the mandrel (leaving the upper portion of the mandrel bare), a six-foot rod with a fast or extra-fast tip would result. Making a six-foot rod on the tip end (leaving the two feet at the butt bare) would result in a smooth-taper parabolic rod, but one with a very strong butt section. Naturally, all of these rods would be for different purposes and have different power, since the diameters throughout would vary.

HOWALD-PROCESS BLANK CONSTRUCTION

The Howald process, used by the Shakespeare Company and named for Dr. Arthur M. Howald, who developed the method, uses a mandrel machined to precise tolerances. The taper and dimensions of the mandrel determine the inside diameter of the resulting rod.

In the first step of the Howald process, the mandrel is coated with a releasing agent — silicone or Teflon — to allow the blank to be removed when finished. Then a machine wraps rod material around the mandrel in a tight spiral. This material can be graphite, glass, other material or combinations thereof, but in the case of Shakespeare is graphite. A second machine, which looks like a lathe, feeds individual longitudinal strands of rod material onto this spiral inner wrap. These strands, which again may be graphite, glass, or other materials, go through a resin bath just before being placed on the wrapped mandrel.

The longitudinal strands are wrapped with clear tape to keep them in place. One important point is that, as the rod is fed through the Howald-process machinery, some of the longitudinal strands are cut in a precise sequence. This results in less rod material at the tip end than at the butt end, resulting in the typical arc or bend in a rod. The action (how a rod blank bends) and power (how it resists bending) are a result of the type of materials used, the amount of material added in each step, the taper and diameter of the mandrel, and the number of strands cut during the Howald process and the position at which they are cut. Cutting most of the strands high up on the rod results in a rod that is stiff but with a very fast tip action. Cutting the strands regularly throughout the blank results in a parabolic-action rod.

BLANK MATERIALS

The cut-and-roll method is used by most rod-blank manufacturers. It uses similar steel mandrels, but instead of individual fibers, sheets of material are cut to specific shapes and then wrapped in place. The materials can be glass, graphite, or combinations, but are always in a sheet form, much like cloth fabric. The fabric used is just like other cloth with a fiber warp and woof going in two directions. (This is usually the case. There are some materials used today that are all longitudinal and use no cross- or right-angle fibers, but to date these are not available in blanks for the home rod-builder.) Materials differ. Typically, fiberglass is a 400 denier cloth, but glass that is finer and coarser is available. The standard glass in the industry, and one used for years, is E glass. A higher-quality glass with a higher modulus

(for stiffer action) is called S glass (T glass by Japanese manufacturers).

Graphite varies as to "modulus," a term used to describe stiffness, or resistance to and recovery from bending. Modulus is really a term for the stiffness of the material — its resistance to breaking or to tearing apart longitudinally (the tensile strength). Ironically, it is this tensile strength modulus that is used by most of the industry in determining low, medium, and high modulus rods and blanks. According to one supplier of graphite fibers to the rod companies, low modulus is in the range of 32 to 35 Msi, medium or intermediate modulus is in the range of 40 to 46 Msi, and high modulus is over 50 Msi. Some companies today are making their rods of 70 Msi (Lamiglas is one example.) Msi is the measurement of modulus. The higher the number, the stiffer and more quickly recovering from bending the rod.

Regardless of the modulus, graphite is manufactured in several different ways. It can be laminated; manufactured with the warp and woof of graphite or with a warp of graphite and woof of glass (this is seldom done); or glass may be laminated to graphite cloth, the glass providing right-angle fibers to the length of the rod and hoop strength. Some of these combinations result in the hybrid or so-called graphite/glass blanks in which both materials are used. Unfortunately, as of this writing, several attempts by the American Fishing Tackle Manufacturers Association to define several grades of graphite and/or glass composition in finished rods and blanks have failed. Thus, a "graphite" blank or rod can be wholly graphite or only ten percent graphite. Generally, you get what you pay for in rods and blanks.

In addition, graphite cloth is made by proprietary processes in which some graphite fibers run perpendicular to the cloth's main fibers. Another proprietary method involves "collimated" fibers, in which all the fibers are parallel, with no scrim or right-angle fibers. This produces a blank in which all the fibers run longitudinally for maximum strength yet without any loss of hoop strength. The finished rod is lighter and has increased sensitivity and power for its weight.

Most of these materials go through a "prepreg" operation in which resins are added to the cloth so that the wrapped cloth on the blank will stick to itself when baked. Polyester or phenolic resins once were typically used with fiberglass; today they still are used, although epoxy resins are also. Epoxy resins, which stick better to graphite, are used with graphite materials. The result with graphite is better bonding and less bubbling than with the phenolic resins. Usually these pre-preg materials are kept chilled to prevent the resins from setting up and curing. If this happens, the cloth becomes stiff and brittle and impossible to wrap on a mandrel.

Other materials are sometimes used in rods and rod blanks. Boron, once widely popular, is rarely used today because it is highly expensive and difficult to work with. Generally, longitudinal fibers of boron are placed with graphite or glass (generally graphite). Silicon carbide, also used as short fibers and "whiskers," resembles a dust in the rod material. Kevlar has been used as an outer coating or scrim on the blank for hoop strength and blank protection.

CUT-AND-ROLL CONSTRUCTION

Construction of the blank begins on the cutting board with the glass, graphite, or composite-fiber cloth. A steel template or pattern outline is placed over the cloth and used to cut the cloth to a precise shape. These templates are basically triangular in shape. One long edge is placed on the edge of the cloth; this edge is tacked to the steel mandrel. The butt end of the material is wider than the tip end, and the taper can be straight, producing an evenly bending rod blank, or complex. For example, a template and material cut with one side in an S shape — the wide end at the bottom, the thin end at the tip — will result in a heavy-butt fast-tip rod. Just where the S curve is placed on the material will determine the action of the rod — moderate, fast, or extra-fast. Moderate rods will have the S curve near the butt end; for a fast-tip rod the S curve will be at the tip end, usually about a fifth to a quarter of the way down from the tip. The degree of curvature in the S will also determine the rod action; a gradual curve results in a gradual change of action, a sharp curve in a rapid and pronounced change of action.

In some cases, extra strength is required in the butt end. While this can be done by widening the rod material (making a broader triangle) this may result in wrinkles in the resulting blank. It also takes more time, resulting in higher labor costs and often in more material waste. A preferred way, and one that allows more economical use of the material, is to add an extra small piece of material variously called a "pennant" or "flag." The pennant may be of a different material, such as a glass reinforcing flag for a graphite blank. The same technique is used to add small pieces

Blanks made by the cut-and-roll method — the most prevalent used today — use mandrels around which the rod material is wrapped. Here, tapered segments of cloth are laid out on large tables and attached to the steel mandrel.

of reinforcing material to high-stress ferrule areas. Often this material is visible on the blank as a spiral line running around the rod for a few inches close to the ferrule, regardless of whether it is a spigot or slip-over (Fenwick-style) ferrule. The spiral is indicative of a small triangular piece of material used to reinforce this area and give it more hoop strength.

Once the material is cut to shape and prepared, a hot iron is used to tack the material to the mandrel. The impregnated resins serve as a glue for this. This mandrel and material then go to a

A rolling table like this will roll the mandrel, in the process rolling the cloth around the mandrel to form the rod blank.

rolling table much like a broad, padded ironing board with a free-swinging, swiveling flat top. The mandrel is positioned, then the top is lowered to push and roll the mandrel so that the material wraps tightly around it. The swiveling and rotating top helps the material roll around the mandrel regardless of the taper or amount of material.

The next step is the cellophaning process, by which a polyester tape is wrapped in a spiral around the blank to secure the material and prevent it from unsticking. Holders on the end of the mandrels then allow the material-wrapped mandrels to be hung vertically in huge high ovens for baking. The blanks are baked for one to several hours at temperatures of from 250° to 350° Fahrenheit. Polyester resins used for glass are baked in the higher range; epoxy resins for graphite are baked in the lower temperature range.

Cellophaning is the process by which tape is wrapped around the rod blank to keep it in place on the mandrel.

The blanks are removed from the oven and special machines pull the mandrel from the blank. The mandrels go back to produce more rod blanks. The rough tip and butt end of the blank are cut off, and the polyester tape is removed from the blank. Some blanks—primarily of glass—are left this way, with the spiral wraps of the tape showing on the blank. Lamiglas manufactures some of their glass blanks this way. Most rods are sanded. This allows the manufacturer to inspect the blanks for any defects; it smooths the blank,

which in the minds of most people makes it more attractive; and when properly done, it will not affect the strength of the rod blank.

Several methods are used to finish the rod blank. Some are given a clear epoxy or poly-urethane finish, others are painted prior to finishing. Most rods have a glossy finish, although some are marketed and advertised with a matte finish, according to the theory that a dull rod will not cause glare on sunny days and thus won't scare fish.

Today, a number of companies make rod blanks for the rod-builer. These include Lamiglas, Sage, G. Loomis, Talon (LCI), American Tackle Ltd., Belvoirdale, Dan Bailey's Wholesale, J. Kennedy Fisher, Orvis, Partridge of Redditch, Powell, Riffle Products, Seeker, Rodcraft, Scott PowR-Ply Co., Shakespeare, and St. Croix. Many of these companies also carry other components, such as

After the rods are baked in an oven, the mandrel is removed using a mechanical puller.

reel seats, grips and handles, guides, ferrules, and glues and finishes.

Blanks that are available include everything from solid glass blanks for heavy fishing through E and S glass blanks, various composite blanks of graphite and glass, and various forms of graphite. Often these various graphites are of different moduluses or stiffnesses. At this writing, for example, G. Loomis manufactures glass blanks for IGFA trolling rods; hybrid blanks that are a blend of regular graphite, woven graphite, and glass; ninety-six percent graphite; IM6 graphite, which has a higher modulus; and IMX graphite, their highest-modulus blank. Similarly, Lamiglas has IM700 high-modulus graphite blanks, G1000 graphite blanks of slightly lesser modulus, and LHS Esprit graphite blanks.

FERRULES

Ferrules vary with rods. Some are of the slip-over type first developed by Jim Green of Fenwick and used exclusively on their rods for years. Today the patents have run out and other companies are using the same system. Basically, it consists of a rod tip that at its lower end is sized precisely in taper and diameter to fit over the upper end of the butt section.

A sort of "reverse" Fenwick-style ferrule is also found in rods, but generally not in rod blanks. In this, the lower section of the tip end is a straight tube (parallel to the outside diameter) that slides into a fitted opening in the upper end of the butt section.

Spigot ferrules are different. These consist of a short section, usually a solid plug of graphite or glass, that is glued and fitted into the upper end of the butt section and precisely sized to fit the inside diameter of the lower end of the tip section. These rod blanks are usually made in one piece, then cut in half (or almost in half — room must be allowed for the ferrule extension on the lower section to have the sections equal overall in length). The butt section then has the plug ferrule glued in place. Naturally, in multipiece rods such as three-piece rods and four- or more-piece travel and pack rods, a plug ferrule is added to the upper end of each section (except the tip) to match the adjoining section. With rare exceptions, almost all blanks available to the rod-builder today have the built-in or "self" ferrule of the spigot or Fenwick style, or a combination of both.

Most rod blanks today are supplied with these self ferrules of glass-to-glass or graphite-to-graphite. Most are also ferruled for equal section lengths, regardless of the number of sections in the blank. Some few two-piece rod blanks are off-center ferruled. In these, the tip section is always the longer, the theory being that placing the ferrule closer to the butt preserves more of the sensitivity of the rod in the tip section or upper end. One disadvantage of off-center-ferruled blanks is that the sections are of different lengths, which requires a longer rod case than equal-section (center-ferruled) rods. From a practical point of view, I find little difference in fishing the two styles of blanks.

Sometimes off-center-ferruled rods are termed butt-ferruled. This term should not be confused with the special ferrules or collets that go onto the butt end of a casting rod and are designed to fish a casting-rod handle. These are at the very end of the rod blank and fit the handle to the blank.

Except on some traditional quality fly rods — usually bamboo — metal ferrules are rarely used. These can be added to any rod because they are tubes that are slipped over the cut blank ends. In addition, ferrules to make a spigot type of ferrule for rods can be constructed from scrap blanks, a procedure described in Chapter 25.

Some anglers insist on one-piece rods without any ferrules, claiming that only these are strong enough and sensitive enough to use and that a ferrule anywhere weakens and desensitizes the rod. This is true with some fly rod blanks that are one piece (primarily those that are short for chalk-stream fishing, or some of the new eight-footers for heavy big-game fishing and specifically made for IGFA twenty-pound class tippets), and some heavy one-piece East Coast surf rods. In all honesty, I find little if any real, demonstrable difference between good one-piece rods and good two- or multi-piece rods. My argument has always been that if you close your eyes and cast any rod without knowing what it is, you cannot tell if it is a one-, two-, or multi-piece model, providing everything else is equal. In fact, fly-rod guru Lefty Kreh points out that sometimes a two-piece or multi-piece rod will be better than a one-piecer because the ferrules will add stiffness to the rod at critical points, improving the action and power. In addition, making long one-piece rods is difficult for the manufacturer. It requires longer mandrels and exponentially increases the possibility of wrinkles and defects. It also makes complex blanks and the addition of flags and pennants and complex S-curve cuts very difficult. In addition, the reject rate (and thus the cost to the consumer) of long one-piece rods goes up rapidly, since the long, lightweight one-piece models tend to have curves, kinks, and twists that are unacceptable to the consumer. Understand that we are not talking about short one-piece bass rods of perhaps five-feet six-inches or so, but long eight-foot one-piece fly rods and nine-foot noodle rods.

BLANK DESIGN

Although most rod blanks are of two or three pieces, travel and pack-rod blanks are available. Most companies carry them in four pieces, such as those by Sage, Lamiglas, Powell, G. Loomis, and others. Also, some rod blanks are designed for specific purposes. For example, G. Loomis IGFA rod blanks are made so that the lower 10 inches have a uniform diameter, and all are designed to fit one of the several Uni-butt handle systems without shimming. They are all 68 inches long, allowing for cutting and modification from 58 inches to 68 inches without affecting the action or power specified for the blank, or the fit into the collet for the handle assembly.

ACTION AND POWER

"Action" and "power" are both terms used to describe how and to what degree a rod bends. In my opinion, these terms are used incorrectly in many cases. Some rod companies refer to their blanks and rods as having a "light action," "medium action," or "heavy action," referring to the range of lure weights possible or degree of stiffness of the rod. Actually, action refers to the *way* in which the rod bends — parabolic, moderate, fast, extra-fast, and so on. These are degrees of stiffness of the *sections* of the rod, parabolic being a gradual bend all along the length of the rod, extra-fast being a stiff rod with a light tip (sometimes called a "worm" action for the action built into worm spinning and casting rods).

Power refers to the rod's resistance to bending. Thus, a stiff rod has more power than a light rod, but both could have a specific action or type of bend when under stress. By the same token, a rod of a certain power or stiffness could be built with completely different actions. Fenwick used to differentiate between these by describing the action and then using a number for the power — the higher the number (usually from about 1 through 7) the stiffer the rod. Two companies that also differentiate between these separate blank characteristics are G. Loomis and Lamiglas, each of which has specific listings for action and power

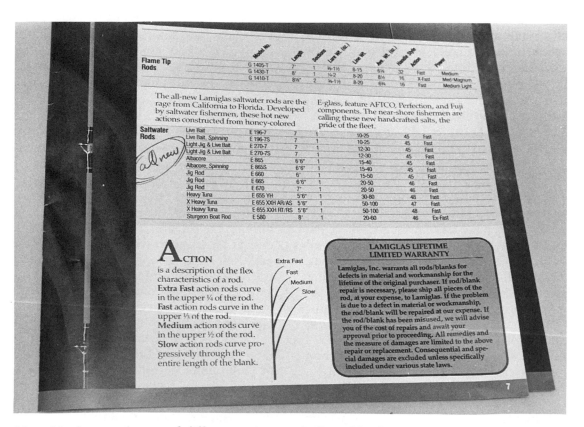

Many blanks come in several different actions, as indicated by this Lamiglas catalog.

in its catalogs. Even so, each company usually describes its rods' actions slightly differently. Thus, Lamiglas describes its as follows:

Extra-fast: bending in the upper quarter of the blank

Fast: bending in the upper third of the blank

Medium: bending in the upper half of the blank

Slow: bending or curving progressively throughout the entire length of the blank

G. Loomis describes their actions as:

Extra-fast: bending in extreme tip of blank

Fast: flexing in upper third of blank

Moderate: bending in upper two-thirds of blank

Slow: flexing or bending in upper three-quarters of blank

Note that in all cases, this does *not* mean that the lower part of the rod is as straight as a poker when under stress, only that the most pronounced bending occurs as described. Note also that the terms light, medium, and heavy have no place in describing action, only in describing the power or relative stiffness of a rod. Note also that it is important to choose a rod or blank by the weight it is designed to cast, or, in the case of offshore and boat rods, the line weight for trolling. Otherwise, the terms light, medium, and heavy are meaningless. A very heavy freshwater spinning rod that might cast a 1 1/2-ounce weight, for example, would still be more flexible and lighter than a light surf rod used off Hatteras, or a light offshore rod.

GUIDES AND TIP-TOPS

Sometimes called "eyes" by novice fishermen, guides force the line to run the length of the rod from the reel, allow for easy casting, and distribute the strain on the rod blank when a big fish is played. They can be broken down into a number of basic styles according to the rod on which they are to be used or the materials from which they are made.

MATERIALS

Guides at one time were virtually all made with wire rings and frames. Some of the better guides were and are made of stainless steel to resist or prevent corrosion. Others are made of carbon steel. Some, such as the Fuji titanium-frame guides, use a titanium/stainless steel alloy. These are rated as being thirty-five to forty percent stronger than stainless steel, more corrosion-

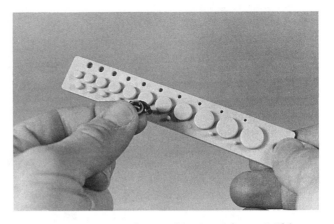

Tip-top gauges, such as this one from Mildrum, make it easy to check tip-top sizes. The sockets in this gauge are designed to fit rod tips for measuring tip top size.

resistant than stainless steel, and more flexible and resistant to metal-fatigue failure (particularly important in one-foot guides) than stainless steel. They are teamed with SIC (silicon carbide) rings and come in a dozen different styles of frame and foot configuration. One company makes their frames of a graphite fill material for lightness and flexibility. However, because more material is needed for strength, they are a slightly bulkier-looking guide.

Snake guides are still made of carbon or stainless steel. Mildrum and Perfection Tip, two of the last companies making these guides, make them only of stainless steel.

Guides and guide frames are sometimes improved with a chrome plating over the stainless steel or carbon steel. The chrome is harder and thus more resistant to grooving and is also smoother and thus reduces friction on the line. Some guides have special coatings, often more for appearance and to match the finish of the rod than for any functional purpose. For example, snake guides can come in black or bright finishes, and sometimes even gold finishes. Perfection Tip also has a snake guide with a Teflon coating for reduced friction. Similarly, frames and outer wire rings or ceramic guides can be chemically finished in gold, black, bright, gunsmoke, and sometimes other colors.

Even roller guides from AFTCO, Mildrum, and Stuart come in different colors to match specific rod and trim colors. Aftco guides, for example, come in a standard chrome-plate finish, a black chrome-oxide finish (both with stainless-steel-finish rollers, screws, and pins), and a black-and-gold finish with frame of black chrome oxide and

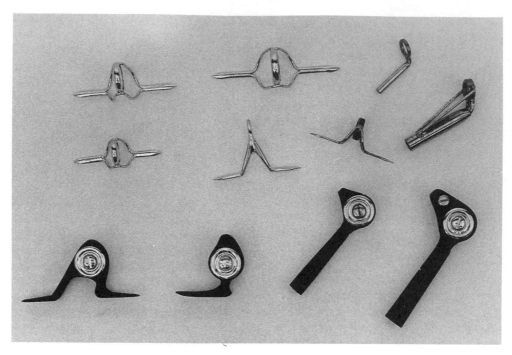

Guides from Mildrum. Guides available include spinning casting and boat/trolling guides.

rollers, screws, and pins coated with gold titanium nitride. All are of stainless steel plated with the specific finish. Mildrum rollers also come in several styles with choices of chrome, black, or gold frames, and side plates (which hold the roller and bearings) of chrome, gold, or black, for up to nine color combinations. Mildrum uses silicon bronze castings for the frame, and stainless steel for the rollers. Stuart roller guides are available in stainless steel, silver, black, or gold anodized-aluminum finishes.

Carbide guides use carbide only in the ring of the guides; the frames are stainless steel, chromed stainless steel, or nickel silver. Carbide, Carboloy, or Mildarbide (the latter two are trade names) are very hard materials, extremely wear-resistant and corrosion-resistant, and like wire rings, these guides are welded or brazed to the frame, eliminating the need for a shock ring.

The popular ceramic guides come in a number of slightly different materials. Unfortunately, "ceramic" can have several meanings. At one point, ceramic meant the less-expensive, poorer-quality white inner-guide ring used on low-quality rods. It can still mean that, but ceramic is a general term for the wide range of a half-dozen or more earth materials used in guide-ring construction. These materials include the original quality guide-ring material, aluminum oxide, along with more recently developed materials such as silicon carbide, silicon nitride, Hardloy (a trade name of Fuji but really an aluminum oxide with an additional ceramic material added), sterite (also called E rings), neo-aluminum (also called O rings), and a U ring that is not currently sold in this country. The white ceramic is often called a "cera ring."

With the exception of the white rings, all of these are dark-colored, although Mildrum does have a white aluminum oxide ring under its Milumina brand. Each of these things has its specific uses. Important factors in guides are hardness (to resist grooving), smoothness (to reduce or eliminate friction and heat), heat dissipation (to prevent line damage during long fights), weight (heavy guides adversely affect rod action, particularly on light rods).

Hardness is one important consideration, since it is a function of how resistant a guide ring will be to grooving by a line. The Vickers scale, used to measure very hard materials (as opposed to the Rockwell C scale, used primarily to measure metals and with a more limited upper range), shows the following range of approximate guide hardness, according to spokesmen from Fuji:

Silicon carbide rings: 2,200 to 2,400 Vickers hardness

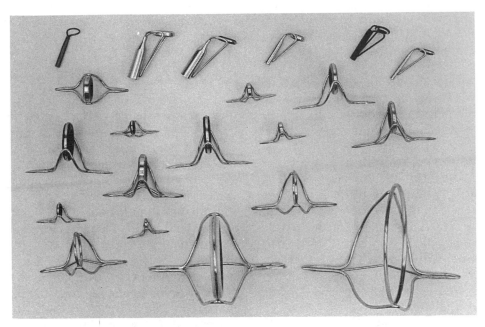

Many types of guides and tip-tops are available. These are just some available from Perfection Tip.

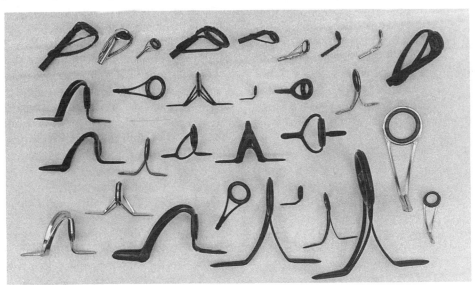

Some of the many types and sizes of Fuji guides available from DNY. They include traditional styles along with heavy-frame boat and trolling guides, high-frame spinning guides and tip-tops to match.

Silicon nitride rings: 1,300 to 1,500 Vickers hardness

Aluminum oxide rings: 1,200 to 1,400 Vickers hardness

Hardloy rings: 1,200 to 1,400 Vickers hardness

Neo-aluminum rings: 1,100 to 1,300 Vickers hardness

Sterite or E rings: 750 to 850 Vickers hardness

White or cera ring: 550 to 650 Vickers hardness

By comparison, knives are considered very hard if they are tempered to a Rockwell C scale of 52 to 54, which is about 600 to 650 on the Vickers hardness scale.

In heat dissipation, silicon carbide also comes out best, followed by Hardloy, aluminum oxide, and silicon nitride (all are similar) and then cera and sterite. Heat dissipation in a guide is important to prevent line damage. Heat build-up in a guide through the friction of line running over it can damage the line, particularly if the fish stops and the line does not move, lying on a hot guide ring.

It is also important to have light guides. Silicon carbide again wins according to Fuji, since with their guides, six identical rings of silicon carbide will weigh the same as one aluminum oxide ring of the same size.

Another important characteristic is the inner diameter of the guide. Initially this was a problem, because the original aluminum oxide guides had (and still have) a shock ring between the wire ring frame and ceramic guide ring. Silicon nitride guides also have shock rings. Silicon carbide and Hardloy guides do not, in part because they are less brittle than the aluminum oxide and silicon nitride, which need a shock ring and slightly bulkier ring for protection.

Shock rings also vary, although most are of a firm but pliable plastic or nylon. They must be firm to hold the ring, which is snapped into the shock ring (the shock ring is held by a groove that secures it into the thin wire-frame ring). Shock rings from Fuji are available in two colors. Light luminous green, which looks like a light cream in daylight and glows in the dark with a light yellow-green color, is used primarily with the aluminum oxide and silicon nitride guides. Black shock rings are used with aluminum oxide and hard-ring economy guides.

Perfection Tip supplies their guides with a black or natural shock ring; the natural is a translucent light gray color. These rings can be colored by dyeing with regular household dyes such as Rit or Tintex to match a rod or trim color on a rod. As a result of the rings' cloudy undyed appearance, any dyed colors will not be pure and bright, but they will be recognizable. The best colors are basic blue, green, or red.

Roller guides typically use stainless steel rollers with a system of bushings underneath for easy turning, and special stainless steel (usually) screws and bushings. Some also have nonconductive and self-lubricating side plates to prevent problems with electrolysis and corrosion.

Tip-tops are just like guides in the materials used for them, including the frame materials, ceramic rings, and shock rings. The only difference is that the tip-top frame and rings are fitted onto a tube; the tube comes in different sizes to fit accurately onto the end of a rod. Usually these tubes have a slight taper to them similar to that on the rod and are constructed of

the same materials—chromed or blackened stainless steel in most cases—as are the guide frames.

RING SIZES

The lack of a shock ring in a guide allows for a larger inner diameter. Originally, all guides were wire rings, and the guide size was the inner diameter of that ring. That was fine at the time, but the same system of measurement was used on the wire-ring frame even with the addition of a nylon shock ring and ceramic inner-guide ring. The result was that a nominally 12-millimeter guide ring would have a true internal diameter of about 8 millimeters.

In part, this is more complicated now as a result of the different sizes of the inner ceramic rings used by some manufacturers (notably Fuji) for the different frame styles of their guides and the purposes of those guides. Thus there are light or standard rings, heavy rings, and flanged rings, the latter with a slight ridge or flange to help prevent the inner ring from popping out. Today, these are used primarily on tip-tops where the line can make a sharp bend the ring. The flange provides line protection throughout the radius of this bend. At one time, inner rings popping out was a problem, particularly for the silicon carbide guides (also called SIC guides), because no shock ring was used. Today, the pressure used to force inner rings into the metal frame ring has been doubled with Fuji guides, and a special glue is also used.

Ring size in guides and tip-tops is very important. It is necessary to consider the true internal diameter of the ring, not just the nominal size of the guide, which is far larger, particularly with ceramic-ring guides, and even more so with those using shock rings. Ring size is important primarily for knot and line clearance. Too small a guide on a rod will impede the line flow, particularly on spinning rods where the line tends to flow off in loops. (An exception to this is when a high-frame, small-ring guide is used for the first of the butt guides, thus removing all the loops at this point and allowing the rest of the line to flow in a relatively straight line.)

There are no real rules on guide size, since line sizes and limpness vary and require different minimum ring diameters. For fly rods it is particularly important, since fly lines are very thick and require good clearance to flow freely through the guides for casting and shooting line.

Knot clearance is equally important to consider for some rods. If you are making a spinning rod, casting rod, or spin-cast rod in which the line will always be tied only to the end of a lure, then this is of no concern. However, for an equally light rod in which you need doubled line through a Bimini twist, or a leader tied with an Albright, or a wire leader, or a shock leader used to cushion the line during the force of casting a surf rod, larger guides and tip-tops are a must. The guides must be large enough not only to clear the knot, but must be extra large because knots tend to jump around as the line goes through the guides and tip-top.

Such considerations are particularly important in the design of surf rods, light-tackle tropical rods for shark and barracuda, muskie rods, or any rod that might be used with a leader at any time. It is equally important for fly rods, because there are knots at the line-leader and line-backing connections. Use a long leader and you might have to bring the leader knot through the top and guides to land the fish. Hook a big fish and it will take the 100-foot fly line plus the backing, zigzagging the line-to-backing knot through the guides several or more times.

Although guides of any ring size can be used on any rod blank (within realistic limits of guide type, size, and rod weight and power), tip-tops are another problem. Most tip-tops are of a specific ring size on a specific tube size. You must use the correct tube size to fit the rod top. Fortunately, many companies have recognized the need for larger ring sizes on some tubes and for fly-rod fishing. Thus, Mildrum manufactures its PMT fly-rod tops with a standard ring in tube sizes 4 1/2 through 8, but also has a PMTL fly-rod top with a larger ring in the same tube sizes. Fuji makes some of its tip-tops in two different ring sizes for the same tube size. These include some light ones for spinning, casting, spin-cast, and even fly, and larger ones such as one style of top that is available in a size 16/64 tube in both a 12 millimeter and 16 millimeter ring.

For those interested in specific sizes, a chart follows for Fuji guides both with and without shock rings. One point of explanation: The outside diameter in the guides refers to the outer diameter of the ceramic ring or shock ring—or the same as the internal diameter of the wire-frame ring. In most cases it is very close to, but not identical with, the nominal size of the guide.

Fuji guides without shock ring				
Size	O/D	I/D light	I/D heavy	I/D flanged
2.5	2.0	1.0		
3	2.4	1.3		
3.5	2.9	1.7		
4	3.4	2.2		
4.5	3.9	2.5		1.7
5	4.6	3.0	2.8	2.6
5.5	5.3	3.5	3.3	2.9
6	6.1	4.1	3.7	3.3
7	7.0	4.8	4.2	3.8
8	8.0	5.6	4.8	4.4
10	9.8	7.0	6.2	5.8
12	11.5	8.3	7.5	6.7
16	14.5	10.6	9.8	8.8
20	18.3	13.7	12.8	12.0
25	23.5	18.1	17.5	
30	29.4	23.2	22.8	
40	35.5	28.5	28.3	

FRAME STYLES

Guides vary widely in frame style. Simple snake guides are nothing more than wire twisted into the guide shape and with flattened ends for easy placement and thread-wrapping. Simple guides for casting, spin-cast, spinning rods, and strippers on fly rods vary widely. They can be double-foot or single-foot, high frame or low frame, reinforced or supported with an additional frame support running from the bottom of the guide ring to the frame end of the guide foot, made with three frame supports (two running to one foot, and one to the other), of light materials or heavy materials

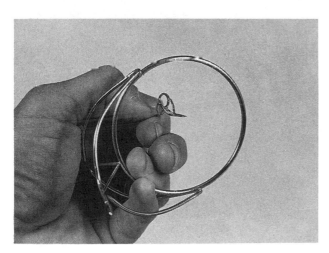

Range of guides is shown in this photo of a 75-millimeter guide (almost three inches) and an 8-mm guide, both from Perfection Tip. The larger size is used on surf-fishing rods.

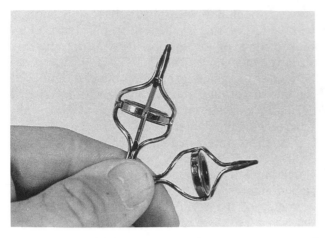

Often the same type of guide can come in several different frame configurations. This heavy-ringed boat and casting style guide is available in standard (right) and reinforced (left) models. The reinforced model has an additional bar under the frame to protect the ring from hard use. This guide also comes with a lighter metal ring holding a lighter shock ring for spinning rods.

(for strength or lightness), in straddle styles in which two feet on one end of the guide bracket the rod blank, or of stamped or round-wire frames. Wire frames running from the foot to the wire ring can be in a U or V shape. Some guides are even completely wire, formed like a snake guide with an additional turn (like the earlier Foulproof sold by Gudebrod). Tip-tops for these guides are similar, with a double wrap or wire for the ring and the two ends of the wire flattened and designed to straddle the rod for wrapping in place.

One important consideration in guides is the width of the guide feet. For example, rod-builders using split-bamboo blanks usually want guides with wide feet so that the guides will set evenly on the flattened side of the blank. In contrast, those

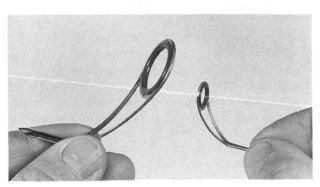

Example of high-frame, one-foot spinning guides from DNY.

using graphite blanks—particularly thin or very lightweight graphite blanks—like guide feet with a narrow width that will not "hang over" the side of the blank when wrapped in place. Naturally, one style of guide is not made in two widths of feet, but any wide-foot guide can be filed to a narrower width for use on a thin graphite-blank section.

TYPES OF GUIDES

Fly-Rod Guides

Snake guides are small guides used on fly rods and presumably are so named because of their twisted appearance when viewed from the top or side. Sizes vary with the few manufacturers that continue to make these guides. There are two different sizing methods—one is used by Mildrum and is called "Mildrum size," and the other is used by other companies. The Mildrum sizes include a small of 4 through a large of 9. The alternate method ranges from a small 4/0 (although 2/0 is generally the smallest made today) through a large of 6. A comparison of these sizes is as follows:

Fuji guides with shock ring			
Size	**O/D**	**I/D light**	**I/D heavy**	**I/D flanged**
5	4.6	2.6		
5.5	5.3	3.2		
6	6.1	3.7	2.8	
7	7.0	4.3	3.3	
8	8.0	5.0	4.1	
10	9.8	6.4	5.2	
12	11.5	7.5	6.2	
16	14.5	9.4	8.8	
20	18.3	12.3	11.4	
25	23.5	16.3	15.1	
30	29.4	21.5	20.1	
40	35.5	26.5	24.6	
50		38.4	35.4	

Size	Mildrum	Other
Small		4/0
		3/0
	4	2/0
	4 1/2	1/0
	5	1
	5 1/2	2
	6	3
	7	4
	8	5
Large	9	6

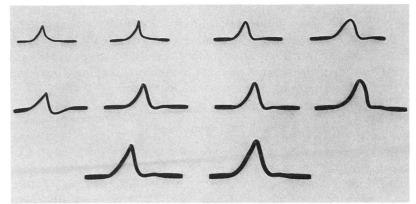

Snake guides come in a variety of sizes, such as this range of guides in sizes 4/0 through 6 from Perfection Tip. Several finishes are available.

Fly-rod snake guides are manufactured by Mildrum and Perfection Tip. Although it is not a snake guide, Fuji manufactures a small-ring, low-frame guide in its SG silicon carbide and BFG aluminum oxide series. Available ring sizes are 5.5 millimeters to 10 millimeters. These are both low-frame, one-foot lightweight models and have matching stripper guides. They are another option for fly rods. Tip-tops have a simple ring—no frame supports—attached to a tube sized to fit the rod tip. Rings are round if of a ceramic or Carboloy, and pear-shaped if of stainless steel.

Casting Guides

Guides for casting rods include any standard style of frames and guide rings in any material. Most are low-frame because the line comes off of the reel in a straight line, not in loops, as with spinning line. Although any size can be used for this, most will range from about 6- through 16-millimeter ring size. Most will be light styles, although heavy frame guides are often used for

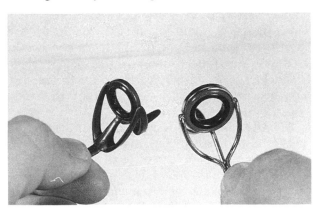

Two styles of guides. The Fuji guide on the left is stamped from one piece of metal with the ring secured in place. The Perfection Tip guide on the rod is welded from wire rods.

saltwater casting or popping rods, muskie rods, and similar heavy-duty rods. Standard sizes for tip-tops for casting models range from 3 1/2/64 up to large sizes used for surf and boat rods, with most for casting rods in the 5/64 to 8/64 range.

Spincast Guides

Spin-cast rods are very similar to casting rods, with the differences sometimes found in the guides and lower-profile reel seats. Since the line comes off the reel in a straight line, the same low-frame, small-ring guides used for casting rods are used for spin-cast rods. Some spin-cast reels do have a very large hole in the nose cone, resulting in some slight looping of the line during the cast. For this reason, spin-cast rods sometimes have a slightly larger butt guide—say a size 16 instead of a size 12. Other than these somewhat subjective choices, the guides used are exactly the same as those for casting rods.

Spinning Guides

Spinning guides are essentially like lightweight casting-rod guides, with light frames and light rings. But they do differ from the former in two important ways: They have much larger rings to accommodate the loops of line that come off the reel, and high frames are a must to reduce or eliminate line slap against the rod blank as the line loops flow off the reel. Sizes will range from a small of 6 millimeters up through a size 75 for the butt guide on a surf-spinning rod. Most for freshwater fishing will range from 6 millimeters through 30 or 40 millimeters. The frame can be U- or V-shaped, stamped or wire, using the same ring materials already covered. Guide weight and thus frame style, ring style, and guide size are very important considerations, particularly with light and ultralight rods. Such rods are light, and the addition of any unnecessary weight makes such a rod sluggish, slow, and "heavy."

One additional thought on spinning guides, that I expressed in the first edition of *Tackle Craft* concerns the large rings used on spinning rods. They may not be necessary, a point I first discovered twenty-five years ago while fishing in Florida, when some expert anglers were using special long-distance spinning rods that incorporated a butt guide with a small Carboloy ring on a very high frame. Since nothing was available commercially at that time, all these special guides were custom-made. The rest of the guides were standard, though small, spinning models. The theory then and now is that the small guide clears the line immediately, and that the line then runs straight through the rest of the guides. Using a series of standard spinning guides with a large butt guide and successively smaller rings, the line usually continues to flow in loops, retaining the possibility of increased guide friction and line slap all the way up the rod.

Shortly after this, Heddon, then still in the rod business, sold spinning rods with small-ring, high-frame guides. Its tests showed that the smaller rings made no difference in casting distance, and in fact might have improved on it over the regular guides. Unfortunately, it could not convince the angling public of this, and so eventually discontinued the rods after several years. Today, Fuji and others are selling guides with the high-frame and small-ring style, and it is being accepted.

Surf rods can be built as spinning or casting (revolving-spool) models. The guides for spinning surf rods are the same as for the standard spinning guides already covered, with the exception that they are larger, unless built according to the small-ring, high-frame theory. Often, revolving-spool surf rods are used for the heaviest of surf fishing, so that these guides are often reinforced and with a heavy or flanged ring. The principle consideration with any surf rod is to use large-internal-diameter guides and tip-tops at the tip end of the rod that are sufficient to allow the smooth flow of knots and shock line through the guides on a cast. Often this means 16- or 20-millimeter rings.

Boat Guides

Typically, boat-rod guides are similar or identical to the heavy revolving-spool guides used for surf fishing. Though spinning rods are used for boat fishing and trolling, traditionally this term means revolving-spool tackle. As such, the guides are low-frame with an extra-heavy frame and heavy rings, and are reinforced for the heavy-duty work required. Since knots, double lines, and leaders are often used with boat fishing, large-ring guides are a must for clearance.

Noodle-Rod Guides

Noodle rods are long and very soft, almost like fly rods in blank design but built as spinning rods and used with very light lines (two-pound test, typically) and spinning tackle. Guides for these rods must be very light and small and typically use the silicon carbide or Hardloy styles in the small-ring, high-frame styles such as are used for match fishing and ultralight fishing.

Roller Guides

Roller guides are just what they seem: guides in a frame with a roller on which the line runs, thus eliminating the friction of the line against an immovable-ring guide. They are used on high-quality offshore trolling rods. All are similar in function, although the four brands available are different in frame design, roller design, bearings and frame materials used, and so on.

The Stuart roller guides have four frame finishes: stainless steel, silver anodized aluminum, gold anodized aluminum, and black anodized aluminum. Mildrum rollers come in chrome, gold, or black on silicon bronze-cast frames, with silver, gold, or black side plates for many finish combinations. There are also several models: the Lite for lightweight fishing (six- to fifty-pound class tackle); the Hi-Rollers, rated for rods of fifty-pound class and heavier; and the Roller Flex, which is of a one-foot design for less of a "foot-print" and greater flexibility on rod blanks used for stand-up fishing to fifty-pound class. Roller Flex is specifically designed for flexible-tip, high-leverage rods such as stand-up rods and West Coast tuna-style rods.

AFTCO roller guides come in several sizes and finishes also. The Super Heavy Duty roller guides and top are available with ball bearings; gold nitride rollers; pin and screw frames of chrome, black chrome oxide, or black-and-gold. There are also regular Super Heavy Duty roller guides and tops with sleeve-type Aftcote bearings. These are ideal for eighty-pound class through unlimited tackle. The Heavy Duty rollers and tops are designed for twenty- through eighty-pound class

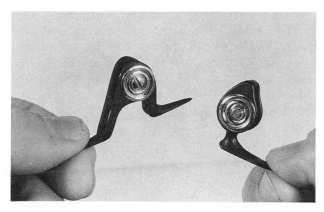

Roller guides from Mildrum are available in both one-foot and two-foot styles. Both are for light-tackle fishing.

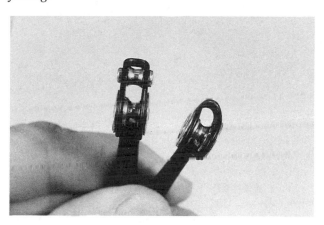

Frames of representative Mildrum tip-tops. The heavy-duty model to the left includes a roller for the line, and a spacer bar above.

rods, and all are available with Aftcote bearings, in chrome-and-black chrome oxide frames with standard stainless rollers, pins, and screws, or in black-and-gold with black frames and gold rollers and fittings. The regular roller guides and tops designed for six- through fifty-pound class tackle come with Aftcote bearings in the same choice of finishes. In addition, rollers are available with special hardened rollers and frames for use with wire line that might in time groove regular rollers. These rollers are also suitable for regular mono and Dacron as well. AFTCO also has a new one-foot roller guide that is very small and designed for fresh water and very light saltwater rods.

The tip-tops for these guides match in materials, finish, and rollers. In some cases, to allow for line and knot clearance, guides are available both with standard and larger heads (in the

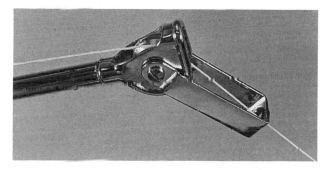

Some guides are designed to prevent the line from rubbing the side of the frame—such as this one by AFTCO used mostly for wire line fishing. The top swivels to keep the line in the center of the roller.

Guides from AFTCO include three different size ranges, each in several finishes. Tip-tops to match are also available.

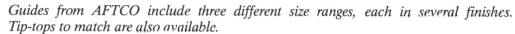

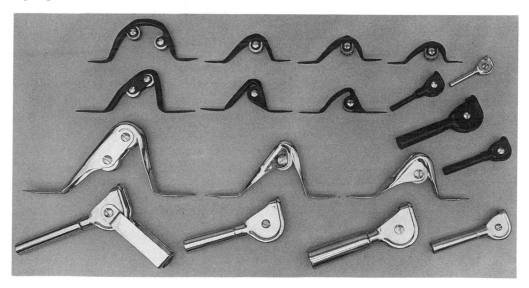

same-size roller) for greater space and knot clearance around the roller. Tube sizes range from 5/64 through 32/64, with different frame and roller sizes based on the top size.

In addition, there are special tip-tops for wire-line fishing in which the tip-top swivels on the tube so that the roller can track the direction of the line. It would not do this, however, without the addition of an extended bail ending in a small carbide ring through which the line travels. This bail travels with the line to cause the roller to turn as the line moves. The sizes for this swivel top, from AFTCO, range from 20/64 to 32/64. The advantage of this for wire-line fishing is that it prevents the wire from wearing against the side of the frame, or in turn wearing grooves in the frame.

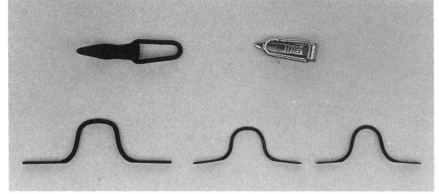

Various types of hook keepers. Traditional styles in three sizes are shown below; a more modern fold up/fold down style from Fuji, in two finishes is above. (Enlarged view.)

REEL SEATS

A reel seat holds the reel in place on a rod. It is a part of the rod and has the simple function of securing the two reel feet. Within this basic function, however, there are many varieties and styles.

SPINNING-REEL SEATS

Spinning-reel seats are mostly simple tubes designed to fit onto the rod with shims that adjust for the diameter differential of the outside of the blank and the inside of the reel seat. A simple reel seat consists of a tube with a fixed hood at one end to hold one of the reel feet and a sliding hood at the other end to fit over the other reel foot. Single- or double-screw collars or locking nuts are fastened finger-tight to hold the reel in place. There is no trigger, as is found on casting-style reel seats, and the hoods and locking nuts are usually made as low-profile and unobtrusive as possible, since in spinning the hand holds the rod at the reel seat with the fingers on either side of the reel shaft and around the reel feet and reel seat.

Basic reel seats like this are made of aluminum, or are more typically molded in nylon or plastic with graphite fibers (often called "graphite" or "graphite fill," or if they lack graphite, "graphite-style"). They come in a wide range of sizes, from a small of about a 16-millimeter internal diameter to a large of about 32-millimeter internal diameter (although sometimes these vary: a Fuji size 16 is really a 15-millimeter internal diameter).

Sizes will vary with the function, with size 18 being about the smallest comfortable for most male adults. A size 16 may be best for some women and children. For freshwater fishing, sizes 18 through 22 are about the best, with the largest sizes of 28, 30, and 32 best for big rods, boat rods, and surf-spinning rods.

There is a wide variety in the quality of such

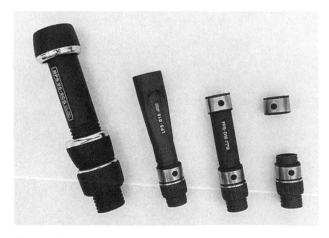

Examples of Fuji reel seats that range from large, heavy-duty models (left) to medium-size models and a skeletal design (right). The skeletal model will require an insert of wood, cork or foam.

Heavy-duty aluminum reel seats. These are skeletal style and require an insert, and come with a specially cut cork ring (left) for hiding the fixed hood.

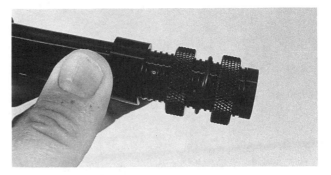

Reel seats for saltwater fly rods usually have double lock nuts. This one from Struble has an additional "O" ring between the locking nuts to help secure the nuts in place.

reel seats, with some having graphite (molded) hoods, others molded hoods covered with stainless steel or gold-plated stainless, and some with a keyway that keeps the sliding hood in line with the reel foot at all times.

In addition, there are skeletal-type spinning-reel seats that consist of the fixed hood and a separate threaded portion, lock nut, and sliding hood. Most often these are anodized aluminum, black or bright. Missing is the smooth, plain barrel in the center. For skeletal reel seats, this missing center is replaced with same-diameter foam, cork rings, wood, or similar material. Often, the same material used for the grips is used here.

In addition, reel seats for spinning rods include various types of skeletal styles, such as simple sliding rings that will slide on a cork or foam grip but will hold securely when slid up onto the sloping reel foot. Some are made in which each ring is really two rings that, when rotated, will lock down the reel foot through a cam mechanism.

CASTING-REEL SEATS

Reel seats for casting (revolving-spool reel) rods have all the same features as spinning models. They have a fixed hood, barrel, sliding hood, and threaded lock nut or nuts. They also have a trigger that is usually fixed to or molded with the fixed hood. These are made of aluminum or molded of plastic (with or without graphite). Several sizes are available, but not usually the full range of sizes of the spinning (no-trigger) reel seats. This does not mean that plain or spinning-style reel seats can't be used with casting rods, only that those with the trigger for an index-finger grip are more typical and standard. Skeletal styles are also available in which the

fixed-hood ring includes a trigger with a separate threaded barrel, hood, and nut.

BIG-GAME, BOAT-ROD, AND TROLLING-ROD REEL SEATS

The basic design of a big-game reel seat is no different from that of a spinning rod. What *is* different is the strength and reinforcement of the reel seat and the hoods. What is required, of course, will vary with the size and type of rod. The graphite-fill reel seat that might work great for a light trolling rod will be completely inadequate for a heavy 80- to 130-pound class offshore trolling rod.

Graphite-fill reel seats do come in boat- and trolling-rod models, with thicker walls and heavier, sturdier hoods. For offshore trolling rods, slip-over aluminum reel seats, such as those from AFTCO, are best because they have the highest

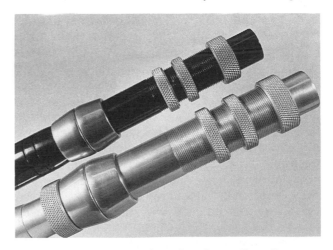

Different sizes and styles of reel seat/handle combinations are available for boat and trolling rods. These are from AFTCO.

Examples of AFTCO reel seats and gimbals for big game rods.

strength-to-weight ratio of any reel seat. These are machined, rather than stamped or rolled, using marine-grade aluminum. The hoods, both fixed and sliding, are heavy, thick-walled, and milled for the reel foot in order to hold under the heavy pressures of this fishing. Double lock nuts hold the sliding hood in place. Aluminum reel seats are anodized: AFTCO reel seats are available in silver-anodized or hard-coat black. Sizes range from 13/16 to 1-3/16.

One important point: The slip-over reel seats described are designed only for one-piece rods in which the rod blank goes completely through the reel seat and the grip is built up on the blank as well. They are not designed for the detachable-butt rods, which require reel seats that include a ferrule that slips into the upper end of the reel seat and into which the butt of the rod blank is fastened. Usually these reel seats are threaded at the upper end to take a special collet nut that fits over the ferrule and that secures the rod-tip section to the detachable butt. One model is available from Fuji in a molded graphite-fill seat; others, made of chrome-plated brass, are sometimes available. In all of these, the reel seat is glued to the rod butt and remains part of the rod butt when the tip is detached. They are also available from Lakeland, and some few might still be found from the remaining stock of Varmac, now out of the component-parts business. Both of these reel seats are chrome-plated over brass, heavily reinforced, and with milled and swaged hood styles.

Other, similar big-game reel seats with ferrules and collet nuts are made as an integral part of aluminum butts and are thus discussed as handles later in this chapter.

FLY-ROD REEL SEATS

Fly-rod reel seats run the full range of sizes, styles, designs, and materials. Their difference from other reel seats is that they are all designed to fit at the end of the rod — at the grip above the reel seat — and thus have a closed end or a plug at one end. The exceptions would be those designed to take an extension butt. Most of these reels seats are designed for butts that screw or slip in and hold with O-ring fittings.

The simplest and least-expensive reel seats are those of aluminum or graphite-fill plastic. For example, the size 16 FPS-style reel seats from Fuji can be used as fly-rod reel seats with the addition of a special rubber plug that fits into the bottom. Other than the plug or a closed fitting at one end, these reel seats resemble small-diameter slip-over reel seats used for spinning rods. Most of those that have a separate or removable plug can be used as up-locking or down-locking types — those that have a permanent fixed plug or closed end cannot. These latter are usually down-locking, with the threads at the upper end and the closed plug or end at the fixed hood.

Those reel seats that allow removal of the plug or fixed-hood end can usually be used either way, and there are advantages to each. Down-locking reel seats are more traditional and are commonly seen on most finished rods. Up-locking reel seats, in which the threaded part of the barrel and the sliding hood are at the base of the rod and the fixed hood is at the upper end, have two advantages. One is cosmetic, in that the upper fixed hood can be hidden under the last of the cork rings (special cork rings with a cutout for the hood are available). The other advantage is more practical, in that locking the reel in place leaves a short extended portion of the reel seat to help prevent the reel from catching in clothing when the rod is braced against the angler's body.

In addition to the basic plain-vanilla fly-rod reel seats, there are also reel seats that are highly individualized, almost custom-crafted, and extremely beautiful. Some are moderately priced, others are relatively expensive. Examples would be those reel seats with cork or wood barrels, such as are available from Lamiglas, Bellinger, REC, RST, Pacific Bay, Winston, Belvoirdale, Barry Kustin, Rodon (Cortland), Powell, and Struble. Some of these have anodized-aluminum threads, locking nuts, and fixed hoods in silver, black, brown, and nickel silver, the latter obviously more expensive. Usually these are made with a recess in the threaded portion of the barrel so that the reel foot rests on a plain metal barrel, not on threads.

Spacers, or the wood inserts, include a wide variety of exotic woods such as bubinga, cocobolo, walnut, English walnut, zebrawood, goncalo alves, imbuya, rosewood, teak, mesquite, ebony, vermillion, bastogne walnut burl, California burled walnut, spalted maple, padauk, bird's-eye maple, snakewood, ash, black ash, butternut crotch, grenadil, thuja, olive, and briar. Naturally, cork is also an option, as are laminated woods and scrimshaw done on bone or plastic.

In addition, some skeletal fly-rod reel seats are nothing more than a cork or wood body that is swelled at the ends to prevent loss of the rings, with sliding rings of nickel silver or aluminum to secure the reel. These reel seats are very attractive and very lightweight, especially when used with a cork spacer or barrel, but they do run the risk of loosening in time during fishing. They also have the disadvantage of the ring slightly cocking at an angle when they are slid onto the reel foot, thus marring the barrel material over time. This is more pronounced on cork than on wood spacers, but it will affect the finish of wood spacers.

Saltwater fly-rod reel seats are similar, but for durability and strength are made mostly of continuous barrel aluminum with up-locking double lock nuts and sometimes with slightly heavier swaged hoods. For the larger reels used in the salt, they are usually longer and slightly larger in diameter than freshwater models. Some have built-in extension butts, which are usually short and sometimes permanent. Others have open ends or removable butts so that a plug-in or screw-in extension butt can be placed in the reel seat when a fish is fought. The easiest and most secure of these have double O-rings to hold the extension butt in place and still allow instant attachment and removal. Also, some of these larger, tougher reel seats have an O-ring between the double lock nuts to help secure them and hold them in place to prevent the reel from becoming loose. One example is in the Struble saltwater fly-rod reel seat.

Steelhead and salmon fly-rod reel seats are similar and are designed to accept extension butts. Some of these are very short—only about 1 1/2 to 2 inches long—while others range up to 6 inches long. Any extension butt of any length can be used, but 6 inches is about the maximum available and is the maximum allowed for IGFA record catches. Just remember that the longer the extension the more likely it is that the fly line will flip around and catch on it at the end of that perfect cast when a tarpon eats the fly as soon as it lands. Typically, the extensions are of the same material used for the barrel insert—cork, or one of the exotic woods.

OTHER REEL SEATS AND REEL-HOLDING METHODS

Skeletal reel seats and rings are really a modification of standard reel seats and have already been discussed. In addition, there are plate-type reel seats such as those available from Fuji through DNY. These fit onto a rod bank in any position, are wrapped or taped in place (special recesses on the plate are designed for this), and hold the reel by means of a fixed hood and a sliding hood that is locked in place with a cam-functioning lever.

REEL-SEAT BUSHINGS

Since reel seats are almost always of a considerably larger inside diameter than the outside diameter of the rod blank, some sort of bushing or shim must be used to fill up this space and to keep the reel seat centered on the blank. Bushings of cork, graphite, fiber, and sometimes fiberglass are available. To fit properly, they must be of the correct internal and outside diameter in order to fit the reel seat and the rod blank. Often they will be available with several outside diameters to fit internal diameters of specific and standard reel seats, but in many internal-diameter sizes for rod blanks.

Although not usually purchased as bushings or bushing material, other materials may be wrapped around a blank to fill up space, including masking tape, paper tape, fiberglass tape, cord, and string. In addition, cork rings and wood or fiber discs can be shaped and sized for bushings. (The details are covered in Chapters 18 and 20.)

GRIPS

We've made the differentiation between grips and handles: Grips fit onto the rod blank and are designed for gripping, while handles incorporate the grips, reel seat, and butt cap. Grips are typically of wood, cork, various types of foam, and graphite tubing. Aluminum is used in offshore rods and is available as a complete handle.

Wood grips are more typically found in complete handles incorporating the reel seat and butt cap, but are also available individually. Most are of hickory and are designed as long rear grips for inexpensive boat rods. Aluminum grips or butts are available with a built-in gimbal knock and a section sized to hold a standard reel seat. In addition, bored aluminum butts are available, again with a gimbal knock and reel-seat bushing, but are bored for through-handle construction of one-piece trolling rods. Both are available from AFTCO.

Cork is used both in ring form and in pre-shaped grips. Rings are widely used to make grips for all types of rod: fly rods, spinning rods, casting rods, boat rods, as foregrips on offshore rods, on downrigger rods, noodle rods, surf rods, popping rods, and so on. Cork is more common in some rod than in others. It is almost a must in fly rods and is popular in spinning, casting, popping, downrigger, noodle, and some surf rods. Foam or leather-covered foam is more prevalent and better as a foregrip on big-game offshore rods.

Cork is a natural material, very light (about a fifth the weight of foam, although this will vary with foam type and hardness), relatively hard, and easy to hold when wet or dry. It comes from Portugal, where it grows as the bark of the cork tree and may be peeled every few years. Cork trees are not a quick crop; they must be ten years old before the cork bark may be harvested. After it is harvested, the cork is cut into cork rings, divided as to quality, and sold as is or used to make preshaped cork grips.

The best cork rings are "specie" cork, in which the natural cork pits run parallel to the handle (the same direction as the center drilled hole in the cork). (Mustard cork rings, rarely seen today, consist of lower-quality cork with the natural pits running at right angles to the drilled hole or handle direction.) Better-quality rods grips and the cork available for custom rod-building are almost always specie cork. There are different grades of specie cork, based on the number and size of the natural pits. The fewer and smaller the natural pits, the higher the quality of the cork, and the more expensive it is. Unfortunately, there is no standard cork-industry rating of grades, so you are dependent upon the reputation of the store or mail-order company from which you buy and the grading system they use. Most will use the grading of the importers from which they buy the cork. Of the importers, Pace uses a system of "Flor" as the best, followed by Super, A, B, and C grades. Other companies use a system of letters, beginning with AAAA through AAA, AA, A, and B; ratings of Super Fine, Extra Fine, and similar descriptions are used by others.

Cork rings are almost always 1/2-inch thick but in different ring diameters for sizing to any rod with minimum waste. (Rod Craft does supply rings 1/4-inch thick, which some rod-builders like because it makes for a different laminated-type look in the finished grip. Most often these are used in fly rods.)

Most rings are available with drilled holes, which also differ in size, although some are available solid and not drilled. Diameters include 1 1/8, 1 1/4, 1 1/2, and 2 inches. The 1 1/8-inch size is typically used for most freshwater fly rods; 1 1/4-inch is used for light spinning and casting grips and noodle rods; 1 1/2-inch is used for light boat rods, saltwater rods, and heavy muskie rods; 2-inch-diameter rings, which often have a large 1-inch hole, are used for thick-diameter surf blanks and some foregrips on big-game rods.

The internal diameters on the rings vary from about .250- to .750-inch; larger rings usually have a larger range of hole sizes. If you buy cork rings for a number of rods, the best way to buy them is in quantities of 100 or a gross, with a large enough outside diameter to make up the grip you want for any rod and a small enough internal diameter to fit the thinnest rod planned. Often it is best to buy rings with a .250-inch internal-diameter hole, since this can be easily enlarged to fit any blank. Building up a blank to fit a larger hole in the cork can be done, but it is far more difficult.

In addition to the individual cork rings that are used to build up a handle of the diameter and length desired, preshaped cork grips are also available. Often these are available through tackle shops or catalog houses, which purchase them from cork importers and wholesalers such as Pace Industries, Cork Products, Inc., C & D Trading, and Cork Specialities. In addition, very high quality preformed grips are available (again through local or mail order dealers) from Lamiglas, Struble, RST, and others. Many of these are in standard fly-rod grip shapes such as cigar, half wells, full wells, and western.

Lamiglas and other companies have cork grips (really handle kits, since these include the reel seat and other parts also) for a variety of other rods, including spinning, steelhead and salmon, casting, muskie, flipping, and popping. Cork grips usually come with a small-diameter hole and are finely finished. Both fore-grip and rear-grip styles are available. Adding them to the blank requires tapering the hole to size to fit the blank and gluing them in place.

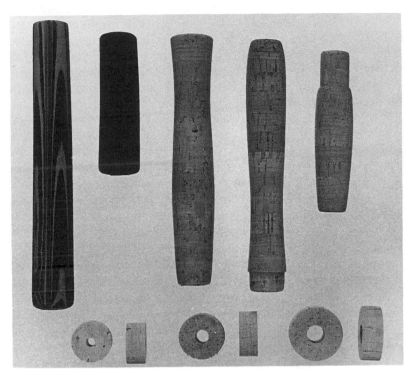

Examples of foam and cork grips and cork rings available for rod-building. The cork rings come in several sizes, as shown.

Foam grips include different materials, as well as foam, under different trade and brand names. All are dense open-cell foams. EVA is a urethane foam that comes in a variety of degrees of softness or hardness adjusted by the manufacturing process. A measuring device called a durameter can measure this. Cork will measure about 60 or 70 on this scale, while the EVA foam varies from about 20 to 80. Hypalon is a similar-looking but different material developed originally for pipe insulation and thus made with a skin on the outer surface. This skin must be removed and the material shaped on a lathe or similar automatic machine to make it into a recognizable rod grip. The shaping is done by the manufacturer or subcontractor so that the final result is a shaped grip that looks and feels similar to the open-foam EVA grips.

Foam is available in a wide variety of colors, although black, brown, and gray are the most popular. Foam grips are available in a wide variety of internal diameters because the proper one is necessary for fitting the grip onto a rod by one of several methods. Considering the extremes, internal diameters will range between 1/4-inch and 1 1/8 inches. Usually only straight sections or grips are available in the largest internal diameters; the shaped grips are not available in as wide a range. The outside diameters also vary, usually between about 1 inch and 1 1/2 inches. Because

these are foam grips, the internal- and outside-diameter measurements are not as precise as measurements on cork, wood, or any other material. There is a certain amount of give in the foam as it is worked. Fortunately, this does not matter a great deal, since the internal diameter must expand to properly fit the grip onto the blank, and the outside diameter can in part be shaped and controlled by the degree of compression or stretch of the foam grip. Straight-grip lengths are available up to about 30 inches long. Shaped grips have shapes similar to those found on cork grips and are often built with a recess at one end for a reel seat or, with rear grips, a recess at both ends for a reel seat and butt cap.

Graphite grips are only rarely used and these usually in the straight-style Tennessee handle in which the reel is usually taped onto the rod handle. The idea is that the straight grip and taping the reel in place leads to greater sensitivity and greater comfort (there is no metal or graphite reel seat to hold), and is better in cold weather because it lacks a metal or molded reel seat that can conduct cold. This type of grip can be made of straight-length cork, but graphite is more common. These are nothing more than straight sleeves of graphite with graphite bushings to center and position the grip. Graphite bushings are mandatory to get optimal transmission of impulses through the rod blank to the grip.

HANDLES

Handles, at least in our definition, differ from grips in that a handle consists of the entire butt cap/rear grip/reel seat/foregrip assembly. Some may not include the foregrip, but the general concept is of a complete unit.

Handles vary as to type as follows:

CASTING

These handles consist of the complete molded unit of a rear grip and trigger reel seat, and are designed for casting and spin-cast rods. They come in two basic styles, each with several variations. One type requires a slip-in or lock-down type of ferrule or adapter. Most require a chuck to lock the adapter in place. The rod blank is glued into the adapter, which then allows the rod to be removed from the handle through this chucking system. These handles come in graphite or fiberglass, are different colors (though black is most popular), with a pistol or straight grip, and are one- or two-handed. The thinner adapters have a series of smaller internal diameters for easier fitting to thin graphite blanks, and the larger outside-diameter adapters have larger internal diameters for larger-diameter blanks. In the Fuji system, the thin-diameter "GA" adapters come in 9- through 10.5-millimeters internal diameters; the larger-diameter "NA" adapter comes in 11- through 14.5-millimeter internal diameters. Similar adapters from other manufacturers have internal diameters as small as 7 millimeters. Handles are specific to a given type of adapter.

Other handles use adapters but are designed so that the rod blank glues into the adapter; the

Examples of cork preformed grips and some casting-rod handles. These require attachment to the rod through a collet; many are also designed for blank-through-the-handle construction.

adapter is glued into the handle. While this might seem to be one extra, unnecessary step, it is not from a cost standpoint. Molds are expensive and it remains far cheaper to the consumer to make one handle type with several different simple molds (only the core rod is changed to make the different internal diameters) than it is to make and inventory different handles. Adapters for Fuji glue-ins range in size from 6 to 11.5 millimeters for the "LA" style, and 9.5 to 15 millimeters for the "EA" style.

In addition, handles are available through-bored for a glue-fitting onto a rod: the result is a one-piece rod in which the handle cannot be removed. Also, for through-handle construction, skeletal type casting-rod-handle kits are available that consist of the preshaped rear cork grip, the trigger/hood section, the cork insert, the threaded barrel, the hood and locking ring, and a short foregrip.

BOAT-ROD HANDLES

Boat-rod handles of wood with a glued-on reel seat and mushroom butt cap are sometimes available; usually hickory wood is used. When available, these come with a ferrule and collet nut to fasten the rod blank to the detachable handle. In addition, they are sometimes available in through-bored models in which the rod blank can be shimmed or the handle sized with a reamer or file so that the two fit together properly.

OFFSHORE TROLLING-ROD HANDLES

Offshore rods are available from several companies, such as AFTCO, Stuart, and Wright. The AFTCO handles come in several styles and models. Most popular are the Unibutts, which incorporate handle and reel seat. The handle is similar to a standard swaged handle, with a built-in gimbal reel seat and ferrule/collet. A pinning system assures that all parts are straight and in line. The hoods are milled from heavy-wall aluminum for strength, and two shouldered nuts hold the sliding hood in place. The ferrules are interchangeable, so that one handle or butt system can be used with several different rod tips. Another advantage is that the ferrule and collet incorporate a rubber O-ring on the ferrule that acts as a watertight seal to keep salt water and corrosion away from the internal parts.

The advantage of the Unibutt system is that the reel seat is an integral part of the handle, thus there are no dissimilar metals that can facilitate electrolysis and corrosion.

The Unibutt system, along with other AFTCO handles and butts, is of high-strength 6061-T6 aluminum. Sizes available include models designed for six-pound class through unlimited-

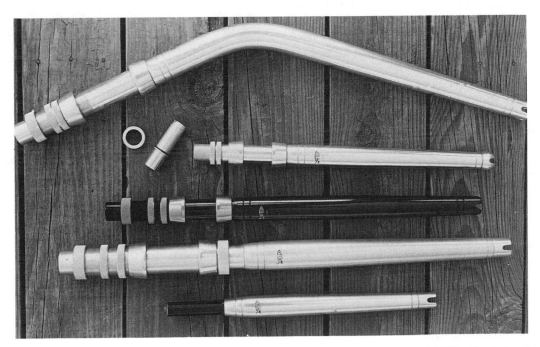

Examples of various sizes and types of offshore trolling handles from AFTCO. Each is of aluminum and designed with a collet (second rod from top) to fit the rod.

class tackle. Both straight-handle and curved-handle models are available; the curved-handle models are designed for heavier tackle such as thirty-pound through unlimited-class. Curved-butt handles are designed to lower the rod tip and allow up to thirty percent more pressure during a fight for the same power and pull on the part of the angler. The result is a quicker fight, a quicker landing of the fish, and less strain on the angler. Finishes available include silver anodized, hard-coat black anodized, and hard-coat black body with gold-anodized hoods and rings. The ferrules allow these butts to take rods with butt diameters of from 0.750 to 1.188 inches. In addition, the rods are available with ball gimbals to reduce deck damage that might occur with the straight gimbal, and the option of slip-over reel-seat sleeves that fit between the reel seat and foregrip to reinforce that area when forward reel braces are used.

While these standard rod butts serve well for most fishing, there are some additional specialized items. One is the Extend-A-Butt by AFTCO, which allows stand-up rods to be used in fighting chairs. Stand-up rods by definition must have a short butt for handling in a rod belt. The Extend-A-Butt slides over this short butt to extend it and make it suitable for a fighting chair.

One additional problem-solver by AFTCO is the Storabutt. This is essentially a handle-and-seat arrangement that not only has a ferrule and collet nut on the upper end for the rod blank but also a ferrule extension of the butt that fits into the reel seat and is secured with a collet nut. In essence, the reel seat is ferruled at both ends. The result is that butts can be removed from rods without disturbing the reel or line/terminal tackle as it runs through the rod guides. It is made with curved or straight butts, in 80- and 130-pound class sizes. It is most useful with the curved butts, since these are more difficult to store or rack in overhead or vertical rod racks.

HANDLE KITS

There are handle kits available for a number of light-tackle fishing-rod styles. For example, Lamiglas lists over forty different handle kits, including those for fly, saltwater fly, steelhead, salmon, casting, two-hand casting, boat, downrigger, Tennessee-handle spinning, spinning, and offshore rods.

BUTT CAPS, GIMBALS

Butt caps and gimbals are designed to finish the butt end of the rod. Butt caps do it on most rods; gimbals or gimbal knocks (two terms for the same item) accomplish this on offshore and big-game rods that are used with fighting chairs and crossbar-style rod belts. Gimbals are longer, sturdier for heavier fishing, and have two crossed slots — like an X — in the bottom to fit the crossbar in fighting chairs, or belt rod sockets. Their purpose is to keep the rod from twisting or torquing under the strain of fighting big fish.

Butt-cap styles range widely. The simplest are those that are a simple rubber or flexible plastic socket — like a crutch tip or chair leg. The rubber crutch-tip type of butt cap is usually available in short and long styles, in black or white, and in diameters of 3/4, 7/8, 1, and 1 1/8 inches. While these are okay, similar but more streamlined butt caps specifically designed for rods are available in dark colors and several styles and diameters to match most rods. One by Fuji has a spread end designed to give extra leverage with forearm support. Even those lacking this specialized shape have some swelling at the butt end. Longer slim tapered butt caps primarily designed for larger rods such as surf rods and boat rods are available in black or brown. They're about 3 inches long and range from about 3/4-inch to a little over 1 inch in inside diameter. Rubber mushroom caps are used on the ends of wood boat rods and also at the ends of some heavy rods, such as some fly-rod extension butts.

Though they are more brittle and thus not as sturdy, small tapered butt caps of a harder plastic are also available. Some butt caps incorporate both metal and rubber or wood, such as the butt

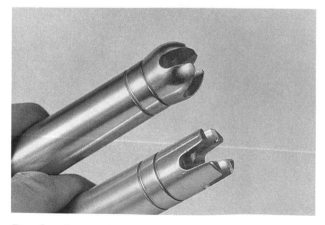

Regular (bottom) and ball gimbals are available on some offshore handles. These are from AFTCO.

caps manufactured by RST. These look more European—they are the type found on some long-handled European-style rods and are readily available for custom rod-building. Those of wood are more attractive, but rubber is durable and doesn't slip, and thus is more practical for most applications.

Some butt caps are simple swaged aluminum sockets, though these are harder to find and seemingly less frequently used. Butt plates of aluminum are popular, mostly as the butt ends on fly rods with short, built-in extensions of 2 inches or less in length, on the ends of fly-rod extension butts, and as the butt ends of ultralight spinning rods incorporating all-cork sliding-ring reel-seat assemblies. Sometimes two sizes can be found: a smaller diameter for fly rods, and a larger diameter for spinning. Most have a short stem by which they are securely glued into a cork handle. Several anodized colors are available, as are some caps in nickel silver.

The most popular gimbals for boat and big-game rods are made of machined aluminum, such as the gimbals by AFTCO that come in silver or hard-coat anodized black in 7/8-, 1-, and 1 1/8-inches in side diameter. Brass gimbals are also sometimes available, as are gimbals of hard molded plastic (nylon), tough polyethylene, or graphite (graphite fill, usually). For true big-game fishing, the machined-aluminum or brass models should be the only choice. For lighter fishing where the stresses, the length of the fight, and the size of the fish are all less, any of the other materials will do fine. Those of molded plastic and graphite are lighter, a sometimes important consideration in lighter rods. Some gimbals are supplied with, or have as an option, a soft-plastic or rubber butt cap that slips over the gimbal and protects decks, boats, and other tackle from damage.

FERRULES, COLLETS, HOSELS, AND WINDING CHECKS

Most ferrules used on rods and blanks today are built into the blank or rod: You buy the blank and the ferrule comes with it. You do need to wrap the female portion of the ferrule for hoop strength, but you get the ferrule as an integral part of the rod blank. Ferrules are available separately, but usually only in two extremes of quality. Nickel-silver ferrules are available for high-quality fly rods and usually used only on bamboo blanks, since the others have built-in ferrules. They are expensive and available in a smaller range of sizes for bamboo blanks.

Chrome-plated-brass ferrules are available from Amtak (American Tackle Limited) in sizes from 9/10 64th, to 49/50 64th (in the smallest size, 9/64) is the internal diameter of the male portion of the ferrule that goes on the tip section; 10/64th is for the larger-diameter butt section. Larger sizes, above 21/22 64th, are reinforced for strength.

Another type of ferrule is used for big-game reel seats. These are designed to fit specific reel seats, such as the ferrules and locking collet nuts on AFTCO Unibutts. Most of these ferrules have a notch to fit a pin in the reel seat, which assures proper alignment of the reel-seat hoods on the handle and the rod guides. Collect nuts fit over the ferrule to lock the rod tip onto the handle and prevent loosening or loss.

Rod hosels serve the same purpose as winding checks in providing a finishing touch between the upper end of the foregrip and the rod blank. Rod hosels are extended or conelike winding checks that are primarily used on big rods, mostly inshore boat rods. Sometimes they are used on offshore tackle, heavy freshwater tackle, downrigger rods, and heavy salmon rods. They are available in larger-diameter internal diameters, usually in sizes of 20/64th through 40/64th.

Winding checks are thin rings of metal, rubber, polyethylene, or nickel silver that serve as trims between grips and rod blanks. They are used on virtually all rods, from fly rods to big-game rods. Depending upon the style, they are sized in 64ths (often from 13/64th to 60/64th) and in millimeters (typically, from 6.5 millimeters to 16 millimeters in nickel-silver rings from RST). Functionally they are not necessary, but they work aesthetically to eliminate an unfinished appearance at the grip-to-blank junction. Aluminum winding checks are available in anodized colors; nickel silver are polished; rubber are almost always black; and the polyethylene are usually available in brown, black, and similar dark colors.

THREAD

Thread is required to wrap the guides in place, make underwraps, and wrap female ferrules, as well as to fashion decorative wraps such as trim wraps at the handle and tip-top and to make any decorative diamonds, chevrons, weaving, or other fancy wraps.

Nylon thread is standard for rod-wrapping and is available from several companies, with Gudebrod the most widely known. Silk thread is available but is not as widely used or available in as many sizes and colors. The advantages of nylon are that it will not rot and break down, and that the slight amount of stretch inherent in the material can be used to place any wrap under tension. Tension helps to get a good secure wrap, so this *is* an advantage.

Nylon thread comes in several sizes and many colors and spools, but not all sizes are available in all colors or spools. Gudebrod thread comes in sizes OO, A, C, D, E, EE, and FF (OO is the thinnest, FF the thickest). Regular nylon does not come in C, however, and the N.C.P. thread (requiring no color preserver) comes only in sizes A, C, and D. The N.C.P. thread is made with special colorfast processes and dyes that resist the color changes caused by the strong epoxies, varnishes, and polyurethanes used on today's wraps. Both the regular and the N.C.P. threads come in dozens of colors. In addition, metallic thread in sizes A and D is made with an aluminized film wound over a nylon core for strength. Metallic thread looks like regular thread in regular colors but has far greater sheen, sparkle, and brilliance. Trimar thread, available in size C only, uses a base of N.C.P. thread twisted with Mylar to make a distinctive sparkle-color thread.

Thread colors currently available from Gudebrod in the regular nylon and N.C.P. include black, white, light blue, cobalt blue, peach, rose pink, spring green, sunburst, garnet, goldenrod, orange, royal blue, dark blue, rust, blue dun, tan, scarlet, candy apple, maroon, gold, dark brown, hot pink, charcoal, purple, medium brown, medium gray, gunmetal, chestnut, dark green, lemon yellow, and medium green. Thread colors in the metallic thread include gold, black, silver, pearl, ole gold, ice blue, lime, fuchsia, aquamarine, royal blue, aqua, red, dusty rose, green, copper, purple, and bronze. Trimar thread colors include black/silver, white/silver, blue/silver, green/silver, brown/silver, red/silver, black/gold, white/gold, blue/gold, green/gold, brown/gold, and red/gold.

The threads are available in spools of 100 yards (50 yards for size FF), 1 ounce, and 4 ounces. Not all colors are available in all thread sizes, nor are all sizes and colors available in all spool sizes. The best spool size for most hobbyists is the 100-yard spool or, for serious rod-builders, the 1-ounce spoon. The 4-ounce spool is primarily for rod manufacturers or commercial jig wrappers because it holds a lot of thread. A 4-ounce spool of size A thread contains 4,800 yards (about 2.8 miles); in size D, 2,300 yards (about 1.3 miles);

and in size E, 1,200 yards (about .66 mile).

Gudebrod recommends the following uses for their various thread sizes (reprinted with permission from the Gudebrod catalog):

Size OO. Wrapping delicate fly rods and ultra-light spinning and spin-cast rods. Also, wrapping and tying jigs from 1/32-ounce through 1/8-ounce.

Size A. Recommended for fly rods, freshwater, spinning, and casting rods. Wrapping and tying jigs from 1/2-ounce through 1 1/2 ounces.

Size C (N.C.P. and D nylon). Wrapping saltwater rods, medium-weight spinning, casting, boat, and trolling rods. Wrapping and tying jigs from 5/8-ounce through 2 ounces.

Size D (N.C.P. and E nylon). Wrapping 80- and 130-pound trolling rods as well as heavy-duty boat and surf rods. Wrapping and tying jigs from 2 1/4 ounces to 3 1/2 ounces.

Size E. Wrapping heavy-duty trolling rods, boat rods, and surf rods.

Size EE. Wrapping extra-heavy-duty trolling rods and extra-long (14 to 16 feet) surf rods.

Size FF. Special wrapping effects on gaffs, outriggers, and antennas. Wrapping heavy-duty rod butts for friction grip. In addition, size FF is the recommended size for wrapping pool-cue handles.

Gudebrod makes a special, heavy rod-butt cord that is used for wrapping rod butts on heavy casting, boat, trolling, and surf rods, and for gaff handles. It provides a colorful and nonslip grip. Colors available include black, blue, brown, white, red, and yellow. Although it's not designed for rod-building, a similar heavy cord is available from craft stores, where it is sold as macrame cord in 1 1/2- and 2-millimeter diameters and many colors.

FINISHES, COLOR PRESERVERS, SEALERS, AND GLUES

Glues are necessary to fasten some rod parts together; color preservers, varnishes, and rod finishes are necessary to protect rod wraps. Glues are used for fastening cork rings together to form a handle on a blank, gluing preformed cork grips into a blank, gluing foam grips to a blank, securing ferrules (where used) onto rods, fastening tip-tops to the end of a rod, gluing reel seats onto rod blanks and handles, gluing butt caps, and assembling reel-seat parts such as the fixed hood, barrel insert, and threaded barrel. Color preservers are necessary when using regular (not N.C.P.) nylon thread, and a final coating of varnish or, more typically, epoxy rod finish, is also applied.

Everyone has their own theories and ideas on the best glues for all the above tasts. Any such glue should be easy to work with, not too thick or thin for the task at hand, waterproof, easy to clean up, not toxic or dangerous to work with, and capable of a secure hold.

My preferences are as follows, but new adhesives and glues are coming out all the time, so be sure to check for the latest available products that will suit your tasks, keeping the above criteria in mind.

GLUED MATERIALS

Butt cap to the rod blank/handle. A good waterproof glue such as Gudebrod Liquid Rod Cement, U-40 Cork Bond, Duco, Devcon, Ambroid, or the various 24-hour epoxies are ideal for this when the butt cap is aluminum, metal, or plastic. For gluing rubber butt caps onto a rod, extension butt, or wood handle, use a glue that will bond with rubber as well as with the other materials.

Gimbal to rod butt. These are going to be under much greater stress than plain butt caps, so use 24-hour epoxy.

Foam grip to rod blank. Foam grips, whether EVA or Hypalon, always use a smaller-diameter hole than the size of the blank on which they are placed, but gluing is still recommended. However, because the grip must be forced over the blank, and because glue is often used both as an adhesive and a lubricant, one that cleans up with water is best. This seeming contradiction, of a water-based glue on a fishing rod, is not as great as it seems, since the glue is under all the foam, and water penetration through the foam would be rare if not impossible. For this reason, I like water-based glues such as Elmer's and various similar craft glues. They glue well and hold well and clean up completely if washed immediately after the parts are set in place. Solvent glues also work well but require more clearup.

Gluing cork rings together to make a rod grip. For this, epoxy glue is not the best, in my opinion. Epoxy glue is so strong and so hard that the necessary filing and shaping of the rings to the handle becomes difficult: Unless you are careful, it is possible to end up taking off more cork than glue between the rings, resulting in a slightly scalloped look. For this use, I like Gudebrod Liquid Rod Cement, U-40 Cork Bond, Elmer's glue, Duco cement, Pliobond, or similar "softer" glues. I have used epoxies for this, but if you do

so, make sure the glue is completely wiped off the cork surface so that you do not have to cut through glue when you try to shape the cork rings.

Gluing preformed cork grips onto the rod blank. For this, epoxy is best: Smear the epoxy onto the rod blank at the proper position, then slide and rotate the cork grip into place. Of course, you first have to check the hole diameter and taper on the cork grip to make sure it fits properly.

Reel seat to rod blank. Reel seats require shimming (in most cases) to fill the space between the rod blank and internal diameter of the seat. Glues should be 24-hour epoxy or other very strong glues.

Tip-top to the tip of the rod blank. There are two possibilities here. For light rods, heat-set glues such as glue-gun materials or stick ferrule cement from Fuji, Gudebrod, or other companies are all ideal. For heavy rods, I like 5-minute epoxy. The epoxy will set up rapidly yet still provide time to work, and will hold far more securely on big rods under extreme stresses when fighting fish. If necessary, you can still remove the tip-top from the rod with heat, as will be described.

Although these suggestions are good for most rods built by hobbyists, rod manufacturers generally use either 5-minute or 24-hour epoxy glue for all their gluing operations (with the possible exception of gluing cork rings together for a grip). They even use it for the often messy job of gluing foam grips onto rod blanks. Commercial rodbuilders have the distinct advantage of having and being able to use acetone or other ketones as solvents for quick cleanups. Extensive use of these solvents should not be used by the home rodbuilder without adequate ventilation and protection. Check with your local Occupational Safety and Health Administration office or similar agency for proper usage and safety requirements.

SEALERS

Sealers are sometimes used with cork grips to seal the cork pores on the outside of the grip, to help give the grip more of a nonslip surface, and to protect it against undue soiling. Several cork sealers are available: U-40 Urethane Cork Seal is one.

COLOR PRESERVERS

Color preserver is necessary on regular nylon thread (not N.C.P. thread). Varnish or epoxy finish used over the thread without a color preserver will result in the thread changing color. Light-colored threads will turn lighter, with white often turning completely transparent. Dark colors will turn darker, and all colors will become translucent, allowing the reel foot to show through in some cases.

Color preserver must penetrate the threads completely to be effective. Often one coat is enough, but occasionally two coats are required. Many companies make color preserver, with perhaps the best known products available from Gudebrod, Flex Coat, and U-40. They are usually available in 1-ounce, 4-ounce, and 1-pint bottles.

FINISHES

Once the color preserver is completely dry, a protective finish must be applied to the thread wraps. Varnish, epoxy, and polymer are all used. Varnish was once the standard but today is used primarily for bamboo rods when an old, traditional look is wanted, or for a quick finish without a two-part epoxy or polymer. Varnish is not as durable as epoxies or polymers and requires more coats to build up the thick, glossy finish that is available with one coat of epoxy. Some brands also have a tendency to yellow in time.

Epoxies and polymers include Gudebrod Hard 'N Fast II, Flex Coat Finish, Flex Coat Lite (designed for a thinner finish of epoxy on fly rods and ultralight rods), Gudebrod Speed Coat rod finish, U-40 Perma Gloss, and U-40 Dura Gloss Polymer Rod Finish.

Most of these types of finishes have the disadvantage of requiring the mixing of two parts (an exception is the Gudebrod Speed Coat and U-40 Perma Gloss), although in some cases the color-coded syringes and bottles (such as those of Flex Coat and U-40) make this easier. The advantage is a one-coat application that will have high build and excellent protection, is highly durable, and will not yellow or turn off-color. One final disadvantage is that most of these finishes are thick and heavy and thus require slow rotation of the rod to prevent sagging and dripping.

Depending upon the brand, these finishes comeee in 1-ounce, 2-ounce, 4-ounce, 8-ounce, 32-ounce, and 64-ounce containers.

MISCELLANEOUS

Some small items, such as protective gloves, razor blades, and ferrule treatments are also handy for rod-building.

Protective gloves, such as the disposable type of surgical gloves (often available from better drug stores and some mail-order companies), are ideal for work with glues, color preservers, and epoxy finishes. They are very thin and easy to work with, allow easy cleanup, and are inexpensive. Skin contact with glues and finishes is discouraged by most manufacturers. In addition, some people are allergic or have reactions to prolonged contact to these materials. If such is a problem for you, gloves are especially recommended.

Razor blades are handy for trimming and cutting operations in rod-building. A razor blade makes it easy to trim excess glue, cut thread when wrapping rods, or scrape a rod to size it into a ferrule or collet. Scalpels and X-Acto knives are also handy, but razor blades are cheaper, disposable, and readily available in "industrial" packs of 100 units.

Some companies (U-40, for example) make a ferrule treatment that is designed to help smooth and hold the self-ferrules (glass-to-glass or graphite-to-graphite) of modern rod blanks. These treatments are fine, but a good substitute is candle wax rubbed over the male portion of the ferrule to aid in fitting and holding.

18

Basic Rod-Building

INTRODUCTION ▪ ASSEMBLING PARTS, MATERIALS, AND
TOOLS ▪ DETERMINING THE SPINE ▪ MOUNTING THE
REAR GRIP ▪ MOUNTING THE BUTT CAP ▪ MOUNTING
THE REEL SEAT ▪ MOUNTING THE FOREGRIP ▪
MOUNTING THE WINDING CHECK ▪ MOUNTING THE
TIP-TOP ▪ PREPARING AND WRAPPING GUIDES ▪
PROTECTING THE WRAPS: FINISHING COATS

Note. Chapter 17 should be read before this chapter is read and before items to build the rod in this chapter are purchased. This chapter will provide detailed information about the parts and materials available.

INTRODUCTION

Building any rod is really an assembly process that is not unlike tying a fly—in which the various materials are added and tied down in sequence—or making a model plane or car. There is some fitting, some sizing, lots of checking, some measuring, a little gluing, a fair amount of cleaning up, and, initially at least, a lot of following directions.

Building a rod is not hard. In this chapter we will construct a 6 1/2-foot two-piece spinning rod with a simple foam grip, graphite blank, aluminum oxide two-foot guides, graphite-style reel seat, and rubber or plastic butt cap. The basics for all the steps in building a rod are essentially the same, regardless of the type of rod. There are some special tips for handling certain types of guides or the different materials used in grips, and so on, but these are easily learned.

Variations of these basics, along with some professional tips and greatly expanded directions and details, are covered in subsequent chapters.

ASSEMBLING PARTS, MATERIALS, AND TOOLS

Before beginning, you will need all the parts, materials, and tools necessary for all steps through the final finish. In this case, we will be making a 6 1/2-foot graphite freshwater spinning rod, and the directions will be generic but applicable to any material brands you might choose.

ROD PARTS

Two-piece 6 1/2-foot graphite spinning rod. Freshwater style, designed for 1/4- through 5/8-ounce lures.

Set of aluminum oxide, silicon carbide, or Hardloy spinning guides. Bought either as a set or individually to match the rod. We will use aluminum oxide for our rod. Six guides are recommended, along with a tip-top. The tip-top tube will have to fit the end of the rod tip, and the guide sizes should be 40, 20, 16, 12, 10, and 8 millimeters. There can be variations in these sizes, particularly if the high-frame small-ring guides currently in vogue are used, since these will allow for good funneling of the line through the guide ring; the high frame helps to prevent line slap and the resulting friction and loss of distance. With these guides, often the largest size is about a 20-millimeter ring. Here a suggested guide set would include a 20-, 16-, 12-, 10-, and 7-millimeter, plus the tip-top.

Rubber or plastic butt cap. These are a simple slip-on, glue-on style that is quite standard on this type of rod. Most are about 3/4- to 7/8-inch in diameter for freshwater model rods.

Foam rear grip. These are Hypalon or EVA or a similar open-cell foam material drilled to fit on the blank and available in many colors. For this rod, we will pick one that is 6 inches long. This must be of the right inside diameter for the blank. Since these are a tight fit (not like cork grips, which must match the taper and diameter of the blank), you must choose a foam grip with the right hole size. The best guide to this is to choose a grip with a hole of about two-thirds to three-quarters the diameter of the blank. This provides for ample gripping of the blank without extreme stresses or mounting problems.

Foam foregrip. This will be of the same material and color as the rear grip, 4 inches long, and sized with an internal diameter to properly fit the rod blank, usually about two-thirds to three-quarters of the blank diameter. Note that with steep-taper rods, this internal diameter of the foregrip might be slightly different from the internal diameter of the rear grip, since they will be separated by the length of the reel seat.

Reel seat. For a light rod like this, a graphite-fill reel seat of about 18 to 20 millimeters is best.

Winding check. Although it's not absolutely necessary, this is a nicety that makes for a decorative trim between the grip and blank.

MATERIALS

Thread. For this example, we will use regular nylon in size A. One small spool will be enough.

Color preserver. This will be necessary to protect the color of the chosen thread and keep it from changing. The color preserver must be compatible with the finish used. A 1-ounce bottle will be sufficient.

Rod finish. For this, we will choose a two-part epoxy finish. The smallest container will be sufficient.

24-hour epoxy glue. Necessary for gluing the tip-top, reel seat, and butt cap.

Water-solvent glue. A glue such as Elmer's will be necessary to serve as an adhesive and lubricant to get the foam grips onto the blank and secure them in place.

Masking tape. Necessary in a 1/4-inch width to hold the guides in place while the threads are wrapped. A larger size (1-inch) is best if the tape is used as a shim or spacer for the reel seat. Other possibilities for these shims are cord, paper tape, cork rings, cork bushings, and fiber bushings.

TOOLS

Rod-wrapping tool and support of some type. As previously described in Chapters 1 and 2. The rod-wrapping device can range from the simplest to the most complex, but it is necessary to do a good job. Features that are a must are the ability to wrap any guide in any position, to support the length of the rod or rod section even when you are wrapping a tip-top or close to one end, and a maintainable and adjustable thread tension.

Razor blade or scalpel. To cut the rod-wrapping thread at the completion of each wrap.

Handle seater. This, or a piece of wood with a hole in it to help push the foam grip down into place on the rod blank. Not absolutely necessary, but it does make this task easier.

File. This is a must to file the ends of the guide

Basic rod-building wrapper for hand-wrapping rods, with two "V" supports to hold the rod blank and a sewing machine-type thread tension device. Courtesy of Flex Coat Company.

feet to slope them and prepare them for the rod wrap.

Brush. Two will be needed, one to apply the color preserver to the wraps, the second to apply the epoxy finish.

Rod-curing motor. This, whether jury-rigged from a barbecue motor or bought as a curing motor, is a must to turn the rod constantly during the curing of the epoxy to prevent sags and drips.

Once the parts, materials, and tools are assembled, you are ready to begin. As with any tackle-building task, make sure you have a completely clean workplace, and that you are familiar with all the following steps of building before beginning.

DETERMINING THE SPINE

Rod blanks made with the cut-and-roll method have glass or graphite material wrapped around them for the equivalent of a thin-wall, hollow jelly roll. The material spiraled around the mandrel during construction results in a slight unevenness in the blank, and thus a slight unevenness in the blank's strength or resistance to bending in different planes. The spine then—sometimes erroneously called the "spline"—is that plane of maximum stiffness, or resistance to bending, on the blank. Generally, the guides are lined up on this spine or plane of stiffness, or on the opposite, or "softer," side.

Because of this construction, all rods of this type of manufacture will vary in stiffness in dif-

ferent planes. Factors controlling this are the diameter of the mandrel and also the number of wraps of material around the mandrel making up the wall. Thus, if you have a blank made with two and a half wraps of material around the mandrel, some parts of the mandrel will have three wraps and the rest will have only two wraps. Thus, one part of the blank will have fifty percent more material than the rest of the blank. On this area, the spine can be pronounced. Conversely, a big-game rod might have twenty and a half wraps of material around the mandrel, resulting in most of the rod having twenty wraps with one section having twenty-one wraps. The result is only a five-percent differential between the various planes, and thus a much less pronounced spine. It would seem that rods made by the pultrusion process (solid-rod blanks) and the Howald process would have equal distribution of material in the blank and thus not have a spine. As a general rule, these processes do come perhaps as close as possible to this ideal, but absolutely even distribution is impossible in any blank. Also, a blank that is not absolutely straight—and very few are *absolutely* straight—will be under tension when it is straightened. Thus, a blank with perfect distribution of material but with a slight curve would have a spine, or plane of stiffness, in line with the concave side of its curvature.

In some cases, the spine will be very pronounced; in other rod blanks it will be very minimal, or almost nonexistent. Some rods will have two spines—one more pronounced than the other—as a result of some of the factors mentioned above. In addition, in all blanks the spine will vary in different sections of the blank. Thus, if you were to cut a blank into four equal parts, the spine could be on a different part of the blank in each part. The spine that we measure is really an average of the total spine distribution and stiffness forces in the rod blank.

It is extremely important to determine the spine in a blank before beginning to build the rod. It is on this plane that the guides must be placed with light-tackle spinning, casting, spinning, and fly tackle. The softest side of the rod, or the side opposite the plane of stiffness (usually, but not always) must be used for big-game rods, trolling rods, and similar heavy tackle.

The reasoning for this is as follows: As just outlined the torque of the rod will always tend to turn the rod to bend on the softest plane. This is countered with rods that have the guides on the underside during casting—spinning and fly rods

—since the rod is light enough and the guides pronounced enough to prevent this from having any great effect. However, some rod manufacturers like to mount their guides for spinning and fly rods on the softest side (the convex side of the rod's natural bend) or the side of natural bending, mounting guides for casting and spin-cast rods on the side opposite this (on the concave side of the rod's natural bend). Trolling-rod guides are mounted on the soft side (the convex side of the rod's naturally roll when it is bent), because these heavy rods, under heavy stresses, will tend to jump and torque if the guides are not lined up to allow the rod to bend naturally on the softest side.

In all cases, even with light rods, it is important to mount the guides in line with this plane of stiffness, since mounting them off to one side by design or accident may result in a rod that casts inaccurately to one side. This is particularly true with spinning rods, since during a normal cast the rod loads as it starts to come forward, and at this point the guides can twist off to the side, causing the lure to cast at a slight angle as the guides torque around on the completion of the cast.

Before determining the spine of the rod, first check to make sure that the butt end is completely smooth, free of any burrs or imperfections, and cut at a right angle to the blank's axis. Wrap a layer of masking tape around the rod blank so that it can be marked with the spine plane. The easy way to check the spine is to place the butt end of the blank on a smooth, laminated countertop, leaning the tip section against your right hand and pressing down on the blank with your left hand to flex the rod. Using your left hand, rotate the rod blank so that it rolls along the counter. As you roll the rod, you will feel a marked difference in its resistance to bending at one point. Mark this side of the rod and make a small note that this is the stiff side. Now allow the blank to roll naturally so that you find the side of least resistance, or the softest side. Mark this side also, with an appropriate designation as to resistance. Often, but not always, these marks will be completely opposite each other. The critical factor with big-game rods is to mount these guides opposite the soft side (or on the convex side of the rod as it naturally rolls with the least pressure) so that the rod flexes naturally as the guides bend when trolling or fighting a fish. Other rods can usually be mounted either way, with the general rule of mounting spinning and fly-rod guides (or for any fishing when the reel hangs underneath during fishing) on the soft side; mount casting and spin-cast

guides (with the reel on top) on the stiff side or opposite the soft side.

In our case of building a 6 1/2-foot graphite spinning rod, check each section separately and mark them so that they are assembled in line with the stiffness. This process of checking each section of two- or multipiece rods is important in any rod, because the spine must be determined for each section for proper guide line-up and so that the rod works most efficiently. In some cases, rod-blank manufacturers or custom component shops may mark the spine on rods and rod sections.

One final note on spines: You may wish to check the spine in different areas of the rod, depending on the rod type and the most important flexion portion of the rod. Thus, for a tippy-action worm rod, you may wish to flex only the upper end of the rod, supporting the very tip end with your right hand and pressing down with your left to check the spine. For a heavy flipping rod or similar rod where the lifting power of the butt end is important, support the rod at the middle and press down at the butt end to check the spine in the lower section of the rod. Naturally, this is more difficult with heavier and stiff rods, because any spine is more difficult to determine on a very stiff rod.

MOUNTING THE REAR GRIP

The rear grip is added to the lower section of the rod first. This provides a basis onto which the butt cap is easily glued. Since we are using a foam grip, there are several mounting possibilities. One is to use air pressure. Manufacturers do this with a special tip on an air hose; they slide the foam grip partially onto the upper end of the blank and insert the hose tip between the foam grip and the blank. Hand-controlled air pressure allows the foam grip to be slid down the blank (the air pressure pushes the foam out to allow it to be positioned on the blank) until the grip is in place.

Another way to mount the grip is to use a water-based glue that will serve both as a lubricant and an adhesive and also allow easy water clean-up. For this, you can use any water-based glue (although I like Elmer's), diluting it slightly with water. I like a dilution of about one-third water to two-thirds glue. Use a dowel or rod to spread the glue evenly on the inside of the foam grip and over the rod blank. As much as possible, try to keep the outside of the foam grip clean. You can cover it with paper towels, taped in place, to help with this.

Place the grip over the rod blank and, using a continuous motion, push the foam grip down on the blank. Do not try to pull the foam grip down, because it will grab the blank and work like a Chinese finger puzzle. Push from the top only. You may wish to use a handle seater, as described in Chapter 2, or you can simply use a scrap piece of wood with a blank-diameter hole drilled into it as a grip-pusher. Either will work fine.

Depending upon the diameter differentials between the outside diameter of the blank and the inside diameter of the foam grip and the firmness of the grip, you may find that the grip retains its shape during this step. Most likely, the foam grip will tend to compress and bunch a little, sometimes even ending up like a little foam football at the bottom of the blank. Don't worry about this—it is easy to "milk" out the foam grip to the desired shape, length, and diameter. Make sure that the foam grip covers the entire butt end of the blank, because you will need the end of the grip to mount the butt cap on.

As soon as you have the grip in place, use warm water to remove all of the excess glue from the blank and especially any that might have gotten on the foam grip. If it dries, glue will be far more difficult to remove from the porous foam grip than from the smooth blank finish. Warm water and a rag is best for removing the excess glue.

The same procedure can be followed using epoxy glue as the lubricant and adhesive. This is what the manufacturers use. It will perform much better, but is also more messy, because the epoxy requires a solvent cleanup—usually acetone or a similar ketone. Some glue manufacturers also sell epoxy cleaners (designed to clean up brushes used with epoxy), and these may also work well.

You can also seat the grip using not glue but various lubricants to help slide the foam grip into place. Gasoline has been mentioned in some magazine articles, and although it will work well, do *not* use it. It is just too dangerous, and can only be used outside under strictly controlled conditions. Better lubricants that work almost as well include soapy water, shaving gel and foam, alcohol, various lubricant sprays, and some demoisturizers. These liquids must be cleaned up, and any left under the grip will in time evaporate and disappear. It does help to use a handle seater or push-board to help slide the foam grip in place quickly, particularly with rapidly evaporating solvents.

Mounting The Butt Cap

We will use a simple socket-type, slip-on plastic butt cap. These are designed to fit onto the rear grip, and make for a finished end to the rod. For an attractive rod, the outside diameter of the butt cap must be no larger than the outside diameter of the rear grip. Often, they are slightly smaller. To properly fit the butt cap onto the rod grip, you must cut a recess out of the end of the rear grip for the butt cap. Because the foam is slightly spongy, this does not have to be a precise fit, but it must be close. (A precise fit would be required if the grip were cork.)

First measure the depth of the butt cap and mark the rear grip with this measurement. The best way to do this is to tape the grip with several layers of masking tape to both mark the grip and protect the exposed portion of the grip while you remove material to make the recess. Measure the inside diameter of the butt cap, then measure the outside diameter of the rear of the grip to determine how much material to remove.

There are several ways to remove the material after you've taped the grip for protection. The best way is to place the rod on a through-center lathe, wrapping the grip material to keep from marring it and using supports to the side of the lathe to hold the rod blank and prevent it from whipping around and becoming damaged. Support the end of the hollow blank with a live or dead center. Then use a simple tool rest (like that used with a wood lathe) to support a wood rasp for removing the material at the exposed area. Be careful not to damage the taped portion of the grip. Use calipers often to check for the diameter, but be sure to take any measurement only after turning the lathe off and waiting for it to come to a complete rest. Make a final check with the butt cap.

If you lack a lathe (as most of us do), there are other alternatives. One is to use a grinder to remove the required foam, holding the grip sideways against the grinder with only the recessed area in contact with the wheel, and turning the grip while applying light pressure against the grinder. Check frequently and make sure that you make complete 360-degree turns to remove material evenly.

Another method is to use a wood rasp and remove the material by hand. Because it is difficult to hold or clamp the grip and use the rasp against it, a better way is to clamp the rasp, flat side up, in a bench vise. Use two boards on the side of the rasp to protect the teeth. Then work the recessed area of the grip against this fixed rasp, rotating the grip slightly while doing so. Work completely around the grip, checking measurements frequently.

One danger of the method just outlined or of working with the grinding wheel is the possibility of taking more foam off one side than another. One way to prevent this is to work in sequence, counting strokes, then rounding off the result. To do this, count several strokes taken on one side of the foam to remove the flat portion. Do not take off to much. Repeat the same number of rasp strokes on the opposite side. Repeat at 90 degrees and then at 180 degrees to the two worked sides to end up with a squared-off area. *Note:* You do *not* have to take the foam down to a square, only slightly square off the sides consistent with the material that you must remove for a good fit. Once you're at this point, square off the corners slightly and check measurements. Repeat if you need to remove more material. Once you're close to the final size, round off the corners and check for a final fit.

Don't worry if this recess is not precise and smooth, because you only need it sized to fit the butt cap properly. The upper edge must be smooth to properly mate with the butt cap, but the rest does not have to be smooth. It does not even have to be completely round—it only has to fit the butt cap properly.

If you cut away too much and the recessed area is too small in diameter, you will have to adjust this. The simplest and best solution is to soak the area with glue and then wrap heavy cord around the butt-cap recess with an even wrap or two to fill up any gap area. Soak the cord with glue and then twist the butt cap in place.

Another problem that sometimes develops is cutting the recess too high up, so that the butt cap bottoms out before the upper edge mates with the handle. To solve this, use a fine-blade hacksaw (32 teeth to the inch) and evenly cut off enough material at the end of the blank and grip to eliminate this gap.

One problem with the above methods is that you may end up with a slight unevenness at the edge of the recess—where the edge of the butt cap meets the rod handle. To smooth off this area after checking for size and fit, remove the masking tape and use medium sandpaper or an emery board to finely polish and dress the area.

Another method of adding a butt cap does not require cutting out a recess in the foam grip.

Instead, it relies on leaving a short length of rod blank exposed at the end of the grip, then fitting a bushing onto the end of the blank that is sized to fit the butt cap. A cork ring or two is ideal for this: First ream out the hole in the cork to fit the end of the rod butt, and then file down the outside of the cork to fit the inside diameter of the butt cap. In neither case must this filing be precise, because the cork will be completely hidden under the butt cap. Use enough cork rings (each 1/2-inch thick) to make up the height of the butt cap. Butt caps vary in size from about 1 to 3 inches, so two to six rings will be required. Once they are sized, spread epoxy glue on the blank end, then glue each cork ring in place. Add glue to the cork faces and twist adjoining rings to assure complete bonding with one another and the rod blank. Once they have cured, and assuming they are sized to the butt cap, the butt cap may be glued in place.

Naturally, other materials can be used for the butt-cap bushings. Wood spacers, wrapped cord, paper tape, and fiberglass tape are just a few. Cork is readily available for rod-building, however, and is easy to work and use.

This step can be done before or after the rear grip is added. If it's done before the rear grip is added, completely assemble and glue the bushings on. Then add the rear grip, sliding it into place against the bushings, which are the same length as the inside length of the butt cap. If the step is done after the rear grip is added, mark the blank for the position of the bushing corks, then slide the rear grip into place at this mark. Clean up as before, then add the cork bushings or spacers for the butt cap as above.

When you are gluing the butt cap onto the bushing, there is one additional step that will make this a professional job and also make it easier and prevent glue from smearing on the butt cap or grip, where it is especially difficult to remove. This step is to add three wraps of regular 1-inch masking tape to the edge of the rear grip and also to the butt cap. This is done right to the edge of these parts—not over them, and not leaving any spots showing. For additional good adhesion, use a rasp, Dremel tool, or rasp bit on a drill to roughen and scar the inside of the butt cap. Make sure that the cork bushings or recessed foam are similarly roughened.

Then, with the masking tape in place, add Gudebrod Liquid Rod Cement or 24-hour epoxy glue, thoroughly mixed, to the sides and bottom of the butt cap and to the sides and bottom of the recess. Do not add too much glue. Then gently twist the butt cap onto the recessed area prepared for it. To prevent air pressure from blocking proper seating of the butt cap, use a slight pinching motion with the butt cap to allow air to escape from one side. Another possibility to eliminate air is to puncture the bottom center of the butt cap with a needle to allow air to escape.

Once the butt cap is in position, glue will ooze from the joint with the grip. This will happen no matter how careful you are with the glue, how evenly it is spread, or how little you use. However, by placing the tape on the edges of the butt cap and grip, you eliminate cleanup problems. To get a clean edge, first use an old rag to remove any excess glue, *then* gently remove the tape. Finally, use a clean rag to touch up and clean any remaining glue.

MOUNTING THE REEL SEAT

Once the foam rear grip and butt cap are in place, the next step is to mount the reel seat. In our case we are using a graphite-fill reel seat. Because the reel seat must sit comfortably under the hand, we have chosen a 20-millimeter diameter seat. This will hold any freshwater reel securely and not cramp the hand. However, the internal diameter of the reel seat is considerably larger than the outside diameter of the rod blank, thus a bushing or shim to build up this space will be necessary. There are several possibilities for this, including cork-ring bushings, special cork bushings, formed-fiber bushings, wraps of paper tape, wraps of masking tape, wraps of fiberglass tape, and wraps of string.

For this basic rod, we will cover the use of cork rings in Chapter 20. You will need one cork ring for each 1/2-inch of reel-seat length, less 1/2-inch. Thus, for a 5-inch reel seat (standard for a graphite-fill seat), you will want nine cork rings to make a 4 1/2-inch bushing. The shorter bushing will allow the foregrip to firmly seat up against the mounted reel seat. A 5-inch-long bushing might be a fraction of an inch longer than the reel seat and would thus create a gap between the reel seat and the foregrip.

Use the poorest grade of cork rings because they will be hidden and are only used to shim the reel seat. You do not need flawless top-quality rings for this. Use a reamer or rat-tail file to ream out the cork rings to fit snugly onto the rod blank. Keep the cork rings in order or number them with a pen, because the degree of reaming will vary from one end to the other with the taper of the rod blank. Once the cork rings are reamed to size, wrap the top of the rear grip with three layers of masking tape to protect against excess glue. Mix some 24-hour epoxy glue and spread a small amount evenly on the rod blank in the area of the reel seat. (More glue can be added while you work, but too much at this point will only drip and cause problems.) Slide the first cork ring into place, and if it's needed, add a small amount of glue to the face that will butt against the top of the foam grip. Check first before doing this, because in most cases sliding the cork ring in place will also push glue down the rod blank. (This is why tape is wrapped around the top edge of the foam—to protect it from excess glue.)

Once the first cork ring is in place, add subsequent rings in order, making sure there is enough (but not too much) glue on the blank and also on the faces of adjoining rings. Twist each ring against the adjoining ring to assure good adhesion and a tight fit. Once all the rings are in place, use a paper towel to clean up any excess glue. Remove the tape from the end of the rear grip and complete any final cleanup. Allow the cork to cure overnight.

Once the rings have cured, wrap the end of the rear grip again with masking tape, but make five or six turns to protect the grip. (If you leave the tape on overnight it may become stiff and difficult to remove.) At this point, you must remove the excess cork in order to size the bushing to fit the reel seat. To do this, use calipers to check the internal diameter of the reel seat against the outside diameter of the cork to get an idea of the amount of cork to remove. There are several ways to remove the cork—by grinding on a wheel, using a wood rasp, or turning on a lathe. Turning on a lathe assures that the cork bushing will be on-center but is not necessarily any better or faster than the other methods. If you use a lathe, mount the rod blank with the rear grip carefully chucked (use layers of tape to protect the grip and butt cap), and secure the free end to prevent it from whipping around as the lathe turns. Use a rasp or file carefully to remove the cork, checking frequently for size with calipers, but only when the lathe is turned off and the work has stopped turning.

To remove cork without a lathe, use the "four-square" system by which you count strokes to remove equal amounts on all four sides, squaring off the cork rings. Check frequently for size so as to not remove too much cork. Once the rings are squared off, take off the corners, then round off the resulting octagon and make any adjustments for size. Counting strokes and removing the same amount of cork on each side is important with this system to keep the bushing on-center with the rod blank. Naturally, you can use a file or sandpaper in place of a wood rasp, but the rasp is quickest and easiest. The same system can be used with a grinding wheel: Remove the cork and check it for size in the process. In this case, use the same number of back-and-forth strokes against the turning wheel to assure equal cork removal.

Once the cork is sized, check it with the reel seat. It should fit snugly, be easy to slip on, but not be tight or loose. At this point remove the old tape from around the end of the rear grip (it was used to protect the grip while you were working on the bushing) and replace with three layers of fresh masking tape wrapped around the end of the grip. Decide if you want the reel seat to be up-locking or down-locking. Most reel seats are up-locking, with the threads at the butt end of the rod. At the same time, make sure you still have the mark indicating the spine of the rod and proper position of the guides, since the reel-seat hoods must line up with this.

Before mounting the reel seat, use a rat-tail file or rasp to roughen the inside of the seat for more "tooth" and better adhesion of the glue. Some reel seats, like those from Fuji, have longitudinal ridges inside the hole for better adhesion, but roughening the inside of any reel seat won't hurt and can only help.

Now, make three tight wraps of masking tape around the end of the reel seat. Use well-mixed epoxy glue and coat the bushing evenly and thinly. Slide the reel seat down the rod (check that the sliding hood is at the end you prefer) and onto the glue-coated bushing. Work the reel seat down onto the cork bushing, twisting and working it up and down as you do so to assure complete distribution of glue. Gradually slide the reel seat to butt against the rear grip. At this point, some glue will ooze out from the two parts. Clean this up with a rag or paper towel, then line up the reel-seat hoods with the spine or guide mark.

There are several ways to line up the hoods with the guide mark. One way is to use a bright overhead light and hold the rod in your lap so that the light makes a streak on the shiny finish of the rod. Without moving your head, rotate the rod so that the guide mark lines up with the light streak. Then, moving your eyes but not your head to check the hoods, line up the reel-seat hood by

rotating the reel seat. Check again. Then remove the tape from around the end of the reel seat and the end of the rear grip. Use a clean rag for a final cleanup of the junction of these two parts. Allow the work to cure overnight.

MOUNTING THE FOREGRIP

The foam foregrip is mounted in the same way as was the rear grip. Various gels, foams, or glue (water-solvent Elmer's or epoxies) can be used to help seat the foam grip in place. As with the rear grip, the internal diameter of the hole in the grip must be smaller than the outside diameter of the rod blank, because the grip will expand to fit tightly in place.

To prevent glue from flowing over onto the reel seat, wrap the top edge of the reel seat with three layers of masking tape to protect it. At the same time, wrap three layers around the butt end of the foregrip. Smear a thin coating of glue onto the rod blank where the foregrip will seat, and begin to slide the grip in place on the rod blank. As with the rear grip, use a push-board or make a board with a hole of about the outside diameter of the blank to help push the foam grip down in place.

Use one smooth motion to push the grip down until it is within about 1 inch of the upper end of the reel seat. Stop at this point and use a clean rag or paper towel to mop up any excess glue. There *will* be excess glue, because the tight grip fit pushes the glue in front of the grip. Note that the short bushing leaves about 1/4- to 1/2-inch of space at the upper end of the reel seat for glue to flow to, but it is still best to mop up any excess. After cleaning this area, work the foam grip down into position, touching the top of the reel seat. "Milk" the grip out, if necessary, to a cylindrical shape. At this point, there may still be some glue that oozed from the reel seat and grip joint junction. Clean this with a clean paper towel. Once the grip is set in place and the joint is cleaned, remove the masking tape carefully. Any excess glue that spilled will have flowed onto the masking tape, demonstrating the value of this protection in keeping the reel seat and foam grip clean.

MOUNTING THE WINDING CHECK

The winding check is not absolutely necessary to the function of the rod, but it's a nice finishing touch. Winding checks are available in aluminum, nickel silver, rubber, and plastic. Any of these will work, but rubber seems to be the most popular at this time. Slide the winding check onto the rod blank and add a tiny bit of glue with a toothpick around the upper end of the foam grip to rod blank joint. Then slide the winding check in place. If it's rubber, it will expand to fit.

MOUNTING THE TIP-TOP

The tip-top must be mounted onto the rod in line with the reel-seat hoods and the spine of the rod. There are several choices of glues for gluing the tip-top tube in place. Ferrule cements (basically heat-set cement) have long been popular, but more and more rod-builders are going to epoxy glue. (Even if you use epoxy glue, a careful application of heat to the tube will allow removal of a damaged tip-top without harming the rod blank.)

Make sure the tip section of the rod is completely clean and round. Sometimes you may find an excess of epoxy as a result of rolling the rod blank. This can be easily removed by sanding with an emery board.

Make sure the tip-top fits and is neither too loose nor too tight. Use a toothpick to spread epoxy glue inside the tube and also lightly on the end of the rod blank. Slide the tip-top onto the end of the rod blank. Some glue may ooze out of the end of the tube and require cleanup with a rag. Also, you may get some glue that oozes through the upper end of the tube. This is because these tubes are tapered and swaged and often have a small gap or hole in the end. If this occurs, there are two ways to clean up the excess glue. One is to use a heavy cord or string and run it through the end of the frame to mop up the excess glue. The other is wait until the glue cures and then use a razor blade to cut away the excess. In any case, it should be removed to prevent it from touching the tip-top ring and possibly damaging the line.

Before the glue sets, line the tip-top up with the spine or reel-seat hoods. The best way to do this is to use the same technique as was used for lining up reel-seat hoods. Use an overhead light that will create a streak of light on the shiny rod blank and line this streak (moving your eyes but not your head) first with the hoods or spine mark and then with the tip-top. Once this is set, make sure you place the rod or tip section horizontally, with the tip-top facing down. Otherwise, the weight of the tip-top will cause it to rotate on the rod blank and become misaligned during curing.

PREPARING AND WRAPPING GUIDES

Before the guides are wrapped in place, the guide feet must be filed to a sharp end. As manufactured, guides do not end in a sharp edge but in a rather blunt end. Without filing the feet, thread will not smoothly cover the end of the foot and will result in a gap as the thread jumps from the smooth rod blank to the guide foot. Often the end of the guide foot will show through. This blunt end also makes it harder to wrap guides, because it is difficult to get the thread up onto the exact end of the foot, even though previous wraps are already on the rod blank.

To prevent these problems, each guide foot must be filed down at the end (not the sides — we are not trying to make a knife edge). Note, however, that you also may wish to file the sides of the guide feet when mounting some guides on very thin tip sections of graphite rods. This will reduce the bulk and width of some guides and make for a more aesthetically pleasing guide and guide wrap without sacrificing strength. File each guide foot with a clean, smooth file until it tapers to a sharp edge. Thus, the size of the file will vary with the size of the guide. A jeweler's file may be all that is needed for a fly-rod snake guide, while a coarser workshop file will be necessary to dress a big-game roller guide.

Although there are definite wrapping advantages to doing this, there are also some disadvantages. For example, with black-frame guides, the finish will be removed, leaving the filed end bright and shiny. Normally this is not a problem, because the thread will cover and hide the guide foot. This may be an aesthetic problem if you use very light colors (white, light yellow) of thin-diameter (size

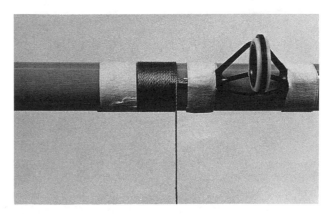

The smooth transfer of thread from the blank to the guide foot usually requires that the guide foot be filed to a knife edge.

Use a regular file to file all guide feet for smooth thread wraps.

2/0 or A) threads, or if you use regular (not N.C.P) thread without color preserver (this will turn light colors lighter and translucent).

There is also a slight problem with plated guides even when the plating is the same color as the base metal. By cutting through the plating, you potentially expose the guide foot to corrosion and oxidation. The possibilities for this are slim, however, and more theoretical than actual because the guide foot is completely covered with thread, which in turn is protected by a thick coating of epoxy rod finish.

When you file the guides, check them over carefully. Check the bottoms of the guide feet for burrs and imperfections that might scar or damage the rod (these could even cause breakage in severe cases), and use the file to remove and smooth any such spurs.

The guide frames should be straight, the guide rings properly seated in the wire frame or shock ring, and the two feet should be in a straight line. If the guide feet are bent slightly up or down, gently bend them in line and check with a straight edge or against the rod blank.

Once the guides are all checked and the feet filed smooth, they are temporarily fastened to the rod for wrapping. Prior to this, of course, proper guide spacing must be determined (See Chapter 21). We will use six guides and place them 5, 11, 18, 26, 35, and 48 inches from the tip. This means that the butt guide will be 30 inches up from the butt end of the 6 1/2-foot rod (30 inches plus forty-eight inches equals 78 inches, or 6 feet 6 inches).

These spots are marked on the rod with a grease pencil or piece of masking tape. Since we are using two-foot guides, these spots will mark the positions of the guide rings. The best way to secure the guides for wrapping is to use thin strips of masking tape. Tape in a 1/4-inch width is best. Buy this in rolls from an art-supply store (some well-equipped component mail-order houses and tackle shops carry this also), or cut short lengths from a standard roll of 3/4- or 1-inch tape. Hold the guide in position in line with the spine (tip-top and reel-seat hoods) and wrap the tape around the foot at the frame end of the guide so that the end of the foot is exposed. This is necessary so that the thread-wrapping can begin on the end of the guide foot without removing the tape, which would loosen the support for holding the guide.

Tape both guide feet on each guide, checking each time to be sure that the guides are lined up properly. If the guides are slightly off, they are easily adjusted by slightly sliding the foot sideways or removing and readjusting the tape.

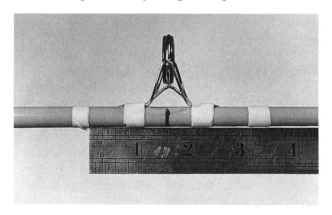

Beginning the thread wrapping by using masking tape to hold the guides in place—with the feet ends exposed for easy wrapping—and tape at the beginning of each wrap. Use a rule or calipers to check measurements on both sides of two-foot guides.

At this point, it helps to discuss ways to properly line up guides, because the methods used will be required when taping the guides down and at each step of wrapping each guide foot. The secret to good guide alignment is to check constantly and to make adjustments as necessary.

It helps to assemble the rod at this point and to exactly line up the spine marks so that the tip-top and the reel-seat hoods, previously aligned on the separate sections, are in alignment when the rod is put together. Then use a strong overhead light as before when making these alignments for the spine. There are several methods, and all should be used at one time as a check against one another.

1. Hold the rod by the butt and sight along it so that the overhead light makes a streak down the length of the rod. Then turn the rod so that the reel-seat hoods and tip-top are straight up or on top of the rod. The guide or guides taped or wrapped on the rod should be in this alignment also.

2. A variation of this, when you have several or all guides taped or wrapped in place, is to sight along the rod and look through the guide ring. If the guides are properly aligned, each smaller guide ring (looking from the butt to the tip end) will appear to be inside and concentric to the larger rings. The guides will be slightly off, but this is because the frame heights vary and also because of the natural curvature from the weight of the rod as it is held horizontally. Also, the tip-top will be slightly off, but this is because the tip-top lacks any frame to hold the ring up and in line with the rest of the guides. Any guide that is out of alignment may be easily adjusted by sighting this way.

3. Often the best way to sight is along the rod with the rod held horizontally as before but with the guides hanging straight down and the hoods and tip-top beneath the rod blank. This allows you to easily check the amount of the ring that appears on each side of the blank. In other words, the blank will hide part of the guide ring but will allow you to see the two sides of each ring. Each ring will have an open area on each side of the blank, and rotating the rod will adjust the butt guide until these two areas, or the amount of the ring showing on each side of the blank, are equal. With the butt guide in alignment, and without moving your head or the rod, run your eyes up the rod to successive guides to check each in turn. Make adjustments as necessary and recheck using this method and the other methods.

Note again that this checking is done with the guides taped in place, and again after each guide foot (not both feet or the entire guide) is wrapped in place.

Once the guides are lined up and taped down, you must make additional markings to indicate where to start the rod wrapping. Note that the wrapping is always begun on the rod blank and progresses up onto the guide foot toward the center of the guide. It helps to use thin strips of masking tape to make these marks. Also, you will want to use calipers or a rule to mark these spots evenly so that they are the same on both sides of

each guide. Also, for a tastefully wrapped rod, the length of the wrap on the blank alone (before reaching the end of the guide foot) will vary with each guide size because the guide feet will vary in length. Usually the best way to think of this is as a proportion of the guide-foot length.

A good general rule is to use a wrap on the blank of about one-half the length of the guide foot, or a total guide wrap of one-and-a-half times the length of the guide foot. Naturally, you can use more or less as desired, but a length of about one and a half, one and a third, or one and a quarter the length of the guide foot is best and makes for a neat wrap. Naturally, this makes each wrap proportional to the guide. A big guide with a 2-inch-long foot would have a wrap of 3 inches under the one-and-a-half ratio, while a smaller tip section guide with a foot length of 1/2-inch would have a total wrap of 3/4-inch long.

Using a rod wrapper or wrapping system as previously described (see Chapters 1 and 2), pick the color you desire in size A thread. Place the rod in the rod wrapper on the support arms or V block and place the edge of the guide directly over the thread-tension device. Adjust the tension so that you will wrap under pressure, but not so much pressure that you risk breaking the rod or forcing the guide foot into the blank, or so little pressure that you can't hold the guide foot securely. (The risk of using tension so tight that you push the guide foot into a thin-walled blank is not an idle fear or an impossibility. I've seen it happen among rod-builders with the philosophy that if a little pressure is good, more is better, and a whole lot is great. The thread should be under reasonable tension, but pull from the thread-tension device as you would pull line off of a reel with a smooth drag.)

Although you must always wrap from the blank toward the guide, you can wrap either from left to right or right to left. Either way works fine. Most right-handers like to wrap from left to right, left-handers from right to left. Doing this does require constantly flipping the rod, so some rod-builders never flip the rod but wrap the left side of the guide feet from left to right, and the right side of the guide feet from right to left.

One other requirement: The rod must be rotated away from you so that the thread laid down on the blank is visible to you at all times. If you wrap with the rod rotating toward you, the thread will be laid down in back — out of sight — and lead to gaps and overlapping. Before beginning, cut a 10-inch length of thread from the end, fold it over, and knot the two ends. This will be needed later to finish off the wrap.

Begin the wrap by taking one turn of thread around the blank with the end of the thread ending on the side of the guide. Wrap over this turn of thread and continue with several more wraps to secure this end of thread. After three or more turns, stop rotating the rod and use a razor blade to cut the end close to the wraps. Continue wrapping evenly and smoothly, covering the rod blank with the thread wrap. One tip to getting a tight wrap with no gaps is to keep the thread at a slight angle so that the thread being laid down is tight against the previous wraps.

Continue the wrap up onto the guide foot. At this point work slowly, since even a smoothed and filed guide foot will at first tend to cause the thread to cross over previous wraps. Once the end of the guide is secured, remove the masking tape. Wrap along the guide foot toward the center of the guide until a point about six to eight wraps or turns away from the end, or at the point where frame or support bars are attached to the foot.

Now pick up the previously made loop of thread and lay it down along the blank with the loop end at the center of the guide. It often helps to tape the knotted end of the loop to the rod blank with masking tape. Carefully rotate the rod and wrap over the loop, making sure that the wraps are tight and even. Continue to the frame or support bars, hold the end of the wrap with a spare finger, and cut the thread several inches from the rod. Tuck the end of the cut thread through the loop and slowly pull the loop tight, gradually pulling the loose thread end along with the loop beneath the thread wraps. This fastens the wrap end in place.

After pulling the loop and all the excess thread through, you must cut the thread to hide it. The method that I like best for this is to alternately work the loose end of thread right and left to open up a gap where the thread exits. Then hold a razor blade parallel to the thread wraps (at right angles to the rod blank) and cut straight down on the thread end. Do *not* use pressure that might harm the rod blank. An easy way to do this is to rock the blade back and forth slightly to be sure of cutting the thread completely with no frays and fuzz. Use a burnisher or the side of a smooth ballpoint pen case to close the gap in the wraps and smooth them.

Once the one guide foot is wrapped down, check the guide for alignment. Make any adjustments as necessary and then replace the rod in the

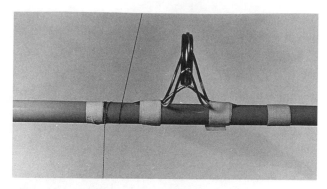

Start the thread by wrapping around the rod with constant tension, crossing over the thread with several turns to "lock" it in place.

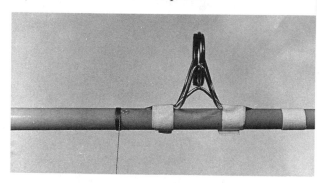

Thread wrapping began with several turns of thread, the excess clipped off and the tape marking the beginning of the wrap removed.

Continue the wrap until the thread begins to cover the exposed guide foot, at which point the masking tape is removed to allow further wrapping.

rod wrapper and wrap the other foot using the same techniques.

Note: There are other ways of wrapping, adding underwraps, and making variations of wraps. There are also variations of tucking the end of the thread under the wrap and finishing the wrap. These are outlined in detail in Chapter 22. Check this chapter for more details and information.

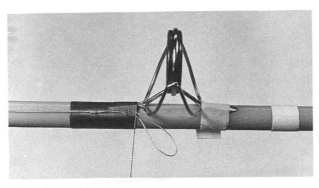

Close to the end of the wrap, a loop of thread is laid down, then wrapped over. It will be used to pull the end of thread under the wraps.

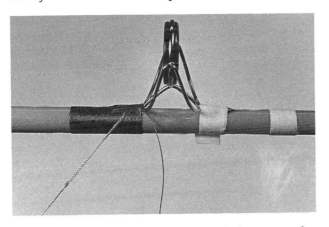

Pulling the loop of thread from under the wraps after the end of the thread is tucked into the loop.

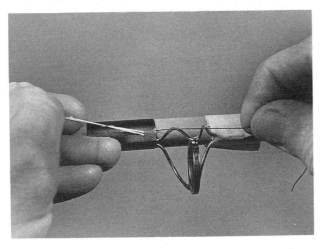

A heavier and different color thread, as shown here, helps to avoid tangles when tucking the thread into the loop and pulling the loop through.

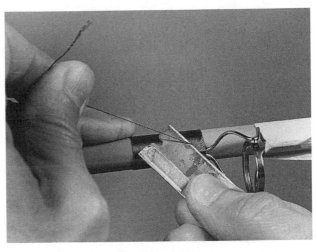

Once the end of the thread is pulled through the wraps, use a razor blade or scalpel to trim the excess. It can be cut flush like this, but there are better methods as outlined in Chapter 22.

OTHER WRAPS

In addition to the wraps made to hold down each guide, other wraps are necessary. A similar wrap, made by the same procedure above, is done at the tip-top. For standard tube tops this is strictly decorative because it is done on the blank, meets but does not go over the tip tube, and does not help to hold the tip-top in place. There are exceptions to this in that some tube tops have slight extensions on the sides that are wrapped down with thread, and the one-piece wire flexible-frame guides have two wire legs that fit on either side of the blank and are wrapped in place, this wrapping serving to hold the tip-top to the blank. There is no tube with this style of tip-top. The length of these wraps must be sized as are guide wraps (about one and a half to one and a quarter the length of the legs on the flex-guide tip-top, or for tube tops about the length of the wrap on the uppermost guide.

A trim wrap is also typically placed immediately above the winding check and handle. This can be fancy (see Chapters 23 and 24), or it can be just a simple wrap of the same color used in the guide wraps. That's what we will do for this first basic rod: Making the wrap the same way as for the guides, finishing with a loop of thread, and making the wrap aesthetically pleasing—usually about 1 to 3 inches long.

For this two-piece rod, one additional wrap is most important and is functional as well as decorative. This is a wrap at the female portion of the ferrule to give the rod additional hoop strength at this important junction. Most manufacturers recommend this, but if not, it should be done anyway. To do this, use normal tension and wrap about 1 to 1 1/2 inches along the blank. If you are using a blank with a spigot ferrule, make a similar, shorter wrap on the male side. In both cases, begin on the body of the blank and work the wrap up to the edge of the blank. To attempt to begin the wrap at the edge of the blank and work in the other direction is too difficult and will not result in the wrap being close to the blank edge. Begin and end the same as for a guide wrap. Although this is a decorative wrap in addition to being functional, some rod-builders like to "hide" it by making it the same color as the blank. To do this, choose a thread color that is close to the blank color, but when finishing the rod do *not* add color preserver. When the epoxy finish is added, the epoxy will cause the wrap to become translucent, causing it to further disappear into the blank.

PROTECTING THE WRAPS: FINISHING COATS

Once all the wraps are completed, the wraps must be protected with some type of finish. Today, the best choices are the various epoxy and polymer resins that provide high-build clear coatings that are very durable. Most are two-part with a 50/50 mix, some are single solutions. Before adding any protective finish, however, you must consider whether or not you want to use color preserver.

COLOR PRESERVERS

Color preservers are often specific to a particular brand of finish (companies that make finishes also produce color preservers) and may or may not work with other brands of finish. Thus, for starters, stay with one brand of finishes.

Color preservers have some advantages and some disadvantages. Color preservers, as the name indicates, will preserve and protect the bright color of the thread used. Thus, the color you see on the spool is the one that you will get on the rod when color preserver is used. Without a color preserver, the thread will become translucent and change color slightly when coated with epoxy or polymers. Dark colors will become darker; light colors will become lighter or in some cases almost transparent.

Second, color preservers will seal the thread against the absorption of the epoxy and thus make it easier to do rod repairs. Preventing the epoxy from soaking into the thread and "gluing" the thread to the blank aids you in removing the wrap with a razor blade.

The disadvantage of using colors preservers is that some rod-builders think the wrap is better protected by the epoxy finish soaking through the wrap, which also provides a protective coating. This is probably true technically, although the practical difference in the durability of epoxy- or polymer-protected wraps with or without color preserver seems to be nonexistent. A more serious disadvantage is that sometimes the use of color preserver can ultimately cause cracking or crazing around the guide feet or at the connection of the foot with the frame. If this is a serious consideration, the only solution is to finish without a color preserver.

The translucency and color changes in the thread caused by using finish without color preserver is preferred by some. This seems to be particularly true with fly-rod builders who like the traditional and muted tones in contrast to the bright colors found on other rods. The translucent wraps resulting from using no color preserver are more like the darkened silk wraps of early bamboo rods.

One compromise solution on rods on which an underwrap is needed is to use the color preserver on the underwrap to make for easy repairs when required, but to use no color preserver on the guide wrap. If good color combinations are chosen, the result can be very attractive, with a light-colored underwrap and a darker yet translucent guide wrap.

There are several ways to apply color preserver. One is to use a small piece of sponge and pat the preserver in place. This is not the best method for the lacquer-based color preservers of some companies but will work fine for others. A brush can also be used for any type of color preserver. You can spread the color preserver with your finger, but this is best for water-based preservers. A paper towel or rag works well but tends to be wasteful.

When coating with color preserver, first follow the manufacturer's directions. But use plenty of color preserver, completely cover the entire wrap, and add enough color preserver to soak well into the threads. This soaking will require more color preserver for heavy-thread wraps, such as for size E or EE, than it will for the thin A thread. Apply evenly and blot up any excess with a paper towel. Even when using N.C.P. thread, one coat of color preserver as additional protection against blotching or uneven finishes is suggested. However, you do not want puddles of color preserver to rest on the wrap and form a skin or thick coating. Add several coats this way, at least two and possibly three on heavy wraps when using regular (not N.C.P) thread. Blot the final coat thoroughly and allow to dry for 24 hours or until you no longer smell any of the solvent or color-preserver odor.

If you work with underwraps or double wraps, add color preserver after each layer of wrap: on the underwrap, after the guide wrap is added, and again after a second guide wrap (double wrap, if used) is added.

FINISH COATS

Finish coats today consist of varnish, two-part epoxies, and similar coatings. Be sure to use only those products designed for rod finishing. Epoxy glue is not the same as epoxy rod finish. Some finishes, such as the Gudebrod Speed Coat Rod Finish and Lamiglas U-40 Urethane Rod Finish, are one solution and require no mixing. Others, such as High Build Polymer Rod Wrapping Finish, Gudebrod Hard 'N Fast II, and Lamiglas U-40 Dura Gloss Finish, are two-part, requiring mixing to produce a thick, clear, one-coat (in most cases) rod finish.

With all of these, follow the manufacturers' instructions, but here are a few tips. For example, all of these work best at least at room temperature, and some mix better at a slightly higher temperature, such as 80° to 90°. Heat thins the liquids and makes for more accurate measuring and easier, faster mixing, and also reduces the possibility of bubbles in the mix.

For easier mixing, use craft sticks, small disposable cups (of the type used for dispensing liquid medicine), and syringes. One point about syringes: Most syringes available for medical use, and thus found in drug stores, have a light silicone coating for better lubrication. However, silicone in any form reacts adversely with epoxy and polymer finishes and may cause the finish to separate from the rod blank and wrap. Flex-Coat manufactures syringes without silicone. Another advantage is that these syringes are color-coded to correspond with the cap colors on bottles of two-part epoxy finishes. Use only these, or obtain syringes that are silicone-free. Avoid paper or wax-coated cups, because these will tend to introduce bubbles into the mix. Use nonporous plastic disposable cups, but check to be sure that the epoxy will not eat through the plastic. I've had this happen with epoxy finishes and paints when using plastic cups. Disposable or artists' brushes for brushing on color preserver and epoxy are useful. (Note that you must use different brushes for each material or clean them thoroughly between uses. Special epoxy cleaners are made for this. The disposable brushes are best because they are inexpensive and allow for one-time use with no possibility of contamination.)

You might also want to prepare a smooth surface on which to spread the epoxy mix. Aluminum foil is often suggested, but I like plastic sheets cut out from the sides and bottoms of disposable plastic food and drink bottles.

To mix the two parts of the epoxy, make sure that the liquids are at room temperature or slightly warmer. Use the graduated mixing cup or syringes to measure equal amounts of the two parts. (If you use syringes, do not attempt to clean them afterward. Just be sure you reserve one syringe for each liquid part used.) Also make sure that you mix *exactly* according to directions, usually in a 50/50 ratio. If the mix proportions are off, you can end up with too brittle a mix or a mix that is soft and even sticky. Ironically, in some cases the terms used for the parts are misleading. With most companies, part A in the finish is the resin; part B is the hardener (catalyst). However, if you get too much hardener in the mix, the result will be a soft or sticky finish. Often, rod-builders try to correct this by adding a second coat with even more hardener, on the theory that the more hardener is added, the harder the resulting finish will be. If you do by chance get a finish that is slightly soft or sticky, the solution is to mix a new batch with exact 50/50 measurements, using at least five cubic centimeters of each liquid, and to apply this over the first finish. This usually solves the problem.

Mix the two parts thoroughly, using a round or flat mixing stick. Roger Seiders of Flex Coat likes a round stick; I prefer a flat craft stick that I think mixes more rapidly and completely. Either is okay, provided that the mix is thorough. Mix evenly and thoroughly but not rapidly or with a whipping motion, because this will form bubbles in the mix that are difficult to remove and will make for an unattractive finish.

When you are sure that the mix is thorough (after several minutes of mixing), pour the solution out on aluminum foil or the plastic sheets cut from bottles and jars. Pouring out this mix will extend its working life. Another way of extending the life is to place the sheet on a tray or dish of ice cubes. Keeping the mix on a flat surface will also allow any small bubbles to pop to the surface easily. Other tips that work for most of the epoxies include:

1. If you have some bubbles in the mix at this point, hold the sheet close to your mouth and blow on the solution slowly and evenly. The purpose is not to make a breeze, but to allow your breath to drift over the puddle of epoxy. Opinions differ as to the reason, but this will usually cause any small bubbles to pop to the surface and dissipate rapidly. (Some think it is because of the carbon dioxide that we exhale; others that it is the moisture in or temperature of our breath.)

2. A hair dryer or heat lamp held over the epoxy briefly will accomplish the same thing.

3. Use at least five cubic centimeters of each solution to get exact measurements and a good mixture.

4. You can sometimes extend the working life of the mixture to about one week by placing the puddle of epoxy into the refrigerator or freezer. In some cases a freezer will ruin the mix, so the refrigerator is the safest choice.

5. Sometimes one part of the epoxy resins will crystallize. Often this occurs when the parts are stored in a cold area. Sometimes the solution can be restored by heating the bottle or jar in hot but not boiling water.

6. If you wish to check the flexibility of your chosen rod finish, mix up a small batch, pour it onto a flat surface, and allow it to cure overnight. You can then peel it off and check for stiffness, flexibility, clarity, and durability (the latter by pushing on it with a thumbnail and subsequently trying harder objects, such as a nail or knife blade).

7. You can sometimes thin epoxy or other finishes with the appropriate solvent or other methods to make a thin coat on light rods. Flex Coat recommends using a stiff brush to spread the epoxy thinly, using heat to thin the epoxy mix, and using solvents. For their products Flex Coat recommends using acetone or epoxy thinner in a ratio of one to four drops of solvent per six cubic centimeters of epoxy mix. Other products may also be thinned but will require experimentation or recommendations from the manufacturer.

Once the epoxy or finish is mixed — or when using a single-solution mix — use a small brush to add the finish to each wrap, with the rod held in a horizontal rack. Often, the rod-wrapping rack is fine for this. Strong light is necessary. I like to begin with the wraps at the tip end of the rod, because the thinner mix will work better on the thin-diameter wraps. That way, if the mix does thicken up slightly by the time you get to the other end, you will be doing the largest wraps and the larger butt decorative wrap, where a thin mix is less important.

Begin by rotating the rod and adding a thin coating of finish to each end of the wrap, in essence making a circular band of clear finish that just barely overlaps the edge of the wrap at each end. After this is done, fill in the rest of the wrap area with the brush, first working around the wrap, then working at right angles to this, parallel to the blank. The result should be complete coverage of the wrap.

To check the coverage, rotate the rod slowly and watch the streak of light that forms on the shiny liquid finish. If there are any gaps, these will immediately show up. Continue working on each wrap this way, from the tip end toward the butt end.

Once you have completed all the wraps, check again with the light to be sure there are no gaps. Also, check the underside of each wrap to see if there is any sagging from the application of too much finish. If there is, remove any excess with the brush and distribute the remainder of the finish evenly from one end of the wrap to the other.

At this point you will need a curing motor to slowly turn the rod so that the finish will not sag and drip during curing over the next several hours. For this, special motors are available, or you can jury-rig a slow-rpm motor from a barbecue grill or old clock motor. Speeds can range from about 1 rpm to about 20 rpm, with 10 rpm a good average.

Chuck the rod butt into the jaws or rod-holder of the device (see Chapters 1 and 2 for details on this), add a support to the rod two-thirds of the way up from the butt (and between guides), and allow the finish to cure in a dust-free environment. The best way to insure this is to use a vacant room or cure at night, when there is little human traffic through the house and the rod can rotate undisturbed. If you allow the rod to rotate without supervision, make *sure* that the rod is chucked so that it will not come out, and that the upper rod support will not move (clamp it down). The finish can be ruined or the rod broken if it slips off the motor or support while the motor continues to turn.

Once the finish has cured overnight, the rod is ready to be fished. For best results, use a small coating of parrafin, candle wax, or U-40 Ferrule Lube on the male section of the ferrule before assembling it for fishing. This coating will aid in keeping the joint tight and will protect the mated areas. Although wax has been widely used, U-40 emphasizes that their Ferrule Lube can be used on any ferrules (including metal ferrules) and does not collect dirt (as does parrafin), which can harm ferrules. It is a thinner material than parrafin or wax, yet it fills the pores of the blank to aid in creating a tight joint when the parts are joined while remaining easy to loosen.

Additional finishing touches can be added to the rod as outlined in Chapter 24.

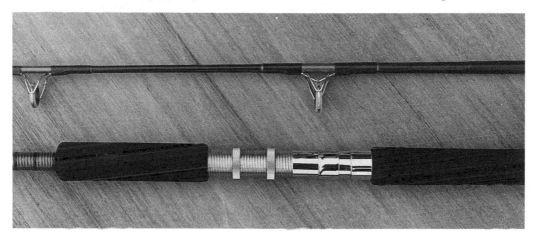

Completed basic spinning rod with simple wraps and foam handle.

19

Building Specific Rod Styles

Note: You may wish to refer to specific sections of this chapter for general ideas for building specific rods after reading Chapter 28. For details on specific aspects of rod construction, check Chapters 20, 22, 25, and 26.

INTRODUCTION

All rods have the same basic parts outlined in the previous chapter: blank, butt cap, grips, winding check, guides, tip-top, essential and decorative wrappings, and protective finishes. These parts all vary quite widely in the wide range of sport-fishing tackle and sport-fishing rods that can be built. All types of rods are built just as easily as

the rods in the previous chapter, although some require slightly different handle treatments, guide wraps, and order of assembly. This chapter discusses differences in turn, with an outline of suggested order of assembly. In some cases, this suggested order can be changed slightly. For example, in the 6 1/2-foot spinning rod of the previous chapter, the butt cap could be put on the rod first and followed by the grip, although this is not recommended. Things like that can be considered somewhat subjective. Putting the handle on the rod before wrapping guides on the same blank section is not, however, because obviously the handle cannot be slid down the blank once the guides are in place.

ONE-PIECE RODS

The differences in building a one-piece rod of any style over a two-piece rod are few. First, you will need a longer bed and working area for the rod-wrapping, because you cannot do the rod in sections, as you can with two-piece rods. You will also need more rod supports for long rods to support the ends and maintain balance as you wrap the rod. Naturally, this length and the number of rod supports will vary with the type of rod. You won't need much space with a one-piece 6 1/2-foot spinning rod; you'll need more for a 9-foot noodle rod or a 14-foot surf rod.

You will not need any reinforcing wraps at the ferrule, since there is no ferrule. Naturally, each style of rod has specific requirements and components. These specifics of components and assembly order are followed with one-piece rods just as they are for two-piece models.

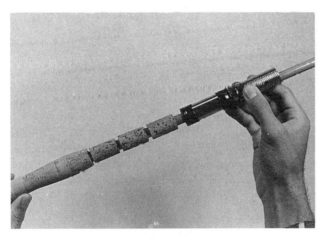

Gluing a reel seat onto a spinning rod, using cork bushings to hold the reel seat in place.

MULTIPIECE RODS

Multipiece rods are in short sections. Most are pack rods in three-, four-, and five-piece models. The difference in building these is that you will need a rod-wrap machine in which the supports can be placed close together to accommodate the short sections. Without this, you can ferrule two or more sections (any adjoining sections) to make for a rod length that is easy to work with on the rod-wrap machine. In addition, you will need to make a reinforcing wrap at each ferrule, at least on the female ferrule for 1 1/2 inches from the end, and it's suggested at the male end for spigot ferrules.

Naturally, careful consideration must be made as to guide placement on multipiece rods. If possible, it is always good to incorporate a guide wrap with a ferrule wrap, because this way you minimize the number of wraps necessary on the rod. It also reduces stiffening because all such pairings of guide and ferrule reduce the number of wraps.

Any style of rod can be built in multipiece fashion, although some require that you cut the blank and build your own ferrules to make a two-piece rod into a four-piece pack rod. (To make ferrules, see Chapter 26.)

The order of assembly in any multipiece rod is the same as for any rod of that style. There is one exception, in that with some multipiece rods there is no guide on the butt section, so the butt assembly can be done before or after you wrap all the guides on the other sections. It does not make any difference, but I like to make the butt assembly of any rod first—including the handle, grips, reel seat, and butt cap—and then wrap the guides. Most multipiece rods are of the light variety, such as light spinning, fly (very popular today), medium spinning, and some casting rods. Rarely will you find a multipiece heavy boat rod or offshore rod, although they are occasionally available and can be made by buying, cutting, and ferruling blanks as outlined in Chapter 26.

ULTRALIGHT SPINNING RODS

Ultralight spinning rods differ from standard spinning rods in that they are generally short; designed for very light reels, line, and lures; and thus built with very light-weight components.

The length of such rods varies, but usually ranges from about 4 feet to 6 1/2 feet. Most are in the 4- to 5 1/2-foot range. The blanks are light and usually designed for lures of about 1/64-ounce to 3/16-ounce. Line weights used with such rods are typically from one- to four-pound test.

As a result, components are light. Butt caps typically are of the lightest plastic or the aluminum butt-plate style. Often the grips are skeletal cork with sliding rings for less weight than the standard reel seats used with larger rods. Usually the grips are short, and 9 to 10 inches is often standard. Foam grips are heavier than cork grips and are usually avoided with these light rods. Guides also are light, with the single-foot silicon carbide style often preferred, or the very light-weight ring flex-guide style. Because of their short length, blanks are usually one piece, reducing both the cost (adding ferrules costs the manufacturer more) and the weight of the blank, as well as the possibility of any dead spots, which would be particularly critical on a light rod like this.

ASSEMBLY OF AN ULTRALIGHT SPINNING ROD

Determine the spine of the rod and mark for guide placement. Although other grip materials (foam, wood), may be used, cork ring grips with sliding rings are standard. Mount the preformed cork grip by first reaming the hole in the grip to fit the blank using a rat-tail file, reamer, or dowel wrapped with sandpaper. Once the grip is sized to fit snugly, add epoxy glue to the blank and slide the grip in place. Often these grips come in two halves (since the end is swelled to prevent loss of the sliding rings) or with a swelled cork for the end. Add one half, or the main part, of the grip and mop up any glue. Add the sliding rings, add more glue to the section covered by the remainder of the grip, slide the grip part or cork ring in place, and add a small amount of glue to the cork faces. Twist the cork pieces together, mop up any excess glue, and allow the glue to cure.

If you make the cork grip from individual cork rings, follow the instructions in Chapter 20 to make and shape the grip, adding the sliding rings at the same time.

Add a winding check with a little glue. Glue the tip-top in place in line with the spine. Place the rod on the wrapping machine and wrap the guides in place, using the spacing chart in Chapter 21. Once the wraps are complete, add color preserver and finish, turn on a rod-curing motor overnight, and the rod will be ready to fish.

LIGHT SPINNING RODS

Building light spinning rods is very similar to building ultralight spinning rods, with some few variations. Light spinning rods by general definition are slightly heavier than the ultralight models and are often longer—5 1/2 to 6 1/2 feet is more typical. They will cast lures ranging from about 1/8- to 1/4-ounce, and a fair number of two-piece models are available. The guides are the same, the grip is typically cork but often with a fixed, glued-on tubular reel seat instead of sliding rings. Foam grips can be used, but they are heavier than cork for the same length and diameter. Wrapping and assembly instructions are otherwise the same as for the ultralight spinning rod or standard spinning rod discussed in Chapter 18.

Spinning-rod handles don't have to be made of foam or cork. This handle is of wrapped heavy cord, with a glued-on reel seat.

Reel seats can be and are eliminated on some rods —the "Tennessee" handles on commercial spinning rods are an example. This similar wood handle uses a taped-on reel.

SURF SPINNING RODS

Surf spinning rods are essentially giant-sized versions of standard spinning rods. Typically called "surf rods," they are also used for coastal fishing from bridges, piers, jetties, and bulkheads. Although length will vary depending upon the application (shorter for pier and jetty, longer for high surf from the beach), most will be between 8 and 12 feet long. Some shorties of about 7 feet are sometimes found—more for pier and jetty fishing —along with some long beach models of up to 15 feet.

Often these rods are two-piece, although those in the 12- to 15-foot range are sometimes three-piece. Some are one-piece, especially those in the

8- to 10-foot range, because some anglers feel this makes a difference in strength or action. In my opinion, it doesn't, but one-piece blanks are found in some beach shops.

As a result of this range, models can be found to throw everything from 1-ounce lures to 10-ounces or more. This heavy-duty purpose requires heavy components. Most of the guides are high-frame two-foot models of aluminum oxide or silicon carbide. Cork is a good grip material, but tends to get chewed up under the harsh conditions of surf fishing and sand-spike use, so foam is often preferred. Other grips can be of wrapped, varnished cord (popular mostly on thick-diameter blanks), leather or synthetic wrapping materials (such as are used on bike grips), and cork tape (also spiral-wrapped around the blank). These thin wrap-on materials are especially good for surf rods because the thick-diameter blanks do not require a large buildup of the blank for comfortable holding, merely the addition of a comfortable nonslip material for gripping. These materials often add only about 1/8-inch to the diameter of the rod.

Reel seats are also a problem, because large-diameter models of the slip-on style are required to fit the large blanks. The graphite-fill style is popular, as is the wrap-on plate style. Because the reel seat is placed so far up the blank for leverage, often the rear grip is divided into two parts, with the bare blank showing between the two. This is more common with foam grips than with cork tape, cord, or spiral wraps. A foregrip, usually of foam, is standard.

ASSEMBLY OF A SURF SPINNING ROD

First determine the spine of the rod or rod sections and mark for guide and reel-seat placement. Although the cork tape, cord, and spiral bike wraps can be added to the blank after the guides are wrapped in place, it is usually best to follow the same order of assembly as for any basic rod. This helps to establish the proper position and alignment of the reel-seat hoods, which in turn aid in lining up the guides.

If you mount cork rings, a preformed cork grip, or a foam grip, follow the instructions previously outlined. Slide the grips down on the blank and glue them in place, leaving enough room to add the butt cap. Note that the shorter length of the two-part rear grip (one section at the butt cap and one immediately beneath the reel seat) will make it far easier to slide in place than if you were using

a full-length rear grip, which often measures up to 22 inches long. Thus, add the lower rear grip, mark the rod for the reel-seat position, and add the second rear grip. (Often, a good way to decide on the spacing for these grips is to hold the rod at arm's length to the side, with the butt end in your armpit and your hand comfortably on the blank. This marks the position for the reel seat; the upper rear grip goes immediately below this.)

Glue the reel seat in place and then add the foregrip. Add the butt cap (which, because of the large diameter of the rod blank, will not usually require shimming).

If you are making a cord-style rear grip, first determine the position of the reel seat, glue it in place, glue the butt cap on, and then wrap the cord on up to the reel seat (which was previously glued in place), using the detailed instructions in Chapter 20. Actually, this is just like making a guide wrap: Wrap over the tag end of the cord at one end and wrap to the other end (butt cap to reel seat), securing the end just as for wrapping a guide or whipping the end of a rope. Gudebrod makes a special butt cord in six colors for this type of wrap, although you can use a macrame cord or a "craft cord," available in craft shops in 1 1/2- and 2-millimeter diameters, also available in many colors.

Most rods with a cord grip still have a foam or cork foregrip for comfort. Follow the instructions just given to wrap on the spiral bike tape or special self-adhesive cork tape. These do have to be secured at both ends with a short (1/2-inch) wrap of heavy thread. A variation of this is to first wrap the entire grip area (from the end of the rod up through the foregrip area) with the cork tape, cord, or spiral tape, and then glue the butt cap over this, using the grip materials as a shim. Similarly, the tubular or wrap-on reel seat is mounted over the grip material. The grip material is secured at the upper end with a short wrap of heavy thread.

Guide-wrapping is best with an underwrap (see Chapter 22). Finish with two coats of color preserver followed by one or two coats of epoxy thread finish, and allow them to cure properly before you use the rod.

CONVENTIONAL SURF RODS

Conventional surf rods are similar to spinning surf rods, except that they are often built on heavier blanks. Often you will not see the excessive lengths used in surf spinning with many conventional surf rods in the 9-foot to 12-foot range. The choice of a conventional surf stick over a spinning rod is often made on this consideration of power and length, with the shorter, more powerful conventional rods used for heavier fishing such as drum fishing or when surf conditions and fishing dictates a heavy sinker and chunk of bait that would be difficult to cast with a spinning outfit.

The basics of building the handle and wrapping the guides are the same, except that the guides are smaller-ring two-foot styles, and one or two more are often added to the blank to reduce line-rubbing (because the guides ride on top of the blank when the angler is fighting a fish). The handle is the same and there is no difference in the reel seat, because these rods do not use trigger-style reel seats, as do shorter casting rods.

BOAT SPINNING RODS

Boat spinning rods can range from fairly simple, inexpensive models used for inshore and Great Lakes trolling to more carefully finished, finely crafted models used for offshore trolling for big game. Most are about 7 feet long, one- or two-piece, built on strong heavy-wall blanks for heavy-duty fishing. The methods of building them are no different from that outlined in Chapter 18, except that all the parts are larger and stronger. They are standard spinning rods in parts, construction, and appearance, albeit heavy "industrial strength" models. Foam grips are typical, along with heavy-duty graphite-fill or chrome-plated-brass reel seats. Guides are typically two-foot heavy-duty models. Often an underwrap, sometimes even a double overwrap (see Chapter 22) is used on these rods.

ASSEMBLY OF A BOAT SPINNING ROD

Determine and mark the spine. Using standard rod-building methods, slide the foam grip in place, then glue the butt cap on the end of the blank. (Although cork grips can be used, they are chewed up rapidly in trolling-rod holders and thus are seldom used on these rods. Even the foam grips take a fair share of abuse from this fishing and the constant pressure on the grip where the edge of the rod holder hits the foam.

Add and glue the reel seat in place, then the foregrip as previously outlined. Glue the tip-top on, add the guides, and wrap them in place. Because this is a boat rod for heavy-duty fishing,

consider using an underwrap (see Chapter 22). Complete the job with color preserver and a wrap finish and allow the finish to completely cure before using the rod.

One consideration is in the style and size of the guides. Large guides are a must, including a large tip-top. This is necessary because these rods are used for inshore and offshore trolling, where it is often necessary when fighting a fish to reel doubled line through the guides. Considering the large-size line in use (thirty-pound, sometimes even fifty-pound), the knots are large and knot clearance is a must. Often a size 16 is the smallest guide that should be used, and the largest tip available should be standard.

NOODLE RODS

Noodle rods can be either casting or spinning style but comprise a general type of design that is similar in both styles. Basically, noodle rods are long, limber rods designed for light-line fishing. Most noodle rods range from about 9 through 12 feet, although this will vary with the manufacturer. Most are very light — some are designed for lines as light as two-pound test — and usually for line no heavier than six- or eight-pound test. They are long and limber so the shock absorbency of the blank can prevent break-offs of big fish on the light tackle and line.

As a result, noodle rods are basically not unlike fly rods but are used for spinning and casting tackle and built like spinning or casting rods. With their light, limber design, they must be built with light components. Building a noodle rod is really like building a light or ultralight spinning rod in component selection, although with the length, more guides must be added to the rod to distribute the stresses and balance the line strain.

The secret is to pick light components, particularly in the guides at the upper end of the rod. Because even on spinning rods the line funnels down rapidly, the guides on the upper end of the rod can be very light small-ring-diameter one-foot guides, such as those made of silicon carbide. The handle is usually cork but often includes a threaded-barrel fixed reel seat rather than the sliding-ring style.

ASSEMBLY OF A NOODLE SPINNING ROD

First mark the spine of the rod sections and mark for guide spacing and handle placement. Assemble the handle just as you would for a standard spinning outfit. Use cork rings or a preformed cork rear grip, and glue and slide them in place. Add the butt cap, then shim the blank above the rear grip for the reel seat and add the fixed reel seat. Add and glue the foregrip. The grips should be cork for lightness. The best reel seats are those that are lightweight graphite-fill or light aluminum. Choose one-foot guides that are light in weight, and get the smallest rings suitable for the tackle. Since the guides are under the rod, you will not need them very close together, but you will need enough to distribute strain. (Check suggested guide spacing in Chapter 21). Use light thread for the wraps, and do not use an underwrap. Protect with two layers of color preserver and one coat of epoxy rod finish.

Making a casting-style (revolving-spool) noodle rod is identical, with some few differences. First, the reel seat will have to be a trigger-style, although the handle length (long rear grip and standard foregrip) will remain the same. The small one-foot guides using light guide wraps are also identical, although you will usually need more guides at the upper end of the rod to reduce line rubbing against the blank because these guides are on top of the rod as you fight a fish. The smallest, lightest one-foot guides with the lightest wrap are thus imperative to keep from ruining the action of these light rods.

CASTING RODS:
DETACHABLE-HANDLE STYLE

At one time, almost all casting rods had detachable handles. Detachable handles were sometimes specific to certain manufacturers of finished rods; in other cases, generic-style handles such as those from the now-defunct Featherweight company were available, by which a special butt ferrule (available in sizes to fit all rods) was available for gluing onto the butt of a blank, the ferrule fitting into a special handle collet. Fuji followed with a similar style and some modern versions of these from DNY (the present offshoot of Lew Childre and Sons — original distributors of Fuji) are readily available. Fenwick had a similar style when it was in the rod-blank business.

In function, what you end up with is a casting rod that might vary from 5 to 6 1/2 feet, with a long one-piece blank and a separate handle. The handle includes the grip, reel seat, and the female ferrule or collet to receive the blank ferrule. Today, most grips are vinyl, with a plastic or graphite-fill trigger reel seat and collet. Grips are

available in pistol grip or straight trigger style, and in one- and two-handed casting lengths. I've seen some handles with cork grips, but they are rare at this writing (these take specific adapters designed for the specific handles). For example, at this time Fuji (DNY) has several handle styles and two different chuck-style ferrules or adapters. The handles and the adapters are specific and can't be mixed, however.

The advantage of these rods is that rod-building involves only wrapping the guides and gluing the ferrule or butt adapter in place. The handle just fits onto the adapter and is not built. There is an important fishing advantage for the traveling angler: Since the handle can be detached, the one-piece rod blank can be placed easily in a travel-rod case or PVC-tubing case. Because the handle is removed (and because the handle makes up most of the bulk in a rod like this), you can get more rods in the case without risk of damage. The handles are easily stored and carried in a duffle bag or suitcase. Construction and assembly of a detachable casting rod is thus simple.

Begin by marking the spine for guide placement. Then, using an adapter that will fit firmly onto the butt end of the rod blank and will also fit the chosen rod handle, glue it in place using a 24-hour epoxy glue. Next, wrap the guides in place and add the tip-top. The guides can be one-foot or two-foot style. Often, this choice is made based on the power of the rod. Light rods are best with one-foot guides; medium to heavy rods will better stand the strain with two-foot guides. Make sure you have enough guides, based on guide-spacing charts. Cover with two coats of color preserver, then one coat of epoxy rod finish. Allow the finish to cure 24 hours before using the rod.

CASTING RODS
WITH PERMANENT HANDLE

Casting rods of this style have the handle glued onto the blank. They might be one-piece or two-piece center-ferruled rods, but the handle is a part of the rod, not separate. There are different choices of handle style. In the simplest, the handles are available from DNY, Amtak, or similar companies, and are simply glued onto the rod. However, because every rod has a different-diameter butt end, an adapter must be used. Thus, these look like the same chuck-style handle and adapter used for the detachable handle style, but in this case the adapter is first glued onto the

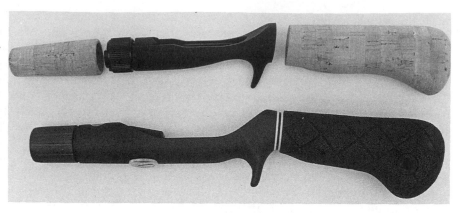

Typical casting-rod handles. The top handle is designed for blank-through-the-handle construction, with each of the parts (grip, reel seat, and foregrip) glued to the blank in turn. The bottom handle, from Fuji, uses an adapter glued to the blank, with the handle remaining detachable.

rod, then the adapter is glued into the handle. (Though some few handles are made in which the rod blank can be glued directly into the handle without the need for an adapter.) The one disadvantage of the handle/glued-adapter style is that the blank does not go through the handle, so you might lose a little sensitivity. Also, if you make a two-piece center-ferruled rod this way you would add to the length of the total rod and also to the length of the butt section. Thus, this method is generally used only with one-piece rods. But there is no handle construction, just these two simple gluing procedures, along with the guide wrapping.

Another way to make permanent-handle casting rods is to use the separate handle components available from manufacturers like Lamiglas and Weibe and glue them onto the blank. In this, the blank runs through the handle (just as for the handle on the basic spinning rod in Chapter 18).

The handle components vary widely. Most grips are cork in the straight or pistol-grip style. The rear cork grips available vary widely, from the short one-hand-casting style to the long steelhead-and-salmon style. Trigger reel seats with or without cork inserts are also available, as are cork foregrips.

Building a rod this way is much like building the spinning rod previously described.

Begin by marking the spine of the rod for the guide alignment. If you are making the rod with a separate handle, glue the adapter onto the rod blank. Then wrap the guides in place, include a trim wrap at the adapter and the tip-top, and finish with two coats of color preserver and a coat of epoxy rod finish. After this is complete, glue the adapter into the rod handle. The reason for varying from the usual instructions of making the handle first is that casting-rod handles are off-balance, either as a result of the trigger or as a

result of the offset handle, in which the grip is at an angle to the axis of the rod blank. Gluing the handle on first would make it very difficult to rotate the rod and wrap the guides in place.

The assembly of a casting rod using handle components is similar to making a spinning rod. First, glue on the preformed cork rear grip (or use foam or cork rings to make your own), then add the butt cap, glue on (with shimming, if required) the reel seat, and finally, glue on the short foregrip and winding check. Because these components are glued onto the blank, usually there is not the imbalance often found with separate handle assemblies. In any case, you can't help this, because the handle must be glued on before the guides are wrapped in place. Add the guides and tip-top, then protect them with two coats of color preserver and one coat of epoxy rod finish.

POPPING RODS

Popping rods are nothing more than very tough saltwater casting rods. They are usually about 6 to 7 feet long with a stiff power and designed for heavy saltwater lures for inshore fishing for big fish such as snook, tarpon, shark, and redfish. Most are in one piece, though some two-piece models are available. They are built just as are the rods using handle components. Any differences between these and standard casting rods of the same construction are in the components, which are tougher and heavier for the rougher fishing. Heavier two-foot guides are a must for the heavier fishing and line stress. Large guides are also helpful, even with these casting rods, because this type of fishing often requires a heavy line and a doubled leader and line and shock leader, resulting in knots that must clear the tip-top and upper guides. Thus, a size 12 ring is often the smallest found and used on these rods. They also have thick handles with a rear grip slightly longer than the one-handed casting grip and large trigger-style reel seats.

SPIN-CAST RODS

Spin-cast rods are very similar to casting rods but often have a slightly larger (by one size) butt or stripper guide. Another difference sometimes found is the use of a recessed or lowered reel seat to better allow for gripping and palming the spin-cast reels used. Thus, they are easier to build with the separate handles that allow for a recessed reel seat, which is not possible with blank-through-handle construction. Other than that, spin-cast rods are about the same as casting rods. They can be in one piece or two pieces, with permanent or detachable handles.

LIGHT FLY RODS

Although there is no real separation between "light" and "heavy" in fly rods, those that are designed to throw up to 7-weight lines can be considered light. Thus, the components must be lightweight and designed for the angler, the rod, and the fishing. Fly-rod reel seats for these rods can be as simple as a graphite-fill or aluminum-barrel seat, or as fancy as those with nickel silver hoods and exotic-wood barrel inserts. Grips should always be cork—foam and other materials do not transfer the energy or make for a good loop on the forward cast. Cork rings or preformed grips can be used in standard shapes as preferred.

Guides can be snake or the small one-foot ceramic-ring guides—traditionalists will opt for the snake guides, though these will wear in time and require replacement. Guide sizes must be chosen with care. Too large a snake guide is not necessary and on the lightest rods will even slow the action. Too small a guide, however, will restrict the flow of the thick fly line through the guides and thus limit casting distance, the ability to shoot the line on the cast, and double-hauling. There is a trend at the present time to make and fish with very light fly rods that will take the lightest possible lines, such as 3- and even 2-weights. For these you need the lightest possible snake guides, thin cork grips, and even skeletal reel seats that consist of a cork base and sliding rings to hold the reel.

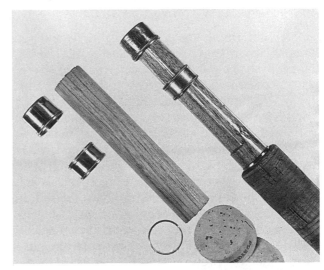

Typical light reel seat used on a very light fly rod. This reel seat uses metal sliding bands to hold the reel instead of locking nuts.

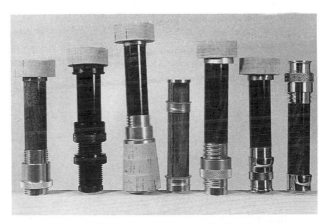

Examples of fly-rod reel seats include downlocking (far right) and uplocking models with aluminum and wood inserts. Some, such as the third from left, have a built-in extension butt. Reel seats are from Struble.

Examples of reel seats by Bellinger.

ASSEMBLY OF A LIGHT FLY ROD

First determine the spine and mark the rod sections accordingly. Then, because a fly rod has the reel seat below the grip, glue the reel seat in place. You will usually have to shim this for most fly rods, although if you use a reel seat with a wood-insert barrel, this is usually minimal. If you work with a wood-insert reel seat in which the parts are separate (that is, the fixed hood, wood barrel, and threaded portion with sliding hood and lock nut), glue the reel seat together first and then glue the completed assembly onto the rod. In all cases, make sure that the butt of the rod blank seats all the way to the bottom of the reel seat. Use a good 24-hour epoxy or similar strong glue. Next, glue the preformed cork handle onto the rod blank, or add and glue the cork rings if you will be making and shaping your own handle. Glue on a winding check. Mark the rod for the guide spacings and wrap the guides in place with light thread. Size A thread would be standard for most rods; if it is available, OO should be used for the very lightest models. Glue the tip-top in place and add trim wraps at the ferrules and just above the winding check. Add and wrap a hookkeeper if desired (this is traditional on most rods). Finish with two coats of color preserver and one coat of rod finish.

HEAVY FLY RODS

Building heavy fly rods (those of size 8 and over, for this discussion) is no different from building light fly rods except in the choices of the components used. For example, heavier reel seats are used, along with stouter (usually thicker and slightly longer) cork grips, larger guides, and more and larger stripper guides. The same reel seats are used, along with similar types of preformed grips. The choice of snake guides or one-foot ceramic-ring guides also remains. Often, you will want to go to a slightly larger tip-top ring (Mildrum makes such a tip-top for this purpose) for better clearance of the line on the cast. Other than this, the steps in building are exactly the same.

There is one exception: the very heavy saltwater or tarpon rod. These rods are designed for sight-fishing, in which a cast is not made until the fish is sighted (usually); thus these rods are built for strength and power, not all-day-long casting ease. They are built on powerful blanks with good lifting power. The reel seats are very heavy-duty, often like the U-7 Struble or similar Beard seats, and are built of anodized aluminum throughout,

with double-locking nuts and extra length to accommodate the longer reel foot of saltwater fly reels. Handles are also thicker and longer to prevent hand cramps during the long fights that entail with any hook-up of a big fish. In some cases, they even have a small additional grip above the handle as an additional grip for lifting big fish to get them out of deep water and into release or gaffing range. There are usually three stripper guides, sometimes beginning with a 16 or 20 ring size for better clearance of the line when the fish is hooked and first takes off and before the surplus line is in the water or on the reel. Snake guides are traditional running size-6 guides attached along the full length of the rod and culminating with the largest tip-top available for line clearance. In some cases, anglers even use the braced-frame tip-tops traditionally used for spinning rods because of their greater strength and larger ring size.

Construction is exactly the same as for light fly rods, including the use of strong 24-hour curing glues for the tremendous pressures and strains exerted on the equipment. Naturally, a lifting grip would be added to the rod immediately after building on the handle and before any guides are wrapped on the butt section.

FLY RODS WITH EXTENSION BUTTS

Heavy fly rods are sometimes built with permanent or removable extension butts. In some cases this is easy, in others a little more care is required. The easy part is when the reel seat purchased includes a permanent extension butt. In this case, the reel seat is glued onto the rod exactly as for any other reel seat. If the extension butt is a removable one that is part of or an option to a reel seat, then you must use care in building the rod.

First, the male portion of the extension butt that fits into the reel seat (it may screw in or slip in with O-ring fit, depending upon style) must have clearance to fit. Thus, the rod blank *cannot* extend all the way to the base of the reel seat, because this will not allow insertion of the extension butt.

First measure the length of insertion of this portion of the extension butt, add about 1/4-inch, and then cut back the rod blank by this amount on the butt end. This is assuming you are working with identical-length sections of two- or multi-piece fly rods. Failure to do this will result in the end of the reel seat extending perhaps 1 to 2 1/2

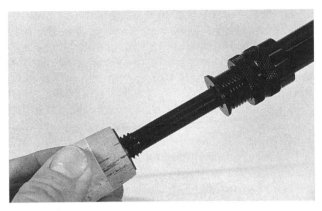

Some reel seats, such as this one from Struble, incorporate adjustable extension butts. This one screws out for a longer extension.

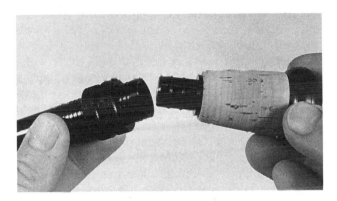

Slip-on extension butts for fly rods often incorporate "O" rings, as shown here, to hold the extension in place when needed. It is normally placed in a pocket while fishing, until hooking a fish.

Example of a homemade extenxion butt made by adding a handle to a wooden dowel, then sizing the dowel to fit into the butt of the reel seat. An open-end reel seat or one with a removable rubber butt cap is required.

inches beyond the length of the other sections. Glue the reel seat onto the rod blank, but be sure that you leave clearance for the extension butt as outlined above. Most reel seats made for this option are all-aluminum-barrel because the wood-insert types with the threaded barrels, even in an up-locking mode, would not be strong enough to hold the extension butt were it really needed.

You can also make your own slip-in extension butt by building up cork rings on a dowel that is in turn cut on a lathe to friction-fit into the open-end barrel of an aluminum reel seat (more on this in Chapter 20). In this case you still have to leave clearance in the barrel of the reel seat for the full insert section of the extension butt.

BOAT RODS

"Boat rod" is a catchall term, since it can be argued that any rod used from a boat is a boat rod. In the parlance of most angling, however, a boat rod is a heavy rod, usually for salt water, often simply built, and designed for a variety of heavy and utility boat-fishing tasks from trolling to bottom-bouncing to chumming to drift fishing.

Often, boat rods have simple wood handles, and it is this style of rod we are discussing. There are two ways to build these rods. One is to use a separate handle in which the reel seat is attached to the wood handle with a mushroom butt cap on the bottom, and a ferrule—with or without a locking collet nut—included to fit the blank to the handle assembly. Construction is just like that for a detachable-handle casting rod.

Glue the ferrule onto the bottom of the rod blank and add a foregrip of foam or cork. Foam is the most common and readily usable for these rods. Finish by wrapping the guides in place. Because ferrules usually come in only one size to fit the upper part or sleeve of the reel seat, you must shim the blank to fit the ferrule (details are covered in Chapter 20). In some cases, the wood butt and the reel seat are separate and the reel seat must be glued onto the wood handle. In this case, use a 24-hour epoxy glue to glue these parts, and make sure that the grain in the wood handle is lined up on a plane with the reel-seat hood for maximum strength. Once the reel seat is glued onto the handle, glue the blank onto the ferrule and wrap the guides in place.

Another possible construction method involves the use of wood handles that have been drilled so that the handle is glued directly onto the blank. Naturally, you must choose the right blank for each of these applications. In making a 7-foot rod, for example, you would choose a blank of about 5 1/2 feet to fit onto a ferrule to make up a 7-foot rod with an 18-inch handle, whereas you would need a 7-foot rod for the straight through-the-handle construction. Naturally, since handles are not drilled for each specific size and taper or rod blank, you must often shim the blank slightly for this fit.

Guides on boat rods are typically two-foot heavy-frame boat-rod guides, although sometimes rollers are found. Also, it is not uncommon to have a boat rod with a double-roller stripper and roller tip-top but with ring guides on the rest of the rod, or a rod with ring guides exclusively but a roller tip-top. When you wrap these guides it is best to use an underwrap, though the functional necessity of this will vary with rod power and function. Heavy rods should have an underwrap; lighter boat rods can have it but generally do not require it. Naturally, the guides must be protected with color preserver and rod finish.

OFFSHORE TROLLING RODS: ONE-PIECE

The construction of offshore trolling rods is really identical to that of boat rods, with some few exceptions. First, in most cases the one-piece rods are about 7 feet long, which is standard for most offshore trolling and boat rods. Second, because they are used for heavy fishing for big fish, they are usually built with aluminum handles, such as the bored aluminum butts from AFTCO. These are about 18 inches long and are bored with varying hole sizes to take anything from six- through eighty-pound class blanks, depending

Making offshore and boat rods requires additional attention to strength in assembled parts. This gimbal butt cap from AFTCO has special grooves on the inside for additional glued strength.

upon the size of the butt. These butts are designed to take AFTCO reel seats, so that the final result is a rod with about 5 1/2 feet of rod showing (the blank must extend to the bottom of the butt for maximum strength) and an aluminum reel seat and butt.

To build a rod this way, first check the rod blank for the spine. Glue the reel seat to the rod butt, using a 24-hour curing-strength glue or one recommended by the manufacturer. (It is easier to do this at this point, because you can smear glue on both the inside of the reel seat and the outside of the reel-seat recess on the butt. To do this after gluing the blank into the butt would risk pressing the reel seat to the blank as you slide it down, marring the blank with the glue. Then the rod is shimmed to fit the drilled hole in the handle; the bottom 18 inches of the blank is smeared with glue and slid into place in the handle. Then glue a foregrip onto the rod just above the reel seat. After this, position the guides. Generally, roller guides are used for offshore trolling rods, with a double roller used for the first or stripper guide and single rollers for the rest. Often these are sold in sets of five and are specifically designed for most trolling rods of this length. Wrapping roller guides requires an under-wrap first, followed by a guide wrap and sometimes even a double wrap for very heavy rods. See Chapter 22 for more details.

Once the guides are wrapped in place, protect them with color preserver and two coats of rod finish.

OFFSHORE TROLLING RODS: DETACHABLE-HANDLE STYLE

Offshore trolling rods with detachable butts are more common than those that are one piece. Many use an AFTCO or similar aluminum butt, either straight or curved (curved only in the heavy-duty models). Naturally, since the detachable handle takes up about 18 inches, rod blanks for this style of rod are about 5 1/2 to 6 feet long. Construction is the same as for a detachable-handle casting rod or detachable-handle boat rod. The butt is usually all aluminum with an inclusive reel seat. Some butts do not include the reel seat, and for them a reel seat must be glued on. In all cases, the handles or reel seat take a slip-on or usually collet locked-down ferrule; the ferrule and collect nut are a permanent part of the butt end of the rod blank. To build this type of rod, first glue the reel seat onto the aluminum butt, if the reel

To guard against corrosion from saltwater, this AFTCO collet on a reel seat/handle assembly has "O" rings and special seals to prevent water intrusion into the collet/reel seat joint.

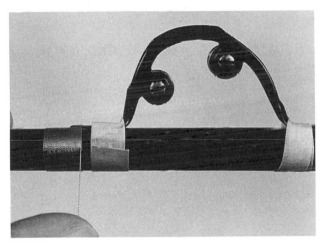

Wrapping an offshore guide is exactly the same as for any other type of guide. Here, a stripper roller guide is being wrapped in place on a light saltwater trolling rod.

seat is not included. Then glue the ferrule (with collet nut and any "O" rings or washers) onto the butt end of the rod blank, shimming at this point with fiberglass tape if required. Use a very strong or epoxy glue for this step, because this joint will be under tremendous pressure and strain during trolling and especially during a fight. Often, the

ferrules used for these heavy rods have a slot that is keyed to a pin in the handle to prevent turning and torquing. If this is the case, make sure that the ferrule is lined up properly so that the spine of the rod is properly aligned for guide placement.

Add a foregrip to the blank. Foam is typically used, although on some very heavy rods a leather wrapping over cork is preferred because it is firmer and provides a better grip.

Once the grip is in place, position the guides on the rod, add an underwrap to the rod at these spots, and then wrap the roller guides in place using a single or double wrap. Coat with color preserver, allow it to dry, and then protect the rod with a rod finish.

STAND-UP RODS

Stand-up rods are a new design of trolling rod in which the angler stands up to fight the fish, holding the rod in a specially designed harness and on a special belt that holds the gimbal at the butt of the rod.

These can be built as one-piece or two-piece rods using the same methods as for trolling rods. There are a few differences, however. First, the rods usually have a different action, with more flex at the tip end. The design is to allow for flexion to place the fish under constant pressure, with power occurring in the butt of the rod for lifting the fish and levering it in when pumping. The result is that the rod requires more guides, particularly at the upper end. Often, seven guides will be used in place of the five typically used with a standard trolling rod. The roller guides, wrap, and underwrap requirements are the same.

The second difference is that the butt sections are slightly shorter for the stand-up fishing than are the butt sections on rods used for fighting fish from a fighting chair. Most are about two inches shorter, but this will vary. The rod-handle manufacturers such as AFTCO have responded to this with models that are designed for stand-up fishing. These usually have detachable handles, and the construction of the rod with these parts is exactly the same as for trolling rods.

20

Handle and Grip Assembly

INTRODUCTION ∎ TOOLS AND MATERIALS ∎
PROFESSIONAL TIPS ∎ GLUE MIXING AND APPLICATION ∎
CORK GRIPS ∎ FOAM GRIPS ∎ GRAPHITE GRIPS ∎ WOOD
GRIPS ∎ ALUMINUM GRIPS ∎ CORD AND WRAPPED GRIPS ∎
CORK-TAPE GRIPS ∎ MISCELLANEOUS GRIPS, REEL
SEATS, AND VARIATIONS ∎ BUTT-CAP ASSEMBLY ∎
REEL-SEAT MOUNTING ∎ FERRULES AND ADAPTERS

INTRODUCTION

It seems as if everyone looks at the guide wraps on a rod, yet little attention is paid to the handle or grip and reel seat assembly. Although perhaps not as decorative as the wraps, these parts are still vital to any good custom rod. A mistake made here can be costly in terms of rod performance and difficult or impossible to repair. For example, a loose reel seat on a rod is almost impossible to repair without tearing apart the whole handle assembly or drilling one or more holes into the reel seat to inject glue. Doing nothing only results in an outfit where the reel will rotate out of line with the guides as the reel seat slides around the rod while the angler is fishing or fighting a trophy. A well-mounted and firmly glued reel seat is a must for solid rod function.

Although there are many handle types used for many different types of rods, there are some basics in construction. Using the right glues, having the right tools (though few are needed), using the right shim materials for reel seats, and taking time for all the steps that are necessary to build the handle correctly are vital to a good job.

TOOLS AND MATERIALS

A complete discussion of tools for tackle-crafting can be found in Chapters 1 and 2. Here is brief rundown of tools you may wish to consider for making handles:

Rod-Handle Seater. These are available commercially, or you can build one as outlined in

368

Chapter 2. It allows seating of foam grips made of EVA, Hypalon, and similar materials. It can be as simple as a piece of shelving board with a hole in the center slightly larger than the diameter of the blank at the point where the grip finally seats. Other possibilities include a board with a series of different-sized holes. A third possibility is an 18-inch-long board in which a long V is cut from one end; this tapered slot is slipped over the rod blank and used to push the foam grip in place. (If you use this tool, however, be sure to leave some clearance around the V — do not shove it up until it fits the blank tightly. The blank is tapered, and pushing down with the V tight at the top can jam the board on the blank or even crack it. Also, do not cut the V close to the end of the board, because this will leave little wood as a frame and the tool might split. A solution to this is to use thick plywood, because the cross-grain of the several layers will prevent splitting.)

A board with holes in it to fit the blank is ideal for pressing foam grips into place. Here a board with a disc holding a series of different size holes is used to push a foam grip onto a rod.

Cork-Handle Gluing Clamp. This also is available commercially, or it can be made by following the directions in Chapter 2. It consists of two boards with holes in the center that are connected by long threaded rods or a combination of chain (adjustable with hitch clip pins) and screw eye bolts. Wing nuts allow adjustment and tightening. This tool allows firm clamping of any cork handle after the rings are glued together. It helps to make for a professional job, eliminates any possibility of gaps between the corks, and also allows easier cleanup because the handle is glued in place.

Wood Rasp. This is the first tool you will need to shape the cork rings after the gluing clamp is

removed. A rasp can be used with a lathe or for removing cork by hand.

File. A number of files can be used for rod-handle work and are used mostly on cork handles where cork removal is necessary after roughening has been done with a wood rasp. Files should be 8 to 12 inches long, flat or half-round, and with a coarse or medium cut. If you don't already have one, buy a file card — a small wire-brushlike tool for cleaning the file teeth. Because the teeth of files fill up rapidly with cork dust, this tool is a must.

Sandpaper. Sandpaper is necessary to finish cork grips and can be used for some shaping of cut lengths of foam grips. For cork grips you will need medium, fine, and extra-fine grades. For foam grips, coarse or medium sandpaper is best for shaping the tapered and rounded ends.

Masking Tape. Masking tape is a must for keeping grips clean while they are glued. Standard 3/4- or 1-inch masking tape is fine for wrapping the ends of reel seats and grips to prevent oozing glue from touching the grip.

Reamer. Reamers are a must only when a cork grip or preformed cork grip must be enlarged to fit onto a blank. Although long commercial reamers are available, they are very expensive. The best reamers for rod-building are those in which a thin strip of coarse or medium sandpaper is wrapped around and glued onto an old scrap rod blank or wood dowel.

Contour Gauge. This is the same contour gauge described for tracing the shapes of plugs and crankbaits for duplicating. It consists of a series of metal rods in a frame: The rods are pushed against the item to be traced to duplicate the item's shape. This tool can also be used for tracing or copying the shape of a cork grip.

Glues. Glues are a must for attaching a grip or reel seat to any blank. A number of different glues are available for rod-building and sold for that specific purpose. In addition, a number of glues for general household or workshop purposes are also readily available from hardware and variety stores.

The best glues for cementing butt caps, reel seats, or grip materials to blanks (directly or through bushings and shims) are the strongest glues available. Usually this means standard epoxy glues, not the quick-set "5-minute" types that are quicker and easier to use but that have less strength.

Good glues include any of the standard epoxies on the market, such as those by Duro, Devcon,

U-40, and Flex Coat. These are all two-part, some are available in double-joined syringes for easy, accurate measuring and mixing, and all to my knowledge are a 50/50 mix.

Five-minute epoxies are similar but not as strong. Different companies rate them differently. Of two consulted for this book, one rated its 5-minute epoxy as ninety-five percent as strong as regular 24-hour epoxy; the other company rated its epoxy as eighty to eighty-five percent as strong as 24-hour epoxy.

Ribbon, paste, and clay-type epoxies are also available. They have been well received in the past by some rod-builders but are generally not as strong as the standard 24-hour epoxy. The reason is that they are paste or claylike, and although they won't run and thus are handy for filling large voids and gluing reel seats in place, they also won't "wet" as well, one of the important characteristics any glue needs to form a good bond.

Paste, clay, or other high-viscosity epoxies, such as PC-7, Duro Master Mend Ribbon, and Devcon 5 Minute Epoxy Gel, can be used for roughly forming bushings that are sized to fit a blank and reel seat. Allow the epoxy to cure and then glue the bushings to the rod blank and reel seat using standard 24-hour liquid epoxy glue.

Another problem with the high-viscosity glues is in the mixing. Even though the two parts of are two different colors to aid in determining a complete mix, they are by their nature difficult to mix completely. In the words of one manufacturing spokesman, if they are not mixed completely, "You have big problems. They don't cure well and are very messy."

Acrylic glues are also very strong—just as strong or stronger than epoxies, according to one manufacturer—but they are more difficult to work with. In short, they allow less working time. They come in two separate parts. One part, the resin, is applied to one surface; the other part, the activator, is applied to the second surface. When the two surfaces make contact, the resin and activator mix and the glue bond is complete. You do have a few seconds to adjust the parts and move them, but this is not normally time enough to adjust reel-seat-hood alignment. These glues would be impossible to use when sliding a foam or preformed cork grip in place on a blank and are best suited for gluing reel seats to bushings or butt caps to blanks or bushings. Thus, instead of mixing different glues for different parts of the assembly process, it is generally better to use epoxies throughout.

PROFESSIONAL TIPS

There are several tips for assembling rod grips and reel seats. One of the best of these is to wrap two to three layers of standard 3/4- to 1-inch masking tape around the end of parts that are to be joined, such as a grip and a reel seat, or a grip and a butt cap. The technique for this is to wrap the tape tightly and to make sure that one edge of the tape touches the edge of the grip or reel seat. In the case of reel seats, it also helps to try to force the tape into various indentations in the reel seat, such as keyways for sliding hoods and the ends of threaded barrels. When you are wrapping around the fixed end of the reel seat, the bulk of the hood may force you to stretch the tape

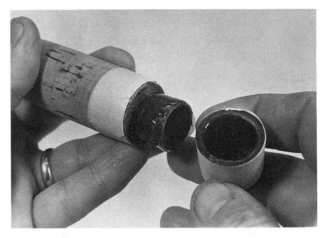

Using tape around both parts when gluing is one of the professional tips to use when gluing parts together. It is ideal for gluing on butt caps (shown), grips, reel seats, and foregrips.

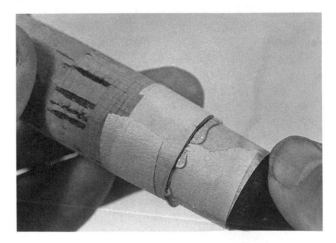

Once pressed together, any excess glue oozes out onto the previously-wrapped parts. A quick clean up with a rag, then removal of the tape, makes for clean joints.

(masking tape is slightly flexible), or you may have to wrap as tightly as possible around the bulk of the hood but then push the masking tape into place at the edge of the reel seat. In some cases, using thinner tape, such as 3/4- or 1/2-inch tape (available in art-supply stores), in place of 1-inch and 2-inch tape will make this step unnecessary.

It also helps to fold over about 1 inch at the end so that you have a tag end to pick up to remove the tape once the two parts are joined together.

This step must be done on both the parts to be joined. The purpose is to prevent glue from marring the parts and to make cleanup quick and easy. As an example of this technique, let's assume that you have a rear cork grip on a blank and are adding a reel seat. Tape several times around the end of both the reel seat and the cork grip. To glue the reel seat in place, you usually must shim the blank with a wrapping of thread or cord. Do this to build the blank area up to the internal diameter of the reel seat and then soak it with a good 24-hour epoxy glue. Slide the reel seat onto the blank and over the shimmed area. As you slide the reel seat in place, rotate it to spread any glue, and work slowly so that air gaps and bubbles are minimized.

Slowly join the two parts, at which time glue will ooze out and usually build up on both the end of the reel seat and the end of the cork grip. This is the reason for the tape — the glue will be on the tape, not the grip or reel seat. At this point, use a soft rag or paper towel to carefully remove any excess glue. Take care that glue does not get on the reel seat or cork grip while you are doing this. Once the excess glue is removed, line up the hoods of the reel seat with the glue alignment marks (the spine of the rod). Then carefully remove the tape first from one part, then from the second. Doing this will remove all of the glue that otherwise would have smeared on these parts or required a cleanup with acetone or fingernail-polish remover. The result is a clean, perfect joining of the two parts that requires no lengthy or special cleanup procedures.

Another tip is to sand or otherwise roughen all parts that are to be glued. First, remove the gloss finish from the rod blank where any grips, butt cap, reel seat, or reel seat shims will be placed. Because almost all rods have a glossy finish, removing this finish with steel wool or light sandpaper will give the rod more "tooth" for a better adhesion of the glue to the blank. Al Jackson, rod designer for Lamiglas, strongly re-commends fine (maroon color) 3M Scotch-Brite, because it will remove the finish without destroying the graphite or glass fibers.

First measure exactly the location of the grip, grips, or reel seat on the blank and mark the spot with a pen or masking tape. To prevent slips and damage to the exposed portion of the blank, cover a few inches of the blank above the grip/reel seat area with masking tape. Then use fine sandpaper or steel wool to remove the gloss. Sand longitudinally, across, and at angles to assure a good roughening of this area of the blank. Do this only until the blank looks dull, because the purpose is not to sand down to the fibers but only to remove the shiny finish.

Also, sand or file the inside of the reel seat. Depending upon the size of the reel seat, there are several ways to do this. For large reel seats such as might be used on saltwater rods, the simplest way is to wrap sandpaper around your index finger and work the finger around on the inside of the reel seat with a rotating motion to thoroughly abrade and scour the finish. Some reel seats, such as the Fuji brand, have longitudinal grooves inside to aid in gluing, but additional abrasion also helps. For small reel seats, you can use a rat-tail file to abrade the inside surface, or use sandpaper wrapped around a file or wood dowel. A rat-tail file can also be used to abrade the smooth surfaces sometimes encountered on the insides of some foam grips and to roughen the insides of preformed cork grips. You can fasten the file or dowel sander in a vise and move the reel seat against the tool rather than try to hold the reel seat (you can't clamp it — it will scratch) and work the tool at the same time.

If you are making a grip from cork rings, usually the hole in the cork will be rough enough from reaming to fit the blank. If not, use a file or reamer. It also helps to slightly abrade the faces of the cork rings, laying the sandpaper and the cork-ring face flat on a work surface and sanding with a rotating motion. Make sure that this is a light sanding only, however — too rough a sandpaper might roughen the adjoining faces so much that they allow noticeable glue gaps between the rings.

Butt caps can also be roughened for better adhesion. Aluminum butt caps are easily abraded with medium sandpaper. Rubber or plastic butt caps are best abraded with a coarse or rough sandpaper moved in a circular motion to scour the inside.

Another tip is to *never* touch the blank, inside the reel seat, inside the butt cap, or inside any other surface that will be glued, after you've removed the gloss finish or roughened the surface. Touching these parts at this point can introduce oils and otherwise contaminate them so that there is poor glue adhesion. Thus, hold the rod blank above or below the sanded point, and do not touch it or the reel seat internal diameter or any other parts to be glued.

Remove any sanding dust with a clean cloth. One good way to thoroughly clean these parts (after sanding and abrading) is to use regular drug-store isopropyl alcohol. Isopropyl alcohol is a cleaning solution for liquid epoxy glue and will not harm the blank or any of it parts or affect the glue or bond. Be sure to allow all of the alcohol to evaporate before using glue.

GLUE MIXING AND APPLICATION

Glues that are in two parts must be mixed thoroughly before use. This includes epoxies, acrylics, and any similar glues. In almost all cases the mix is 50/50, but in all cases follow the manufacturer's instructions as to percentages or proportions by volume or weight. Most glues include mixing and application instructions in the package.

For any glue, hold the tube or syringe upright (tip up) to allow for any air bubbles at the tip to rise. Puncture the tip or cut off the end (in the case of the syringe-types).

There are several options for mixing surfaces. One is to use paper or cardboard. Some rodbuilders like to use the larger size Post-It notes from 3M, because these are large enough for mixing and will peel off easily for a new surface with each new mix. Cardboard is also good, and because it is stiffer than paper, it will not wrinkle or fold on you, as might occur with paper. I like to use small sheets of scrap plastic I cut from the sides and bottoms of milk, juice, and other disposable food and drink containers. They are smooth, easy to mix on, do not allow absorption of the glue into the mixing surface, and cost nothing.

Begin by spreading out two equal ribbons of each part of the glue on the mixing surface. If you are using the syringes, the glue is measured for you. If you are using glue supplied in separate tube containers, it's easy to roughly measure the same amounts of resin and catalyst. If you are mixing a lot of glue, spread the glue in several double ribbons instead of one long ribbon, be-

cause this will concentrate the glue and make it easier to mix.

Once the glue is spread out, your working time will be about 5 minutes for the 5-minute epoxies, and about 30 minutes to 1 hour for the 24-hour epoxies. The best spreaders are tongue depressors (though they are a little wide for this), Popsicle sticks (also called craft sticks and sold for this purpose in craft and hobby shops), craft picks (small and thin, almost like a toothpick, but about 3 to 4 inches long), and cooking skewers (available in food markets for kabob and skewer cooking and ranging from 4 to 12 inches long). I like the craft or Popsicle sticks best, because they are flat and allow for easy folding, blending, and mixing. Use the mixing stick to fold back and forth, mix in circles, and even to scrape along the mixing surface to thoroughly mix both parts of the glue.

Once the glue is mixed, apply it to both the surfaces to be glued. Apply it evenly but use a thin coat, because otherwise the glue might drip and run even before you get the two parts together. This method is best for gluing butt caps to rod blanks and bushings, and reel seats to bushings. It is not good for gluing cork rings or foam grips to the rod blank or when the reel-seat internal diameter is close to the outside diameter of the blank. In these cases, adding glue to the lumen of the part to be slipped on will only end up smearing glue on the rod blank, which will have to be cleaned up before it sets up and hardens. For these cases, the best procedure is to add a little excess glue to the blank or bushing and then use a rotating and reciprocating (back and forth) motion on the slip-over performed grip, reel-seat cork ring, or other part to assure good wetting of that part and a good glue bond.

In gluing parts, be sure to use the taping method to keep excess glue from the blank, reel seat, or grip materials.

Once the parts are glued, it is important to *immediately* line up critical parts such as the reel-seat hoods, tip-top, and perhaps the grain of wood handles. Line these up with the spine of the blank and future position of the guides. Once this is done, *do not* touch or move these parts, because the glue bond will begin to gain its strength almost immediately and will gain sixty to seventy percent strength within the first few hours, in the case of 24-hour epoxies. Often, it is best to prop the rod blank straight up, using masking tape to tape it to a workbench temporarily while the glue cures overnight.

Heat has often been suggested for increasing

strength and decreasing curing time with glues. Heat will decrease curing time because it will increase the catalytic reaction. It may also *slightly* increase the strength, though glue technicians differ in their opinions on this. Some suggest there is no real strength advantage; others claim there is a slight increase in strength with the molecular changes caused by the heat. The decrease in curing time is generally not important because overnight curing is not really an inconvenience. It is important that all glue technicians agree that *too much* heat will *decrease* the strength of a bond. Most who recommend heat suggest using temperatures of from 100° Fahrenheit to 120°. Higher than that will weaken the bond and cause it to become brittle and shrink somewhat — causing the two parts to separate. Some ways to heat include using heat lamps, any light bulb at close range, a 250-watt photoflood lamp kept several feet away, and even a hair dryer propped to blow on the glued area.

Epoxy cleanup can be easily accomplished when it is still liquid with acetone or isopropyl (regular rubbing drug-store) alcohol. Of the two, acetone is more expensive, more difficult to get, more dangerous to use (because of the fumes and the chance of skin contact), and when used in excess can dissolve or react with the resins used in the gel coat of a rod blank, possibly ruining the blank. Alcohol will not create such a reaction and will clean up any spilled glue equally well. Use a rag dampened with alcohol (or acetone) and wipe rapidly and firmly to remove the liquid glue *before* it sets up.

CORK GRIPS

Cork grips are made from cork rings 1/2-inch thick (most of the time — some 1/4-inch rings are available) and are available in diameters of 1 1/8, 1 1/4, and 1 1/2 inches. Occasionally, rings of 2 inches in diameter are available for extra-heavy rods and surf rods. Buy the best quality cork rings possible. There are no standard cork-industry terms for the best-quality rings, but catalogs will usually indicate quality, as will the price of the rings. Naturally, cork can be used for shimming reel seats, in which case poorer-quality, less-expensive rings can be used.

Buy cork rings that are larger than the diameter of the cork grip you intend to make. Regardless of the care you exercise, the cork rings will not line up exactly and will have to be rasped and sanded into final form and shape. Use 1 1/8-inch-

diameter cork rings for fly rods; 1 1/4-inch-diameter rings for spinning, casting, spin-cast, and most freshwater rods, some heavy fly rods, and light-tackle saltwater rods; 1 1/2-inch-diameter rings for heavy boat rods, medium to heavy saltwater rods, and medium surf rods; and 2-inch-diameter rings for the heaviest of offshore rods (80- and 130-pound class) and very heavy surf and specialty rods. It is best to choose rings with the smallest possible available hole size, because it is far easier to ream out a ring to fit a blank than to build up or shim the blank to fit a large-hole ring. The exception to this might be with heavy rods or heavy surf rods because the diameters on these are large, and a larger ring hole will mean less reaming and rasping.

Steps in adding cork rings to make a grip are simple, yet some tips will make it easier. Begin by selecting top-quality rings, two for each inch of grip length. Slide the ring over the blank to the handle area to check for size. Remove the ring and ream it to fit, checking frequently on the blank to get a snug but not loose or too-tight fit. Use a pencil or pen to number this ring (number it 1) on its face. Repeat with each ring in turn, and continue numbering to keep the rings in order. The rings should be kept in order because the taper of the rod blank will dictate a slightly different internal diameter for each ring.

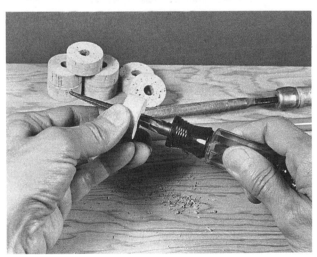

Using a reamer to ream out each cork ring to fit the rod blank.

Once all of the rings are reamed to fit, they are ready to slide in place, usually butting up against a butt cap (as with a rear grip) or reel seat (as with a foregrip). Wrap several layers of masking tape around these parts so that the glue will not touch the reel seat or butt cap and the joint can be cleaned as outlined.

Use a good bonding glue, such as 24-hour epoxy glues, Gudebrod Liquid Rod Cement, Flex Coat Rod Builders Epoxy Glue, U-40 Rod Bond, or U-40 Cork Bond. I like the epoxies best for the general bonding of all handle, reel-seat, and grip parts. After mixing the glue (if necessary) according to directions, smear a light coating onto the blank in the grip area. Do *not* place any on the cork rings or into the cork-ring hole, because this will only smear glue onto the blank as you slide the ring in place.

Gluing cork rings onto a rod blank.

With the glue *on the blank,* slide the first ring onto the blank, twisting and rotating it to assure good glue adhesion to the blank. Once the first ring is in place against the reel seat or butt cap, use a cloth or paper towel to wipe any excess glue off the masking tape. This will prevent the glue from flowing onto the covered part and making cleanup more difficult. Slide the second ring in place, but before seating it against the first ring, smear a small amount of glue onto the adjoining faces of the two rings. Bring the rings into contact with each other and twist them together to assure good bonding. It also helps to use a push-board such as that used for pushing foam grips into place. This tool can be made with the hole in the center of the board, with different-sized U-shaped slots in a side, or with a long V slot cut into the long side. Any of these variations will work well.

Continue with each ring in its turn until the grip is complete. At this, point wipe up any excess glue from the cork rings, wipe again the glue from the masking tape, and then remove the masking tape.

While it's not absolutely necessary, it helps to use a gluing clamp on the grip during the curing process. The clamp can be used just on the grip itself or it can be extended from the upper end of the cork-ring grip to the end of the rod. Tighten the grip and wipe it free of any glue that oozes out from between the cork rings. Do *not* overtighten, because this will squeeze glue out from between the cork faces and lessen the strength of the glue bond.

An additional step can be followed for more

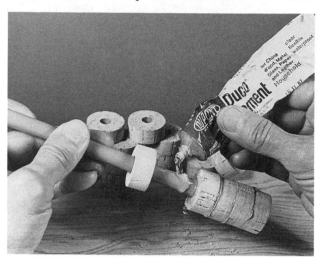

For proper gluing, each cork ring must be glued to the rod blank and to adjacent cork rings. Once all the corks are added, excess glue must be wiped off and the grip allowed to cure.

strength in the grip, if desired. Cut each cork ring with a slight bevel or taper on each face for an additional gluing surface in this area. To do this, size and ream each cork ring and then, using a countersink or small half-round file, cut a bevel into each ring face. This slight bevel allows for a buildup of glue for greater bonding strength. Be sure to add a little (not too much) glue to this area and to twist each new ring against the adjoining one to spread the glue for maximum bonding.

Another similar and equally good tip is to use a triangular file to cut several (three or four) grooves on the inside of the hole in each cork ring so that there is a buildup of glue in this area to keep the bond from breaking free and the ring from rotating on the rod blank. Naturally, both of these steps can be used for additional bonding. Just be sure that you do not make too much of a

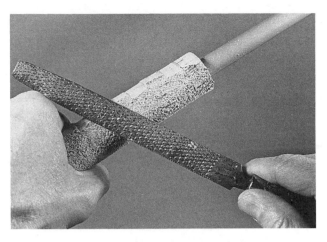

Methods of assuring that cork rings are securely glued to the rod blank include cutting three or four grooves into the hole in the ring (left) or cutting a bevel (right, using a countersink as shown) into the two edges of the ring. Both methods assure a bead of glue at these points to lock the cork ring in place.

Using a rasp is one easy way to remove excess cork when shaping the grip. Follow directions in the text to remove cork evenly around the perimeter of the grip.

bevel or too deep a groove, which will prevent contact of the cork internal diameter with the blank.

Once the cork grip is cured, remove the clamp. There are several ways to finish the cork grip. One is to place the rod into a lathe, making sure that you have plenty of rollers to support the rod blank and prevent it from whipping around (and breaking) as you turn the grip down. Also, even though you have rollers on a lathe, wrap the blank with several layers of masking tape at the blank/roller contact point to protect the blank finish. The taped blank, not a bare blank, runs on the rollers. Naturally, it helps if you have a lathe with rollers that surround the blank to prevent it from coming loose. The usual arrangement is to have two rollers for the blank to ride on, with an additional one or two above the blank to hold it down and prevent it from jumping out. Turn the lathe on at the lowest possible speed to see if the rod blank will run without whipping. Then gradually increase the speed. Once the lathe is running at the right speed, begin shaping the cork.

Note: Although any speed in the lathe can be used, manufacturers use about 3,500 rpm for shaping cork. Keep in mind that cork is an extremely abrasive material that will dull cutting tools quickly. If you are using a cutting tool, be sure to check it frequently and to keep it sharp.

One of the best ways to shape cork is with a rasp or file. To do this, with the blank secured in the lathe first use a rasp or coarse file along the length of the cork grip to bring the rings to a uniform diameter. Then use the same tools to lightly shape the cork grip into the desired shape. For spinning and casting rods, this will likely be a smooth uniform cylinder or fat cigar shape. For fly rods, there are a number of choices of grip shape, including full Wells, half Wells, cigar, reverse half Wells, western, and Payne. Do *not* take the cork down to the final diameter desired. Since the rasp or file is rough, you will need to use successively finer grades of sandpaper to smooth the grip. Stop the initial shaping when the grip is about 1/8- to 3/16-inch larger in diameter than the final size desired. Also, be sure to stop the lathe before checking the diameter with a template, calipers, or rule.

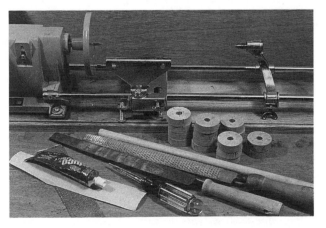

A small simple lathe can also be used for making cork grips. Here the tools and materials needed are shown.

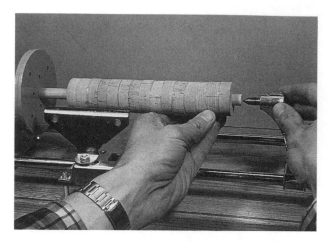

Cork rings glued to a wood dowel are mounted in the lathe.

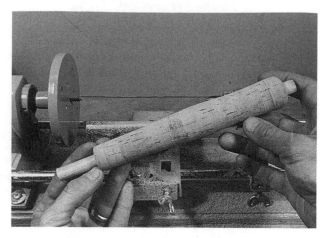

Finished shaped cork grip on wood dowel. The dowel is then removed to glue the grip onto a rod blank.

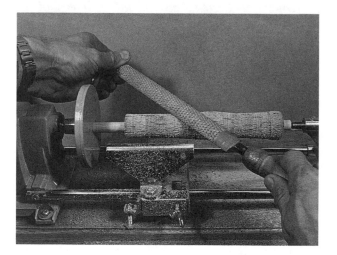

Using a rasp for initial shaping of the cork grip.

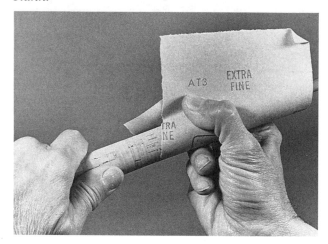

Successively finer grades of sandpaper are best to polish the cork grip.

Once you have the general shape, start the lathe again and use medium sandpaper on the grip, then switch to finer grades until you are using the finest possible grade for the smoothest finish. In fact, a tip from lathe woodworkers is to finish by using the lathe dust and the backing of the sandpaper to get the smoothest finish.

One tip, which I hope will not be necessary, involves the possibility of uncovering a pit in the cork while initially turning the cork to shape. If this occurs, stop and fill the pit with a mixture of cork dust and glue, but do not use the very hard glues, such as epoxies. (I like Gudebrod Liquid Rod Cement.) Mix the dust and glue and fill the pit to slightly overflowing to allow for some shrinkage. Allow this to cure overnight and then continue the shaping, using the lathe tools and sandpaper. Use care, because some glues are so hard that the cork around the filling will cut away,

leaving a "bump" of filler in the grip. If the repair is done right, the patched area will be as smooth and level as the rest of the grip.

Another way to do this is to wait until the cork grip is complete and smooth and then fill the pit with the cork-dust-and-glue mixture and allow it to cure overnight. Then sand to shape using an emery board. The stiff emery board allows sanding in the immediate area so that you do not affect the previously shaped grip, as well as rapid shaping and finishing. Begin with the coarse side of the emery board; finish with the fine side.

If you do not have access to a lathe, you can shape a cork grip with hand tools. Use a rasp first and remove cork using even strokes from one end of the grip to the other. Do this along one part of the cork grip so that you slightly flatten that side. Then turn the grip over 180 degrees and do the same on the opposite side. Now turn the cork grip

90 degrees and remove cork again to slightly flatten the area, and then turn this 180 degrees for more removal of cork. The result at this stage is a cork grip with four slightly flattened sides. Now remove cork from the "corners" to make a grip that is slightly octagonal. Then use the rasp to knock off these corners to make the cork grip truly round. Working this way assures that the cork grip will not end up either angled or off-center.

Once the grip is roughed out this way, use the same technique to shape and taper the ends or middle, depending upon the type of grip you want. Finish by hand-sanding with successively finer grades of sandpaper, beginning with a medium grade and working to the finest grade available.

Preformed cork grips are available in a variety of styles and lengths for spinning, casting, spincast, fly, noodle, and saltwater rods. These do not require any finishing but do require slightly different mounting methods.

First, buy the grip with a hole diameter similar to—but smaller than—the diameter of the blank where the grip will be mounted. Slide the grip onto the blank to check for size.

If the grip does not fit, remove it and use a long reamer or sanding reamer to taper the hole in the grip to size and shape. Remember that you must remove more material from the butt end of the grip than from the forward end due to the taper of the rod. Take care in doing this, because a natural tendency is to end up removing more from each end than from the middle. Try to work evenly and smoothly to remove cork from all parts of the hole uniformly. Since you will be sliding the entire grip into place, it is generally best to have a slightly looser fit than you would with individual cork rings. Otherwise, the tendency of the cork grip will be to act as a squeegee and push the glue ahead of it down the blank.

Another solution here is to wait until the epoxy glue is fairly close to setting up, so that the glue will be stiffer and less likely to be pushed along the blank. Naturally, this is also a little more hazardous, because you do not want to get to the point where the glue is so stiff that it will not adhere to the cork or so close to setting up that you can not push the cork grip completely into place.

Once the grip is sized to fit, cover the adjoining butt cap or reel seat with masking tape to protect it. Smear glue onto the blank and then slide the grip onto the blank. Slide it over the glued area, working it back and forth and rotating it to get complete glue distribution and good adhesion.

Another possibility, although it's seldom done, is to make your own preformed grips by building up cork rings on a dowel, old scrap blank, or threaded rod, and then remove the grip for gluing onto the blank. Do *not* add glue to the mounting surface, because this will not allow removal of the grip from the dowel, blank, or rod. The main advantage of this method is that you can make grips in advance. You can also turn the grips on a lathe for easy, quick shaping without fear of damaging the rod blank. It is an additional advantage if you wish to make a preformed grip that is completely different from one commercially available—one with insert rings of plastic or wood or of an unusual shape, for example.

FOAM GRIPS

Foam grips of EVA, Hypalon, and similar dense-foam materials are readily available. They are used for rod-blank grips, bike handlebar grips, and some tool-grip applications. They are heavier than cork grips (sometimes up to five times heavier) and thus are not recommended for ultralight and light rod blanks, nor are they recommended for fly rods where a firm grip is required to punch forward on the final cast.

In some cases you may find that you have to ream out a foam grip to fit a blank. As stated earlier, foam grips should be bought with a hole diameter about two-thirds to three-quarters of the blank diameter where the grip is to fit. This allows for expansion of the foam grip onto the blank for a solid fit. If the hole in the foam is too small, however, it will not fit, will not allow the grip to go on completely, and may split or crack the blank, particularly light-wall blanks. To prevent this, ream out any foam grips that may be too small. One easy way to do this is to get a drill-bit extender and some rotary-rasp drill rasps. The bit extender is usually about 12 inches long and will fit into any 1/4-inch chuck electric drill. The other end will hold (by means of a set screw adjusted with an Allen wrench) any 1/4-inch-shank of a rotary bit or file. Start the drill and slowly run the rotary rasp in and out of the hole in the foam. The foam will expand around the bit (you can feel it under your hand as you do this) but the bit will in time ream out the entire length of the grip. If the grip is longer than 12 inches, work alternately from both ends.

The best way to add a foam grip to a blank is to use a lubricant—preferably of glue, which will also hold the grip in place — and to push the grip down the blank using a pushing board. Another solution is to use a lubricant of isopropyl alcohol on the foam grip (with glue on the blank) and immediately slide the foam grip in place. Because the alcohol is a solvent for the glue, the effect on the glue will be minimal. The alcohol will, however, aid in lubricating the blank-to-foam-grip surface, particularly if the foam grip starts to "grab" the blank above the glue. Once it reaches the glue, the glue will serve as additional lubricant.

Naturally, this will push glue ahead of the foam grip, because the grip will act as a squeegee on the blank. Tape both the end of the foam grip and the adjoining part (usually a butt cap or reel seat) so that the glue ends up on the masking tape for easy cleanup, not on the rod component.

GRAPHITE GRIPS

Graphite grips are available from some component-parts houses. These are essentially cylindrical tubes of graphite material — almost like parallel-side graphite blanks — that are used for the popular tape-on Tennessee-style handle used in the South to tape spinning reels to rod handles. (Standard clamping-type reel seats are not used.) Although the same thing can be done with cork grips, one of the advantages of graphite is that it will provide greater sensitivity through the handle, provided that graphite or hard bushings are used. Some kits are available that include the graphite tube, two end caps (one is either drilled for the blank or must be drilled for the blank), and graphite bushings that must be drilled to fit the blank but that are sized for the grip. Some, designed for removal of the reel, include two slip-on bands to hold the reel foot.

Building these is a simple two-step operation: First glue the bushings in place and then glue the graphite tube or sleeve to the bushings. Measure the position of the grip and mark it on the blank. Then mark the positions of the bushings, because these usually are not as long as the handle. Use regular 24-hour epoxy glue to glue the bushings onto the blank. Allow the glue to cure overnight and then glue the graphite grip to the bushings. In both cases, use plenty of glue for a secure bond.

In some cases, bushings may not be available and must be made. In this case, use the tips suggested on page 387. Be sure to use firm bushing materials, such as graphite material (this is best) or cork rings, wood bushings, or molded epoxy

bushings (made from paste-type high-viscosity-epoxy glues).

WOOD GRIPS

Although wood grips can be used on any rod, they are generally used for the rear grip on boat and inshore trolling saltwater rods. This is because these rods are primarily used in rod holders and are not held except during the fighting of a fish, and then are held mostly by the foregrip, which is usually more comfortable cork or foam. Wood is durable and a good grip material from that standpoint, but it is too hard to be comfortable for rods that are held and cast.

Wood grips are available drilled straight through for through-handle construction, or undrilled. In the latter case, they are primarily used with reel seats that have a built-in slip-on or screw-down ferrule; the end of the rod blank stops at the ferrule, and the rod breaks down at this point.

Most of these wood grips are about 18 inches long and include some sort of recess at the bottom for a gimbal knock or mushroom-style butt cap and a recess at the upper end to hold the reel seat. Often they are made specifically for certain reel seats, which will glue on without shimming or requiring the recess to be cut to a smaller diameter.

To glue the drilled wood grips onto a blank, first check the fit of the blank and grip. If the blank is too large to go completely through the hole in the grip, use a long reamer, rat-tail file, or 12-inch drill bit (known as electricians', aircraft, or extended bits) to drill out the wood grip close to the size of the blank. Often this means drilling the top end with one size bit and using a larger bit to drill the butt end. Use calipers first to check the diameters of the hole in the grip and the outside diameter of the blank before drilling.

Once the grip is drilled and sized properly (with no play or slack), measure the wood handle's length on the blank, remove it from the blank, and spread mixed epoxy glue thoroughly over this measured portion of the blank. Slide the grip down into place, using a rotating motion to assure a good wetting of the inside of the grip and a good bonding of the two parts. Do this over old newspapers, because excess glue will be squeezed out during this procedure. Once the grip is in place, mop up any excess glue and rotate the grip so that the wood grain is in line with the spine of the rod blank for maximum length. Allow the glue to cure overnight.

Wood grips that are not drilled are intended to be used with blanks that end in the ferrule/reel-seat combination. These require no installation and are covered later in this chapter.

ALUMINUM GRIPS

Aluminum grips are available straight or curved, bored (for blank through-construction) or unbored, with reel seats (such as the Unibutt) or without, in sizes to fit any saltwater fishing need, and in anodized finishes of black, silver (natural), and black-and-gold.

Most of these grips have been described in Chapter 17. Assembly of the unbored grips involves gluing the rod butt into the ferrule that comes supplied with the reel seat. Because these assemblies are used on heavy saltwater rods and because of the excessive strain to which these rods are subject, matching the rod butt to the ferrule is critical. For example, many rod manufacturers include special bushings as an integral part of the butt end of trolling-rod blanks; these bushings fit specifically into special ferrules from AFTCO, Fin Nor, and other manufacturers. In turn, manufacturers of the reel seats and grips usually have specific ferrule internal diameters so that rod manufacturers can match them or so that rod-builders can cut down the rod-blank butt end, if necessary, to precisely fit the reel seat. Thus, ferrule internal diameters on AFTCO Unibutts measure 0.750, 0.875, 1.000, and 1.188.

Occasionally you have to fit a rod blank with a small butt end into a ferrule with an internal diameter that is too large for the blank. In these cases the best solution is to get a boat repair kit of fiberglass resin and tape and build up a bushing around the butt end of the blank, allow it to cure overnight, and then rasp, file, or lathe it down to size and a smooth cylindrical shape. After this, it is a simple matter to use 24-hour epoxy glue to glue the butt into the ferrule. Other bushing materials, such as epoxy putty, epoxy glues, and synthetic tapes built up with epoxy glue around the butt of the rod, can also be used. In all cases, these *must* be firm and solid. Never use string, masking tape, or similar materials for bushings, even with epoxy glue.

The best way to glue a blank into a bored aluminum butt is to drop the rod blank into the bored butt, making sure that the blank goes all the way through to the bottom of the butt section.

Use a pen or masking tape to mark the point where the blank exits the butt section. If the blank is loose at this point (it usually is), remove the blank and use the previous methods (fiberglass boat tape and resin, epoxy and synthetic cloth, epoxy putty) to build up the blank at this point to precisely fit the hole in the butt section. If necessary, build this oversized, allow it to cure overnight, then work the section down to size and shape with a rasp, file, or lathe.

Next, add enough liquid epoxy to the rod butt through the hole in the top to fill up the bottom to a level of several inches. (If there is a hole in the bottom, tape this over temporarily.) Usually an ounce or two is enough. Then smear glue on the bushing that has previously been sized to fit the bored butt snugly. Slide the rod blank down into the butt and mop up any excess glue.

CORD AND WRAPPED GRIPS

On thick rod blanks, such as those for surf rods and other heavy rods, wrapped grips are possible. In all cases, you must start with a blank that has a diameter that will be comfortable to hold, because the wrapping will not add much to the diameter —only to the gripping quality. In most cases, this will vary between about a 1- and 1 1/4-inch blank diameter. Adding a foam, cork, or wood grip will make the diameter too large to be held comfortably.

One simple solution is to use cord, wrapping it around the blank using the same technique as for wrapping guides in place. Several types of cord are available for this. Gudebrod makes Butt Cord, which is specifically designed for wrapped grips. It is available in black, white, blue, red, yellow, and brown in 50-yard tubes. In addition, craft stores, hobby shops, and sewing shops often carry hard cords that are used for craft work, macrame, or similar hobbies. Some that I have seen are 1.5 or 2 millimeters in diameter and ideal for wrapping grips. In some cases, larger-diameter cord is available.

Regardless of your choice of cord, it must be hard and stiff so that it will not stretch and will allow a firm grip. Also, if color is important, the cord must be colorfast, because most anglers do not coat cord with color preserver or rod finish. Doing so would make for a slick surface, something that would not allow a firm, comfortable grip. Other anglers like to soak the grip with varnish (several coats until it soaks in and builds up on the grip) or thin epoxy glue.

If you use anything other than the Gudebrod cord, be sure to check samples by soaking them in water or exposing them to the elements for a few weeks before wrapping on the rod.

To wrap cord on the rod, first choose the area to be covered. In the case of surf rods, often this is from the butt cap all the way up to the top of the grip area. In some cases, it is easiest to wrap the entire grip area and then use the grip as a shim on which to mount the reel seat. In other cases, it is best to mount the reel seat directly on the rod blank and then add wraps both above and below this for a rear and foregrip.

The technique of wrapping is the same as that used for a guide. Begin by crossing over the main thread, continue for several turns, and then cut the excess thread. Continue the wrap until you are about four to six wraps from the end, then lay down a separate loop of the same cord or of heavy monofilament. Continue wrapping, cut the thread, pull the end through the loop, and pull the loop from under the wraps. Open up a gap where the thread exits between two wraps, cut the thread off by cutting straight down with a razor blade, and then close the gap formed.

Fraying out the end of a cord wrap for a rod handle makes for less of a lump at this point. Here, Gudebrod rod cord is used.

There is a technique to avoid lumpiness in the wrap where the cord ends are wrapped over. This can be used with any cord and should definitely be used with heavy cords. To do this, start with a wrap of heavy thread: Fray out the several strands of the cord (usually there are three strands), spread these ends out around the blank, and wrap these cord ends down with the thread. Finish the thread wrap as you would a guide wrap, making sure you end where the three strands combine into the one cord. Then begin the cord wrap next to the thread wrap. Continue to wrap. At the end cut the cord with several inches of excess, fray out the ends into three strands, and begin a thread wrap to wrap over the cord ends. Continue the thread wrap, cut the ends of the cord strands, and finish the cord wrap as for a guide wrap, with a loop of thread or mono. By fraying out the strands of the cord, you will reduce any lumpiness under the wrap, which makes for a smooth grip. The same thing can be done without the thread wrap by starting with the cord frayed out and wrapping the cord around the frayed strands (like whipping the end of a rope). Finish by pulling the strands through the wrap after first fraying them out to diminish their bulk—this is just like a guide wrap but with frayed ends.

CORK-TAPE GRIPS

Cork tape will serve the same purpose as cord: as a thin grip material on blanks that are of large diameter. As with cord, the cork tape can be run the length of the area of the rear grip and foregrip, and then the reel seat can be placed over this with the cork tape used as a shim. In most cases, the reel seat is mounted and then the cork tape is added. Most cork tape comes with a self-adhesive backing.

Before starting, be sure the blank is clean. To get complete coverage without gaps, achieving the proper angle of attachment is a must. To get this for each individual rod, leave the backing paper in place and wrap the tape several times around the blank. This will adjust to the correct angle with only a short length of the tape. Make several turns, making sure the cork-tape edges abut. Now hold the wrap and unwrap several turns at the blank end. Peel off the backing paper from the unwrapped tape. Rewrap the peeled cork tape around the rod. Then unwrap the tape that still has backing paper and peel the backing off a few inches at a time, wrapping the cork tape on the blank as you do so. The result is that you get the exact taper and angle the cork tape must take when it's wrapped around any particular rod.

Once you finish this wrap, cut both ends of the tape so that they are square with the butt end of the rod. To keep the ends from unwrapping, add some masking tape temporarily to hold each end down. For the butt-cap end, remove the masking tape, add some epoxy glue to the cork tape and

Method of making a cork tape grip on a rod. The spiral is formed on the rod with the backing in place and then the backing removed while holding some of the tape in place to maintain the correct spiral without gaps or overlapping. Here, the lower part of the cork tape has been fastened to the rod; the backing is being removed from the rest of the tape.

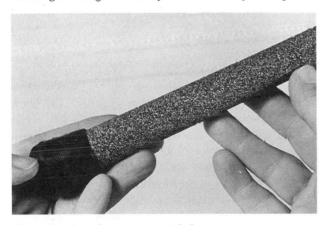

Completed cork tape grip with butt cap.

the butt cap, and slide the butt cap in place. To finish off the wrap below a reel seat or at the end of a foregrip, hold the end of the cork tape in place with masking tape. Use a razor blade or a coarse emery board to taper the end of the cork tape all the way around the blank. This will serve as a base for the wrap that will hold the end of the cork tape down. Use heavy cord or thread (E or EE) and begin a wrap around the blank just as you would with a guide wrap. Continue wrapping up onto the tapered cork tape but use a very light pressure to avoid cutting into the cork tape with the thread. Continue wrapping for a dozen turns or so, and then finish with a loop of thread as you would any other wrap. These wraps must be coated with color preserver and epoxy finish, as

must any other rod-guide or ferrule wrap.

MISCELLANEOUS GRIPS, REEL SEATS, AND VARIATIONS

The grips already mentioned are standard, but nonstandard grips are possible. They can be made of almost anything that can be fitted to a rod blank and that will provide a good gripping surface. Possibilities include drilled acrylic rod (clear or in colors), fancy woods (for casting-rod pistol and straight grips), bicycle handlebar tape over a cork base, wood dowels, and so on. Construction for most of these is the same as for typical rod grips in terms of measuring, sizing, and gluing. Some, such as the bicycle or leather tape over cork grips, are sometimes used for the foregrips on big-game rods and can be used on other rods. The best method is to glue the cigar-shaped tapered cork grip to the blank, taper it sharply at each end, and then wrap the tape around the cork grip, holding it in position with a band of rod-wrapping thread.

Variations of grips most often include inserts of other materials in the grip. The techniques are pretty basic and the possibilities endless, including the following:

Inserts of plastic or wood into a cork grip. These are most often small discs of contrasting-color material such as plastic and exotic wood. You can include these inserts into a grip you are making from cork rings, or into a preformed cork grip. However, if you are using a preformed cork grip, you will need to make the grip slightly longer (the length of the insert material) or you will have to remove that much cork from the insert position to keep the same length.

If you use a preformed cork grip, carefully and accurately cut the cork grip through at the point where you want the insert material. Use a fine saw, and if the shape of the grip allows it, a small mitre box. Once you make the cut, use sandpaper to smooth the surface and correct for any inaccuracies.

Next, pick out the insert material. This can be slices of wood; clear, translucent, or opaque plastic; or similar materials. Drill the material to fit the blank at the position where it will be placed. Another good method is to use a hole saw, which will not only drill the hole but will also cut the plastic or wood to the diameter you want for the rod grip. Shape the diameter of the material close to, but not exactly the size of, the grip (if you have not already done this with the hole saw). You will have to wait until the grip is glued on the blank to do the final shaping.

Glue the cork rings in place one at a time, as for making a standard cork ring grip, or glue on the lower half of the preformed cork grip. Add the insert material, making sure that you get a good glue bond to the blank and also to the adjoining cork surfaces. Glue the rest of the rings or the remainder of the grip in place. Once this is done, allow the glue to cure overnight.

Next, you must shape the insert material to the diameter and form of the grip. For best results, roughly file and shape the cork grip (if it's made from cork rings) until it is close to the final diameter. Then use a hard file, sandpaper backed by a board, or a stiff emery board to shape and size the insert ring. You can't just sand the cork and the insert ring at the same time because the softer cork will be sanded away faster than the hard insert. The result would be a scalloped or dished appearance to the cork on each side of the insert. Once the insert is shaped, sand the cork grip to meet this diameter. When working with a preformed cork grip, use a layer or two of masking tape to protect the cork on each side of the insert, then use the hard files and sanders to sand the insert to shape and size. Remove the masking tape and do any final sanding with fine sandpaper.

An alternative is to use a hole saw and saw out insert materials to the exact diameter needed, then polish the edges, enlarge the hole to fit onto the blank, and glue the insert in place when gluing the foam or cork rings onto the rod blank. Assuming the cork rings are larger than the insert, the cork can then be shaped and sized to the diameter of the insert ring, using methods previously described.

Inserts can be of one, two, or more materials. One common method is to use a cork grip with one or more insert materials, with each insert area composed of alternating material bands. Often, white material is used for light bands. One variation is to use insert materials in colors that will match or blend with the color of the thread to be used in the guide wraps.

Another popular and easy insert can be composed of burnt cork, a dark brown cork that is available from most tackle-component suppliers. It can be inserted as a single ring or thinner slice of contrasting cork in a reel-seat insert or grip on spinning, casting, or fly rods.

Inserts of rubber foam in foam grips. Rubber foam comes in several colors, and inserts of contrasting colors can be cut in short sections and then inserted into foam grips. Cut the foam grip where you want the insert, then trim the insert accurately with a razor blade. For an accurate lineup of the two foams, which must be glued together, you must use the same material and the same internal and outside diameters. The best procedure is to glue the parts together with rubber cement and then glue the completed grip onto the blank with epoxy glue. Use care, however, because the glued grip will be more fragile than will a solid, uncut grip.

In addition to using different colors of foam, you can cut foam from the center of old thong-type sandals. Many of these are colorful, with several layers of bright color, and can be added to grips for a decorative touch. For best results, use a hole saw run at a very slow speed to cut out the rings of material from the sole.

In addition, any inserts of wood, plastic, foam, or other material can be placed into the grip at an angle by cutting the grip on an angle and allowing for the change in dimensions in the insert material. The insert material will require an oblong hole — or a hole cut at an angle to the axis of the material, and must be oblong in shape to fit the angled cut.

Skeletal reel seats. Skeletal reel seats can be bought and they can also be made. Start with a plain reel seat of aluminum or graphite fill. Then use a fine-blade hacksaw (32 teeth per inch) to cut out the barrel section between the fixed hood and the threaded barrel holding the adjustable hood. After cutting these, use a fine file to smooth the cut edges and remove any burrs. If you are working with an aluminum anodized reel seat, use a permanent felt-tip marker of the same color as the reel-seat anodizing to touch up the edges. You can then make an insert of wood or cork. For a wood insert, the best procedure is to turn the wood on a lathe until it is of the right diameter and length and has a slight recess to go under the fixed hood, with a longer recess to go under the threaded barrel. The outside diameter of the wood insert should be the same as for the aluminum or graphite. The recesses at both ends must fit snugly into the remaining reel-seat parts. If you are making an insert of cork, glue several rings together on a threaded rod and shape them as an insert to fit the reel seat. It is possible to place insert discs in these for added decoration. In making these inserts for skeletal reel seats, be sure you make them the correct length, because once the barrel is cut out you will have no reference as to the proper length that will accommodate the feet of reels you plan to use with the rod.

Wood handles on casting and spinning rods. Exotic woods can be used for handles, although for most tastes these are too hard and firm for comfort. If you wish to try them, do it on one rod and fish with it before changing all your rods or building a whole new stock of tackle with wood handles.

Any exotic wood can be used. Some exotic woods are available from well-stocked lumber-yards, and special wood-carving and wood-hobby shops can carry any type of wood. Popular woods include those that are used for fly-rod reel-seat inserts, such as walnut, cocabola, mesquite, and ebony. To make a spinning or straight handle — such as that for a trigger-stick-style casting rod — use a lathe to shape the wood.

You will have to drill a hole for the blank, and there are two ways this can be done. One is to drill the hole first, using a drill press and a long-shank drill bit. These bits come in 6- and 12-inch lengths so that you can make any but the longest grips. Make a jig for your drill press that will hold the wood stock (usually square in cross section) perfectly vertical and in line with the drill bit. Essentially this jig is nothing more than a precise corner of wood scraps. By clamping the base of this corner onto the drill-press table, the two sides will be made vertical. Placing the wood stock into this corner assures vertical drilling. To drill long grips, you will probably have to position the wood stock in this jig on the drill press, place the drill bit into the chuck, and then position the drill bit in line with the center of the wood stock. Then drill as deeply as possible, periodically raising the drill bit to clear the wood chips and dust. Because most drill presses will not feed a bit a full 12 inches, you will probably have to stop the drill press with the bit still in the wood, raise the drill-press table in line with the bit, and then continue drilling. Once the wood stock is drilled, place it in a lathe and shape it to size.

An alternative method is to drill with the wood in the lathe. Usually this is easily accomplished by using a drill in a chuck in the tail stock, with the wood stock held in a four-jaw or three-jaw universal chuck.

Once the wood is shaped and drilled, a reamer or other drill bits can be used to further drill the hole to the proper taper to fit the rod blank.

To make pistol-grip casting-rod handles, first decide on the type of wood you want and on the length required. A general size would be about 5 to 6 inches long, about 3 inches wide, and about 1 1/2 inches thick. First drill a hole through the wood, gradually enlarging it to fit the blank. Once this is done, trace the general shape of the grip on the wood. Often a good way to start is by using a pistol grip you like as a template. If you wish, you can make the grip unique by adding finger-grip indentations. Once you are satisfied with the shape, cut the wood on a band saw. Once the grip is cut out, use a rasp, sanding belt, or files to roughly shape the body of the grip, finishing with various grades of sandpaper. For those with the inclination and tools, checkering, such as is done for gun stocks, will add security to the gripping surface and also make it more decorative.

Extension and fighting butts on fly rods. Extension butts on fly rods can be made of varying lengths, permanent or detachable. They are available commercially with some reel seats such as those by Beard, Cortland, and Struble. They can also be made using standard fly-rod reel seats. The purpose is to provide for extending the fly reel from the body when fighting big fish. Usually the rod butt is held against the body for leverage in fighting such fish, and the extension butt allows this while keeping the turning reel away from clothing.

To make a permanent extension butt, you must use an open-end reel seat (open at both ends) so that the blank can fit straight through. Begin building such a permanent extension butt by first deciding on materials. Classic design dictates a small aluminum butt cap or butt plate, above which is mounted several cork rings to make up the extension butt. (If you will be mounting a socket type of butt cap, first mount the cork rings, sand them to size and shape to form a recess for the butt cap, and then glue the butt cap in place. If you will be mounting a plate-type butt cap, add the cork rings and then glue the plate in place.) You can make any length of extension butt you want, using one cork ring for each 1/2-inch of butt length.

If you ever plan to use the rod to catch or try to catch a world-record fish, the extension butt must be limited to 6 inches, the maximum allowed by current IGFA rules. In most cases this is longer than you would want anyway for any extension butt, especially a permanent butt. Longer extensions will catch the fly line more, get caught in sleeves of shirts and jackets, and get in the way of casting. Lefty Kreh states that each inch over two inches of extension butt adds another problem to casting and fishing. A short permanent extension butt of about 2 inches is far better, because it will still extend the reel away from the body yet not be so long as to interfere with casting.

After gluing on the cork rings to make the extension butt, add the reel seat or reel-seat bushing to hold the reel seat. In this, you have a choice between up-locking or down-locking seats. Up-locking (locking up toward the tip of the rod) seats are better, because they will add another inch or so of space between your clothing and the reel. Down-locking seats push the reel down toward the extension butt.

Add the reel seat, first gluing together any component parts (wood or cork insert, fixed hood and threaded barrel with adjustable hood), and then ream out the reel seat to fit snugly on the blank. Make sure you use the masking-tape method of protecting the parts from glue. Allow the parts to cure, and then glue the completed, assembled reel seat onto the rod blank and seat against the corks making up the extension butt. Align the hoods with the spine of the rod. Then add the adjoining cork to finish the rest of the handle. Cover the reel seat with several layers of masking tape to protect it and then, using hand or lathe methods, shape and size the cork grip and the short cork extension at the same time.

You can make an extension of other materials, such as foam or wood. I do *not* recommend using foam for the fly-rod grip because foam, regardless of type, is too flexible and gives too much on the forward part of the cast for you to maintain good loop size and line control. Foam or wood can be used for the extension fighting butt, because this is nonfunctional on the cast. For this, proceed as above, adding the foam or wood in place of the cork. The foam should have an outside diameter approximately equal to that of the rear of the reel seat, and an internal diameter slightly smaller than the outside diameter of the rod blank for smooth fitting. Fit the foam on with epoxy, using the same methods as for adding a foam grip on other rods.

Wood extensions of exotic woods to match the fly-rod reel-seat-insert wood can be made also. The best technique is to drill a short length (the best extension butts are only about 2 inches long, so this does not require long drill bits) and then place it on a lathe. Shape the exposed portion of the extension butt and then make any appropriate recesses to fit into a butt cap or halfway into the open-end fixed-hood reel seat. If you are using a skeletal-type reel seat like this, you will also have to cut off a portion of the recess of the wood-barrel insert to allow for the partial recess of the extension butt.

Note that if you build the rod this way, you will move the grip and reel seat slightly forward (the length of the extension butt), but both sections of the blank (or several sections) will all remain the same length. If you do not wish to shift the position of the reel seat and grip, you can add a permanent extension to the end by using a scrap of blank epoxy-glued into the butt end of the rod, on which you can build the extension. If you do this, make sure the tapers are identical or similar and that at least four inches of the scrap blank fits into the rod blank. Substitutes for a tapered rod blank include tapered wood dowels. This method is not really recommended for permanent extensions because it does add to the overall length of the butt section of the rod.

I like removable extension butts best. You can leave them off when you don't want or need them but can still carry them in a hip pocket or fly-fishing vest to plug into the rod when desired. And, if you make your own, you can make and carry several different lengths, say 2- and 6-inch lengths.

There are several ways to make a removable extension or fighting butt. They all must use an open-end reel seat, so that there is an opening into which the extension butt can slide. In essence, all are made using some sort of ferrule system, even though it may be very crude when compared to a rod ferrule. For example, one simple way to make an extension butt is to build the rod normally, with the butt of the rod blank extending all the way to the end of the reel seat.

An exception to this would be if you are using a special button or butt cap—such as the button for the Fuji FPS 16 fly-rod reel seat—that requires fitting to the reel seat, not to the blank. In this case, leave space for the button, with a little extra for clearance. You *must* clear all of the glue from this open end so that the butt cap or button will fit. This means not only the glue on the inside walls of the reel seat but also any bulge of glue at the end of the rod blank that might interfere with proper full seating of the button. If you use this method, cut off as much of the rod blank as you plan to recess the blank for clearance for the button. Naturally, check and measure against the tip section first—some rod sections are not exactly identical and you may not have to cut off any rod blank at all.

Once the reel seat and grip are glued in place, you can add a removable extension butt using a scrap of blank or a tapered wood dowel. Either the scrap blank or tapered wood dowel must have the proper size and matched taper to fit securely into the blank for about three or four inches. If you have a piece of scrap blank that is not exactly the right taper, a little sanding will quickly match it to the rod-blank taper. Wood dowels must be tapered with sanding or scraping methods to get the insert portion of the dowel shaped and sized to fit. This is easy to do but requires a little work and trial-and-error fittings. One way to check your work is to insert the extension into the rod blank end and twist it several times with moderate pressure. When it's removed you can usually spot the glassy rub marks, indicating high points that must be sanded more.

Once you have a good fit, build the cork, wood, or foam body on the extension butt, add a butt cap, and shape the cork or foam if necessary. Once the extension is glued and completed, add a little paraffin or candle wax to the plug-in part (this helps it to grip and hold), and you are ready to fish.

An alternative, for use with a regular aluminum open-end fly rod or light-spinning-reel seat (with no wood or other inserts), is to measure the reel seat and cut off half of this amount from the end of the rod blank. In many cases, these reel seats are about 5 inches long. Thus, cut off about 2 1/2 inches of the butt end of the rod blank. Naturally, check the length of the butt section against the length of the tip section to make sure the two remain equal.

Then glue the rod blank into the reel seat (see page 387 for suggestions), making sure the rod blank leaves about 2 1/2 inches of clearance at the end. Completely clean the end of any excess glue.

You then have a straight shaft, 2 1/2 inches long, into which you can insert a straight-sided plug holding an extension butt. You can use a straight dowel, cut for a snug fit on a lathe, to fit into the end of the reel seat and serve as a base for the removable extension. Build as before with cork, foam, or wood.

Because the size of the dowel is critical for this friction fit, a variation is to make for a slightly looser fit and then cut two or three grooves around the dowel, using a pointed parting tool and a lathe. This will place two or three even grooves, into which you can stretch small O-rings that will serve to make a tight friction fit. Naturally, this does require some trial and error in getting the right depth to the grooves for the size of the O-ring used. Small O-rings for this purpose

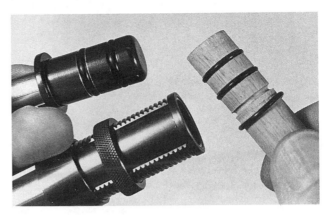

This method of making an extension butt for a fly rod involves cutting grooves around a dowel (a lathe is best for this) as shown; "O" rings, available at hardware store, are placed in the grooves for friction and centering. In essence, the insert becomes similar to a commercially available insert (left top). One of the "O" rings on the wood dowel has been moved to show the groove. Fit is trial and error, and the wood dowel is then built up with cork rings.

are available at all good hardware stores. In essence, this is a homemade copy of the same O-ring fitting of the removable extension butts available from some commercial reel seat manufacturers, such as Beard.

Though I do not like it as well, you can also make a threaded fitting. There are several ways to do this. One of the easiest is to get a 1/4-20 or 5/16-20 threaded rod fastener. These are like a nut but long—usually about 1 to 1 1/2 inch. Use epoxy glue to glue this inside the blank at the end of the reel seat (if it will fit), or in the reel seat if the blank is cut and recessed. Then glue a same-size bolt with the head cut off or a short section of threaded rod into the center of the blank used for the extension or into a straight hole drilled for the purpose into a wood dowel.

Another, though heavier, alternative is to use a short bolt of the right length, building the extension onto the bolt with the threaded end exposed to fit into the reel seat. In all cases, extend the threaded rod (bolt) about 1/2 to 1 inch, enough so that it will thread into the rod fastener. Then build up the extension butt so that the forward end of the butt meets the beginning of the threaded rod. For best results, use a sander or grinder to carefully point the end of the threaded rod so that it will be easier to begin to thread the extension butt into the end of the rod.

If you add this type of screw-in extension butt

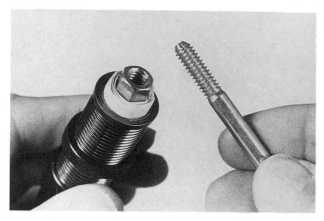

Method of making an extension butt for a fly rod. A nut extension is glued into the reel seat end (not yet glued at this point) and the cork rings built up on a shoulder bolt. Best size for this is 1/4 inch by 20 threads, although any size can be used. Cork rings are built up on the shoulder bolt and the extension threaded into the end of the rod when needed.

before fishing, it is easy, but it has no real advantage over previously described systems. Trying to do this after hooking a big fish — say a tarpon jumping all over the county — is almost impossible. Some commercial reel-seat/extension-butt combinations use this system, but in my opinion there are better, simpler ways.

Fly-rod fighting grips. These are commonly used on the largest fly rods, such as those used for billfish, tarpon, big sharks, and other large game-fish. These are nothing more than slim cigar-shaped grips mounted forward of the standard grip. They are usually about 5 to 6 inches long and slimmer than a normal grip, because they are only used for a second hand-support to help raise the rod to lift a big fish from the depths or in a sideways motion to turn the head of a big fish.

They are built just as are standard grips on a fly rod. Cork rings are built up on the blank and then are shaped on a lathe (preferably). Usually they are mounted about 2 to 4 inches above the standard grip, with a decorative trim wrap and hookkeeper in between the two grips. Some big-game anglers do not add a hookkeeper, avoiding anything that might interfere with the line or smooth landing of big fish.

BUTT-CAP ASSEMBLY

Butt caps are easy to add to any rod handle, but there are some tricks and considerations with them. Some butt caps are designed to fit over the

end of the handle, so that the process is one of simply gluing the butt cap onto the end of the handle with a strong epoxy glue. Be sure to use a file, sandpaper, or rasp to roughen the outside of the end of the handle to be covered by the butt cap and the inside of the butt cap. Use a layer or two of masking tape around the open edge of the butt cap and also around the handle *at the point where the butt cap will stop.*

Some butt caps require — or look better with — a recess in the handle so that the edge of the butt cap is flush with the edge of the handle rather than slightly overlapping it. These type of grips can be done with any rod, any style butt cap, and any style handle. Cork handles can be sanded, cut, or turned to allow for such a recess. Some preformed cork handles and some foam handles are made with specific recesses for butt caps and reel seats. The gluing procedure is exactly the same for this type of handle. Roughen the glued surfaces and add a layer of masking tape to the butting edges of the handle and butt cap.

Some butt caps are really butt plates, in that they are aluminum or plastic buttons with a plug in the center; the plug is designed to be glued into the hole in the rod blank that extends to the rear of the rod handle. Most often these are used on cork handles for ultralight or light spinning rods, although they can be used on any type of rod and any type of material. Use sandpaper to roughen the inner flat surface and also the extending plug. Roughen the flat end of the rod handle. Then add a good quantity of 24-hour epoxy glue to the hole in the rod blank and smear some glue on the end of the rod handle and on the inside surfaces of the butt plate. Push the butt plate into place, wipe up any excess glue around the edges, and stand the rod absolutely vertically.

One good way to do this is to stand the rod vertically alongside a bench and hold it in place, using masking tape to tape it to the bench edge. Often it helps to add some weight to the rod to keep pressure on the bond as the glue cures. One way to do this is to add a reel to the rod (if the reel seat has been mounted) or to slide some weights down the rod blank so that they jam at the handle. If the guides are in place, you can hang weights over the rod where they will jam at the guide frame.

REEL-SEAT MOUNTING

Reel seats require specific methods of mounting on a rod blank, because the outside diameter

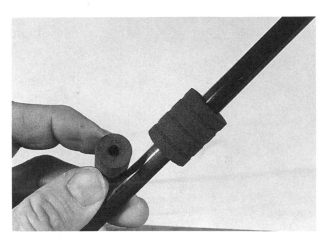

Graphite bushings are available for shimming reel seats when there is a lot of space to fill. These are ideal since they transmit any impulses from the rod blank to the grip and reel seat. Several sizes are available, and all can be reamed or drilled to fit any rod blank.

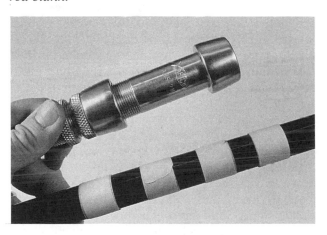

In some cases, only a very slight shimming of a reel seat is required such as this fitting of a heavy-duty reel seat onto a rod blank. Masking tape is ideal for this, but space should be allowed for a direct glue bond of the blank to the reel seat—not just gluing the reel seat to a solid layer of masking tape.

of the rod blank on which they are mounted is almost always thinner than the reel-seat barrel. (Exceptions today in commercial rods are the skeletal reel seats that are specifically designed for a given blank diameter and thus are glued directly to the blank. At the present time, however, these are not available to the rod craftsman.)

In essence, what you have to do is to add a bushing of some sort to the rod blank, with the internal diameter of this bushing sized to the outside diameter of the blank and the outside diameter of the bushing sized to the internal diameter

of the reel seat. In some cases bushings or shims can be drilled, tapered, and sized to fit; in other cases tape and cord can be used to build up the area on the rod blank to fit the reel seat. Some possibilities for bushings of all types include materials that are slid and glued in place and those that are wrapped around the blank to build it up to the reel-seat diameter. Those that can be wrapped around the blank include thread, cord, masking tape, paper tape, self-adhesive cork tape, and fiberglass tape. Those that are slipped onto the blank include cork rings, cardboard bushings, graphite bushings, wood bushings, and old thread spools sized to fit.

Although you can wrap thread or cord around the blank using the standard rod-guide-wrapping method to start and finish, it is not necessary. One easy way is to smear epoxy glue onto the blank, lay

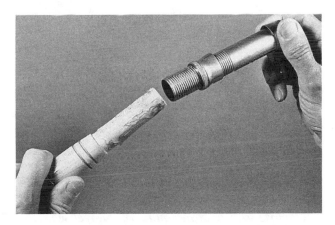

Adding a reel seat to a wooden boat-rod handle. For best results, these parts should be taped, as previously outlined, to prevent smearing of glue.

Some bushings or fittings for reel seats require shimming. On this wood handle, this is done by adding crossed cords to take up space between the wood and the reel seat. The ends of the handle and reel seat are taped, glue added and the reel seat slid on.

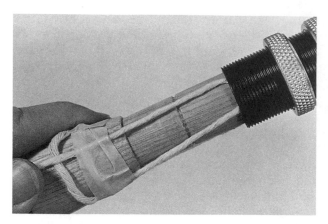

Checking a bushing for fitting after the cords are added as a shim.

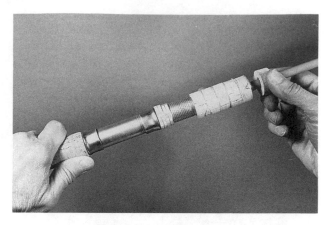

The reel seat glued in place, with corks added to make the foregrip on this spinning rod.

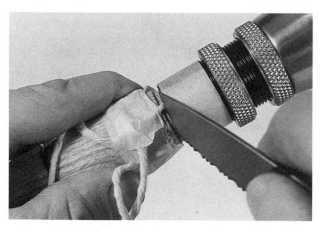

Once close to a final mounting of the reel seat, any excess cord is cut away, then the reel seat pushed home on the handle.

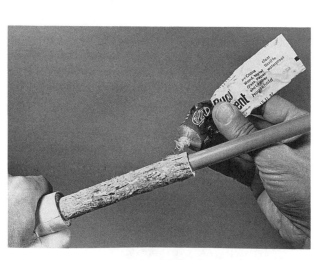

Additional cork rings or cork bushing (or other types of bushing) are added to the rod blank above the rear grip to glue the reel seat in place.

a short length of cord parallel to it, then start with light pressure to wrap around the blank and cord. The glue holds the cord in place. After each wrapped layer, add more glue to make a solid cement bond of the cord or thread bushing. Once the layers produce the thickness prescribed by the reel seat internal diameter, finish with a half-hitch or two, cinching them down to hold them in place and to prevent ridges in the finished bushing. Finish with a final layer of glue.

Another method I like is to spiral-wrap up and down the section of rod blank so that large latticelike gaps are left in the wrap, to be filled with glue as the wrap progresses. This goes rapidly, reduces the bulk of the cord, and also makes for a solid epoxylike bond and bushing. Paper tape can also be used: Glue the paper to the blank (or use self-adhesive or glue-back tape), and then wrap tightly around the blank until the paper wrapping is the diameter of the internal diameter of the reel seat. Similarly, fiberglass tape can be used in the same way: Wrap it around the blank, but in this case use epoxy glue or fiberglass resin to glue it in place.

Regardless of the type of bushing used, a good permanent bond of the reel seat to the blank through the bushing requires a solid bushing properly glued to the blank and reel seat, or made from cord, thread, paper tape, or other tape but with a solid bond of epoxy glue from the blank all the way out to the reel seat. Thus, for "soft" materials such as cord, paper tape, and especially masking tape, the bushing material can only serve to keep the reel seat centered on the rod blank, while the epoxy, resin, or other glue forms the solid base for a permanent reel-seat mount.

An additional suggestion, particularly if you use tape products, is to use thin bands of tape around the blank so that you have a series of three or four or more bands, each about 1/2 to 1 inch thick and an equal distance apart. That way, a lot of glue can be added to these spaces between the bands while the reel seat is being slid onto the blank. The glue then bonds the reel seat to the blank.

If you are building up a solid bushing of any type, allow it to cure overnight. Then add glue to the bushing and slide the reel seat gently and slowly onto it. Make sure you first wrap the end of the grip and the lower end of the reel seat with several layers of masking tape to make a smooth, clean joint when the tape is later peeled off, along with any oozing glue. Slide and rotate the reel seat back and forth several times when adding it to the bushing to get a good distribution of glue. If you use a bushing made up of several bushing bands, add glue to them, slide the reel seat onto the bushing until the first bushing ring is hidden, then add as much epoxy glue as possible and slide the reel seat on farther. Continue until the reel seat is in place, and then allow the glue to cure overnight with the rod held vertically. This allows the liquid glue to flow and form a block of epoxy between the rod and reel seat.

FERRULES AND ADAPTERS

Methods used to add ferrules and adapters are similar to but far simpler than the methods used to add reel seats. First, the ferrules we are talking about here are not the self-contained ferrules found on most center-ferruled rod blanks but are the metal ferrules that used to be found in all rods and are today most common in older or older-style rods and in bamboo fly rods. At one time, companies such as Allen, Featherweight, and others made ferrules in a wide range of sizes and materials. Today, ferrules for general rods are available from AmTak (American Tackle Limited) in chrome-plated brass (in sizes from 9/10/64ths to 49/50/64ths. The first (smaller) of the two numerators is the diameter of the tip section; the larger is the diameter for the butt section.) In addition, Cortland/Rodon carries fine—but also expensive—Super "Z" nickel-silver ferrules in sizes from 9/64ths through 17/64ths. Although they can be used for any rod, they are primarily used for bamboo rods. Ferrules—at least these styles—are in two pieces: one piece is permanently fitted to the tip section and the other to the butt section to allow the joining and separating of the two sections.

Adapters are similar to ferrules, but by my definition at least include only one part, which fits into a reel seat or collet fitting of some sort in the rod handle or reel seat. Examples would be the adapters that are permanently glued to rods and are designed to allow the rod to fit into a specific Fuji or AmTak reel seat or handle, as well as the adapters (though they call them ferrules) glued to offshore rods and designed to fit into the Unibutt handles by AFTCO. In most cases these ferrules or adapters are available in 1/64th size increments, so that no special sizing of the blank or parts are needed.

If additional sizing is needed, there are some tips to make this easy. First, do not count on building up the space between a ferrule and rod blank with excess epoxy glue. It might work, but a bond with only a thin amount of glue is better and stronger. (Though you can go too thin with the glue. Because the blank and ferrule are made of impervious materials, you must count on a surface coating of glue for proper bonding. It is important to lightly sand the blank to give it some roughness and tooth to hold the glue. If the ferrule or adapter is large enough to do so, it also helps to roughen the inside of the hole with a rat-tail file, rasp, or sandpaper strip glued to a dowel chosen for the purpose.) There are several steps to take in checking and correcting any looseness of these parts:

1. First recheck the size of the blank or ferrule and make sure that a smaller-size ferrule or adapter will not fit. A proper fit is one that will slide on snugly without any appreciable looseness but also without requiring forcing or pushing to get the ferrule completely on the rod.

2. If the ferrule or adapter is not the best size for the rod (and the next size smaller is too small), then you can correct the situation in one of several ways. The first is to wrap a single tight layer of thread around the rod—just like a guide wrapping—to build up the thickness of the blank in this area. Soak the area with glue and slide the ferrule or part in place.

3. A second method is to make a thread wrap. Spiral the thread for most of the wrap, keeping it tight only at both ends, where you start and finish. That way the thread wrap serves as a shim to keep the ferrule or adapter centered on the blank; the gaps in the spiral wrap allow glue to bond the rod blank to the ferrule. In other words, you are not

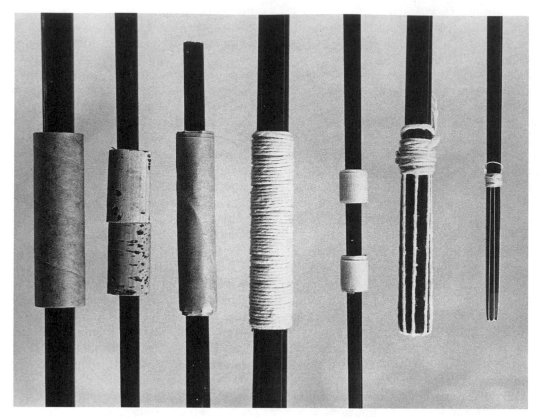

Types of bushings for reel seats and metal ferrules. Left to right, fiber bushing, cork bushings, wrapped paper tape, wrapping of cord, built-up rings of masking tape, spines of cord over the end of the rod, and spines of thread over the end of the rod.

running the risk of just gluing the ferrule to the surface of the thread wrap.

4. Another method, which I like very much, is to obtain thread or cord and lay it longitudinally along the blank, taping it in place several inches above the end, running it over the end and up the opposite side, and taping it again. Repeat this several times so that you end up with four (the minimum), six, or eight taped-down strings, threads, or cord. Soak the cord and blank with glue and slide the ferrule in place. The advantage of this method, particularly if the fit is tight, is that there is no way to push the thread wrap out of place, as might occur with circular wraps. If the fit is too tight, the ferrule won't go on, but the cord can't dislodge, as can a wrapped-thread shim.

5. Another method to use, if the fit is slightly loose on a butt section, is to cut the blank back slightly. This produces an increased blank diameter as you slide the ferrule on, as on the upper (tip) end of a butt section. However, it pays to take some careful caliper or micrometer measurements before you do this; otherwise you can get into a situation where you cut the blank back too far and thus shorten that section of the blank and possibly even change the action of the rod at this critical ferruled point. The rationale, of course, is that with the increasingly larger diameter of the blank, you will get to a point where the ferrule will fit perfectly.

Once the ferrule or adapter is glued onto the rod blank, clean any excess glue with a solvent-soaked rag and, if necessary (as with the longitudinal-cord method), trim off any exposed shim material. Then the ferrule or adapter can be wrapped with thread (see Chapter 22) as desired. Note that some metal ferrules have a slight shoulder or recess acting as a stop point for a thread wrap that begins on the blank and partially wraps up over the ferrule. In some cases, the ferrules are wrapped completely as part of the decoration of the rod or to hide the shiny metal portion. If this is the case, the male portion that slides into the sooe female ferrule must be kept clean and free of any thread work.

21

Guide and Part Spacing

INTRODUCTION ▪ TOOLS AND MATERIALS ▪ USING OTHER
RODS FOR SPACING ▪ GENERAL CONSIDERATIONS ▪
OTHER SOURCES FOR GUIDE SPACING ▪ FORMULAS ▪
GUIDE-SPACING CHARTS ▪ CHECKING GUIDE SPACING

INTRODUCTION

An important note: All guide spacing should be checked before the guides are wrapped down and coated with epoxy. After this it is a little late to make easy adjustments. After you are sure of the guide spacing, check anyway, using one or more of the methods at the end of this chapter. Then, when you're finally satisfied, proceed to the wrapping bench.

Guide spacing is critical in making a custom rod. If the guides are spaced wrong, casting distance, accuracy, and pleasure can be hindered severely. Poor guide spacing can turn a good blank into a terrible rod. If you have too many guides on a light rod, or the wrong guides, you can make the rod sluggish and unusable. If there aren't enough

guides on a rod, the line can rub against the rod excessively or, because the stresses haven't been distributed evenly, the rod can break.

There are, however, no absolutes in terms of the exact number, size, or position of guides. There are some general rules and there are guide-spacing charts. That's what this chapter is all about: understanding the concept of guide spacing and getting the best spacing available for the rod blank and type you have chosen.

TOOLS AND MATERIALS

Tools for guide spacing are few. You will want some masking tape to mark the location of the center of each guide. Also, you will want an accurate ruler to measure the distances on the rod blank you've taken from rod charts or other formulas to determine guide spacing. For this, a straight metal or wood rule is best. The roll-up tapes will work but are sometimes a little awkward to work with, particularly if you are determining the space from a tip-top to a butt guide for proper spacing of the intermediate guides.

If you plan to make a number of rods of the same design with the same guide spacing, you may want to make an additional tool of a board or strip that serves as a template for the exact measurement of all the guides on that rod. As an example, a length of wood with the blank number marked at the top and marks measured from the top for the position of each guide will serve as a good template. You do not have to have a strip of wood as long as the rod—only one that is as long as the distance between the first and last guides. You can include information as to guide size and type, if desired. Thus, the strip of wood would contain a list of numbers beginning with the distance from the tip-top to the first guide and followed by guide information and, for safety, the measurement in inches. An example might look like: #1-SHG 10-6 1/4". Another easy way to do this is to use a discarded venetian blind and mark the measurements with a permanent felt-tip pen. In use, the curve of the blind will serve to cradle the rod blank while you are transferring the measurements from the blind to the blank.

USING OTHER RODS FOR SPACING

Once you have the handle glued on, or the exact measurements for the length of the handle, one of the easiest ways to determine guide spacing is to copy it from a *good* existing rod. I emphasize the word good, because a poor rod, or one made with compromises, or one with too few guides or the wrong type of guides will result in an equally poor copy. A good rod with good guide spacing and good guides that was made with attention to quality and performance should result in a rod equally good or better when you copy the same dimensions. Naturally, the rod must be of the same power (the strength, or resistance to bending), the same action (the way in which the rod bends—parabolic or fast-tip), the same length, and must have the same type of handle assembly.

Assuming these things, copying guide spacing is a perfectly acceptable way to start. I say start, because even with the same type of rod, it pays to tape guides in place and then bend and cast the rod to assure that it works the way you want. If not, some adjustment of the guides may be required.

GENERAL CONSIDERATIONS

If a rod to copy from is not available, you can start from scratch, assuming some general considerations. The first step in any such calculation is to determine the position, or approximate position, of the butt or first guide up from the reel seat. The best way to figure this is from the center of the reel seat, or center of the reel, to the guide. This is the only unchanging measurement and the only one that counts. The presence of long or short rear grips or the length of the foregrip does not matter. What does matter is the distance from the reel, where the line leaves and travels along the rod, to the first guide, where it is gathered (thus the term "gathering guide," which is sometimes used) to continue through the rest of the guides.

This location can be critical. Some years ago I did some testing for a major rod and rod-blank manufacturer in which I was asked to start from scratch and determine the best possible guide spacing and size for its line of fly rods. In the process I tried some ridiculous butt- or stripper-guide positions, including some as close as about 20 to 24 inches above the center of the reel seat.

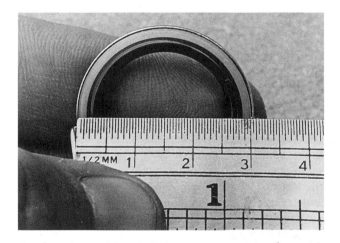

In choosing guides, it is important to note that with the new ceramic guides, the true size of the opening in the ceramic ring is often far smaller than the nominal stated size. This 30-mm guide, for example, actually has an interior diameter of about 23 millimeters. Ring diameter is important for line flow and knot clearance, particularly in small guides.

Tip-tops must also be chosen for line clearance. The two on the left both are the same tube size to fit the same diameter blank, but the center guide has a larger ring than the one on the left. When possible, choose tip tops with the largest ring size.

In these cases, the first guide is only about 11 to 15 inches above the top of the handle. Usually, up to about 27 inches from the center of the reel seat, the guide position would cause line waves and rod shock to the point that you could not effectively cast the rod. The rod blanks were first-rate designs, but this extreme of guide positioning made them impossible to cast. I also tried placing the first guide much higher than normal — ranging from about 35 inches or more from the reel-seat center. In these cases, the line slap was so great that it also reduced casting distance and accuracy. It did not create the same line shock, line waves, and rod shock as did the shortened distances, but it did adversely affect an otherwise fine rod. Naturally, these tests were done with the guides taped on, the way you should do them also, until I was absolutely sure of the guide spacing.

Other types of rods are also affected by extremes of butt-guide placement. Thus, the position of this guide is really the most important of all. It can control how well your rod casts and will also determine in part the amount of spacing between the rest of the guides used, and thus the distribution of stress.

There are some approximate figures for positioning the butt guide. These are as follows, all measured from the center of the reel seat to the butt guide:

Fly rods: 28 to 32 inches. Use the shorter distance for light, short fly rods; the longer distance for larger, longer, and heavier fly rods.
Ultralight spinning rods: 16 to 24 inches. Short-en the distance with very light 4 1/2-foot rods, lengthen with longer ultralight rods.
Freshwater spinning rods: 19 to 27 inches.
Saltwater spinning rods: 20 to 27 inches.
Bait-casting rods: 17 to 25 inches.
Popping rods: 18 to 26 inches.
Boat rods: 22 to 26 inches.
Trolling rods, East Coast style: 20 to 25 inches.
Trolling rods, West Coast style: 22 to 26 inches.
Surf rods: 27 to 33 inches.

Once the basic butt-guide location is determined, the positioning of the rest of the guides can be determined. For this there are also some general considerations as to the location of the guides and the number of guides used on each type and length of rod. Note however, that these are *general* considerations. There can be and are exceptions to all of the following based on a specific rod, rod action, rod power, handle length, type of rod, and so on. These basic considerations are:

1. In all rods, the number of guides are important but not critical. Thus, if you have one too many or too few guides (according to some-one else or a formula) it is not the end of the world. However, it is best to have the "right" number. Too many guides and the rod can become sluggish. Too few and the rod won't distribute stresses properly.

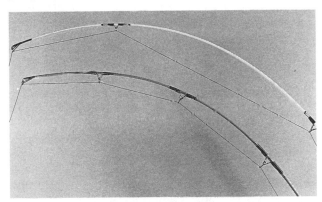

Guide spacing is important on all rods. Here, the top rod has too few guides, resulting in uneven stresses on the blank and extreme "bowing" of the line between guides. More guides distribute rod stresses evenly for casting and fighting fish.

2. Fast-tip rods will need more guides than even-bending parabolic rods, and these guides will have to be closer together, with more at the tip end. This will help distribute the stresses of the light-rod action better. In the case of revolving-spool tackle in which the guides are on top of the

rod, it will help to minimize line contact with the rod blank between the guides.

3. For fly rods, use one guide for each foot of length or fraction of a foot of length, exclusive of the rod's tip-top. Thus, an 8-foot rod would have eight guides, an 8 1/2- or 9-foot rod would have nine guides.

4. For spinning rods, use one guide for each foot of length, not including fractions of a foot but exclusive of the tip-top. Thus, a 4 1/2-foot ultra-light would have four guides, a 6- or 6 1/2-foot medium spinning rod would have six guides, and a 7-foot rod seven guides.

5. Casting and spin-cast rods should have one guide for each foot of rod length or fraction of a foot of rod length. Thus, a 5-foot casting rod would have five guides; a 5 1/2- or 6-foot casting rod would have six guides.

6. Surf rods should have one guide for each two feet or fraction of that of rod length, exclusive of the rod tip-top. An 8-foot surf or jetty rod would have four guides, a 9- or 10-foot rod would have five guides, and a 12-foot rod would have six guides.

7. Offshore and heavy boat trolling rods of standard lengths of about 6 1/2 to 7 1/2 feet would have five guides plus the tip-top.

8. West-Coast-style and action trolling rods in which there is a pronounced tip action but the same lengths as standard or East-Coast-style trolling rods (6 1/2 to 7 1/2 feet) would require six or seven guides plus the tip-top. The greater number of guides is required to help distribute the stresses of the tip-action rod, and the extra guides are located in this tip area.

9. Stand-up rods would have one or two more guides than trolling rods as a result of their fast tip actions and usage.

10. Long, thin, light so-called noodle rods would have more guides than similar-length casting or spinning rods to help distribute stress and reduce line rubbing. Generally, most noodle rods would have one guide for each foot of length or fraction of a foot in length, plus two or three additional guides, plus the tip-top. Thus, a noodle rod about 9 feet long would have eleven or twelve guides. These guides would be very small and lightweight, in keeping with the rod's power and action.

OTHER SOURCES FOR GUIDE SPACING

If you are experienced in fishing and rod-building, then perhaps the easiest way to

determine guide spacing is to simply lay the rod blank on a flat surface and determine the number of guides needed and to begin to position the guides along the blank, adjusting as you go. The best way to do this is to first position the butt guide where you think it belongs, then position the rest of the guides, with less spacing at the tip end and more at the butt end to adjust for the rod taper and type of bend. I do this but still check with a rule and make any adjustments as required, then I tape the guides in place and check them.

Other information for guide spacing is available. If you don't have a rod from which to copy spacing, often specific guide information is available from the source from which you bought the rod blank. Mail-order companies will often provide guide spacing for the specific rod you buy. Others will sometimes determine guide spacing for you, based on the rod blank, the guides chosen, and the type and length of handle to be used. Tackle shops will often have the same information or provide the same service.

Fishing clubs that are heavily into rod-building as a club project or as a service to members also sometimes keep information on guide spacing for specific rods.

Some mail-order catalogs and rod-blank-manufacturer catalogs also include guide-spacing information. In mail-order catalogs this information is often obtained from the rod manufacturers and then reproduced in the catalog.

There are two important factors to consider in using any such information. The first is that although the information is accurate, it is based on the rod being built to specification. Thus, if you begin with a six-foot casting-rod blank and use charts for blank through-handle construction with a short pistol-grip handle but modify it for a long flipping- or steelhead-type handle with a 12-inch-long rear grip, the guide spacing will change. In effect, the longer handle moves the entire grip and reel-seat assembly forward about 4 or 5 inches on the rod blank, and thus shortens the distance between the reel and the first or butt stripper guide by this much. The effect may make for more line friction on the cast and when line is retrieved, particularly when a wide-spool reel is used. Conversely, a rod designed for a through-the-handle construction with a long steelhead-type rear grip that is built with a short 5-inch rear grip will have increased distance between the reel and first guide, thus increasing the possibility of line-slap and rod friction.

The second factor is that you do not have to

match the exact same brand and power of rod if you use a chart from a ready built commercial or custom rod. For example, a rod built on a blank by manufacturer A will generally work fine with the guide spacing taken from the same length, action, and power of a rod built by manufacturer B. Similarly, most rod-blank manufacturers will have rods of the same length and action but in several different power ranges, for instance, light, medium, and heavy. In general, the same guide spacing will apply to all three rod blanks, even though you might want to go with a light one-foot guide on the light-power rod, a two-foot guide on the medium-power rod, and a reinforced, braced two-foot guide on the heavy-power rod.

The same rule may not apply to rods with different actions. For example, a manufacturer may have a rod blank of the same length, basic purpose (say, casting), and power (designed for the same general range of lure weights), but of an even parabolic action, different than the second rod, which has a stiff butt and fast-tip action. This often requires different guide spacing for the two rods. The parabolic rod will require even guide spacing from the tip to the butt (though the distance between guides will increase from tip to butt). The fast-action rod may require closer guide spacing at the tip end to better distribute stress at this light, whippy area, requiring greater distance between guides at the butt end, or perhaps one more guide than the parabolic rod of the same length.

One method that was used years ago to determine guide spacing and that is still accurate as a starting point is to use a deflection chart. Admittedly, this is something that most rod-builders will not want to use, because it involves the use of a large wall-mount chart against which to check rods. This chart must be as long as any rod you will test and generally several feet wide, or high, since it will be placed vertically. The chart is placed on a wall.) It must be exactly horizontal, checked with a level.

The chart must have horizontal stripes or lines to determine guide position. You can make such a deflection chart from a wide strip of paper. The 54-inch-wide background paper used by photographers (and available from good photo-supply stores) is ideal for this. Pick white or a light color and draw in the lines you need. A more colorful and easier alternative is to pick wallpaper with even vertical stripes and attach it to the wall horizontally. Narrow stripes about 1 inch wide are ideal, but any even striping will give you an easy

way to check the points where the bent rod blank intersects with the chosen line measurement.

The deflection chart must have a bracket or pegs on which to hold a rod horizontally with the handle *exactly* straight and horizontal. This can be done with a series of adjustable pegs or by using a tube or rod holder (such as those that fit onto the side of a boat for fishing or trolling) to hold the handle.

With the rod in the horizontal position, hang a weight from its end. This can be done by first gluing the tip-top in place and then tying a weight to it, or by taping cord or line to the tip end of the rod and then a weight to that. The weight will vary with the rod but should place a pronounced curve in the blank similar to what it would get during casting or playing. Often this will result in the tip end pointing straight down or almost straight down, with the rest of the rod curving until gradually becoming horizontal at the handle. You want a weight that will arc the rod, not be so heavy that it will only bend the butt end while pulling the top end straight down for several feet.

Guide positioning can be done in one or two ways. One way is to determine a deflection measurement — say, 5 inches — that you wish to use between the tip-top and the first guide. Measure 5 inches straight up from the position of the tip end or tip-top to a horizontal line that will intersect the bent rod blank. This intersection is the point for the first guide. Measure 5 inches to the next line. Continue doing this — measuring 5 inches (or whatever measurement you determine best) to where the horizontal lines intersect the rod blank. Do this until you are at or close to the position for the first (butt) guide. Naturally, this measurement will vary with the rod and will be determined by the rod type. A surf rod might have an initial distance of 8 to 12 inches; a freshwater spinning rod about 6 inches; a fly rod about 5 inches; and a very light noodle rod about 4 inches.

An alternative method is to place the rod on the chart, hang a weight from the tip, and then measure along the rod from the center of the reel seat to determine an approximate placement of the first guide (see the lists on page 397 for suggestions here). With the weight hanging from the rod tip, mark this point on the deflection chart, then measure straight down the chart to a point where the bent tip end intersects a horizontal line. Measure this distance and divide it by the number of guides you plan to use. Thus, if a particular rod had 30 vertical inches between the tip end and the position of the first butt guide and you were planning to use five guides, then the *vertical* distance between guides (not the distance on the rod blank) would be 6 inches. This method eliminates the possibility of getting a butt guide positioned too high or low on the rod blank and having to redo the measurements and calculations.

A simpler way is to mount the rod horizontally with a bracket or clamp, and then stretch a string horizontally (check it with a level) so that the handle and reel seat are centered on the string. Then hang a weight from the rod to bow it and, using a straight rule, measure down from the string to the tip end. Move up a set amount (based on the rod type) and then measure down, moving the rule until the second measurement intersects with the bowed rod blank. Repeat this until you are at the first position for the location of the butt guide. Alternatively, you can use the second method, measuring along the rod blank to position the butt guide. Measure straight down to this point, take a second measurement to the end of the rod, and then divide the distance between the two by the number of guides to determine the first spacing.

Perhaps the most important point is that all formulas for guide spacing should be considered as starting points. All guide spacing should be checked, as will be outlined later in this chapter.

FORMULAS

There are formulas for determining guide spacing, or at least to serve as starting points for guide spacing. Some of these are simple, some are quite complex. Some take into account the positioning of ferrules and make allowances for them, others do not and thus sometimes require adjustment of guide positions.

One simple formula calculates the distance between guides after the position of the butt guide is located. It also allows for the gradually increasing distance between the guides as they progress from the tip to the butt. The simplest way to understand this is to consider a standard spinning rod 6 feet long with six guides and a tip-top. Assuming the butt guide to be 2 feet up from the end of the rod, this would place the bottom guide 4 feet, or 48 inches, below the tip-top. This then creates six spaces between the adjacent guides, starting with the space between the tip-top and the first guide. If we assume this first distance to be a constant factor — "X" — then we can figure the remaining guides by adding to this X factor. Using the addition of 1 more inch

per guide is a good starting point. Thus, the position between the tip-top and first guide would be X, the distance between the first and second guides would be X plus 1, the distance between the second and third would be X plus 2 (1 plus 1), the distance between the third and fourth would be X plus 3 (2 plus 1), the distance between the fourth and fifth would be X plus 4 (3 plus 1), and the distance between the fifth and sixth or last guide would be X plus 5 (4 plus 1). This formula would look like this:

$X + (X + 1) + (X + 2) + (X + 3) + (X + 4) + (X + 5) = 48$ inches (the space between the tip-top and butt guide)

If we subtract the inches from the formula, it becomes:

$$6X + 15 = 48$$
$$6X = 48 - 15 = 33$$
$$6X = 33$$
$$X = 5.5$$

Going back to the formula, we then see that the distances between the guides are as follows: Between the tip-top and the first guide, 5.5 inches (X); between the first and second guide, 6.5 inches (X + 1); between the second and third guide, 7.5 inches (X + 2); between the third and fourth guide, 8.5 inches (X + 3); between the fourth and fifth guide, 9.5 inches (X + 4); and between the fifth and sixth or last guide, 10.5 inches (X + 5).

Naturally, you can use any additional spacing factor you desire. Thus, while the formula is simple by using the addition of 1 more inch with each guide spacing, you could just as easily use 1 1/4 inches, 1 1/2 inches, or 2 inches (though you would not use such large spaces on this standard medium freshwater spinning rod.) If you used 1 1/2 inches, for example, using six guides, then the spacing would be X, X + 1 1/2, X + 3, X + 4 1/2, X + 6, and X + 7 1/2.

The three factors involved in this that would change the guide spacing and positions would be the length of the rod (or the length between the tip-top and butt guide), the number of guides, and the constant number that would be added to the spacing of each previous guide. Naturally, this can be done using millimeters or centimeters as well as inches. Just be sure you keep all numbers in the same measuring system.

Note that the above does not take into account the number or positioning of ferrules. In some cases with two- or multiple-piece rods you may have to adjust the position of a guide slightly to avoid it sitting right over a ferrule. It is permissible to place a guide just above or below a ferrule so that the guide wrap also becomes the ferrule wrap, reinforcing the blank for hoop strength. This change is position usually requires some slight adjustment of guides above and below the guide in the ferrule area.

GUIDE-SPACING CHARTS

The following companies have been most helpful in providing guide spacing charts for all of their rod blanks. Unfortunately space limitations allow only a small sampling of these listings. All of these companies make more rods for a variety of line sizes and weights that those listed. When choosing between different rods of the same length but of different power (line size in fly and lure weight in others), I usually chose the lighter. In most cases, the guide spacing would be identical or very similar to that of heavier rods, although the guide sizes might change. Realize that you *must* use the same style handle and position of reel seat as used by the manufacturer in their finished model or the guide spacings will be invalid. Naturally, complete information on any rod blank is available directly from the manufacturer or from vendors selling the rod blank. (See appendixes F and G for complete addresses)

J. KENNEDY FISHER, INC. ™ GUIDE SPACING CHART

All measurements are from top of tip top to center of each guide.
For all 2pc and 4pc rods, except models listed on other chart.

LENGTH OF ROD

GUIDE #	7'	7 1/2'	8'	8 1/2'	9'	9 1/2'	10' OLD	10' NEW	10 1/2'	11'
GUIDE #1	4	4	4	4	4	4	4	4	4	4
GUIDE #2	9 1/4	8 3/4	8 1/2	8 1/2	8 1/2	8	8	8	8	8
GUIDE #3	16	14 3/4	14	14	15 1/4	13 1/2	13 1/2	13 1/2	13	13 1/2
GUIDE #4	23 1/2	22 1/4	20 1/2	20 3/4	22 3/4	20	19 3/4	19 3/4	19	19 3/4
GUIDE #5	30 1/2	31	28	28 3/4	31 1/2	27	26 3/4	26 3/4	26	26 3/4
GUIDE #6	38	40 1/4	36 1/2	37 3/4	41 1/4	35 1/4	34 1/2	34 1/2	34 1/2	34 1/2
GUIDE #7	46 3/4	50 1/4	45 3/4	47 3/4	52	46	43 1/4	43 1/4	44	43 1/4
GUIDE #8	56 1/2	60	55 1/2	58 3/4	63 3/4	56	52 3/4	52 3/4	54 1/2	52 3/4
GUIDE #9			66	70 3/4	76 1/2	68 1/2	63	64	66	64
GUIDE #10						82	74 1/4	77 1/4	78 1/2	77 1/4
GUIDE #11							86 1/2	93 1/2	92	93 1/2
GUIDE #12										105 3/4

J. KENNEDY FISHER, INC. SPECIAL MODELS GUIDE SPACING GRID

	FL25692	FL25604	FK25672	FGT3 — 81	STERLING	STERLING	STERLING	STERLING
GUIDE #	7'8"	8'8"	6'	81"	107"	108"	109"	115"
GUIDE #1	4	4 1/2	4 1/8	4	4	4	4	4 3/8
GUIDE #2	8 3/4	9 1/4	8 3/4	9	8 1/2	8 1/2	8 1/2	9 1/4
GUIDE #3	14 3/4	15 3/4	15 1/2	15 1/2	14 1/2	14 3/4	14 3/4	15 1/2
GUIDE #4	22 1/4	23 1/2	23 1/2	23 1/2	21 1/4	21 1/2	22	22 1/4
GUIDE #5	31	32 1/2	32 7/8	32	29	29 1/2	30	31
GUIDE #6	40 1/4	43 1/2	44 1/2	41	37 1/2	38	38 1/2	40
GUIDE #7	50 1/4	57		50 1/2	46 1/4	47	47 1/2	49 1/2
GUIDE #8	61 1/2	73		60 1/2	56 1/8	57	57 1/2	59 3/4
GUIDE #9					66 1/2	67	68	70
GUIDE #10					77 1/2	78	79	81 1/2

▪ LAMIGLAS, SUGGESTED GUIDE SPACING CHART (Guide Measurement in Inches From Tip) ▪

TYPE & LENGTH		1st	2nd	3rd	4th	5th	6th	7th	8th	9th	10th	11th	12th
FLY:													
7'	(84")	4	9	14	20	27	35	44	55				
7 1/2'	(90")	4	9	15	22	30	39	49	61				
8'	(96")	4	9	15	22	30	40	52	66				
8 1/2'	(102")	4	9	15	22	30	39	49	59	71			
9'	(108")	4	9	15	22	30	39	49	61	76			
9 1/2'	(114")	4	9	14	20	27	35	44	54	66	81		
10'	(120")	4	9	15	22	30	39	48	58	70	86		
10 1/2'	(126")	4	9	14	20	26	33	41	50	61	74	90	
SPINNING:													
4 1/2'	(54")	4 1/2	10 1/2	19	28								
5'	(60")	5	12	22	35								
5 1/2'	(66")	5	11	18	26	38							
6'	(72")	6	13	21	31	44							
6 1/2'	(78")	5	11	18	26	35	48						
7'	(84")	5	11	18	27	38	53						
STEELHEAD SPINNING:													
8'	(96")	4	9	15	22 1/2	31 1/2	42	56					
8 1/2'	(102")	5	11	18	26	36	48	62					
9'	(108")	5	11	17	24	32	41	52	67				
STEELHEAD CASTING:													
8'	(96")	4	9	15	22	30	38	46	59				
8'4"	(100")	4	8	13	24	31	39	47	62				
8 1/2'	(102")	4	9	15	22	30	39	48 1/2	64				
9'	(108")	4	9	15	22	30	38	47	57 1/2	70			
10 1/2'	(126")	5	10	16	22	29	36	43	51	59	67	78	90
FLIPPING (TELESCOPING HANDLE):													
7 1/2'	(90")	5	11	18	26	35	66						
CASTING:													
5'2"	(62")	4	9 1/2	16 1/2	24	34							
5 1/2'	(66")	5	11	18	26	37							
6'	(72")	5	11 1/2	19 1/2	29	42							
6 1/2'	(78")	5	12 3/4	21 1/4	30 3/4	41 3/4							
7'	(84")	5	11	18	26	36	50						
7 1/2'	(90")	5 1/4	10 3/4	17 1/4	27	38 1/4	51						

G. LOOMIS ™ GUIDE PLACEMENT CHART

BASS CAST

C661	5'6"	4 1/4 — 8 7/8 — 14 5/8 — 21 1/2 — 29 5/16 — 37 3/4
721	6'0"	4 1/2 — 9 1/4 — 14 3/4 — 21 1/4 — 29 1/4 — 38 1/4
MB783	6'6"	5 — 10 5/8 — 17 — 24 — 33 — 44
802x	6'8"	4 — 9 — 15 — 22 1/4 — 31 — 42 1/4
FS904x	7'6"	5 — 10 1/2 — 16 1/2 — 23 — 19 3/4 — 38 1/4 — 48 3/8
MB844	7'0"	4 1/4 — 9 — 14 5/8 — 21 5/8 — 29 5/8 — 38 3/4 — 48 7/8

STEELHEAD AND SALMON

BB964	8'0"	3 1/4 — 6 3/4 — 11 — 16 1/4 — 22 3/4 — 30 1/4 — 38 1/2 — 47 1/2 — 57
HS9000	7'6"	4 — 8 5/8 — 13 5/8 — 19 1/2 — 25 1/2 — 32 — 40 3/4 — 51 1/4
981	8'2"	3 1/4 — 7 — 11 1/4 — 16 1/2 — 23 1/4 — 31 1/4 — 39 1/2 — 48 3/4 — 58 3/4
1021	8'6"	4 — 8 3/8 — 13 3/8 — 19 1/8 — 25 3/8 — 32 3/8 — 40 3/8 — 50 1/8
1082	9'0"	4 1/2 — 9 1/2 — 15 1/2 — 22 1/2 — 30 1/2 — 39 — 48 — 58 1/2 — 70 1/2
1141	9'6"	5 — 11 1/4 — 18 1/8 — 26 — 34 1/8 — 43 1/8 — 52 1/2 — 63 3/4 — 75 3/4

LIGHT SALT

L844-2	7'0"	4 1/4 — 8 3/4 — 13 3/4 — 19 7/8 — 26 1/4 — 33 1/2 — 42 — 51 1/2
F783	6'6"	3 — 8 1/2 — 13 1/2 — 19 — 25 — 32 1/2 — 41 1/4 — 50 1/4
904	7'6"	4 — 9 — 15 — 21 3/4 — 29 1/4 — 37 3/4 — 47 1/4 — 58 3/4
932	7'9"	4 — 9 — 15 — 22 — 30 — 38 1/4 — 46 3/4 — 55 1/2 — 65 1/4
963	8'0"	4 — 9 — 15 — 22 — 29 1/2 — 37 1/2 — 46 — 55 — 65 1/2
1024	8'6"	4 — 9 — 15 — 22 — 29 1/2 — 37 1/4 — 45 3/8 — 54 1/4 — 63 1/4 — 72 3/4
1083	9'0"	4 — 9 — 15 — 22 — 29 1/2 — 37 1/2 — 46 5/8 — 56 3/4 — 67 1/4 — 78
1145	9'6"	4 — 9 — 15 — 22 — 29 1/4 — 37 — 44 — 53 1/4 — 62 3/8 — 72 3/4 — 84
1204	10'	4 — 9 — 15 — 22 — 30 — 39 — 48 — 57 1/2 — 68 3/8 — 79 3/8 — 90 3/4
1328/9-3	11'	4 — 9 — 15 1/8 — 22 1/8 — 29 3/4 — 37 7/8 X 31 1/4 — 13 1/4 — 23 3/4 — 34 3/4 X 3 — 14 5/8
1569/10-3	13'	4 3/8 — 10 — 17 — 26 — 36 — 46 7/8 — 58 5/8 — 71 5/8 — 85 5/8 — 100 5/8 — 116 7/8
1801/11-3	15'	4 1/2 — 9 1/2 — 15 3/4 — 23 — 31 1/2 — 41 1/2 — 52 1/2 — 66 — 82 — 99 3/8 — 117 3/8 X Butt 19

SPIN JIG

SJ 720	6'0"	4 3/4 — 11 1/4 — 18 3/4 — 28 1/4 — 39

SPIN TROUT

S541	4'6"	5 1/2 — 11 3/4 — 18 3/4 — 27 1/4
6010	5'0"	5 3/4 — 12 1/2 — 20 13/16 — 30 1/16
661	5'6"	4 1/2 — 9 1/2 — 16 1/2 — 24 1/4 — 34 1/4
782	6'6"	5 — 11 — 18 — 26 1/2 — 36 1/2 — 48
842	7'0"	5 1/2 — 12 1/2 — 20 1/2 — 29 1/2 — 40 — 50 7/8

POPPING SPIN

P842	7'0"	4 1/2 — 10 1/4 — 17 1/2 — 26 — 36 1/2 — 48 1/4

STEELHEAD SPIN

HS9000	7'6"	5 — 11 — 18 — 27 3/4 — 38 1/2 — 53 1/2
ST1023	8'6"	5 1/16 — 11 1/16 — 18 1/16 — 26 7/8 — 36 7/8 — 48 1/4 — 62 1/4
1141	9'6"	6 3/4 — 13 7/8 — 22 7/8 — 32 7/8 — 43 3/4 — 56 13/16 — 72 5/8

NOODLE

13825	11'6"	tip 5 7/8 — 12 3/4 — 21 3/4 — 31 3/4 — 42 7/8 — 55 7/8 — 69 butt 14 3/4 — 30 1/8

SAGE GUIDE SPACING

(Measure from TIP TOP to center of guide)

ROD MODEL	BUTT (length)	BUTT (GUIDE SIZE / GUIDE SPACING)										TIP
LL												
379LL	7'9"	10 / 64 7/8	3 / 55 1/2	1 / 46 1/4	1/0 / 37 1/2	1/0 / 29 5/16	1/0 / 21 1/2	1/0 / 14 7/8	1/0 / 9 1/4	1/0 / 4 1/8		
389LL	8'9"	12 / 72 7/8	4 / 62	2 / 52 1/8	1 / 42 7/8	1/0 / 34 7/8	1/0 / 28 1/8	1/0 / 21 1/2	1/0 / 15 3/8	1/0 / 9 1/4	1/0 / 4 1/8	
469LL	6'9"				10 / 51 3/4	1 / 40 1/2	1 / 31 5/16	1 / 22 7/8	1/0 / 15 1/2	1/0 / 9	1/0 / 4	
473LL	7'3"			10 / 60 3/4	3 / 51 1/2	1 / 43 7/8	1/0 / 35 1/2	1/0 / 27 1/2	1/0 / 20	1/0 / 13 3/8	1/0 / 8	3 1/2
4711LL	7'11"		10 / 66 13/16	10 / 57 7/16	3 / 47 1/2	1 / 39 1/4	1/0 / 31	1/0 / 22 15/16	1/0 / 15 15/16	1/0 / 10	4 13/16	
486LL	8'6"		12 / 70 3/8	4 / 60	2 / 50 7/8	1 / 41 5/8	1 / 31 1/8	1/0 / 25 1/8	1/0 / 17 3/8	1/0 / 10 3/8	4 1/2	
490LL	9'0"	12 / 76 5/8	4 / 64 5/8	3 / 53 7/8	2 / 45	2 / 29 5/16	1 / 22 3/16	1/0 / 15 13/16	1/0 / 9 7/8	4 1/2		
580LL	8'0"		10 / 66 5/16	3 / 57 1/16	1 / 47 13/16	1 / 38 3/4	1 / 30 9/16	2 / 22 3/4	1 / 15 3/8	9 11/16	4 7/16	
RPL												
461RPL	6'11"		10 / 56 5/8	3 / 46 3/4	1 / 37 3/4	1/0 / 30 3/4	1/0 / 24 1/4	1/0 / 18 3/16	1/0 / 12 7/16	1/0 / 7 1/4	1/0	1/0
490RPL			12 / 76 5/8	4 / 64 5/8	2 / 45	2 / 36 11/16	2 / 29 5/16	1 / 22 3/16	1 / 15 13/16	1 / 9 7/8	1	2 7/8
576RPL	7'6"			3 / 53 1/8	2 / 45 1/8	2 / 36 3/8	2 / 28 3/8	2 / 20 3/4	1 / 14 1/4	1 / 8 3/4	1	1
596RPL	9'6"	12 / 80 3/4	4 / 70 3/16	4 / 60 7/16	3 / 51 7/16	3 / 42 3/4	2 / 35 1/16	2 / 28	2 / 21 1/4	1 / 15 1/8	1 / 9 1/4	4 1/2
5100RPL	10'0"	12 / 91 3/8	4 / 80 3/4	3 / 70 7/16	3 / 60 7/16	3 / 51 7/16	2 / 42 3/4	2 / 35 1/16	2 / 28	2 / 21 1/4	1 / 15 1/8	4 3/8
583-4DS	8'3"	4 / 80 5/16	10 / 69 3/4	10 / 59 7/8	3 / 50 15/16	2 / 42 3/4	2 / 35 1/6	2 / 27 3/4	1 / 21 3/16	1 / 15 3/16	1 / 9 11/16	4 7/16
GFS576B (FLIPPING)	7'6"		10 / 68 3/4	59 / 20	49 7/8 / 12	40 3/4 / 10	31 7/8 / 10	22 1/8 / 10	15	9	1	1
GSH1798	7'9"		76 5/8 / 47	38 1/2 / 16	31 / 24	18	12 1/2	8	8	1	3 7/8	8
GIISH186B	8'6"			43 1/4 / 8	58 / 6	32 1/2 / 6	22 1/4 / 6	13 1/2 / 6	6	3 1/2	6	
GIISH286B				10 / 57 3/4	44 7/8 / 8	35 5/9 / 6	27 1/4 / 6	20 1/2 / 6	14 1/2 / 9	6	6	
GIISH386B												6
GSH286B												
GSH486B												4
GIISH290B	9'0"		10 / 62 3/4	49 / 8	37 3/4 / 8	28 / 6	20 1/2 / 6	14 3/8 / 6	8 7/8 / 6	6	6	
GSH290B												4 1/8
GSH390B												
GSH490B												
GSH590B												

SAGE GUIDE SPACING (continued)

(Measure from TIP TOP to center of guide)

ROD MODEL	BUTT	GUIDE SIZE / GUIDE SPACING (butt → tip)										TIP
GSH2100B	10"			10 / 74 1/2	8 / 59 5/8	8 / 48 1/4	8 / 28 1/4	6 / 20 1/4	6 / 14 5/8	6 / 9 1/8	6 / 6	6
GSH4100B	10'6"	8 / 83 1/2	8 / 72 1/2	6 / 62 1/2	6 / 52 3/4	6 / 44 1/4	6 / 36 3/4	6 / 29 3/4	6 / 23 1/4	6 / 17	6 / 6	4 3/8
GSH3106B		10 / 90 1/2	10 / 77 1/4	8 / 65 1/2	8 / 55 1/4	8 / 46 1/4	6 / 38	6 / 30 1/2	6 / 23 1/2	6 / 17	6 / 11 / 6	6
GSH4110B	11'											5 1/4
GSH3113LB	11'3"	12 / 84 1/4	10 / 72 1/2	8 / 61 3/8	8 / 50 3/4	8 / 40 3/4	8 / 31 3/4	8 / 23 1/2	8 / 16 1/2	8 / 10 1/2	8 / 8	5 1/4
GSH3113MB		10 / 96 1/2										5
GSH4120	12'	12 / 102	10 / 77 1/2	10 / 69 1/2	10 / 66 1/4	8 / 55 1/2	8 / 45 1/2	8 / 36 1/2	8 / 28 1/2	8 / 21 3/8	8 / 15 / 9 1/4	4 1/2

SPINNING STEELHEAD

ROD MODEL	BUTT	GUIDE SIZE / GUIDE SPACING (butt → tip)						TIP
GSH179B	7'9"	30 / 58	16 / 43 1/4	12 / 32 1/4	10 / 22 1/4	8 / 13 1/2	8 / 8	8
GIISH186B	8'6"		30 / 58 1/4	20 / 44 3/4	16 / 34	12 / 25 1/4	10 / 17 1/2 / 10 5/8	6
GIISH286B								8
GIISH386B								4 1/4
GSH286B								
GSH486B								
GIISH290B	9'0"	30 / 61 1/2	20 / 48	16 / 36 1/2	12 / 26 1/2	10 / 18	8 / 11	8
GSH290B								5
GSH390B								
GSH490B								
GSH590B								

SPINNING FRESHWATER

ROD MODEL	BUTT	GUIDE SIZE / GUIDE SPACING (butt → tip)					TIP
GSP153B	5'3"	25 / 25	16 / 10	10 / 8			7
GSP159B	5'9"	25 / 48 1/2	25 / 35 1/2	16 / 25 1/2	10 / 17 1/2	8 / 10 1/2	5
GSP160-1B	6'0"	25 / 43 1/2	20 / 31 1/8	12 / 20	8 / 10 / 8		7
GSP260-1B		16 / 41	16 / 28 1/2	10 / 18 1/2	8 / 10 3/4		5
GSP360-1B							7
GSP460-1B							5
GSP269B	6'9"	25 / 48 1/2	20 / 35 1/4	16 / 24 5/8	12 / 17	10 / 10 1/4	
GSP273B	7'3"	25 / 54 1/4	20 / 39 1/2	16 / 27 3/4	12 / 19	10 / 11 3/4 / 10	4 3/4
GSP473B							8
GSP276B	7'6"	20 / 16 / 12	8			7 / 8	5 1/4
GSP366B	6'6"	20 / 55 3/4	25 / 43 3/4	20 / 32 3/4	16 / 23 3/4	16 1/4 / 16 / 10 1/4	7 / 5
SP370B	7'	25 / 49 1/2	25 / 45 1/4	20 / 37 1/2	20 / 27	16 / 18 1/8 / 11	8 / 5

TALON 1992 GUIDE PLACEMENT SPECIFICATIONS

MODEL #	LENGTH	PIECES	LINE WT.	LURE WT.	BUTT DIA	TIP TOP	BLK WT. (OZ.)	SUGGESTED GUIDE PLACEMENT, IN INCHES, FROM TIP; SUGGESTED GUIDE SIZE ( )
CAIRNTON AND PROFESSIONAL								
Fly								
C7'9"F-2	7'9"	2	2		0.285	4.0	0.80	5(1), 10 1/4(1), 16 1/8(1), 22 3/8(1), 29 1/8(2), 36 3/8(2), 45 7/8(2), 55 3/4(3), 67 1/2(10)
C8'0"F-5	8'0"	2	5		0.325	4.0	1.50	5(1), 10 1/4(1), 16 1/8(1), 22 3/8(1), 29 1/8(2), 36 3/8(2), 44 7/8(2), 54 1/4(3), 65 1/2(10)
C8'6"F-5	8'6"	2	5		0.350	4.0	1.60	5(1), 10 3/8(1), 16(1), 21 3/4(1), 28(2), 34 3/4(2), 41 3/4(2), 49 5/8(3), 59 5/8(3), 71(10)
C9'0"F-4	9'0"	2	4		0.340	4.0	1.20	5 1/2(1), 11 1/2(1), 18(1), 25(1), 32 1/2(2), 40 1/4(2), 48 1/4(2), 57(3), 66 3/4(3), 78 1/4(10)
C9'6"F-9	9'6"	2	9		0.400	4.5	2.00	5(2), 10 1/2(2), 16 1/4(2), 22 1/2(3), 28 7/8(3), 35 1/2(3), 42 3/4(4), 50 1/2(4), 58 1/2(4), 67 1/4(10), 77(12)
Casting								
P5'6"C-MLF	5'6"	1	6-17	1/4-5/8	0.430	1.8	1.10	4(8), 8 5/8(8), 14 1/2(8), 21 1/4(10), 29(10), 37 5/8(12)
P6'0"C-MLF	6'0"	1	6-17	1/4-5/8	0.450	1.8	1.70	4 1/2(8), 9(8), 14 1/4(8), 21 1/4(10), 29 1/4(10), 38 3/4(12)
P6'6"C-MLF	6'6"	1	6-17	1/4-5/8	0.485	2.0	2.20	4 1/2(8), 10(8), 16 1/2(8), 24 1/4(10), 32 1/2(10), 42 3/4(12)
P7'0"C-MXF	7'0"	1	6-17	1/4-5/8	0.460	2.0	1.70	5 9/16(8), 12 1/4(8), 20 1/16(8), 28 3/4(10), 38 3/4(10), 50 3/4(12)
P7'6"C-MXF	7'6"	1	10-20	3/8-4	0.520	1.8	2.50	3 1/2(6), 7 1/2(6), 11 3/4(6), 16 1/2(8), 22 3/4(8), 31(8), 41 1/4(10), 53 5/8(12)
P8'3"C-MLXF	3'3"	2	6-10	1/4-1/2	0.430	1.8	1.80	4 1/4(6), 8 5/8(6), 13 5/8(6), 19 1/2(6), 25 1/2(8), 32 3/8(8), 40 1/8(8), 49 1/2(10), 59 7/8(12)
P8'6"C-MF	8'6"	2	6-15	3/8-3/4	0.440	1.8	2.00	4 3/4(6), 10 1/2(6), 17 1/4(6), 24 1/8(8), 32(8), 40 7/8(8), 51 1/8(10), 63 1/2(12)
Spinning								
P5'6"S-UM	5'6"	1	2-8	1/16-3/8	0.275	1.8	0.80	5 1/2(10), 12(12), 20(16), 29 1/2(20), 42(30)
P5'8"S-MLF	5'8"	1	10-20	1/4-5/8	0.375	1.8	1.40	5 1/2(10), 12(12), 20(16), 29 1/2(20), 42(30)
P6'0"S-LF	6'0"	1	6-12	3/16-3/8	0.385	4.8	1.40	5 1/2(10), 12(12), 20(16), 29 1/2(20), 43(30)
P6'6"S-MLF	6'6"	1	6-17	1/4-5/8	0.475	1.8	1.90	5 1/2(10), 13(12), 23(16), 34(20), 46(30)
P7'0"S-MF	7'0"	1	8-17	3/8-3/4	0.470	1.8	1.90	5(8), 10 7/8(10), 18 1/2(12), 27 1/2(16), 37 1/2(20), 49 1/2(30)
EXCELON								
Fly								
E5'7"F-3	5'7"	1	3		0.240	4.0	0.6	4 (1/0), 9 1/4(1/0), 15 1/4(1/0), 21 1/2(1), 28 1/2(1), 35 1/2(2), 42 1/2(8)
E6'6"F-2	6'6"	2	2		0.255	4.0	0.8	4 1/2(1/0), 9 1/2(1/0), 15 1/4(1/0), 21 3/4(1), 29 1/4(1), 38 1/2(2), 49(8)
E7'6"F-4	7'6"	2	4		0.275	4.0	1.1	5(1), 10 3/8(1), 16 3/8(1), 23 1/8(1), 30 3/4(2), 39 1/2(2), 49 5/8(3), 61 1/4(10)

TALON 1992 GUIDE PLACEMENT SPECIFICATIONS (continued)

MODEL #	LENGTH	PIECES	LINE WT.	LURE WT.	BUTT DIA.	TIP TOP	BLK WT. (OZ.)	SUGGESTED GUIDE PLACEMENT, IN INCHES, FROM TIP; SUGGESTED GUIDE SIZE ( )
Casting								
E5'6"C-MLF	5'6"	1	6-17	1/4-5/8	0.480	2.2	1.7	4(8), 8 5/8(8), 14 1/2(8), 21 1/4(10), 29(10), 37 5/8(12)
E60"C-MLF	6'0"	1	6-17	1/4-5/8	0.510	2.2	1.7	4 1/2(8), 9 (8), 14 1/4(8), 21 1/4(10), 29 1/4(10), 38 3/4(12)
E6'6"C-UF	6'6"	1	4-8	1/8-5/16	0.405	2.0	1.7	5 9/16(8), 12 1/4(8), 20 1/16(8), 28 3/4(10), 33 3/4(10), 50 3/4(12)
E70"C-LF	7'0"	1	6-12	1/4-3/8	0.425	1.8	1.9	5 9/16(8), 12 1/4(8), 20 1/16(8), 23 3/4(10), 38 3/4(10), 50 3/4(12)
E7'6"C-LF2	7'6"	2	6-12	1/4-3/8	0.465	2.0	2.1	47/8(8), 9 7/8(8), 15(8), 21(10), 28(10), 36(10), 44 1/2(12), 53 5/8(16)
E83"C-MLXF	8'3"	2	6-10	1/4-1/2	0.470	2.0	2.4	4 1/4(6), 8 5/8(6), 13 5/8(6), 19 1/2(6), 25 1/2(8), 32 3/8(8), 40 1/8(8), 49 1/2(10), 59 7/8(12)
E8'6"C-MF	8'6"	2	6-15	3/8-3/4	0.485	2.0	2.2	4 3/4(6), 10 1/2(6), 17 1/2(6), 24 1/8(8), 32(8), 40 7/8(8), 51 1/8(10), 63 1/2(12)
E90"C-LMF	9'0"	2	4-8	1/8-3/8	0.455	2.0	3.1	4(6), 8 5/8(6), 13 3/4(5), 19 1/2(6), 26 5/8(8), 35 1/4(8), 46(8), 57 3/4(10), 70 3/4(12)
Spinning								
E5'6"S-US	5'6"	1	2-6	1/8-1/4	0.310	1.8	0.7	5 3/4(10), 12 1/4(12), 20 1/4(16), 29 3/4(20), 43(30)
E5'8"S-MLF	5'8"	1	6-12	3/16-3/8	0.490	2.0	1.7	5 1/2(10), 12 12), 20(16), 29 1/2(20), 42(30)
E60"S-LF	6'0"	1	6-12	3/16-3/8	0.445	2.0	1.9	5 1/2(10), 12(12), 20(15), 29 1/2(20), 43(30)
E66"S-LF	6'6"	2	6-12	3/16-3/8	0.525	2.0	1.9	5 1/2(10), 13(12), 23(16), 34(20), 45(30)
E70"S-LF	7'0"	1	6-12	1/4-3/8	0.425	1.8	1.9	5(8), 10 7/8(12), 18 7/16(12), 27 1/2(16), 37 1/2(20), 49 1/2(30)
E8'6"S-MF	8'6"	2	6-15	3/8-3/4	0.485	2.0	2.2	6 3/4(8), 15 7/8(10), 26 1/8(12), 37 3/8(16), 49 1/2(20), 64 1/2(30)
S5'8"C-XHF	5'8"	1	100#		0.735	4.0	6.3	5 3/8(R-2), 11 1/4(R-2), 17 3/8(R-3), 25 3/4(R-4), 35(R-5)
S5'9"C-XHM	5'9"	1	15-40	3/4-4	0.585	4.5	4.0	5 1/16(10), 12 1/8(10), 19 3/16(12), 28 (16), 36 7/8(20)
S80"C-XHF	8'0"	1	15-30	1-6	0.665	2.6	5.3	4(6), 8 1/4(6), 13(6), 18 1/2(8), 25(8), 33 1/2(8), 44(10), 56 3/4(12)
S90"C-LMF	9'0"	2	4-8	1/8-3/8	0.445	2.2	3.1	4(6), 8 5/8(6), 13 3/4(6), 19 1/2(6), 26 5/8(8), 35 1/4(8), 46(8), 57 3/4(10), 70 3/4(12)
S116"C-US	11'6"	2	4-6	1/8-3/8	0.375	1.8	2.2	5(6), 11(6), 18(5), 26(6), 35(8), 45(8), 56(8), 69(10), 83(10), 98(12)
Spinning								
S46"S-US	4'6"	1	1-4	1/16-3/16	0.235	1.8	0.6	5(8), 12(10), 20-16), 32 1/2(25)
S50"S-US	5'0"	1	1-4	1/16-3/16	0.250	1.8	0.7	6(8), 13 1/2(10), 22 1/2(16), 34 3/4(25)
S5'4"S-MLF	5'4"	1	4-10	1/8-5/16	0.285	2.0	0.8	5(8), 11(10), 16 1/2(12), 25(16), 37(25)
S5'9"S-LS	5'9"	1	2-8	1/8-3/8	0.395	2.0	1.7	5 3/4(10), 12 1/4(12), 20 1/4(15), 29 3/4(20), 43(30)
S8'6"S-MF	8'6"	2	6-15	3/8-3/4	0.430	2.0	2.8	6 3/4(8), 15 7/8(10), 26 1/8(12), 37 3/8(16), 49 1/2(20), 64 1/2(30)
S9'0"S-LMF	9'0"	2	4-8	1/8-3/8	0.445	2.2	3.1	6 5/8(8), 14 1/2(8), 23 7/8(10), 34(12), 45 1/4(16), 57 1/4(20), 70(30)
S116"S-MHM	11'6"	2	10-30	2-6	0.750	4.0	7.5	6 1/8(10), 14 3/8(10), 23 13/16(12), 37 1/4(16), 51 1/8(20), 68 15/16(30), 86 1/8(40)
Striker-Saltwater								
S5'6"R-MF	5'6"	1	20#		0.565	110	5.6	5 1/8(R-2), 11 5/8(R-2), 19 7/8(R-3), 29 5/8(R-4), 40 3/8(R-5)

CHECKING GUIDE SPACING

Note that in all checking of guide spacing, you should work with the guides taped in place. By using narrow masking tape you can change guides or guide positions easily until the guides are positioned properly and the rod is exactly right.

There are several ways to check guide spacing. In fact, some of these can be used to determine guide spacing. One of the easiest ways is to first determine the guide spacing by any method you prefer. Then tape the guides in place at these locations and glue the tip-top in place. Mount a reel on the rod (the handle and reel-seat assembly will be complete at this point), thread the line through the guides, and tie on a practice plug. Pick a sunny day and make a practice cast at right angles to the direction of the sun. Make this a gentle cast, because the guides are only taped in place. Do not watch the plug (a natural tendency) but instead hold the rod out and look in the direction of the sun (not *at* the sun) as the line comes off the reel and goes through the guides. This shows up best against a dark background, but in any situation the glint of the sun on the line shows exactly what the line is doing during the cast. It is best to have an experienced angler cast while you watch the line flowing through the guides. That way you can adjust your position to best see the line at different angles. Do this several times, so that on each cast you can examine closely the line flow through and around each guide. For example, you might find that there is excessive line slap on the rod between the reel and the first guide on a spinning rod, indicating either too low a frame on the first guide or too much space between the reel and the guide. By changing the guide position, or the guide itself, you will see the results of your adjustments.

If you want to check the degree of friction coming through a set of guides in comparison with a similar rod of the same length, you can do so but must have (or beg or borrow) two identical spinning reels and spool them with identical (in brand, type, and line-test) line and have two identical practice plugs or sinkers. You will also need to find a spot with a straight drop where you can drop the sinkers or practice plugs. Ideally, this drop should be 20 feet or more. This is sometimes called a "drop test" and is used by some manufacturers to test their spinning rods against the competition. (You can also test spool-lip friction on a spinning reel in two different reels by using identical rods.)

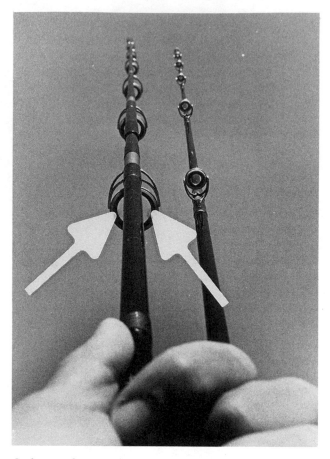

Sighting along rods to check guide alignment. Two methods are shown: left, with the rod guide under the rod; right, with the guides on top of the rod. Note that on the left rod, more of the guide ring can be seen to the right (note arrows) than to the left. This would have to be adjusted, and then this guide used as a check against all the other guides without moving the rod.

On a place with a straight vertical drop, fasten the rods horizontally by clamping the rod handles or otherwise supporting them. I find an easy way to do this is out of a second- or third-story window in a home. Run line through both rods and tie the identical practice plugs to the line. With the plugs hanging down 6 inches from the tip end, lift both lines above the horizontal rods between the reel and the first guide. Then, holding the line, open the bails. With the bails open, release both lines at once (hold both lines between your index finger and thumb). The practice plug that hits the ground first from the high drop will have experienced the least guide friction. Check this several times to be sure. The principle is that because the reels, line, and practice plugs are all identical, any differences in the drop will be the result of friction as the lines run through the guides.

A third method of checking rod guides is to use a deflection test. In this, you would use a chart as previously described for positioning the guides. Mount a reel on the rod, run the line through the guides, and tie a weight to the end of the line. This should be slightly heavier than the weight of a lure or sinker balanced for the rod. This will bend or deflect the rod, and you can check visually for evenness in the distribution of stresses and of bending.

Once you are completely satisfied with the positioning, size, and type of the guides on the rod, tape them down securely and proceed to wrap the guides in place.

22

Guide Wrappings and Variations

INTRODUCTION · TOOLS · MATERIALS · MOUNTING
THE TIP-TOP GUIDE · PREPARATION · MEASUREMENTS ·
WRAPPING METHODS · UNDERWRAPS · DOUBLE AND
TRIPLE WRAPS · VARIATIONS AND SPECIAL EFFECTS AND
WRAPPINGS · WRAPS ON PARTS OTHER THAN GUIDES

INTRODUCTION

Careful guide wrappings are a must for any custom rod. Although some inexpensive manufactured rods have been and are being made with slip-on guides, wrapped-on wire guides, and taped-on guides, these would never be used on a custom rod. Guides are wrapped on with thread on virtually every type of rod, from ultralight spinning and 3-weight fly rods up to heavy surf and 130-pound IGFA-class offshore rods.

The technique of wrapping guides is the same on all rods, although variations and additions to this technique abound. The important thing to remember is that once the basic guide-wrapping technique is learned—and it can be learned in only a few minutes—it is basic to any wrap for any

guide, using any size thread, and may be applied to any of the many variations that can be used.

TOOLS

Tools for rod wrapping can be costly and complex, inexpensive and simple, or you can make uncomplicated tools from scraps in only a few minutes that will suffice for one or two rods. The main tool of course is the rod wrapper or rod winder.

The simplest tools consist of no tools but rather of a methodology of wrapping. One method involves dropping a spool of thread into an empty cup or bowl, then running the thread between several sheets of clean typing paper placed in the center of a phone book. The phone book—or books piled on top of it—creates the necessary tension, while the bowl or cup keeps the thread secure. By placing the spool of thread on a table and resting the phone book on the near edge of the table, the thread can be brought straight up and over the front of the rod blank for wrapping. This is best, because bringing the thread up behind the rod does not allow you to see the position of the thread to prevent gaps or overlapping.

A better way is to make a rack or supports to hold the rod blank while you are wrapping it. There are several ways to make racks. One is to use a heavy-wire (all-wire) coat hanger. Pull the wire out straight, then bend it so that it will clamp onto a worktable; the hook will support the rod. At least two of these are needed, and for long rods a third or possibly even a fourth hanger will be needed to support the long end of the rod blank.

A rod support can also be made from a cardboard carton. Use a large, sturdy carton and cut off the top to the level on which you want the rod to rest. Then cut out the front, but leave a margin around the two sides and bottom so that the box will retain its shape. Cut V-shaped notches into the two sides to serve as guides to support the rod. If the box is large, you may wish to place the phone book and the cup with the spool in the box. If the box is not large enough for that, cut a hole in the back of the box, place the phone book and bowl outside the box, and run the thread through the hole. Hold the box in place by C-clamping it to the table or holding it down with heavy books. To keep the thread in front, where you can see it when the cup is in or in back of the box, tape a guide to the C-clamp and run the thread through it. This brings the thread straight up in front of the rod blank for easy wrapping, regardless of the position of the thread spool.

A third variation is to use scraps of wood to make a support rack that can then be clamped to the table. Although any size of wood can be used, a good start is with old shelving, 4 inches or more wide. Make a base about 18 inches long and two end supports about 8 to 12 inches high. Nail or screw the upright supports to the base. For added permanence and strength, use metal corner brackets. Cut a V-shaped notch into the top end of each upright support. To protect the rod, line this notch with self-adhesive felt or with a strip of plastic cut from a plastic bottle, or wrap the rod with masking tape where it will touch the wrapping support. The first two methods are the best because they are one-time solutions, whereas the wrapping position changes with each new guide; thus the masking-tape protection must be constantly changed. You can still use the cup and phone book, but mount a spare guide to the center base of the wood support through which to run the thread while you are wrapping.

Simple rod-wrapping tools are sold commercially and are widely available. Most of these consist of a clamp-on support with two arms to hold the rod, in the center of which is a small combination thread holder and tension device. These are fine for one or two rods, provided they are lightweight freshwater rods. The small distance between the two supports makes these supports impractical for building large or heavy rods or long sections of rods. They can be used for long and heavy rods with an additional rod support, such as one made from coat-hanger wire.

Other simple and inexpensive rod-wrapping tools consist of finished models very similar to the scrap-wood tool just described. Usually there is a base with two upright supports. Often, one or both of these upright supports are adjustable, as is the center thread holder and tension device. In addition, it is easy to cut a cardboard box to size to hold one end of a long or heavy rod to be placed in these tools, since they are used on top of the worktable, not clamped to it.

Larger and more complex rod winders are available. Often, these have longer bases on which to make larger, longer rods, have rollers to help turn the rod without potential damage to the rod blank, and have adjustable blank supports and thread-tension devices.

Homemade, adjustable rod wrapper with rollers to support the rod. The thread-tension device is adjustable for any size thread spool.

Rubber rollers such as those on this rod wrapper prevent scratching or damage to the rod blank. If using plastic wheels, cover them with several layers of masking tape to protect the blank.

The next stage of rod winders incorporates motors to control the thread-wrapping. The motor is controlled by a foot-operated rheostat. Most of these have rollers both above and below the rod blank, so as to both support and hold down the rod blank. They are available with extensions for extra-long rods (such as one-piece surf rods), and some have an option of standard or self-centering chucks to hold the rod. These are expensive and thus are best suited as a purchase for a fishing or rod-building club, for the serious angler, or for a small-scale rod-builder.

Other tools will help to make the wrapping task easier. A file is required to file the ends of the guides to make them into a sharp point for easy transition of the thread from the blank up onto the guide foot. A fine or medium file works best for this. It is also good for removing any burrs on the base of the guide foot to prevent damage to the rod blank.

Masking tape is required both to hold the guide in place and to mark the ends of the wrap, at which point the thread wrap is begun. The best sizes are 1/8- or 1/4-inch. Masking tape is available from art-supply stores and some tackle and mail-order companies specializing in rod-building supplies.

Scissors are necessary for general thread work: cutting thread for wrapping and making up the loops of thread used to pull the end of the thread through the wraps. Almost any type of scissors will work, although special rod-wrapping scissors are sold by firms like Gudebrod. Fly-tying scissors are also fine for this purpose.

A thread puller, described in Chapter 2, consists of hook-and-loop strips (Velcro) joined at one end by a rivet or grommet, to which is attached a loop of mono of about eight- to fifteen-pound test. Use finer sizes of mono for finer thread, such as size A; and larger mono for larger thread, such as sizes D, E, and EE. In use, the thread-puller hook-and-loop strips are separated and attached around the rod with the loop of mono pointing to the center of the guide. The cut thread is placed through the loop and the loop is pulled through. Unlike thread loops, this tool is reusable, although in time the mono loops do have to be replaced.

A scalpel or razor blade is needed to cut the end of the thread after it has been pulled under the end wraps. Either will work, although disposable razor blades are more readily available and less expensive.

A burnisher is suggested for rubbing over the wrappings to remove any small gaps or unevenness that might have occurred during wrapping. Burnishing tools are sold by Gudebrod and others, but the same tool is also available from art and stationery-supply stores. Any smooth round tool can be used for this purpose. Plastic pen barrels are ideal—avoid aluminum or metal that might discolor the thread.

A simple rule helps to measure rods for guide positions, wrap lengths, equalizing wraps on both sides of a two-foot guide, and so on. One of the best of these is sold in stationery stores as a center rule. C-Thru Ruler Company is one manufacturer. One side of the rule is a standard metric rule measuring from 0 to 15 centimeters from left to right. The other side has a grid pattern in tenths of an inch, with the edge of the scale measuring from 0 to 6 inches. The important part of the rule for rod-builders is the center of the transparent plastic, which has an O in the center of the rule with measurements in tenths of an inch in both directions from this central point. This makes it easy to determine equal wrapping positions for a two-foot guide by taping the guide in position, holding the rule against the rod blank and guide with the center O of the rule on the center of the guide ring, and then measuring from each side to mark the beginning of the wrap.

MATERIALS

The main material for wrapping guides is special rod-wrapping thread. The company making such thread today is Gudebrod, although sometimes threads are available from Kreinik, D. H. Thompson, E. Veniard, and Universal Vise Corporation. Some of these are strictly fly-tying threads, and because they are very thin would be suitable only for the lightest rods (Gudebrod has both fly-tying and rod-wrapping threads.)

Rod-wrapping thread comes in a variety of sizes, ranging from 00 through FF. Suggested uses for these, as per recommendations from Gudebrod, are:

Size 00. Wrapping delicate fly rods and ultralight spinning and spin-cast rods. Also, wrapping and tying jigs from 1/32-ounce through 1/8-ounce.

Size A. Recommended for fly rods and freshwater spinning and casting rods. Also, wrapping and tying jigs from 1/2 ounce through 1 1/2 ounces.

Size C (N.C.P. and D nylon). Wrapping saltwater rods and medium-weight spinning, casting, boat, and trolling rods. Also, wrapping and tying jigs from 5/8-ounce through 2 ounces.

Size D (N.C.P. and E nylon). Wrapping 80- and 130-pound trolling rods, as well as heavy-duty boat and surf rods. Wrapping and tying jigs from 2 1/4 ounces to 3 1/2 ounces.

Size E. Wrapping heavy-duty trolling rods, boat rods, and surf rods.

Size EE. Wrapping extra-heavy-duty trolling rods and extra-long (14 to 16 feet) surf rods.

Size FF. Special wrapping effects on gaffs, outriggers, and antennas. Also, wrapping heavy-duty rod butts for friction grip. In addition, size FF is the recommended size for wrapping pool-cue handles.

Because Gudebrod is the main supplier of wrapping thread, we'll deal primarily with their products. Of the thousands of thread colors that Gudebrod (or any company) can make, they currently have over thirty available in basic solid colors. In addition, they make a metallic thread that consists of a high-sheen aluminized film wound over a nylon core for strength. The result is a very bright metallic-look thread. Trimar thread from Gudebrod is made with colors contrasting with a silver or gold base color thread, so that the result looks like a shimmering wrap on a rod.

Basic solid colors available from Gudebrod at this writing include: black, white, light blue, cobalt blue, peach, rose pink, spring green, sunburst, garnet, goldenrod, orange, royal blue, dark blue, rust, blue dun, tan, scarlet, candy apple, maroon, gold, dark brown, hot pink, charcoal, purple, medium brown, medium gray, gunmetal, chestnut, dark green, lemon yellow, and medium green.

Metallic thread colors include gold, black, silver, pearl, ole gold, ice blue, lime, fuchsia, aquamarine, royal blue, aqua, red, dusty rose, green, copper, purple, and bronze. Trimar threads come in black/silver, white/silver, blue/silver, green/silver, brown/silver, red/silver, black/gold, white/gold, blue/gold, green/gold, brown/gold, and red/gold.

To add to this complexity, not all colors and styles of thread are available in all sizes. Thus, the basic solid-color nylon thread is available in 00, A, D, E, EE, and FF in 100-yard spools (FF comes in 50-yard spools), 1-ounce spools, and 4-ounce spools. The metallic thread is available in A in all colors, and gold and silver is available in size D. Trimar threads are available in size C only. The basic nylon thread is available in sizes A, C, and D in an N.C.P. style. The thread is processed with a color preserver so that it will resist the damaging effects of epoxy rod finishes and varnishes. Thus, rod finish may be applied directly over this thread, although many rod-builders will add at least one coat of color preserver to the thread just to be sure.

Note: For more details on yards per spool and the break strength of Gudebrod threads, see the Thread Specification Chart in Appendix D.

MOUNTING THE TIP-TOP GUIDE

The tip-top, or tip guide or top guide, as it is variously called (I like, and most manufacturers use, the term "tip-top") should be mounted before the guides are wrapped in place. Although this is really a gluing operation, it is considered here with the guides because sometimes the glues used are different from those used for handle and reel-seat assembly. Also, it is a guide and does get a wrapping, even though this wrapping is strictly decorative. (Though there is one exception where it is functional, which we will discuss.)

Tip-tops must match the guides. All manufacturers make tip-tops, which match their guides in color, style, and construction. Some manufac-

Adding tip-tops. One easy way is to melt the ferrule and tip-top cement, smear on the rod tip and immediately add the tip-top.

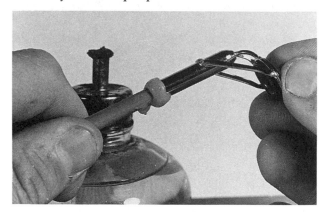

If liquid enough, the hot rod-tip cement will flow as the tip-top is added and ball up at the base of the tip-top tube.

turers, such as Fuji, have different tip-tops to match different guide styles. Almost all tip-tops consist of a ring and frame that is mounted on a tube. The tubes are available in different sizes to fit the tip end of different-sized rods. The tube should fit the rod tip firmly but not tightly or loosely. It should slide on easily, without any slack or play. Naturally, you must first check the tip end of the rod to be sure that it is even, not splintered, flattened, or damaged in any way. If it is, you may have to cut it back slightly. This may require cutting back the tip section anywhere from a fraction of an inch to an inch. Cut back more and you are into the custom cutting and chopping of the blank. For details on cutting see Chapter 26. Briefly, however, the technique requires a fine triangular file to groove and then cut through the blank where you wish it cut, or a fine-tooth hacksaw blade (preferably with 32 teeth per inch) with light pressure applied to drag the blade toward you to prevent the teeth from catching on

the thin-diameter graphite blank. Rotate the blank until the blade or file cuts through.

For a good bond of the tip-top to the end of the blank, use steel wool or fine sandpaper to roughen the end of the blank. To prevent scratching the blank, wrap the end with masking tape to expose to the sandpaper only that portion that will be glued into the tip-top tube.

You can use 24-hour epoxy glue for gluing the tip-top, or you can use other glues. One caution in gluing on the tip-top is that these are subject to breakage and damage. Thus, they sometimes have to be replaced. And if they must be replaced, the tip-top must be removed from the end of the rod without damaging the rod blank. For this reason, I like glues that are not quite as strong as the 24-hour epoxies. Thus, for light freshwater rods and light fly rods, I like to use a stick-ferrule or tip-top cement such as Gudebrod Stick Ferrule

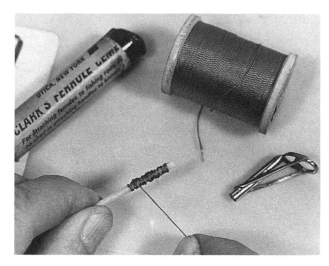

If some shimming is required, it is possible to wrap the rod blank at the tip, or lay threads over the end and along the sides of the blank.

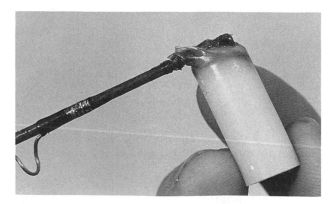

Adding melted tip-top cement to the wrapped rod blank.

Cement. For heavier freshwater rods, heavier fly rods, and light saltwater rods, I use a 5-minute epoxy glue that will be stronger than the heat-set cements but only about eighty to ninety percent as strong as the 24-hour epoxy glues. One advantage is that these 5-minute epoxies, according to the glue manufacturers, will break down under heat more rapidly than the stronger epoxies and thus will be easier to remove from the rod tip. For heavy surf rods, heavy trolling rods, and other heavy tackle, I use the regular 24-hour epoxy glues such as are best for handle assembly.

When you use the ferrule cements or other heat-set cements (the glue sticks from craft stores also work well), you will need a heat source. A butane lighter, match, or similar *small* heat source will work fine. In all cases, use the side of the flame to melt the glue or heat the tube. If you hold the rod end or tip-top over the flame, the heat will cover a broad area and is more likely to damage the rod or shock ring in the tip-top. Also, there is the increased possibility of smoking or darkening the blank parts from any soot or unburned particles.

There are several ways to add a tip-top using heat set cements. First use the flame to melt the end of the ferrule cement or cement stick. When the cement is molten, coat the end of the rod tip with it. Don't worry if you get too much on the end of the rod. Do *not* use the flame around the rod tip. Once the molten cement coats the rod end, you can immediately slide the tip-top tube onto the rod blank, making sure that the rod tip goes completely to the end of the tube and that the tip-top is immediately lined up with the spine and guide placement on the rod blank.

If you are not quick enough, the cement might solidify on the end of the rod. If this happens, there are two possibilities to consider. One is to use the side of the flame previously used to heat the cement and bring the rod tip close enough to the flame to melt the cement. Rotate the rod while doing this to assure complete melting. Then slide the tip-top on the rod blank. The second possibility is to hold the tip-top gently with pliers and heat the tube with the flame. Then, when the tube is hot, slide it onto the rod tip. The hot metal tube will melt the cement on contact and glue the tip-top to the rod.

A completely different method involves using a knife blade to shave off fine slivers of the ferrule cement and slip these into the metal tube of the tip-top. Once you have the tube filled, heat it with the flame and immediately slide it onto the end of

the rod. Heating the tube causes the cement to melt and to glue the tip-top to the rod.

In using any heat-set cement, do not try to wipe up the glue while it is still molten. It can burn and usually only strings out and makes a mess. Instead, wait until the cement is completely cured and cool. At this point the cement will be hard and it can be easily peeled or knocked off of the rod end.

Although I haven't seen any yet, the possibility exists that someone will produce a tip-top with a composite tube instead of a metal tube (guides with composite graphite/glass/resin materials are produced at this time). If this happens, then naturally you cannot use heat on the tube when gluing with heat-set cement but must rely on the other methods just described.

Using 5-minute epoxy is simple. Mix the epoxy as described in Chapter 20, and then smear the glue on the roughened tip section of the rod. At the same time, use a toothpick or straightened paper clip to smear a little glue inside the tip-top. Then slide the tip-top on the rod tip, use a rag to remove any excess glue, and align the tip-top with the guide alignment. One problem with this is that the liquid glue often allows the tip-top to rotate on the rod blank if the blank is not placed exactly vertically (held against a workbench with masking tape) or laid at an angle (butt down, tip up, and with the guide position facing down) so that gravity will hold the tip-top in line with the guide/reel-seat position. As an alternative you can just hold and check the tip-top until the glue sets up, in about 5 minutes.

The technique for using 24-hour epoxy glue is exactly the same, only additional care must be taken to keep the tip-top in line with the position of the guides during curing, which is much longer.

Some few tip-tops do not come with a tube but instead are made of a double-wrapped wire; the ends of the wire extend parallel at an angle to the loop to form "legs" that are wrapped in place. These are filed to a smooth edge, taped in place with thin masking tape, and wrapped down using the same thread size, color, and proportion as is used for the guides on the rod.

Tip-tops are sometimes damaged and must be removed. If the tip-top is one of the rare types that is wrapped in place, the technique for removal is the same as that for a guide. Use a razor blade to plane down the threads and finish until the blank is reached. Then peel the wrap off just as if you are peeling the shell from a steamed shrimp. Wrap the new tip-top using standard guide-wrapping methods.

Tube tip-tops, by far more common, require a different technique. Heat must be used — use the least heat necessary for the ferrule-cement/heat-set cements and the most possible for the 24-hour epoxies.

You must use care in all steps of removing tip-tops, because failure to follow exact directions can result in damage to the rod blank. First, you must shield the wrapping and the exposed portion of the rod blank from the heat. This can be done in several ways. One is to make a shield that you can hold against the rod so that only the tip-top is exposed. A shield can be a groove cut into a scrap piece of wood, a small wood angle made for this purpose, or a similar device. A simpler method is to use several layers of masking tape wrapped around the blank, beginning the tape right at the edge of the metal-tube tip-top. Build this up to serve as insulation against the heat.

Use a small flame and heat the metal tube on the tip-top, rotating the rod as you do so. Use only the side of the flame (a flame under the tip-top will produce too broad a heat source) and try to keep the flame toward the end of the tip-top. You might melt or damage any glues or shock rings holding the ring in place, but this won't matter because the tip-top is damaged anyway.

Keep some pliers handy and check frequently for looseness on the tip-top. Using pliers (the metal tip-top will be hot enough to burn you), remove the tip-top as soon as possible to avoid applying any more heat to the rod blank than is necessary. In the case of all glues, the heat will break down the resins and allow removal of the tip-top.

Once the damaged tip-top is removed, the blank can be cleaned and a new tip-top added using gluing methods or the wrapping method. Once the old tip-top is off, remove the shield or the masking tape as soon as possible. Use alcohol to clean up any remaining masking-tape adhesive. If the tip-top is the tube type and the wrap is properly protected, you will not need to rewrap the thread. Just use a new tip-top of the right size and glue it in place, butting the new tip-top down on the thread wrap. Clean up the glue and the rod is ready to use as soon as the glue cures.

PREPARATION

Before you begin to wrap the guides in place, there is a little preparation. First, you must check the position of the blank's spine. Naturally, at this point, you will have the handle assembly in place with the reel-seat hoods lined up with the spine and the tip-top in place. Both will help determine the alignment of the guides. An exception to this would be those rods in which the handle is separate from the section with the guides, such as offshore two-part trolling rods where the handle separates from the blank, pack rods in which the butt handle section is so short that it does not include any guides, casting rods in which the handle separates from the blank, and spinning rods with a sliding-ring reel-holding system that is not lined up with the guides. For these types of rods, it is necessary to retain the masking tape or mark that indicates the spine and guide alignment, or to determine the spine location again.

Once you have the spine and alignment of the guides located, you may wish to clean the rod with alcohol. This will remove any greases, dirt, hand lotions, or body oils that would later harm the wrapping or cause blotching or mottling of the thread wrap. To be honest, in building many rods without taking this step, I have never seen a problem, but theoretically at least, it is probably best to observe it. The next few steps should be done while you are wearing light cotton gloves, such as are available for camera and darkroom work, or rubber gloves, such as are available for lab and medical workers. These are generally readily available through camera shops and medical-supply stores.

A final preparation involves checking the guides for wrapping. Basically this involves filing the ends of the guide feet, checking and filing the bases of the guide feet, and, if necessary, adjusting the guide feet for straightness.

Filing the guide feet is necessary to provide a smooth, gradual "slope" for the thread to follow as it is wrapped from the bare blank up onto the guide foot. For this, the feet must be ground down. A fine flat file is perhaps the safest tool to use for this because it is hand-held and can thus be controlled at all times. However, instead of working the file against the guide, I find it best to work the guide against the file. I also find it easier to slightly twist or rotate the file to follow the convex curvature of the top of the guide foot while filing it to a knife edge. To do this, place the file in a vise, protect it with scrap wood or rags, and work the guide foot against the flat file face.

Other methods of filing guide feet include using a small rotary grinding tool such as a Dremel Moto-Tool. These tools come in several different styles and models and will chuck small diamond-wheel points, aluminum-oxide grinding stones, aluminum-oxide abrasive wheels, silicon-carbide grinding stones, and various drum sanders.

Standard bench-type grinders can also be used, although in most cases the stones supplied with them are too coarse and the motors too fast for good control. In fact, although any motor-operated grinder will work faster than hand-filing, the danger is in loss of control and excessive cutting, which might ruin the guide foot. I do like the drum sanders used with the Dremel Moto-Tool, because these are small enough for me to hold easily while I'm working on the guide and allow good control and guide-foot shaping. In addition, small bench-type belt sanders, fitted with a fine sanding belt, will work fine. They are perhaps the best of the motorized tools because they allow one to hold the guide securely with both hands and work the foot against the moving belt.

In addition to sanding the top of the guide foot, you should at the same time check the guide foot for straightness. Hold the guide on a tabletop, strip of wood, or rod blank to check the guide feet. If the two feet are not straight, slightly bend them up or down until they are straight and parallel to each other.

Once the guide feet are straight, rub the bottom of the two feet lightly over a piece of sandpaper to remove any slight burrs that might have occurred in manufacture. Most guides have a crosswise concave curvature on the bottom of the foot, so be sure to check this also for any slight burrs or imperfections. If you do feel any, remove them with a slim round file run along the length of the guide foot.

MEASUREMENTS

Guide spacing was covered in Chapter 21. However, for a careful, neat job, you still must establish the measurement of the wrap for each guide, considering factors such as underwraps, trim wraps, and so on. Let's consider a standard two-foot guide. You will want the guide wrap to look right, you'll want sufficient wrap to begin on and hold the blank before being taken up on the guide foot, and you'll want the guide to be proportional to the wrap, the size of the guide, and the size and type of the blank.

In all cases, you must wrap over the entire guide foot. Also, you must begin the wrap on the blank. There are two methods of considering such measurements. In the one that I prefer, I make

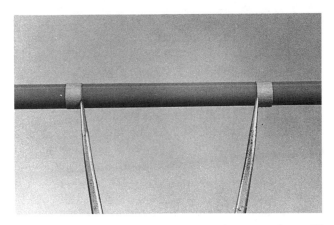

Measurement must be made for underwraps that will match the guide wraps to be placed on top of them. Calipers or a rule help to check these dimensions.

the entire wrap proportional to the length of the guide foot. This also becomes proportional to the diameter of the blank, because smaller guides with shorter feet are used on the thinner tip end than on the butt end of the rod. I measure the distance between the ends of the two guides and multiply this by a constant factor, usually about 1 1/4. Thus, for a large butt guide measuring 2 inches between the end of the feet, the total length of the guide wrap would be 2 1/2 inches. The total length of the wrap on the blank would be 1/2-inch, or 1/4-inch on each end. For a smaller guide that would measure about 1 inch between the guide feet, the total length of the guide wrap would be 1 1/4 inches long, a total length of 1/4-inch — or 1/8-inch on each end. Naturally, you can adjust this to any constant factor you desire, depending upon your preference for the total length of the wrap and the length of the wrap on the blank before it reaches the end of the guide foot. Some rod-builders prefer to use a constant of 1 1/2, thus doubling the amount of wrap on the blank in the above examples.

If you use an underwrap, you must figure this first, in addition to the length of the guide wrap, which should also be in proportion. Thus, for the above examples to be wrapped with an underwrap, I would use a constant of 1 1/2 for the underwrap and a constant of 1 1/4 for the guide wrappings. This allows a small portion of the underwrap to show at the end of the wrap in addition to providing a smooth base on which to wrap the guide. Again, such constants can be anything you wish, but the constant for the underwrap must always be a larger figure than that for the guide wrapping. Also note that these constants are figured on the basis of a simple one-color wrap or a simple wrap with a simple trim wrap, and include the total length of the wrap. If you use these figures for the base wrap alone and then add a trim wrap, the underwrap constant factor will have to be larger to allow for the additional trim on the end of the wrap.

Where you will be making fancy or multiple-thread trim wraps at the end of a guide wrap, you may want to make the constant far larger to accommodate these additional wraps. Because this is often difficult to plan initially, one solution is to first measure the length of the guide feet on the largest guide to be wrapped (the butt guide) and to wrap that guide in place, using whatever fancy trim wraps, multiple-thread wraps, or additional wraps you wish to make.

Note that if you get very fancy, you may have to count and note thread colors and turns in order to maintain symmetry on both sides of the guide. Do one side of the guide and then measure the total length of this wrap with an accurate scale or rule. Make the same measurements on the other side of the guide, measuring from the junction of the foot and the frame. Mark the end of this measurement with masking tape. Then measure the total length of this distance—from the masking tape on the one side to the end of the wrap on the other side. The proportion of this figure within the length of the guide feet is the constant you will use.

As an old-timer, I prefer a slide rule (remember them?) to figure this constant, but other proportional rules and methods are available. If you can't find your school slide rule or other proportional scales, you can always revert to basic math, as follows:

In this hypothetical example, we will use a total guide-foot length of 1 5/16 inches and a total guide wrap of 1 29/32 inches. The formula then becomes:

1 is to 1 5/16 inches as X is to 1 29/32 inches
1 is to 21/16 as X is to 61/32
1 is to 42/32 as X is to 61/32
42/32X = 61/32
42X = 61
X = 1.4523 or 1 29/64 inches

This also points out why it is far better to develop a basic, simple constant first, because using a constant of 1 3/8, 1 1/2, 1 1/4 or the decimal equivalents of 1.375, 1.5, or 1.25 is far easier than using an awkward constant multiplier such as 1.4523 or 1 29/64.

Although I like this method best and think it

makes for attractive wraps that are proportional to the size of the guide and the diameter of the blank, it does have some problems if fancy trim wraps or single-thread trims at the end are wanted. Since the length of the wrap on the bare blank changes with the guide (the foot length, really), it also might change the proportions of the number of rotations of the thread around the blank in fancy or detailed trim wraps. Thus, if you had a trim wrap of four turns on a large guide, this might have to be reduced to three turns or two turns on the smaller guides and shorter wraps to remain in proportion to the rest of the guide wrap. The same would apply to inlaid wraps.

An alternative method of determining measurements is to use a constant measurement of the length of the wrap extending beyond the guide feet. In this method, you would use a constant in inches or millimeters that would be added to the total length of the guide feet for any wrap. Thus, using a constant measurement of 1/4-inch of wrap on the blank alone at the end of each guide, you would have a total of 1/2-inch. Thus, for a larger guide in which the total length of the feet might measure 2 inches, the total guide wrap would be that 2 inches plus 1/2-inch, for a total of 2 1/2 inches. For a smaller guide used farther up the blank in which the total length of the guide feet might be only 1 inch, the total length of the guide wrap would still be that 1/2-inch plus the 1-inch guide-feet length, for a total of 1 1/2 inches. Personally, I feel that the proportional method is best, though this second method does have some advantages. The main advantage is that the proportions or number of thread rotations of trim wraps and inlaid wraps do not have to be changed with the guide, because the space for this remains constant regardless of which guide is being wrapped in place.

WRAPPING METHODS

Any guide-wrapping or wrapping associated with a guide is simple, although there are some variations to finishing and adding trim wraps and single-strand wraps inlaid in a guide wrap. For the basics, I'll first describe a simple guide wrap—no underwrap, no trim wraps, no fancy inlays.

Once guide spacing is determined, you must tape the guides on the rod blank. For this, use thin masking tape. I like 1/8-inch-wide tape, although 1/4-inch-wide tape will work for large guides and for guides on large rods. If tape in these widths is not available, measure out several inches of standard masking tape (usually 1 inch wide) on a plastic base (a standard kitchen cutting board works well) and use a razor blade to cut thin longitudinal strips.

Once you have the strips cut, place each guide on the rod blank at the predetermined position, line it up with the spine of the rod, and tape it in place. Tape the guide down close to the frame using the thin strips. In other words, leave the end of the guide exposed. By doing so, it will be easy to leave the tape in place until after the guide wrap begins on the guide foot to hold it securely and in line with the spine. If you tape over the end of the foot, you will have to remove the tape before the thread gets to that point, in effect negating the purpose of the tape.

Although it is a small point, you should also wrap the tape in the same direction in which you will rotate the rod when wrapping. Many rod-builders turn the rod for each guide foot on two-foot guides (so that they always wrap from left to right, for example). If you do this, then the wrap for each side of the rod must be opposite the previous wrap. A final tip is to fold over the end of the tape so that you have a small tag end to grab when you wish to remove it. This makes tape removal easier if you are also controlling the tension and position of the guide-wrap thread.

Tape both guide feet, making sure they are lined up with the rod blank and with the spine of the rod. Usually, with the flexibility of masking tape, you can make slight adjustments as required at this point. Tape all the guides in place, but remember that you can make final alignment adjustments immediately before wrapping each guide.

Similarly, use the measurements for each guide (determined by previously mentioned formulas), mark the center position of the guide with a rule, and use strips of masking tape to mark the beginning point for each wrap. Alternatively, some suggest using a small scratch mark in the rod finish or a felt-tip marker or grease pencil. I don't like any of these methods. I don't like scratching the blank at any time and the various marking pens either leave a permanent mark or are too broad and wide to be accurate for fine custom rod work. The taping method allows for precise measurements, leaves no mark once removed, and can be adjusted infinitely until it's exactly right.

Once the guide is taped in place, place the rod in your rod wrapper with the guide centered over the thread-tension device. Make sure the rod will rest without you having to hold it. If necessary, use extra end supports to hold the rod securely. After all, you want to concentrate on wrapping the guide, not on holding one end of the rod down.

Most rod-builders like to wrap from left to right, meaning they always wrap the left-positioned guide foot. Some like to wrap from right to left, others will wrap in either direction, wrapping from left to right for the left-positioned guide foot, then, without moving the rod, wrapping from right to left for the right-positioned guide foot. Any of these methods is satisfactory. Choose the one that is most comfortable for you.

I'll assume we'll be wrapping from left to right on the left-positioned guide foot in these directions. First bring the thread up from the thread-tension device and over the rod blank. At this point, you may want to check the tension, adjusting it for the thread and the type of blank. Naturally, you will want more tension for a larger guide on a heavy-wall surf blank when using size D thread than you will for wrapping a snake guide on a fly-rod tip section using size A thread. Although you will want enough tension to hold the blank, do not use too much tension. With the strong threads available today and the thin-wall graphite blanks, you can use too much tension, which will compress the wrap and in effect push the guide foot into and through the wall of the rod blank, ruining the blank. Be particularly careful of this with thin-walled graphite and thin-walled S glass blanks.

Once the thread tension is correct, bring the thread up over the blank next to the tape marking the beginning of the wrap. Bring several inches of the thread around the blank until this first wrap makes at least a 360-degree circle. Keep tension on the end of the thread and push the thread with your thumb so that it crosses over the thread underneath. Continue with tension on the end of the thread, and rotate the rod so that the thread wraps around the rod and over the thread end. Continue maintaining tension until about four to six wraps are completed. At this point, cut the end of the thread close to the wrap and continue the wrapping. One tip here for all wraps is to maintain the wrapping thread at a slight angle so that it is constantly pulled in toward the existing wrap and thus is wrapped tightly, with no gaps.

Continue wrapping by rotating the blank. When you reach the end of the guide foot, slow down, because even with the smooth taper to the end of the foot, care is required in this area. Make sure the thread is tightly wrapped, does not have any gaps, and traverses smoothly up the slope of the guide foot.

At this point, grab the tag end of the masking tape and pull the tape off while making a rotation of the rod. (This is why you want the tape wrapped in the same direction as the rod rotation. It will come off as you rotate the rod.) Once the masking tape is removed, continue wrapping as before until about six to eight wraps from the end of the guide foot and the beginning of the frame.

You must lay down a loop of thread or monofilament to finish off the wrap. To do this, prepare a loop of mono or of thread. If you use thread, it should be the same size used for wrapping. If you use mono, use approximately the same size as the thread. Although monos vary widely today based on purpose, the following comparison chart, based on Gudebrod thread, should show clear similarities:

Thread Size	Thread Diameter	Monofilament Size
00	.0045	two-pound test
A or N.C.P. A	.0070	four-pound test
D or N.C.P. C	.0104	eight-pound test
E or N.C.P. D	.0132	twelve-pound test
EE	.0154	fifteen-pound test
FF	.0175	twenty-pound test

I rarely use anything lower than six-pound test and usually stick to about six-, twelve-, and twenty-pound test for most mono loops. You can lay these loops down on the rod and just wrap over them, or you can tape them down with a small square of masking tape, or, in the case of the mono loop, you can buy or make a hook-and-loop fastener that will hold the mono loop to the rod blank while you continue wrapping. Make sure the end of the loop faces the center of the guide.

Wrap over this loop until you reach the end of the guide foot. Use your thumb or finger on the thread wrap to maintain tension and cut the end of the thread. Tuck this end into the loop and pull the loop up slowly. Make sure the thread is straight as you pull the loop snug. At this point, you can release the tension on the thread, hold the blank with one hand, and slowly pull the loop under the previous wraps. This also pulls the end of the thread free, securing the end of the wrap.

There are several ways to cut the end of the thread. One is to pull the end of the thread snug and use a razor blade to cut the end of the thread close to the thread wrap and parallel to the axis of the blank. Although this will hold the thread wrap securely, it is the poorest way to finish a wrap because it leaves the end showing between the two thread wraps.

A better way is to pull the end of the thread snug and then work it back and forth to open up a slight gap where the thread exits between the wraps. Then use a razor blade or scalpel blade to cut straight down on the blank, using a slight rocking motion with the sharp blade to cut cleanly through the exiting thread. Take care that you use only enough pressure on the blade to cut the thread. Do *not* use hard pressure that might score or cut the blank. This is extremely important in order to avoid cutting through the resin coat and into the blank's longitudinal fibers, which affect the rod's action and power. Also, if you make a guide wrap over an underwrap, then you *must* be very careful when cutting down with the razor blade to avoid cutting into the underlying threads. If there is an underwrap, you will find it more difficult to open up a gap to trim the thread. The thread beneath the guide wrap will prevent side movement of the guide-wrap threads.

Another method involves a slightly different technique. For this, it is best to make about eight to ten wraps over the thread loop instead of the six to eight previously suggested. Cut the end of the thread, tuck it through the loop, and pull the loop snug. At this point, use fine-point scissors to cut the end of the thread so that the length extending from the snug loop to the end of the thread is slightly *less* than the distance between the end of the wrap and the exit point of the loop. Once this is done, pull the loop slowly through. The loop pulls the end of the thread under the wraps, but the short thread end never exits through the wrap with the loop. There is no end to cut or stubs of thread to worry about. There is a slight gap in the thread wrap from the loop, but this may be burnished closed easily.

A fourth method of finishing can involve any of the first two methods of cutting but does not involve the use of a loop to pull the thread through. I first learned this years ago at the Leonard rod factory, which had used this method for years for wrapping split-bamboo fly rods. In all honesty, I don't think this method offers any great advantage over the loop method. The steps are the same for wrapping the blank and guide foot in

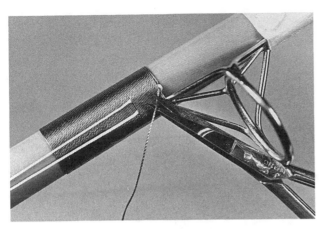

Another method of finishing a wrap with a loop is to pull the loop snug as shown, then clip the end of the thread so that it will be completely hidden under the thread wrap. This eliminates any cutting or trimming after the loop has been pulled through, since the end is too short to pull all the way through the wrap.

place up to the point at which the thread is pulled through. Do not use a loop of thread at this point. Instead, place your finger on the wrap to maintain tension and remove the thread spool from the tension device.

Spool off some thread and then lay a length of this thread over the blank toward the far side of the guide. Then bring the spool of thread around the blank in the same direction as the previous thread wraps, but wrap inside this length of thread and back toward the guide. Make a number of turns equal to the number of turns you want around the blank to secure the thread. Once you reach this point, bring the spool of thread back over the original length of thread to the side of the guide being wrapped, but now reverse the thread direction. If you were wrapping over the rod blank and away from you on the far side of the guide, you would now wrap over and toward you. Make turns equal to the number of turns on the other side of the guide.

Set the thread spool down on the workbench, and with your free hand grab the loose thread at the point immediately above where you are holding the wrap to maintain tension. Holding this end, rotate the rod to wrap over the portion of thread you just crossed to the opposite side of the guide.

Continue doing this and you will notice that you are decreasing the excess loops on both sides of the guide wrap. Ultimately, you reach the point where all the loops are removed (by rotating the rod), and you have only to maintain tension and

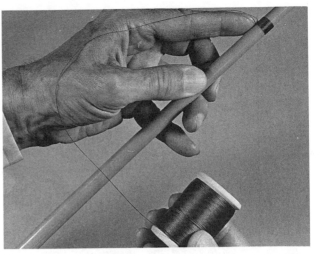

Making the Leonard style of finish on a thread wrap, here shown without guides for clarity. When within several turns of completing the wrap, make a larger loop of thread well ahead of the main wrap.

Continue by wrapping back around the rod blank toward the guide or wrap, wrapping in the same direction as the thread wrap.

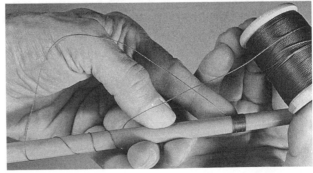

After several turns, bring the excess thread back across the thread wrap and make several turns around the rod blank in the opposite direction of the thread wrap.

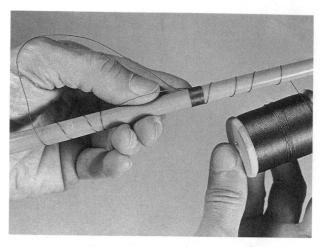

Turns around the rod blank in opposite direction of the thread wrap.

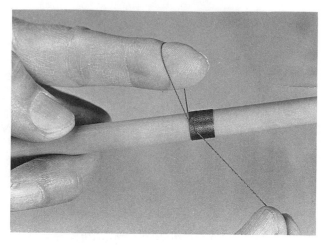

Hold the loop of thread and pull the excess thread through the wrap.

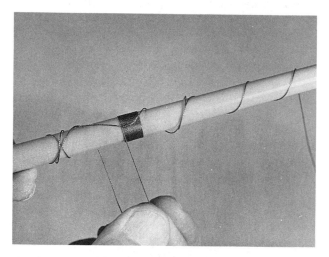

At this point continue the thread wrap, using the loose wraps made above the guide wrap as shown.

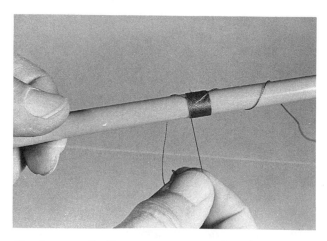

Continue until all turns are removed and the thread is completely wrapped around the blank.

pull the loose end of the thread through the wraps.

The end result is exactly the same as with other finishing methods, except that it does not involve a loop. The excess thread must be cut off by one of the several methods already suggested. The one main disadvantage to this method if you are wrapping anything other than fly rods where small snake guides are used is that the larger guides of other rods are sometimes awkward to make the thread wraps over while turning the rod. The larger the guides, the more thread you need for this step.

In all of the above methods, use a burnisher to polish the wrap and close up any slight gaps that might have occurred during the wrapping process. An ideal tool for this is the Gudebrod burnishing tool and plastic-letter-transfer tool made by C-Thru Ruler Company and sold in art, stationery, and now tackle-component shops. Plastic ball-point pens and similar smooth-plastic tools are ideal for this. You can use anodized-aluminum crochet and knitting needles, but make sure you do not use anything that might leave a stain or mark on the thread wrap.

These methods are basic for any rod, any wrap, any size thread, and any type of guide. However, there are some special tips you may wish to consider. These include:

1. If you use heavy thread, such as sizes E, EE, or FF, you may wish to cut the end at the beginning of the wrap and then fray out the cut end so that there is a smooth transition of the thread wrap over the cut end. In most cases this will not be noticeable, however.

2. When using standard nylon rod-wrapping

thread, you should have no problem with "frizzes" — tiny fibers of the thread. However, in some cases, some of these will interfere with a perfect wrap and epoxy finish. To remove them, use a flame from a cigarette lighter and hold the side of the flame against the finished wrap while rotating the blank. The flame will burn off any of these fine fibers to leave a smooth surface. Make sure you rotate the rod, and use only the side of the flame to avoid damaging the wrap or soiling it with soot.

3. Do not finish the thread so that the wrapped-over portion ends up in the gap alongside the guide foot. By necessity, this is a small space and the thread end will not be held tight there. You must snug it up under a tight wrap on the top of the guide foot or on the blank.

4. When it is examined carefully, the beginning and end of any wrap can be seen — both where the end tucks through and also at the beginning of the thread wrap. You can't eliminate this, but you can position it where it will not normally be seen during fishing. For example, on a fly rod or spinning rod, you can position the beginning and end of every wrap in line with or on top of the guide foot. Because the guides hang under the rod during fishing, this will place the ends of the wrap out of view. For casting rods, traditional trolling rods, and revolving-spool tackle, place these spots directly opposite the guide foot and thus away from view during fishing. The same thing can be done with any part of any wrap — underwraps, trim wraps, inlaid wraps, and single- and multiple-thread wraps.

Using the side of a flame to singe any thread fibers remaining after wrapping. Usually this is not necessary. Use only the side of the flame; otherwise the thread might burn or become soiled from smoke.

Completed thread wrap with finish added.

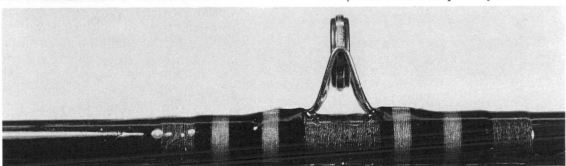

UNDERWRAPS

Underwraps are wraps placed on a rod prior to the guide wraps. They are directly underneath each guide wrap and have several purposes. They are decorative because they are almost always a different color than the guide wraps and thus provide contrast and additional color. They are also functional in that they provide a cushion between the blank finish and the metal foot of the guide.

Underwraps are made using exactly the same

techniques as guide wraps, except that no guide is wrapped down. An underwrap is usually a plain, continuous wrap, although decorative wraps to make the center ring of the guide or to dress up the end are also possible, just as they are on any guide wrap. Naturally, an underwrap must be slightly longer than the guide wrap, thus the need for care in measurements for underwraps previously mentioned. An underwrap must be exactly centered for guide positioning. Thus, you will usually mark the center position of the guide and

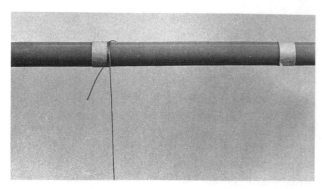

Beginning an underwrap by wrapping around the blank and over the previous thread wraps several times.

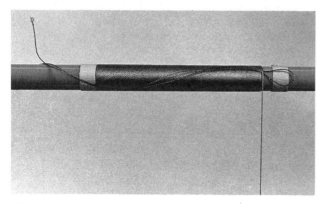

The wrap is completed Close to the end where a loop of thread is laid down to finish the wrap.

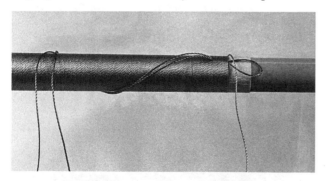

Here, the thread has been wrapped to the end, over the loop and the thread cut and tucked into the loop.

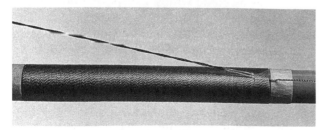

Pulling the loop through eventually pulls the end of the thread under the wrap to secure the thread.

then use this mark and a center rule to mark both ends of the underwrap (use masking tape). Begin as for a guide wrap, wrap the whole length of the underwrap, and finish as described. You can begin and end underwraps so that you will not see these areas while fishing.

Color choice in underwraps is important. Generally, it is always better to use light colors for underwraps and darker colors for guide wraps. Using a dark color for the underwrap and a lighter color for the guide wrap can result in a show-through of the darker-color underwrap. It would be the same as using one layer of light paint over a dark-color paint—the darker color would affect the lighter color. Any effect of the underwrap color—light or dark—will be accentuated unless color preserver is used on the underwrap *before* the guide is wrapped in place. Often one coat is best over N.C.P. thread (though you are probably reasonably safe without it), and two or three coats over regular nylon thread. Be sure to use a color preserver that will match the final finish used. In most cases, this means using the same brand of color preserver and finish.

Some rod-builders go even further, adding one coat of epoxy rod finish to the underwrap before wrapping the guide wrap. There are several advantages and some disadvantages to this. The advantages are that the underwrap is completely protected from any show-through or blotching of color, the smooth finish provides a smooth working base on which to wrap the guide, and if you make this smooth base of finish you can then use the same size of thread used for the underwrap. Otherwise, you should use different thread sizes for the underwrap and the guide wrap—say, size A for the underwrap and D for the guide wrap, or size D for the underwrap and size E or EE for the guide wrap on a large rod. Doing this when you do not use the epoxy rod finish prevents the guide-wrap thread from wedging in between the underwrap threads, as would happen with threads of the same size and no finish. A larger thread size for the guide wrap spaces the wraps differently, preventing this problem.

Although finishing wraps is covered in Chapter 25, we must consider finishing here before adding guide wraps over underwraps. One of the problems with underwraps is a splotching or mottling if the underwrap shows through the overwrap, particularly if the guide wrap is a medium rather than a dark shade.

One way to prevent this is to use N.C.P thread on the underwrap or to use one or two coats of color preserver on the underwrap before adding the guide wrap. This seals the underwrap colors and prevents any show-through.

One other possible cause of blotching and mottling is contaminants on the wraps. Before beginning any wrap, make sure your hands are clean, that you use no hand lotion or other lotions, and that you do not handle or come in contact with any chemicals that could cause problems. If you have very sweaty hands, consider using cotton gloves during wrapping operations.

DOUBLE AND TRIPLE WRAPS

Guide wraps can be made single (as previously described) or they can be made double or triple. Usually multiple wraps are done for added strength when using light thread on heavy-duty rods or just as added insurance, even with heavy thread, on heavy-duty rods. It can also be decorative if separate thread is used of a different color than the basic guide wrap.

There are several ways to do double and triple wraps on a guide. The simplest way is to continue using the same thread as for the main guide wrap. For this technique, begin and proceed as for the single guide wrap, but do not lay down a loop of thread near the end. Instead, proceed to the end of the guide foot and, at this point, cross back over the thread to begin making a wrap of thread on top of the wrap just completed. You are only reversing the direction of the thread on the guide foot — the rotation direction continues the same. Often you can begin within about one or two wraps of the end. You may find that you will have to use a slightly reduced thread tension during this step to prevent the thread from pulling through the previous wraps and into the gaps between. Thus, the problem here is similar to that of making a guide wrap on top of an underwrap. Continue wrapping as far as you like. Some rodbuilders like to stop about halfway along the guide foot; others continue along the guide foot almost to the original beginning of the wrap. If you continue this far, remember that you will be going down the slope of the end of the guide foot. Use care here to prevent gaps, although this won't cause as much of a problem as it would on a bare guide foot. The previous thread wraps provide a base that will grip the next layer of threads.

Regardless of where you plan to stop, lay down a loop of thread or mono about six to eight wraps from where you want to end, with the loop pointed away from the guide center. Wrap over the loop for six to eight turns, cut the thread end while maintaining the tension, tuck the end through the loop, and pull the loop through. Cut the end using one of the methods described for the single guide wrap.

Although I still like the method best, there is an additional problem and danger if a razor blade is used to cut straight down between the wraps. First, the thread base here will make it harder to spread the wraps apart. Second, you must cut carefully so as not to cut the thread beneath, which comprises the first layer of the guide wrap. The problems are easily handled once you understand them and are no different from cutting through a single wrap made over an underwrap.

A triple wrap is done in the same way, by first making the single wrap from the blank up to the frame end of the guide foot, reversing the wrap, and then reversing it a second time to begin a third wrap, this time going back toward the center of the guide. Finish as for any wrap, using a loop of thread or mono.

In addition, double and triple wraps can be made as separate wraps: The first, second, and third layers of the wraps are made with separate thread colors for a decorative as well as strengthening effect. The advantage is that all the guides can be wrapped in place and color preserver can be added as is done for underwraps to prevent blotching. Then the second-color wrap is added, with more color preserver, and finally a third-color wrap is added if desired. The color preserver helps to seal the wraps and make for a more solid and level base on which to make the subsequent wrap. In most cases, a small edge of the previous wrap is left exposed at each end, or at least at the outer end of the guide wrap, for decorative purposes.

VARIATIONS AND SPECIAL EFFECTS AND WRAPPINGS

The foregoing describes some good but basic ways to make single wraps, double wraps, triple wraps, and underwraps. There are a number of variations that will not hold the guides any more securely but that will make the guide wraps more decorative and with more of an unusual custom look.

Some of these are as follows:

Wrapping a single-foot guide. The technique for wrapping a single-foot guide is really the same as for wrapping two-foot guides, whether by using a basic bare-bones method as previously described, using a double or triple wrap, or using some of the fancy techniques to be covered here. The one concern is that since there is only one foot, it is not stabilized as easily when taped in place, so that there is a greater likelihood of its being wrapped at a slight angle to the rod axis. There is no real way to prevent this other than to check the guide and guide-foot alignment frequently while wrapping. The wrap beginning, wrapping method, wrap ending, and finishing methods are all the same as for two-foot guides.

One variation of this that I have sometimes done is to add a small "bumper" of thread in front of the guide foot, both for decoration and to prevent the guide foot from sliding out from beneath the wraps. If the guide is wrapped tightly, this is not really a problem, but I still like to add the bumper. One way to do this is to wrap up to the end of the guide foot and then jump the thread over the front of the guide and finish on the bare blank in front of the guide foot. You will have to work at a slight angle to get the thread around the guide because all of the frames lean slightly forward. Sometimes I will end this way; other times I go about four wraps and then reverse the thread, laying down a loop at the same time, to double-wrap this bumper area.

An alternative is to make a short wrap (four to six turns of thread) first, butt the guide foot against it, tape the guide in place, then finish with the same thread or a different color or size thread. To do this, you must lay down the loop first and make the whole wrap over the loop; otherwise, the wrap is too short to finish. If you double-wrap this bumper, do not lay down the loop until the first layer is complete.

Trim wraps. Trim wraps at the end of the guide wrap or at the end of the underwrap are generally several thread wraps in width, although they can be more or less. They can be done in several ways. The basic wrap (the guide wrap or underwrap) can be completed and the trim wrap then can be added to the end. Or, you can make the trim wrap first, then begin the basic guide wrap or under-wrap at the end of the trim wrap. In both cases, it helps to mark the end of the wraps with masking tape to help in proper alignment and accurate spacing.

One problem with trim wraps is that they are generally very short and thus are perceived as difficult to begin and finish because there is a very narrow wrap under which to pull a loop of thread for finishing. If the wrap is fairly wide — say, six or eight turns of thread — you can begin as with a regular wrap, continue for a turn or two, then trim off the thread end and lay down a loop of thread or mono, continuing to the end of the wrap (another four to six turns). Then cut the end and tuck it through the loop, pulling the loop through. Make sure you burnish this well but lightly. Too heavy a pressure on these wraps can sometimes pull threads loose. Also, for best results with any burnishing, burnish *toward* the center of the wrap, not away from it, which might create gaps in the last turn of thread.

It is also possible to make several trim bands at the end of the wrap with different colors of thread. Treat each of these the same way to begin and end, using separate loops for the endings but keeping the loops close together so that the endings are all in line.

It is also possible to make two or more bands using one finishing loop. To do this, wrap down two different additional colors of thread when making the beginning of the main guide wrap. For most wraps, use threads about 12 inches long. Finish the main wrap and then begin the trim wraps. Take the thread to be used for the end trim band and tape it down to the blank at the end of the thread. Tape down a loop of thread or mono at the same time with the loop pointing away from the guide center. Then wrap the first thread around the loop and taped-down thread for several turns. Cut the end and run it through the loop. Pull it back toward the guide and tape this end down. Then tape down the end of the loop to help maintain tension on this wrap. Begin the second wrap with the previously taped-down thread, wrapping over the loop. Continue for several turns and then cut the end, tucking it through the loop. Take up the tape over the loop and pull the loop slowly through. In doing this, the loop will first pull through the end thread and then pick up and pull through the first thread. Both threads will exist through the same gap in the main-wrap threads. Cut and finish.

A variation of this is to use thread for the trim wrap that is one size smaller than the wrap thread. When used at the ends of the wrap, this makes for a more tapered effect with the wrap and also allows for the thinnest possible wraps, including the single-thread wrap as described next.

Single-thread trim wraps. For a delicate look, you can make a trim wrap of only one or two threads at the end of the main wrap. Naturally, these are too narrow to finish with a loop of thread in the traditional way, so an alternative method must be found: There are two. One is to first lay down a loop of thread pointing away from the guide center. Do this so that the loop is at the location of the beginning of the wrap. Then lay down a length of thread that will be the one- or two-turn trim wrap. Then begin the main guide wrap or underwrap with a different color of thread, wrapping over the loop and the thread to be used for the single-thread trim. After about five turns, cut the end of the main-wrap thread, cut the end of the trim-wrap thread, and flip the knotted end of the loop up and over so that subsequent wraps will not be over the loop. Continue the main wrap to the end and finish.

To complete the trim wrap, make one, two, or as many turns as you want around the blank. Then cut the end of the thread, tuck it through the loop, and pull the loop through. Because the loop has several turns under the main wrap in addition to the trim wrap, the end of the thread will be completely secured. Cut the end and finish.

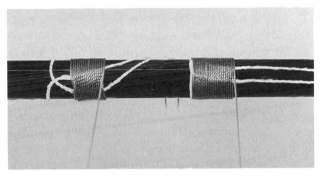

Making a single wrap of thread at the end of a guide wrap. Left, the single contrasting-color thread is held in place (using masking tape) to the blank and the main wrap begun over it. Note that the thread is crossed over itself. After the wrap is complete, or after several turns are made, the single wrap can be pulled tight against the main wrap. Right, the single thread pulled tight, but before the ends of the thread are cut.

A second method does not involve loops. Instead, before making the main wrap, use tape to secure one end of the trim-wrap thread. Use another piece of tape to hold the thread about 2 inches away from the beginning of the wrap and make one or more turns around the blank. The number of turns you make here will determine the number of turns the trim wrap will make around the blank upon completion. Then lay the thread down parallel to its end and tape it in place. These wraps must be loose at this point because you will be rewrapping them when the main wrap is completed.

Begin the main wrap between the tapes holding the thread and at a predetermined point — preferably marked at this time with tape after measuring. Continue the wrap for six to eight turns, cut the end of the main-wrap thread, remove the tape from the trim-wrap thread, and pull these two threads out so that they are free of subsequent wraps. Continue the wrap to the end and finish and cut the thread. At this point, make sure that the two parallel threads cross over each other at the point where they were wrapped around the rod. Keep them in this position and then wrap the topmost thread around the wrap so that it is tight against the main wrap just completed. Continue wrapping, and the loose wrap will unravel until you are at the point where the thread goes under the main wrap. Gently pull this thread while maintaining light tension on the loose thread loop. Pull tight, tighten both threads, and then cut them with a razor blade.

Note that this wrap can be done on the end of a guide wrap or underwrap and can be one, two, three, or more threads in width when complete. It is very important to have the parallel wrapped-over threads crossing each other at the end, particularly for a one-turn wrap. This will prevent the two ends from being pulled apart when they are pulled tight, thus eliminating part of the "circle" of this single-strand wrap.

Naturally, this same method of making one- or two-turn wraps in the center of a wrap can be applied anywhere along a guide wrap or underwrap for decorative effect. Often, such wraps are placed near the end of a wrap to give a decorative or trimmed look to the wrap.

Guide-center single-thread wraps. Guide center wraps are sometimes added to an underwrap to indicate in a decorative way the center of the guide or position of the guide ring. These are often single- or double-turn wraps and thus require care.

Begin the underwrap in the normal manner and proceed until within about six to eight turns from the center. Check the exact position of the center with a rule or caliper and mark the spot with a pencil. Once you are several turns from the center, cut a 12-inch length of thread to be used for the center wrap. Lay down one end of this thread. Continue wrapping over this thread with the main underwrap thread until it's right at the center. Check again for the center position at this point. Now make one or more turns of the center thread around the rod blank, wrapping over the main-wrap thread at the same time. Once you have made the desired number of complete turns, use the main-wrap thread to wrap over the loose end of the center thread. Continue for several wraps and then make sure the center wrap is tight, or adjust it by slightly pulling the wrapped-over thread. Cut this thread and then continue to the end of the wrap. The effect is to secure both ends of the center wrap, with one end on each side of the center mark and wrapped over by the main wrap.

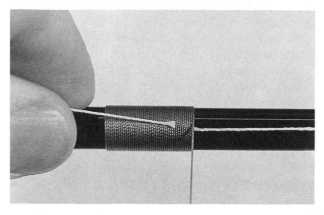

Beginning a center thread in the middle of an underwrap. Here the contrasting thread is wrapped down.

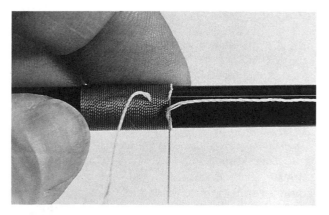

The contrasting thread is wrapped around the rod and over the other thread, then the main thread wrapped over this.

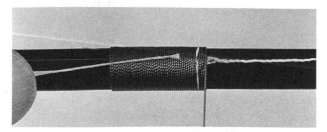

Completed center wrap in place. Both ends of this contrasting thread must be cut at this point.

False underwraps. Sometimes you might want the look of an underwrap within the extra layer of thread. This is easily done by creating what has been called a false underwrap, which is nothing more than a wrap underneath the center of the guide covering what would be an open exposed area.

First measure the distance between the inside ends of the guide feet: This will be the length of the false underwrap. Measure on the blank the center position of the guide and mark the blank there. Place a tape marker on both sides of this mark, each marker to be at one-half the inside guide foot spacing. Make this wrap, which can be plain or a center-guide wrap. Once this wrap is complete, position the guide on the top center of the wrap, tape it in place, and mark the beginning point of each guide. Complete each guide wrap, making sure you wrap up to the frame edge to meet the previous false underwrap. The completed effect is just like an underwrap, particularly if you add a simple, short trim wrap to the outside end of the guide wraps. This is ideal for light rods where you do not want or need the added weight and stiffness of the underwrap.

Double-, triple-, or quadruple-thread wraps. You can use more than the four threads indicated, but most rod-builders do not. In effect, what you are doing here is wrapping with two, three, or four threads, all of different colors, at the same time. The effect is an almost shimmering look. Once started, this wrap is no problem other than in the handling of several threads at one time and in keeping them from crossing. One way to simplify this is to use a comb to keep the several threads in the proper relation to one another.

There are several ways to start this thread wrap. Let's assume a wrap of three threads, although the same principle would apply with fewer or more threads. One way to begin is to treat all three threads as one and wrap them around the blank and then cross them over to lock them down. Make several turns while holding the ends of the threads to maintain tension, then cut the excess and continue wrapping.

This type of wrap can be finished off using a loop of mono or thread. To do this, wrap until you are several turns from the end (this can be just one or two turns because one turn will be three threads for a trim wrap and two turns will be six threads). Lay down the loop, wrap two turns over it, and then cut all three threads while continuing to maintain tension. Keep the threads in order (do not mix or cross them), and tuck all three into the

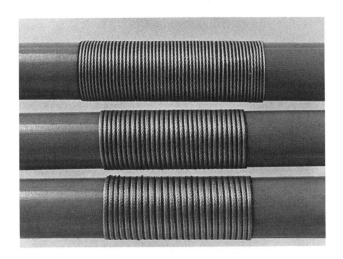

Wraps using two or more solid-color threads at one time: top, a wrap with two threads; center, a wrap with three thread colors at once; bottom, a wrap with four color threads at one time. Such wrapping is tedious, since all threads must remain parallel and remain under equal tension.

loop. Arrange the threads in order and pull the loop to pull the threads through. Cut as before and burnish to close the resulting gap. Obviously, two threads will be easier to pull through than three, three will be easier than four, and so on.

Another method is to begin with one thread and make two wraps, then add the second thread (by wrapping over it with the first wrap) and make two more wraps, then add the third thread (by wrapping over it with the first two wraps) and continue. After several more wraps, cut the excess thread and continue to the end, where you reverse the process with three loops, all close together. Use one loop to tuck under the closest thread, make two more wraps or turns with the remaining two threads, and use the second loop for tucking in the second thread. Then, with two more wraps, finally finish the last thread by tucking it into the remaining loop and pulling it through. Cut the exiting threads as outlined.

Variations of simple guide wraps. Variations of simple guide wraps (with one thread color) are easy to do using several techniques. These include spiral wraps, spiral wraps over tape or mylar, and band wraps. A spiral wrap is a single thread spiraling over a bare blank or underwrap. Begin it as for a standard wrap, but after about six turns of thread begin to spiral the wrap toward the guide. Stop spiraling before the end of the guide foot is reached, and return to the standard wrap. Finish normally.

This same wrap can be made over a band of mylar or tape. The mylar or tape provides underlying color to the spiral part of the wrap. First measure the position for the wrap, then add tape to that point that will be exposed by the spiral wrap. Make sure the end of the wrap is located on the side opposite where it will be viewed during fishing. Begin as above, starting and ending the spiral wrap over the top of the mylar or tape. Finish normally.

A band wrap is like a spiral wrap, but instead of a continuous spiral, one spiral turn is made, then the thread is wrapped tightly to make a short band, a second spiral is made, another band is wrapped, and so on. The number of separate bands is limited only by the total length of the wrap.

One final method of making a wrap is to begin at one end, but instead of finishing at the frame/foot junction, the thread is "jumped" around the base of the guide and continued on the other side. The difficulty here is that it is hard to maintain tight wraps on the down-slope of the second guide foot. It can be done, but it requires less tension in order to avoid pulling the threads down the slope. Finishing is accomplished as for any wrap.

Spirals, bands, and similar wraps are not usually found on custom rods. They are more common on less-expensive factory rods but are included here for those who would like to try them.

Wraps on Parts Other Than Guides

The basic wrappings just described are used in other ways than wrapping guides. In all cases, the wraps are made in exactly the same way as for guides. The same techniques, the same variations, the same several methods of finishing are all applicable.

As previously described, the tip-top is always wrapped. This is for decoration only in the case of the tube-type tip-tops, because the tubes are glued in place. The wrapping does not hold anything but only covers the last inch or so of the rod blank below the edge of the tube.

Ferrules also have to be wrapped, even when they are built into the rod. This is necessary to give the rod blank hoop strength in order to prevent the tubular blank from splitting under the pressure of bending. In most cases, an inch or two here is enough of a wrap, but in all cases follow the specific directions of the individual rod-blank manufacturer. There are several types of self-ferrules, but all should be wrapped.

The spigot type is made by cutting through a one-piece blank and then inserting into the larger butt section a short plug or ferrule. This plug is usually solid, and must be of the same taper as the lower end of the tip section or upper section (in the case of multiple-piece rods) in order to fit and mate properly. Wrap on both sides of the ferrule to reinforce both the lower male end with the plug, and the upper female end. The "Fenwick style" (so-called because Fenwick developed this ferruling system back in the early 1960s) or slip-over style involves a blank made on two mandrels —the upper end has an internal diameter that will match the outside diameter of the lower section for an easy slip-over and mating. Naturally, the tapers must be the same. Most of these require wrapping only for the female section to give it hoop strength, because the female section provides hoop strength for the male end.

Making these wraps is just like making an underwrap or making a guide wrap without the guide. In any of them, begin on the body of the blank and work up to the edge. This will allow you to make the wrap much closer to the edge of the blank than would be possible if it were started at the edge.

If you will be using metal ferrules (as when rebuilding an old rod or when making a bamboo rod, which requires a metal ferrule), these too must be wrapped. This is more for decoration than strength, but it does help to impart some strength to this joint. Begin as for a guide wrap on the blank and wrap up to the ferrule. Ferrules vary in manufacture. Most will have a slight shoulder about 3/8- to 1/2-inch above the end, which is a marking for the end of the thread wrap. Thus, wrap up to and finish off at this point. The wrap will completely cover the end of the ferrule and provide for a decorative touch. If you wish to hide a metal ferrule or prevent glare from a bright ferrule, you can wrap the entire ferrule. Most female ferrules have a rolled edge, and the thread can be wrapped up to that point. The male ferrule should be wrapped to the point where the male section enters the female ferrule.

Some rods will also have a hookkeeper. These are small loop- or hooklike holders that are wrapped to the blank just above the foregrip and are used to hold the hook of a fly or lure to prevent it from catching anglers or objects when not in use. Some of these are small, two-foot wire devices with a separate ring that are wrapped on just like two-foot guides. Others have only one foot and are wrapped on as a one-foot guide would be. They are easy to do. Alignment is a matter of choice, but most rod-builders place the hookkeeper in line with the guides. Some in the past have placed the hookkeeper to the side or directly opposite the side with the guides. Although it rarely happens, I have seen situations where a hookkeeper opposite the guides can cause casting problems. With both fly and spinning rods, sometimes the line will loop around or fly up to catch the hookkeeper and slow or stop the case. With the hookkeeper in line with the guides, this can't happen. Hookkeepers are wrapped exactly as are guides, following all the same steps. The hookkeeper feet must be filed and polished, in proper alignment, and the foot must be taped down to the rod blank with the end of the foot showing to receive the first thread wraps.

Examples of spiral wraps (top) and band wraps (bottom) with basic solid-color thread.

Rods also have a wrap immediately above the foregrip. This is again strictly decorative and tends to finish the look of the rod and to cover any roughness or unevenness that might have occurred when the grip or the winding check was mounted. In all cases where a hookkeeper is used, these wraps are usually combined.

Begin the wrap at the winding check, using a burnisher to push the beginning wrap well back against the winding check or grip to eliminate any gaps. Then continue for an inch or so until you've wound up onto the foot of the winding check. An alternative is to start an inch or so above the winding check and wrap down to the winding check to make sure the threads are tight against it, with no gaps.

These simple thread wraps are completely different from the decorative wraps used on the butt section of some rods, as will be described in the next two chapters.

23

Simple Butt Wraps and Decorative Wraps

INTRODUCTION ▪ TOOLS AND MATERIALS ▪ SIMPLE BUTT WRAPS ▪ BASIC THEORY ▪ ROD PREPARATION ▪ UNDERWRAPS ▪ LAYOUT OF DECORATIVE WRAPS ▪ BASIC WRAPPING TECHNIQUES ▪ DIAMOND WRAPS ▪ CHEVRON WRAPS ▪ CROSS WRAPS ▪ FLAG WRAPS ▪ CHECKERBOARD OR SNAKESKIN WRAPS ▪ OTHER VARIATIONS OF SIMPLE WRAPS

Basic Safety Requirements
  Safety goggles
Basic Tools
  Flat, sturdy workbench
  Rod-wrapping supports; thread-tension device
    or rod-wrapping tool
  Ruler
  Razor blades
  Burnisher
  Masking tape
Helpful Tools
  Circle template and angle aluminum or plastic
  Proportional-scale ruler
  Bobbins for holding thread, particularly when
    making multiple-thread-color simple and
    complex wraps

INTRODUCTION

Decorative wraps on rods are just that—strictly decorative. Decorative wraps can be placed at the butt of a rod just above a foregrip, between the hand grip and lifting grip of a saltwater fly rod, above the adapter or ferrule of a bait-casting rod, filling the space between the foregrip and first guide on an offshore rod, or even woven in between the frame and foot of guides to make a "mini diamond" (or similar wrap) on each and every guide. All such wraps are decorative and as such contribute nothing to the strength or function of the rod. They are, however, beautiful, and if done tastefully and well contribute to the appearance of the rod and mark it as truly a work of individual craftsmanship.

Such decorative wraps are not hard to do but require careful planning, particularly when laying out and designing unique custom wraps that involve intricate placement and order of the threads. They also require layout and careful thread work throughout the wrap. Other than that, all they require is thread, a lot of time, and some simple tools that are easily obtained or made.

The time required must be emphasized. To make a simple diamond wrap might require only an hour. More complex wraps with more thread, more colors, and more intricate designs can require much more time—hours and hours. As with any aspect of tackle craft and rod-building, decorative wraps can be as simple or as complex as you like.

If you have not made a decorative wrap before, start simple before going on to designing your own patterns or getting into complex multiple wraps or weaving. One suggestion is to add a simple diamond or chevron to an existing rod, whether that rod is custom-built or factory-made. Existing simple butt wraps—usually just a band of thread above the foregrip—are easily removed using a razor blade as a carpenter's plane to shave off the thread and peel off the finish to expose the bare blank. A simple basic diamond wrapped here can help you determine your level of interest in making other wraps. Some rod-builders love—almost live for—the custom wraps and touches they can create on their rods; others are interested only in plain, serviceable, highly functional rods that have little in the way of decoration—and nothing in the way of decorative wraps.

TOOLS AND MATERIALS

Tools and materials for underwrapping are few and simple. Most often, they are found in craft and stationery stores and then adapted for decorative wraps. Some possibilities include:

Circle template. This is a clear-plastic template sold in stationery stores and used for drawing circles. It consists of a series of differently sized circles, in inches or millimeters (both are available). One I use has holes in millimeters, from 2 through 10 millimeter in half-millimeters, and then from 11 through 30 in full millimeters. Another measures from 1 millimeter (about 1/25-inch through 45 millimeters (about 1 3/4 inches). These tools help in proper alignment of the decorative wrap, but you must buy the right kind. Such templates *must* have quadrant marks that

mark each 90 degrees of every circle. This is mandatory to properly line up a wrap.

Clear right-angle plastic strip. This is nothing more than a strip of the clear-plastic corner protection sold in hardware stores and designed to protect outside corners of walls in heavy-traffic areas. They are popular with young couples to protect household walls from bicycles, tricycles, and abuse by young children. They can be cut into strips of any length. They are used with the circle template for laying out the wrap and later checking it for straightness. Several strips of about 6, 9, and 12 inches are ideal for most work and can be cut with a hacksaw from a standard 4-foot strip of this material.

Proportional rule. This is a clear-plastic rule that, in addition to having an inch rule on one side and a millimeter rule on the other (the rule is very wide), has grooves cut into the middle for easy measurement of odd increments. The ones I use from C-Thru Ruler Company are unfortunately no longer made, although you might occasionally find a leftover in a stationery store. One is for architectural work (model AR46 or AR56), the other for engineering (EN46 or EN56). The central grooves have no other markings than the incremental marks. Standard marks include not only 1/4-, 1/2-, and 1-inch but also 3/16- and 5/8-inch (in the architectural model). Because these are the only marks on the grooves, the layout of the design is easy. Otherwise, you would almost have to calculate as you go along. With 3/16-inch, for example, such calculations would be 3/16, 3/8, 9/16, 3/4, 15/16, 1 1/8, 1 5/16, 1 1/2, and 1 11/16.

You can make your own proportional rule if you do a lot of this type of work. My suggestion is to obtain a cheap, readily available clear-plastic rule and use a permanent felt-tip marker to mark those incremental measurements you want for a given decorative wrap. You could use a different rule for every different set of incremental measurements, or a different color felt-tip pen for different measurements. Using a standard rule in which the measurements are marked will make for far more accurate spacing than will using cardboard and marking it, although this is another, less-expensive, possibility.

Standard rule. A standard ruler will work for making measurements along a rod for proper layout of the design—just be sure to measure very carefully.

Rod-wrapping support. You will not need the tension device used for standard guide-wrapping, but you will want a support to hold the rod while you rotate it when spiral-wrapping the thread up and down to make a decorative wrap. You will need the thread-tension device when you make the band wrap at the end of each decorative wrap. These band wraps are made with the same method used for guide wraps and are used to hold spiral wraps securely in place.

Other rod-wrapping tools. You will also want the other tools associated with guide-wrapping, such as a razor or scalpel to cut the thread, a loop of thread or mono to pull the binding thread through, and a burnisher to smooth threads.

Materials are not complex, and about the only requirements here are masking tape to hold the thread at the end of each wrap and double-stick tape, which will serve as a substitute for the masking tape and will also hold threads in place.

SIMPLE BUTT WRAPS

Simple butt wraps by our definition do not involve crossing threads or weaving. They are variations of the basic guide wrap in which the thread is wrapped around the blank, begun, and finished in the same way as a guide wrap. These butt wraps can involve all of the variations of guide wraps, such as one-color wraps; trim wraps at the end; two-, three-, four-, and more-color wraps; spiral wraps; spiral wraps over mylar; spiral wraps over an underwrap; band wraps; band wraps over mylar; band wraps over an underwrap; and so on.

There are other variations. For example, most butt wraps (and, for that matter, other decorative wraps) are combined with the wrap for a hook-keeper, if one is placed on the rod. In addition, butt wraps are sometimes separated so that there is a wide band just above the foregrip, then information about the blank, rod, or blank manufacturer, then another short band wrap. This latter band wrap, when applied, serves to "frame" the written information on the blank. (See Chapter 25 for details about adding inscriptions to the blank.)

These wraps can be made over the bare blank or over a contrasting-color underwrap or over mylar tape, allowing the tape to show through band or spiral wraps.

Other possibilities include short bands, usually only about three to five threads wide, that serve as measuring points for fish caught with that rod. This is most common on fly rods for trout fishermen, with the marking on the blank serving as a measurement for a minimum size when measured up from the upper end of the grip; for a per-

sonal size limit; for a trophy-trout size limit; or for a slot-limit size where applicable on certain waters. Other anglers will mark other rods—casting or spinning—with small bands of thread, using different colors for the size limits of different species. This is particularly popular with wade fishermen, who are less likely than boaters or shore anglers to have a rule or tape for quick reference.

Other than that, these simple butt wraps are no different from basic guide wraps. The same methods of starting and finishing are used, as are the procedures listed in Chapter 22.

BASIC THEORY

The basic execution of decorative wraps (other than the simple wraps that are like guide wraps) is to cross threads that make up a decorative pattern on the blank. Thread is spiraled up the blank, then back down the blank. As the thread is spiraled down the blank, it crosses over the threads made on the up-spiral. This causes intersections of thread that are the basis of all decorative wraps, except in weaving. These crossing threads are used to form and develop diamonds, double diamonds, chevrons, double chevrons, flags, Maltese crosses, plaids, snakeskin patterns, and so on. How the threads are run up and down, their position in relation to previous wraps, and what colors are used when determine the ultimate pattern and design.

Naturally, these crossing wraps must be straight—the intersection in line with the rod blank—and the measurements between each intersection of thread must be accurate and identical in order for the completed wrap to look right. This points out one of the basics of any decorative wrap: The intersections of the first thread wrap must be properly aligned with the rod and must be accurately measured. If it is properly aligned and accurately measured, all the rest of the thread wraps will follow in proper alignment and accurate measurement. If the measurement or alignment of the first thread (intersections) is off, all the rest of the threads will be off.

The basic design involves alternately crisscrossing one thread after another alongside the basic initial spiral wrap or adjacent threads. The added threads may be positioned either at the tip end of the previous thread crossing, at the butt end, or to one side or the other. In almost all cases, one thread is used at a time, although two, three, four, or more (if you can handle them) threads can be wrapped at once. Doing so imparts a different look to the wrap and also makes for wider bands of color where this is done. Using several threads at one time speeds up the wrapping process as well. Even if wide bands are made with single threads, the two methods make for completely different looks in the final wrap.

ROD PREPARATION

There is little rod preparation for making butt or decorative wraps other than in the basics of any wrap. The rod should be clean, smooth, free of dirt and any previous wraps or finish (should it be a previously wrapped rod), and without any marks or lettering. Lettering, however, can be a problem. Many rod blanks have silk-screened or stamped lettering to indicate manufacturer, model number, and specifications such as blank weight and length, action, lure, and line range. Depending upon the length of the handle, this lettering may end up just above the foregrip, where you will want to frame it with simple butt wraps or a complex decorative wrap and forward band wrap. Or you may wish to remove or cover the lettering completely.

The removal of lettering and covering have their problems, although they are possible. Removal may be easy or difficult. Some rod manufacturers have a clear stick-on label for the specification information. If this is the case, it is usually easy to pull off the label and then clean the blank with alcohol, acetone, or ligher fluid.

If the label is silk-screened onto the blank, you may be able to remove it with lighter fluid or acetone. If you use acetone, be very careful: Use it outside or with good ventilation, keep it away from flames, and use it rapidly to avoid damaging the resins in the blank. This will *not* work if the lettering is covered with a clear-epoxy rod finish. A clear epoxy finish over the lettering will require either repeated scrubbing with acetone or the use of another solvent, and this could damage the resins in the rod blank. It is best to avoid this.

A better procedure is to sand or scrape the finish off, removing the lettering at the same time. You can use regular sandpaper, a fine file, or similar abrasives, but take care to work only in the area of the lettering to be removed. One way to prevent damage to the rest of the blank is to mask the area with several layers of masking tape. When this step is necessary, I use a small emery board that is stiff enough to work one small area and that has both coarse- and fine-grit sides.

Another removal method is to use a sharp knife blade, but instead of cutting with the blade, scrape the blank by holding the blade in such a way as to scrape off the finish coat and ultimately the lettering.

Once the lettering is removed, a general sanding with a very fine sandpaper will remove any lumps or imperfections and will make it easy to wrap and finish the blank.

You may choose not to remove the lettering but to wrap over it, particularly if it is in an area that will be wrapped anyway. However, this is best only if the wrapping thread is dark enough to cover any possible show-though of the lettering. Thus, if you will be working on a white rod blank with black lettering, a wrap of light yellow or light blue would probably not work because the black lettering would likely show through. Using a dark blue, dark green, dark brown, or black wrap would likely prevent this show-through. Light-colored lettering (white lettering on a dark blank) is easily covered by any wrapping, although for a dark rod a dark wrap would be a must (to prevent the blank from showing through and marring the color of the wrap). If a medium-colored wrap is to be used on a dark blank, a light or white underwrap should be placed first.

To minimize show-through, you can paint over the lettering with a latex or acrylic paint. The paint should be the color of the blank or white, which will help prevent the blank color from bleeding through light-color wraps. Use paints that will not react with the epoxy rod finish.

UNDERWRAPS

Some rod-builders like underwraps, some do not. Underwraps have advantages and disadvantages. The advantages are:

1. An underwrap helps to keep the blank color from affecting the thread-wrap colors. By using an underwrap—which will usually be light in color—the blank color is visually separated from the decorative wrap color and allows more of the true color of the wrap to show. It is like giving a dark-colored object a light or white base coat before painting it, or like painting lead-head jigs white before adding bright colors or fluorescent colors.

2. An underwrap will give more tooth to the blank, and thus will hold or grip crisscrossing threads more easily. On a bare blank these threads will tend to slide, making it more difficult to keep them accurately aligned and measured.

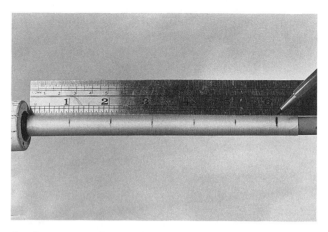

Laying out a basic decorative wrap. If making a diamond wrap, the marks made will be hidden. If making a chevron, the marks must be as small as possible to prevent them from being seen at one edge of the wrap. Marks are laid out at even intervals on one side of the blank, at equally even intervals on the opposite side but spaced halfway between the original marks.

3. An underwrap will show through the spaces left in any decorative wraps (unless the entire blank area is filled with the decorative wrap, as with snakeskin wraps). This allows an additional color in the decorative wrap. Also, when the underwrap is in a strongly contrasting color to the decorative wrap (as they usually are), this allows the decorative wrap to stand out far more than it would on the blank alone.

The disadvantages of using an underwrap are:

1. The advantage of the underwrap providing tooth for overlying crisscrossing threads can also be a disadvantage. If the wrapped threads are tight, this makes it difficult to move or change the position of the crossing threads to adjust alignment. A wrap over the bare blank—which is somewhat slippery—makes this easier.

2. If you will be making a wrap in which all of the spaces will be filled in, there is no decorative advantage to using an underwrap, because it will be completely hidden. This won't apply, of course, if the light underwrap helps to preserve and maintain the bright colors of the decorative butt wrap.

Underwraps for decorative wraps are done exactly as are underwraps for guides, only for the butt decorative wraps they are longer. They must be slightly longer than the decorative wrap, so you must first measure and decide on the length of the decorative wrap (including any tie-down wraps at the butt end and possibly the tip end) and then calculate the length of the underwrap. This does

not have to be a complicated calculation—just one that will allow you to make the wrap of the length you want. Often, this is more a feel or estimate than an actual measurement—at least that is how I do it most of the time.

You can begin the underwrap either at the winding check to work up the rod, or at the upper limit of the wrap to work down to the winding check. Either way will work fine. Note that if you are going to do an underwrap and also add a hookkeeper, do the underwrap first and then add the hookkeeper, incorporating it as a part of the butt-thread wind-off to hold the decorative wrap in place.

Begin by using rod supports and thread tension, just as for guide wraps. Use a light color (preferably) with darker colors for the overwrap, because this will reduce the possibility of blotching, mottling, or show-through. Wrap the thread around the blank, cross over this first wrap, maintain tension, and then continue for several turns. Clip off any excess thread. Then continue to wrap the full length you decided upon with this underwrap. Although this can be done with any method of rod wrapping, it is one procedure for which a motorized wrapping tool is very handy. Otherwise, wrapping around the blank for 6 or 8 inches gets monotonous in a hurry.

Once you're at the end, lay down a loop of thread, wrap over it for about five or six turns, hold the last wrap in place, clip the thread, tuck it through the loop, and pull the loop through, along with the thread end. Open up a gap and use a razor blade to cut straight down through the gap (parallel to the thread wraps—at right angles to the rod blank) to cut the thread beneath the surface of the underwrap.

As mentioned earlier, underwrap colors should be lighter than the overwrap to prevent problems of show-through. Good colors include white, light blue, tan, yellow, light green, orange, and any very light shade of any color. It also helps to give the completed underwrap a coat or two of color preserver before continuing with the decorative wrap. Some rod-builders go even further, applying an additional coating of epoxy rod finish to completely protect and finish the wrap, before they proceed with the decorative wrap. To do this, follow the suggestions in Chapter 25. The advantage of color preserver on the underwrap before adding the decorative wrap is that it helps to seal the wrap to the blank and also reduces or eliminates the possibility of show-through. The epoxy finish gives even more protection, but it also adds a layer of finish to the wrap and makes the area slightly slippery—reducing in part the advantage of the extra tooth that holds decorative wraps in place while the thread is wrapped in the up-and-down spirals.

LAYOUT OF DECORATIVE WRAPS

Whether working on the bare blank or with an underwrap, you must lay out the alignment and crossing points of the decorative wrap. This applies to everything from the simplest wrap to the most complex. The first step of laying out the wrap is to determine a straight line on the blank or underwrap that is also in line with the guides and reel-seat hoods. There are several ways to do this, as follows:

1.   One of the easiest ways to determine a line on the rod, and one that requires no tools, is to sight along the rod. Place one band of masking tape at the butt just above the winding check, with a second band above the underwrap or where you plan to end the decorative wrap. Support the rod horizontally directly under a strong overhead light. Long fluorescent lights that are hung in line with the rod are ideal for this. Then, from directly over the rod, close one eye, and with your open eye rotate the rod until the guides are straight up. If your eye is directly over the rod, the glare from the light should form a streak on the blank precisely in line with the guides and reel-seat hoods. Mark the position of the light streak on the tape at both ends. The glare won't be visible on the tape, but it will extend to the tape.

(One note if you are using an underwrap. An underwrap won't reflect the light, and the streak might be difficult to see. To adjust for this, place a long strip of cellophane tape on the blank. This shiny surface will reflect the glare, and the resulting streak can then be transferred from the clear shiny tape to the masking tape bands.)

Once you have marks on these two bands, it is easy to line them up with thread or a rule so as to mark the rest of the decorative wrap area. Once you do this, however, you must turn the rod over and position the guides directly down (you can position butt guides so that equal parts of the guide rings are visible on either side of the rod blank), then repeat the marking procedure.

If you plan to make double diamonds (see Chapter 24 for details) you must make additional alignment marks on the sides of the blank so that you have four alignment marks—all 90 degrees apart. For single diamonds and chevrons, such as

are discussed in this chapter, two marks 180 degrees apart are all that is needed.

2.   An alternative to sighting these separate streaks is to determine the first streak or line, and then work from this. Place another band of masking tape around the rod, making sure that the tape overlaps a little and that the overlapping is a little out of line, and that this overlapping occurs where the alignment has already been determined. (Do not remove or use the original masking tape for this, or you will have to start all over.) Mark the second tape band with the same alignment mark, (based on the first mark) making a permanent mark on both parts of the overlapping tape. Remove the second band of tape, lay it out on a rule, and determine the distance between the two marks that indicate an O point on the rod. Mark this tape halfway between these marks for single wraps, in quarters for double wraps. Then carefully replace the tape on the rod at its original position, making sure the original overlapping marks are in line with the originally determined line.

Do this at the other end of the wrap also six-or eight-inches up from the handle since the taper of the rod will preclude using the same tape or measurements at both positions. Once this is done, it is easy to use a rule or thread to line up the 90-degree or 180-degree marks for single or double decorative wraps.

3.   Another method of laying out decorative wraps involves the use of circle templates and a short length (about 6 inches is good) of right-angle aluminum or plastic. The circle template *must* have quadrant marks on each circle in order for this method to work. First make a tight wrap of masking tape at both ends of the decorative wrap. Then slide the appropriate-sized circle on the template onto the rod blank. (*Note:* This is possible on many two- or multipiece rods that do not have guides on the butt section. If the rod does call for a guide on the butt section, this method can only be done prior to wrapping the guide or guides in place, because it requires that you slip the circle template onto the rod.)

Make sure the circle used is closest to or identical with the diameter of the rod at the winding check. If you can't get an exact fit, wrap several layers of masking tape around the rod blank until the fit is snug. Once the circle template is in place, sight down the rod section from tip end to butt end and line up the quadrant mark on the circle with the hoods of the reel seat. Sometimes it helps to place a reel in the seat to get an exact alignment. Once this is done, mark the position of the required two or four quadrant marks on the masking tape (two should be 180 degrees apart if you are making a single decorative wrap; four should be 90 degrees apart if you are making a double wrap).

Once these marks are made, use a short length of right-angle aluminum or plastic and place it on the blank. Line up the sharp bend of the angle with the main quadrant mark on the circle template. Place a mark on the upper masking tape wrap (which should be positioned at the end of this strip or angle) in alignment with the angle of the metal or plastic strip. Remove the angle, remove the circle template, and replace the template on the rod blank using another, slightly smaller, circle that will fit onto the blank or masking-tape wrap. Line one of the quadrant marks on this circle with the mark on the masking tape and then make the other mark or marks on the tape for single or double decorative wraps. You can also double check this second mark by aligning the circle quadrant mark with the reel on the reel seat.

Once these marks are made, you can make straight lines with a rule or thread. White thread is good because you can use a black felt-tip marker to mark it at the cross-over points and then tape the thread onto the rod in line with the previously made marks. After the first several spiral wraps up and down have been made (and thoroughly checked and measured in the process), the thread can be pulled out and the wrap completed.

Another method is to make small marks with a lead pencil at the cross-over points. If you do this, make these as small as possible, particularly when making a chevron. All marks should be small for accuracy; this is especially important for chevrons, in which the first wrap—where the mark is located—is at the edge of the decorative pattern, not at the center, which will be covered, as with the diamond pattern.

Because the threads spiral and create a pattern on both sides of the blank, those on the reverse side are exactly half the distance of those on the top side. Thus, if the marks on the guide side of the rod were at 1, 2, 3, 4, 5, and 6 inches, then those on the opposite side would be positioned at 1/2, 1 1/2, 2 1/2, 3 1/2, 4 1/2, and 5 1/2 inches. If you will be making a double wrap, the wraps would be the same when on opposite sides of the rod (say at 0 degrees and 180 degrees) and half way in between at the halfway positions at 90 degrees and 270 degrees.

The positioning of these marks is relative to the diameter of the rod, but can be adjusted so that the patterns are tight together and bunched up, or spaced far apart and stretched out. Naturally, the closer together the marks are, the smaller the pattern will be, while the more stretched out they are, the larger the pattern that can be made.

Although there are no rules as to spacing, a general guide is to use spacing that will be about double the diameter of the rod blank. Thus, for a rod blank about 1/2-inch thick at the handle, the marks to indicate the first crossed thread should be about 1 inch apart.

Once the wrap is laid out, we are ready to begin.

BASIC WRAPPING TECHNIQUES

Before considering types of rod wraps, some basics must be discussed and are applicable to all decorative wrappings. The basic technique is to spiral or wrap thread up and down the blank to form crossing threads that will develop into a colored pattern. You begin on the handle or just above it and spiral thread up and down. When the spiraling is complete, a simple band wrap around the blank finishes off the decorative wrap, and the excess thread used to begin each thread wrap is cut away in the process. The upper end of the decorative wrap can be finished off the same way, or you can make a turn of the threads there to bring them back down the blank so that no finishing wrap at the upper end is necessary.

Let's look at beginning the wraps. You have a choice of wrapping thread crudely around the blank or grip and then cutting it away or of using masking tape or double-sided tape to fasten the thread down at this point. Both methods work well, but if I begin on the handle, I like to use tape, while I will usually wrap the thread down if I start just above the handle on the blank. The reasoning here is that if I wrap around the handle, in time there will be enough thread and enough pressure to cut or scar the rod handle. This is particularly true of cork handles but can apply to any handle. If you are at all concerned about this, begin on the blank or lay down a layer of tape before wrapping the thread in place on the handle (the tape will protect the grip). The reason for beginning on the handle in the first place is that it allows for a shorter "back wrap" of thread to secure and finish the spiral wraps. If you start on the blank, this is more difficult to do.

If you will be making the turn at the upper end

of the wrap to avoid finishing there, it is best if you work with an underwrap. The underwrap gives some tooth to the surface so that you can make the turn easily. Trying this over a bare blank will often result in thread slippage and problems later on in the wrap. One solution to this is to use a little color preserver on the first wrap of thread or two, because this will tend to "tack" these threads down. Once the first thread is down, all the rest will follow. Naturally, this requires that the first threads to be tacked down are in perfect alignment and measurement, because it will be very difficult to move them later.

DIAMOND WRAPS

Once the wrap alignment and thread crossings are laid out, it is easy to begin a simple diamond wrap. In fact, one of the simplest does not involve regular thread but instead uses a kind of wide-band thread. Gudebrod used to make Butt Wind thread for simple decorative wraps. A similar material can be found in craft and sewing stores. Some I found is labeled Soutache Braid. I have no idea what a "soutache braid" is, but it is wide (about 1/8-inch), and when wound up and down the rod (taking care for proper alignment and measurement), the effect is like a several-threads-wide diamond or chevron wrap of one color. Additional colors will build up a very wide diamond wrap quickly, although it will have a different look from those done with just one thread. In using this or similar materials, follow the same directions as for the basic diamond, but you will not have to make repeated runs with the thread, because one wrap up and down per color with this wide thread is sufficient. Test the material on a scrap blank for any reactions to color preserver or epoxy rod finish. These threads are not made by rod-component or thread-supply companies and often are combinations of cotton and rayon, and thus they must be tested for color reactions to finish coats.

Regular decorative diamond wraps with thread are simple, though time-consuming. For illustrative purposes, we will use a white underwrap and make a diamond with a red center over it, bordering it with bands of white, blue, and a final outline thread of black. We'll begin by using masking tape to secure the end of the red thread to the blank just above the grip. If possible, use a fly-tying bobbin for this wrap. These are available to fit small, 100-yard spools of thread from any fly-tying shop, and Gudebrod makes a larger bob-

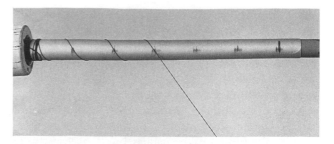

Beginning the wrap by tying down the center thread (for a diamond) and then wrapping up the blank, crossing all the marked points.

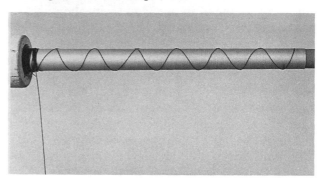

At the top, the thread can be turned to come down the blank (as shown here) or wrapped up on to the blank where it can later be wrapped down. This is a side view, showing the first thread up and down and tied off at the handle.

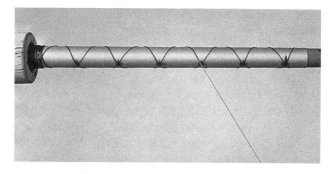

Beginning the second wrap of thread up the blank. Two courses up and down the blank are needed for each successive wrap of thread — one on each side of (or above and below) the original central thread.

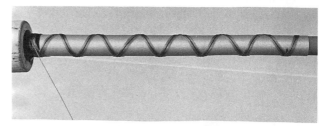

Continuing the wrap of thread in one color up and down the blank. Care must be take to prevent gaps.

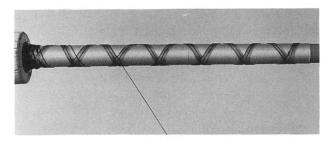

Continuing with another color thread. One course of thread has been made up and down the blank; this is the second wrap which, when completed, will bracket the other thread colors.

Beginning the band wrap that will hold the decorative wrap in place. This is identical to a guide wrap or underwrap, begun on the decorative wraps and worked down to the rod handle.

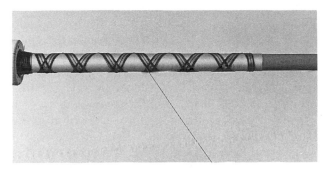

Continuing the wrap to broaden the bands of color.

Once the wrap is complete and the loop pulled through (it is finished the same as a guide wrap), the excess thread is cut. The wrap is now complete and adjustments in the thread or thread gaps can be made.

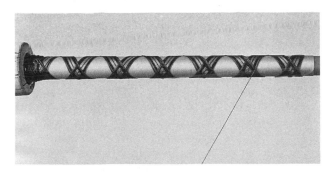

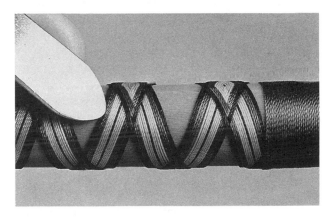

Another color thread added. Diamonds formed this way can thus be as small or big as desired and as simple or complex as the number of color threads used.

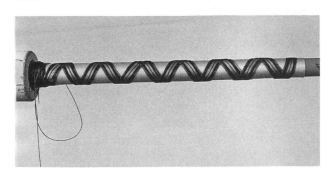

A scalpel handle or Gudebrod burnisher can be used for adjusting threads and closing any gaps that might have occurred while wrapping.

Once the thread wraps are complete, all the thread is tied off at the end. Each thread color must be tied off in turn as the wrapping proceeds.

Examples of simple wraps made on a wood dowel to check patterns and wrapping techniques. This is a method used by master rod builder Cantwell Clark in teaching and to show wraps to clients. Wrap by Cantwell Clark.

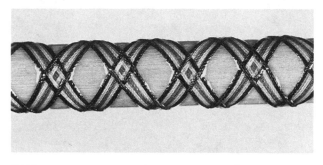

Different spacing in these wraps will result in a different look. This is the same wrap as above, but with a closer spacing. Wrap by Cantwell Clark.

bin for their 1-ounce spools, as well as one for their 100-yard spools. Using bobbins eliminates the necessity of handling the thread, and they are particularly useful for working with several colors simultaneously, as with complex wraps.

Spiral the red thread up the blank, making sure that the thread crosses exactly in the center of each previously made mark on both sides of the rod. We'll wrap off at the upper end, so above the underwrap we'll make a couple of turns and then reverse the direction of the thread and spiral back down the blank, crossing over the previous wraps exactly where the measured markings are located. Once at the butt (just above the grip), make several turns around the blank and then spiral up the blank again, making sure the thread is laid down next to the previous wrap with no gaps. Bring the thread down the same way, wrap around the butt end a few times, and then spiral up again. This time, however, keep the thread on the *other* side of the first wrap. Thus, the first wrap is below — on the butt side — of the initial thread crossing, the second wrap is up and above — on the tip side — of the initial threads. Wraps continue this way

—up and down — always using the first thread as the central thread on any diamond.

At the end of these wraps, tie (with half-hitches) or tape the thread to the rod. Then start with a white thread, again in a bobbin if possible, and wrap up and down the blank, first on one side and then with a second up-and-down wrap on the other side to bracket the red band. Continue this two more times to make a frame of three threads of white around the central red band. Tie this thread off, tie down a blue thread, and wrap up and down with the blue thread to bracket the white band. Continue this to make three thread wraps around the white thread, and then tie off. Finally, tie down a black thread and spiral up and down twice with it to finish and frame the completed red, white, and blue diamond wrap.

At this point the diamond is completed, but it must be finished with a regular wrap (rotating around the rod, like a guide wrap or underwrap). This is a critical step, because a slight mistake here can cause some of the diamond threads to loosen and ruin the wrap. One way to reduce this possibility is to coat the diamond with one coat of color preserver and blot it dry. The color preserver will tack the diamond wrap to the rod and help prevent loosening.

If, or once, this is done, place the rod on a regular rod wrapper and wrap thread around the wrap at the butt, but above where the threads are no longer lined up properly. Begin this wrap and make about five to six turns before cutting off any excess thread. At this point, maintain constant tension on this wrap and begin to carefully cut away the tie-down threads and tape of the diamond. (One way to maintain tension on the rotary wrap is to secure it and tape it in place tightly with masking tape. Another way is to use a heavy rod anchor — a tapered hook that fits over the rod with a heavy weight (heavy sinker) on the end to hold the rod and keep it from moving. For best results, the tapered hook should be rubber-coated to prevent the rod blank from sliding.)

Use scissors, a razor blade, or a scalpel to cut away all threads to a point above the winding check. Then remove the masking tape or rod anchor from the rotation wrap and continue wrapping, working all the way to the winding check. About six turns before the winding check, lay down a loop of thread and wrap over it to the end. Maintain tension, cut the end, and tuck it through the loop. Pull the loop through, and with it the end of the thread, then open up a gap and use a razor blade to cut down into this gap to cut the thread end. The technique is just like finishing a guide wrap.

Alternatives to this are to wrap down to the winding check and then double back, finishing by making a double wrap of thread. Another possibility is to wrap down a hookkeeper at the same time, finishing off on each side of the hookkeeper or spiraling the thread around the hookkeeper to finish in one wrap.

Make a similar wrap on the upper end of the rod, beginning on the decorative wrap and working up (away from the wrap) to secure the thread. Tape the thread down and then carefully cut away the excess thread of the diamond wrap. Finish as described. The final result will be a fine single diamond (diamonds on the top and bottom of the rod — but not on all four sides) finished by a band of thread between the winding check and the diamond and a band of thread wrap at the upper end.

Naturally, the various combinations of thread colors and types and the spacing of diamonds, make for endless possibilities.

CHEVRON WRAPS

Chevron wraps are started and completed in the same way as are diamond wraps. The main difference is in the method and order of working with the threads to form the chevron pattern. Making this wrap is just like making one-half of a diamond. To begin, first decide whether or not you will work with an underwrap, then lay out the wrap as previously described. The layout of this wrap is exactly the same as for a diamond. For our example, we will pick the same colors as for the diamond and make a red, white, and blue chevron.

Begin by tying or taping the black framing thread to the rod and run up and down the blank with that thread, making sure it is exactly aligned and measured. Tie the black thread off and then tie down the first red thread. Wrap up and back down again with the red thread, just as with the diamond wrap. Make sure this first red wrap of thread is to the *tip side* of the first black thread. Continue with four more wraps to make a total of five wraps, all placed to the tip side of the previous wraps. Tie the red thread off, tie in a white thread, and repeat the wrap to the *tip side* of the previous wrap. Tie the white thread off and then tie in the blue thread. Continue with five wraps of this thread, again to the tip side of the previous wraps.

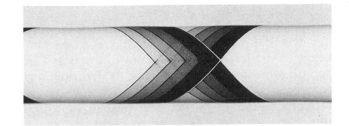

A simple but attractive chevron wrap. This is done just like half of a diamond — all thread wraps are sequentially on one side of the first thread. This wrap progressed from the first dark thread on the left through the successively darker wrap, and finished with the white thread on the right. Wrap by Cantwell Clark.

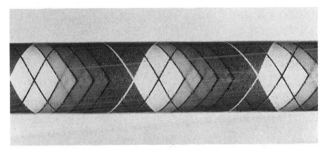

Example of a simple chevron with an additional single thread wrap (the black thread crossing in the white space) to make it look more complex. The black crossing thread is added last. Wrap by Cantwell Clark.

To frame or block off the finished wrap, use a black thread to go up and down, to the tip side again, of the previous wraps. This, together with the first black thread, will bracket or frame the wrap. Tie off, then make the finishing band wraps on the butt end just above the winding check to hold down the chevron-wrap threads. The result will be a chevron of red, white, and blue, just like the colors in the diamond. The difference will be that the diamond is diamond- or square-shaped, while the chevron is an inverted V shape as you look from the butt of the rod toward the tip.

There are several variations to this basic wrap. The first is to make all the wraps described, but to make them on the *butt side* of each previous thread, not on the *tip side*. This will result in a chevron that is V-shaped, in essence running in the opposite direction (toward the butt) of the original design.

Another possibility, one seldom if ever seen, is to make a chevron that points sideways. For this, continue as described, but always make each wrap to one side of the previous wrap, so that the V is worked to the side. If you make wraps to the right as you look from the butt to the tip end of the rod, the V will point to the right. If you make the wraps to the left, the V will point to the left. The one disadvantage of the right- or left-pointing chevrons is that they might not seem lined up properly on the top of the rod. To correct for this, you might wish to make four quadrant marks on the rod, as if you were making a double wrap, and begin the right- or left-pointing chevron at the appropriate 90-degree quadrant mark, then work around the rod to end up with the final thread making the point of the V at the top center of the rod, or at the position of the mark aligned with the guides and reel-seat hoods.

Just as with diamond wraps, there are endless thread combinations. And chevrons can be made pointing in any of four directions. Also, as with the simple diamonds made with the wide Soutache Braids, simple chevrons using this or similar materials are a possibility.

CROSS WRAPS

A cross is essentially a diamond done backward —from the outside threads working to the inner or central thread. The layout can be the same, but the wrap is a little more difficult because you must lay down the outside and then work to the center. The two outside threads must be parallel throughout the wrap so that there are no gaps when the wrap is complete. To use the three colors of red, white, and blue, begin with two wraps up and down with the red thread to bracket the wrap area. These wraps must be parallel, and you must try to figure out the total width of the wrap with five threads each of red and white on each side, and then five threads of blue in the center. Five plus five red, five plus five white, and five blue, for a total width of twenty-five threads. (If you don't get this spacing exactly, don't worry, because any of the thread bands can be made with more or less thread as desired. Also, if you have too little space, you can use a thread pick or pointed burnisher to open up the wrap for an additional thread wrap or two, or use the burnisher to close up the total wrap if you have too much space and some gaps.)

Once these threads are in place (using one thread on the markers on the underwrap or blank) and parallel, continue with the rest of the four red threads up and down twice, always laying down the thread on the inside of the bracketed wrap. Tie off and then tie down the white thread and

continue with two bands each of five threads. Finally, tie off and finish with a five-thread wrap of blue for the center. If the spacing was calculated correctly, there will be room for all the thread wraps and no gaps in the process. However, this is one wrap you might want to do a little loosely so that you can use a burnisher to tighten up the wraps, if desired. The other possibility is to allow for some adjustment in the number of thread wraps as you work, adjusting as you go along so that you end up with a tight no-gap wrap with no overlapping. One possibility if you have too much space at the end but not enough for an additional double up-and-down wrap, is to wrap with two threads at the same time to fill in gap areas. Combinations in threads (including the wide-braid materials), in the number of wraps, in the thread types, and in the thread colors lead to unlimited possibilities in these various cross patterns.

FLAG WRAPS

Flag wraps that look like an American flag are popular and attractive. They are done using standard solid red and white Gudebrod thread along with blue Trimar thread to create the sparkle of the star-filled upper left corner of the flag. These wraps require the same precise layout methods of other wraps, because the area around the flag is usually filled in with a background-color thread. The marked point in this case will be the lowermost right corner of the blue, star-filled portion of the flag.

Begin by laying out the wrap. One variation is that you can work with several or more threads at once if you want to make this wrap quickly—it will not affect the appearance. You can also work one thread at a time if you wish, or one color in three or four threads, depending upon the width of each band of red and white.

Let's assume you will be working one band of color at a time, with three threads. Tie or tape down a band of three strands of solid red (Gudebrod Scarlet 326) and spiral them up the blank, going from left to right around the blank as you look toward the tip end. Make sure that the lower part of this band just touches the measurement mark. Once at the top of the wrap area, do not come back down, but tie or tape off and cut the thread. Continue this way, working alternately with three strands of white (Gudebrod White 002), three strands of red, and so on, until you have a solid field of four red bands and three white bands.

At this point, begin the blue star field, working with Gudebrod Blue/Silver Trimar thread 245S. Again, you can work with one thread or several at once. We'll work with three at a time again, because this will help us determine the correct proportions of the parts of the flag. Begin by spiraling three strands of the blue/silver Trimar up the rod, working from right to left as you look toward the tip. Make sure that the upper edge of this thread just touches the measurement mark. Thus, at this point, each of these marks will be in a corner made by the lower part of the lowest red band of color and the upper part of the blue. Continue with the blue/silver Trimar until you have twenty-seven strands laid down. Since the red and white bands make up twenty-one bands (three each of four red and three white), this will make the proportions correct. All these wraps are tied down or taped off at the top of the wrap area — not continued down the rod.

Return to the three strands each of white and red. Begin with white, spiraling up the rod from left to right so that the white thread covers the lower part of the blue and just touches the red band previously made. Alternately lay down three strands of white and red to finish the flag colors (for total of thirteen horizontal stripes — seven red and six white). The flag is blocked off by using another color of thread to border first the bottom and left side of the flag and then the top and finally the right side of the flag. The right side of the flag is done last, because the position of the border wrap here will determine the proportions of the flag.

Roughly, the flag is in a proportion of 3 X 5. Exact dimensions can't be given, because much would depend upon the size of thread used (though if Trimar is used, it only comes in size C and presumably the other colors would be in size D, which in Gudebrod thread is the same diameter as C), how tight the wraps are, how many threads are used for each band of red and white,

This American flag wrap appears far more complex than it really is. First three bands of red and white are spiraled up the rod to make the top of the red and white stripes of the flag directly opposite the blue field. There are four red and three white to this band. Next a spiral wrap of blue or Gudebrod Trimar blue is laid down to form the blue field with "stars." More bands of red and white follow, these parallel to the first bands and consisting of three bands each of white and red. Finally a gold "flag pole" band is added to the left. The wrap is completed by boxing in the rest of the wrap with a wrap of contrasting color. Wrap by Cantwell Clark.

Another "flag" pattern done with spiral wrappings of thread.

and so on. The border can be broadened a little to outline the flag and the rest of the wrap can be exposed, or the rest of the wrap can be completely covered with a border. Usually this latter method is used to make the flag stand out.

An alternative to this is to lay down a gold band of two or three threads on the left of the blue field to resemble a flagpole. Then block in the rest of the flag with a background color.

CHECKERBOARD OR SNAKESKIN WRAPS

Checkerboard or snakeskin wraps are simple. They are not really a checkerboard but a solid color broken up into small squares by single threads in a contrasting color. To make this wrap, lay out the design as previously described. The wrap simply involves wrapping several bands of a chosen color up and down the rod, as with a standard diamond or chevron. There are several techniques that can be used to obtain the final result. One is to make a solid block of color and then to come back with a contrasting color, and with a single thread go up and down the rod to lay out small squares with every few threads. These must be equal in size for the wrap to look right. Once this is done, the whole block can be bracketed with a border of the same color as the individual threads, or with a third color. The result is that the individual threads of contrasting color sit on top of the base-color wraps.

Another method of doing this is to first make the base-color wraps under lessened tension. The secret here is to make them slightly slack but not so much that they are noticeably loose. Then, when the individual contrasting color thread is laid down it can be forced in between the existing threads. Because these individual threads are laid down under more tension, it is important to being at the center of the wrap and then to work out; forcing the individual threads into place will slightly push the base-color wraps to both sides. The wrap is bracketed as previously described.

A third method is to make the base-color wraps with bands of two, three, four, or five threads, separating each such band one thread's width from the next. After this is complete, it is easy to lay down one thread to block out the checkboard pattern.

OTHER VARIATIONS OF SIMPLE WRAPS

Variations of these simple wraps are endless. Some possibilities include:

1. Making individual thread cross-wraps between any of the above wraps—diamonds, chevrons, Maltese crosses, flags, or checkerboards. You can measure for these, but if you do them after the main wrap is complete, it is easy to estimate measurements. These can be a simple single-thread wrap or two or three threads of the same or contrasting colors. If you do these before the main wrap is made (which will cover some of this thread work), you will want to measure for them.

2. Another variation is to build up this cross-wrap into a mini-diamond, mini-chevron, or other wrap. This is completely different from the technique of double wraps as described in the next chapter, because it will add another row of wraps on the rod, but in the same line and on only two sides, as with any single wrap—not at 90-degree angles, as with the true double wrap.

3. Another variation is to make the mini-wrap of a diamond or chevron on the wrap, but at 90 degrees to the main wrap so that it will closely simulate a double wrap. It won't be exactly like it, because this variation is done with the two wraps completed separately, as opposed to double wraps, which are done simultaneously.

4. Decorative wraps can be mixed, as in making a chevron and then adding cross-wrap threads between the original threads and building up these cross-wraps to make a mini diamond, for example. Any combination of these is possible.

5. The end result, look, and effect of a wrap is completely changed when one thread at a time is used. Working with one thread gives more of a detailed, intricate look to most wraps; although with some, such as the checkerboard, it will not

Decorative wraps can be made using simple spiral bands, tied in using a basic guide-style wrap at both ends. Such wraps' avoid complex spacing and the necessity of lining up crossing threads. Wrap by Cantwell Clark.

make a noticeable difference. In fact, for the checkerboard wrap, working with bands of threads may even make the wrap easier, with a better final appearance.

As with any decorative wrap, there is no limit to the number of wrap combinations, band widths, thread colors, or number of colors that may be used. And there is no distinct separation between simple decorative wraps and complex decorative wraps, as will be discussed in the next chapter. They are all accomplished by a buildup of knowledge and experience, just as each wrap is accomplished by a buildup of thread.

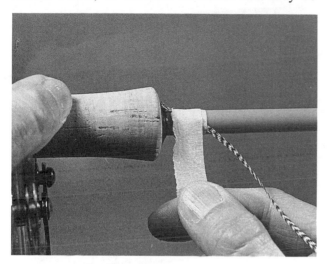

A simple wrap of wide, flat sewing materials called "soutache" will make for a simple butt wrap. Begin by taping this material in place and spiraling up and down the rod.

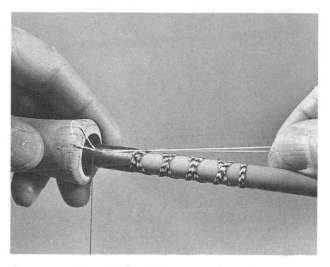

Once complete, the braid is wrapped in place using a basic guide wrap as shown.

24

Complex Butt Wraps and Decorative Wraps

INTRODUCTION ▪ TOOLS AND MATERIALS ▪ LAYOUT AND
DESIGN ▪ MULTIPLE WRAPS ▪ PLAIDS ▪ SPLIT DIAMONDS ▪
SPLIT CHEVRONS ▪ WEAVING LETTERS AND NUMBERS ▪
WEAVING SCENES ▪ DECORATIVE WRAPS ON GUIDES

The safety equipment, basic tools, and helpful tools for making complex wraps are exactly the same as for the simple wraps described in Chapter 23. Consult that chapter for details. To understand complex wraps, read Chapter 23 before reading this chapter.

INTRODUCTION

Complex decorative and butt wraps are essentially an extension of simpler wraps. In fact, there is no clear separation between the two, even though a separation is created by the two chapters here. Complex wraps are just that—more complex in design and execution than the simpler wraps, but where you draw the line between the two is a subjective decision. Complex wraps are for the most part built on the same concept as are simple wraps: intersecting threads that in turn are built up into designs and patterns.

As with simple wraps, complex wraps are not difficult, but they do require care and planning, and particular attention must be paid to the first crossing wraps, which will determine the accuracy and spacing of all subsequent wraps.

In addition, the more complex a wrap becomes, the more planning must go into it and the more care in design and step-by-step production must be taken to make sure it results in the color scheme and design desired. The method of weaving is another aspect of complex wraps, and woven wraps take on a totally new design methodology. For weaving letters and numbers, the design and layout of each letter and number must be planned in advance in order to know how many wraps to make over and under each horizontal thread.

Weaving scenes is almost a matter of trial and error, because you have to have a basic concept of what you want to do, of the scene you wish to make, and of the thread colors and arrangements possible for the scene. In all such cases, it helps to keep notes so that designs can be repeated if desired. In the case of numbers and letters, simple charts are available that will allow you to repeat figures of the same size and shape.

TOOLS AND MATERIALS

Tools and materials are exactly the same as those for simple wraps. The only addition might be some chart tape, such as is available in stationery stores and art-supply shops. This tape is ideal for testing designs before beginning the actual wrapping process. An alternative is to use various colors of construction paper cut into strips.

The fly-tying bobbins mentioned in the previous chapter become even more useful here, because many of the more complex wraps involve different thread colors. The use of a bobbin for each color makes wrapping easier.

LAYOUT AND DESIGN

The layout and design of complex wraps are exactly the same as for simple wraps. You still have a choice of wrapping on a bare blank or over an underwrap, still must measure the center stripe of the rod for proper alignment with the guides and reel-seat hoods, and still must accurately measure the position for the crossing threads that are the basis for any subsequent wraps.

To use the chart tape as a guide for wraps, first make an X on a sheet of paper or white cardboard (cardboard is better, because you can keep the resultant design for reference). Then use this X as the basis for the first crossing threads. From this it is possible to lay down subsequent wraps of any color of chart tape in any order to make any pos-

sible design or to test any design. It is really better for the latter — testing designs where you are unsure of the final result. Also, it helps to make accompanying notes that list in order the wraps made and the color used.

A good and more readily available substitute for chart tape is construction paper. I buy assorted-color packs, use a paper cutter to cut the paper into 1/4-inch-wide strips, and use the various strips to lay out and plan wraps. Unlike chart tape, which has a sticky side, this paper allows you to lay down strips and remove them to start over if you don't like the result. If you do like the result, it is easy to use clear tape to secure the edges of the strip to make it stationary.

One simple way to keep a permanent record of your designs is to use 8 1/2 × 11 inch paper for the base, plan the wrap as above, tape on the paper base, trim off any strips that extend beyond these borders and place the taped-down result into a clear plastic sheet protector. These are designed for three-ring notebooks, so you can make up your own book of designs. In most cases, the strips of paper can substitute for a general idea of the design appearance, if not the exact number of threads you might use. On the same paper, you can write notes as to the number of threads used for each band in an actual wrap, the suggested number of threads in a planned wrap, and even the exact thread colors by stock numbers. (Gudebrod has a number for each thread color.)

In addition, it is important to understand the basic differences between making a single diamond or chevron wrap, as described in Chapter 23, and making double or multiple wraps. With a single wrap, one spiral of thread up and down the blank serves as the basis for all other thread wraps and the formation of the pattern being developed. The ultimate effect is that of a series of patterns forming on the two sides of the rod, 180 degrees apart. With double or multiple wraps, the thread must be spiraled up and down several times to form the basic thread wrap. Note that this effect is completely different from the effect described in the last chapter, in which a single wrap is made, and additional cross-wraps or mini-wraps as additional decoration are added later. The effect there is of two separate wraps, one made over the other. The effect of the double wrap or multiple wrap is that of a totally integrated set of patterns.

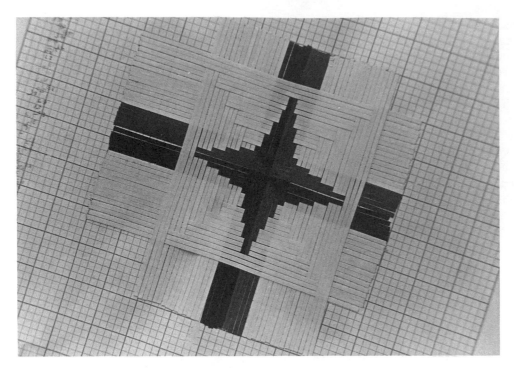

Complex designs are often best laid out first using chart paper or strips of different color paper. This is a design to show the sequence of wraps for a cross pattern done by Cantwell Clark.

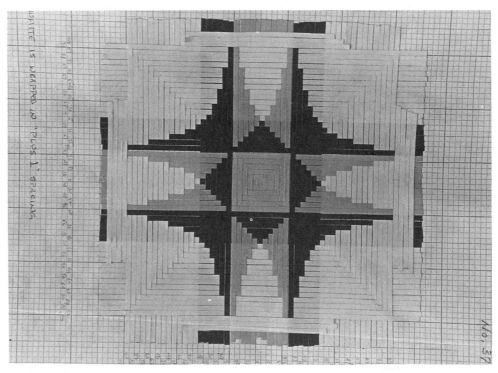

Another complex design by Cantwell Clark. Making such designs on paper helps to develop the sequence of wraps and to help define widths of bands and colors used.

Another design by Cantwell Clark, this of a stylized fish.

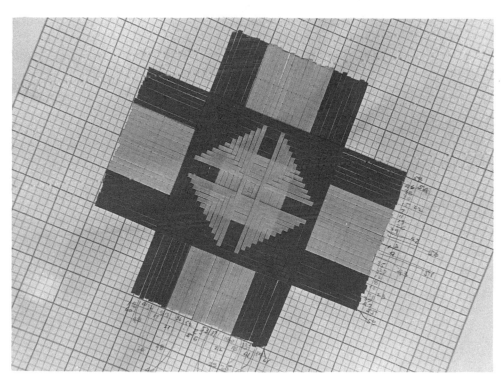

Notes along the margins of wraps serve as helpful reminders of wrapping steps and procedures. Wrap by Cantwell Clark.

MULTIPLE WRAPS

Double and multiple wraps involve the same turns of thread up and down the blank, as was outlined for single wraps, to get identical band widths, but several turns up and down the blank are made with each thread. Thus, while one spiral turn up and down is required for a single wrap in which patterns end up on both sides of the rod, two turns up and down are required for a double wrap, three turns up and down are required for a triple wrap, and so on.

The difference in these wraps is both in the number of turns made and in the position of the patterns. Thus, with a single wrap, although the patterns on the two sides of the rod are 180 degrees from each other, they are not directly opposite. If the position of the top patterns, measuring from the foregrip, are 1, 2, 3, 4, and 5 inches, the position of the patterns on the opposite side of the rod will measure 1/2, 1 1/2, 2 1/2, 3 1/2, 4 1/2, and 5 1/2 inches.

In making a double wrap, the thread is wrapped up and down twice. This results in a layout such that the wraps at 0 degrees and 180 degrees are directly opposite each other (at the 1, 2, 3, 4, and 5 inch positions), and those on the sides, at 90 degrees and 270 degrees, will be at the halfway spots: 1/2, 1 1/2, 2 1/2, 3 1/2, 4 1/2, and 5 1/2 inches.

For this double wrap, you have to lay out the straight lines not only on the top and bottom of the rod (0 degrees and 180 degrees), but also on the sides (90 degrees and 270 degrees). This is easily done using the circle quadrant marks on circle templates or the marked-masking-tape method, both outlined in Chapter 23. After this layout is done, then lay out and measure the position of the crossing thread. In making the marks for these patterns, we can think of the four lines as 1, 2, 3, and 4 heading clockwise around the cross section of the blank at 0 degrees, 90 degrees, 180 degrees, and 270 degrees. Making the wrap requires two spiral wraps up and down the rod—the first wrap crossing at 0, 2, and 4 inches on top, and 1, 3, and 5 inches on the bottom or underside. The second wrap up and down will fill in these areas, crossing on top at 1, 3, and 5 inches, and on the bottom at 0, 2, and 4 inches, all measured from the foregrip.

Making quadruple wraps is similar, because you end up with eight instead of four patterns around the rod. The lines, based on the cross section of the blank, will be at 0 degrees, 45 degrees, 90

Methods of laying out simple and complex wraps. Here the first thread wrap of these patterns is shown. Top to bottom: a single wrap (patterns on opposite sides of the rod), double wrap (two courses of thread up and down to result in patterns on four sides of the rod), triple wrap (three courses of thread up and down the rod to result in patterns on six sides of the rod or every 60 degrees), and quadruple wrap (four courses of thread up and down the rod to result in eight patterns around the circumference of the rod). Note that these wraps are not precisely measured, but simply spaced by eye — often a good way to check the complexity and "business" of any wrap to be developed. Spacing, or distance, along the axis of the rod, can be adjusted for any of these wraps.

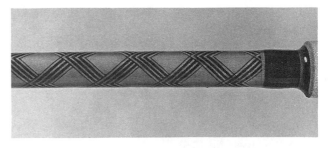

Multiple wraps (this is a chevron) require two wraps up and down the rod for each band of color. The result is a wraps that cross at the side so that a double chevron will have chevrons at each 90 degrees rather than the chevrons at only 180 degrees, as with a simple wrap. Six-sided and eight-sided wraps can be made similarly.

degrees, 135 degrees, 180 degrees, 225 degrees, 270 degrees, and 315 degrees.

If we think of these lines as traveling clockwise and numbered 1 through 8, the number 1, 3, 5, and 7 lines will pattern at the same position, as measured lengthwise from the rod grip; those at the 2, 4, 6, and 8 positions will pattern at the same position as well, although this second batch of patterns (lines 2, 4, 6, and 8) will intersect halfway between lines 1, 3, 5, and 7. Thus, if we are to make all the patterns 1 inch apart, the markings on lines 1, 3, 5, and 7 would be 1, 2, 3, 4, 5, 6, 7, and 8 inches. Those for lines 2, 4, 6, and 8 would be at 1/2, 1 1/2, 2 1/2, 3 1/2, 4 1/2, 5 1/2, 6 1/2, 7 1/2, and 8 1/2 inches. The markings for each line remain 1 inch apart, they just vary in comparison to the adjacent lines. (In all of these examples, the measurements are only hypothetical—you will often need more or less space between wraps, based on the appearance of the wrap and the diameter and type of rod used.)

For a quadruple wrap, four spirals in the first wrap are required, beginning at 0, 4, and 8 inches (measuring from the top of the rod). A second wrap at 3 and 7 inches is followed by a third at 2 and 6 inches, and a fourth at 1 and 5 inches. Only then are the crossing threads for all eight wraps complete. Subsequent thread wraps must follow the same pattern up and down the rod four times for each wrap.

Making this many wraps creates unique problems. First, because the distance between the marks for each course of the thread is somewhat far apart (four inches in the example we have been using), the resulting patterns tend to get a stretched-out look. You can move all the markings closer, but this then causes the patterns to fill up the allotted area and cover the underwrap or bare blank. Often this can be used to advantage in filling up the rod area completely to make a snakeskin effect of repeated patterns, usually diamonds (similar to that found on some snakes) or chevrons (similar to scales on a reptile) or a latticelike diamond or checkerboard. The easiest way to think of this quadruple wrap, however, is as an extension of the double wrap previously described. In essence it is, with additional wraps of thread used to fill in the blanks that occur on a standard double wrap.

If you will be making triple wraps, a different layout has to be planned. You must plan for crossing thread wraps to allow for three turns up and down the rod to make three different crossing points on three different locations on the rod blank.

For this, there are six lines of patterns around the rod. These will be positioned at 0 degrees and each successive 60 degrees (thus, at 0 degrees, 60 degrees, 120 degrees, 180 degrees, 240 degrees, and 320 degrees). There are also different measurements for the start of each pattern. Let's assume a final position where the wraps are 1/2-inch apart. Marks made on the three straight lines will have to be 1/2-inch apart; however, not all will have the same positioning, even though all of the measurements will be the same length apart. If we envision a cross section of the rod blank, we can number the straight lines used for the crossing threads at the 0-, 60-, 120-, 180-, 240-, and 320-degree positions around the blank. If we number these in a clockwise direction, we would have patterns on lines 1, 2, 3, 4, 5, and 6. The markings for the 1, 3, and 5 line positions will be at 1/2-, 1, 1 1/2, 2, 2 1/2, 3, and 3 1/2 inches. Those for the lines in the 2, 4, and 6 positions will similarly be 1 1/2- to 2-inches apart *but will begin with a 1/4-inch measurement, then follow with the successive 1/2-inch measurements.* Thus, the measurements for this second set of wraps will be 1/4-, 3/4-, 1 1/4 inches, and so on. An easier way to think of and measure these is to make the first 1/4-inch measurement and then reset the rule so that all subsequent measurements are 1/2-inch apart.

The first thread wrap up and down the rod will not be at each crossing point, but at every *third* crossing point. To continue with our final measurements 1/2-inch apart, the first course of the single thread wrap up and down will be at 0, 1 1/2, 3, 4 1/2, and 6 inches, and so on. Once the first course is made, the second course up and down will be at 1, 2 1/2, 4, and 5 1/2 inches, and so on. The third course will be at 1/2-, 2, 3 1/2, and 5 inches, and so on. Any sequence of order can be made, provided that the constant distance of 1 1/2 inches is maintained between all wraps.

At this final point, all the threads will have crossed all the measurements made on the wrap to complete the first, single-thread, stage of the wrap. Subsequent wraps of thread will be made up and down the rod in the same sequence, using three courses up and down the rod for each thread color (unless several threads are used at once).

Any multiple wrap is finished the same as is a single wrap. Thus, you first have a choice of turning a corner at the upper end of the wrap, in which no locking-thread wrap is used at the upper end, or of continuing up onto the rod blank and finishing off both ends of the wrap with a simple band wrap to lock the threads in place. As with any wrap of this type, it often helps to add a coating of color preserver before laying in the band locking-thread wrap. Doing this does not allow you to just rip away the excess thread, but it does allow you some insurance that threads will not loosen as you make the band wrap at the rod handle, and at the upper end, if required.

PLAIDS

Plaids are made by using a combination of N.C.P. thread and standard thread. You must have a white base, which you can create by using a white blank, by using a white underwrap, or by painting the blank white. Working with a white rod is the easiest. If you paint the blank, paint it only in the area of the plaid wrap and use only a latex or acrylix paint that will not react with the epoxy rod finish. If you use a white underwrap, use N.C.P. white thread and add one coat of color preserver, or use regular white thread and two or three coats of color preserver. The color preserver or N.C.P. thread and color preserver is necessary to prevent the white thread from showing through when you add epoxy finish to the main wrap.

Once the white base is prepared, lay out your cross marks for a double diamond and begin to build the double diamond. Usually these plaid wraps look best if they closely simulate Scottish tartans, so you might wish to check a fabric pattern or a book of tartans from the library. Tartans can be of any color combination but are often blue and green, green and red, red and black, yellow and red, and yellow and blue. Build up the double diamond, and in doing so try to use as little tension as is necessary, because you might have to adjust some thread positions later.

Once the diamonds are complete, use regular white thread in between to build up and cover all of this blank area. Here is where you might have to adjust some thread positions and push some threads around, because the taper of any blank seldom allows for an easy fill-in of this area between decorative wraps. Assuming everything else to be equal, the taper of the blank allows for less room between the perimeters of the diamonds at the upper end of the wrap than at the lower end. Use continuous up-and-down spirals of white to fill this in completely, using the point of a burnisher or similar tool to push threads out of the way and to allow for threads with no crossover or overlapping.

Once the regular white thread is completely covering all of the space between the diamonds, coat the area with a thin epoxy finish such as Flex Coat Lite or some other thinned rod finish. This

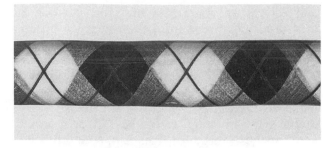

Plaid wrap, by Cantwell Clark, using different colors and regular and N.C.P. thread.

allows for complete penetration into the wrap and a bleed-through of the darker colors in the plaid. Once this coat is complete and cured, finish with trim wraps of individual N.C.P. threads, generally using a white over the dark diamond as an accent point, and dark over the white wrap in between the diamonds. Once these are completed to your satisfaction, protect the entire wrap with a final coat or coats of epoxy rod finish.

SPLIT DIAMONDS

Diamonds can be split so that they develop a completely different look, that of two different colors. This can be done around an existing diamond (usually made small) or as a completely separate pattern in which the splits become the central block, which in turn are blocked in with other color wraps. They can also be done so that the split occurs along the axis of the rod or at right angles to the axis of the rod.

Let's first consider a split of diamonds across the axis of the rod. For this, first lay out a central crossing thread, using one of the two colors you want for the diamond. Let's assume red for this example. Then you lay out to one side (above, toward the tip, or below, toward the butt) of this diamond crossing wrap a second up-and-down wrap of the other color—let's say green. Standard diamond wraps are made with one central thread and separate bracketing threads on each side, so that you always have an odd number of threads. I prefer to think of these first two threads as a set and add equal numbers of same-color thread on each side of this set. I think of this as starting with one color and ending with the second color. Thus, if your first color is red, the last color—regardless of the size of the pattern—will be green (in this example). This, then, keeps the diamond equal in size on both sides and also does away with any separate-color central threads, as are used with

A Cantwell Clark split wrap in which different colors are used on each side of the original thread wrap. Side-to-side split wraps can be made by using a different color thread going up the rod than that coming down the rod.

standard diamonds. (The central thread may not always be a separate color—in fact, it is often the same color for several wraps to build up a central block of one color, to be surrounded by separate-color diamonds.)

Once this basic set of thread colors is laid out—one color up and down as an initial thread followed by one contrasting color up and down on one side—you have the basis for the rest of the wrap. For the rest of the wrap, continue laying down one red thread up and down, always on the red side, and one green thread up and down, always on the green side. The result ultimately is a diamond consisting of the shapes of two abutting triangles of different colors.

To finish this diamond, you can bracket it with a third color—let's say black. This bracket can be one or two threads, or as thick or thin as you wish it to be. You can also make additional diamonds of uniform colors (as with a standard diamond wrap), so that the split diamond becomes blocked in with successive bands of contrasting colors.

You can develop a split diamond with the split along the axis of the rod. To do this, first lay out the initial crossing thread (we'll use red for the first color, green for the second, as before). Then wrap the second color (green), making the course up the rod *below* the initial red thread, the course down the rod *above* the red thread. Continue this way, with the next red thread kept above the red thread going up, and kept below the red thread going down. The colors continue this way, with the green always next to the green, the red always next to the red. In essence, you are working to the side of the rod from the center axis, keeping green on one side and red on the other. Once you have the split diamond sized as you desire, bracket it

with a third color to frame the pattern, or build up other bands of color as previously described.

Although the above description is for simple split diamonds using one color on each side of the split, you can also make multicolored patterned diamonds by building up a split diamond and then, after a given number of thread wraps, changing colors. This is how a standard diamond is usually done: starting with a block of color and then one or more times shifting to different colors and band widths of colors to make the diamond more decorative. For this you can use totally new colors for each of the new bands or simply reverse the colors so that a split diamond that starts with red above (toward the tip) and green below would reverse to a second band of green above and red below. Naturally, when using reversed bands or different colors, you can continue as many times as you wish, using as many colors as you wish, with identical- or different-sized band widths.

An alternative is to make each band up and down of a different color, but keep the colors consistent for each side of the diamond. The result will be a four-sided diamond with each of the developing sides a different color. Thus, you can have a diamond in which each little triangle that makes up the diamond is different—say red, green, blue, and yellow. Of course, any combination of colors is possible.

SPLIT CHEVRONS

Just as diamonds can be split, so can chevrons. Chevrons are really easier, because they are only half of a diamond. To make a split chevron, you will work with two colors (let's use red and green again), but in this case one color (let's say red) spirals up the rod, and the second color (green) spirals down the rod. Thus, for the initial wrap, the two crossing threads will not be the same color but will be red and green. After these threads are properly checked and positioned on the premarked underwrap, the rest of the wrap is easy and involves nothing more than running the same colors up and down the blank: red up and green down.

But unlike a diamond, in which the central threads or sets of threads are bracketed on both sides, for a chevron all of the subsequent threads are to one side (above or below—toward the tip or the butt) the initial wrap. If all of the wraps are below the initial wrap, then the point of the chevron will be aimed toward the butt of the rod. If all the wraps are above the initial thread, then the point will be aimed toward the tip. As described in Chapter 23, you can also make a chevron to the right or left simply by tracking all the threads after the first thread to the right or left. If you make all of the wraps to the right, the point will aim right; if you make all the wraps to the left, the chevron will point left.

Regardless of the direction to which the chevron points, you can also make additional bands of color, just as you would on a standard chevron. One way I like to do this is to reverse the colors, so that if there is a split chevron with red left and green right in an initial band, I can switch to green left and red right in a second band, then back to red left and green right in a third band, and so on. These bands can be of the same width each time or of varying widths each time, although each side is identical in the number of threads used.

A variation is to make the bands of different widths and colors on each side or to vary their positioning so that there is a more fragmented zigzag pattern to the chevron. One easy way to do this is to start with the red and green to make two bands up and down with each color, then to continue with two more bands of green on the one side, white on the other. Continue the white for two more on one side, with two of blue on the other, then two more of blue on one side, red on the other. The final look is of a chevron, but with the two stripes on each side not lining up exactly.

Another way to get a similar effect, even if the bands are lined up, is to work with bands of threads rather than individual threads. The individual threads will make a neater wrap, but bands will make for a different zigzag look.

If you wish to frame these chevrons, the best way to do it is to first lay down a framing thread (let's say black) and then lay down the chevron threads, finally framing with black threads again. If you place the entire frame after completing the wrap, it will have a diamond frame and lose some of the chevron look, although this is a matter of personal taste.

WEAVING LETTERS AND NUMBERS

Weaving letters and numbers can be tedious but is relatively easy once the principles are understood. The purpose for weaving numbers and letters is to provide a way by which various information can be added to the rod. In most cases, the owner's name is added to the blank. Other information, such as the rod-maker, rod

Simple chevron by Cantwell Clark, boxed in with white thread separates the wrap from the crossing threads required to make it.

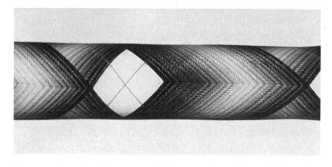

Sometimes simple wraps appear more complex than they really are. This three-dimensional looking "box" pattern is really a multiple chevron in which different colors are used in each direction (a light color in one direction, dark color in the opposite direction) to make it appear shaded. Wrap by Cantwell Clark.

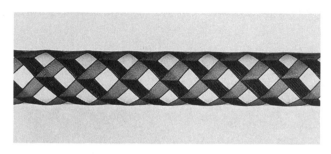

Long simple chevron with crossing threads in the open white space.

Complex wrap developed by Cantwell Clark.

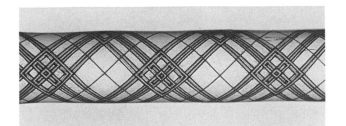

Another complex wrap by Cantwell Clark.

Example of letter weaving on a rod blank. Wrap by Cantwell Clark.

Cantwell Clark at his rod-building table.

length, rod weight, line and lure size, and date is written onto the blank of one of the several means outlined in Chapter 25.

To weave numbers, letters, and scenes, you will want not only the rod supports used for making various diamonds, chevrons, and other decorative wraps, but also the thread-tension device you use for making regular guide wraps. This is a must for making a rotary wrap of base thread as you work the horizontal threads back and forth along the rod to form the letter, number, or scene.

The technique of weaving letters and numbers involves a basic wrap like an underwrap, and longitudinal threads (parallel to the rod blank) that are wrapped over the base wrap to form the letters and numbers. Weaving is not like making diamonds, chevrons, or other decorative wraps in which threads are spiraled up and down the blank.

Thus, in weaving all the letters are made of threads that are laid down parallel to the blank, over the base wrap, which is formed by a tight wrap around the blank. The number of parallel

threads used determines the height of each letter, and the number of wraps around the blank behind the parallel threads determines the width of each letter. Although you can make any letters you want by stretching or compressing them in width, a general rule would be to make the letter width about eighty percent of the height.

The letters can be made any height, but are usually made in proportion to the type of rod and to the rod-blank diameter at the butt. Thus, for a freshwater spinning rod you might want a letter height of only 1/8-inch and for a big-game rod you might want larger letters of about 1/4 inch. Usually the height is determined first, because the width is proportional to the height, not the other way around.

Just how high the letters will be depends upon the size of thread used. Different rod-builders have different views on this. Ted Bingham, writing in an excellent series on the subject in *The Fisherman* magazine, for Atlantic Coast anglers, notes that he likes a height of fifteen threads and a width of twelve threads. Dale Clemens, in his book *Advanced Custom Rod Building,* suggests seven threads high and eight wide, although the eight-thread width is used primarily for wider letters, such as M, N, Q, T, V, W, X, Y, and Z.

The point is that you can vary the height and width of letters and numbers, but you must have a plan for what you want to do and how you will do it. If you will do a lot of weaving, make up your own outline of letters and numbers using graph paper. I use ten-by-ten graph paper (ten squares in each direction per inch) on which to draw out the letters. I use one horizontal line for each horizontal thread and one vertical line for each wrapping thread, keeping the scale of the width to about eighty percent of the height. Naturally, I draw only the horizontal threads that will make up the letters.

One way to determine a reasonable arrangement for threads is to figure letter size based on the width of the thread. This won't hold up completely, because thread will become slightly compressed when wrapped, but it will provide a starting point. Gudebrod, the major manufacturer and supplier of rod-building thread, provides the width of its threads in both decimal inches and millimeters. From this we can figure out the width of a band of a certain number of threads or the number of threads that will make up certain band widths. For inches, the chart would look like this:

N.C.P. Thread	Regular Thread	Diameter	10 threads	20 threads
A	A	0.0070	0.070	0.140
C	D	0.0104	0.104	0.208
D	E	0.0132	0.132	0.264

In millimeters, the same chart would be:

N.C.P. Thread	Regular Thread	Diameter	10 threads	20 threads
A	A	0.175	1.75	3.50
C	D	0.260	2.60	5.20
D	E	0.330	3.30	6.60

From such a chart, it is also possible to multiply the number of threads that will be required for a certain height in inches or millimeters. A chart showing also the approximate width of the letter based on the eighty percent formula (height/width) would be as follows:

Letter Height	Thread Size		
	A	C(N.C.P.)/D	D(N.C.P.)E
0.125-1/8 inch	18/14	12/10	9/7
0.250-1/4 inch	36/29	24/19	19/15
5 milli- meters	29/24	19/15	15/12
10 milli- meters	57/48	38/30	30/24

Naturally, in some of the above there will be just too many threads to handle. This would apply to most thread wraps where more than twenty horizontal threads would have to be handled. You could work with larger thread sizes—EE for example—but often this makes for a coarser-looking wrap and should be avoided if possible.

In principle, weaving letters and numbers is easy. In practice, there are a couple of tips that will help. Begin by deciding where you will make your lettering wrap. Often this is just above the foregrip and done in conjunction with or in place of a diamond or some other crossing wrap. Use masking tape to tape to the rod blank the number of horizontal threads to be used. Do this close to the foregrip or on the left side of the wrap, because we write and read from left to right. Then, about 2 inches to the right (or leaving enough space for the writing you have planned), tape down the threads again. In doing this, make sure they are all parallel. Also, because you will constantly lift and tape down these threads, using double-sided tape is better than using masking tape. Double-sided clear tape and masking-type drafting tape are available for this operation. To hold the threads to the left as you lift them up for making the thread letters, place another strip of double-sided tape to the left of the original tape and at the beginning of the wrap.

One trick I use to make this easier is to tape the left side in two steps. First, I just gather a short length of the correct number of threads and tape them down in a bunch. Then, immediately to the right of this, I straighten out the threads so that they are parallel and tape them a second time, making sure they are all touching in a straight, flat bundle. If you are worried about getting close enough to the foregrip, you can tape the bundle down on the foregrip, straighten out the threads, and make the second taping (with the threads parallel) on the blank just above the foregrip.

Once these threads are in place, run them between the teeth of a comb to keep them parallel for taping down straight and parallel on the right side.

Once this is done, begin wrapping with a base wrap around the rod, just as you would for an underwrap. Begin on the left, over the parallel threads, leaving the taped ends exposed. Make several turns, or wrap until you wish to begin the letters. At this point, let's assume you will make an L—certainly an easy letter to make using 15 horizontal threads. Where you wish the letter to begin, remove all the parallel threads from the right side (which is why the double-sided tape is better here) and place all 15 threads completely to the left. Continue the base wrap for three complete turns. Bring parallel threads 1 through 12 (counting from the top) back to the right and wrap over them with the base wrap. Make nine complete turns (which now gives you 12 complete turns of thread from the beginning of the letter L) and then bring the last three threads (13 through 15) back to the right. Wrap over these threads to complete the L. Now all of the parallel threads are wrapped over, and after making several more

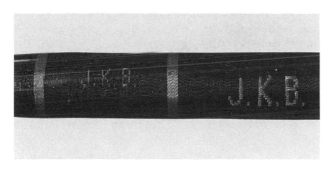

Sample letters by Cantwell Clark, woven into a rod. Note the two sizes used in this sample.

Example of extreme skill by Cantwell Clark in this script lettering for a rod-blank manufacturing company. Wrap is a sample, built on a wood dowel.

turns of the base wrap (usually about one-half of the letter's width, or six turns in this case) you begin the next letter.

Other letters would be made similarly. A C would be just like an L except that the top three threads in addition to the bottom three would be held to the left and brought over at the same time as the bottom threads. An O is the same as a C except that the right stroke of three threads is made to complete the letter. A U is the same as an O except that the top is left open. H, A, E, F, and P are similar. Other letters are pretty obvious and follow suit, once you understand the principle. That principle, of course, is that any thread flipped to the left will ultimately be exposed, any to the right will be hidden.

Note that in the L, with a 15/12 size configuration, we have arbitrarily chosen three threads as the width of the lettering. That lettering can be made narrower with only one or two thread widths, or wider with four or five threads for the width. (In our example, the lettering can't be wider than four or five threads, because in an H, for example, a width of five would only allow for a space of two threads between the two vertical strokes—each vertical stroke would be five, for a total of twelve threads in width.)

It is also possible to get into funny letters, such as letters with very thin vertical strokes (one thread) and very thick horizontal strokes (up to four threads), or very thick vertical strokes (up to five threads) and very thin horizontal strokes (one thread). This is not usually done.

It is always best to first outline on graph paper a complete alphabet or those letters you plan to use. This will quickly point out any problems you have in spacing or planning before you start to wrap—and possibly get into trouble. Also, for some letters you will have to plan on making a series of small connected blocks of thread for diagonal lines, as in K, M, N, Q, R, V, W, X, Y, and Z. Often these will have to be considered "extra width" letters, requiring a little more space to complete them properly and proportionally.

In some cases, you can partially round off letters, as when leaving out a corner for the right side of a D, B, P, or R, or you can round off all the corners of an O or Q, the top of an A, or the corners of a G. This is done by flipping over (to the right) the top and bottom threads in these spots so that they are wrapped down and thus are hidden.

Numbers are made the same way and are best blocked out first on graph paper to determine the best shape and appearance before the wrap is begun.

Some tips in making letters and numbers are as follows:

1. Proper alignment of the completed name or message is extremely important. One way to aid this process is to make alignment marks on the blank. Hold the rod blank in a horizontal position and place a piece of masking tape at each end of the letter area. Then, with a strong overhead light and without moving your head, use the streaks of light cast by the overhead light to mark the pieces of tape. Then rotate the rod to the bottom of the lettering area and mark the tape again. When you wish to check the alignment, use a rule to line up the top and bottom marks to serve as a guide.

2. Leave the end of the parallel threads out until you are finished. That way, you can pull on all of the threads together to tighten the lettering, or you can pull individual threads to help straighten and smooth the resulting letters. For this reason, do not make the base wrap too tight or it will be difficult to move any of the parallel threads. If you can move the parallel threads, you can sometimes shift them back and forth enough to remove any crossed threads that might have resulted while making a letter. Such crossing should be avoided, but if it does occur, pulling the thread back and forth may help to remove it.

3. Use contrasting-color threads for the base and lettering wrap. It is best if you do not use a very light thread color for either wrap. It you were to use white or a very light color for the base wrap and a very dark color for the parallel threads, you could end up with a wrap in which the dark strands of thread would show through the base wrap. For this reason, try to use similar shades of contrasting colors—red and blue, yellow and light brown, gray and pink, orange and light blue, green and red, and green and blue.

4. If you wish to get fancy, you can use different colors for the parallel threads. Thus, you could have green letters with a red central thread or threads, red letters with a black top and bottom border to each letter, letters that are dark blue on top and light blue on the bottom, a similar-color Trimar (Mylar metallic shimmering) thread in the middle of each letter, and so on. Remember, however, that you will have to consider the colors in order to avoid any show-through once the wrap is finished.

WEAVING SCENES

Scenes and figures can be woven just as letters and numbers are woven—although making scenes is more of an advanced method. Master lettering first to understand completely what is involved in weaving.

Some possible figures involve stylized fish, a fisherman with an arched rod and a fish on the end of the line, dock scenes, and boats (particularly offshore rods on offshore boats). Some custom-rod-builders are so adept at this that they can make very lifelike fish of different species on a blank using the same basic threads.

Any number of threads can be used. In most cases, the colors used, the number of threads of each color, and the arrangement of each color will depend upon the scene desired. Most fish, for example, have dark-colored backs blending into light bellies. Thus, the top of a wrap depicting a fish would use dark colors, and these colors would gradually change into lighter colors near the bottom of the weave. The thread colors chosen will depend upon the fish and personal preference. For making a bonefish, you might start at the top with a light gray, then shift to a blue-silver Trimar and end up with a white-silver Trimar thread. Thus, the appearannce will be of a bone-

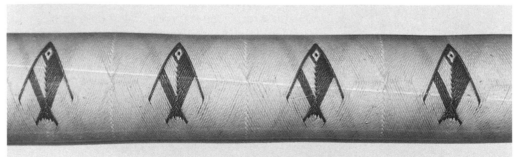

Stylized fish wrap by Cantwell Clark.

fish with a gray back, blue-silver sides, and a white-silver belly. A blue marlin might have a medium or dark blue top with a light blue belly. A channel bass or redfish might have a medium brown back and gold or tan belly. A shark might be a uniform medium gray or gunmetal gray.

Other scenes, such as that of a river and sky with a boat and fisherman, would more typically use light blue threads at the top to simulate the sky, and other colors in the middle and bottom to simulate other subjects in the scene.

Unlike the various formulas and charts some-

times seen for weaving letters and numbers, there are few if any charts for scenes or figures. As with developing patterns for letters and numbers, the best method for working out a pattern for scene is to draw it out on graph paper, using one vertical graph line for each vertical base thread and one horizontal graph line for each horizontal thread used in the scene. Often, it is best to first sketch out the scene with a pencil and then to come back with crayons, colored pencils, or colored felt-tip markers to draw in threads of each color.

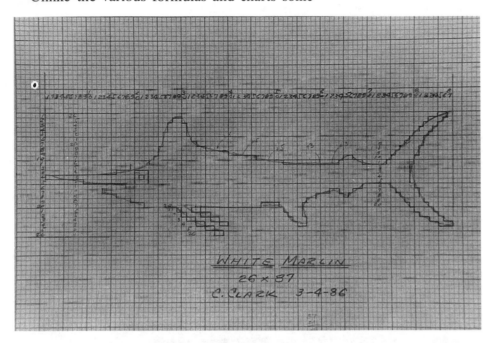

Design layout for weaving a white marlin into a butt wrap. Each thread and step is laid out on graph paper. Design by Cantwell Clark.

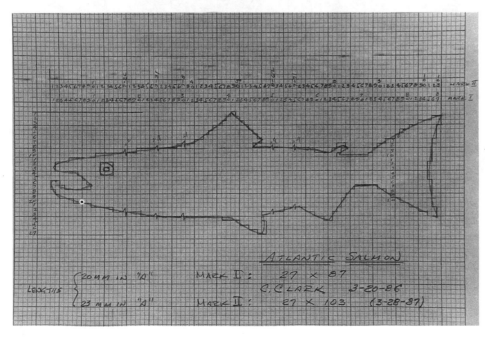

Another Cantwell Clark design, this for an Atlantic salmon.

Weaving notes, this for a Cantwell Clark design for a sperm whale. Notes are a must for designs to be repeated.

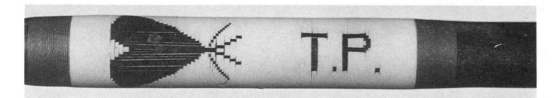

Example of stonefly and letters by Cantwell Clark.

Woven fishing scene of two fishermen in a boat. Design by Cantwell Clark.

Sample fish designs by Cantwell Clark.

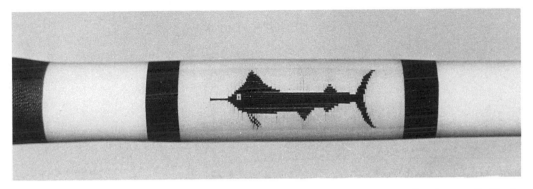

Marlin design by Cantwell Clark.

DECORATIVE WRAPS ON GUIDES

Some anglers like the look of custom decorative wraps on guides. These are basic wraps to hold down the guides and are used as underwraps for subsequent wrapping techniques. A standard diamond, chevron, or double diamond would be placed over this underwrap. This is a very tedious wrap to create, however, because it is relatively short (the length of the guide wrap), and each one must be finished off with a band wrap at each end of the guide. This is not normally done with separate wraps on each guide foot but with a long underwrap that is completed by running the decorative wrap from one end of the guide wrap to the other. Because these are tedious and time-consuming, they are usually done on large rods, such as fancy offshore big-game rods and IGFA-style trolling rods.

They are tedious also because the threads used for making the diamond or chevron must be laced through the frame and around the guide feet. This requires careful planning, because the guide size and type used must allow for the size, style, and positioning of the pattern. Too large a pattern, for example, might run into the frame or not allow proper positioning at the sides of the rod or under the center of the guide. Although I have seen such wraps where the diamonds or chevrons matched those on the butt of the rod above the foregrip, most of these have been on offshore and similar large rods.

25

Finishing Touches and Finishing Rods

INTRODUCTION ▪ TOOLS AND MATERIALS ▪ FINISHING TOUCHES ▪ COLOR PRESERVER: PROS AND CONS ▪ APPLYING COLOR PRESERVER ▪ MIXING ROD FINISHES ▪ APPLYING ROD FINISHES ▪ FINISHING PROBLEMS AND SOLUTIONS

Basic Safety Equipment
Safety goggles
Cotton or rubber gloves
Respirator mask

Basic Tools
Mixing cups
Flat stirrers, such as Popsicle sticks, craft sticks, or wood skewers
Brushes
Smooth, flat surface onto which to pour epoxy
Good light (for viewing rod finish on rod)

Helpful Tools
Rod supports   Hair dryer or clean torch
Rod-curing motor   Fine nibs and pen holders

INTRODUCTION

The guide wraps and decorative wraps of the most elaborate and well-built rod in the world won't last long if the rod is not protected with a long-lasting finish. That finish usually involves a color preserver (to preserve the thread colors) and an epoxy (to protect the wraps with a clear coating).

In addition, sometimes additional finishing touches are made to dress up a rod and impart a custom look. Executing these final steps well by working carefully and following all manufacturers' directions can make the difference between a fair-looking rod and a beautiful one.

TOOLS AND MATERIALS

Tools and materials for rod finishing are specialized yet simple. Tools can include mixing cups to combine the two-part epoxy finishes. Throwaway or good-quality brushes are used for applying the color preserver and the epoxy finish. Flat craft sticks or wood kitchen skewers can be thrown away after mixing the epoxy. A curing motor is not completely necessary but will help in getting a good, smooth, drip-free finish on any rod. A drying box is a simple or fancy long box in which a rod can be placed to cure completely. These boxes have curing motors built in or a hole at one end to allow the butt end of the rod to extend into the box. They allow complete curing in a relatively dust-free environment. A hair dryer or torch may be used to heat the epoxy in order to remove bubbles after the finish is applied to the rod.

The materials used for finishing involve several different brands of color preserver and epoxy finish. Popular brands include Flex Coat, Gudebrod, U-40, and Classic Rod Coat (from B.D. Classic Enterprises). Often these vary as to type. Some companies, such as Flex Coat, offer both high-build epoxy rod finishes for larger and heavier rods and a lighter, thinner finish for light rods, such as light and ultralight spinning and all fly rods. Gudebrod manufactures several different finishes, including a two-part epoxy rod finish with a high build-up (Hard 'N Fast II), a one-part high-speed rod finish (Speed Coat Rod Finish), and a traditional rod varnish. All of these, along with finishes from manufacturers such as U-40 and B.D. Classic Enterprises, have matching color preservers available. In most cases you will need both a color preserver and a finish coat. Other finishes, such as varnish, are available, although varnish is most often used for finishing traditional bamboo rods.

If you are adding an inscription of any type to your rod, you will want some ink you can use to write on the blank. A good ink is often one that will contrast with the color or finish of the blank. White ink is a good contrast to a dark brown or black glass or graphite blank; black ink contrasts well with white, honey-color, yellow, or other light-colored blanks. Good possibilities include india ink for the dark ink and diluted typewriter correction fluid or water-based latex paint in light colors for the light-colored "ink."

In addition to tools and materials, you will need a good, flat, clean work area, particularly one that

Example of slow-turning curing motor to prevent sagging of epoxy rod finishes. Courtesy of Flex Coat Company.

Homemade curing motor, using a rotisserie motor and chuck to hold a butt cap that holds the rod. Different size butt caps (all screwed on a bolt) can be interchanged for different rods.

is dust-free. In most homes, the best time to apply a finish is in the evening, when human activity in the home has lessened, and in a room or part of a basement that is clean and out of the way of human traffic.

A good strong light is also a must, because a light helps you to detect any gaps in the finish and aids you in adding an inscription to the finished rod.

FINISHING TOUCHES

In addition to decorative wraps and weaving, there are other finishing touches that can be added to a rod before the protective wrap finish is applied.

One of these finishing touches is the addition of information on the rod. Typically, it includes the length and weight of the rod, line range, lure-weight range, the date the rod was completed, and so on. In some cases, some of this information is on the blank already and can be left in place if it has not been covered by a decorative wrap. In other cases, you might want to add to it, including your name and address, or if you're making the rod for a friend, a notation as to the maker and recipient. An example of a typical inscription would be: "Custom-built for John Doe by Tom Smith, March 3, 1992."

This information can be inscribed on one line, but more typically is inscribed on several lines around the circumference of the rod, with each line printed on the rod's longitudinal plane. Thus, a typical arrangement would be:
Custom-built for
John Doe
by Tom Smith,
March 3, 1992.

Usually these lines would be sized to be placed about ninety degrees apart around the rod, with the recipient's name on the top of the rod where he or she will see it. If the blank is of a thin diameter, then these four lines might be too much to include. If this is the case, another possibility would be:
Custom-built for John Doe
by Tom Smith, March 3, 1992.

All of these lines provide the same information and vary only in the arrangement for the given rod and the information to be included. Of course it is also possible to inscribe simply "Custom-built for John Doe" on one line.

There is a variety of ways to add such information to a rod. Perhaps the best and easiest is to write on the rod. Naturally, such information must be printed on the bare blank and must be covered with a clear rod finish to protect it.

One problem that can occur is that the clear finish added to the rod can smear the writing. Often this occurs with water-based ink combined with a water-based finish, or a solvent-based ink and solvent-based finish. The similarity of solvents —whether water- or chemical-based—seems to cause the problem, with the solvent in the finish

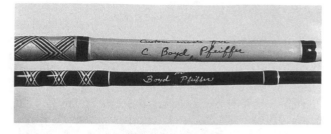

Examples of writing on rod blank. Both white and black inks can be used, depending upon the color of the blank.

Example of using dry transfer letters for labeling a rod blank. Sample by Cantwell Clark.

loosening and smearing the writing. One simple solution to this is to use a water-based ink for writing and a solvent-based finish, and vice versa. Most finishes are chemical-solvent-based. This includes Gudebrod Hard 'N Fast II, Flex Coat, Flex Coat Lite, Classic Rod Coat, U-40 Perma Gloss, and U-40 Dura Gloss. Some are water-based finishes, such as Gudebrod Speed Coat.

Writing can be done with any type of pen, but usually a small fine-point pen is best, because the writing must be delicate. You may find, however, that certain pens or pen points work with certain inks or fluids, so it does pay to experiment.

Although any ink can be used, a water-based black or dark ink is best for light-colored blanks. For dark blanks, light-colored writing is a must. I like slightly diluted (about one part water to two or three parts of fluid) water-based typewriter correction fluids. These are available in a water base or a solvent base (the trend is to water-based correction fluids—be sure to get the water-based kind if you will be using a chemical-solvent-based finish coat) and are available in a wide variety of colors. Companies making such fluids include Wite Out, Liquid Paper, Pentel, Universal, and Benchmark. In addition to white, colors include blue, canary, yellow, goldenrod, regular green, ledger green, ivory, gray, pink, and buff. Another advantage to using the water-based fluids is that mistakes can be easily wiped up with a wet paper towel and inscriptions can be redone until they are perfect.

If there is a key to all of this, however, it is to experiment. You must experiment with the best dilution formula for writing. Add a small amount of water at first, because it is easier to add more water and increase the dilution than it is to add more fluid to a too-watery solution. By the same token, it helps to experiment with pens. I like the inexpensive pens with detachable nibs best, and those with a slightly rounded end seem to write best on blanks—but perform your own experiments to find the best writing combination. Pens are available individually (this is the best way to get them) or in sets that include a variety of nib styles and are designed primarily for calligraphy.

It is also necessary to experiment to make sure that the finish will not smear the writing. Practice on a scrap piece of blank, although any similar surface will do. Write on the scrap piece, allow the solution to dry completely, and then carefully add a coating of rod finish.

Once the solutions are tested, some tips will make any inscriptions easier:

1. Place masking tape around the area of the blank to be inscribed, and lightly roughen this blank area with fine steel wool. Do this only enough to take the sheen and gloss off the blank—not enough to cut into the blank or damage the underlying fibers. This will make it easier for you to write on the blank, because the pen will not slip, or will tend to slip less. Use a tack cloth or similar means to completely wipe the blank free of all steel-wool dust. Also, it helps to wipe the blank in this area with acetone or alcohol to completely clean it.

2. It is always easier to write on the same level on which the hand rests. Thus, use a small support—a stack of cardboard, a block of wood, an old book—that is approximately the same thickness as the blank. If the blank is 1/2-inch thick, use a support for the heel of your hand that is 1/2-inch thick. This will prevent many mistakes and slips that might otherwise occur.

3. Plan each line of the inscription, as well as the size of the writing. This is especially important for thin blanks, such as those of light fly rods and ultralight spinning rods.

4. If you have trouble lining up your writing or writing on a straight line, use a strip of masking tape along the axis and write above its edge. Keep the writing about 1/32-inch above the masking tape—do not let the ink touch the masking tape

or it will bleed. An easy alternative if the blank is relatively thin is to split or cut in a straight line a two-inch length of plastic straw, then slip the straw around the blank and line up one of the straight edges to serve as a bottom guide for writing. As with the masking tape, the writing does not touch the straw, the straw serving only as a guide to maintain relatively straight lines. Two straws can be used—one to serve as a guide for the bottom, the other to serve as a guide for the top edge of the writing.

Another alternative is to use the glare from an overhead light to form a streak on the rod and thus a line (this only works if you do not move your head), or to inscribe a faint line with a pointed awl. The scratch formed will be filled in with the finish coat.

5. Another alternative is to use a commercially available lettering guide. Both the C-Thru and Alvin companies make them of clear plastic and both have slots that provide guides for various sizes of lettering. Both metric and fractional sizes are available, and the fractional Alvin model TD-1119 includes slots for 1/8-, 5/32-, 3/16-, and 1/4-inch.

6. Once you write on the blank using a previously tested formula of ink or correction fluid, allow the inscription to dry completely.

7. Often, inscription areas are bracketed with thin thread wraps or are placed at the upper end of a decorative wrap (the other side is bracketed with a simple wrap). Such wraps can be added before or after the inscription. Often they are best added before, after proper planning of the size and space needed for the given inscription.

8. Once the inscription is completely dry, and when you are coating the rest of the rod wraps with rod finish, coat this area of the blank with rod finish also. To prevent any possibility of smearing, do this early, with the application of the rod finish, to make sure the finish is completely liquid and not beginning to get stiff. Use a clean brush and the lightest possible touch of the finish to the blank to prevent too much contact with the inscription.

A good way to do this is to pick up a large blob of finish on the brush and add it immediately over the inscription, then lightly use the brush on top of the finish (not enough to drag the bristles of the brush over the inscription) to spread the finish over the area and any bracketing thread wraps.

9. As with rod finish on thread wraps, use a strong overhead light to create a glare on the shiny finish and help detect any missed spots. Use

care and a light touch in filling in any such spots.

The same basic techniques are applied when using calligraphy or india-type inks, such as those from Higgins (Faber-Castell) or Stradtler. Colors generally available include red or black, and all of these so far seem to be chemical-solvent-based. Use a small-nib pen for the writing.

In addition to writing inscriptions, there are other ways in which information can be added. One is to use gold or silver foil that is usually sold with a small round-point burnisher (not a pen) with which the foil can be laid on a surface, taped or held in place, and, by means of the burnisher, transferred by pressure to the writing surface, in this case a rod blank.

Dry-transfer letters and numbers are also available from stationery stores in sizes from about 1/8-inch and larger. These come on sheets that include both capital and small letters and numbers, and some punctuation marks. These are transferred to the rod blank by holding the sheet containing the letters on the blank and using a burnisher (such as one made by Gudebrod or in the same style from a stationery store) to transfer the letters to the rod blank. The rod must be clean and dry for this. Use care, because the rod is round and the letter must be transferred completely to the blank. Once the letters are burnished completely, a finish coat of epoxy will hold them in place and protect them.

One way to add transfer letters easily is to first lay down a strip of masking tape in a straight line to serve as a guide for the bottom of the letters.

Another possibility is to use the gold or silver foil that is transferred by means of a heated pen used for bookbinding or woodworking.

As when writing with ink, it helps to use some of the previously mentioned tips, including sanding the rod blank and working from a surface at the same level as the surface of the rod blank.

Other ways in which information can be added include the use of stick-on or self-adhesive labels. The information is written on the label, which is then applied to the rod blank. This label is then coated with a rod finish.

The one advantage to a label is that all the information can be written on a flat surface, thus making it easier to get straight lines of script. It is also possible to use small ink stamps with a name or name and address and a label for a printed effect. If you do this, make sure the ink pad is new and the stamp is thoroughly covered with ink for a good, dark impression. If you have an ink pad with your name and address and you wish to use

only your name, it is easy to mask the address lines with a sheet of paper or index card.

Another possibility, particularly if you have trouble writing on the curved surface of a rod blank, is to write on a piece of clear tape (cellophane tape or similar tapes) with the tape stretched out onto a smooth surface, such as a laminated countertop. Make sure you do not touch the adhesive side of the tape. Once the information is written on the tape and the writing has dried, lift the tape, trim any ends, and apply it to the blank. Finish with a regular rod-finish coat.

One potential problem with these systems is that not only that the ink from the stamp pad or the pen might smear, but the label, once applied, must not lift up or curl around the edges. Experiment with a scrap blank to check the results of these methods.

COLOR PRESERVER: PROS AND CONS

Color preserver has both fans and critics. On the plus side, color preserver is designed to do exactly what it says—preserve and maintain the color of the thread wrap. One or two coats of color preserver on a rod wrap will do this, even though the wrap will turn darker when it's wet. When the color preserver dries, the wraps will return to the original color.

Another plus is that the use of color preserver will help in removal of the thread wrap, should this be necessary. The color preserver prevents penetration of the epoxy into and through the wrap to bind the thread to the rod, and thus makes removal easier. Color preserver does help in cementing the thread wrap to the blank, although not as securely as does epoxy finish. In this respect, color preserver helps in fancy thread work, because it will bind the wrap to the rod and thus prevent mishaps in which threads are moved or jostled out of position.

Color preserver also soaks into the thread and thus dispels air bubbles from the wrap, making it easier to get a perfect finish without a haze of bubbles in the finish coat. By soaking into and coating the thread, color preserver provides a smooth base on which to add rod finish, unlike the spongelike base of untreated thread wraps.

Detractors of color preserver correctly say that color preserver will prevent the penetration of the rod finish (usually epoxy) into the thread, and that this penetration of the epoxy rod finish into the thread to bind the wrap to the rod blank and protect and coat the surface is what is important.

In essence, without color preserver the rod finish glues the wrap to the blank, as well as coating and protecting it. Critics of color preserver feel—probably rightly from a technical standpoint—that the lack of color preserver makes for a stronger, more durable wrap and finish. Countering this is the fact that even the finest threads are plenty strong (2.8 pounds break strength in size A Gudebrod) when formed into a tight wrap.

Naturally, there is a reason for the use of color preserver, because a lack of it will result in permanent thread-color changes when varnish or epoxy finish is applied. In most cases, dark-color threads (blue, red, green, purple, brown) will become darker than the original color, while lighter-color threads (white, yellow, goldenrod, pink, orange, light blue) will become lighter in color. And all thread will become translucent, allowing a partial show-through of the guide foot. In some cases this is not bad, and some rod-builders deliberately omit color preserver to get this effect. For example, among traditionalist fly-rod builders some years ago, and even with some companies and custom-builders today, this technique is used and the bright feet of the snake guides and matching stripper guides are allowed to show through the wraps. It does look funny though, on black frame guides in which the end of the guide foot has been polished or filed to a knife edge for a smooth transition of the thread from the blank onto the guide foot. One solution to this is to use only bright finish guides, or to color the filed end of the guide foot with a permanent felt-tip marker. Allow this coating to dry completely before wrapping the guide in place.

APPLYING COLOR PRESERVER

Color preserver comes in two styles: water-based and chemical-solvent-based. At one time, most color preservers were solvent-based, but the water-based styles are becoming more popular and prevalent. If there is one key to using color preservers, which must be covered with a rod finish, it is to stick to the same brand for both products or to be *sure* that the two products are compatible. For example, Flex Coat cautions against using a lacquer color preserver under its Flex Coat Rod Finish; U-40 Color Lock can be used under its urethane one-part Perma Gloss rod finish and Dura Gloss epoxy resin finish; Gudebrod Color Preserver can be used under its Hard 'N Fast II or Speed Coat Rod Finish; and its Speed Coat Color Preserver and Sealer can be

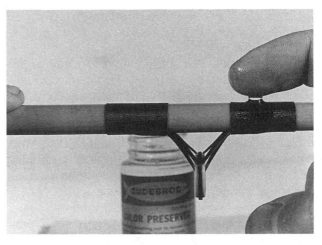

Using color preserver. Solvent color preserver can be added with a fingertip as shown here. Avoid too much solvent contact.

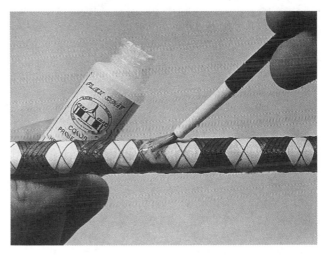

Using a brush to brush on water-base color preserver. Such white color preserver will dry clear, but must be blotted after allowing it to soak into the wrap.

used under Speed Coat Rod Finish or Rod Varnish. The lesson in all of this is to follow the manufacturer's directions for application and compatibility of products. Naturally, no manufacturer is going to recommend the use of another brand's product with his, but such combinations often work. If you wish to try, conduct compatibility experiments.

There are different ways to apply color preserver. Often the best, neatest, and cleanest is to use a brush, mix the color preserver well if required (it sometimes is with the water-based preservers), and then liberally coat the rod wrap with the color preserver. To keep the color preserver from building up and causing blushing or mottling of the wrap when the finishing coat is applied, blot off any excess with a paper towel. Blot—don't rub. Rubbing may move some of the threads (particularly with decorative wraps), and some of the towel might come off onto the wrap and into the color preserver.

For how much to apply, follow manufacturer's directions. Some suggest one coat, others two coats, and some even suggest three coats for heavy threads. Some suggest using one coat as a protective measure even when using N.C.P. thread, and two coats for regular thread.

Other debates concern the use of color preserver: how much and when, and when to apply on underwraps and double and triple wraps. One method is to complete the entire wrap and then add several coats of color preserver, allowing each to sink in before adding the next. Often it is best to wait at least an hour for the water-based color preservers and overnight for the solvent-based types. One key, especially for the solvent types, is to smell the color preserver. When there is no smell, it means the color preserver has cured or all of the solvent has evaporated.

When creating several layers of wrapping, make the underwrap and then apply one or two coats of color preserver, allowing it to cure completely before adding the guide and wrapping it in place. Then the guide wrap (single, double, or triple wrap) can be protected with color preserver and later coated with rod finish. This same technique can be used with decorative wraps: First coat the underwrap and allow it to cure, then add the decorative wrap, coat it with color preserver again, and finally add the finish coat.

An alternative is to leave the color preserver off the guide wrap (after adding it to the underwrap) and coat only with rod finish. This allows for color protection of the underwrap and easy removal of the wrap, should it be necessary, while also providing for the durability and extra strength of the bond on the overwrap and slight translucency in the colors.

Once the final coat of color preserver has been added, wait overnight (24 hours) to be sure of complete curing before adding the final rod finish. If you use water-based color preservers, the time to clean up the brushes is immediately after finishing wrap coatings. Wash them thoroughly to remove all color preserver and then rinse and allow the brush to dry. I even do this with so-called disposable brushes with no problems.

MIXING ROD FINISHES

Some rod finishes do not require mixing. Rod varnish and some one-part finishes are ready to use from the bottle. Examples are U-40 Perma Gloss, Gudebrod Rod Varnish, and Gudebrod Speed Coat Rod Finish. Usually these are not epoxy, and the U-40 Perma Gloss is described as being a nonyellowing, flexible, noncracking, thin-coat aliphatic urethane polymer.

Other finishes are in two parts that must be mixed. These include Gudebrod Hard 'N Fast II, Flex Coat Polymer Rod Finish, Flex Coat Lite Rod Finish, U-40 Dura Gloss, and B.D. Classic Enterprises Classic Rod Coat. Fortunately, most of these two-part mixes have cap coding systems to help you avoid placing the wrong cap on the wrong bottle, a situation that could cause contamination and hardening of the bottle contents.

All of the two-part mixes I know of for custom-rod builders are a 1:1 mix, because this makes for easy mixing. There are two ways of mixing these finishes. One is to use small mixing cups, the other is to use syringes. The syringes are best for very small amounts of finish, while the mixing cups that hold an ounce or more are best for larger quantities of finish.

It should be noted here that some rod-builders have advised against using plastic in any mixing process for epoxies. This would include mixing cups, syringes, flat working surfaces, and nylon- or plastic-bristle brushes. Although it is a good practice not to use odd or offbeat plastic products in the mixing process, I have never had a problem using plastic, provided that I apply common sense. I use medical mixing cups, medical syringes, nylon-bristle brushes, disposable brushes, sometimes plastic brush handles for mixing sticks, and plastic coffee lids and plastic mixing surfaces cut from drink and milk containers. In fact, many finish manufacturers use plastic and sell plastic products for use with their epoxy or other rod-finish resins. Gudebrod offers nylon-bristle brushes; Flex Coat has plastic brushes, mixing cups, and syringes; U-40 has plastic mixing syringes; B.D. Classic Enterprises has plastic brushes, syringes, and mixing cups.

One key to using any solution is to keep it warm. One easy way to do this is to place the bottles into a pan of hot water for about 15 minutes, checking the temperature from time to time. Other possibilities include use of a hair dryer, or placing the solution in the sun on a warm summer

Two-part epoxy finishes require a mixing cup, as shown, for accurate measuring and mixing.

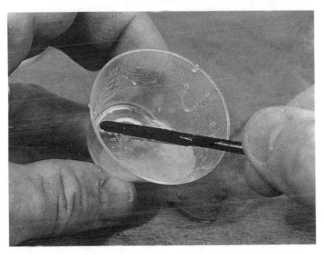

Thorough mixing of all epoxy is necessary to assure a good finish. Avoid whipping the finish, since this will add bubbles that must be removed later.

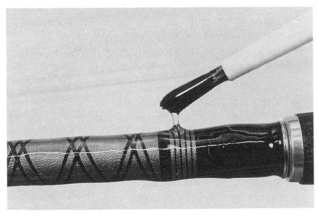

Adding two-part epoxy to a decorative wrap. When wet, the finish will be very shiny and a bright light will help to show any gaps, bubbles or missed spots.

day. Just a hand check for temperature will do— you don't need a thermometer. Warmer temperatures make the solutions more fluid and thus aid in pouring and mixing. Other advantages are that the hotter fluids will help to dissipate any bubbles that form, and heated finish will soak better into wraps to protect them. Flex Coat recommends at least 75° Fahrenheit for its rod finishes, with an ideal of about 80° to 90°.

The best way to add epoxy to a mixing cup is to hold the cup level with your eye against a light background that allows you to clearly see the measurement markings. Then add one of the two solutions to the mixing cup until it reaches the mark indicating one-half of the total amount needed. Make sure you add the liquid to the center of the mixing cup and that none splashes on the sides of the cup above the marks, because this will make the mix inaccurate. Also, make sure you pour slowly, because thick viscous liquids often require a little time to self-level for accurate measurement. Once the first solution is added, close the bottle, open the second bottle, and add that liquid until the full measure is reached. Close this bottle and mix the solution.

There are varying theories as to mixing. Roger Seiders of Flex Coat likes a rounded stick for mixing, arguing that the round stick is less likely to create bubbles, which must be removed at some time in the future. I like flat sticks, such as some craft sticks, that allow folding of the mix onto itself and a thorough scraping of the sides and bottom of the mixing cup to assure that all of the solution is completely mixed. Small, flat craft sticks and kitchen skewers are ideal. Some of the stiff little plastic coffee stirrers are ideal because they are flattened but with rounded edges. They are available everywhere and are disposable.

Obviously, a disposable mixing stick is best, as are disposable mixing cups. However, avoid the use of paper cups, waxed cups (the wax can come off and contaminate the mix), and aluminum (some recommend it, and it is disposable, but I find it difficult to mix in without tearing or puncturing). Also, the epoxies will sometimes dissolve some food service disposable cups.

Mixing with syringes is easy, because two identical syringes are used to pull up identical amounts of the respective resin and hardener or catalyst. But be careful. According to Roger Seiders of Flex Coat, silicone and epoxy will not mix, and medical syringes available at drug stores often have a silicone coating. These cannot be used with epoxy, or not, at least, with Flex Coat.

Flex Coat syringes do not contain silicone.

Once the syringes are filled with the right amounts of solution, slowly discharge the contents into a mixing cup. An alternative is to spread the liquid on a flat mixing surface, but this often makes mixing more difficult.

Once the syringes are empty, don't try to clean them. Keep them separate and marked (if they are not already marked with some code) for use the next time. Do not allow the tips to touch, because then the two solutions will mix slightly and "glue" the syringes together or contaminate them.

To mix the solution, use the mixing sticks of your choice to fold and stir. Do not try to beat the solutions into a lather, which will only create bubbles in the mix that may be difficult to remove later.

At first, the solution formed with most brands will become cloudy, and often you can see the combining of the two parts as they begin to mix. Ultimately, the solutions will turn clear and will be completely mixed. In all parts of the mixing, make sure you fold the mix over and over, side to side and top to bottom, and that you scrape the sides completely as you fold. This assures a good mix.

You will need a flat surface on which to pour the rod finish once it is mixed. Ideal surfaces include scraps of paper, glossy cardboard stock (like poster cardboard — not skirt cardboard that might fray and contaminate the mix), aluminum foil (though I don't like it, because it has a tendency to tear), or plastic sheets. I like plastic surfaces the best, because they can be bent in order to pop off the dried mix and used repeatedly. One good source are well-cleaned plastic surfaces from juice, milk, drink, and food containers. I use milk containers, cutting out the sides and bottoms and stacking several for use when needed. The thin sides are ideal for rod finish, the thicker and tougher bottoms for rod glues.

As soon as the finish is completely mixed, pour and scrape the complete solution onto the flat surface. This accomplishes several things. First, it prevents the mix from curing too rapidly. As you end the mixing process and hold the cup, you may feel some buildup of heat. This is a result of the solution being in a confined space and indicates the catalyst is reacting with the resin and beginning to cure the mix. Pouring the solution out on a flat surface will slow this reaction and allow you a reasonable working time. Also, pouring the solution out onto a flat surface makes for a much shorter distance any bubbles will have to travel to get out of the mix. And you must remove the bubbles to prevent them getting into the finish on the rod.

Another way to further slow the curing process (and extend the solution's working life, if necessary) you can place the flat surface on a tray of ice cubes to cool it. This extends the solution's working life longer than the typical 30 minutes of most standard mixes.

An added advantage to pouring the mix on a flat surface is that it will then be easy to accomplish one of the methods of removing bubbles. This method is to exhale onto the mix. Manufacturers don't seem to know why this works, but it does, and as you do this you can see bubbles rapidly popping to the surface. Theories on this are that the dispelled bubbles are caused either by the carbon dioxide in your breath, the moisture in your breath, or the warmth of your breath.

Another way to remove air bubbles is to use a hair dryer. Even though it's often recommended, I don't like it because a hair dryer blows air, and air contains dust. I don't want to blow dust into my finish before it goes on a rod. (Or after it is on the rod but not yet cured, for that matter.) Another method is to use a flame, because the heat of an alcohol lamp or propane or butane torch will cause bubbles to escape. This works great, but I don't like the idea of an open flame around epoxies. Use extreme care if you try this, and move the flame constantly to avoid any heat buildup or danger. I find that breathing on the mix and stabbing the occasional large stubborn bubble with a bodkin seems to work fine.

APPLYING ROD FINISHES

Once the solution is bubble-free after having been completely mixed, it is ready for applying to the rod wraps. For this, you will need a good-quality brush or a disposable brush. Neither kind must shed bristles when being used, because any bristles must be picked out of the mix, for they might dry in the mix if not detected in time. A number of companies, such as Gudebrod, B. D. Classic Enterprises, and Flex Coat have good brushes (ox hair and disposable from Gudebrod, disposable from Flex Coat, sable from B.D. Classic Enterprises), and brushes are available from craft stores and hobby shops.

Before beginning, make sure the rod is on a rack that is ready to be attached or plugged into a slow-rpm curing motor. Some companies, such as K & K Rod Turner Company, make motors just for this, or you can use any low-rpm motor provided you can jerry-rig it to hold the rod. Good ways to do this include using different sizes of butt caps or crutch tips to hold the rod butt, or using a 2-inch-diameter PVC cap with thumb screws tapped (a 1/4-20 tap and thumb screw works well) into the edges and set equally around the perimeter to grip the rod butt. Both connectors have to be attached to the motor shaft, and the best system uses a small coupling or threaded rod coupler as required. Often some imagination is required for this, though. Good motors are AC, although if you don't mind the expense of batteries, DC hobby motors are available also. In any case, make sure the motor is sufficiently powerful to turn the largest rod you wish to make. A good speed for such motors is about 10 rpm, although anything from 1 to about 60 rpm will work.

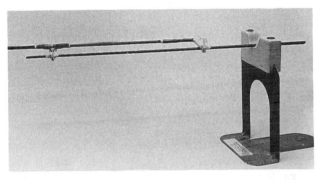

When an entire rod finished or refinished, sometimes the tip section can not ride on a support. For this, an additional dowel or blank, stuck through and taped to the guides, will allow turning the rod without making contact with the rod.

An alternative to the above is to use several swivels (preferably ball-bearing) and a snap to attach the rod tip-top to a vertical stand for complete turning without rod contact.

Begin by dipping the brush into the epoxy. Take care to avoid creating more bubbles with the bristles. Load the brush well. Then add the epoxy to the rod wraps while rotating the rod. Begin with a band of epoxy around the outside edge of each wrap. This band of epoxy should cover the wrap and just barely overlap the edge so as to touch the blank and thus seal the wrap from the elements. Ideally, the finish will completely coat the wrap so that there can be no intrusion of water or moisture. Pay particular attention to the area around the open gaps formed by the thread going over the guide feet. Try to fill these gaps with epoxy, and make sure this area has a complete seal of finish for complete protection. One way to do this is to push the brush bristles into the small tunnel formed by the thread wrap bridging from the guide foot to the rod blank.

Once this is done, continue to add finish to the wraps as needed until you fill in the entire area between the two "bands" of finish first applied. This allows you to completely fill in each wrap as you rotate the rod after you've made sure the bands around the end seal the rod wrap. Be certain to add equal amounts of finish to each wrap, based on the surface area of the wrap. Thus, you want an even thickness of finish, so that more finish will be added to a wrap on the butt guide that has more surface area than to the wrap at the tip end of the rod.

Also, make sure that the finish is evenly spread around the blank and from one end of the wrap to the other. Failure to do this can sometimes produce a wrap finish that looks slightly pregnant. Thus, after brushing around the blank, brush along the axis of the rod to even out finish buildup in any one area.

Because the finish will begin getting slightly stiffer as you add it to the blank (though in most cases this will be almost unnoticeable), I find it best to begin adding finish to the tip end of the rod and then work down to the butt guides and finally to the decorative wraps just above the handle. That way, if any stiffness does begin to occur, it will be on the heavier butt end where it is easier to spread rapidly with broad strokes, not on the tip end. And naturally, cover all wraps—not just guide wraps but also the wraps at the tip-top, ferrules, or hookkeeper, and decorative wraps and wraps bracketing inscriptions.

For best results, rotate the rod as you work (this will be necessary anyway to get the finish on all parts of each wrap) to keep the finish from sagging and beginning to drip. Once you are through, you can place the rod on the curing motor if the rpm's are slow, or closely examine each wrap under the glare of a strong light. The strong light makes it possible for you to detect any gaps in the finish. When you spot these areas, add finish and brush it out to blend with the existing finish. Check with the light several times on each wrap to assure that there are no gaps.

Then place the rod on the curing motor and allow it to cure for several hours. In most cases, it will cure enough to allow you to stop the motor in about three or four hours, but be sure to check the manufacturer's directions for details. If you don't have a completely dust-free environment in which to cure the rod, build or use a drying box. This can be nothing more than a long cardboard box or a couple of boxes with the ends mostly cut out, which completely cover the curing part of the rod. You do not have to cover the curing motor or the rod-handle section.

Other suggestions are to finish rods late at night when house traffic is lowest and when pets and children are not around. Make sure you have enough humidity (you can spray the area with a water mister before curing any rods).

If you do not have a curing motor, sometimes you can jerry-rig something from AC barbecue motors that come with grills. Most of these motors turn at about 10 rpm and are ideal for rod-curing. If you don't have one, you can hand-turn the rod, but continous hand-turning gets old in a hurry. One solution is to hand-turn the rod about 90 degrees every 5 minutes for the first 20 minutes, and then about every 15 minutes for the next 2 hours. Often a good way to do this is to watch a miniseries on TV and turn the rod each time there is a commercial break. Often you can judge the amount of turning needed by the tendency of the finish to sag between turns. Exact figures can't be given, because the variables include brand of finish, epoxy, or urethane; ambient temperature; humidity; and the amount of finish on each wrap.

In some cases, one coat of epoxy rod finish is enough. With other finishes and other rods, you may want to add two or three coats. If this is the case, repeat the mixing and adding of finish after allowing the previous coat to cure for 24 hours. Often, the lighter finishes used on fly rods or light spinning rods require only one coat, but any coating should lightly but completely cover each thread wrap.

Not all finishes are two-part. Those that aren't, such as Gudebrod Speed Coat Rod Finish and U-40 Perma Gloss, are one-part, and other than

mixing are added just as the previously outlined steps indicate. Because these finishes are often thinner, you may need more than the one coat that is often enough with epoxy finishes. For example, U-40 recommends using two coats of its Perma Gloss over two coats of its Color Lock on A thread, and two or three coats of Color Lock followed by four coats of Perma Gloss on size E thread wraps. Most of these finishes also cure or dry quicker; Perma Gloss is tack-free in half an hour, and Gudebrod Speed Coat Rod Finish sets up in one hour. Naturally, both finishes require more time to cure completely.

FINISHING PROBLEMS AND SOLUTIONS

Sometimes problems occur when rods are finished. Some of these, along with possible causes and suggested solutions are:

1. In some cases the finish will still be tacky even after it should be completely dry. Often this is caused by an inaccurate mix of two-part finishes, so that the finish never really cures. If this tackiness is just borderline, often a wait of a day or two can help, as can adding heat to help the finish cure. In other cases, nothing can be done. One solution is to mix new finish and coat the rod a second time. Often this will solve the problem, but only if you make an accurate mix. One tendency (I did it once) is to figure that if the finish is not cured, it needs more hardener. So the second mix contains more hardener—which is exactly the wrong thing to do. Although many brands call one part of the mix "hardener," it is really a catalyst, and more of it will make the finish even stickier the next time. Mix the two parts exactly, and if you have to err, do so on the side of slightly less hardener.

2. If the cured finish is smooth and hard in some areas and tacky or sticky in others, this indicates incomplete mixing. In other words, some parts of the epoxy were thoroughly mixed (and thus are hard and smooth) and other parts had too little resin (and thus are still sticky). The solution here is to make up a new batch of finish, mix it thoroughly this time, and recoat the blank to solve the problem.

3. In some cases blotching or mottling of the rod wraps will occur. This can be caused by several things. One possibility is contamination of the wraps by oils from your skin, hand lotions, or various other substances that are passed from your hands to the wraps while you wrap the rod. To avoid this, clean your hands thoroughly before

wrapping or wear cotton gloves (available from photos stores for handling negatives) or rubber gloves (available from surgical-supply houses and some drug stores).

Another possible cause is the use of too much color preserver and allowing it to puddle on the rod wrap. To avoid this, add a coat of color preserver and allow it to soak in completely, then blot to remove the excess. Do this with each coat of color preserver added.

A third possible cause of blotching is incompletely applying color preserver to the wraps, so that some areas of the wrap receive more than others. Thus, the underlying threads will react differently when coated with rod finish.

4. Sometimes finishes look lumpy. Usually this is a result of the rod not being turned evenly enough after the finish was applied, resulting in some sagging, which then cures that way. The solution is to use a curing motor or to turn the rod more rapidly. Sagging can also be caused by adding too much finish to the wraps or by not smoothing the finish out completely. To solve this problem, use less finish and add several coats, if required. Also, be sure to smooth the finish out with the brush. If the finish is excessively lumpy, use an emery board to sand down the high lumps, then recoat. Even though the sanded areas appear opaque and are not shiny, they will completely fill in with a new coat and will not show.

5. Bubbles on the surface or in the finish are another problem. As previously mentioned, this can be caused by not using a color preserver (which expels bubbles), by too rapid mixing of the epoxy finish, or by not expelling the bubbles by breathing on the finish before adding it to the rod. Once the finish is on the rod, a torch can be used, along with breathing, to expel bubbles when the finish is still wet and uncured.

6. Dimples on the surface are caused by large bubbles that escape to the surface and then break open. If this happens when the finish is close to setting up, the resulting dimple will not float out and become smooth. If you have a larger bubble that will not dissipate from your breath, use a toothpick or bodkin to break it, and then use a finish-filled brush to flood this area and smooth it. If you notice this problem only after the finish is cured, roughen the area slightly with steel wool and recoat with a new batch of finish.

7. Some two-part epoxy finishes are too thick for light rods such as light fly rods and ultralight spinning rods. For this, there are several solutions (although this is best recognized *before* adding the finish, to prevent cutting off the wraps and rewrapping. There is no easy way to remove the finish from a wrap.) One possibility is to use some of the lighter finishes available. Flex Coat produces Flex Coat Lite for a thinner two-part epoxy finish on light rods; Gudebrod Speed Coat Rod Finish is a one-part thinner coating, as is U-40 Perma Gloss. Thinning thick finishes with a solvent (acetone for most epoxies, such as Flex Coat) is a possibility. Although no manufacturer really recommends this, try acetone in a ratio of 1 drop to 1 to 5 cubic centimeters of rod epoxy mix, but be sure to test first on a scrap wrap or blank to check for any adverse reactions or problems.

8. An oily or waxy appearance is often caused by high humidity. To prevent this in the first place, do not coat a rod under very high-humidity or low-temperature conditions. The ideal temperature is between 70° and 85° Fahrenheit for most finishes. To solve this problem after it has occurred, you usually must apply a second coat of finish.

If you notice this oily or waxy look on the finish while it is still wet, one suggested solution is to use a torch to heat the entire area. Wait 30 minutes and torch it again. The oily slick will disappear.

9. If you mixed up too much finish and don't want to waste it, try sealing it and storing it in the refrigerator. Often finish can be stored this way for about a week or more, and if it's frozen it can be stored for a month or more. Obviously, the refrigerated finish will require some warming or heating up before use.

26

Chopping Blanks and Making Ferrules

INTRODUCTION ▪ TOOLS AND MATERIALS ▪ CUTTING
BLANKS: PURPOSES ▪ CUTTING BLANKS: METHODS ▪
MEASURING FOR FERRULES ▪ MAKING SLEEVE FERRULES ▪
MAKING SPIGOT FERRULES ▪ REINFORCING FERRULES ▪
SEATING METAL FERRULES ▪ WRAPPING FERRULES

Basic Safety Equipment
Safety goggles
Shop apron

Basic Tools
Fine-tooth (32-inch) hacksaw blade and handle
Triangular file
Centering miter box

Helpful Tools
Ruler
Calipers
Marking pen

INTRODUCTION

Most custom rods are built on blanks that are used the way the manufacturer supplies them. That's great, because rod and blank manufacturers try to build blanks that are designed for a specific purpose, fishing method, action, and power. It is to their advantage to have each of their blanks bought by as many anglers as possible.

There are good reasons for chopping blanks, however. In some cases you may want a shorter, heavier rod built from a blank on hand, or you may want to modify a one-piece rod into a two-piece rod or a two-piece rod into a four-piece rod by ferruling, or you may need to remove a damaged or broken tip from an existing rod to rebuild the rod with a slightly shorter tip section.

In this context I am referring to making self-ferrules — ferrules of glass or graphite for glass or graphite rods. Also, however, it is important to realize some of the basics of adding metal ferrules to blanks, even though this is rarely done today. Obviously, there is no point in adding ferrules to a rod other than to make it easier to transport. Installing ferrules takes time, something manufacturers understand. Often, blank manufacturers will offer the same blank in one- and two-piece styles — the two-piece model is always more expensive. This is a reflection of the additional materials and labor costs associated with two-piece blanks.

TOOLS AND MATERIALS

Tools for chopping and modifying blanks and making ferrules are relatively simple. The only tools really required include:

A fine-tooth hacksaw blade. The only ones that should be considered for cutting blanks are those with 32 teeth to the inch. If I ever find a hacksaw blade with more teeth to the inch — or if one comes out in the future — I'll buy it, because it should be even better. The reason for the fine-tooth blade is that you want to cut through delicate material. When cutting any material, the larger the teeth of the saw, the more likely it is that those teeth will tear and splinter the material being cut. You obviously don't want to splinter the graphite or glass materials you are cutting. Thus, the fine-tooth blade is a must.

Fine-tooth triangular file. This is really a substitute for the above, because blanks can be cut with a saw or with a file. The triangular file should also be fine, so as to avoid tearing the material.

Centering miter box. This is a homemade mitering tool that will aid you if you frequently cut and modify blanks. It is nothing more than a wood miter box with a V shape, instead of a U or square shape inside, in order to center the blank for cutting. The easiest way to make one is to rip a 1-foot long board in half lengthwise at a 45-degree angle, flip one piece end to end to make a V, and nail this securely to a second board. Then, using a right-angle square, cut through the top part of the miter box (the V part at right angles to the length of the board). In use, the blank can be centered in the V, and the hacksaw blade fits into the slot to cut through the blank.

Materials are as follows:

Masking tape. It helps to wrap several layers of masking tape around the blank where the cut is to be made to prevent splintering.

Epoxy glue. You will need this for gluing ferrule parts to the rod, whether you use metal ferrules or make ferrules from rod-blank parts.

Sandpaper. A little fine sandpaper is handy for dressing and smoothing cut blanks and also for roughing the blank and ferrule surfaces that are to be glued together.

Scrap blanks. You will need some scrap blanks if you are making sleeve or spigot ferrules. Sources are broken rods that you or a buddy might have accumulated over the years, and scraps are available from dealers at no or low cost. These scraps must be about the same diameter as the blank you are planning to chop and ferrule.

CUTTING BLANKS: PURPOSES

You cut blanks for different purposes. In some cases cutting is necessary to finish a rod properly. For example, I have seen blanks that are rough at the tip and butt ends (more often at the butt end), a result of some of the rough blank materials being left on the rod when the mandrel is pulled out of the blank. In most cases, this is easily trimmed by removing just a few inches of the rough area. Often this is extra length anyway — not really a part of the measured length of the rod blank — and thus there is no loss to the rod. Although this can happen on any rod, most manufacturers check carefully to prevent blanks with untrimmed ends from getting out of the factory. Although this can happen on any style of rod blank, I have seen it mostly on big surf rods and offshore trolling blanks.

Another reason for cutting blanks is to remove a broken tip if you lose a few inches due to a fishing mishap. By cutting the blank back, it is possible to salvage the rod. As an example, my longtime friend Norm Bartlett built a beautiful split-bamboo fly rod, splitting the culms himself and making the rod from scratch. It had one of the finest actions of any bamboo rod I've ever tried. Unfortunately, he lost a few inches off the tip end in a fishing accident, cut down the rod, added a new tip-top, and went on to use the rod to take a new IGFA record on a two-pound test tippet for striped bass with a 6-pound 11-ounce fish. The lost tip might have affected the rod aesthetically, but not functionally.

You also would need to cut a rod blank when customizing a rod or blank to make it easier to pack. One-piece rods can be made into two or more pieces, two-piece rods can be made into four-piece pack rods, and so on. Naturally, if you wish to keep all sections of a two-piece or three-piece rod the same length, you must end up with double the number of pieces you currently have. (Thus, you would make a two-piece rod into a four-piece rod, although you could also make it into a six- or eight-piece rod if desired, and a three-piece rod into a six-piece rod.) When starting with a two- or three-piece rod, you can't end up with a three-, five-, or seven-piece rod or some other odd number of pieces unless you plan on one section being longer than the others, which defeats one of the main purposes of ferruling.

An exception to this would be if you are working with a one-piece rod that you can cut into three, five, or seven pieces as well as into two, four, or six pieces.

CUTTING BLANKS: METHODS

There are two basic ways to cut a blank. One is with a file, the other is with a fine-tooth hacksaw blade. Most of the manufacturers recommend using a triangular file, but I have never had any problem with the hacksaw blade. If there are basic guidelines that apply to both methods, they are to measure carefully to be sure you are cutting in the right place, to use care in all steps, and to not force the cut in any way. A gentle touch is required throughout the process.

To cut through a blank using a file, first measure the blank carefully and mark it. Recheck this measurement. Then wrap several layers of masking tape around the blank and remark the measurement on the center of the tape.

Support the blank on a flat surface and, using a fine-cut triangular file, begin stroking the corner of the file back and forth on the tape mark. Once you cut through the tape, move the rod blank slightly and continue until you have a groove in the tape all the way around the rod. Continue around a second time, gradually cutting a slight groove into the skin of the blank. Use the lightest possible pressure, because bearing down hard will tend to splinter the blank and may even crush it as you come close to cutting through. Continue in

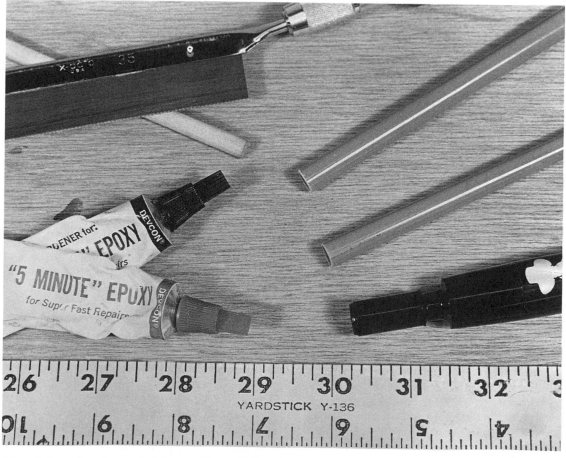

Materials and tools needed for making self-ferrules.

this way, working slowly and carefully, until the blank is completely cut through. This method will work on all hollow-glass and graphite rods (and also on the solid thin tip ends of some of the newer rods), but it will not work on thick solid-glass blanks. Solid-glass blanks should be cut with a hacksaw.

To cut through a hollow blank using a hacksaw, first make sure you have a fine-tooth hacksaw blade with 32 teeth per inch. Do not attempt to cut blanks with a coarser blade, or you may tear or splinter the blank. It helps if you have a small handle to hold the blade, but do *not* use one of the standard bracket-style frames that stretch the blade between two ends. They are too bulky, heavy, and difficult to control for this purpose. If you don't have a small handle, hold the blade in your hand (wear a glove) or wrap one end of the blade with tape to make a handle. You can arrange the blade in the small handle with the teeth pointing toward or away from you. The secret in using the blade, however, is to begin by dragging the blade backward (pushing or pulling, as the case may be). Note that this is contrary to the way you were taught in shop class in high school, but it will protect the blank from splintering. Do not use any appreciable pressure. Let the weight of the blade and the dragging of the teeth make the cut.

You may wish to use a miter box, as described earlier. This will help to center the rod blank and position the blade at right angles for an easy cut. For best results, place the miter box in a vise to secure it and to hold the rod blank securely in the V slot.

The technique for cutting is almost the same as for using a file. Measure the blank and mark it, then tape the blank with masking tape and mark the tape. Pull or push the blade so it drags backward over the mark, and rotate the rod so you work completely around the blank. After cutting through the tape, cut through the skin of the blank and continue on to deepen this groove.

Once part of the blank is cut through, rotate the blank to cut through the rest of it. It is always best to work so that you are cutting from the surface of the blank toward the center and constantly rotating the rod blank, rather than to begin at one spot and cut straight through as you would do with a piece of wood. By cutting through the blank skin first, you minimize splitting the material fibers. If you cut straight through, you risk tearing some of these fibers on the sides and bottom of the blank.

Proper cutting of rod blanks is a must. Failure to do so can result in split or torn ends, as shown here.

Using a homemade miter tool for cutting rod blanks (see directions in Chapter 2). When used with a fine-toothed saw blade, such a box will not damage the rod blank.

Example of a smooth cut around the rod. The entire perimeter should be scored or cut before cutting through.

Once the blank is scored, the rod can be cut through with a fine-toothed saw.

You will want to sand the end of the blank after cutting, but sand only from the outside to the center to avoid the possibility of splintering the blank fibers.

MEASURING FOR FERRULES

Blanks must be measured precisely and cut accurately when you make or add ferrules. There are three types of ferrules that can be added to rods. They include the metal ferrule that used to be common before the self-ferruling system was developed by Fenwick; the sleeve-type of slip-over ferrule, in which a sleeve is glued to the butt end of the tip section to friction-fit with the butt section; and the spigot ferrule, which consists of a plug glued into the upper part of the butt section to friction-fit with the tip section.

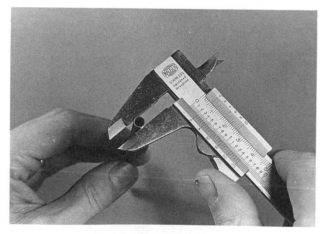

Using a caliper to check the diameter and wall thickness of a blank, for choosing an insert spigot ferrule or external sleeve ferrule.

MEASUREMENTS FOR METAL FERRULES

Metal ferrules don't really require any measurements if the blank is already cut or supplied in sections. In most cases, the extension of the female portion of the ferrule matches or closely approximates in length the extension of the male ferrule. Thus, although the ferrules will add perhaps an inch or two of length to the broken-down rod, the measurement of the rod sections before these ferrules are added will not be affected. On some ferrules, the butt end of the upper section (the tip section in two-piece rods) fits all the way down into the end of the male ferrule, so that to match lengths of the separate sections, the upper end of the butt section must be cut back the length of the male extension, or the butt end of the rod must be cut off. Often, this latter suggestion is better, particularly if there is a snug fit of the female ferrule to the blank. Cutting back the upper end of this section may make it impossible to fit the ferrule in place. Cutting back the butt end for one or two inches does not affect the action.

MEASUREMENTS FOR SLEEVE FERRULES

With sleeve ferrules, you will be using a sleeve that is an identical taper to the blank. This sleeve is slipped over the blank and glued in place so that there is a sleeve extension of 1 to 2 or more inches beyond the bottom end of the tip section, or the butt end of multisection rods. If a two-piece blank is cut exactly in half and the sleeve extension to the tip end adds 2 inches, then the tip end will be 2 inches longer than the butt section. This isn't a problem functionally but rather aesthetically, and makes it more difficult to case and pack the rod with unequal sections.

To solve this in order to measure for the point at which to cut the blank, you must first decide on the length of extension of this sleeve. (This is the extension beyond the end of the blank—not the total length of this sleeve. Obviously, the sleeve must be longer than these figures to include 1 or 2 inches to be glued to the blank.) For a light rod, it might be no more than 1 1/2 inches. For a heavy rod, it could be 3 inches. To properly measure the rod for cutting, first mark the rod at the exact halfway point. Then make the cutting mark exactly one-half the length of the ferrule extension to the tip side of the rod. As an example, let's use a 6-foot-long spinning rod to be cut into 2 pieces with a 2-inch ferrule extension. For this 72-inch-long blank, the halfway point is at 36 inches from each end. The blank should be cut 1 inch to the tip side of this mark (one-half of the 2-inch extension) so that the tip section is 35 inches long and the butt section is 37 inches long. Then, when the sleeve ferrule is added to the tip section and extends 2 inches from the butt end, the total of this section becomes 37 inches (35 inches + 2 inches), or the length of the butt section. Both are identical.

Another way to think of this is to add the 72-inch length and the 2-inch extension together to make 74 inches as the total length of the two separate sections (even though they are not cut yet). Divide by two to equal 37 inches, or the length of the butt section and the position of the cut. The tip section becomes 37 inches through the addition of the 2-inch extension onto the 35-inch blank-section length.

This method also helps when you cut a blank into three or more sections, because the more sections, the more additions of ferrule-sleeve extensions that must be added. For cutting a 72-inch blank into three sections, you use a slightly different method of adding the blank length to the length of the two sleeve extensions. Using 2 inches for this again, it becomes 72 inches + 2 inches + 2 inches = 76 inches, or a total of 76 inches for the rod plus the two ferrule extensions. Divide this by three and you get 25 1/3 inches, or the position of the first mark from the butt of the rod. The next mark will be 23 1/3 inches up (25 1/3 inches - 2 inches), leaving a final upper section of 23 1/3 inches. The 2-inch sleeve additions to these two upper sections bring them back to a 25 1/3-inch length, the same as for the butt section. For a four-piece pack rod made from a one-piece 72-inch blank, the formula is 72 inches + 2 inches + 2 inches + 2 inches, or 78 inches total. Thus, each of the four sections (with the 2-inch sleeve ferrules added to the upper three sections) will be 19 1/2 inches. This means that the cut on the butt section will be at 19 1/2 inches, the next cut will be at 17 1/2 inches, and the third cut will be at 17 1/2 inches, leaving a 17 1/2-inch upper section, for a total of 72 inches.

The same formulation can be applied to any length or type of rod, any length of ferrule extension, and any number of pieces. Just remember that you must always subtract the extensions from any marks and cuts and that it is extremely important to measure, check, and recheck several times until you're sure of the results when you cut. If you are not sure, or don't understand the formula, don't cut!

You can even use this formula for making ferrules of different lengths for different sections of the rod, such as a four-piece rod that might have a 3-inch sleeve in the butt for strength, a 2-inch sleeve in the center of the rod, and a 1-inch sleeve in the tip end, where less strength is required. Just be sure to add the respective extensions to any total length and to make the marks on the blank relative to and compensating for the different extension lengths. As an example of this, let's assume that same 72-inch-long blank is cut into four sections, but with a 3-inch extension sleeve for the butt sections, a 2-inch sleeve for the center of the rod, and a 1-inch sleeve for the tip sections. The formula would still be 72 inches + 3 inches + 2 inches + 1 inch = 78 inches, divided by 4 = 19 1/2 inches for the butt section. The next cut would be at 16 1/2 inches (19 1/2 inches - 3 inches for the extension that will be added to this section), the third cut would be at 17 1/2 inches (19 1/2 inches - 2 inches of sleeve extension), leaving a final section of 18 1/2 inches long that with the 1-inch extension will measure 19 1/2 inches. Use this formula and all sections of any multipiece rod will be equal when the rod is finished.

MEASUREMENTS FOR SPIGOT FERRULES

Spigot ferrules are made as self-ferrules to fit on any blank, but unlike the sleeve ferrule, which is glued to the butt end of each section to fit over the tip end of the next section, spigot ferrules consist of a plug of blank material glued into the tip end of each section to mate with the inside diameter of the next upper section. Thus, the

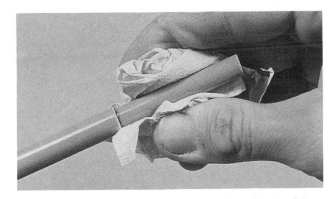

A spigot ferrule uses a short section that is glued into the upper end of the butt section to mate with the lower end of the tip section of the rod. Here, a spigot has been pushed and pulled into place and is being cleaned with a rag.

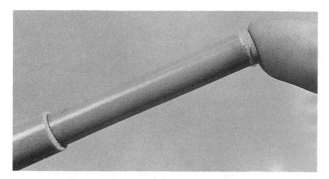

Spigot ferrule with a cork added to the end to seal the rod. Both sleeve ferrules and spigot ferrules must be wrapped to give them hoop strength.

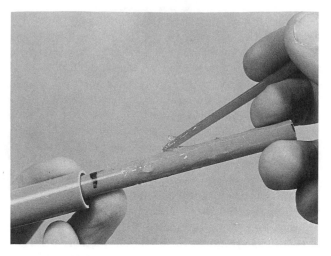

An external sleeve ferrule is made by gluing a sleeve over the tip section of the cut rod so that the sleeve will mate with the upper end of the butt section. Here, glue is added to the butt end of the tip section so that the sleeve can be slid and glued in place.

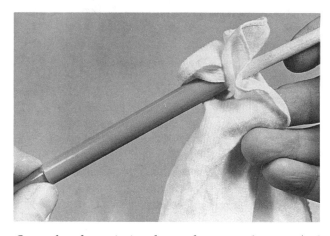

Once the sleeve is in place, glue must be removed from the ferrule. A small dowel or rod blank and rag work well for this. All glue must be removed for proper seating of the sleeve on the rod section.

measurements for these will be just the opposite of the sleeve ferrules.

As an example, a 72-inch rod cut exactly in half and with a 2-inch plug inserted into the butt section would have a butt 38 inches long and a tip section 36 inches long. To prevent this, measure the exact center for a two-piece rod, then mark *toward the butt side* exactly one-half the length of the plug ferrule. (As with sleeve ferrules, this is not the total length of the plug, because there must be 1 or 2 inches that will be glued to the inside of the blank. This is just the length of the extension.) Thus, for a 2-inch plug, a cut 1 inch to the butt side will result in a butt section that will be 35 inches long and a tip section 37 inches long. When the 2-inch plug extends from the butt end, both sections will be 37 inches long.

To expand this to a four-piece rod from a 72-inch blank, the formula would be 72 inches + 2 inches + 2 inches + 2 inches = 78 inches, divided by four = 19.5 inches. But in this case, the 2-inch plug is *subtracted* from the butt section to make a section of 17 1/2 inches. The next two sections will be the same length. The final, uppermost section will be 19 1/2 inches, which will be the length of the three lower sections when the 2-inch plug ferrules are added to each. The formulas for each of these are simple—just remember in which direction you are cutting, which end gets the extension, and which section remains full length, to be matched by the others when the sleeves or plugs are glued in place.

MAKING SLEEVE FERRULES

To add sleeve ferrules to a rod, you will need a minimal number of tools, but you will need some scrap blank material that has an internal diameter that is approximately the same as the outside

diameter of the blank where the ferrule will be placed. The scrap blank must be the same taper as the blank you are fitting, although this can be adjusted slightly.

Begin by measuring and cutting the blank. Once the blank is cut and the ends are sanded, cut a section of the scrap blank to slide down over the upper or tip section of the rod blank. If the taper of the scrap blank is the same as the rod blank, then you can avoid cutting out any sections, and simply slide the scrap over the blank. The purpose here is to determine the approximate area where the scrap will fit snugly onto the end of the blank.

Because the scrap blank will cover and hide the end of the rod blank, the best way to do this is to measure the rod-blank section, slide the scrap blank in place, and then measure down to determine the approximate position of the end of the rod blank. Mark this spot on the scrap blank and remove it. If the taper of the blank and the scrap are the same, you can then cut about 4 inches on each side of this mark on the scrap. If you're unsure of the amount of play between the two sections, or of the tapers, cut about 4 inches below the mark and about 6 inches above the mark. This will allow room for adjustment with a second fitting.

Slide the scrap sleeve onto the blank again to check for fit, remark the position of the end of the blank on the scrap, and trim the scrap to fit. At the same time that the scrap is fitted snugly to the tip end, slide the butt end into place to see if you get a match as to taper and fit. You will probably have to cut about 1/4- to 1/2-inch off the end of the butt section or the lower end of the tip section. This assures a tight fit of the sleeve to the butt section. Failure to do this may result in the two rod sections "bottoming out" against each other, making for a loose fit. Ideally, I like to cut abut 1/4-inch from the butt end of the tip section, to glue the ferrule on, and then to make any additional cuts and trimming of the butt section if needed.

At this point, check to make sure the tapers are compatible. First, the scrap sleeve should fit snugly onto the end of the tip section without any play at either end. If there is play, use a rat-tail file or sandpaper wrapped around a dowel to lightly sand the tight end, checking frequently until you get a tight, snug fit with no play. Once this sleeve fits the upper end, check for play and fit with the butt end lightly fitted into the sleeve.

Cut the sleeve so that there is about 2 to 3 inches of sleeve to be glued onto the blank, the final length depending upon the blank's diameter and power. Use longer sections for strength, shorter sections for light rods and tip ends. Mark the blank at the upper end of the sleeve and remove the sleeve. Use steel wool to lightly roughen the blank for better gluing. Also, use sandpaper or a fine file to shape a tapered angle on the sleeve, which will make it easier to wrap thread onto this ferrule section for hoop strength.

To glue the sleeve onto the blank, coat the end of the rod section with epoxy rod glue or any good 24-hour epoxy glue (not epoxy rod finish!) and slide the ferrule down the blank. When you reach the glued section, slide the sleeve rapidly over the glue, and as it starts to seat, twist several times to assure a good glue bond. Do *not* pull too much, because the glue will serve as a lubricant, and too much tension could split the sleeve at this point.

Once the sleeve is glued on, use a cotton swab, a dowel covered with a paper towel or thin rag, or a similar probe to thoroughly wipe the glue out of the end of what is now the female ferrule. This is most important, because any glue residue will prevent the proper seating of the ferrule onto the butt section. Allow the glue to cure overnight. Once the glue is cured, check for a tight, proper fit of the ferrule onto the butt section, but do not force, because the ferrule still needs wrapping to provide hoop strength. If the butt end bottoms out, remove and cut it back by 1/4-inch and try again. (It is a must to have some small space between the butt end of the tip section and the tip end of the butt section so that the friction of the ferrule maintains the tight joint during the action of fishing.)

At this point, the ferrule is ready to wrap to provide hoop strength. Naturally, this method can be used for any number of ferrules on a rod of any diameter and any material.

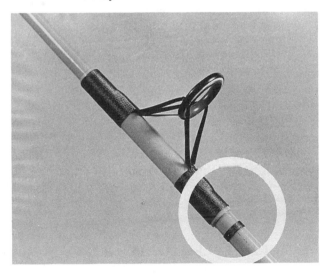

Example of sleeve ferrule with a guide mounted on the ferrule. The wrap thus has two purposes — to hold the guide in place and to provide hoop strength to the ferrule.

MAKING SPIGOT FERRULES

The technique of adding a spigot ferrule to a rod is not unlike that of adding sleeve ferrules — only in this case you are adding a separate plug into the butt section rather than a sleeve over the tip section. For this you will also need sections of scrap blank, in this case scraps that will have an outside diameter that is the same as or similar to the internal diameter of the upper end of the butt section.

Begin by measuring and cutting the rod blank as previously described. Then slide the scrap section up through the butt end in the lower rod section and out the upper end. If you have a short section of scrap blank, you might need a dowel or straightened-coat-hanger pusher to push the scrap out of the end. Pull snug and mark the end of the blank on the scrap. Remove the scrap and cut about 4 inches on each side of this mark. Replace this scrap in the butt end of the blank and check the mark again, and check, too, for any play of the scrap in the blank. If there is play at either end, remove the scrap and sand and file it, rechecking frequently until the play is removed and the scrap fits precisely and snugly. Check for the fit of the tip end over this plug. If the two ends of the rod meet, cut back the butt end about 1/4-inch.

Lightly sand the scrap for a better fit on the blank and into the tip section. Use a thin dowel or skewer to spread 24-hour epoxy or rod-building epoxy into the end of the blank. Make sure you use plenty of glue and spread it thoroughly into the blank for about 3 or 4 inches. Using the pusher, push the plug up into the butt section and out the end. Pull it snug, but do not pull too tight and risk splitting the blank. Use a rag to immediately wipe up any glue on the exposed plug ferrule. Allow the glue to cure overnight. Once it's cured, check the fit with the tip end, and if necessary cut back about 1/4-inch so that a firm fit onto the ferrule still leaves a gap of about 1/4- to 3/8-inch between the rod-section ends. This is necessary to maintain a firm fit and to allow for some wear.

This type of ferrule can be used for any type of rod and on any diameter of rod blank. At this point, the ferrule is ready to wrap.

REINFORCING FERRULES

Sometimes the section of blank used in the above ferrules is not strong enough for the rod. This is more typical of spigot ferrules than of sleeve ferrules, but it can occur in either type. Part of this is because we are all dependent upon getting and using scrap-blank sections for these sleeves and plugs, and there is no way to judge beforehand the thickness and strength of these sections.

One way to adjust for this is to reinforce the sleeves and plugs. To do this with a sleeve, use an additional sleeve over the initial sleeve, repeating the steps described above. You can do this after the first sleeve is added to the blank, or you can make up the double-wall sleeve, then glue it onto the blank. In most cases it is easier to add the second sleeve to the first after the first is glued to the blank.

Similarly, additional smaller-diameter plugs can be glued into the main plug that forms the plug spigot ferrule in rods. I find it easier to make up a thicker, reinforced double- or triple-walled plug, then to trim this reinforced plug to length and finally glue it into the blank. This seems to be more important in the spigot ferrules, because the plug is thinner than the rod blank and thus has less strength for this critical area.

In some cases, you can find solid plugs for spigot ferrules. Some mail-order companies have sold these in the past, and sections of solid-glass blanks are often used for this. This is ideal, because there is less work involved (no building of double-or triple-wall ferrules) and the strength is unquestioned.

SEATING METAL FERRULES

Metal ferrules are measured in sixty-fourths of an inch internal diameter, sometimes sized slightly larger for the female section that is fitted onto the upper end of the butt section or the upper ends of sections of multipiece rods. To fit them to a rod, first cut the blank. Check to see if the blank fits all the way into the male section or stops where the male section fits into the ferrule. The difference will determine how to cut the blank, because otherwise the blank section with the female section will be longer than the other section.

A snug fit is a must. You may have to sand slightly to get a proper fit. For example, a female ferrule that just fits onto the tip end of a butt section but does not seat all the way down (measure to check) might require light sanding of the blank below this area to accommodate the ferrule. If the ferrule just barely fits on, or if the rod is of a steep taper that will require a lot of sanding (and possibly weakening), try going to the next larger size ferrule.

Male ferrules that fit onto the tip section of the rod have the opposite problem, because the taper is thickest at the end of the blank. Thus, sand

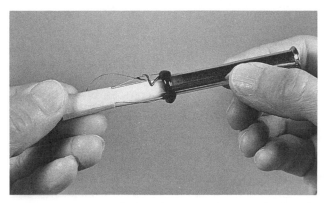

Mounting a metal ferrule using heat-melt ferrule cement. Thread shims have been used here for an accurate mounting.

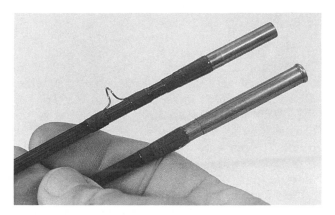

Example of ferrule set on a bamboo rod. Ferrules must be glued in place and wrapped as shown, for both strength and appearance.

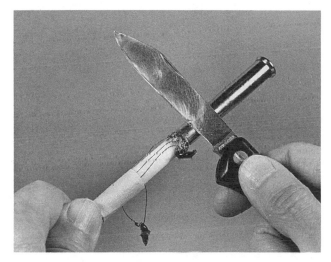

Once the ferrule cement hardens, it can be cracked off with a knife blade, as shown. This is better than trying to remove it while hot.

lightly only at this tip end, because it is likely that the ferrule will fit fine if the blank sides are made close to parallel.

Once the fit is correct, lightly sand the blanks in this area (protect the rest of the blank here with masking tape), add 24-hour epoxy glue to the blank and also to the inside of the ferrules, and slide the ferrules in place. Rotate slightly to assure a good glue bond and immediately wipe up any excess glue. Allow the glue to cure overnight. At this point, the ferrules are ready for wrapping.

Below: Examples of adapters for rod blanks, showing shims used for accurate sizing to the rod blank. Such adapters usually are designed for casting-rod handles.

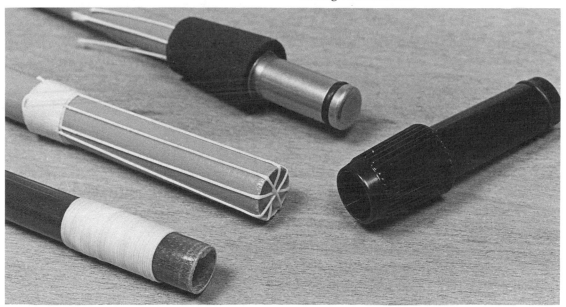

Wrapping Ferrules

Wrapping directions are described completely in Chapter 22, but some tips specific to ferrules are included here. Metal ferrules have a shoulder area that should be wrapped. Begin the wrap on the blank and wrap up and over the end of the ferrule to the end of this shoulder area. It is usually obvious as a slight visible ridge on the ferrule. The wraps are coated with color preserver and rod finish along with the guide wraps.

Self-ferrules that are built into blanks must also be wrapped to provide hoop strength to the female ferrule. Follow the manufacturer's directions. If such directions are not available, wrap manufactured sleeve ferrules (such as the Fenwick style) completely with a thread wrap, beginning on the blank and running up to finish as close as possible to the end. Use the same tension as for guide wraps to provide hoop strength.

Plug ferrules that are built in by the manufacturer or installed by you should also be wrapped. In this case, wrap not only the female section (the butt end of the tip section) but also the area where the plug is glued into the butt end. This butt end is the equivalent of a female ferrule in construction and does require the wrapping for hoop strength. In both cases, begin on the body of the blank and work as close to the end of the blank as possible.

Sleeve ferrules do not require a wrap on the butt section, although often rod-builders add a slight band here as a decorative addition. They do require a complete wrap of the sleeve beginning on the blank and wrapping up over and onto the sleeve and to the end of the sleeve. This presents some problems, however. Earlier it was suggested that you might want to taper the end of the blank end of the sleeve. The reason is that it will thus be easier to control the thread as you make this step up from the blank to the sleeve.

One tip here is to slightly lessen the tension on the thread during this critical step so that you can run the thread up the steep taper of this area and get it onto the flat sleeve without overwraps or gaps. If the thickness of the sleeve is too much for this, there is another tip. This is to first lay down a separate wrap on the blank that ends at the sleeve. Then begin the regular wrap on the blank, go up over the short band wrap, and from that up onto the sleeve. The short band provides an additional step to make this transition easier. An alternative to this is to begin the wrap right next to the sleeve, wrap back down the blank, and then reverse the wrap as a double wrap to go back up and over the sleeve to the end.

27

Rod Variations

INTRODUCTION ▪ TWISTED-GUIDE RODS ▪ PACK RODS ▪
ICE-FISHING RODS ▪ RIGHT-HAND AND LEFT-HAND FLY
RODS ▪ RIGHT-HAND AND LEFT-HAND SPINNING RODS ▪
MIXED-MATERIAL RODS ▪ ROD BUTT-SECTION
REINFORCERS ▪ TELESCOPING RODS ▪ OTHER
POSSIBILITIES

Basic Safety Requirements
Safety goggles
Rubber gloves for epoxy

Basic Tools
Coat hangers
Book and cup
Razor blade
Burnisher
Masking tape

Helpful Tools
Rod-wrapping tool, thread-tension device
Rod miter box
Rod-handle seater
Cork-grip clamp

Ruler
Brushes
Reamers
Tip-Top gauge
Curing motor
Diamond wrapping tools

INTRODUCTION

The basics of rod-building are covered in Chapters 18 and 19. Details on specific parts of rod-building are covered in Chapters 20, 21, and 22. These chapters should be checked for details on the specifics of rod-building. This chapter is meant to describe some of the odd variations possible. However, basic and standard rod-building methods and procedures, along with basic safety considerations, apply to all of the rods listed in this chapter.

Some of these rods have very specific applications. Some are more widely applicable to a wide range of fishing, and others are simply unusual variations that can be applied—or not—to any type of rod or type of fishing.

As an example, pack rods are useful primarily for traveling anglers, especially those traveling by plane or needing a short rod pack for a western pack trip. These rods would be less useful for anyone traveling by car, and of very little use to an angler traveling exclusively by car or living on a lakefront, whose tackle is from taken from garage to a boat.

Casting rods with twisted guides—guides that rotate around the blank and end up on the opposite side of the rod from the reel—have their champions, primarily among anglers who want something slightly different and those who fight big fish on light tackle and don't want line rubbing against the rod.

Ice-fishing rods are highly specialized and are made with specific ice-fishing requirements in mind.

TWISTED-GUIDE RODS

These rods go by several names—in fact, some anglers on their own have "invented" and named them. In essence they are all casting (revolving-spool) rods where the guides rotate around the rod in progression from butt to tip. The rationale for this evolves from one of the typical problems of light-casting tackle where, even with a normal complement of guides, the stress of fighting a big fish will result in line rubbing against the rod. These rods bend so much under extreme stress that the rod section between each two guides arches enough for the line to hit it. One solution to this, of course, is to use high-frame guides—more like spinning guides than casting-rod guides—but this can also increase the torque on the rod, twisting the blank.

The solution of "twisting" the guides eliminates the problem of line-to-blank contact completely and also minimizes the torque problem. Building a casting rod with twisted guides is the same as building a normal casting rod until the guides and tip-top are fitted. First the tip-top (usually added to the rod blank before the guides

are in order to aid in lining up the guides) is placed on the blank 180 degrees from the normal position. When the tip-top is glued, it must be positioned on the opposite side of the rod from its normal position. The guides are positioned so that when the line comes off the reel it will run in a spiral around the blank to exit directly under the rod.

There are several ways to position these guides, but the best way is to first calculate the position of each (this will not vary from the guide positions on a normal rod) and then to tape the guides in place. Begin with the butt guide at about a 30-degree angle from the normal position; the second guide will be about 120 degrees from the normal position, and the remaining guides will be directly under the rod. Some rods will require one more guide at an angle, so that the first guide might be at 20 degrees from normal, the second guide at 80 degrees from normal (60 degrees from the butt guide), the third guide at 140 degrees from normal (60 degrees from the second guide and 120 degrees from the butt guide), and the rest of the guides at 180 degrees from the normal positions. Occasionally, you may have to keep the butt guide in the normal position and vary the other guides. Usually you can get away with only two additional guides traversing the blank, with the second guide after the butt guide at 45 degrees, the third at 135 degrees, and the rest at 180 degrees.

Naturally, you will have to check the rod to be sure you accomplish the goal of not allowing any line-to-blank contact at any time under any circumstances. With the guides only taped in place, you can't run line through the guides and stress the rod to check. So you must attach a line to the tip-top (make sure it is securely glued in place and cures overnight) and at the same time run a line off the attached reel and through the guides and tip-top ring. Attach a light weight (or less than an ounce) to the end of this line. Then stress the rod by bending it, pulling against the line tied to the tip-top. At the same time, reel in the line through the guides until the sinker used is hanging free.

Check the rod at this point for any contact of the line with the rod blank. There will be enough tension from the weight to indicate the path of the line through the guides, but not enough to twist the guides away from their taped-on positions. Make any adjustments as necessary to be sure the line clears. Once you are satisfied with the positioning of the guides, remove the lines carefully and wrap the guides in place.

Such guides can be used for any type of re-

Example of twisted-guide rod; arrows show the guides as they spiral around the rod. Such design is used only on casting rods and most often on downrigger rods.

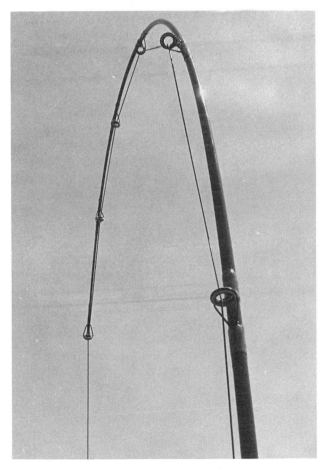

Another view of the above showing how the guides spiral around the rod.

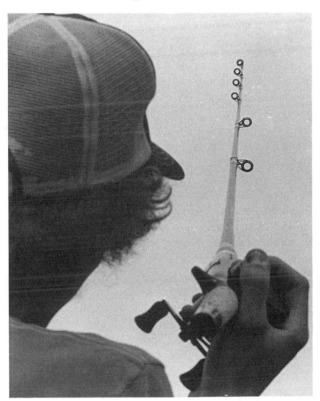

View of casting rod with spiral guides.

volving-spool rod, not just casting rods for bass or walleye or light-tackle saltwater rods. They are ideal for downrigger rods that are bent into a sharp arc as a result of the tension put in the line from downrigger fishing. They are also ideal for casting-style noodle rods and long-handled steelhead and West Coast salmon rods. In all cases, it only takes two or three guides to route the line from on top of the rod to completely underneath — the rest of the guides can run straight in line with the tip-top.

Although the guides can route the line around either side of the rod, I prefer to run it to the left as I hold the rod. My slight argument for this is that because I am a right-handed caster and because this means that my casting rod is turned 90 degrees to the left (counterclockwise) when I make a cast, any gravity during the cast will pull the line away from the blank, not toward it. Admittedly, this effect will be minimal and the force of gravity will only be at the end of the cast, when any such drag of the line on the rod blank would be minimal anyway.

PACK RODS

Pack-rod blanks for fly rods and sometimes light spinning rods are available from a number of manufacturers. Some are three-piece, most are four-piece, and a few have even more pieces. The techniques for building these are no different from building any fly or light spinning rod, except for some new additional thoughts, as follow:

1. With pack rods, it does help to pinpoint the spine of each section of the rod if this is not already marked on the blank sections by the manufacturer. This is a little more difficult on shorter sections, because the reduced length makes it hard to bend the section enough to determine jumping or stiff and soft sides. Bending will be easiest to do on the light tip section and most difficult on the heaviest and stiffest butt section. Thus, you can usually determine the spine where it is most helpful — on the tip and upper sections. If possible, mark every section's spine.

2. The ferrules must be wrapped in accordance with manufacturer's directions. If there are no directions, then the female ferrules must be wrapped. If the blank has spigot ferrules, the blank portion of the male ferrule should also be wrapped.

3. The additional ferrules (three instead of one on a four-piece rod) require additional concern in guide placement. Often you can reduce

stiffening in the blank by combining the ferrule wraps with the guide wrappings; by adjusting the position of the guides so that they will fall on the female ferrule, where one wrapping will suffice for the guide wrap; and by wrapping to give the ferrule hoop strength.

In addition to making rods that are supplied in pack-rod versions, you can also make your own by cutting a blank to make it into the pack rod desired. Your choices as to section length and number of pieces are limited by the length of the rod and what you start with. Start with a one-piece rod and you can cut and ferrule it any way you wish — into two, three, four, five, or more sections. If you start with a two-piece rod, you are limited to four or six pieces, depending upon whether you cut each of the two sections into two or three pieces. If you start with a three-piece rod, you can only end up with a six-piece pack rod, because each piece must be cut into two pieces.

In working with two- or three-piece rods, it is better if you stick to the same type of ferrule the manufacturer supplied. This will be impossible if the rod has a female ferrule built in as part of the rod blank — as Fenwick does with Fenwick Feralite Ferrules. Because this is a slip-over type of ferrule, however, you can make the other ferrules sleeve-style, which will most closely imitate the manufacturer's ferrule. Similarly, if the rod has a spigot ferrule, it is easy to make additional spigot ferrules.

Naturally, before you begin any of this, make sure you have or can get the appropriate-sized plugs or sleeves to fit the rod where the ferrules will be required. Also, if you are planning a certain type or length of rod to break down into a certain length to fit a rod case, suitcase, or satchel, the ferrules will add approximately 2 inches to the section length. Thus, an 8-foot one-piece blank, when cut and ferruled into a four-piece rod, will have sections measuring about 26 to 27 inches, not 24 inches. The additional 2 or 3 inches will be a result of the plugs or sleeves added to make the ferrules. Because there are definite formulas to aid in cutting blanks for the type of ferrule used, the number of ferrules, and the length of the rod, check Chapter 26 for details and instructions.

Because good fly and light-spinning blanks are often readily available, many rod-builders concentrate on other styles for their pack rods. Thus, rods for every conceivable type of fishing have been made into pack rods. Casting, popping, heavy spinning, spin-cast, surf, boat, and offshore rods have all been successfully converted into or built as pack rods. One caution with all of these involves the strength of the ferrule. The heavier the rod, the heavier the required ferrule. Thus, with the heaviest rods, such as those for offshore or surf fishing, the ferrules must be reinforced hollow sections of blank (as described in Chapter 26), or must be of the solid-glass or graphite-plug type, properly tapered and securely glued into place.

The other instructions and guidelines for making manufacturer-ferruled pack rods also apply to those you ferrule on your own.

ICE-FISHING RODS

Ice-fishing rods are very specific rods for very specific fishing. Although you could argue that one can use any type, style, size, or length of rod for ice fishing (and you would be right in one sense), ice-fishing rods are typically short and very light in power. They are designed this way so that an angler can sit in an ice-fishing shanty or on a sled, poised over an ice-fishing hole. This provides more control of the rod and the lure than would be possible if the angler were sitting back 8 feet and trying to work or control a long casting or spinning rod with the line dangling through a small hole in the ice. In addition, the short rod allows for far greater close control and action of the lure or bait, as well as the quickest possible response from the angler on each bite or tap on the line. If a float is used, it also provides the closest view of the float.

Some ice-fishing-rod blanks are available, but most are cut down from damaged or scrap blanks. The tip sections of these damaged standard casting or spinning rods are used. Most ice-fishing rods measure about 24 to 36 inches, and thus may be cut from old or discarded freshwater fishing rods.

Ice-fishing rods can be built as casting, spin-cast, or spinning rods, with the appropriate guides added. Naturally, because of the shorter length they require only two or three guides and a tip-top, and because the line is dropped straight down into a hole—not cast—special guides or guide sizes are not needed to funnel the line. Most guides are small—about 10 to 12 millimeters; this is not so small that ice in the guides would be more of a problem than it is for any other type of rod.

The main changes come in the way the handles are made and used, because ice fishing implies severe weather conditions. Thus, avoid metal reel seats and spinning-rod rings and other parts,

because metal transmits cold. Under extremely cold conditions, your skin can freeze to the metal reel seat—not a happy situation. All-graphite reel seats are ideal, and for spinning where rings are to be used, graphite rings are available. (Naturally, if you can't avoid metal, you can cover the metal parts with several layers of masking, duct, or electricians' tape after the reel is attached. But it is better to build for the cold rather than to try and adjust for it later.) Grips and handles of cork, foam, and graphite (ideal for sensitivity) are best.

If you are building the handle onto the tip-section blank, you will build it just as with any other handle. The only difference is that the thin diameter of the tip section of a thin blank will require handle materials with very-small-diameter holes. Cork or foam with 1/4-inch holes is best, and even this might require shimming in some cases. If necessary, shim with paper tape, a tight thread wrapping, or cord or thick thread. (See Chapter 20 for details.)

One additional concern when building casting- or spin-cast-style ice-fishing rods using a standard casting-rod handle is that they require a fixed or removable adapter to fit into the handle; the adapter is glued onto the rod. Even though adapters are made to fit different sizes of blanks, they are sometimes not small enough to fit the thin blanks used for ice fishing. Thus, adapters range from a small size of about 9 millimeters (a little larger than 1/3-inch) to 7 millimeters (a little larger than 1/4-inch), depending upon the adapter style. Some blanks could be thinner than that. If you will be using an adapter in these cases, it will be necessary to shim the adapter by wrapping the rod blank with cork, thread, paper tape, masking tape, or fiberglass tape, as described in Chapter 20.

One final thought on ice-fishing rods is that some anglers eschew standard grips and handles and simply drill the end of a 1-inch or larger dowel, glue the blank tip into the dowel, and drill the side of the dowel to accept two short pegs. The pegs serve as a simple line winder. Thus, these anglers don't use a reel at all, but simply run the line through the few guides from the line winder and store line by running it back and forth between the two wooden pegs.

RIGHT-HAND AND LEFT-HAND FLY RODS

According to a tip I first learned from Lefty Kreh, fly rods can be right-handed and left-handed. This has more to do with the line as it comes off the deck of a boat when an angler shoots a long cast than it does with the hand that holds the rod. The theory here is that the thick line coming up off of the boat deck — or from the water surface — at a high rate of speed, and often a high incidence of tangle, will benefit by going through a larger guide that is angled to the side. Most of us, when shooting long casts, will funnel the line through a circle made with our line-hand index finger and thumb. A large guide (16 or 20 millimeters in most cases) canted slightly to the line-hand side will more easily funnel the line from the line hand and up through the rest of the stripper and snake guides. The handle is no different, even though the rod when built must have the guide canted and wrapped to the left for right-hand casters and to the right for left-hand casters.

In making a right- or left-handed fly rod, the wrapping techniques, other guides, grip, and reel seat are no different from those of a standard fly rod. It should be noted, however, that this method of building a fly rod is best primarily on larger rods that will be used with heavy lines and long casts. Largemouth-bass rods, saltwater fly rods, and salmon rods will be the prime beneficiaries.

RIGHT-HAND AND LEFT-HAND SPINNING RODS

Though it's rarely done, it is possible to build rods with grips specifically for the right or left hand. This is easier for spinning rods than for casting rods, because spinning rods stay in one hand for casting and retrieving. Casting rods are more difficult because they are usually cast with one hand and then switched to the other for retrieving.

The technique of making these grips involves individual finger grooves. Finger grooves are sometimes built into custom-made knives and other outdoor equipment, but rarely into rod grips. And such grooves for the fingers are not made straight across but at a slight angle. Thus, a rod grip made with grooves on an angle for the right hand would make impossible a good grip by the left hand.

Admittedly, grooves on rod grips will not be pronounced, because on most spinning rods the reel seat will interfere with all but those for the ring and little finger. Using spinning rings on a straight cork grip will allow for more extensive grooves, but it is still best to leave a flat spot on which to seat the reel foot.

The best way to make these grooves on a cork grip is to first leave the grip slightly oversized. You don't have to sand it smooth at this point, but it should be close to a final finish. Because the reel seat or spinning rod rings will already be mounted, place a rod in the reel seat. Then grab the rod with the preferred hand, holding it in a comfortable position. To mark the ridges between the finger grooves, lift each finger in turn and draw a line against the adjoining finger. Do this with all the fingers, then remove your hand and check the marks. It helps to regrasp the rod several times, lifting one finger at a time to see if the original lines are accurate.

Once you are satisfied with the position of the lines, use a rasp to lightly cut in between them, keeping the finger grooves on a slight angle as indicated by the lines. Use successively finer sandpaper to shape, smooth, and polish the grip, as per instructions in Chapter 20.

MIXED-MATERIAL RODS

"Mixed-material" in this case does not refer to rods or blanks of a mixture of graphite and glass and/or other materials. It refers instead to rods — usually two-piece — that are composed of one material for the butt section and of a second material for the tip end. First popularized by rod-builder Russ Peak, these rods have been built by the large rod manufacturers. Rods have been made with graphite butts for power and fiberglass tips for slow flexibility. The theory here is that when fishing crankbaits (for which these rods are usually made) the slow-reacting fiberglass tip allows a bass to inhale the crankbait deeper, thus producing deeper, surer hooking as opposed to fast-reacting graphite, which can pull a lure from the fish's mouth. Not all anglers agree with this theory, but that is the concept behind the slow tip and fast, powerful butt.

Building these rods is no different from building any other two-piece spinning or casting rod. The main concern is to acquire one blank with the combination of materials or to combine two blanks into one rod. For the latter, the only possibility, and admittedly it's an expensive one, is to find a graphite rod with a butt section that will fit the fiberglass tip section of another rod, and to buy both. Even if you are willing to pay the price to do this, it is best done at a local store where you can check the accuracy of the fit of the two parts or determine the degree of adjustment by sanding and fitting that will have to take place.

ROD BUTT-SECTION REINFORCERS

At one time, Fenwick produced a fly rod that was used extensively for big-game fly fishing. Basically it was a heavy fly rod with a removable butt cap and a separate long, insertable section that fit into the butt section. The rod was used without the insert for casting and during the hook-up, but after that the insert was added to increase the rod's butt-section strength. In essence, it provided a double-wall butt section to provide more lifting power for big fish on heavy tippets. This was in the days of glass rods, when heavy graphite rods were not available for big-game fishing.

Although this insert method of strengthening rods was criticized by some, it accomplished its stated purpose well and allowed the landing of big fish that might otherwise have been impossible. Admittedly, then and now, many serious fly anglers are opposed to modifying a rod during the act of fishing. Regardless, such an insert for a fly rod (or for that matter, a spinning or casting rod) is relatively easy to make.

If you wish to try something like this, it can be done by building any big-game fly rod (or any other rod) in the traditional manner, with special attention paid to a removable butt cap and access to the hollow end of the blank at the base of the reel seat. Naturally, any rod for which this is being considered must have blank-through-the-handle construction in order for the insert to fit properly. The insert usually has a small butt on the end of a short section of an inch or two, or a couple of cork rings ending in a butt cap. Ideally, the insert blank should friction-fit into the base of the rod-blank butt. If it fits too loosely, the insert blank can be shimmed with a layer or two of fiberglass tape about 4 inches wide. The tape should be well soaked with resin and then sanded and shaped to fit the rod blank after complete curing. Naturally, any such insert will have to be shorter than the butt section of the rod, since the insert cannot extend beyond the plug used in some spigot ferrules.

TELESCOPING RODS

Telescoping rods are one form of the pack rod but are built so differently that they deserve a section of their own.

Telescoping rods are just that—rods whose several sections slide out of one another from the butt end just like a telescope or a camera-tripod leg. In all honesty, I don't care for them much, but they are sold commercially and can be built by the tackle-crafter—although building them is not easy.

You can cut blanks so that each piece fits inside another for as many sections as you want based on the length of the rod. The upper end of each blank section must be wrapped to provide hoop strength. Because usually one one guide is added to each section, often this guide's wrap is incorporated into the hoop-strength wrap, or the wrap for hoop strength is used as an underwrap beneath the rod wrap.

While building a telescoping rod is simple in theory, in practice you often need two blanks to make up the rod, because simply cutting a blank into several pieces and sliding each one into a larger section will result in too much net loss of blank length. It also results in too much extra blank length inside the rod, although with measuring, marking, and trimming this can be reduced.

Unfortunately, there is no way to plan all of this out, because there is no easy way to measure the inside diameter of the rod blank at several points on the rod. You just have to cut and hope for the best. For this reason, it is best to use this method only if you have a scrap blank that you care little about, or if you wish to experiment just for the sake of experimenting.

To measure and check the rod, you just have to cut—say, a 6-foot rod into four pieces—and then slide each section into the next larger section and see how long a rod you get when the sections are pulled out. Obviously, a rod with a shallow gradual taper is better suited for this, because a steep taper will result in too much rod being "lost" inside the previous section.

Once you have pulled the rod sections out so that they are snug inside the previous sections, use a felt-tip marker to mark each blank section at its exit point from the previous section. Then remove the blank sections and check for the mark that will indicate the exit point of that section. If you are satisfied with the result you had and are confident you will not be losing too much length, cut off any excess butt ends but leave about 4 to 5 inches below the marks on each section.

Then reinsert the sections and check for any looseness or play. If there is some, you might have to sand slightly or remove the section and add some epoxy glue to build up the blank for sanding and precise fitting to the inside of the larger section. If you add glue, use the 5-minute kind or rotate the rod section—just as you would do on a curing motor with rod-wrap finish—to produce an even coat of epoxy that will be easier to sand and size later on.

Once you are ready to build the rod, add the handle components to the butt section first, because you will not be able to do this after the internal rod parts are assembled. You can make any kind of rod you want, using any handle components previously described to make casting, spin-cast, or spinning rods. Once the handle is built on, insert the sections, and at the end of each, apply a hoop-wrap underwrap followed by a guide wrap, or just use a guide wrap at the end of the rod, which will also give the rod hoop strength. Glue the tip-top to the end, pull the rod out to full length, and coat it with epoxy rod finish. Rotate the rod while the finish is curing, and the rod is ready to go.

An additional thought is that there is only one guide for each section on a telescoping rod, which is often too few for a good distribution of stress. Naturally, you can't wrap another guide on each section, because this would prevent the rod from collapsing—the very reason for making it tele-scope in the first place. You can, however, use scrap sections of blank that were cut away, cut small 2- to 3-inch lengths that will fit onto the rod in the appropriate places, and wrap a guide to these. This then creates sliding friction-fit guides in the middle of the sections; thus these guides can slide free and still allow the rod to telescope after fishing. Naturally, the guides will take up a little more space, so the resulting collapsed rod will be longer with these sliding guides than with-out, but the action and stress-distribution will be much improved.

Add these short lengths to each rod section, then slide the rod sections in place (all after build-ing the handle), wrapping the guides in place on the ends of the sections and on the short sliding-guide sections. Finish as previously described.

OTHER POSSIBILITIES

There are some other rod variations. One, which seems to get reinvented every ten years or so, is the idea of avoiding guides completely and running the line off the reel, up through the center of a hollow blank and out through a special tip-top that is almost like a ceramic tip on a fly-tyer's bobbin. One company several years ago even had a rod in which the line flowed off the casting or spin-cast reel normally, but then at the upper end of the rod went through a short (perhaps 2 feet long) length of blank that was spliced to, but did not make a continuous tunnel with, the lower portion of the blank.

The problem with any of these methods is that basically they will not work well, at least as far as current development in rods is concerned. To make them, you have to drill a hole in the blank—which then has to be reinforced—a foot or two up the handle in order for the line to flow from the reel into the blank. Then you must figure out how to make a tip-top, since nothing appropriate is commercially available. Assuming you overcome all this, the main problem is that the line running through the blank creates excessive friction, and the inside of the blank rapidly chews up the line. As great as this idea sounds, avoid it and stick to rods with guides.

Another rod variation that is difficult or im-possible for the home tackle-chafter is to make pack rods with several extra sections that make up a rod of varying lengths and even varying actions, depending upon which section is used where. Although manufacturers have done this success-fully, the difficulty for the home craftsman is in finding the right length, taper, and fit of short blank sections or in being able to cut and fit sections to achieve these. In essence, this rod is like a pack rod with extra sections. One possibility if you ever end up with extra butt sections or with scraps that can be made into extra butt sections is to make one butt section with a spinning grip and reel seat and another with a casting handle. Us-ually there will have to be a compromise on the guides so that the rod will work with either handle, but this is a good workable variation for a double-duty rod if you have an extra butt section.

Appendix A

Rod and Tackle Care

To cover the basics of tackle care would require a book of its own, and indeed one has been written on the subject. My book *Tackle Care: The Tackle Maintenance Handbook* (Lyons and Burford, 1987) describes not only tackle you can build but also other types of tackle, including reels, boots and waders, accessory equipment, all types of lures and hooks, field tool kits, and more. The 151-page book contains extensive photos that illustrate various phases of tackle care and repairs. For detailed information on care and repair of all types of tackle, consult *Tackle Care.*

This appendix will provide some general information on the types of problems you can encounter when fishing with your home-crafted rods, lures, and miscellaneous equipment. Obviously, tackle care is important. Once you build lures or a custom rod, you want them to stay nice—that's where proper care comes into play

Proper care begins in the home by properly storing rods in cases or racks and avoiding over-stressing the rod by standing it in a corner or piling equipment on top of it. Lures should be stored properly, which means that hard baits should be separated from soft-plastic lures to prevent the solvents and plasticizers in the soft plastics from harming the finish of other items. Similarly, soft-plastic lures should be separated by color, because mixed colors will bleed into one another and ruin the lures. If you store soft plastics you have molded (or purchased), make sure they are stored in "worm-proof" containers. Almost all modern tackle boxes made today are worm-proof.

During travel, keep lures properly separated and stored, and keep your rods cased and protected. When fishing, make sure that lures are hung in racks on a boat or are kept in tackle boxes until they are needed. Rods should be similarly racked or stored so that they will not cause accidents or get stepped on.

Once fishing is done, tackle should be checked and cleaned. This is necessary to prevent corrosion if the tackle has been used in or around salt water. Clean rods with a good soaking from a garden hose or by rinsing in a shower. Scrub the rod lightly with a brush or washcloth and allow it to dry thoroughly before casing or racking it. Pay particular attention to the threads and hoods of reel seats and around the frames of guides. Check guides for any chipping, grooving, or cracking of the guide ring, and replace guides if necessary. A new finish coat can be added over the old. Tip-tops often break more frequently than other guides, yet are easy to replace. Mark the rod blank to protect it, heat the tip-top tube, slide it off, add more heat-set cement, and fit on a new tip-top.

If desired, smooth and clean the cork grip with fine sandpaper. Butt caps sometimes come off but are easily glued back on.

Rod blanks are often rejuvenated by the use of paraffin, candle wax, or a lubricant (such as U-40 Ferrule Lube) to get a good friction fit of the two sections. Rod wraps on guides should be checked and the finish replaced if it is chipped or scratched.

Reels, though they are not covered in this book, should be rinsed, and the drags should be backed off to preserve the soft drag washers. Once the reel is clean, spray its metal parts with a demoisturizer. Check the line capacity and respool with new premium line if necessary.

It also helps to rinse off lures and to allow them to dry before being stored. If the tackle box is noticeably damp from wet lures or a drizzle, open the box to allow it to dry thoroughly before storing lures and closing it up again.

Check hooks and sharpen them with a good hook sharpener. Lures that have chipped finishes can be repainted following the methods outlined in Chapter 15.

Specific lures need specific care. Often it helps to polish spinners, spinnerbait blades, buzzbait blades, and spoons with a metal or silver polish. The life of skirts on jigs and spinnerbaits is often prolonged by cleaning and drying them thoroughly, then coating them with talcum powder, cornmeal, or cornstarch to prevent the rubber from sticking to itself.

Fur skirts, such as are found on some jigs, should be washed gently, combed out, and allowed to dry.

Check the hardware on all lures: Jump rings, split rings, hook harnesses, screw eyes, and so on should all be checked for strength and durability. If there is any sign of weakness or corrosion, remove and replace the part.

Lures can be washed, but do not drop them in hot or boiling water. Hollow-plastic crankbaits in particular can be deformed by the heat. Check wood plugs for any cracks that can lead to warpage and repair them by coating the area with a clear epoxy finish.

Appendix B

Sales of Tackle

This book is meant to be a handbook for the tackle and fishing hobbyist — not a business manual for the fledgling manufacturer. However, it is likely that some readers will sell or attempt to sell the tackle they've made following the methods outlined. Several things must be considered before beginning such a venture. First, most manufacturing processes are different from those outlined here not so much in the methods used but in assembly-line procedures and some of the manufacturing equipment. For example, many jig and sinker manufacturers use expensive centrifugal molding machines in which two-part molds are in the shape of a wheel. The wheel is spun at high speed and the molten lead is poured into a central cavity and is moved by centrifugal force to the mold cavities in the outer edges. Soft-plastic worms are made in similar two-part aluminum molds that create a number of worms at one time: The molds are fed from 55-gallon drums of liquid plastic.

A more important consideration is in dealing with the legal aspects of manufacturing tackle. Some of these are the laws requiring the payment of excise tax on tackle items, the result of the Wallop/Breaux Act and the previous Dingall/Johnson Act. The original act of 1951 required a tax on most fishing tackle; the 1984 W/B Act supplemented this and broadened it. Officially, the act is known as the Federal Aid in Sport Fish Restoration Fund, noted by a small logo.

YOUR PURCHASE SUPPORTS

Your purchase of fishing equipment and motor boat fuels supports Sport Fish Restoration and boating access facilities

The two acts and their resultant laws require the collection of a ten percent excise tax on most fishing tackle (three percent on depth finders, but ten percent on the rods and lures that would be applicable here). This tax is then apportioned to state fisheries agencies using a formula based on license sales (sixty percent) and land and water area (forty percent).

Such a regulation makes it important to have licenses, for such licenses, regardless of the amount, count in this formula. There are minimum and maximum figures to prevent inequities.

The system is the finest example of a user tax. Almost all revenues (about ninety-four percent) go to the states, with a bare minimum (six percent maximum by law) earmarked for administration. For 1991, the account hit $209 million, with about thirty-nine percent of the funds coming directly from the sale of fishing tackle.

The funds go to hatcheries, fish restoration projects, fisheries protection, boat ramps, and boating safety programs (some of the money comes from a formula for paid boating taxes), and thus is returned to the fisherman. All manufacturers and importers are required to pay this tax. If you are considering manufacturing or selling tackle, consult the booklet *Dingell-Johnson/Wallop-Breaux: The Federal Aid In Sport Fish Restoration Program,* available free from the Sport Fishing Institute: 1010 Massachusetts Avenue NW, Washington, DC 20001; (202) 898-0770. Another manual, *GUIDE TO THE PAYMENT OF FEDERAL EXCISE TAXES ON SPORT FISHING EQUIPMENT,* has been published by the American Fishing Tackle Manufacturers Association: 1250 Grove Avenue, Suite 300, Barrington, Il 60010; (708) 381-9490. Contact the association for availability and price.

One final point: There seem to be constant raids or threats of raids on this fund from Congress. It is important to remind our congressmen that these taxes are *user fees* creating dedicated funds for fisheries from fishermen and manufacturers. Such funds should not be appropriated for the general revenue or to reduce our deficit-spending problems!

An additional consideration is the increasing importance of trademark registration by manufacturers of their products. More and more manufacturers are applying for and being granted trademark protection. This protection applies to specific rods, reels, lures, and terminal tackle. Zebco has trademark protection on the shape of the Zebco 33/202/404 reels, Shakespeare has it on the clear-tip Ugly Stik rod, Arbogast has it on its Hula Popper and Jitterbug, Sampo has it on the shape of its swivel,

AFTCO has it on the shape of its roller guides, Red Eye Tackle has it on its Red Eye Wiggler and Evil Eye spoons, and Wheatley has it on its sixteen-compartment fly box.

This protection makes it illegal for anyone to manufacture, distribute, or sell (at any level) counterfeit products that might be confused with the original protected item. These are not patents, and unlike utility patents, which run out in seventeen years, or design patents, which run out in fourteen years, a trademark registration lasts forever.

What this means to the budding tackle designer and manufacturer is that you cannot—upon threat of severe penalties—copy for sale a product already in existence and readily identifiable as a product with a particular name and made by a particular company. Technically, some experts tell me, you can't even make one item for your own use, even if you have no plans to make more, or sell that one, or give it to a friend. The making of an exact copy *by appearance* (this is how the item is protected) is a violation of the trademark registration law. Other experts indicate that you can make particular items for your own use—you just can't sell any. From a practical standpoint, no manufacturer is likely to go after you for this, but the best rule is to stay away from exact copies of existing tackle. Making exact copies anyway would be somewhat self-defeating, because part of the joy of tackle-crafting is in making new tackle of original design.

For additional information on this aspect of tackle manufacturing, contact the American Fishing Tackle Manufacturers Association: 1250 Grove Avenue, Barrington, Il 60010; (708) 381-9490. AFTMA has information on member-registered and common-law trademark names and shapes.

Basic Facts About Trademarks is a brochure available from the Superintendent of Documents: Government Printing Office, Washington, DC 20402.

Other helpful brochures include *A Guide to Proper Trademark Use* and *A Trademark Is Not A Patent,* both available from the Publications Office: U.S. Trademark Association, 6 East 45th Street, New York, NY 10017; (212) 986-5880. There is a cost for these publications—inquire about current prices.

Naturally, as with any business, you must also become familiar with and conform to the laws affecting your business, including those from local municipalities, counties, states, and the federal government. For more information, check with your local tax office or your accountant or business consultant.

Appendix C

English-Metric Conversion Table

INCHES DEC.	MM	INCHES DEC.	MM	INCHES FRAC.	DEC.	MM	INCHES FRAC.	DEC.	MM
0.01	0.2540	0.51	12.9540	1/64	0.015625	0.3969	33/64	0.515625	13.0969
0.02	0.5080	0.52	13.2080						
0.03	0.7620	0.53	13.4620	1/32	0.031250	0.7938	17/32	0.531250	13.4938
0.04	1.0160	0.54	13.7160	3/64	0.046875	1.1906	35/64	0.546875	13.8906
0.05	1.2700	0.55	13.9700						
0.06	1.5240	0.56	14.2240	1/16	0.062500	1.5875	9/16	0.562500	14.2875
0.07	1.7780	0.57	14.4780	5/64	0.078125	1.9844	37/64	0.578125	14.6844
0.08	2.0320	0.58	14.7320						
0.09	2.2860	0.59	14.9860	3/32	0.093750	2.3812	19/32	0.593750	15.0812
0.10	2.5400	0.60	15.2400	7/64	0.109375	2.7781	39/64	0.609375	15.4781
0.11	2.7940	0.61	15.4940						
0.12	3.0480	0.62	15.7480	1/8	0.125000	3.1750	5/8	0.625000	15.8750
0.13	3.3020	0.63	16.0020						
0.14	3.5560	0.64	16.2560	9/64	0.140625	3.5719	41/64	0.640625	16.2719
0.15	3.8100	0.65	16.5100	5/32	0.156250	3.9688	21/32	0.656250	16.6688
0.16	4.0640	0.66	16.7640						
0.17	4.3180	0.67	17.0180	11/64	0.171875	4.3656	43/64	0.671875	17.0656
0.18	4.5720	0.68	17.2720	3/16	0.187500	4.7625	11/16	0.687500	17.4625
0.19	4.8260	0.69	17.5260						
0.20	5.0800	0.70	17.7800	13/64	0.203125	5.1594	45/64	0.703125	17.8594
0.21	5.3340	0.71	18.0340	7/32	0.218750	5.5562	23/32	0.718750	18.2562
0.22	5.5880	0.72	18.2880						
0.23	5.8420	0.73	18.5420	15/64	0.234375	5.9531	47/64	0.734375	18.6531
0.24	6.0960	0.74	18.7960	1/4	0.250000	6.3500	3/4	0.750000	19.0500
0.25	6.3500	0.75	19.0500						
0.26	6.6040	0.76	19.3040	17/64	0.265625	6.7469	49/64	0.765625	19.4469
0.27	6.8580	0.77	19.5580	9/32	0.281250	7.1438	25/32	0.781250	19.8437
0.28	7.1120	0.78	19.8120						
0.29	7.3660	0.79	20.0660	19/64	0.296875	7.5406	51/64	0.796875	20.2406
0.30	7.6200	0.80	20.3200	5/16	0.312500	7.9375	13/16	0.812500	20.6375
0.31	7.8740	0.81	20.5740						
0.32	8.1280	0.82	20.8280	21/64	0.328125	8.3344	53/64	0.828125	21.0344
0.33	8.3820	0.83	21.0820						
0.34	8.6360	0.84	21.3360	11/32	0.343750	8.7312	27/32	0.843750	21.4312
0.35	8.8900	0.85	21.5900	23/64	0.359375	9.1281	55/64	0.859375	21.8281
0.36	9.1440	0.86	21.8440						
0.37	9.3980	0.87	22.0980	3/8	0.375000	9.5250	7/8	0.875000	22.2250
0.38	9.6520	0.88	22.3520						
0.39	9.9060	0.89	22.6060	25/64	0.390625	9.9219	57/64	0.890625	22.6219
0.40	10.1600	0.90	22.8600	13/32	0.406250	10.3188	29/32	0.906250	23.0188
0.41	10.4140	0.91	23.1140						
0.42	10.6680	0.92	23.3680	27/64	0.421875	10.7156	59/64	0.921875	23.4156
0.43	10.9220	0.93	23.6220	7/16	0.437500	11.1125	15/16	0.937500	23.8125
0.44	11.1760	0.94	23.8760						
0.45	11.4300	0.95	24.1300	29/64	0.453125	11.5094	61/64	0.953125	24.2094
0.46	11.6840	0.96	24.3840	15/32	0.468750	11.9062	31/32	0.968750	24.6062
0.47	11.9380	0.97	24.6380						
0.48	12.1920	0.98	24.8920	31/64	0.484375	12.3031	63/64	0.984375	25.0031
0.49	12.4460	0.99	25.1460	1/2	0.500000	12.7000	1	1.000000	25.4000
0.50	12.7000	1.00	25.4000						

For converting decimal·inches in "thousandths," move decimal point in both columns to left.

Courtesy: The L.S. Starrett Company

492

Metric-English Conversion Table

MM	INCHES	MM	INCHES	MM	INCHES	MM	INCHES	MM	INCHES
0.01	.00039	0.41	.01614	0.81	.03189	21	.82677	61	2.40157
0.02	.00079	0.42	.01654	0.82	.03228	22	.86614	62	2.44094
0.03	.00118	0.43	.01693	0.83	.03268	23	.90551	63	2.48031
0.04	.00157	0.44	.01732	0.84	.03307	24	.94488	64	2.51968
0.05	.00197	0.45	.01772	0.85	.03346	25	.98425	65	2.55905
0.06	.00236	0.46	.01811	0.86	.03386	26	1.02362	66	2.59842
0.07	.00276	0.47	.01850	0.87	.03425	27	1.06299	67	2.63779
0.08	.00315	0.48	.01890	0.88	.03465	28	1.10236	68	2.67716
0.09	.00354	0.49	.01929	0.89	.03504	29	1.14173	69	2.71653
0.10	.00394	0.50	.01969	0.90	.03543	30	1.18110	70	2.75590
0.11	.00433	0.51	.02008	0.91	.03583	31	1.22047	71	2.79527
0.12	.00472	0.52	.02047	0.92	.03622	32	1.25984	72	2.83464
0.13	.00512	0.53	.02087	0.93	.03661	33	1.29921	73	2.87401
0.14	.00551	0.54	.02126	0.94	.03701	34	1.33858	74	2.91338
0.15	.00591	0.55	.02165	0.95	.03740	35	1.37795	75	2.95275
0.16	.00630	0.56	.02205	0.96	.03780	36	1.41732	76	2.99212
0.17	.00669	0.57	.02244	0.97	.03819	37	1.45669	77	3.03149
0.18	.00709	0.58	.02283	0.98	.03858	38	1.49606	78	3.07086
0.19	.00748	0.59	.02323	0.99	.03898	39	1.53543	79	3.11023
0.20	.00787	0.60	.02362	1.00	.03937	40	1.57480	80	3.14960
0.21	.00827	0.61	.02402	1	.03937	41	1.61417	81	3.18897
0.22	.00866	0.62	.02441	2	.07874	42	1.65354	82	3.22834
0.23	.00906	0.63	.02480	3	.11811	43	1.69291	83	3.26771
0.24	.00945	0.64	.02520	4	.15748	44	1.73228	84	3.30708
0.25	.00984	0.65	.02559	5	.19685	45	1.77165	85	3.34645
0.26	.01024	0.66	.02598	6	.23622	46	1.81102	86	3.38582
0.27	.01063	0.67	.02638	7	.27559	47	1.85039	87	3.42519
0.28	.01102	0.68	.02677	8	.31496	48	1.88976	88	3.46456
0.29	.01142	0.69	.02717	9	.35433	49	1.92913	89	3.50393
0.30	.01181	0.70	.02756	10	.39370	50	1.96850	90	3.54330
0.31	.01220	0.71	.02795	11	.43307	51	2.00787	91	3.58267
0.32	.01260	0.72	.02835	12	.47244	52	2.04724	92	3.62204
0.33	.01299	0.73	.02874	13	.51181	53	2.08661	93	3.66141
0.34	.01339	0.74	.02913	14	.55118	54	2.12598	94	3.70078
0.35	.01378	0.75	.02953	15	.59055	55	2.16535	95	3.74015
0.36	.01417	0.76	.02992	16	.62992	56	2.20472	96	3.77952
0.37	.01457	0.77	.03032	17	.66929	57	2.24409	97	3.81889
0.38	.01496	0.78	.03071	18	.70866	58	2.28346	98	3.85826
0.39	.01535	0.79	.03110	19	.74803	59	2.32283	99	3.89763
0.40	.01575	0.80	.03150	20	.78740	60	2.36220	100	3.93700

For converting millimetres in "thousandths" move decimal point in both columns to left.

Appendix D

Size Charts

SIZE CHARTS FOR CONNECTOR SLEEVES

Cat. No.	Inside Dia.	Length	Fits-Wire Multi-Strand	Fits-Wire Nylo-Strand	Fits Mono-Filament
11	.027	.215	90	30	40
21	.038	.215	150, 210	45, 60	60, 80
31	.048	.310	275 "49"-Str.	90, 150	100, 130
41	.063	.394	480 "49"-Str.	210	150, 200
51	.075	.394	600 "49"-Str.		200
61	.087	.470	800 "49"-Str.		300
71	.115	.550			525

Courtesy: Mason Tackle Co.

Cat. No.	Inside Dia.	Outside Dia.	Lgth.	Fits-Wire Multi-strand	Fits-Wire Nylo-strand	Fits Mono Filament
1	.033	.062	.187	30	10	10, 15
2	.046	.086	.250	45, 60	15	20, 30
3	.055	.094	.250	90, 100	20, 30	30, 40
4	.070	.125	.250	125, 150	45, 60	50, 60
6	.082	.156	.375	210	90, 125	80
7	.106	.190	.400	210	150, 210	100, 130
8	.116	.190	.400	275 ("49" Str)	210	150
9	.125	.190	.400	480 ("49" Str)		180
10	.140	.215	.500			200
12	.159	.250	.500	600 ("49" Str)		200
14	.203	.312	.500	800 ("49" Str)		300

Courtesy: Mason Tackle Co.

494

SIZE CHARTS FOR CONNECTOR SLEEVES

SLEEVES

Copper Connector Sleeves 1A 2A 3A 4A

Silver/Black Connector Sleeves 2 3 4 5 6

Silver/Black Monofilament Connector Sleeves 1 2 3 4

	Description	Size	Inside Diameter	Length	Steelon® Lb. Test	Steelstrand Lb. Test	Nylon Lb. Test
	Copper	1A	.025	.250		20	4-10
	Connector	2A	.033	.250		30	12-15
	Sleeves	3A	.044	.250	10-15	45	17-25
		4A	.058	.250	20-45	60-100	30-40
	Silver/Black	2	.040	.375	10	20-45	12-20
	Connector	3	.062	.375	15-45	60-140	25-50
	Sleeves	4	.080	.375	60-80	210	60-80
		5	.098	.500	120		90-125
		6	.137	.625	210		150-225
	Silver/Black	1	.055	.250			60-100
	Monofilament	2	.065	.375			125-160
	Connector	3	.080	.562			200-250
	Sleeves	4	.095	.562			300-400

Courtesy: Berkley and Co., Inc.

Sleeves

Wire Sleeve Stock No.	Fits Sevenstrand Wire Sizes	Fits Sevalon Wire Sizes	Fits Duratest Wire Sizes	Fits Monofilament Sizes
A1	8, 12, 18, 27 lbs.			
A2	40, 60	8, 12, 18, 27 lbs.		10 lbs.
A3	90	40		15 & 20
A4	135			30 & 40
A5	170	60		50 & 60
A6	250		175 lbs.	80
A7		90	275	100 & 125
A8			400	150
A9		135		165
A10		170	480	185
A11		250	600	200
A12			800	220
A14				250

Courtesy: Sevenstrand Tackle Corp.

Selecting the correct size guide

Determine the Perfection guide size for your rod building requirement by referring to the chart. When sizing a guide needing replacement, simply use the chart to match its outside ring diameter to the corresponding Perfection size.

Lay your rod on this page as shown. Look straight down on the guide ring from above and match it with the Perfection Guide closest in size.

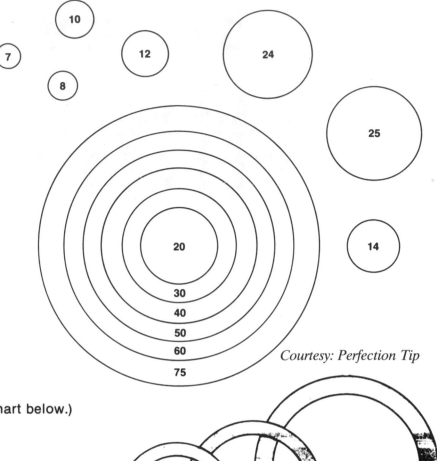

Courtesy: Perfection Tip

(Ring sizes and dimensions are shown in chart below.)

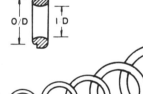

light duty ring   heavy duty ring   flanged ring

O/D   I/D

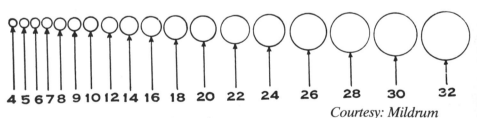

Courtesy: Fuji — DNY

64th OF AN INCH SCALE FOR TOPS

½"

Place your rod tip on this ½" mark.

Courtesy: Perfection Tip

4 5 6 7 8 9 10 12 14 16 18 20 22 24 26 28 30 32

Courtesy: Mildrum

5	5½	6	6½
7	7½	8	9
10	12	14	16

NOTE: When mounting Aftco guides, the "Size No." stamped on the guide frame should face the reel seat or rod butt.

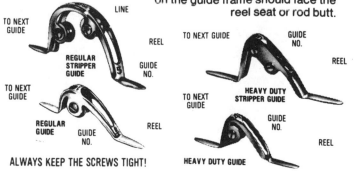

LINE

TO NEXT GUIDE   REEL

REGULAR STRIPPER GUIDE   GUIDE NO.

TO NEXT GUIDE

REGULAR GUIDE   GUIDE NO.   REEL

ALWAYS KEEP THE SCREWS TIGHT!

TO NEXT GUIDE   GUIDE NO.

HEAVY DUTY STRIPPER GUIDE   REEL

TO NEXT GUIDE

HEAVY DUTY GUIDE   GUIDE NO.   REEL

Courtesy: AFTCO

GUIDE SIZE CHART
(mm)

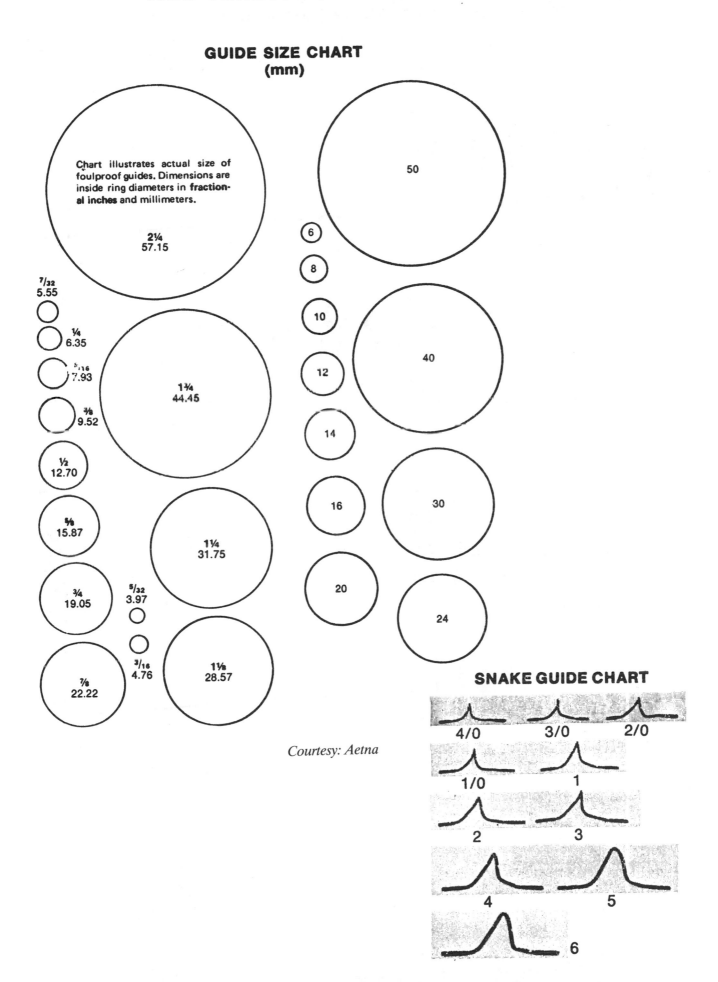

Chart illustrates actual size of foulproof guides. Dimensions are inside ring diameters in fractional inches and millimeters.

2¼
57.15

50

6

8

⁷/₃₂
5.55

10

¼
6.35

12

⁵/₁₆
7.93

40

1¾
44.45

⅜
9.52

14

½
12.70

16

⅝
15.87

30

1¼
31.75

20

¾
19.05

⁵/₃₂
3.97

24

³/₁₆
4.76

⅞
22.22

1⅛
28.57

Courtesy: Aetna

SNAKE GUIDE CHART

4/0   3/0   2/0

1/0   1

2   3

4   5

6

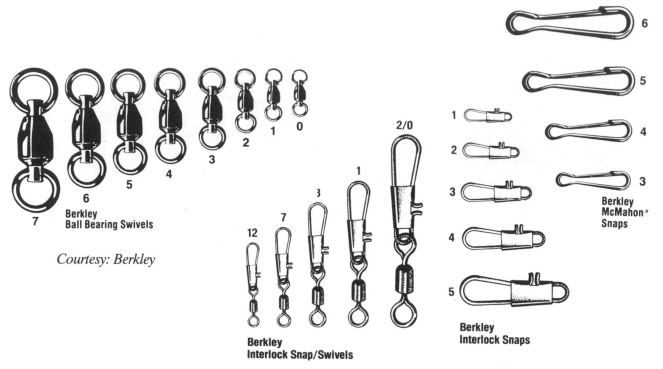

Berkley
Ball Bearing Swivels

Courtesy: Berkley

Berkley
Interlock Snap/Swivels

Berkley
Interlock Snaps

Berkley
McMahon® Snaps

BALL BEARING CROSS-LOK® SNAP/SWIVELS

Size	0	2	3	5	6	7
Lb. Test	25	75	125	175	175	275

McMAHON® SNAP/SWIVELS

Size	10	7	3	1	2/0	4/0
Lb. Test	18	40	80	80	110	150

CROSS-LOK® SNAP/SWIVELS

Size	12	7	5	3	1	1/0	3/0
Lb. Test	40	65	100	100	150	175	275

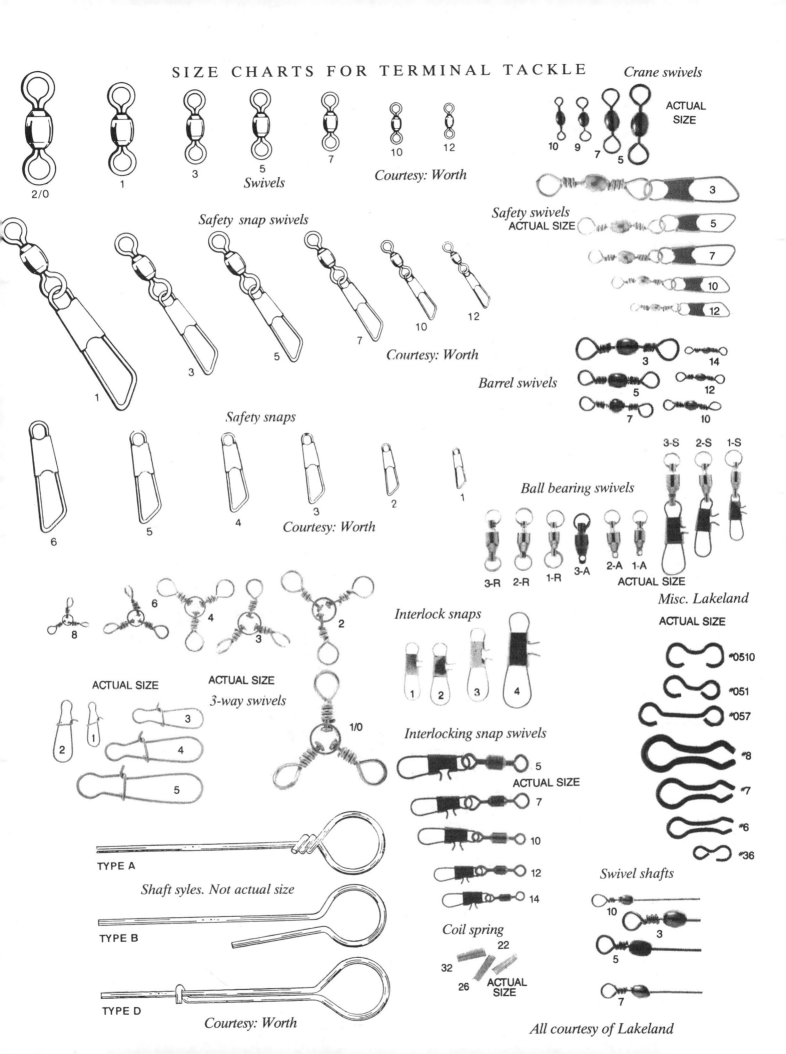

SIZE CHARTS FOR TERMINAL TACKLE

Crane swivels

ACTUAL SIZE

10 9 7 5

Swivels

2/0 1 3 5 7 10 12

Courtesy: Worth

Safety swivels
ACTUAL SIZE

3 5 7 10 12

Safety snap swivels

1 3 5 7 10 12

Courtesy: Worth

Barrel swivels

3 14
5 12
7 10

Safety snaps

6 5 4 3 2 1

Courtesy: Worth

Ball bearing swivels

3-S 2-S 1-S

3-R 2-R 1-R 3-A 2-A 1-A

ACTUAL SIZE

Misc. Lakeland
ACTUAL SIZE

#0510
#051
#057
#8
#7
#6
#36

8 6 4 3 2

ACTUAL SIZE

ACTUAL SIZE

3-way swivels

2 1 3 4 5

1/0

Interlock snaps

1 2 3 4

Interlocking snap swivels

5
ACTUAL SIZE
7
10
12
14

Swivel shafts

10
3
5
7

TYPE A

Shaft styles. Not actual size

TYPE B

Coil spring

22
32 26
ACTUAL SIZE

TYPE D

Courtesy: Worth

All courtesy of Lakeland

SIZE CHARTS FOR TERMINAL TACKLE

Courtesy: Berkley

BALL BEARING SWIVELS

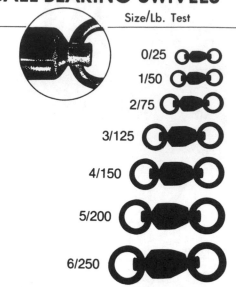

Size/Lb. Test
0/25
1/50
2/75
3/125
4/150
5/200
6/250
7/300

McMAHON® SWIVELS

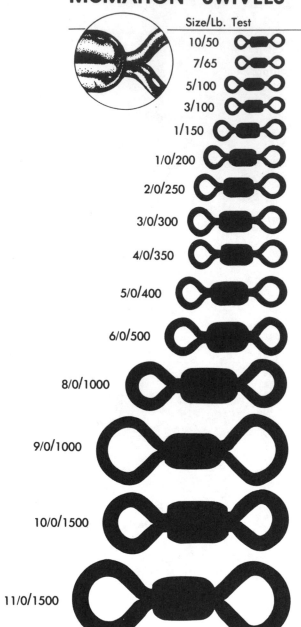

Size/Lb. Test
10/50
7/65
5/100
3/100
1/150
1/0/200
2/0/250
3/0/300
4/0/350
5/0/400
6/0/500
8/0/1000
9/0/1000
10/0/1500
11/0/1500

CROSS-LOK® SNAPS

Size	1	3	6	9	10
Lb. Test	40	75	125	175	275

McMAHON® SNAPS

Size	3	4	5	6
Lb. Test	80	80	110	150

SIZE CHARTS FOR TERMINAL TACKLE

Courtesy: Sampo

FRESH WATER SERIES

General usage: nos. 1 and 2, light spin fishing; no. 2, casting also; no. 3, spinning, casting and trolling; no. 4, casting and trolling; no. 5, heavy casting and trolling; no. 6, extra heavy trolling. The pound designation figure below each number indicates swivel test.

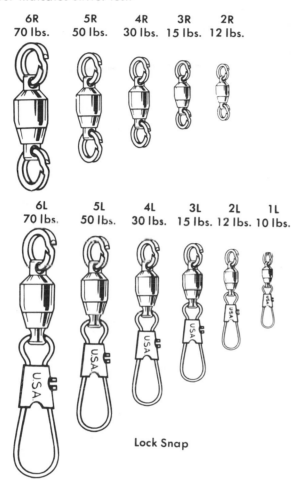

6R	5R	4R	3R	2R
70 lbs.	50 lbs.	30 lbs.	15 lbs.	12 lbs.

6L	5L	4L	3L	2L	1L
70 lbs.	50 lbs.	30 lbs.	15 lbs.	12 lbs.	10 lbs.

Lock Snap

SALT WATER SERIES

Designed for use in all types of salt water fishing. Different riggings are available for local fishing requirements and preferences.

The pound designation figure below each number indicates swivel test.

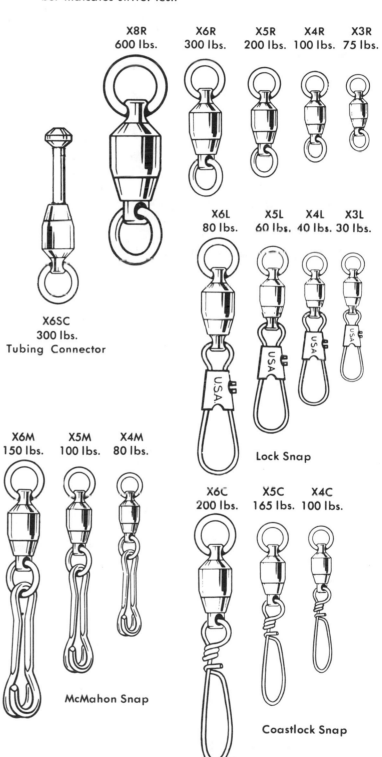

X8R	X6R	X5R	X4R	X3R
600 lbs.	300 lbs.	200 lbs.	100 lbs.	75 lbs.

X6SC
300 lbs.
Tubing Connector

X6L	X5L	X4L	X3L
80 lbs.	60 lbs.	40 lbs.	30 lbs.

Lock Snap

X6M	X5M	X4M
150 lbs.	100 lbs.	80 lbs.

McMahon Snap

X6C	X5C	X4C
200 lbs.	165 lbs.	100 lbs.

Coastlock Snap

SIZE CHARTS FOR TERMINAL TACKLE

BEAD CHAIN
Deluxe NATURAL ACTION Flexible Spinners
"EVERY BEAD A SWIVEL"

SINGLE SPINNERS

2/00   3/0   6/1   6/2   6/3

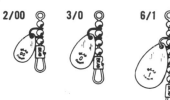

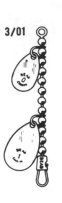

DOUBLE SPINNERS

3/01   6/12   6/23   10/45

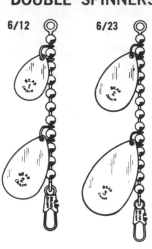
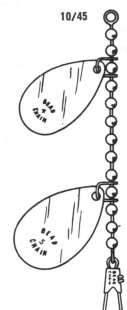

BEAD CHAIN
Monel Swivels
"EVERY BEAD A SWIVEL"

ITEM NO.	LBS. TEST
PLAIN	
21	25
61	35
101	75
131	175
SINGLE SNAP	
22	25
32	30
62	35
645	45
102	75
132	120
LOCK TYPE SNAP	
62L	35
102L	75
132L	150
DOUBLE SNAP	
63	35
103	75
133	120

Stainless Steel SAFETY SNAPS

 #1A   #1X   #4X   #5X

KEEL LEADS

ITEM NO.	LBS. TEST
1/16 oz.	30
1/8 oz.	30
1/4 oz.	35
3/8 oz.	35
5/8 oz.	35
1 1/4 oz.	75
2 1/4 oz.	75
4 oz.	150

CASTING & TROLLING LEADS

ITEM NO.	LBS. TEST
1/4 oz.	35
1/2 oz.	35
3/4 oz.	35
1 oz.	75
1 1/4 oz.	75
1 1/2 oz.	75
1 3/4 oz.	75
2 oz.	75
3 oz.	75
4 oz.	150
6 oz.	150
8 oz.	150
16 oz.	150

SIZE CHARTS FOR TERMINAL TACKLE

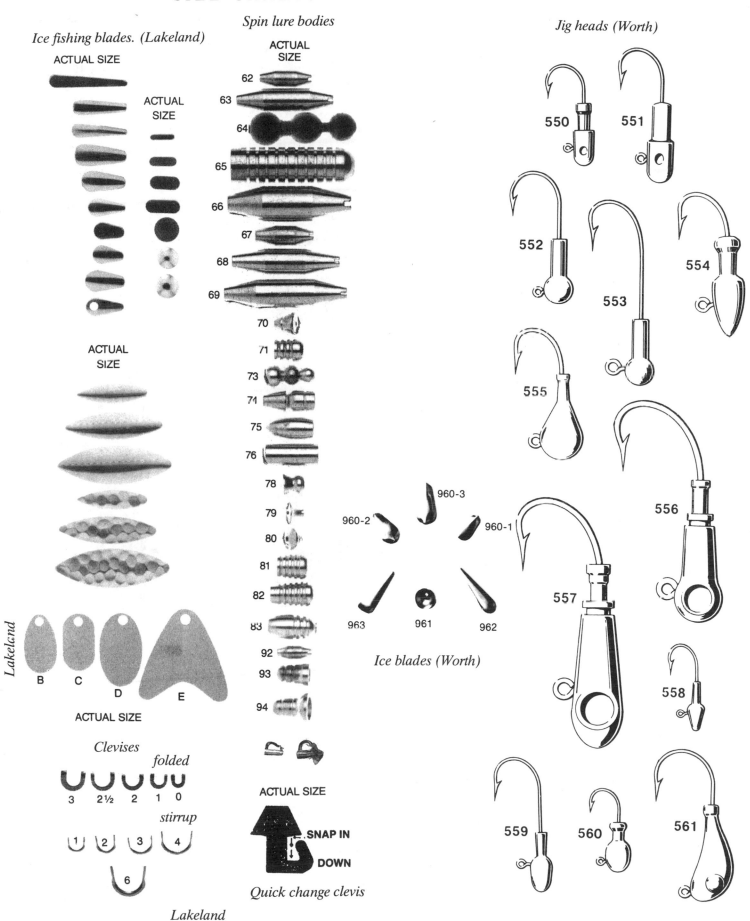

Ice fishing blades. (Lakeland)
ACTUAL SIZE

ACTUAL SIZE

ACTUAL SIZE

Lakeland

B   C   D   E

ACTUAL SIZE

Clevises

folded

3   2½   2   1   0

stirrup

1   2   3   4

6

Lakeland

Spin lure bodies
ACTUAL SIZE

62
63
64
65
66
67
68
69
70
71
73
74
75
76
78
79
80
81
82
83
92
93
94

ACTUAL SIZE

SNAP IN

DOWN

Quick change clevis

960-3
960-2
960-1
963   961   962

Ice blades (Worth)

Jig heads (Worth)

550   551

552
553
554

555

556

557

558

559   560   561

SIZE CHARTS FOR SPINNER PARTS

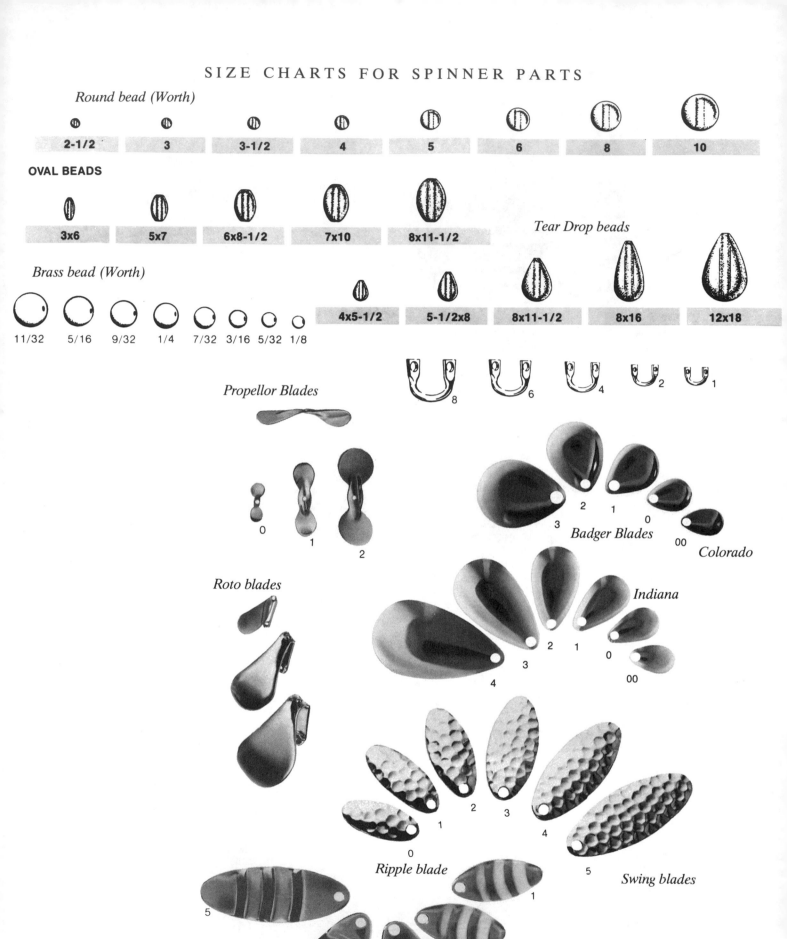

Round bead (Worth)

| 2-1/2 | 3 | 3-1/2 | 4 | 5 | 6 | 8 | 10 |

OVAL BEADS

| 3x6 | 5x7 | 6x8-1/2 | 7x10 | 8x11-1/2 |

Tear Drop beads

| 4x5-1/2 | 5-1/2x8 | 8x11-1/2 | 8x16 | 12x18 |

Brass bead (Worth)

11/32   5/16   9/32   1/4   7/32   3/16   5/32   1/8

8   6   4   2   1

Propellor Blades

0   1   2

Badger Blades

3   2   1   0   00

Colorado

Roto blades

Indiana

3   2   1   0   00

4

0   1   2   3   4   5

Ripple blade   *Swing blades*

1   2   3   4   5

All courtesy of Worth

SIZE CHARTS FOR SPINNER BLADES

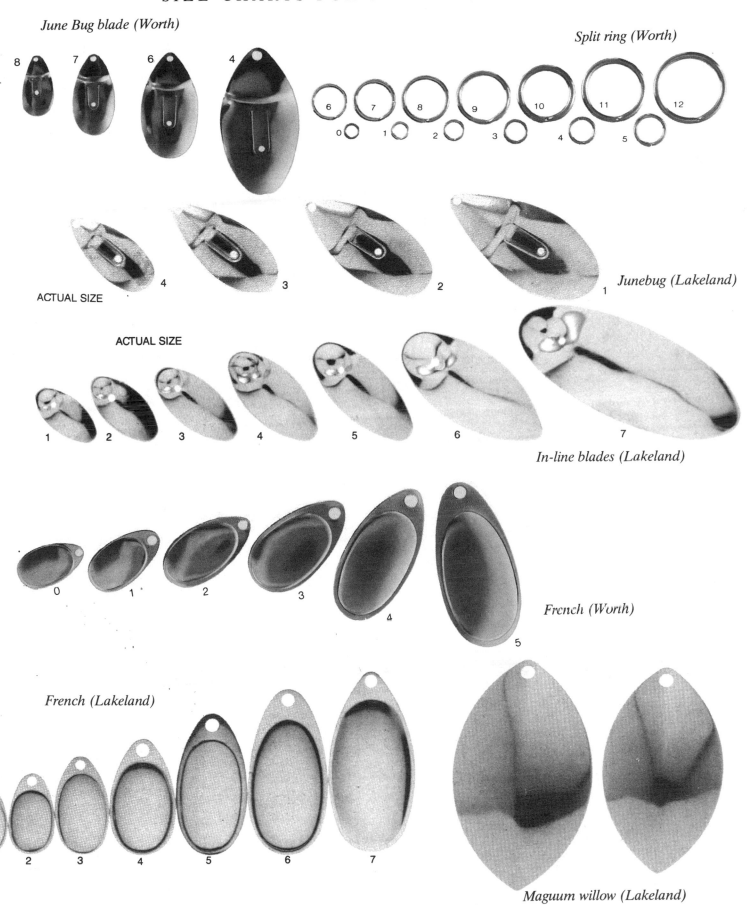

June Bug blade (Worth)

8 7 6 4

Split ring (Worth)

6 7 8 9 10 11 12

0 1 2 3 4 5

ACTUAL SIZE

4 3 2 1

Junebug (Lakeland)

ACTUAL SIZE

1 2 3 4 5 6 7

In-line blades (Lakeland)

0 1 2 3 4 5

French (Worth)

French (Lakeland)

2 3 4 5 6 7

Maguum willow (Lakeland)

SIZE CHARTS FOR SPINNER BAIT, BUZZBAIT, AND JIG SPINNER WIREFORMS

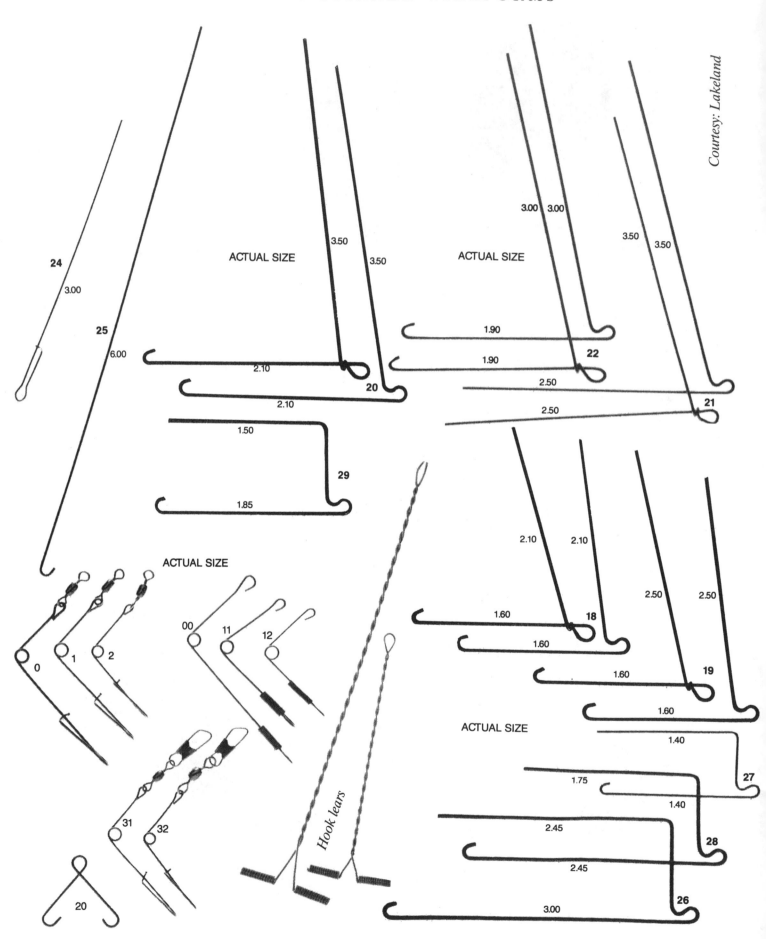

Courtesy: Lakeland

SIZE CHART FOR BUZZ BLADES, DELTA BLADES, BODIES

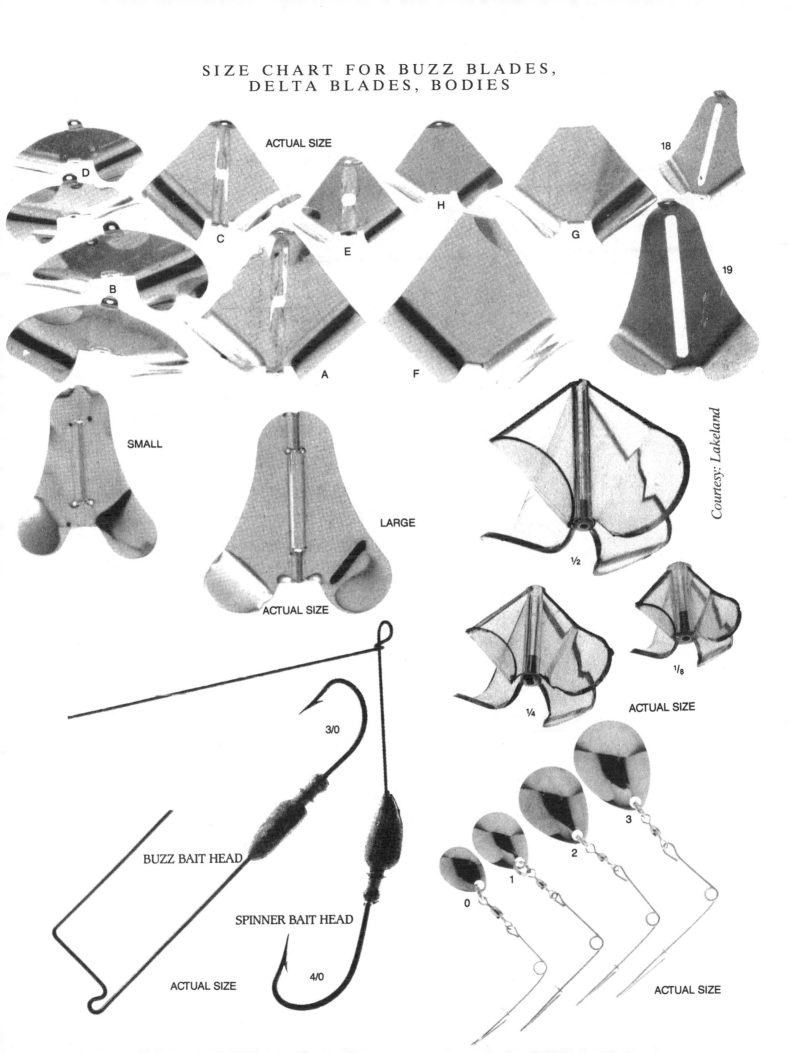

ACTUAL SIZE

D

B

C

A

E

H

F

G

18

19

Courtesy: Lakeland

SMALL

LARGE

ACTUAL SIZE

½

¼

⅛

ACTUAL SIZE

3/0

BUZZ BAIT HEAD

SPINNER BAIT HEAD

4/0

ACTUAL SIZE

0

1

2

3

ACTUAL SIZE

SIZE CHARTS FOR SPINNER BLADES AND TROLLING BLADES

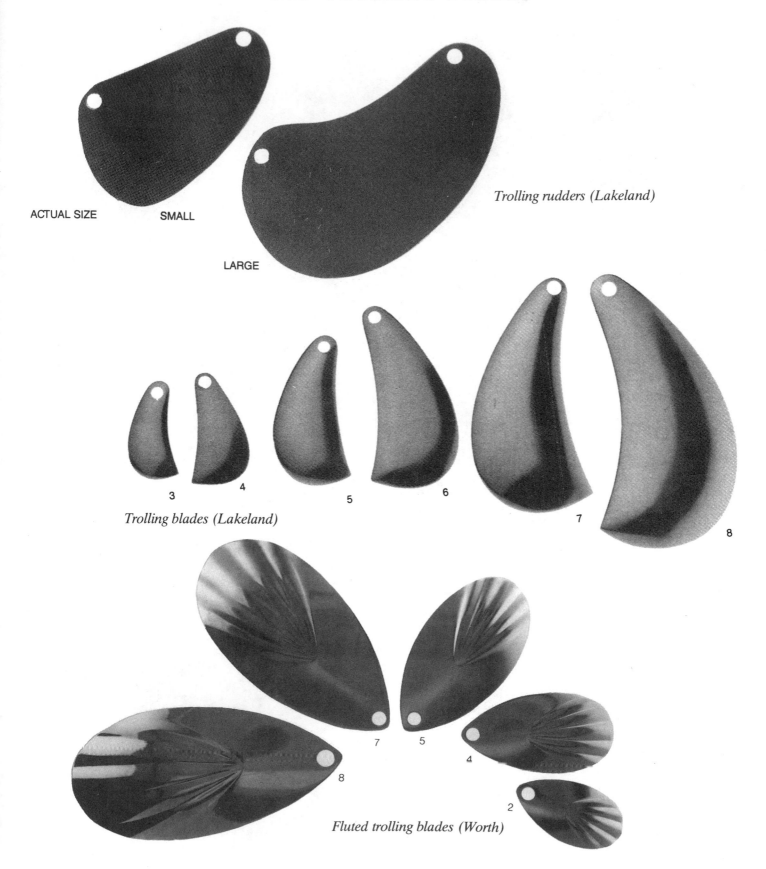

ACTUAL SIZE

SMALL

LARGE

Trolling rudders (Lakeland)

3   4   5   6   7   8

Trolling blades (Lakeland)

7   5   4

8   2

Fluted trolling blades (Worth)

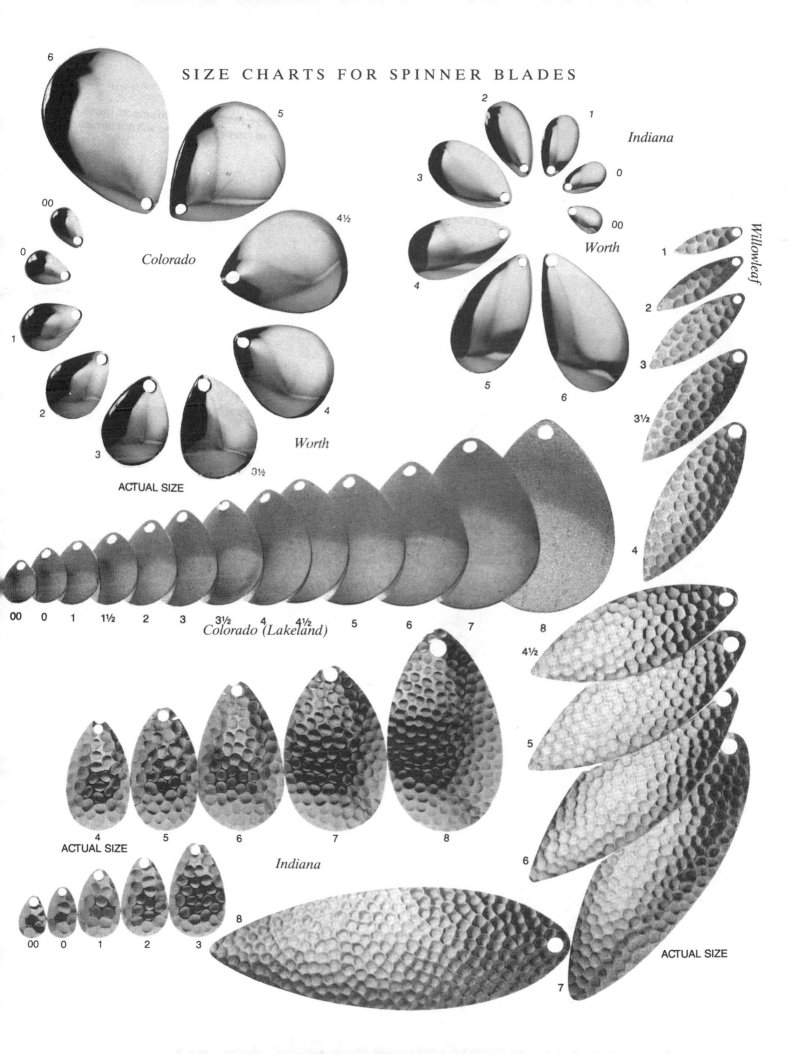

SIZE CHARTS FOR SPINNER BLADES

Colorado

6
5
00
0
1
2
3
ACTUAL SIZE

4½
4
3½

Worth

Indiana

2
1
0
00
3
4
5
6

Worth

Willowleaf

1
2
3
3½
4
4½
5
6
7

ACTUAL SIZE

Colorado (Lakeland)

00   0   1   1½   2   3   3½   4   4½   5   6   7   8

Indiana

4   5   6   7   8

ACTUAL SIZE

00   0   1   2   3

8

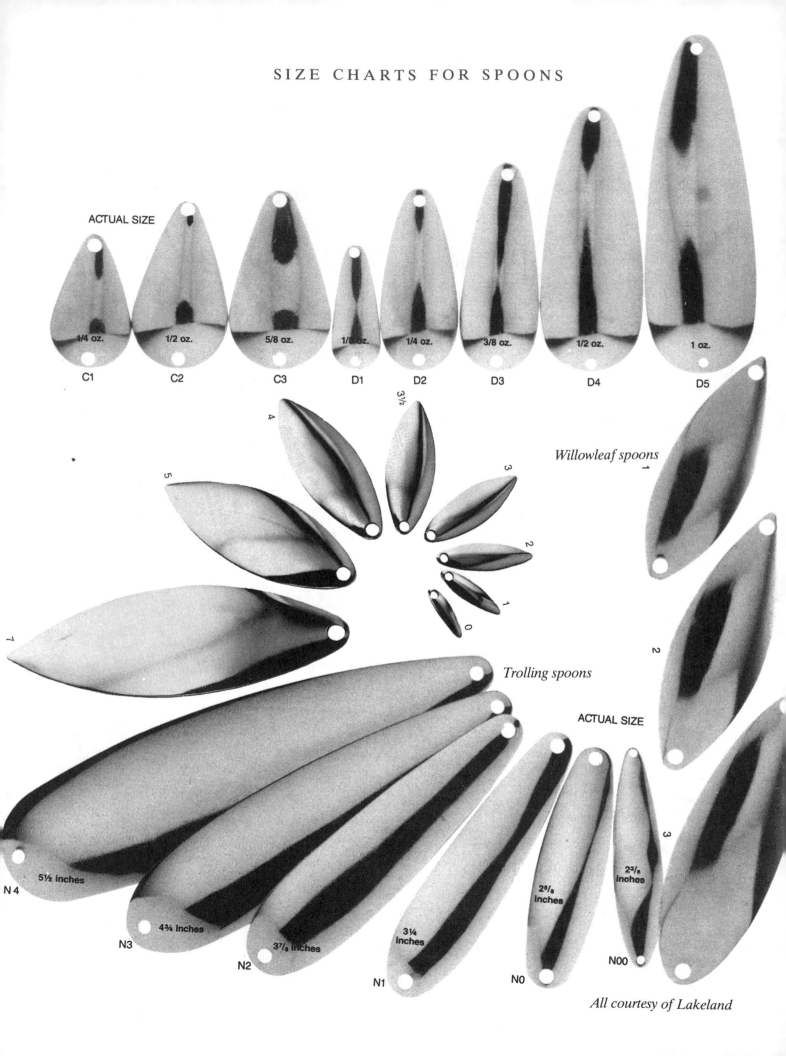

SIZE CHARTS FOR SPOONS

ACTUAL SIZE

| 1/4 oz. | 1/2 oz. | 5/8 oz. | 1/8 oz. | 1/4 oz. | 3/8 oz. | 1/2 oz. | 1 oz. |
| C1 | C2 | C3 | D1 | D2 | D3 | D4 | D5 |

3½
4
5
3
7
2
1
0

Willowleaf spoons

Trolling spoons

ACTUAL SIZE

1
2
3

5½ inches
N4

4¾ inches
N3

3⅞ inches
N2

3¼ inches
N1

2⅝ inches
N0

2³/₈ inches
N00

All courtesy of Lakeland

SIZE CHARTS FOR HOOKS

SHANK BENT DOWN SUPERIOR MUSTAD-O'SHAUGHNESSY HOOKS

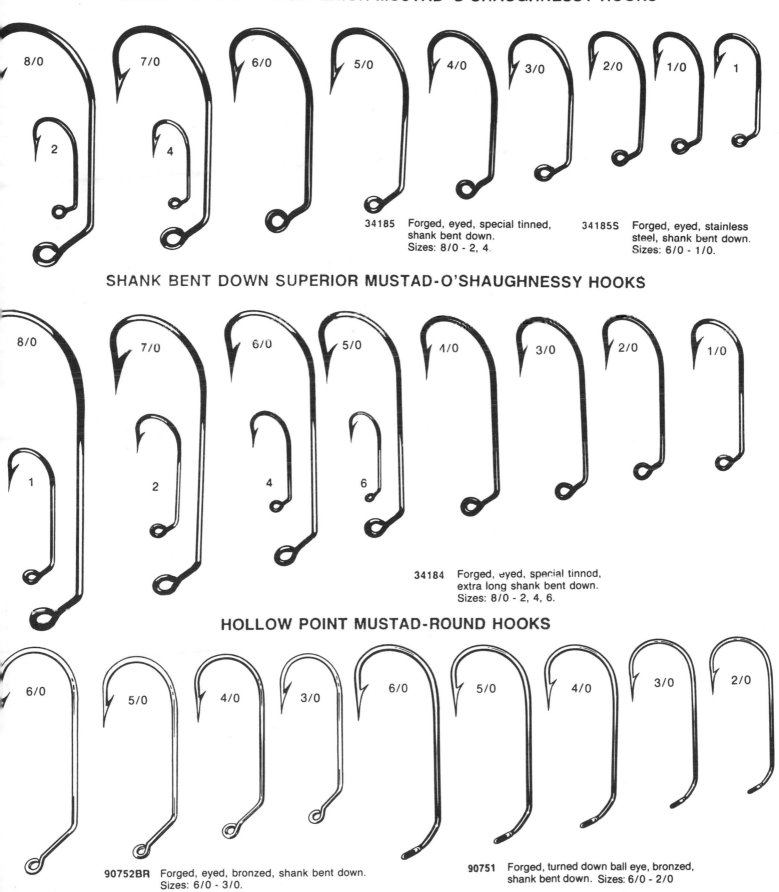

34185 Forged, eyed, special tinned, shank bent down.
Sizes: 8/0 - 2, 4.

34185S Forged, eyed, stainless steel, shank bent down.
Sizes: 6/0 - 1/0.

SHANK BENT DOWN SUPERIOR MUSTAD-O'SHAUGHNESSY HOOKS

34184 Forged, eyed, special tinned, extra long shank bent down.
Sizes: 8/0 - 2, 4, 6.

HOLLOW POINT MUSTAD-ROUND HOOKS

90752BR Forged, eyed, bronzed, shank bent down.
Sizes: 6/0 - 3/0.

90752CT Forged, eyed, special tinned, shank bent down, special sizes: 6/0 - 3/0.

90751 Forged, turned down ball eye, bronzed, shank bent down. Sizes: 6/0 - 2/0

Courtesy: Mustad

SUPERIOR MUSTAD-ABERDEEN HOOKS-EXTRA SHORT SHANK BENT DOWN

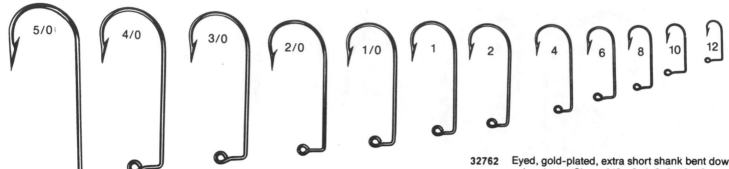

32760   Eyed, bronzed, extra short shank bent down, extra strong. Sizes: 5/0 - 2, 4, 6, 8, 10, 12.

32762   Eyed, gold-plated, extra short shank bent down, extra strong. Sizes: 4/0 - 2, 4, 6, 8, 10, 12.

32763   Eyed, tinned, extra-short shank bent down, extra strong. Sizes: 3/0 - 2, 4, 6, 8, 10.

SUPERIOR MUSTAD-ABERDEEN HOOKS-SHORT SHANK BENT DOWN

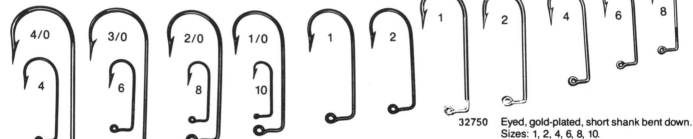

32755   Eyed, gold-plated, short shank bent down, extra strong. Sizes: 4/0 - 2, 4, 6, 8, 10.

32756   Eyed, bronzed, short shank bent down, extra strong. Sizes: 4/0 - 2, 4, 6, 8, 10.

32750   Eyed, gold-plated, short shank bent down. Sizes: 1, 2, 4, 6, 8, 10.

32751   Eyed, bronzed, short shank bent down. Sizes: 1, 2, 4, 6, 8.

SHANK BENT DOWN SUPERIOR MUSTAD-O'SHAUGHNESSY HOOKS

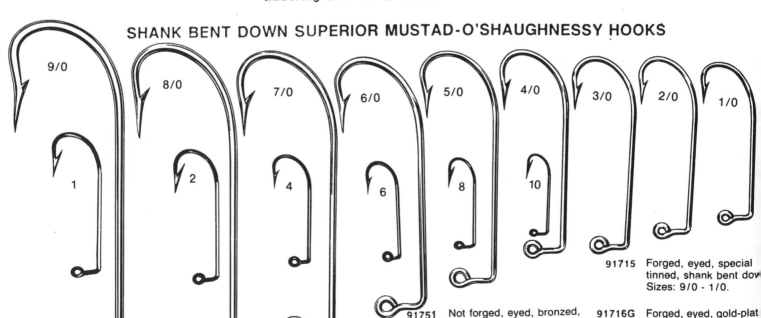

91750ST   Not forged, eyed, special tinned, shank bent down. Sizes: 9/0 - 2, 4, 6, 8, 10.

91751   Not forged, eyed, bronzed, shank bent down. Sizes: 4/0 - 2, 4, 6, 8.

91753   Not forged, eyed, gold-plated, shank bent down. Sizes: 5/0 - 2, 4, 6, 8, 10.

91715   Forged, eyed, special tinned, shank bent dov Sizes: 9/0 - 1/0.

91716G   Forged, eyed, gold-plat shank bent down. Sizes: 4/0-6.

91718   Forged, eyed, nickel-plated, shank bent dov Sizes: 3/0, 2/0, 1/0.

Courtesy: Mustad

SUPERIOR MUSTAD-TREBLE HOOKS

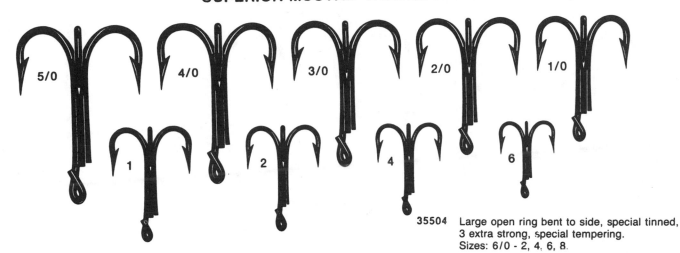

35504 Large open ring bent to side, special tinned,
3 extra strong, special tempering.
Sizes: 6/0 - 2, 4, 6, 8.

7790X Open ring and shank, bronzed.
Sizes: 2, 4, 6, 8, 10, 12, 14, 16.

35517 Open straight ring, special tinned, 3 extra strong,
special tempering. Sizes: 7/0 - 4, 6, 8, 10.

35517B Open, straight ring, bronzed, 3 extra strong,
special tempering.
Sizes: 4, 6, 8.

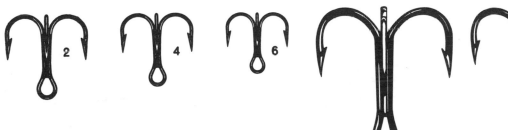

35657 Ringed, round bend, nickel-plated
extra short shank, extra strong.
Sizes: 1, 2, 4, 6.

35657BR Ringed, round bend, bronzed, extra
short shank, extra strong.
Sizes: 2, 4, 6, 8, 10, 12, 14.

35657D Ringed, round bend, Duratin, extra
short shank, extra strong.
Sizes: 2, 4, 6, 8.

35656BR Ringed, round bend, extra strong,
bronzed.
Sizes: 5/0, 3/0, 1/0-14.

Courtesy: Mustad

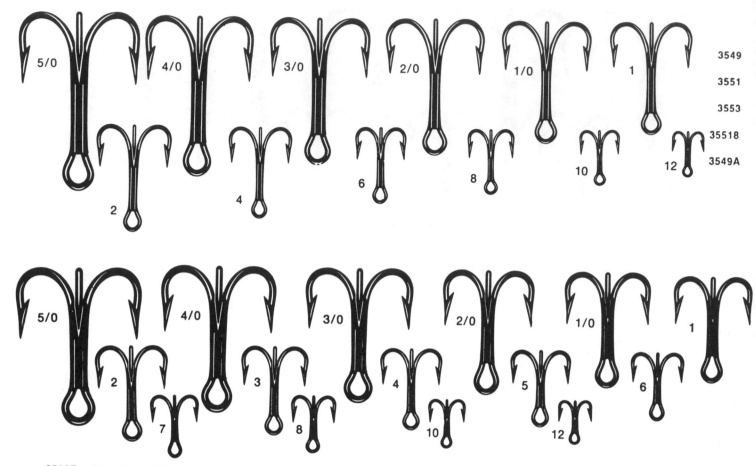

3549
3551
3553
35518
3549A

3565B — Ringed, special tinned, short shank, 2 extra strong. Sizes: 3/0, 2, 4, 6, 8, 10, 12.

3566A — Ringed, nickel-plated, short shank, 2 extra strong. Sizes: 7/0 - 6, 8, 10, 12, 14.

3567B — Ringed, bronzed, short shank, 2 extra strong. Sizes: 6/0 - 2, 4, 6, 8, 10, 12, 14, 16.

7794B — Ringed, special tinned, short shank, 3 extra strong. Sizes: 6/0 - 6, 8, 10, 12.

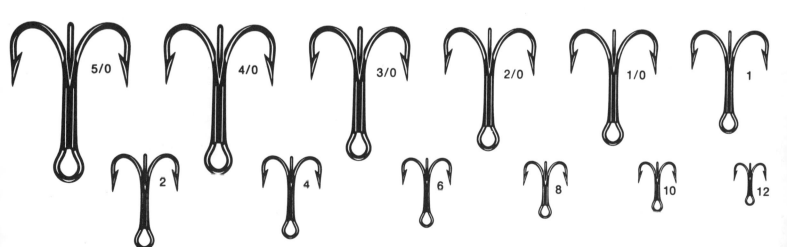

3551A — Ringed, bronzed, short shank. Sizes: 3 - 8, 10.

3553A — Ringed, nickel-plated, short shank. Sizes: 1/0, 2 - 10.

3553B — Ringed, special tinned, short shank. Sizes: 2 - 6, 8, 10.

3562E — Ringed, special tinned, short shank, extra strong. Sizes: 2 - 4.

Courtesy: Mustad

SUPERIOR MUSTAD-TREBLE HOOKS

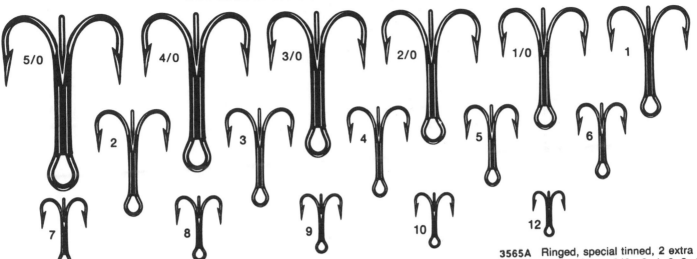

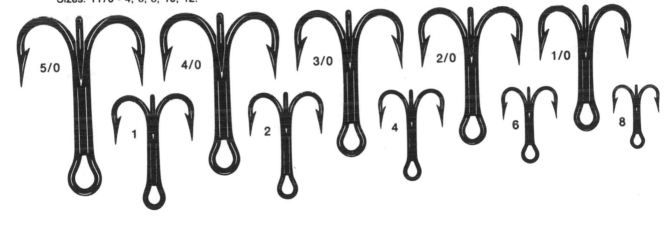

3561C Ringed, nickel-plated, 3 extra strong. Sizes: 6/0 - 2, 4, 6, 8, 10, 12.

3561D Ringed, bronzed, 3 extra strong. Sizes: 2/0 - 2, 4, 6, 8, 10, 12, 14.

3561E Ringed, special tinned, 3 extra strong. Sizes: 11/0 - 4, 6, 8, 10, 12.

3565A Ringed, special tinned, 2 extra strong. Sizes: 8/0 - 2, 4, 6, 8, 10, 12, 14.

3566 Ringed, nickel-plated, 2 extra strong. Sizes: 6/0 - 4, 6, 8, 10, 12, 14.

3567 Ringed, bronzed, 2 extra strong. Sizes: 3/0 - 6, 8, 10, 12.

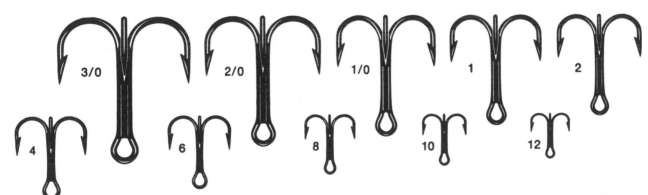

35647 Ringed, round bend, bronzed. Sizes: 3/0 - 4, 6, 8, 9, 10, 12, 14, 16, 18.

35648 Ringed, round bend, nickel-plated. Sizes: 2/0 - 2, 4, 6, 8, 10, 12.

35648A Ringed, round bend, gold-plated. Sizes: 1 - 6, 8, 10, 12, 14, 16, 18.

Courtesy: Mustad

POINT BENT IN MUSTAD-ABERDEEN HOOKS

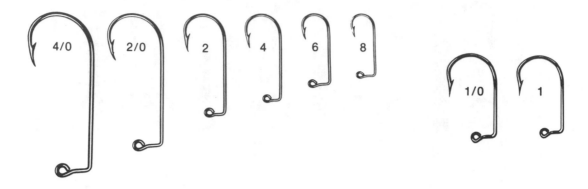

37400 Eyed, bronzed, extra short shank bent down, extra strong. Sizes: 4/0, 2/0 - 2, 4, 6, 8.

37402 Eyed, gold-plated, extra short shank bent down, extra strong. Sizes: 2/0 - 2, 4, 6.

32761BR Eyed, bronzed, 5 extra short shank, bent down, extra strong. Sizes: 1/0-1.

ROUND BEND MUSTAD-ABERDEEN HOOKS

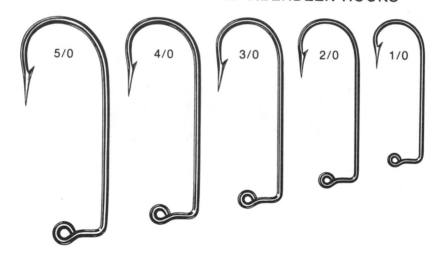

32771BR Eyed, bronzed, short shank, bent down, 4 extra strong, special. Sizes: 5/0 - 1/0.

32771CT Eyed, special tinned, short shank, bent down, 4 extra strong, special. Sizes: 5/0 - 1/0.

SUPERIOR MUSTAD-ABERDEEN HOOKS

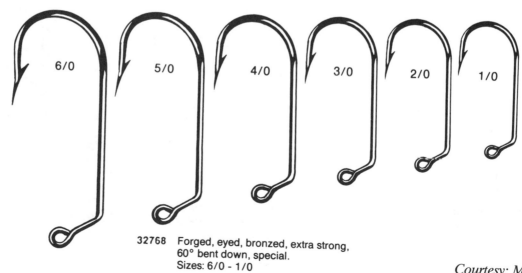

32768 Forged, eyed, bronzed, extra strong, 60° bent down, special. Sizes: 6/0 - 1/0

Courtesy: Mustad

SIZE CHART FOR HOOKS

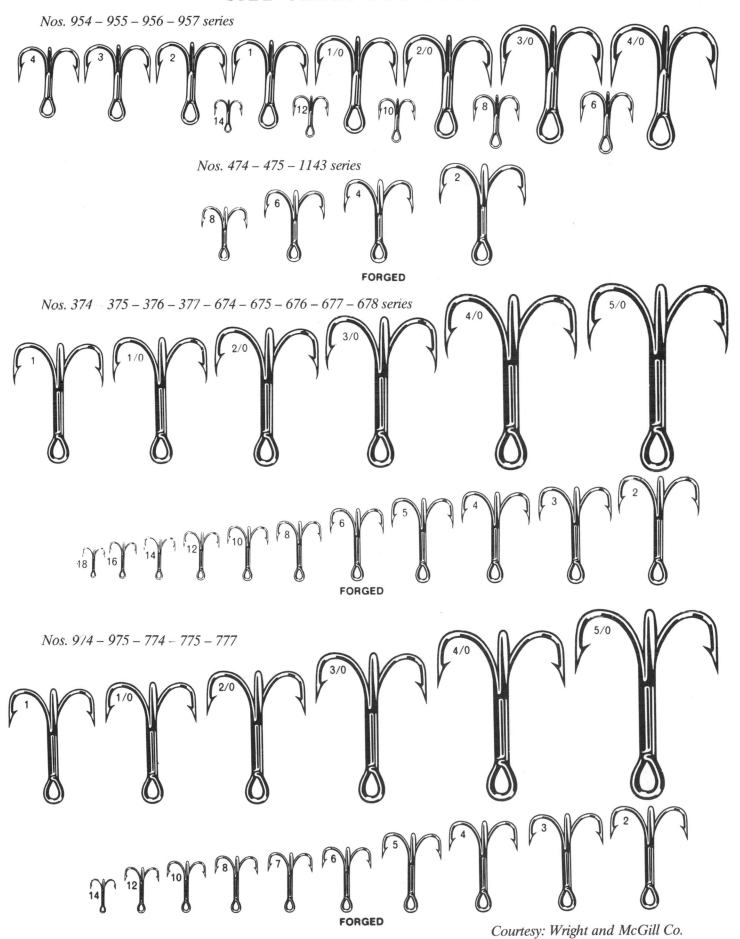

Nos. 954 – 955 – 956 – 957 series

Nos. 474 – 475 – 1143 series

FORGED

Nos. 374 – 375 – 376 – 377 – 674 – 675 – 676 – 677 – 678 series

FORGED

Nos. 974 – 975 – 774 – 775 – 777

FORGED

Courtesy: Wright and McGill Co.

SIZE CHARTS FOR WORM HOOKS

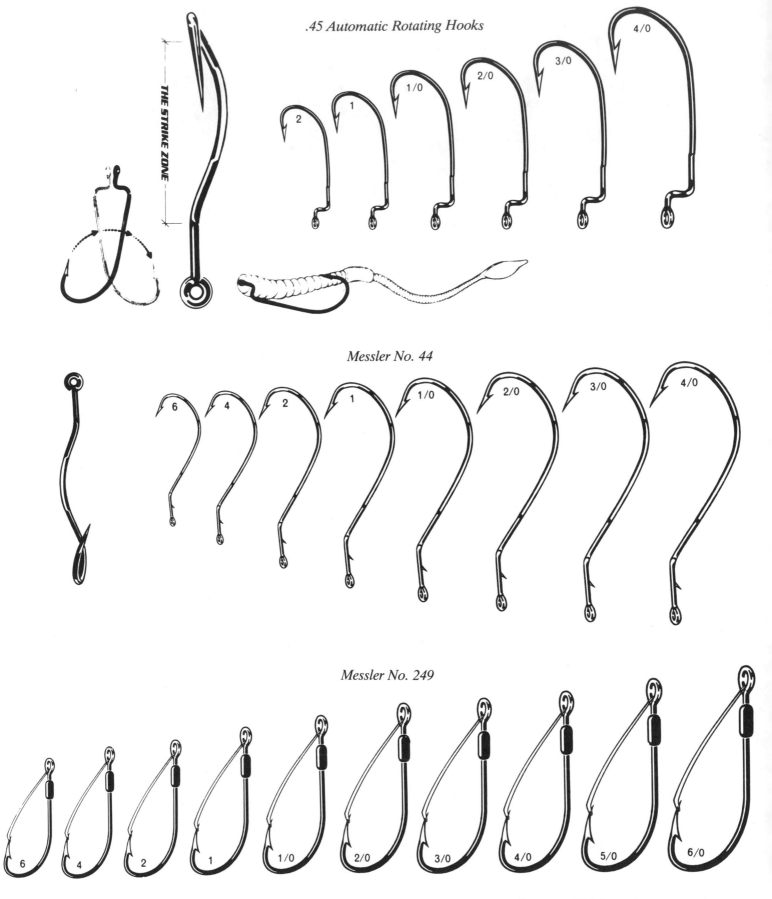

.45 Automatic Rotating Hooks

THE STRIKE ZONE

4/0 3/0 2/0 1/0 1 2

Messler No. 44

6 4 2 1 1/0 2/0 3/0 4/0

Messler No. 249

6 4 2 1 1/0 2/0 3/0 4/0 5/0 6/0

Courtesy: Wright and McGill Co.

SIZE CHART FOR HOOKS

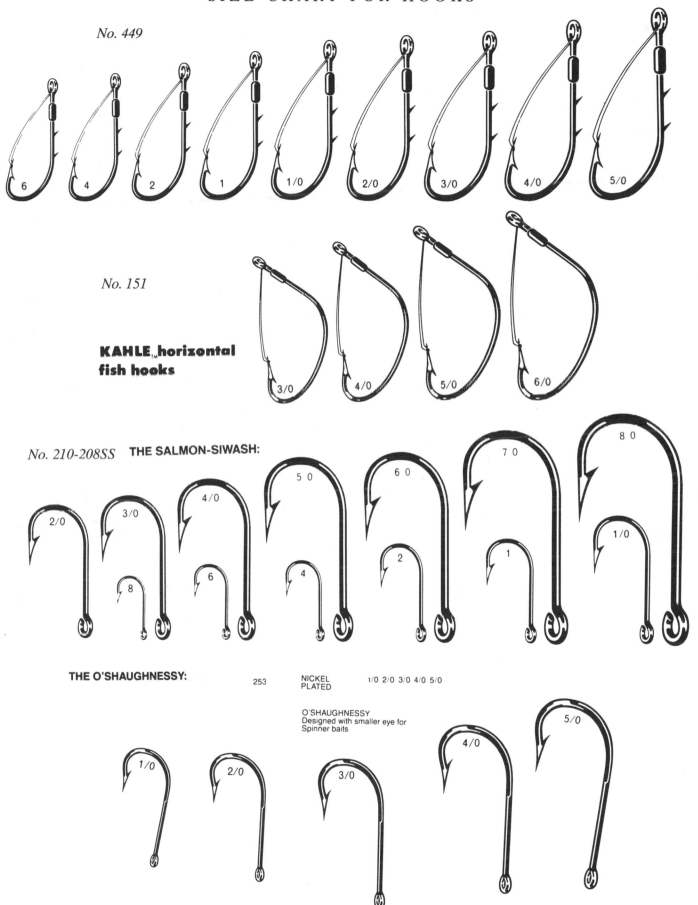

No. 449

6 4 2 1 1/0 2/0 3/0 4/0 5/0

No. 151

KAHLE™ horizontal fish hooks

3/0 4/0 5/0 6/0

No. 210-208SS **THE SALMON-SIWASH:**

2/0 3/0 4/0 5/0 6/0 7/0 8/0

8 6 4 2 1 1/0

THE O'SHAUGHNESSY: 253   NICKEL PLATED   1/0 2/0 3/0 4/0 5/0

O'SHAUGHNESSY
Designed with smaller eye for
Spinner baits

1/0 2/0 3/0 4/0 5/0

Courtesy: Wright and McGill Co.

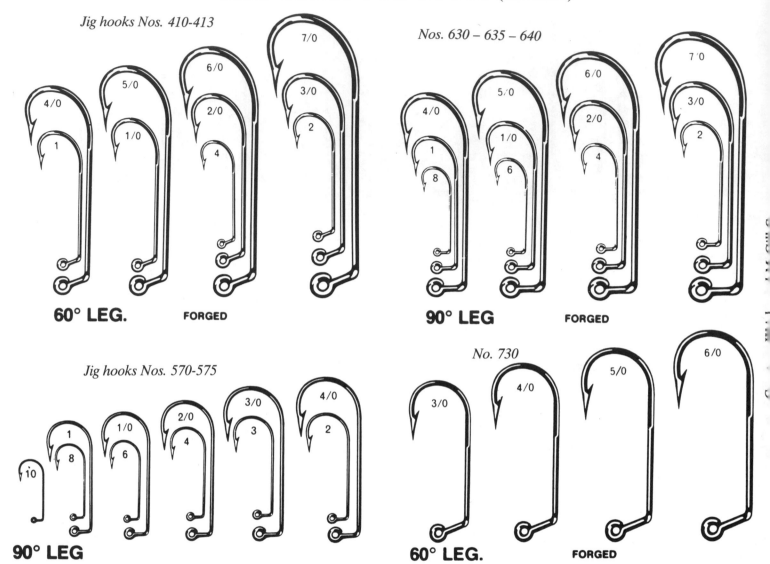

Jig hooks Nos. 410-413

Nos. 630 – 635 – 640

60° LEG. FORGED

90° LEG FORGED

Jig hooks Nos. 570-575

No. 730

90° LEG

60° LEG. FORGED

GUDEBROD ROD WRAPPING THREADS

Thread Specification Chart

REGULAR NYLON THREAD

Size	Diameter	MM	Yards Per Spool			Break Strength
			521	524	519	(Pounds)
OO	.0045	.113	100	NA	NA	1.8
A	.0070	.175	100	950	4800	2.8
D	.0104	.260	100	450	2300	6.0
E	.0132	.330	100	350	1200	9.0
EE	.0154	.385	100	220	1065	11.8
FF	.0175	.438	50	NA	NA	17.5

N.C.P. NYLON THREAD

A	.0070	.175	NA	950	4800	2.8
C	.0104	.260	NA	450	2300	6.0
D	.0132	.330	NA	350	1200	9.0

TRIMAR THREAD

C	.0104	.260	100	450	2300	6.0

METALLIC THREAD

A	.0070	.150	100	350	4800	0.85
D	.0104	.260	100	300	2300	3.1

Courtesy: Gudebrod, Inc.

7312 BZ

A wide gap 90° offset shank worm hook forged for strength used for Texan style large bait rigging in sizes 5/0 to 1/0.

5/0   4/0   3/0   2/0   1/0

7650 BZ-PS
ROUND TREBLE

's round bend design has me very popular with the ros across the country ecause of its increased oking capabilities. Made bronze and perma steel in sizes 3/0 to 8.

3/0   2/0   1/0   1   2

4   6   8

7255 BZ-NI

The VMC O'Shaughnessy SPINNER BAIT HOOK is forged for strength to resist the initial force exerted by fish using the spinner as leverage.

5/0   4/0   3/0   2/0

7161 BZ
ROUND JIG

Round bend "wide gap" flippin jig hook with a 60° eye bend forged for strength in sizes 5/0, 4/0 and 3/0.

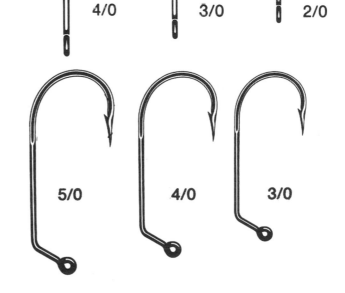

5/0   4/0   3/0

LOOSE-SIZES 2-5/0
100PACK-SIZES 2-5/0

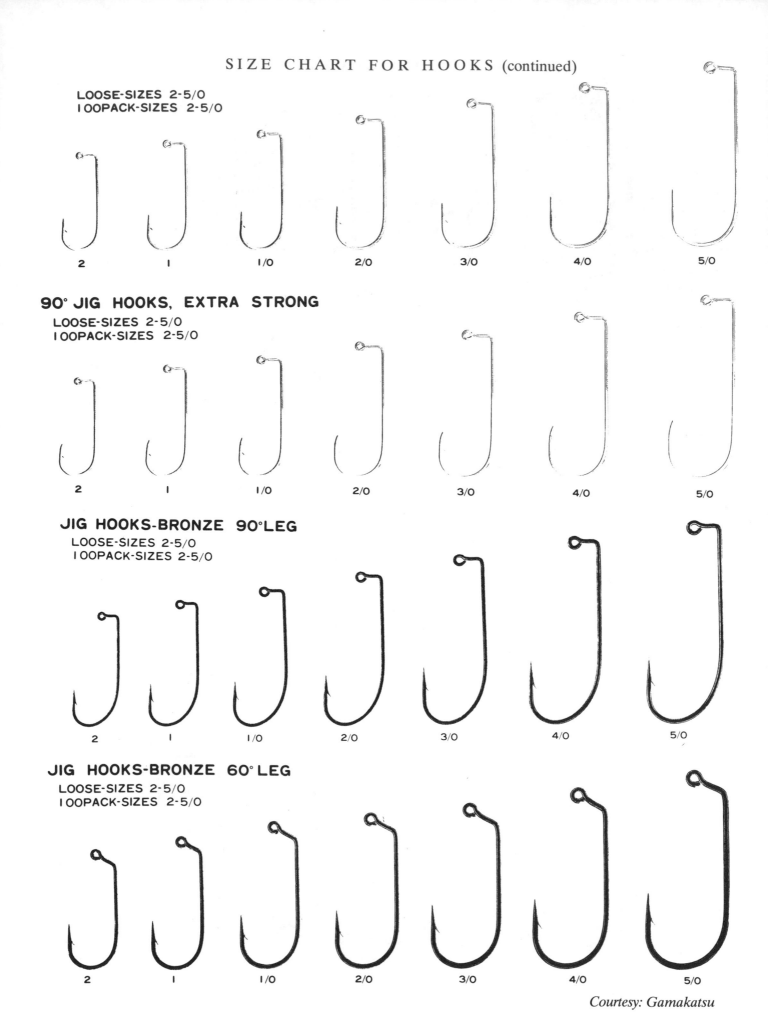

2	1	1/0	2/0	3/0	4/0	5/0

90° JIG HOOKS, EXTRA STRONG

LOOSE-SIZES 2-5/0
100PACK-SIZES 2-5/0

2	1	1/0	2/0	3/0	4/0	5/0

JIG HOOKS-BRONZE 90°LEG

LOOSE-SIZES 2-5/0
100PACK-SIZES 2-5/0

2	1	1/0	2/0	3/0	4/0	5/0

JIG HOOKS-BRONZE 60° LEG

LOOSE-SIZES 2-5/0
100PACK-SIZES 2-5/0

2	1	1/0	2/0	3/0	4/0	5/0

Courtesy: Gamakatsu

SIZE CHART FOR HOOKS (continued)

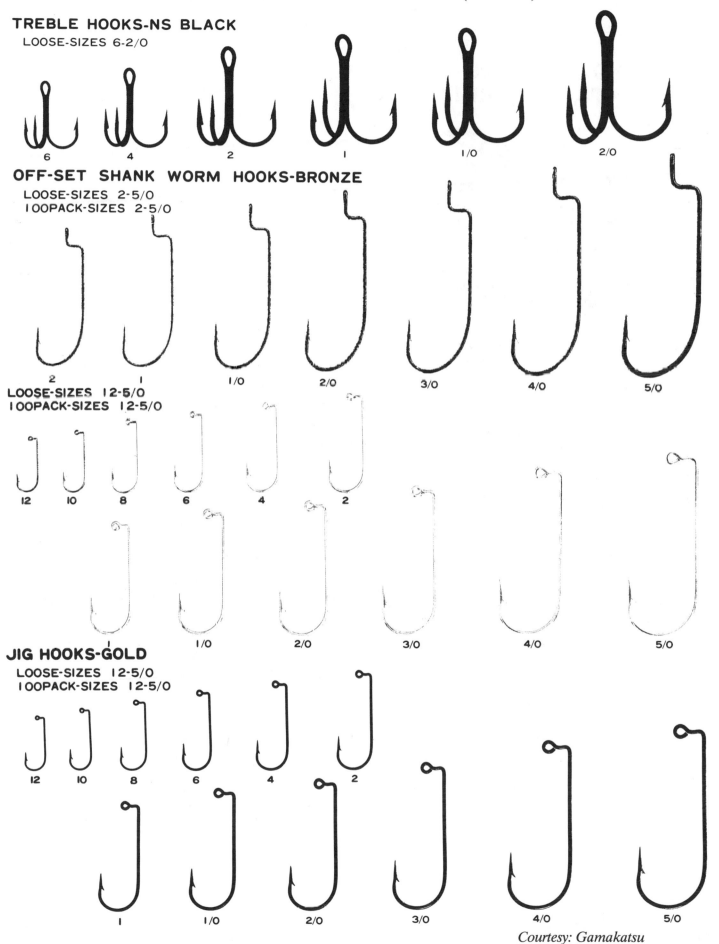

TREBLE HOOKS-NS BLACK
LOOSE-SIZES 6-2/0

6   4   2   1   1/0   2/0

OFF-SET SHANK WORM HOOKS-BRONZE
LOOSE-SIZES 2-5/0
100PACK-SIZES 2-5/0

2   1   1/0   2/0   3/0   4/0   5/0

LOOSE-SIZES 12-5/0
100PACK-SIZES 12-5/0

12   10   8   6   4   2

1/0   2/0   3/0   4/0   5/0

JIG HOOKS-GOLD
LOOSE-SIZES 12-5/0
100PACK-SIZES 12-5/0

12   10   8   6   4   2

1   1/0   2/0   3/0   4/0   5/0

Courtesy: Gamakatsu

HOW TO MAKE A PROPER CRIMP

1 Thread end of leader material through sleeve forming a loop, do not allow end to protrude. To avoid the possibility of slippage, be certain to use the proper size sleeve.

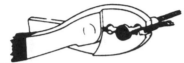

2 Hold the loop in a horizontal position - be careful not to cross wire inside sleeve - apply the crimping tool in a horizontal position to the sleeve, and crimp in one or more places depending on the length of the sleeve.

3 NOTICE HOW FIRMLY AND COMPLETELY The Sleeve Strand Swadges Around All Strands Of The Wire! IMPORTANT

We recommend the use of two sleeves spaced one inch apart on the 90 - 400 lb. test leader material.

TO GAIN A STRONGER LOOP WHEN APPLYING SLEEVES TO SEVALON AND DURATEST

1 Thread Sevalon thru sleeve and hook eye.

2 Make overhand knot.

3 Go thru hook a second time.

4 Make second overhand knot thru sleeve, draw up loop and crimp twice.

Courtesy: Fenwick

A P P E N D I X   E

Knots, Splices, and Snells

IMPROVED CLINCH KNOT

1. An old standby. Pass line through eye of hook, swivel or lure. Double back and make five turns around the standing line. Hold coils in place; thread end of line through first loop above the eye, then through big loop, as shown.

2. Hold tag end and standing line while coils are pulled up. Take care that coils are in spiral, not lapping over each other. Slide tight against eye. Clip tag end.

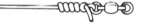

PALOMAR KNOT

1. Easier to tie right, and consistently the strongest knot known to hold terminal tackle. Double about 4" of line and pass loop through eye.

2. Let hook hang loose and tie overhand knot in doubled line. Avoid twisting the lines and don't tighten knot.

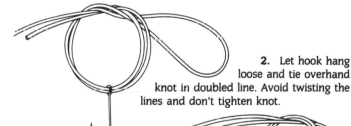

3. Pull loop of line far enough to pass it over hook, swivel or lure. Make sure loop passes completely over this attachment.

4. Pull both tag end and standing line to tighten. Clip about 1/8".

The Uni-Knot System

One basic knot which can be varied to meet virtually every knot tying need in either fresh or salt water fishing. That was the objective of Vic Dunaway, author of numerous books on fishing and editor of "Florida Sportsman" magazine. Here is the system which resulted.

TYING TO TERMINAL TACKLE

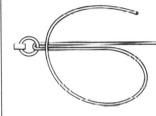

1. Run line through eye of hook, swivel or lure at least 6" and fold to make two parallel lines. Bring end of line back in a circle toward hook or lure.

2. Make six turns with tag end around the double line and through the circle. Hold double line at point where it passes through eye and pull tag to snug up turns.

3. Now pull standing line to slide knot up against eye.

4. Continue pulling until knot is tight. Trim tag end flush with closest coil of knot. Uni-Knot will not slip.

LEADER TO LINE

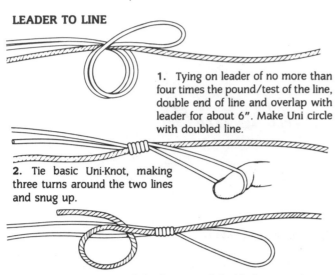

1. Tying on leader of no more than four times the pound/test of the line, double end of line and overlap with leader for about 6". Make Uni circle with doubled line.

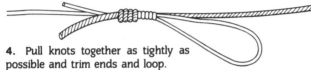

2. Tie basic Uni-Knot, making three turns around the two lines and snug up.

3. Now tie Uni-Knot with leader around double line. Again, use only three turns.

4. Pull knots together as tightly as possible and trim ends and loop.

SNELL KNOT

The Snell Knot provides a strong connection when fishing with bait and using a separate length of leader. (You can only use a Snell Knot with a leader.)

1. Insert one end of the leader through the hook's eye extending one to tow inches past the eye. Insert the other end of the leader through the eye in the opposite direction pointing toward the barb of the hook. Hold the hook and leader ends between thumb and forefinger of your left hand. Leader will hang below the hook in a large loop.

2 Take the part of this loop that is closest to the eye and wrap it over the hook shank and both ends of the leader toward the hook's barb.

3. Wrap for 7 or 8 turns and hold wraps with left hand. Grip the end of the leader that is through the eyelet with your right hand and pull it slowly and steadily. Hold the turns with your left hand or the knot will unravel. When knot is almost tight, slide it up against the eye of the hook. Grip the short end lying along the shank of the hook with a pair of pliers. Pull this end and the standing line at the same time to completely tighten the knot.

Trim the tag end.

LOOP CONNECTION

Tie same knot to point where turns are snugged up around standing line. Slide knot toward eye until loop size desired is reached. Pull tag end with pliers to maximum tightness. This gives lure or fly natural free movement in water. When fish is hooked, knot will slide tight against eye.

JOINING LINES   The Uni-Knot System

1. Overlap ends of two lines of about same diameter for about 6". With one end, form Uni-Knot

circle, crossing the two lines about midway of overlapped distance.

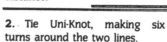

2. Tie Uni-Knot, making six turns around the two lines.

3. Pull tag end to snug knot tight around line.

4. Use loose end of overlapped line to tie another Uni-Knot and snug up.

5. Pull the two standing lines in opposite directions to slide knots together. Pull as tight as possible and snip ends close to nearest coil.

SNELLING A HOOK

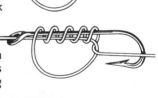

1. Thread line through hook eye about 6". Hold line against hook shank and form Uni-Knot circle.

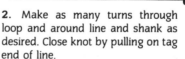

2. Make as many turns through loop and around line and shank as desired. Close knot by pulling on tag end of line.

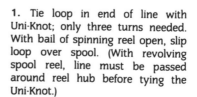

3. Tighten by pulling standing line in one direction and hook in the other.

LINE TO REEL SPOOL

1. Tie loop in end of line with Uni-Knot; only three turns needed. With bail of spinning reel open, slip loop over spool. (With revolving spool reel, line must be passed around reel hub before tying the Uni-Knot.)

2. Pull on line to tighten loop.

Knots to tie line to line — Line to leader

The two most often used knots to join line. The simplified Blood Knot for two lines of about the same diameter — the Surgeon's Knot to join a leader to line where the diameters vary considerably.

SIMPLIFIED BLOOD KNOT

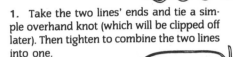

1. Take the two lines' ends and tie a simple overhand knot (which will be clipped off later). Then tighten to combine the two lines into one.

2. Form a loop where the two lines meet, with the overhand knot in the loop.

Pull one side of the loop down and begin taking turns with it around the standing line. Keep point where turns are made open so turns gather equally on each side.

3. After eight to ten turns, reach through center opening and pull remaining loop (and overhand knot) through. Keep finger in this loop so it will not spring back.

Hold loop with teeth and pull both ends of line, making turns gather on either side of loop.

4. Set knot by pulling lines tightly as possible. Tightening coils will make loop stand out perpendicular to line. Then clip off the loop and overhand knot close to the newly formed knot.

SURGEON'S KNOT

1. Lay line and leader parallel, overlapping 6" to 8".

2. Treating the two like a single line, tie an overhand knot, pulling the entire leader through the loop.

3. Leaving the loop of the overhand open, pull both tag end of line and leader through again.

4. Hold both lines and both ends to pull knot tight. Clip ends close to avoid foul-up in rod guides.

DOUBLE SURGEON'S LOOP

The Double Surgeon's Loop is a quick, easy way to tie a loop in the end of a leader. It is often used as part of a leader system because it is relatively strong.

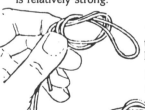

1. Double end of line to form loop and tie Overhand Knot at base of double line.

2. Leave loop open in knot and bring doubled line through once more.

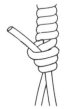

3. Hold standing line and tag end and pull loop to tighten knot. Size of loop can be determined by pulling loose knot to desired point and holding it while knot is tightened. Clip end 1/8" from knot.

Knots to form double-line leaders

Used primarily for offshore trolling, double-line leaders create a long loop of line which is stronger than the single strand of the standing line.

BIMINI TWIST

1. Measure a little more than twice the footage you'll want for the double-line leader. Bring end back to standing line and hold together. Rotate end of loop 20 times, putting twists in it.

2. Spread loop to force twists together about 10" below tag end. Step both feet through loop and bring it up around knees so pressure can be placed on column of twists by spreading knees apart.

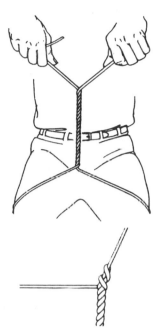

3. With twists forced tightly together, hold standing line in one hand with tension just slightly off the vertical position. With other hand, move tag end to position at right angle to twists. Keeping tension on loop with knees, gradually ease tension of tag end so it will roll over the column of twists, beginning just below the upper twist.

4. Spread legs apart slowly to maintain pressure on loop. Steer tag end into a tight spiral coil as it continues to roll over the twisted line.

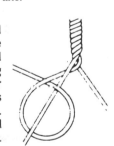

5. When spiral of tag end has rolled over column of twists, continue keeping knee pressure on loop and move hand which has held standing line down to grasp knot. Place finger in crotch of line where loop joins knot to prevent slippage of last turn. Take half-hitch with tag end around nearest leg of loop and pull up tight.

6. With half-hitch holding knot, release knee pressure but keep loop stretched out tight. Using remaining tag end, take half-hitch around both legs of loop, but do not pull tight.

7. Make two more turns with the tag end around both legs of the loop, winding inside the bend of line formed by the loose half-hitch and toward the main knot. Pull tag end slowly, forcing the three loops to gather in a spiral.

8. When loops are pulled up neatly against main knot, tighten to lock knot in place. Trim tag end about ¼" from knot.

These directions apply to tying double-line leaders of around five feet or less. For longer double-line sections, two people may be required to hold the line and make initial twists.

SPIDER HITCH

This is a faster, easier knot to create a double-line leader. Under steady pressure it is equally strong but does not have the resilience of the Bimini Twist under sharp impact. Not practical with lines above 30-lb test.

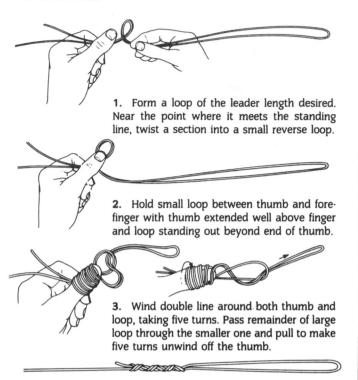

1. Form a loop of the leader length desired. Near the point where it meets the standing line, twist a section into a small reverse loop.

2. Hold small loop between thumb and forefinger with thumb extended well above finger and loop standing out beyond end of thumb.

3. Wind double line around both thumb and loop, taking five turns. Pass remainder of large loop through the smaller one and pull to make five turns unwind off the thumb.

4. Pull turns around the base of the loop up tight and snip off tag end.

HOMER RHODE LOOP KNOT

For trolling lures or jigs, this is a good knot because it allows the lure to work freely at the end of the line.

1. Tie an overhand knot in the fishing line a few inches above the end but don't snug it up. After passing the end of the line through the eye of the lure, push the end back through the opening of the overhand knot.

2. Tie another overhand knot above the first, making sure to tie the knot around the line. Finally, snug the overhand knots together.

ARBOR KNOT

The Arbor Knot provides the angler with a quick, easy connection for attaching line to the reel spool.

1. Pass line around reel arbor.
2. Tie an overhand knot around the standing line.

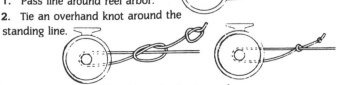

3. Tie a second overhand knot in the tag end.
4. Pull tight and snip off excess. Snug down first overhand knot on the reel arbor.

IMPROVED BLOOD KNOT

The Improved Blood Knot is used for tying two pieces of monofilament together of relatively equal diameters.

1. Overlap the ends of your two strands that are to be joined and twist them together about 10 turns.

2. Separate one of the center twists and thrust the two ends through the space as illustrated.

3. Pull knot together and trim off the short ends.

ALBRIGHT KNOT

The Albright Knot is most commonly used for joining monofilament lines of unequal diameters, for creating shock leaders and when a Bimini Twist is tied in the end of the lighter casting line. It is also used for connecting monofilament to wire.

1. Bend a loop in the tag end of the heavier monofilament and hold between thumb and forefinger of left hand. Insert the tag end of the lighter monofilament through loop from the top.

2. Slip tag end of lighter monofilament under your left thumb and pinch it tightly against the heavier strands of the loop. Wrap the first turn of the lighter monofilament over itself and continue wrapping toward the round end of the loop. Take at least 12 turns with the lighter monofilament around all three strands.

3. Insert tag end of the lighter monofilament through end of the loop from the bottom. It must enter and leave the loop on the same side.

4. With the thumb and forefinger of the left hand, slide the coils of the lighter monofilament toward the end of the loop, stop 1/8" from end of loop. Using pliers, pull the tag end of the lighter mono tight to keep the coils from slipping off the loop.

5. With your left hand still holding the heavier mono, pull on the standing part of the lighter mono. Pull the tag end of the lighter mono and the standing part a second time. Pull the standing part of the heavy mono and the standing part of the light mono.

6. Trim both tag ends.

Attaching swivel or snap to double-line leader

OFFSHORE SWIVEL KNOT

1. Slip loop end of double-line leader through eye of swivel. Rotate loop end a half-turn to put a single twist between loop and swivel eye.

2. Pass the loop with the twist over the swivel. Hold end of the loop,plus both legs of the double-line leader with one hand. Let swivel slide to other end of double loops now formed.

3. Still holding loop and lines with one hand, use other to rotate swivel through center of both loops, at least six times.

4. Continue holding both legs of double-line leader tightly but release end of loop. Pull on swivel and loops will begin to gather.

5. To draw knot tight, grip swivel with pliers and push loops toward eye with fingers, while still keeping standing lines of the leader pulled tight.

CRIMPING POINTERS

Here's how to make a crimp correctly. The procedure works with one sleeve or two:

1. Put the end of the wire through the sleeve and then through the eye.

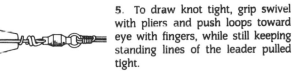

2. Bring the end back through the sleeve. There shouldn't be any excess sticking through.

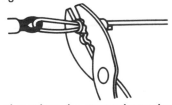

3. Using a crimping tool and matching the correct slot on the tool to the sleeve, crimp down as hard as you can near the bottom end of the sleeve. Then move up near the top of the sleeve and crimp it at a 90-degree angle to the first crimp.

HEAVY-DUTY CRIMPING

Big game anglers often use this rigging technique when they're crimping a wire cable or heavy-duty monofilament leader to a lure hook.

1. Slip two crimping sleeves over the cable or mono, then pass the cable or mono through the hook eye twice.

2. After the second loop is made, pass the tag end through the loop in three overhands.

3. Snug up the loop, pass the tag end through the two sleeves and crimp both close together as shown.

UNDERSTANDING HOOKS

Today's sophisticated sportsman knows that there's a lot more to catching fish than just tying any type hook to the line. Hooks just may be the most important part of your arsenal, and if you skimp in this area, your results may suffer accordingly.

That's why it's important to find the hooks that work best for you, and stick with them. Hook size is determined by its pattern, and is given in terms of the gap widths in the hook. The two important dimensions of the hook are its gap and throat, as illustrated by the Mustad-Viking hook below.

Note the width of the gap, clearance between point and shank and the depth of its throat. These generous dimensions make for a bigger bite, deeper penetration and better holding power.

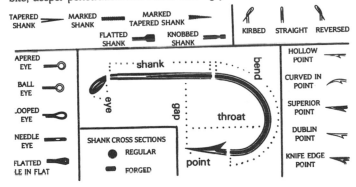

World's fair knot

Created by Gary L. Martin of Lafayette, IN, this terminal tackle knot was selected by a panel of outdoor writers as the best new, easy-to-tie, all-purpose fishing knot from 498 entries in the Du Pont Great Knot Search. Martin named it the World's Fair Knot because it was first publicly demonstrated by him at the Knoxville '82 World's Fair.

1. Double a 6-inch length of line and pass the loop through the eye.

2. Bring the loop back next to the doubled line and grasp the doubled line through the loop.

3. Put the tag end through the new loop formed by the double line.

4. Bring the tag end back through the new loop created by step 3.

5. Pull the tag end snug and slide knot up tight. Clip tag end.

Appendix F

List of Suppliers

The following is a partial list of suppliers of tackle-crafting supplies. Obviously, the first place to look for supplies is to your local tackle shop. Often it will have a lot of what you need or will be able to get it on short order for you. Tackle shops exist to help you—it pays to give them your business where possible. Mail-order companies like those listed here often specialize in do-it-yourself items more than can most tackle shops. Some even specialize in certain areas, such as tools and materials for soft-plastic lures, general lures, spinners, rods, and so on.

In addition, it often pays to check out craft stores, art-supply stores, hobby shops, and similar outlets.

These places often sell items that, while not specifically designed for tackle-crafting, can be adapted to it. Examples would be various types of glitter for finishing lures, moldable plastic, glue guns, various glues, beads, doll eyes, plastic parts that will serve as spinner bodies, and so on. Hobby shops have casting plastic, tubing with which spoons and lures can be made, glues, and lots of neat tools. Art-supply stores have air brushes, paints, and stencils. Fly tying supply houses are also excellent sources for materials like furs, feathers, threads, and other soft goods for tying on bucktails and finishing other lures.

Angler's Workshop
1350 Atlantic
Woodland, WA 98674

Angling Specialties
19520 McLoughlin
    Boulevard
Gladstone, OR 97027

Barlow's Tackle Shop
451 North Central
Expressway
Box 369
Richardson, TX 75080

Bass Pro Shops
1935 South Campbell
Springfield, MO
65898-0123

Bunda's Quality Tackle
    Components
Box 162
Nashotah, WI 53058

Cabela's
812 13th Avenue
Sidney, NE 69160

Custom Tackle Supply
2559 Highway 41-A South
Shelbyville, TN 37160

Dakota Tackle
2001 Bismarck
Expressway
Bismarck, ND 58504

Dale Clemens
444 Schantz Road
Allentown, PA 18104

Do-It Molds
501 North State Street
Denver, Iowa 50622

E. Hille
The Angler's Supply House
Box 896
Williamsport, PA 17703

El Capitan
1590 NW 27th Avenue
Miami, FL 33125

Feather-Craft
P.O. Box 19904
St. Louis, MO 63144

Gander Mountain
Box 248
Wilmot, WI 53192

Great Rip Tackle
Box 3646
Cranston, RI 02910

Hilts Molds
1461 East Lake Mead Drive
Henderson, NY 89015

Industrial Art Supply
5724 West 36th Street
Minneapolis, MN 55416

Jann's Sportsman's
    Supplies
Box 4315
Toledo, OH 43609

Jerry's Tackle Shop
604 12th Street
Highland, IL 62249-1820

JoCo
2301 Galilee
Zion, IL 60099

Kaufmann's Streamborn
Box 23032
Portland, OR 97223

Mac's Shark River
    Tackle
1301 Highway 35
Neptune, NJ 07753

Madison River Fishing
    Company
Box 627
109 Main Street
Ennis, MT 59729

Midland Tackle
    Company
66 Route 17
Sloatsburg, NY 10974

Netcraft Fishing Tackle
2800 Tremainsville Road
Toledo, OH 43613

Reed Tackle
Box 1250
Marshalls Creek,
PA 18335

Shoff Tackle Supply
P.O. Box 1227
Kent, WA 98035-1227

Sportsmans Guide
965 Decatur
Avenue North
Golden Valley,
MN 55427

The Surfcaster
113 Maywood Road
Box 1731
Darien, CT 06820-1731

Tackle Craft
1440 Kennedy Road
Box 280
Chippewa Falls,
WI 54729

Tackle Service Center
246 East Washington
Mooresville, IN 46158

West Falmouth Tackle
Box 873
West Falmouth,
MA 02574

Appendix G

List of Manufacturers

The following is a list of manufacturers that make materials, supplies, or tools for the tackle-builder. Many have catalogs they will send to you on request. Almost none will sell direct but will instead refer you to their nearest dealer. Dealers are usually local tackle shops or mail-order firms, such as those listed in Appendix F. Many of these manufacturers make far more fishing tackle than the brief notes here can indicate. For example, Berkley sells a broad line of tackle accessories, line, fishing rods, and marine products, and Hildebrandt sells a complete line of finished lures in addition to several styles and sizes of spinner blades.

To buy specific products, refer to your local tackle shop or check a good mail-order company, such as those listed in Appendix F.

AFTCO Manufacturing Company
17351-B Murphy Avenue
Irvine, CA 92714

Manufacturer of high-quality rod components, including offshore roller guides, tip-tops, reel seats, and butts.

American Fishing Wire
205 Carter Drive
West Chester, PA 19380

Manufacturer of leader wire and trolling wire and cable, crimping tools, and sleeves.

American Import Company
1453 Mission Street
San Francisco, CA 94103

Importer of lure-component parts.

American Sabre, Incorporated
15622 Chemical Lane
Huntington Beach, CA 92649

Manufacturer of glass and graphite rod blanks.

American Star Cork Company
33-53 62nd Street
Woodside, NY 11377

Manufacturer and importer of cork products and rod components.

American Tackle Limited
940 Old Post Road
Box 1270
Cotuit, MA 02635

Manufacturer of rod components, including guides, tip-tops, reel seats, butt caps, handles, and grips.

Barry Kustin Rods and Components
8589 Nevada Avenue
West Hills, CA 91304

Manufacturer of reel seats and tools for rod-building.

B.D. Classic Enterprises
Box 2445
Santa Fe Springs, CA 90670

Manufacturer of rod-finishing supplies, including two-part epoxies and color preserver.

Bead Tackle Incorporated
600 Main Street
Monroe, CT 06468

Manufacturer of bead-chain swivels and snaps and parts for lures and riggings.

Bellinger Reel Seats
3482 El Dorado Loop S.
Salem, OR 97302

Manufacturer of reel seats.

Belvoirdale
Box 176
Wyncote, PA 19095

Manufacturer of rod blanks and components for rod-building.

Berkley
One Berkley Drive
Spirit Lake, IA 51360

Manufacturer of line, wire, terminal snaps and swivels, and rigs.

Braid Products
Box 1305
Woodland Hills, CA 91364

Manufacturer of rod parts and accessories.

C & D Trading
Box 21072
Minneapolis, MN 55421

Manufacturer of rod components, importer of cork rings and handles.

C & H Lures Ultimate Tackle, Incorporated
142-A Mill Creek Road
Jacksonville, FL 32211

Manufacturer and distributer of hooks, wires, sleeves, riggings, and skirts for offshore lures.

C Beard
355 Hawthorne Drive
Loveland, CO 80538

Manufacturer of fly rod handle components.

Coburn Corporation
1650 Corporate Road W
Lakewood, NJ 08701

Manufacturer of lure-conversion kits.

Cork Specialties
1454 N. W. 78th Avenue
Miami, FL 33126

Importer of cork products and rod components.

Cortland/Rodon
Cortland Line Company, Incorporated
Box 5588, 3736 Kellogg Road
Cortland, NY 13045

Manufacturer of rod components.

C. Palmer Manufacturing Incorporated
5 Plummer School Road
West Newton, PA 15089

Manufacturer of sinker and bucktail molds.

Dan Bailey's Wholesale
Box 1019-G
Livingston, MT 59047

Manufacturer of rod blanks and components.

The Danielson Company
755 North Central
Kent, WA 98064-6030

Manufacturer of various rod components, bottom rigs, and general fishing tackle.

D.H. Thompson, Incorporated
11 N. Union Street
Elgin, IL 60123

Manufacturer of fly-tying vises and tools.

The Diamondback Company
Route 100 South
Box 308
Stowe, VT 05672

Manufacturer of rod blanks.

DNY Marketing
110 East Azalea Avenue
Foley, AL 36535

Manufacturer of rod components, including guides, tip-tops, reel seats, and handles.

Do-It
501 N. State Street
Denver, IA 50622

Manufacturer of high-quality molds and accessories for making sinkers, jigs, and other lead fishing items.

Dremel
4915 21 Street
Racine, WI 53406

Manufacturer of small power tools for hobbies, including tools useful for rod-building and lure-making.

Duin Greve Industries, Incorporated
121 East Avenue S.
Box 164
Rushmore, MN 56168

Manufacturer of spinner blades and lure parts.

DuPont Fishing Line
1007 Market Street
Wilmington, DE 19898

Manufacturer of fishing line and leaders.

Ed Hain Company
551 Stracks Dam Road
Myerstown, PA 17067

Manufacturer of lure- and sinker-component parts.

Fish Hair Enterprises, Incorporated
1484 W. County Road C
St. Paul, MN 55113

Manufacturer of synthetic fur for flies and jigs.

The Fishin' Worm Company
5512 S. Florida Avenue
Lakeland, FL 33803

Manufacturer of rattles and soft-plastic lures.

Five Star products
P.O. Box 7479
Torrance, CA 90504

Manufacturer of self-adhesive tape.

Flex Coat Company, Incorporated
Box 190
Driftwood, TX 78619

Manufacturer of rod-finishing products (color pre-servers, epoxies) and rod-finishing tools.

The Gaines Company
Box 35
Gaines, PA 16921

Manufacturer of epoxy and plastic jig and fly heads for making lures.

Gamakatsu Sporting Resources Company
Box 3730
Kent, WA 98032

Manufacturer of hooks.

Glenn Struble Manufacturing
1382 Duke Avenue
Sutherlin, OR 97479

Manufacturer of reel seats and rod components

G. Loomis
Box E
Woodland, WA 98674

Manufacturer of graphite rod blanks.

G. Pucci and Sons, Incorporated
43 Park Lane
Brisbane, CA 94005

Importer of hooks and guides.

Graphite-USA
7569 Convoy Court
San Diego, CA 92111

Manufacturer of fishing rods.

Gudebrod, Incorporated
Box 357
Pottstown, PA 19464

Manufacturer of threads for rod-building, jig tying, and fly tying, along with accessories for making fishing rods.

Hackle and Tackle
1 West Bridge Street
Saugerties, NY 12477

Manufacturer of reel seats.

Hildebrandt Corporation
Box 50
Logansport, IN 46947

Manufacturer of spinner blades for making lures.

Hi-Seas Industries, Incorporated
18-22 Minetta Lane
New York, NY 10012

Manufacturer of line and crimping sleeves and swagging tools and pliers.

Hilts Molds and Manufacturing Company
1461 E. Lake Mead Drive
Henderson, NV 89015

Manufacturer of high-quality molds and accessories for making sinkers, jigs, and other fishing items.

Hobbs Feather Company, Incorporated
202 West 4th Street
West Liberty, IA 52776

Manufacturer and supplier of feathers, fur, and artificial materials for fly tying and jig tying.

J & L Tool & Machine Incorporated
Box 367
Shelbyville, IN 46176

Manufacturer of self-adhesive tape for lures.

J. Kennedy Fisher, Incorporated
Box 3147
Carson City, NV 89702

Manufacturer of rod blanks.

K & K Rod Turner Company
Angler's Covey, Incorporated
917 West Colorado Avenue
Colorado Springs, CO 80905

Manufacturer of rod-finish curing-motor tool.

Kreinik Manufacturing Company Incorporated
Box 1966
Parkersburg, WV 26102

Manufacturer of rod-wrapping and fly-tying threads.

Kurachi Manufacturing Company
1323-A Canal
Modesto, CA 95354

Manufacturer of spinner and spoon parts.

Lakeland, Incorporated
1 Lakeland Drive
Isle, MN 56342

Manufacturer and distributor of lure and spinner parts.

Lakeland Manufacturing
RFD 11, Box 153
Mahopac, NY 10541 Secor Rd.

Manufacturer of brass and aluminum reel seats, gimbals, and other component parts.

Lamiglas, Incorporated
Box U
Woodland, WA 98674

Manufacturer of graphite and glass rod blanks.

Landmark Company Incorporated
4350 Ryan Way #1
Carson City, NV 89706

Manufacturer of rod tubes.

Li'l Mac Sinker Molds
27770 SW Parkway Avenue
Wilsonville, OR 97070

Manufacturer of sinker molds.

Luhr-Jensen
P.O. Box 297
400 Portway
Hood River, OR 97031

Manufacturer of prism tapes and other lure components.

Magnuflex
American Rod Manufacturers Incorporated
2147 NW 32rd Avenue
Miami, FL 33142

Manufacturer of rod blanks.

Mason Tackle Company
11273 Center Street
Box 56
Otisville, MI 48463

Manufacturer of wire and leader riggings.

M-F Manufacturing Company Incorporated
Box 820442
Fort Worth, TX 76182-0442

Manufacturer of worm- and soft-lure-making molds and supplies.

Micro-Mark
340 Snyder Avenue
Berkeley Heights, NJ 07922-1595

Specialists in small tools and materials for hobby crafts.

Mildrum Manufacturing Company
Napier Park
Meriden, CT 06450

Manufacturer of rod guides for all types of rods.

Missouri Boat Products
18048 Manchester Road
Glencoe, MO 63038

Manufacturer of Wormizer worm melding tool.

Moldcraft Company
501 NE 28 Street
Pompano Beach, FL 33064

Manufacturer of skirts, tails, bubblers, and rattles for offshore lures.

Nationwide Lure Manufacturing Company Incorporated
119 N. Main Street
Beaver Dam, KY 42320

Manufacturer of soft-lure molds.

O. Mustad & Son, Incorporated (USA)
Box 838
Auburn, NY 13021

Importer of all types of hooks.

The Orvis Company
Historic Route 7
Manchester, VT 05254

Manufacturer of rod blanks and components.

Owner American Corporation
17165 Von Karman, Suite 111
Irvine, CA 92714

Importer of hooks.

Pace Industries, Incorporated
Box 5127
Fort Lauderdale, FL 33310

Importer of cork products, including cork rod rings

Pacer Technology
Rancho Cucamonga, CA 91730

Manufacturer of Zap glue.

Pacific Bay, Incorporated
540 S. Jefferson
Placentia, CA 92670

Manufacturer of rod wrappers and component parts for rod-building.

Palsa Outdoor Products
Box 81336
Lincoln, NE 68501-1336

Manufacturer of self adhesive lure tapes

Partridge of Redditch
Mount Pleasant
Redditch, Worcestershire, England B97 4JE

Manufacturer of rod blanks.

Perry Design
7401 Zircon Drive SW
Tacoma, WA 98498

Manufacturer of small tools for the rod-builder, including a rod wrapper.

Perfection Tip Company
Box 16725
Denver, CO 80216

Manufacturer of all types of guides and tip-tops for fishing rods.

PFC Fishing Wire
Prindle Fabbri Corporation
4103 Clark Road
Sarasota, FL 34233

Manufacturer of all types of wire for fishing and riggings.

Powell Rod Company
Box 4000
Chico, CA 95927-4000

Manufacturer of rod blanks and components.

Profisherman Tackle Company
Box 422
40 Kingsway Road
Pierre, SD 57501

Manufacturer of spinner and lure components, including the Quick Change Clevis.

Rail Rod Rapper
Box 6034
San Clemente, CA 92672

Manufacturer of wood and metal rod wrapping machines.

Riffle Products
HCR 62, Box 140
Renovo, PA 17764

Manufacturer and importer of rod blanks and components.

Rodcraft
6445 Lyndale Avenue South
Richfield, MN 55423

Manufacturer of rod blanks and components.

RST North America Limited
1636 S. Fairway Drive
Pocatello, ID 83201

Manufacturer of grips, reel seats, and components for fishing rods

Sage
8500 Northeast Day Road
Bainbridge Island, WA 98110

Manufacturer of fly-rod blanks.

St. Croix
Box 279
Highway 13 North
Park Falls, WI 54552

Manufacturer of rod blanks.

Sampo
Rome Specialty Company, Incorporated
Box 328
Barneveld, NY 13304

Manufacturer of swivels, snap swivels, and terminal tackle.

Scott PowR-Ply Company
707 B Heinz St.
Berkeley, CA 94710

Manufacturer of rod blanks.

Seeker Fishing Rods
Box 14744
Long Beach, CA 90803

Manufacturer of graphite and glass rod blanks.

Sevenstrand Tackle
899 West Cowles Street
Long Beach, CA 90813

Manufacturer of wire, crimping sleeves, and crimping tools.

Sevier Manufacturing, Incorporated
2200 Clermont Street
Denver, CO 80207

Manufacturer and distributor of rod components.

Shakespeare Company
3801 Westmore Drive
Columbia, SC 29223

Manufacturer of glass and graphite rod blanks.

South Bend Sporting Goods Incorporated
1950 Stanley Street
Northbrook, IL 60065

Manufacturer of terminal tackle, riggings, and accessories

Stuart Industries, Inc.
526 N.E. 190th St.
N. Miami beach, FL 33179

Manufacturer of components for big game reels

System Tackle
503 Front Street
Lake Park, MN 56554

Manufacturer of lead-head jigs and soft-body jig heads.

Talon
Box 907
Woodland, WA 98674

Manufacturer of graphite rod blanks.

Tri-Peek International, Incorporated
1447 Parker Road, Suite 700
Conyers, GA 30207

Manufacturer of EasyWeld micro-flame torch and soldering iron.

Tru-Turn
Drawer 767
Wetumpka, AL 36092

Manufacturer of unique shank-bent hooks.

Tycoon/Fin-Nor Corporation
2021 SW 31 Avenue
Hallandale, FL 33009

Manufacturer of rod components and guides.

Umpqua Feather Merchants
P.O. Box 700
Glide, OR 97443

Manufacturer and importer of feathers and fur for fly tying and lure-making, and of other fly-fishing equipment.

Venom Manufacturing
Box 275
Lithopolis, OH 43136

Manufacturer of worm and lure rattles.

VMC Incorporated
1901 Oakcrest Avenue, Suite 10
St. Paul, MN 55113

Importer of fishing hooks.

Walker International
1901 W. Lafayette
Detroit, MI 48216

Manufacturer of rod components and general tackle.

Wapsi Fly Incorporated
Route 5, Box 57E
Mountain Home, AR 72653

Manufacturer and importer of feathers and fur for fly tying and lure-making.

Wiebe Manufacturing Company
431 Kensington Way
Lodi, CA 95242

Manufacturer of reel seats and rod components.

Witchcraft Tape Products
Box 937
Coloma, MI 49038

Manufacturer of self-adhesive tape products in tapes, sheets and precut shapes.

The Worth Company
Box 88
Stevens Point, WI 54481

Manufacturers of all types of lure, spinner, and spoon parts, and of wire-forming tools.

Wright and McGill Company
Box 16011
Denver, CO 80216

Manufacturer of hooks.

Zak Tackle Manufacturing Company Incorporated
10910 26 Avenue
Tacoma, WA 98444

Manufacturer of lure-component parts.

Zing Products
Box 1407
Fall River, MA 02722

Manufacturer of lure-component parts and surgical tubing.

Glossary

ABS. A type of plastic used to mold hard-plastic-plug bodies. Used extensively by modern manufacturers. Other plastics used include **butyrate** and **tenite.**

Action. Describes the type of bend a rod makes during casting or fighting. Some manufacturers still refer to action when they mean not only the way in which a rod bends but also the resistance to bending. Resistance to bending is better referred to as **power.** The action is the bend the rod makes as a result of the mandrel and the cut of the graphite or glass fabric used to wrap around the mandrel. The result can be a rod that bends almost evenly from tip to butt (**parabolic**), one that has more of a tippy action or bend (**fast action**), or one that is very tippy (**extra-fast action**). Other terms are sometimes used, and some manufacturers refer to a "worm" action when describing a fast or extra-fast-tip-action rod. A rod can have a given action and still be light or heavy power.

Aetna Guide. A guide that used to be popular and is sometimes still found on the market. It is made with a strand of wire that is bent into a complete circle to form a ring for the line flow; the ends form the guide feet. Similar wire guides in different brand names are available.

Airbrush. A special type of painting tool used primarily by artists, in which air is sprayed through a nozzle along with paint to create a smooth feathered effect. Ideal for painting some lures and used by many lure manufacturers.

Aircraft Cable. A very-large-diameter twisted wire leader used in big-game fishing. Often consisting of wire made by first twisting seven strands of single-strand wire into one cable, then twisting seven of these cables into one aircraft cable.

Airplane Cable. Another name for **aircraft cable.**

Aluminum Oxide. A ceramic material used in guide rings. The material is very hard, essentially nongrooving, and is one of several ceramic materials used in guide rings.

Artificial Fur. Synthetic fur that is used in fly tying and lure-making. It can go by any number of names, perhaps the earliest of which was FisHair. Craft fur, available in large sheets from hobby shops, is similar and is often used by fly

tyers and lure-builders. Many colors are available.

Attractor Tubing. A round hollow tubing, usually composed of vinyl or a similiar plastic, that is cut into short lengths and added to the shaft of hooks (usually treble hooks) that are placed on spinners and similar lures. It is used to create an attraction for fish and comes in bright colors, including fluorescent and standard red, yellow, orange, and green.

Ball-Bearing Swivel. A swivel in which tiny ball bearings are used between the swiveling surfaces. Used primarily in big-game fishing and trolling, where freely moving and rotating lures are a must and line twist must be reduced or eliminated. More expensive than regular swivels.

Ball-Head Jig. A lead-head jig with a spherical head that is often used for making crappie jigs and lures.

Banjo-Eye Jig. A large bucktail with bulging eyes. Usually the eyes are molded into the lure but sometimes are made of glass or plastic and then added to the finished lure.

Bank Sinker. A teardrop-shaped sinker with hexagonal sides, designed to be used in rocky areas. The shape of the sinker resists hanging up on rocks.

Barrel Swivel. A simple two-eye swivel in which the central part resembles a small barrel.

Bass-Casting Sinker. A pear-shaped sinker with a molded-in swivel eye. Also called a dipsy doodle sinker, dipsy sinker, or bell sinker.

Basswood. One of several woods used to carve fishing plugs. It is easy to carve, fine-grained, and popular. Other woods used for plugs include **cedar** and fine-grain clear pine.

Beads. Various types of beads are used in spinners and lures, both as attractors and also as bearings or swiveling surfaces for spinner-blade clevises. Beads are available in glass, plastic, and metal; in faceted, plain, and patterned surfaces; and in a wide range of opaque and translucent colors.

Bell Sinker. Another name for **bass-casting sinker.**

Belmar Frame. See **Belmar Guide.**

Belmar Guide. A rod guide in which the frame that supports the guide ring is much longer and more extended than in a standard guide. Also called a bridge guide, it is found mostly on big-game and trolling rods.

Bent Handle. A special type of offshore-rod handle that is made of aluminum. The handle is bent below the reel seat to provide greater leverage and fish-fighting ability when the angler is working from a fighting chair.

Bib. A small, short, wiggling-plate lip, usually attached by small screws to the front of a wood crankbait or plug.

Blade. The flat, rotating part of a spinner or the wobbling part of a spoon, sometimes called "spinner blade" or "spoon blade," before hooks are added or before being built into a lure. Sometimes also called **blank,** although this can be confused with a rod blank.

Blank. The fiberglass, graphite, or bamboo stick or "pole" used as the basis of a fishing rod. The blank is a plain pole without any of the appointments of the finished rod, such as a reel seat, butt cap, grips, guides, and tip-top. The term may also refer to a metal (sometimes plastic) blade for a spinner or spoon.

Body. The entire part of the female ferrule (separate from the blank), except the cap onto which the thread windings are adjusted. Also the center-drilled solid piece of metal (usually brass or steel), tapered or bullet-shaped, that fits onto the shaft of a spinner to provide most of the weight of the lure.

Boxing-Glove Jig. A large bucktail with a head similar in shape to a boxing glove. Used mostly in saltwater fishing.

Box Swivel. A simple two-eye swivel in which the center swiveling part resembles the sides of a box. Not commonly used today.

Brass Lure Wire. A heavy wire, usually about 0.060-inch in diameter, that is used for making through-wire riggings for plugs, hook lears, bottom rigs, and the like because it is both strong and easy to form.

Bridge Frame. See **Belmar Guide.**

Bridge Guide. See **Belmar Guide.**

Bucktail. The fur from the tail of a deer that is often used for tying flies and jigs; the jigs are often called "bucktails" for this reason. Also, another name for a jig, but one that has only fur for a tail, usually bucktail from the tail of a deer. Often "bucktail" is used in saltwater and "jig" is used in fresh water, but this distinction is blurring.

Bullet-Head Bucktail. A lead bucktail with a head shaped like a bullet.

Bushing. Most frequently used to describe the cork, fiber, wood, or similar material that is used to fill up the space between the rod blank and the reel seat on a fly, spinning, popping, surf, or similar rod, where the reel seat is placed over the rod blank and where there is a size differential between the two. Special bushings are sometimes available for specific reel seats and to fit certain sizes of rod blank. Also called a reel-seat bushing.

Butt Cap. A plastic, metal, or rubber cap that fits onto or over the butt end of a rod handle and is designed to give the rod a finished look while at the same time protecting the rod end from damage. Some lightweight butt plates serve the same purpose for ultralight rods and are glued in place.

Butt-Ferruled. A term sometimes used to describe a two-piece rod in which the ferruled sections are of two different lengths, with the tip section the longer. As a result, the ferrule is closer to the butt. Seldom seen anymore, the purported advantage of this system was to prevent a deadening of the action at the center of the rod, but the disadvantage was that the rod would not fit easily into a rod case. Also a term used to describe rods, usually spin-cast or casting models, in which the rod blank separates from the handle by means of a butt ferrule or adapter that serves to allow the joining of the rod blank to the handle. The ferrule or adapter fits into a collet in the rod handle.

Butt Guide. A term sometimes used for the first guide, through which line flows as it comes off the reel.

Butt Plate. A small, lightweight metal plate that is screwed or glued onto the end of the handle of a rod. Most often used on light or ultralight tackle.

Butt Section. The lower or butt portion of the rod, that which incorporates the rod handle. In a two-piece rod, it is the lower and heavier of the two sections. In a multipiece rod, it is the lowest of the several sections. In some cases, the term "butt section" or "end" is used to refer to the lower or butt end of any rod piece. Thus, the center section of a three-piece rod might have its two ends referred to as the "butt section" (or end) and the "tip section" (or end).

Butyrate. A plastic used for molding hard-plastic plugs by modern manufacturers. Other plastics used for this include **ABS** and **tenite.**

Buzz Blade. This is a blade specifically used on buzzbaits. It is usually available in right- and left-rotating styles, in short and larger, triangular delta-wing blades, sometimes called by this name.

Calcutta Cane. One type of cane used for rods, not as popular as the **Tonkin cane** used for split-bamboo rods. It is no longer used but was once highly thought of for rods, particularly long, stout surf rods. It was never split to make split-bamboo rods.

Cam-Action Hook. The first was from Tru-Turn,

although other companies have now followed with the same or similar designs. These hooks, most often used for bass fishing, have a sideways bend in the shank that theoretically causes the hook to turn in the fish's mouth for better, deeper hooking.

Cap. That part of a male or female metal ferrule onto which decorative thread windings are wrapped.

Carboloy Guides. Any of a number of types of guides in which the ring is made of **tungsten carbide.** Carboloy is a trademark of General Electric. Mildrum calls its guides of this material Mildarbide.

Cedar. A wood used for carving plugs. Other good woods include **basswood** and fine-grain pine.

Center. That portion of a male metal ferrule that fits into the female ferrule.

Center-Ferruled. Applies to two-piece rods in which the ferrule (any type of ferrule) is in the exact center of the rod. Almost all two-piece rods and blanks are built this way.

Chemically Sharpened Hook. A hook made by many manufacturers that is chemically sharpened by a slow, controlled drip of acid. These are very sharp hooks as they come from the box.

Cigar Grip. See **Phillippe Grip.**

Clamp-Type Mold. A bucktail, sinker, or jig mold in which the two mold halves are separate and are clamped together in use with built-in pinned clamps.

Class Rod. A rod that is designed for a certain category of fishing line or class line. Such rods are usually offshore rods and designed in the various IGFA line-class categories, typically beginning with about 12-pound class rods and going through 16, 20, 30, 50, 80, and 130.

Clevis. The small U-shaped wire or sheet-stamped devices used to attach spinner blades to the spinner shaft. The clevis is run through the eye of the spinner blade, then the spinner shaft is run through the holes in the ends of the clevis. See also **folded clevis** and **wire clevis.**

Coastlock Snap. A very long snap, designed for maximum strength and used extensively on the East Coast.

Coil-Spring Fastener. The tightly coiled spring that is used to close and fasten the loop shaft of a spinner.

Collet. The chucklike device at the fore end of a casting or spin-cast rod handle that is tightened on the butt ferrule or adapter of the rod to hold it securely.

Colorado Blade. A slightly tapered spinner blade, rounder than an **Indiana Blade.**

Color Preserver. A thin, watery finishing liquid that must be used over thread wraps before any final finish coats are added if the original color of the thread is to be preserved. It is not a must for protecting the wraps (the epoxy of varnish does that) but must be used to preserve thread color. If color preserver is not used, epoxy, acrylic, or varnish coating will turn light thread colors lighter and dark thread colors darker and will make all threads slightly translucent. Color preservers are available in solvent types and with a water base for easy cleanup.

Connecting Link. Looks almost like a very long link of chain with a sliding locking sleeve in the center to keep the ends from springing apart, yet opens for adding and removing parts. Sometimes used as the line-tie for plugs.

Core Pin. See **Core Rod.**

Core Rod. A brass or steel rod placed in a sinker mold to form a hole in egg-sinker molds, plastic-worm slip sinkers, and molds for spinner bodies.

Cork Grip. The handle used for most fine rods. The grip is formed of round, usually 1/2-inch thick, center-drilled rings of cork that are glued together on the blank and shaped to form the grip.

Cork Ring. A round, drilled, 1/2-inch thick ring (a few are 1/4-inch thick) used to build up a handle on a rod blank. It comes in either **specie cork** or **mustard cork** based on the way the cork plugs are cut out of the bark. Specie cork is by far the best, although many different grades of specie cork are available. The rings come in several outside diameters and many inside-hole sizes.

Crimping Pliers. Specially made pliers with jaws for crimping different sizes of leader sleeves. Several sizes and types are available, and some have built-in wire cutters.

Crossline Swivel. A swivel with three eyes in which two are in a single plane and the third is at a right angle to them—almost like a T. Used for hanging drop sinkers in trolling.

Cup Washer. A small cupped washer, about 1/8-inch in diameter, used under a screw eye in a plug for a finished appearance and also to limit the movement of the hooks to prevent tangling. A deeper washer, used principally under screw eyes holding hooks, is often called a **derby washer** because of its resemblance to a derby hat.

Dart Jig. A small, tapered jig with a flat face. Also called a **quill-dart jig** or shad-dart jig.

Decal Eyes. Fishing-plug eyes that are decals. These eyes are placed on the finished plug and covered with a clear coat of epoxy or varnish.

Decorative Winding. See **Windings.**

Deep-Cup Spinner Blade. This is exactly what it seems: a spinner blade that has a deeper concavity in the blade than does a normal blade. These are preferred by some anglers for the different wobbling action they have in the water.

Delta-Wing Blade. This is a large trianglelike or delta-shaped blade that is used on buzzbaits. Sometimes it is called simply "delta blade."

Derby Washer. Similar to a cup washer but deeper. Designed to go under the screw eye holding the hook on a plug, these deeper washers limit the movement of a hook to prevent it from scarring the plug finish ot tangling with other hooks or the line.

Dipsy Doodle Sinker. See **Bass-Casting Sinker.**

Doll Eyes. These are also called "rattle eyes" or "movable eyes," because the pupil is loose in a cuplike clear bubble with an opaque back. Many sizes are available. Most are round, but oval eyes are available, as are various styles in many colors.

Down Gate. See **Sprue Hole.**

Drail. A heavy, large L-shaped sinker used in deep trolling. The shape works as a keel and prevents line twist.

Double-Snap Swivel. A standard snap swivel, to which a second snap is attached to the free eye.

Dry-Fly Action. A fly-rod action in which the tip does most of the bending. Designed for dry-fly fishing when the fast action of the tip end (in the days of the very slow bamboo rods) was required to dry a fly between casts. (This is the opposite of a wet-fly action, in which the action extends well down into or toward the grip of the rod.) Today, rods are seldom characterized by this term, even though there is a recent return to labeling rods by the type of fishing they are designed for. In some cases, these labels refer to a type of action or bend.

Duo-Lock Snap. A simple single-wire snap, the construction of which makes it possible to unhook the snap at either end. It has a double-locking arrangement that makes it strong but does not swivel. It can be combined with a swivel. It predates the similar Berkley Cross-Lok snap, also a single-wire double open-end snap.

Ear-Grip Sinker. See **Pinch-On Sinker.**

Egg Sinker. A round or torpedo-shaped sinker with a hole running through its long axis. Designed for bottom fishing, the line running through the sinker prevents the fish from detecting the sinker weight while it's mouthing or running with the bait.

Electric Lead Pot. A pot with a built-in or built-on AC heating element. Available in small, simple, inexpensive styles as well as large, bottom-feeding, sophisticated styles.

Epoxy Glue. Probably the best glue type today for most tackle-building. These are two-part glues, usually in a 1:1 mix. They are easy to use, have a high bonding strength, and are completely water-proof.

Epoxy Rod Finish. Several brands are available for this; they are generally less viscous than the glues. They also often have special additives to release bubbles, to prevent ultraviolet-ray damage and yellowing, and to keep the finish flexible. Epoxy rod finish can be used as a glue but will take much longer to dry than will regular epoxy glue. Epoxy glue should not be used as a rod finish.

Eyed Shaft. A spinner shaft that comes with a closed eye formed in one end for line attachment. Available in several lengths, it is the most popular spinner shaft for making spinners.

Faceted Bead. A bead that has flat surfaces to reflect light; sometimes used in place of round beads in a spinner body.

Fast Tip. A rod action in which the tip bends sharply while the butt remains relatively straight. Also called worm action. See also **Action.**

Female Ferrule. That half of a ferrule set that has a hollow center into which the male ferrule fits. In a set of metal ferrules, the female is fitted to the butt section of the rod, and the male ferrule is fitted to the tip section. In self-ferrules of the Fenwick style (graphite to graphite or glass to glass), the female ferrule is really an extension of the tip section, and the butt section ends with the male ferrule. This is also true of spigot ferrules, though that construction method is different.

Ferrule. The metal built-in or built-on glass or graphite part that allows the joining of different sections of rods. Metal ferrules are glued to the rod, and self-ferrules such as the Fenwick style are built into the rod as a part of blank construction. Spigot ferrules are added to the rod during manufacture but include a separate plug of glass or graphite in the butt section of the rod —this plug is the male part of the ferrule.

Ferrule Cement. A resin- or plastic-based cement in stick form that must be heated to be used. It can be used to glue ferrules and tip-tops to a rod blank and allows for easy replacement of damaged ferrules and tip-tops by the application of heat to the part to be removed, which melts the ferrule cement.

Figure-Eight Attachment. A figure-eight-shaped piece of wire for lure attachments and line-ties. Often attached to the metal wiggle lip of a plug.

Flash. The excess lead, lead alloy, or tin that leaks out along the joint between two mold halves during the pouring of lead or tin bucktail heads, squids, or sinkers. It forms a line that runs through the center plane of the lure or sinker. Ideally, it should not occur in better molds, but when it does it must be removed by cutting or filing. It will not interfere with sinkers, but is usually removed from them.

Flat Sinker. A sinker that may come in several

shapes—all flat—that is designed to be snagless. It is shaped much like a flat spinner blade.

Folded Clevis. A clevis stamped from sheet metal in the shape of an O and folded over to make a U-shaped clevis. See **Clevis.**

Foregrip. That part of a cork or wood handle that is in front of or above the reel seat. Casting-rod handles come with or without a foregrip, and all spinning-rod and boat-rod handles have a foregrip of some type.

Foulproof Guide. Still sold in some areas, this is a guide formed of wire that is bent into a circle. The ends of the wire form the guide feet.

French-Type Blade. Used in popular spinners, this blade has an egg-shaped raised surface on its convex side.

Full Wells Grip. Used on fly rods, this is a grip with a cigar-shaped swollen center that narrows before flaring out at both ends.

Gathering Guide. Another term for stripping guide or butt guide.

Gimbal. A heavy, solid butt cap primarily for big-game rods, in which the bottom of the metal butt cap is slotted (or double-slotted in an X) so as to fit onto a bar placed in the gimbal socket of a fighting chair or on a belt. Usually made of aluminum or heavy chrome-plated brass. Sometimes called a "gimbal knock" or "knock."

Glass Eyes. Glass eyes come paired on a long wire and are used to finish wood fishing plugs. The wire is cut off 1/2-inch from the eye, and the short wire is inserted with pliers into the wood body. An advantage to these eyes is that they can be painted any desired color around the blank pupil.

Gordon Grip. A fly-rod handle similar to the **Phillippe tapered-style grip,** except that the rear grip flares out instead of remaining straight.

Grip Check. See **Winding Check.**

Hardy Grip. A cigar-shaped grip with a flare at the rear, really a reversed **Half Wells Grip.**

Half Wells Grip. A fly-rod grip, almost a reversed **Hardy Grip,** in which the front is flared, is followed by a swelled area, and is then tapered at the rear of the grip.

Hammered Blade. A lure blade that has been hammered or given a hammered finish. Can apply to any type of spinner or spoon blade.

Hammerhead Jig. A bucktail or jig with very pronounced protruding eyes on each side of the head, much like a hammerhead shark.

Handle. That part of the rod held in the hand as the rod is cast. Fly rod handles are above the reel seat, spinning rods have fixed or sliding-ring reel seats in the middle of the handle, and casting rods have built-on or separate handles that include a reel seat. Depending upon who is using the term, "handle" can mean only the grip

that is held (though "grip" is a more accurate term for this), or it can mean the entire grip, reel seat, and butt cap assembly.

Handled Mold. A bucktail, sinker, or lead-head mold that is hinged on one side with handles on the opposite side of each of the two halves. It has the advantage of making lead molding a quick and easy operation.

Hardy Grip. A modified **cigar** or **Phillippe** grip used on fly rods, in which the rear part of the grip flares out slightly.

Hold-Down Clamp. The small, flat piece of metal found on the reel seat of some casting or spincast handles that holds the foot of the reel.

Hook Hanger. A small metal device, shaped like a bent garden trowel, by which hooks are added to a plug or crankbait. Hangers are fastened to the plug with very small round-head screws. The advantage of hangers over screw eyes is that hangers limit the forward movement of the hook to prevent tangling with the line or other hooks.

Hook-Hanger Spreader. A small wire device, first popularized in early plugs (primarily the Helin Flatfish), by which treble hooks are held away from the body of a lure, presumably to aid in hooking fish that are short-strikers.

Hookkeeper. A small device that is wrapped down on the rod blank just in front of the foregrip and by which hooks and lures are fastened in place.

Hosel. A large, usually plastic, device designed to serve the same purpose as a winding check but usually found only on larger saltwater rods. Center-drilled, hosels fit over the rod blank and up against the rod handle.

Ice-Tong Snap. A special type of terminal rigging snap, the end of which resembles a pair of ice tongs. Often used in attaching sinkers with bottom rigs for saltwater fishing. Preferred mainly on the West Coast. Also called a "McMahon snap."

Indiana Blade. A pear-shaped spinner blade. Not as fat as a **Colorado Blade.** Available in many sizes and finishes.

Ingot Mold. A mold for making ingots or bars of lead or tin. Most molds make about four bars of approximately 2 pounds each.

Injection Mold. A mold into which the molding material is injected with pressure. It is used primarily by manufacturers to mold liquid plastic into worms and other soft-plastic lures. This method can be used by the tackle-crafter with a Hilts worm mold, which has a special syringe system to inject the liquid plastic.

Jigging Spoon. A heavy-blade spoon that is used for vertical jigging and is similar to the metal thrown by surf casters. Also called a structure spoon by bass anglers to differentiate it from the weedless spoons used in grass and weeds.

Jig Hook. A special hook designed to be used in molding jigs and bucktails. It has an upward bend (toward the hook point, because the jig rides with the hook up) in the hook shank and an eye that is parallel to the hook bend for easy placement and removal in the mold. The bend in the hook shank is usually at right angles but can be sixty degrees for some hooks and some molds.

Jigs. Another name for a **bucktail** or bucktail lead head. This term is more commonly used for freshwater fishing, while the term bucktail is more common in saltwater fishing, but such distinctions are blurring. A jig is also a device used to hold materials or to form materials. Examples in tackle-crafting would be special jigs used to hold plug bodies upright for through-wire drilling in a drill press, jigs used to bend wire for making bottom rigs and hook lears, and jigs for bending tubing for making landing nets.

Jointed Plug. A plug or crankbait that is jointed. These plugs are usually in two parts, occasionally in three or more.

Jump Ring. A small open ring sometimes used to attach hooks or swivels to spoons and spinners. In use, the parts to be attached are placed in the ring and the ring is closed with pliers and welded or soldered for strength. Not as easy to use as a split ring.

June Bug Spinner. A spinner using a blade with a cut-out central portion that forms a leg that attaches to the spinner shaft. The leg running from the center of the blade holds the blade at a certain angle from the spinner shaft. June Bug spinners are often used in conjunction with bait.

Keeper Ring. A **Hookkeeper.** Designed to hold a hook or lure and wrapped onto a rod blank just above the handle.

Knock. See **Gimbal.**

Latex Tubing. A pure-rubber tubing, used for making lures fished primarily on the Atlantic Coast. The resulting long lure presumably resembles an eel. Shorter lengths of hose are used in some lures. The tubing comes in a variety of colors and sizes for making lures.

Lead-Cutting Pliers. More a cutter than pliers, this tool is used to cut lead sprue from molded lures and sinkers and to cut lead and other soft wire.

Lead Dipper. A small, deeply cupped, specialized pouring ladle.

Leader Sleeve. A small metallic cylinder used to fit over leader wire to form loops and eyes and to make leader and riggings. Leader sleeves come in different sizes for use with different wire (there are also specialized leader sleeves used for mono) but cannot be used with single-strand wire. Also called a sleeve fastener.

Lead Pot. A large pot for melting lead, it is often made of cast iron. Lead is not poured into the mold from these large pots but is transferred to smaller, long-handled pouring ladles. The capacity of these pots varies from about 5 to 20 pounds of lead.

Lima Bean Jig. A jig or bucktail shaped like a lima bean so that it will drop rapidly and still have a noticeable profile when seen from the side.

Loop Shaft. A shaft for spinners that comes with a loop eye formed in one end. Used to make some types of spinners (such as the French-style spinner) where the hook is added to the loop shaft and followed by the body and other parts, with the line-tie eye formed last. Also used with coil-spring fasteners to change hooks and parts. Used on June Bug and similar spinners with long-shank hooks for bait fishing.

Mandrel. The tapered steel rod used as a core when making hollow glass or graphite rod blanks. The cloth used to make the rod is wrapped around the mandrel and baked, then the mandrel is pulled out and a tapered, flexible fishing rod blank results.

Mask. A term used in finishing, when a lure is painted selectively with dots, streaks, stripes, or similar patterns. A "mask" of paper, tape, plastic, or similar material prevents the sprayed-on paint from hitting other parts of the lure. The term can also refer to the materials used for the masking process.

McMahon Snap. See **Ice-Tong Snap.**

Mesh Gauge. A gauge used to measure the size of the mesh squares in landing and fishing nets. Gauge sizes range from 1/2-inch to 3 inches, although any long rectangular piece of plastic, metal, wood, or stiff cardboard can serve as a mesh gauge.

Mildarbide. Trademark of the Mildrum company for tungsten-carbide guide-ring material.

Modulus. The degree of stiffness with which a rod rebounds from a bent position. This term became important to the rod and blank industry with the introduction of graphite, and various companies strive for high-modulus rods and blanks with increased performance, casting distance, and sensitivity.

Mold Furnace. A special furnace used mostly by bullet-casters. It is electric and varies widely in cost, capacity, and style. Some models are bottom-feeders, others take lead from the top. Most have thermostatic temperature controls for melting lead. Although some are designed for bullet-casting, they are also ideal for molding sinkers and jigs.

Multiple-Cavity Mold. A bucktail, jig, sinker, or worm mold with more than one cavity.

Mustard Cork. A low-quality cork (see **Cork Ring**)

seldom used today in cork handles.

Netting Knot. A special knot used for making the mesh squares in fishing nets. In essence it is a sheet bend.

Node. The swollen part of a bamboo pole or culm. In making split-bamboo fishing rods, nodes are planed down and usually staggered along the rod blank so that the weaker node points will not all be in the same place. Also, when a rod is shaken, that point where the two curves of the rod intersect is called a "nodal point."

Nylon-Coated Leader Wire. Twisted leader wire coated with nylon for easy handling.

Off-Center-Ferruled Rod. A two-piece rod in which the sections are cut in unequal lengths; the butt section is always the shorter of the two. The theory is that the action and power will be less adversely affected with the ferrule closer to the butt. A disadvantage is that the rod will need a longer rod case to accommodate the longer tip section. Also called **butt-ferruled,** but this is not to be confused with rods (primarily casting and spin-cast) with separate handles that are ferruled at the blank-to-handle joint.

Open-Face Mold. A one-piece mold for making tin squids, plastic worms, and lures in which the molten metal or liquid plastic is poured into the open mold. Because the mold is in one piece, the lure shape is formed on one side only; the top side is flat. Also called a one-piece mold.

Open Screw Eye. A screw eye used for lure-making in which the eye is open to allow the addition of hooks. In use, the screw eye is partially screwed into the lure, then the hook is added and the eye is closed with pliers. Finally the screw eye is completely seated into the plug body.

Pack Rod. A rod, usually a spinning, fly, or casting model, which by means of multiple sections and ferrules breaks down easily for packing and travel. Once rare in good blanks, the lightness of the self-ferrule has made the pack rod more popular, and many blanks are available, although most are in the fly and spinning category. Also called a travel rod.

Parabolic Action. Rod action in which the rod bends evenly and uniformly from the tip to the handle. This is the best type of action for casting accuracy but often lacks the power for fighting big fish.

Payne Grip. A fly-rod grip similar to the **cigar** or **Phillippe** style, except that the rear of the grip has straight parallel sides. Only the front is tapered like a cigar.

Phillippe Grip. A round fly-rod grip that is large in the middle and tapered at both ends, similar to a fat cigar.

Phillippe Tapered Grip. A tapered fly-rod grip with straight sides. The forward end of the grip is thicker than the rear.

Pinch-On Sinker. A long tapered sinker with a slot cut into into the long axis for the line and small ears or projections at each end to clamp the sinker to the line.

Pistol Grip. A large grip used on casting and spin-cast rods used primarily for bass-fishing. It is usually made of wood, cork, or foam and is sometimes called a "comfort grip" or "bass grip."

Pompanette Snap. A very long snap usually made in extra-heavy wire and designed primarily for big-game use. Comes in large sizes only, with 100-pound test the usual minimum size.

Pouring Ladle. A long-handled ladle, usually made of cast iron and used for pouring molten lead into jig and sinker molds. It comes in various sizes and styles with capacities from about 1 to 6 pounds.

Prismatic Tape. A self-adhesive tape that is embossed with prismatic patterns and added to lures. The tape comes in a variety of prismatic patterns, finishes, and colors and is available in sheets of various patterns, bars, and eyes. All are designed to resemble fish scales and to increase the attractiveness of the lure to which they are added.

Propeller Blades. Blades similar to a plane propeller: The two blades are on a center hub through which the spinner shaft or screw eye runs. Usually used for top-water plugs.

Quill-Dart Jig. See **Dart Jig.**

Rattles. Many different types of rattles are available for lure-making. Small rattles originally designed for insertion into plastic worms are available in glass, plastic, and aluminum, and each has a slightly different sound. Larger rattles are available for saltwater lures. In addition, medium- and large-sized rattles can be built into some lures using BB's and shot.

Reel Bands. See **Spinning-Rod Rings.**

Reel Seat. A tubular device fitted with hoods to hold a reel foot and with locking threads to hold a sliding hood in place. It comes in a number of styles, colors, sizes, and finishes for fly, spinning casting, spin-cast, boat, surf, and big-game rods. Some have a trigger (casting rods), some have incorporated ferrules (big-game rods), some are skeletal (ultralight spinning rods), and some have slip-in extension-butt sections (saltwater fly rods).

Reel-Seat Bushing. See **Bushing.**

Ripple Blade. A spinner blade with a rippled surface almost like the surface of corrugated cardboard.

Rod Hosel. See **Hosel.**

Rod Tip. The upper section of a two-piece or multipiece rod. Can also refer to the uppermost end of any rod, or the "tip end" of any section.

Rod Winding Check. See **Winding Check.**

Roller Guide. A big-game rod guide in which the guide is fitted with a smooth roller or pulley, over which the line runs. The advantage of roller guides is that the roller will prevent wear during the strong fast runs of a large fish and will also prevent line damage when the run stalls and the friction-caused heat buildup in a ring guide could cause line damage and weakening.

Ruby-Lip Bucktail. A bucktail or jig with pronounced lips molded into the lure. Usually the lips of the finished lure are painted bright red, thus the name.

Safety Snap. A small snap that closes and locks almost like a safety pin. Used for attaching lures to line.

Scale-Finish Netting. A small-mesh, hexagonal-hole netting designed for use in painting scale finish on lures. Such netting is available from fabric stores. In use, the lure is painted a base color, held tightly against the netting, and paint is sprayed over the netting in the finish color. The base color shows through the finish as scales.

Scoop. A term sometimes used for a large type of wiggle plate or lip that causes a lure to dive deeply.

Screw Eyes. Either open or closed small-wire screw eyes used in plug construction. The closed-eye screws are used for plug heads (where the line is tied on), and open-eye screws are used where the hooks are to be added to the lure. Both styles come in several wire thicknesses and lengths.

Self-Lock Snap Shaft. A type of spinner shaft in which the open loop end of the eye can be closed in a manner similar to fastening a safety pin. It makes the use of coil-spring fasteners on a loop-eye shaft unnecessary and still allows hook-changing.

Shoulder. That part of a male ferrule extending from the center portion (which fits into the female ferrule) to the cap. The cap is the tapered end onto which the thread windings are wrapped. No longer a widely used term.

Shuttle. The plastic device used to hold net-making twine so that it can be passed easily through the net to make rows of net meshes. Shuttles come in different sizes and lengths for use with different net twines and for different sizes of mesh squares.

Single-Cavity Mold. A bucktail or jig mold that makes only one lure at a time. This type of mold is usually found only in the highly finished professional-type molds that mold lures with little or no flash. This terms can also apply to an open-faced worm mold that has only one cavity,

for making one worm at a time.

Slag. The waste material found in most lead and lead alloys used for molding lead-head lures and sinkers. It floats to the surface of the molten lead and can be skimmed off before the lead is poured into the mold.

Slip Sinker. A bullet-shaped sinker used with plastic worms. See **Egg Sinker.**

Snake Guide. A small guide used on fly rods that is made from a single length of wire and looks almost like a twisted snake. Comes in different sizes and finishes.

Snell. The technique of wrapping line around a hook shank to secure it to the line; a substitute for a knot in the hook's eye. The eye of the hook does not have to be used, but if it is used should be a turned-up or turned-down eye. Also a term sometimes used for a hook with a snell-attached mono leader.

Solid-Brass Rings. Small solid-brass rings used in lures and terminal riggings when a high degree of strength for size is needed.

Specie Cork. The better of two methods by which cork rings are cut from cork bark. In specie cork, the natural pits in the cork run parallel to the central hole drilled in the cork ring. Even specie cork comes in a number of grades, however, from excellent down to lesser grades.

Spine. The stiffest plane of the rod blank. The spine of a rod blank should be determined for guide placement.

Spinner. A lure in which a blade rotates around a central shaft by means of a clevis; the central shaft holds a body or beads and the lure, ending with the hook.

Spinner Bearing. A small bearing used between the clevis and the body of a spinner that allows less friction from the rotating spinner blade. Without a spinner bearing of some sort, the clevis will have a tendency to bind on the spinner body. Also called a "unispin" or "uni." Small plastic and glass beads can substitute for this.

Spinner Body. A small, usually tapered, body with a hole through the long axis, used in building spinners. Available in brass and other metals as well as in painted lead. Molds for making these bodies out of lead are available as well.

Spinning Guide. A guide with a larger-diameter ring (at least in the butt guides used) to be used on spinning rods. The smaller sizes are often used on casting and spin-cast rods. The theory of the large ring for the butt guides is that the rod will cast better because the line is coming off the spinning reel in large loops. One theory claims that the first butt guide on the rod should be about two-thirds of the diameter of the spinning-reel-spool lip. The guide rings decrease in size toward the tip-top.

Spinning-Rod Rings. These are rings placed over the spinning-rod cork grip (sometimes over foam grips as well) to hold the reel in place when a fixed reel seat is not used. The two rings fit snugly on the handle and are usually tapered or swaged to hold the foot of the reel.

Split-Ring Pliers. These small pliers have a tooth at the end of one jaw for use in opening a split ring to make spinners and spoons. Indispensable for the spoon- and spinner-maker. Both inexpensive and better high-quality models are available.

Split Rings. Like miniature key rings, these round rings make possible easy attachment of hooks, swivels, and other fittings to the body of a spoon or spinner. Also used to attach hooks to some plugs and to make other terminal riggings. A half-dozen sizes are available.

Sprue Hole. The funnel-shaped opening into a two-piece mold cavity through which the molten lead or liquid plastic is poured to make sinkers, lead-head jigs, and soft-plastic lures. Also called a "gate" or "down gate."

Stainless Steel Leader Wire. Single-strand leader wire made from stainless steel. Used in salt water.

Straddle Mounting. A special type of guide that uses four feet—two at each end of the frame. These feet straddle the rod blank. Used mainly one big-game rods, these guides are wrapped as are other guides.

Stripping Guide. The lowest or butt guide on a fly rod, this guide is not a snake guide or single-foot fly-rod ceramic guide (such as are commonly used on the rest of the rod) but is instead a lightweight small-ring spinning or spin-cast guide. It is also called a **butt guide.** Light fly rods will have only one stripper guide, larger fly rods will have two or three. Larger stripper guides are more common today than in years past.

Swing Blade. A narrow elliptical spinner blade used in popular spinners.

Swivel Shaft. A spinner shaft in which half of a swivel is built into the end used for line attachment. It helps to prevent line twist.

Tail Tags. Small bright pieces of plastic drilled with a hole at one end and attached to the eye of a spinner shaft along with the hook. Used to make a spinner more attractive to fish and to provide a visual "strike point."

Template. A paper, cardboard, steel, or plastic sheet cut into the outline shape of a plug, spoon, spinner blade, rod handle, or similar item. The template makes it easy to duplicate tackle parts.

Tenite. A tough plastic sometimes used for injection-molding or plastic fishing lures. Most plastics used today are of this material, **butyrate,** or **ABS.**

Three-Way Swivel. A swivel with three eyes for tying line. All three are equidistant around the central ring that holds them.

Through-Wire Construction. A method by which all the hooks of a plug, as well as the eye to which the line is tied, are connected together through the center of the plug by a heavy wire. Used primarily on saltwater plugs where the chances are far greater that a fish may shatter the plug on a strike or during a fight, there are several construction methods that use wire and also metal plates.

Tip Action. Rod action in which most of the bending is in the tip of the rod. Also called fast action or extra-fast action (depending upon degree); used to be called **dry-fly action** on fly rods.

Tip-Top. The correct term, although this is sometimes called the "top guide" or top eye." It is the topmost line guide on the rod and is attached to the rod by means of a small metal tube sized to fit onto the end of the blank. There are tip-tops that are specific for spinning, casting, surf, big-game, and other rods.

Tonkin Cane. One of the two thousand species of bamboo, a member of the grass family, and the only one used seriously for split-bamboo rods. (**Calcutta cane** was once used intact for rods, often for cane poles or surf rods.) Comes from the Tonkin Province in China.

Top Guide. See **Tip-Top.**

Travel Rod. See **Pack Rod.**

Trim Windings. See **Windings.**

Trolling Sinker. A sinker made specifically for trolling. These can be crescent-shaped, L-shaped (this is often called a "**drail**"), keeled to prevent twisting, or a simple torpedo shape. Those intended to minimize twist are most often used in trolling.

Tube Heads. These are special lead heads used with tube lures. Molds in these shapes are available to tackle-crafters. A tube head has a smooth rounded shape that will easily fit into and conform to the shape of a tube lure.

Tungsten Carbide Guide. A guide in which the ring is made of tungsten carbide, very hard and tough—though slightly brittle—material. The tungsten carbide called Carboloy is a trademark of General Electric. The tungsten carbide called Mildarbide is a trademark of the Mildrum company.

Twisted Leader Wire. This is leader wire made from number of smaller strands. Often these are twisted around one another, and several strands make up one wire. Cable is composed of these twisted strands to make up heavier leaders.

Two-Part Plug. A plug with a front half and a rear

half that is joined in the middle with two screw eyes or a plate-and-pin coupling. These plugs wiggle more in the water as a result of the jointed sections. They are also called **Jointed Plugs.** The term also refers to plastic-plug blanks that come in two halves and must be glued or welded together (usually with acetone) before finishing or use.

Two-Piece Mold. A mold for making sinkers, bucktails, or plastic lures in which the two mold halves are joined by hinges, are locked by clamps, or are pinned together to assure proper registration. Molten metal or plastic is poured into the mold cavities through a gate or **Sprue Hole.**

U-Frame Guide. A spinning, casting, or spin-cast guide in which the frame holding the guide ring looks like a U when viewed from the end of the guide. See **V-Frame Guide.**

Underwrapping. A thread wrapping placed on the rod before a guide is seated and wrapped in place. Not often used on light or ultralight rods. On heavier rods, the underwrapping helps protect the finish of the rod blank, cushions the blank from the metal guide feet, and provides a more secure base for the guide foot.

Uni. See **Spinner Bearing.**

Unispin. See **Spinner Bearing.**

Varnish. A clear protective finish for rods and rod wrappings. At one time the standard for finishing wraps, today it has been replaced by various epoxy rod finishes. It is still used on bamboo rods, where tradition is important.

V-Frame Guide. A spinning, casting, or spin-cast guide in which the frame holding the guide ring looks like a V when viewed from the end. See **U-Frame Guide.**

Vinyl Skirt. A soft, flexible skirt of plastic strands that can be attached to a plug, spinner, bucktail, or other lure either as a primary skirt or as an additional attraction. Skirts may be molded and made in large sizes for saltwater lures and off-shore trolling lures.

Weed-Guard. A wire, plastic, or nylon device that extends over the hook to prevent it from catching weeds while being retrieved. Many styles are available for single, double, and even treble hooks, and for a variety of baits and lures.

Welt. The thicker outer lip of a female metal

ferrule (separate from and added to the rod blank) that is designed to protect the lip from expanding or splitting under the strain of the flexing rod.

Wet-Fly Action. A slow or parabolic type of action in a fly rod. This is an almost obsolete term and is applicable primarily to older bamboo fly rods. Years ago this action was desired for wet-fly fishing.

Wiggle Eye. A small plastic bubble with a flat back (to be glued to a plug or lure) and a loose, dark central pupil. Because the pupil is loose in the plastic bubble eye, it rolls around as the lure moves through the water. Sometimes called **doll eyes.** Available in many sizes and several colors.

Wiggle Lips. Metal or plastic lips (the latter primarily of Lexan) that are glued or screwed into a plug to make it dive under water. Available in several shapes and sizes.

Willowleaf Blade. A spinner blade that is long and slender with pointed ends, like a willow leaf.

Winding Check. A small, round, dish-shaped piece of plastic, metal, or rubber with a hole in the center that is designed to fit snugly over a rod blank and up against the foregrip. Primarily decorative. Sometimes also called a **grip check.** Larger plastic fittings like this for saltwater rods are sometimes called rod hosels. See **Hosel.**

Windings. The wraps of thread that are used to hold guides in place on a rod or to reinforce the ferrules—also, any decorative wraps in front of the foregrip or at the tip-top. There are a number of types of windings, such as the single wrap, double wrap, underwrap, trim wrapping, spiral wrap, spiral wrap over Mylar, and decorative wraps such as diamonds and chevrons. Winding are usually made with nylon thread, which is available in several sizes and many colors.

Wire Clevis. A clevis formed from round wire. The ends are flattened and drilled with holes to fit onto the spinner shaft.

Wire Former. A tool used for bending and forming wire for spinners and riggings. Some are simple tools, and there are also large bench tools for making complex wraps and rigs that are designed for near-production work. The simple tools are best for simple wraps, eyes, and loops.

Selected Bibliography And More Information

Some of the following books are out of print; however, they are listed for those who, like me, browse old book stores and college book sales for books on fishing. Some of these old books have unique tips for and approaches to building tackle. Some of the older books are available in libraries or from used-book mail-order lists.

BARNES, GEORGE W. *How to Make Bamboo Fly Rods.* New York: Winchester Press, 1977. Out of print. Good book on the subject of making bamboo rods from raw culms of bamboo. Recommended for those interested in this aspect of rod making.

BATES, L. VERNON. *Tackle Making for Anglers.* London, England: Herbert Jenkins, 1958. Out of print.

BREINING, GREG and STERNBERG, DICK. *Fishing Tips and Tricks.* Minnetonka MN: Cy DeCosse, Inc. Mostly fishing tricks and tips, modifications of lures, etc., but some material on tackle care and repair.

BURCH, MONTE. *The Outdoorsman's Workshop.* New York: Winchester Press, 1977. General book on making outdoor equipment; some fishing.

CLARK, NANCY and CUTTER, THOMAS and MCGRANE, JEAN-ANN. *Ventilation.* New York: Lyons & Burford, 1984. An excellent book on all aspects of ventilation for craftsmen and the subject of dealing with working materials and their potential fumes.

CLEMENS, DALE P. *Custom Rod Thread Art.* Wescosville, PA: RodCrafters Press, 1982. A book of detailed instructions on complex thread wraps and weaving.

_____. *Fiberglass Rod Making.* New York: Winchester Press, 1974.

_____. *The New Advanced Custom Rod Building.* New York: Winchester Press, 1987.

EMERY, JOHN. *How to Build Custom-made Handcrafted Fishing Rods.* Miami, FL: Windward Publishing, 1977.

EVANOFF, VLAD. *Basic Bottom Rigs.* Patterson, NJ: Athletic Activities Publishing Co., 1968. Out of print.

_____. *Fishing Rigs for Fresh & Salt Water.* New York: Harper and Row, 1977. An excellent book on the many possible riggings for fish and the various terminal tackle parts needed for this.

_____. *Fresh Water Fishing Rigs.* Coral Springs, FL: Catchmore, 1984.

_____. *How to Make Fishing Lures.* New York: Ronald Press Company, 1959. Out of print.

_____. *Make Your Own Fishing Lures.* New York: A.S. Barnes, 1975.

FINNYSPORTS. *Bait Makers Bible.* Toledo, OH: Finnysports. Out of print.

FRAZER, PERRY D. *Amateur Rodmaking.* New York: The Macmillan Co., 1949. Out of print.

GARCIA-VELA, LUIS AGUSTIN. *Handcrafting a Graphite Fly Rod.* Lakewood, CO: The Rodcrafter, 1978.

GARRISON, EVERETT (with Hoagy B. Carmichael). *A Master's Guide to Building a Bamboo Fly Rod.* Katonah, NY: Martha's Glen Publishing, 1977. An excellent book on the subject of making the blanks for split-bamboo rods from the raw culms of Tonkin cane. Recommended for those interested in this aspect of rod making.

GRAUMOT, RAOUL and WENSTROM, ELMER. *Fisherman's Knots and Nets.* Cambridge, MD: Cornell Maritime Press.

JONES, ROBERT H. *Make Your Own Fishing Tackle, vol. 1—Lures.* Vancouver, BC: Special Interest Publications, Maclean Hunter Ltd. 1884.

HERTER, GEORGE LEONARD. *Professional Fly Tying, Spinning, and Tackle Making Manual and Manufacturing Guide.* Waseca, MN: Herter's Inc., 1961. Out of print, but a fascinating book on the subject and far underrated considering its time. Mostly on fly tying, however.

_____. *Professional Glass and Split-Bamboo Rod Building Manual and Manufacturer's Guide.* Waseca, MN: Herter's, 1953. Out of print, but interesting on the varieties of early bamboo rods made.

KIRKFIELD, STUART. *The Fine Bamboo Fly Rod.* Harrisburg, PA: Stackpole Books, 1986. Primarily on restoration and repair.

KREH, LEFTY and SOSIN, MARK. *Practical Fishing Knots.* New York: Lyons Burford. Out of Print. Excellent books on fishing knots.

KREIDER, CLAUDE M. *The Bamboo Rod and How to Build It.* New York: The Macmillan Company, 1951. Out of print.

LAMBUTH, LETCHER. *The Angler's Workshop.* OR: Champoeg Press, 1979. General book on making fishing equipment; some material on tackle, rods.

LUDGATE, H.T. *Make Nets—Here's How.* Toledo, OH: Netcraft Co., 1976. Currently available from Netcraft.

_____. *Popular Netcraft.* Toledo, OH: Netcraft Co., 1948. Details on all types of nets and how to make them.

_____. *Tackle Tricks with Wire.* Toledo, OH: The Netcraft Co., 1969. Details on wire formers, fishing, tackle, and rigs made with wire. Currently available from Netcraft.

MAJOR, HARLAN. *Salt Water Fishing Tackle.* New York: Funk and Wagnalls Company, 1955. Out of print, but good information on early tackle design.

MARSHALL, MEL. *How to Make Your Own Fishing Rods.* Harrisburg, PA: Stackpole Books, 1978.

_____. *How to Make Your Own Lures and Flies.* New York: Outdoor Life Books, 1976.

MAYES, JIM. *How to Make and Repair Your Own Fishing Tackle.* New York: Dodd, Mead & Company, 1986.

MOHNEY, RUSS. *The Complete Book of Lurecraft.* New York, 1987.

MORRIS, SKIP, *The Custom Graphite Fly Rod—Design and Construction.* New York: Lyons & Burford, 1989.

PFEIFFER, C. BOYD. *Tackle Care.* New York: Lyons & Burford, 1987. Completely covers all aspects of tackle care, maintenance, and repair.

_____. *Tackle Craft.* New York: Crown Publishers, 1974. Out of print, and the original of *this* completely rewritten book.

SAINDON, GARY L. *The Off-Season Angler.* Whitefish, MT: Gary Saindon, 1985. General book on making some fishing equipment, some tackle.

STINSON, BILL. *Do It Yourself Rod Building.* Portland, OR: Frank Amato Publications, 1983.

SOSIN, MARK and KREH, LEFTY. *Practical Fishing Knots II.* New York: Lyons & Burford 1991. A current update of the above book and also excellent.

SOUCIE, GARY. *Hook, Line, and Sinker—The Complete Angler's Guide to Terminal Tackle.* New York: Holt Rinehart and Winston, 1982. Excellent book on the subject of terminal tackle.

_____. *Soucie's Fishing Databook.* New York: Lyons & Burford, 1985. An excellent small handbook on all types of terminal tackle, tests and specs on same, etc. Highly recommended.

TAPPLY, H.G. *Tackle Tinkering.* New York: A.S. Barnes and Company. Out of print.

VARE, ALAN and WHITEHEAD, KEN. *Rod Building.* London, England: Rod and Gun Publishing, Ltd., 1975.

WALKER, J.B. *Rods—How to Make Them.* London, England: Herbert Jenkins, Ltd., 1959. Not readily available.

WATSON, BILL. *Floatmaker's Manual.* London, England: Ernest Benn Ltd. A small but definitive book, all 96 pages on the making of floats.

WILSON, LORING D. *The Handy Sportsman.* New York: Winchester Press, 1976. General book on outdoor equipment; some fishing.

In addition, several booklets are available from tackle component manufacturers. Most are available from tackle shops or mail-order supply catalogs. They include:

CARSON, WALLY. *Rod Building by Lamiglas.* Woodland, WA: Lamiglas, Inc.

FLEX COAT CO. *Decorative Rod Wrapping, Step By Step, Book I.* Driftwood, TX: Flex Coat Co. Fold out instruction guide including fish, boxes, American flag, and diamonds.

_____. *Decorative Rod Wrapping, Step by Step, Book II.* Driftwood, TX: Flex Coat Co. Fold out instruction guide including tuna, cross, maze, and thunderbird.

GUDEBROD, Inc. *How to Build and Wrap a Rod with Gudebrod.* Pottstown, PA: Gudebrod.

SEIDERS, ROGER. *Flex Coat Step by Step Rod Building.* Driftwood, TX: Flex Coat Company.

Several videos have also been produced covering tackle building. Those available include:

Build Your Own Rod (Dale Clemens). St. Paul, MN: 3M/Scientific Anglers, 1985.

Creative Rod Crafting (Dale P. Clemens). St. Paul, MN: 3M/Scientific Anglers, 1985.

Creativity of Custom Rod Design. Anglers Video, 1985.

Fundamentals of Custom Rod Building. Anglers Video, 1985.

Fundamentals of Weaving (Cam Clark). Wescoville, PA: Rodcrafters Press, 1990.

Hilts Molds How-To Video (Sean Foxen). Santa Ana, CA, 1984.

Make Your Own Bass Lures. Fish Tale Productions, 1989.

Index

The following is not an expansive or cross-indexed reference; it is intended to be an aid to guiding you through this book. The book follows in logical, progressive order, and each chapter treats a specific subject—either a lure type or rod construction method. These chapters and the subheadings that are listed at the head of each chapter make it easy to discover the contents of each chapter. The following is meant to help point you to a specific page for a specific process or tackle-making item.